A SONG OF WAR
READINGS FROM VERGIL'S *AENEID*

Roman mosaic, 3rd cent. A.D.

I half fancy I can trace the origin of this personal affection for Virgil . . .. When I was at school we met every morning for prayer, in a large circular hall, round which, on pedestals, were set copies of the portrait busts of great ancient writers. Among these was "the Ionian father of the rest," our father Homer, with a winning and venerable majesty. But the bust of Virgil was, I think, of white marble, not a cast (so, at least, I remember it), and was of a singular youthful purity and beauty, sharing my affections with a copy of the exquisite Psyche of Naples.

Andrew Lang (1844–1912), letter to Lady Violet Lebas

A SONG OF WAR

READINGS FROM VERGIL'S *AENEID*

RICHARD A. LAFLEUR

ALEXANDER G. MCKAY

A Prentice Hall Latin Reader

PEARSON

Boston, Massachusetts
Chandler, Arizona
Glenview, Illinois
Upper Saddle River, New Jersey

Cover photo: Gian Lorenzo Bernini (1598–1680), *Aeneas and Anchises* (marble statue), Galleria Borghese, Rome, Italy © NewsCom.

Acknowledgments appear on page 461–462, which constitute an extension of this copyright page.

ISBN–13: 978–0–13–320520–6
ISBN–10:   0–13–320520–7
3 4 5 6 7 8 9 10 -V063- 17 16 15 14 13 12

CONTENTS

For additional resources, go to PHSchool.com and enter the
web code **jwk-1000** to access the Companion Web Site.

PREFACE

Both volumes of *A Song of War*, the student text and the Teacher's Guide, have been a joint endeavor from the very beginning. Originally we were to have a third collaborator, our dear colleague Jane Harriman Hall, but when Jane had to withdraw early on for personal reasons, the two of us were left to oversee the production of this new edition of readings from Vergil's *Aeneid*, a venture—indeed, an adventure—at which we have labored with ever-increasing enthusiasm and intensity over the past three years. Our aim has been to produce a vibrant and occasionally provocative introduction to this monumental poem via an array of exploratory and critical essays, explanatory notes, and detailed discussion questions, all informed by the best scholarship of recent decades (which is abundantly catalogued in the bibliography and other materials included in our Teacher's Guide and on the book's student and teacher Companion Web Sites, the latter important new ancillaries to this expanded edition) and enlivened by dozens of illustrations that offer a visual and imaginative feast to enrich the reader's appreciation of the epic. Now, at the end of our task, we hope that students and teachers alike will agree that we have in some measure succeeded in providing a guided tour into the creative genius of Vergil as poet-artist-storyteller, a genius in which images and words unite to produce a powerful, enigmatic, and often cinematographic portrait of war, and passion, and the human condition.

In this Preface we should like first to thank jointly the several colleagues and associates who have assisted us in so many ways over this very fruitful triennium, and then each of us separately will offer a brief personal expression of gratitude to other friends and loved ones who have lent us their support individually during the course of our work on the two volumes. The most richly merited thanks go to Mary Wells Ricks of the University of Georgia for her inspired and inspiring vigilance, Muse-like, over the myriad technical details involved in the preparation of the manuscript, for her expert editorial advice, and for her unflagging good cheer: *dux femina facti*. Likewise of inestimable help was our research assistant, University of Georgia M.A. graduate Brandon Wester, who labored intelligently and meticulously for hundreds of hours on countless facets of the project, not least the very detailed work involved in constructing the end Vocabulary and compiling the toponym list for the book's several newly designed maps. And of course we are enormously grateful to our four very special friends at Prentice Hall—Bill Fleig, Keith Fry, Matthew Shimkus, and Cathy Wilson—who have assisted us throughout this odyssey, providing not only spiritual support but also the resources needed for the student edition's numerous illustrations, the hardcover binding, and the resplendent printing.

Thanks are due also to: Jim Anderson, Clyde Austin, Gail Polk, Dan Robie, and Sallie Spence, for field-testing portions of the student text in their classes;

Tim McCarthy of Art Resource, Frances Van Keuren of the University of Georgia School of Art, and Tricia Miller of the Georgia Museum of Art, for their generous assistance in identifying appropriate and attractive illustrations; and finally Jared Klein, Ginny Lindzey, John Nicholson, Matt Payne, and Jim Yavenditti, for help with a variety of editorial matters.

Finally, we would like to acknowledge the wide range of editions and commentaries that were employed both in establishing our own Latin text (which we have newly edited with careful attention to such matters as punctuation, capitalization, paragraphing, and important manuscript variants) and in composing the accompanying notes and discussion questions; most often consulted were the following volumes, for which full bibliographical citations appear on the teacher's website: the Oxford Classical Text of R.A.B. Mynors; the Loeb Classical Library edition and translation of H.R. Fairclough and G.P. Goold; the commentaries of R.G. Austin (on Books One, Two, Four, and Six) and R.D. Williams (on Books One–Six and Seven–Twelve); and the school texts of H.E. Gould and J.L. Whiteley (Books One, Two, Four, and Six), R.H. Jordan (Book Ten), Keith Maclennan (Book Six), W.S. Maguiness (Book Twelve), and Clyde Pharr (Books One–Six, with revisions plus notes for Books Ten and Twelve by Barbara Boyd).

RICHARD A. LaFLEUR
ATHENS, GEORGIA

ALEXANDER G. McKAY
HAMILTON, ONTARIO

Much of my work on this project was completed in the aftermath of the terrible national tragedy of September 11, 2001, and the ensuing international conflict (which resonated daily in my engagement with Vergil's "song of war"), as well as during my own struggle with a devastating personal crisis. I am profoundly grateful to a host of family members and close friends who provided their love and support throughout this very difficult period, especially to my three beloved children, Jean-Paul, Caroline, and Kimberley, for their unbounded affection, and to the following very dear friends, each of whom contributed immeasureably and in innumerable ways to my emotional survival: Frank Erhardt, Ginny Lindzey, Gretchen Mosier, Evelyn Ramsey, Mary Ricks, and most especially Alice Tipton. Thanks are due also to my department head Bob Curtis and my dean Wyatt Anderson for their constant support of my endeavors in teaching, research, and professional service—and to all the students in my undergraduate and graduate Latin classes: my hours with them, as with Vergil himself, have been among the high points of all my days throughout the many months of this sojourn in the world of Aeneas.

ADDENDUM TO THE REVISED EDITION: Laboring alone on the revisions to our book presented a sorrowful reminder of the passing of my friend and co-author Alexander McKay, whose death August 31, 2007, was mourned by countless family members, friends, and readers of Vergil throughout the world; the endurance of our modest text is but one of myriad *testimonia* to Sandy's far-reaching and monumental contributions to the study of Rome's greatest poet.

I must thank for their assistance with this *Song of War* revision my editor Jennifer Creane, my colleague David Perry (whose authorship of the AP Latin companion volume for Caesar's Gallic War, *A Call to Conquest*, provided several helpful ideas for my Vergil revision), my former department head Naomi Norman, my graduate research assistant Derek Bast, friend and editorial assistant Kay Stanton, and again, for their constant support, my children, Jean-Paul, Caroline, and Kim, and my dear wife Alice, *uxor carissima atque amatissima.*

RAL

To McMaster University, Hamilton, and York University, Toronto, I offer an expression of undying gratitude for many years of genial and productive encounters with students, scholars, and professional colleagues across Canada and the United States, and particularly for the enriching experiences of teaching and learning during the Vergilian Society's Overseas Summer Sessions at the celebrated Villa Vergiliana in the heart of Vergil's Campania and in the *Rus Maronianum* which embraces Italy and Sicily.

I am likewise deeply grateful: to friends and mentors past and present, to librarians, and correspondents, *hic undique,* who have made teaching, research, and writing such rewarding activities; to my faithful allies at home and abroad, for contributions and enlightenment at regional classical meetings across North America; and to my beloved family for constant support in all times and places.

AGM

A Song of War
Readings from Vergil's *Aeneid*

For additional resources, go to PHSchool.com and enter the web code **jwk-1000** to access the Companion Web Site.

"Virgilio," pen and ink with wash on tan paper, ca. 1855–60
Pietro Nicoli (Italian, died 1883)
Ceseri Collection, Georgia Museum of Art, University of Georgia

INTRODUCTION

Publius Vergilius Maro ("Vergil," as he is commonly called today) was born near Mantua on 15 October 70 B.C. His boyhood familiarity with the north Italian landscape of the Po Valley colored his three masterworks: the 10 pastoral poems called *Bucolics* or *Eclogues;* the *Georgics*, his treatise on farming in four books; and his epic *Aeneid* in 12 books. After primary and secondary schooling in Mantua, Cremona, and Milan, Vergil left Cisalpine Gaul for Rome, where he studied medicine and mathematics, possibly astrology, and continued his education in courtroom oratory, rhetoric, and philosophy. Although he maintained a house on the Esquiline Hill in Rome, his preferred residence was at Naples in the shadow of Vesuvius, where he composed his *Georgics* and *Aeneid* and continued his studies in Epicurean philosophy with Siro and with Philodemus of Gadara at nearby Herculaneum. He had a marvelous sense of the diversity of Italy and a deep respect for its mosaic of traditions and cultures. He moved comfortably in the bicultural, Graeco-Roman society of writers and intellectuals in Naples, which was renowned for its philosophical schools and theater, and for its seductive high-life that attracted national leaders, jaded politicians, self-indulgent aristocrats, wealthy traders, and financiers. Tall, dark, and "rustic" in appearance, with a chronic throat ailment and stomach complaint, Vergil must have enjoyed the luminous atmosphere of Campania, where he could visit the celebrated mineral baths along the shoreline.

VERGIL'S EARLY POETIC CAREER:
THE *ECLOGUES, GEORGICS,* AND MINOR WORKS

The poet's lifetime, at least until he was 40-something, was spent in tumultuous times; civil war was prevalent and almost everyone had to endure some measure of disturbance and dislocation. The shepherds and goatherds of his pastoral poems, properly called *Bucolica,* composed between 42 and 37 B.C., show the strain of war's disruptions in their melancholy love songs and consoling meditations on friendship.

The 10 poems of the collection generally offer dialogues on public and private issues, the impact of civil war on individuals (*Eclogues* 1 and 9), along with passionate love and stressful love affairs (2, 6, 8, 10), artfully interspersed with poetic competitions (3, 5, 7). Although the poems' settings and scenery are generally Sicilian, they sometimes include Mantua, Cremona, and the river Mincius of Cisalpine Gaul, where Vergil grew up. Contemporary poets and statesmen, both directly and indirectly, appear often in the "cast" of Vergil's performers and references in these poems. The Fourth *Eclogue,* called "Messianic," which recalls the prophecies of Isaiah, foretells the birth of a wonderful child who will rule a world at peace. Who will it be? Perhaps the child of Antony and Octavia (Augustus' sister), or, in the Christian tradition, Jesus Christ. These brief poems, today commonly called "Selections" *(Eclogae),* were eminently suitable for stage reading and for mime performance in private or public theaters. Theocritus, a third-century Alexandrian poet who composed 30 pastoral *Idylls,* provided models for Vergil's adaptations and determined the basic shape of the entire European pastoral tradition, where Vergil holds pride of place.

The "Georgic Book," Vergil's verse treatise on farming (which Dryden called "the best poem of the best poet"), was modeled after Hesiod's eighth-century *Works and Days,* a sort of poetic almanac for farmers that detailed what to do and what not to do, and underscored the moral value of hard work. In very many respects Vergil's *Georgics* are closely analogous, but they also reflect peninsular Italy in a time of civil war, when the land and its cultivators were laid waste and ravaged, when the Italian peninsula was repeatedly demoralized and anarchic. Composed between 36 and 29 B.C., the *Georgics* preached a sermon of regeneration and of salvation by hard work *(labor)* in the pursuits of agriculture, tree cultivation, animal husbandry, and bee-keeping. Several passages are particularly memorable and repay close reading: Book 1.463–514 portrays the civic and cosmic disorder after Caesar's assassination in 44 B.C.; Book 2 is remarkable for its praise of Italy, in lines 136–76, and for its eulogy of the farmer's life, verses 458–74; 3.440–566 provides a chilling account of plague among animals and humans; and 4.453–527 recounts Proteus' song of Orpheus and Eurydice, which has been an inspiration for musicians and artists through the ages.

A collection of 14 poems, known as the *Appendix Vergiliana,* has also survived from antiquity. Because the manuscripts are late and the textual problems are legion, their authenticity has been questioned. The ancients were inclined to regard them as youthful Vergilian poems. The *Catalepton* (a collection of "trifles"), *Copa* ("The Hostess"), *Culex* ("The Gnat," which recounts the experience of a poor dead bug in the Underworld!), and *Moretum* ("The Salad," whence came the phrase *e pluribus unum*) had a substantial following, and probably these and others were classroom fare. Some of the shorter poems may be autobiographical (e.g., *Catalepton* 5 and 8), but *Culex* seems the most Vergilian, with its praise of country life, description of a serpent, its tripartite structure, and its portrayal of an Underworld with heroes, both mythological and Roman. Vergilian or not, the *Appendix* provides an engaging complement to our poet's serious verse.

VERGIL'S NATIONAL POEM: THE *AENEID*

The *Aeneid,* written largely at Naples between 29 and 19 and still incomplete at the time of Vergil's death (21 September 19 B.C.), is a monumental national epic. "Arms and the man" are the primary focus of this magnificent poem, which resonates from beginning to end with Homer's *Iliad* and *Odyssey.* The first six books, in fact, depict by design the "Odyssey" of the Trojan prince Aeneas, a refugee from devastated Troy, led by divine prophecy (Apolline) and divine interventions (Venus) to the Promised Land of Italy. His adventures include storm, shipwreck, and disappointments, the loss of Creusa, his exceptional wife and mother of their son Ascanius (known also as Iulus), a Tunisian interlude which highlights Dido, another refugee from a distracted Near Eastern realm (Tyre and Sidon), now youthful queen of Carthage, the death of his father Anchises, and a sensational passage through the Underworld, which is marked by revelations, instruction, and exhortation by the shade of Anchises. The last six books, Aeneas' "Iliad," center on the Trojan leader's adventures in Italy, his encounter with the site of Rome, his alliance with Greeks and Etruscans, and his conflict with Latin and Rutulian resistance forces, most notably with Turnus, the Rutulian prince. Turnus' death, in conflict with Aeneas at the close of Book 12, consolidates Aeneas' victory and signals the advent of Rome's dispensation. The parade of Roman heroes (Book 6.756–886) and the scenes on Aeneas' shield (8.626–731) together signal the achievements and the greatness of past and future: *famamque et fata nepotum,* "the fame and the fortunes of his descendants" (8.731).

Echoes of Greek tragedy are constant throughout the poem, of Aeschylus and Euripides particularly, and of Roman adaptations for the Republican tragic stage. Vergil's "tragic" orientation highlights the motivations and psychology of his characters, their emotions, dilemmas, and inner conflicts. Overall the epic's emphasis is on qualities of leadership and on the painful progress and transition from chaos to order, from old to new values. Loss, divorce, and separation seem essential for progress and self-realization; they are part of Aeneas' progress toward the realization of his personal destiny as father of a new nation and of Rome's rise to power and dominion in the peninsula and in the Mediterranean. Vergil's hero is heavily indebted to Homeric characters of action and self-determination, to Achilles and Hector in the *Iliad* and to Odysseus in the *Odyssey.* However, Julius Caesar and Octavian-Augustus were also never very far from Vergil's mind in the designing of his Trojan hero, and Dido's tragedy carries the imprint of Cleopatra's short-lived career.

HEROES AND HEROINES

Homeric heroes were for Vergil imperishable figures; so too were the protagonists, both men and women, of Greek tragedies which dealt with the Trojan War. Both influenced Vergil's shaping of his own "players," newly designed and modified for a more civilized age than Homer's, and for an age far removed from Periclean democracy. The episode of Dido and Aeneas owes much to Odysseus' adventures with Calypso, Nausicaa, Circe, and Arete in Homer's *Odyssey.* Heroes and heroines of Greek tragedy were equally magnetic and formative: Hecuba and Andromache, Paris and Helen, Orestes and Clytaemnestra, Odysseus and Philoctetes, and the

Trojan Women, are all involved in Vergil's epic text. The Hellenistic epic of the third-century scholar-poet, Apollonius of Rhodes, the *Argonautica,* in four books, was another major influence. Repeatedly Vergil finds models and modes of poetic expression in the Hellenistic epic, particularly in its love story of Jason, the Argonaut, quester for the Golden Fleece, and Medea, the young sorceress and barbarian princess of Colchis at the farthest end of the Black Sea.

THE EPIC QUEST

Aeneas' objective is to establish a new home for his son and for his refugee companions from ruined Troy. Dido's career as refugee from Sidon shares the same task and commitment. The central theme of "the quest" is not only relevant to the antique heroic tradition, with its search for a home, a prize, and a wife; it is also relevant to Vergil's epic and to Italy's experience, where renewal and rebuilding, both moral and physical, for the future were watchwords of the Augustan order after 27 B.C. Although Octavian, Caesar's adopted son and grandnephew, won a decisive victory over Antony and Cleopatra at Actium on the Adriatic in 31, the countryside of the war zones and the morale and spirit of the Roman people were ravaged and inert. The nation had been divided and exhausted by a century of civil war, from 133–30, and there was little cause for a sense of security when Vergil began his national epic.

MELPOMENE AND CLIO: TRAGEDY AND HISTORY

The story of Dido and Aeneas is heavily imbued with the hostilities of Rome's past history. Three separate conflicts between Rome and Carthage (264–41, 218–01, and 149–46 B.C.) had been traumatic and left a legacy of dread, resentment, and hatred in Roman minds. Vergil's narrative, centered on Dido's Carthage, offers hints sometimes of the tradition that Carthaginians were monsters of arrogance, wealth, and cruelty. Punic perfidy and guile *(fides Punica)* were deeply imbedded in Rome's prejudice against Carthage and the Carthaginians. The name of their most celebrated and punitive general, Hannibal (247–183), inspired terror in children centuries after the Second Punic War. The ultimate victory and pitiless destruction of Carthage in 146 seemed to many Romans to be just retribution for the barbaric cruelty and martial frenzy *(furor)* of the Punic enemy. The after-effects of Dido's suicide (*Aeneid* 4.667–71) bring the fall of Carthage all the more vividly into the foreground. Many of our poet's readers must also have sensed behind the romantic liaison of Dido and Aeneas reflections of more recent history involving Julius Caesar (100–44) and Mark Antony (82–30) with Cleopatra (69–30), the last of the independent Ptolemaic rulers, who committed suicide in Egypt.

The story of Aeneas and Turnus is also emphatically colored by the travails of Italy's progress towards unity and peace during late Republican history. During

Vergil's boyhood, the Roman political stage was in constant turmoil. When Cicero gained the consulship in 63 (the birth year of Octavian and his lieutenant Agrippa), he uncovered and suppressed the conspiracy of Catiline against the government. The Roman renegade was defeated and killed during the hostilities. To guarantee some measure of equilibrium, the three leaders of the age, Pompey, Crassus, and Julius Caesar, formed in 60 B.C. an extra-constitutional alliance which we call the First Triumvirate. During these momentous times, Horace was born at Venosa (8 December 65) and Catullus' love for Lesbia/Clodia (61–58) excited matchless lyrics. Pompey and Crassus were consuls in 55; thereafter Crassus was sent to the East against the Parthians, and was slain at the battle of Carrhae. The aftermath was chaos and anarchy at Rome; Pompey was designated sole consul in 52 to restore order. Caesar defied senatorial demands to demobilize his Gallic veterans and crossed Italy's Rubicon River in 49, and so civil war was renewed. Pompey fled to Greece, where he was defeated by Caesar in the Battle of Pharsalus (9 August 48), and when Pompey sought asylum in Egypt, he was killed by the order of an ungrateful pharaoh.

Adherents of Pompey continued to provide resistance to Caesar overseas, but Caesar was victorious at Thapsus (Africa) and at Munda (Spain), and returned to Rome in 46 as its master, its perpetual dictator, honored like an oriental ruler, determined to bring about constitutional reforms and to march against the Parthians in Mesopotamia. He was assassinated on the grounds of Pompey's theater on the Ides of March, 44; his murderers, Brutus and Cassius, and their fellow assassins fled Italy for Greece. Antony appeared as Caesar's moral heir but had to share the limelight with young Octavian, adopted by Caesar in his will. By 43 a state of war existed, pitting Octavian, allied with the two consuls of the year, Hirtius and Pansa, against Antony. After Antony had been defeated and the two consuls perished, the two enemies made peace and formed a constitutional arrangement, the Second Triumvirate, with the consular and pontifex maximus Marcus Aemilius Lepidus as their colleague. Proscriptions, involving the confiscation of enemy property, and political murders ensued, with Antony as prime offender. Cicero, Antony's outspoken enemy, was murdered on 7 December 43, close to the time when Vergil began his *Bucolics*.

When the army of Antony defeated the tyrannicides Brutus and Cassius at Philippi in 42, the ensuing distribution of lands to the triumviral veterans and expropriations affected both Horace and Vergil. By 40, the date assigned to Vergil's *Bucolic* Four, when Asinius Pollio was consul, Antony had married Octavian's sister Octavia, in order to safeguard peace for the future, and Vergil forecast the birth of a marvelous child who would make peace a universal reality. The publication (and performances) of his pastoral poems brought Vergil into the circle of the literary patron Maecenas during 39, and by 38 Vergil and Varius, his poet/dramatist friend, introduced Horace to the same circle. Vergil began his *Georgics* during a time of war between the Triumvirate and Sextus Pompey, the ambitious and aggressive son of Pompey the Great, who sought retribution for his father's disgrace and the restoration of his father's estates. Vergil and Horace accompanied Maecenas on a diplomatic mission to Brundisium in 37 to gain Antony's support against Sextus Pompey. Meanwhile, Cumae, near Naples, the ancient Apolline sanctuary site, and in earlier times Italy's answer to the Apolline oracle and temple site at Delphi, was radically militarized; a new harbor, Portus Julius, was constructed by uniting two adjacent volcanic lakes, Avernus and Lucrinus, and Campania was put on a wartime footing. Octavian and his admiral Agrippa defeated Sextus Pompey at Sicilian Naulochus in 36, and Lepidus was eliminated from the Triumvirate for questionable behavior. A year later, Antony, married already to Cleopatra, officially repudiated Octavia, Octavian's sister, and a state of war existed between Octavian and Antony. On 2 September 31, at the battle of Actium, Octavian routed Antony's fleet. By 30 both Antony and Cleopatra had committed suicide and Egypt became a Roman province.

Vergil read his *Georgics* to Octavian when he had returned from the East and was preparing to return to Rome to celebrate his triple triumph in Rome (29). By then Vergil had begun his *Aeneid.* During 27, Octavian regularized his role by constitutional reform, and was named Augustus. Caecilius Epirota opened a private school in Rome in 25, and Vergil's works were prescribed material. Horace published his *Odes,* Books 1–3, in 23, the same year that Marcellus, son of Augustus' sister, husband of his daughter Julia, and his heir-designate, died at Baiae in his 20th year. Agrippa married the widowed Julia in 21. Horace published his first book of *Epistles* in 20. Vergil contracted fever in Greece during 19, and died at the Italian Adriatic port city of Brundisium on 21 September, leaving his epic to be edited and published by his poet friend Varius. Although Vergil's will directed that his epic, which had not yet been finally revised and polished, should be burnt in the event of his death, Augustus intervened and the epic was saved. Augustus celebrated the Ludi Saeculares in 17, a major festival to mark Rome's anniversary, and Horace's *Carmen Saeculare,* enriched by allusions to Vergil's posthumous published epic, was given a public performance.

Cruelty and reprisals, criminality, proscriptions, dislocations, executions, and murders during the Civil War era had left a lasting impression on the poet and affected his sensitive response to the tides of war in Books 7–12, his "Iliadic" epic. The War of the Trojans in Latium is basically a civil war. Since the Trojans claimed Italian ties through their ancestor, Dardanus, their war against Italians and Rutulians is in fact a war against distant relatives, a civil conflict where families are matched against families, leaders against leaders, Aeneas (in the name of his dead comrade Pallas) against Turnus. Premature deaths, especially those of young men who fail to save their fathers or one another, but also deaths of fathers who fail to save their sons, are ubiquitous and a source of intense grief for the "actors" and for the narrator-author himself. The roll-call of untimely deaths and sacrifices is overwhelming: Laocoön and his sons, Priam and Polites, Cassandra's lover Coroebus, Polydorus in Thrace, *infelix* Dido, Daedalus and Icarus, Augustus' nephew and son-in-law Marcellus, Nisus and Euryalus, Mezentius and Lausus, Evander (with Aeneas as his surrogate) and Evander's son Pallas. Many of these figures are tragic victims in a war that echoes the conflicts of the late Republic. The concluding duel between Aeneas and Turnus is in a sense "gladiatorial," but it also marks the end of a civil conflict. Revenge and retaliation are keynotes of the final enactment. Aeneas' memory of the dead Pallas, which is aroused by Turnus' baldric (*saevi monimenta doloris / exuviasque* 945–46) transforms him, spiritually, into Pallas and provokes his retaliation, spurred by wrath and rage (*furiis et ira* 946). The Rutulian prince Turnus is thus, in the end, sacrificed by his own victim, Pallas, with the Trojan Aeneas as the youth's enraged and vengeful agent.

ASPECTS OF VERGIL'S STYLE

Vergil can generally be read without great difficulty, and most of the peculiarities of his poetic style are addressed early on in the notes accompanying the text, as well as in the list of poetic and rhetorical devices included at the end of this Introduction; as a convenience to readers, however, the following summary comments are provided, along with references to the text or to the definitions that are included below in the Poetic Devices section (here abbreviated "PD").

WORD ORDER: Word order is certainly one of the greatest challenges for students coming to Vergil with little or no prior experience in reading Latin poetry. You should be aware from the outset that word order in verse, though by no means random, is nevertheless much freer than in prose and that attention to word-endings which signal such syntactical relationships as adjective-noun agreement is accordingly all the more crucial to comprehension and translation. Noun and adjective are often widely separated (*Tyrias . . . arces* 1.20, *aeternum . . . vulnus* 1.36); words are sometimes positioned outside their clauses (*Troiae* 1.1); initial conjunctions, relative pronouns, and other words that would ordinarily introduce a clause, are frequently delayed (*sed* 1.19, *quae* 1.20); closely connected or coordinating words occasionally "frame" a verse by being positioned first and last in the line, often in order to achieve some sort of emphasis (*quam . . . unam* 1.15). Other special arrangements of words are frequently employed for imagistic or rhetorical effect; see PD "anastrophe," "chiasmus," "enjambement," "framing," "golden line," "hyperbaton," "interlocked word order," "word-picture."

ELLIPSIS: Words are more frequently omitted in verse than in prose, including forms of *sum,* speech verbs, conjunctions, and prepositions (1.11, 37). PD "asyndeton," "ellipsis."

NOUNS: Vergil frequently employs case usages less common in prose, e.g., the genitive of specification or respect (*opum* 1.14), appositional genitive (*formae* 1.27), descriptive/predicate genitive in place of a predicate nominative (*tantae molis* 1.33), dative of direction (*urbi* 2.47), dative of agent with any passive verb form (*ulli* 1.440, *sorori* 4.31), dative of purpose (*excidio* 1.22), adverbial accusative (*grave* 6.201, *torva* 6.467), accusative of specification/respect (especially with reference to body parts, *oculos* 1.228, *genu* 1.320), ablative of route (*Averno* 6.126), ablative of manner without an adjective or a preposition (*cumulo* 1.105), locative with the names of countries (*Libyae* 4.36) and with *terrae* (6.84) and *animi* (4.203). The "poetic plural" for singular (*terris* 1.3), and singular for plural (*capite* 2.219), are common, as are Greek noun and adjective forms, including patronymics and other names (*Troas* 1.30, *Cymothoe* 1.144, *Tydide* 1.97).

VERBS: Often used are the third-person plural perfect form *-ere* for *-erunt* (*tenuere* 1.12) and perfect-system forms with the intervocalic *-v-* and other letters or syllables omitted (*audierat* 1.20, *accestis* 1.201); simple for compound form (*verteret* for *everteret* 1.20); the so-called Greek middle voice, essentially a passive form with active or reflexive sense (*suffusa* 1.228); the historical present (*perflant* 1.83); participles instead of regular verbs or in place of nouns (*summersas* 1.69, *exacta* 1.309), the future active participle sometimes indicating purpose (*ventura* and *inspectura* 2.47), and the perfect passive participle with the force of a present (active) tense (*proruptum* 1.246); *ne* + imperative instead of *noli(te)* + infinitive for negative commands (2.48); historical infinitives (*prodire* 6.199), exclamatory (accusative +) infinitives (*desistere* 1.37), infinitives used to indicate purpose (1.527), and infinitives dependent on nouns (*cognoscere* 2.10) and on adjectives (*videri* 6.49).

OTHER PARTS OF SPEECH: Adjectives are often used in place of a proper noun in the genitive (*Hectorea* 1.273) or with adverbial force (*laeti* 1.35) or as transferred epithets (*memorem* 1.4); prepositions are often omitted (*Lavinia . . . litora* 1.2); *-que* is extremely common and is often employed in polysyndeton (*tenditque fovetque* 1.18). See PD, "asyndeton," "polysyndeton," and "transferred epithet."

ARCHAISMS: Archaic forms are frequently employed by Vergil, sometimes for metrical convenience but also lending an "antique" quality to the poem (*quis* for *quibus* 1.95, gen. pl. *-um* for *-orum* 1.4, *ast* for *at* 1.46, *olli* for *illi* 1.254, *lenibat* for *leniebat* 6.468).

SPELLING: Besides the archaic and Greek spellings and shortened perfect system verb forms noted above, Vergil employs a wide range of syncopated and contracted forms and alternative spellings (*Dardanidum* for *Dardanidarum* 2.242, *curru* for *currui* 1.156, *mi* for *mihi* 6.104). See also PD, "syncope."

RHETORICAL STYLE: Vergil (who, like all well educated Romans, had studied oratory) often employs a highly rhetorical style, especially in speeches; for favorite devices, see PD "anaphora," "apostrophe," "irony," "litotes," "oxymoron," "polysyndeton," "rhetorical question," "tricolon crescens."

FIGURATIVE LANGUAGE: Vergil is a consummate master of figurative language and imagery, of word-pictures and even cinematographic effect; for some of his favorite devices, defined with passage references, see PD, "allegory," "hendiadys," "metaphor," "metonymy," "personification," "simile," "synecdoche," and "transferred epithet" (and see above on word order).

SOUND EFFECTS: One of the most lyrical of Latin poets, Vergil often manipulates such devices as alliteration and assonance simply to add musical effect to his verse, but in other instances the intent is to enhance meaning onomatopoetically; he employs both internal and end-line rhyme (*clamorque . . . stridorque* 1.87, *mella . . . cellas . . . mella* 1.432–36), uses dactyls for rapid or violent action (1.45, 116, 418) or spondees to suggest slow or solemn action or for emphasis in some dramatic moment (1.32, 44, 157). See PD, "alliteration," "assonance," "dactyl," "onomatopoeia," "spondee," and the section below on meter and scansion.

SCANNING AND READING VERGIL'S HEXAMETERS

Ancient poetry was composed to be read aloud (or, in certain instances, to be sung or chanted to musical accompaniment) and with the listening audience, at least as much as the reading audience, in mind; we know that Vergil on occasion recited his verse to Augustus and the imperial family. The Latin poet hoped to appeal at once to the intellect and to the emotions—in varying proportion, depending upon the particular genre—and his approach to both was through the ear. Both the "music" and the "message" of poetry derived in part from its sound effects and its delivery, which was as important to a poet as to a trial lawyer or a politician; rhythm and assonance and such devices as alliteration and onomatopoeia contributed much to the overall effect of a poem. When we read silently, therefore, or aloud but unexpressively, we are neglecting altogether an important aspect of the poet's artistry, just as surely as if we were to experience an opera of Mozart's without the music or the colorful paintings of Gauguin or Picasso only through the medium of black and white photographs.

CORRECT PRONUNCIATION

The late Professor Gareth Morgan (in his review of the excellent Latin audio package by Stephen Daitz, cited on the Teacher's Companion Web Site) imagined a student, perhaps reading the *Aeneid* for the first time, who complains to his teacher,

"How do I put the meter in?" The wise instructor replies, "You don't: Vergil put it in. All you do is bring it back to life again." This "revival of the text" is the fundamental meaning of the term *recitatio,* which is related to the words "incite" and "excite"; and all that is required, as Morgan suggested, is to read the Latin correctly and with attention to what it means.

The first and most important step in any beginning language course is to learn the sounds of the language, that is the correct pronunciation, and to exercise that knowledge through listening and speaking activities every day. Very straightforward rules for pronouncing Latin are provided in the introduction of every beginning Latin text, and more detailed discussions can be found in W. S. Allen's *Vox Latina* and Stephen Daitz' *Pronunciation and Reading of Classical Latin* (cited in the bibliography on the Teacher's Companion Web Site). The first step in reading Latin poetry aloud is simply to read each sentence from beginning to end, following those rules and thinking about what the sentence is saying.

METER, SCANSION, AND THE DACTYLIC HEXAMETER

As you read, and especially if your pronunciation is careful and accurately reflects the differences between long and short vowels, the proper sounds of diphthongs (*ae, oe, ei, ui, au,* and *eu*), and so forth, you should detect a certain rhythmical pattern in the arrangement of the words. This, of course, reflects what Roger Hornsby has called "a vital, indeed a primordial, aspect of poetry," meter (from Latin *metrum,* Greek *metron,* meaning "measure"), which may be defined as the measured arrangement of syllables in a regular rhythmical pattern. In English verse, meter is determined by the patterned alternation of accented and unaccented syllables, an accented syllable being one that is spoken with greater stress or emphasis, such as the syllables "-pon," and "mid-" in "Ónce upón a mídnight dréary" (which is here "scanned," the "scansion" indicating schematically the accented syllables [´] that alternate with unaccented syllables).

In classical Greek, normal word accent was based upon pitch rather than stress (the language was therefore by nature more "musical" than either Latin or English) and was not the prime determinant in verse rhythm. Rather than being "qualitative" (i.e., based on the stress quality of a syllable), Greek meter was "quantitative" (i.e., based on the quantity, or length, of a syllable); and, though this Greek system was not entirely suited to their own language, the Romans abandoned the stress-accented poetry they had at first experimented with and adapted the use of quantitative meter to their verse from the time of the early epic poet Ennius (239–169 B.C.) and throughout the classical period.

That syllables may be defined in terms of quantity, i.e., that some may be "long" and others "short," is clear enough even from English: compare the time required to pronounce *e, be, beak, beach, beached.* Though the length of Latin syllables might vary considerably, as in these English examples, the Romans thought in terms of only two grades, short and long; a long syllable was felt to take about twice as long to pronounce as a short syllable (in musical terms, one might compare the half note and the quarter note). Latin quantitative meter is based upon the patterned alternation of long and short syllables, and the second step in reading Latin poetry aloud is to read each verse metrically, with an eye (or one should say, an ear) to this quantitative rhythm.

With practice a student can read a Latin poem metrically at first sight, simply because the quantities are inherent in the language. Beginning students, however, should learn the mechanics of scanning a line on paper, i.e., of marking the long and short syllables and separating off the feet in each verse (a "foot" is the smallest characteristic group of syllables in a particular rhythmical pattern, e.g., a short syllable followed by a long one constitutes a foot in iambic meter—a "verse" is the smallest characteristic grouping of feet in a particular meter, e.g., a series of five iambs is an iambic pentameter verse). Such scansion is a simple, mechanical exercise and involves the following steps:

A. *Mark the long and short syllables using the macron (ˉ) and the breve (˘), respectively.* In their initial introduction to Latin pronunciation, students learn to identify a syllable as either long or short because syllable quantity determines placement of the stress accent in ordinary Latin speech. The rules are essentially the same in scanning poetry: a syllable is long only if it contains a long vowel or a diphthong or if the vowel, though itself short, is followed by two or more consonants (except where the second of the two consonants is *h*, including the aspirates *ch*, *ph*, and *th*, or where the only two consonants are *qu* or, *sometimes*, a "stop," especially *b*, *c*, *d*, *g*, *p*, or *t*, followed by one of the "liquids," *l* or *r*). In this last instance, however, when attempting to determine the quantity of a syllable occurring *at the end of a word within* (not at the end of) *a verse*, one must take into account any consonants occurring *both* at the end of the word *and* at the beginning of the next word; consider *Aeneid* 1.4:

vī superum, saevae memorem Iūnōnis ob īram

Here the first syllable *vī* is long (as the first syllable of a line always is in Vergil's hexameters), because the vowel -*ī* is long (as indicated by the macron); the *su-* syllable is short because the vowel itself is short and is not followed by "two or more consonants" (sometimes called the "consonant cluster" rule); the next syllable, -*pe-*, is short for the same reasons (thus the opening foot is a "dactyl," i.e., a long-short-short, ˉ˘˘). The next syllable, -*rum,* is long, however, even though the vowel -*u-* is short, due to the fact that the vowel is followed by two consonants (here -*m* + *s*-), when taking into account the ending of *superum* itself and the beginning of the next word *saevae*. The same principles make the -*rem* long (i.e., the -*e*- is short but is followed by the two consonants -*m* + *I*-, so the syllable itself is long). The long and short syllables in the entire line would be marked as follows:

vī sŭpĕrŭm, saēvaē mĕmŏrēm Iūnōnĭs ŏb īram

Note that this line has a total of 15 syllables, one for each vowel and diphthong (remember that *ae* is one of Latin's six diphthongs, not two separate vowels, and so makes a single, long syllable). A line of verse, like an individual word, generally has as many syllables as it has vowels and diphthongs, but there is one exception: when a word in the verse ends with a vowel or a diphthong, or a vowel followed by -*m*, and the following word begins with a vowel or a diphthong, or a vowel or diphthong preceded by *h*-, the final syllable of the first word and the beginning syllable of the next were usually collapsed, or "elided," into a single syllable. The quantity of the single syllable resulting from such "elision" was usually that of the second syllable (suggesting that, in some cases at least, the preceding vowel or diphthong was in pronunciation actually dropped altogether, as the term "elision," from *elidere* "to compress or strike out," might suggest). In writing out the scansion of a verse, any elided syllables should be bracketed and the macron or breve should be centered above the space between the two words, as illustrated by *Aeneid* 1.7 and 11:

Ālbānīquĕ pātrēs āt[quĕ ăl]taē moēnĭă Rōmaē

īmpŭlĕrĭt. Tāntaē[nĕ ă]nĭmīs caēlēstĭbŭs īrae?

The elided syllable in 1.7 is long because the second syllable *al*- is long (the short *a*- being followed by the consonant cluster -*lt*-), whereas the elided syllable in 1.11 is short because the second syllable *a*- is short (containing a short vowel with only one consonant following); the actual classical pronunciation of elided syllables was variable, but here the pronunciations were probably *atqu'altae* and *tantaen'animīs*. Occasionally the conditions for elision will exist but the poet will choose for metrical or other purposes not to elide; this phenomenon is called "hiatus" (see definition and examples cited in PD below), from the Latin word for "gaping" or "yawning" (a very apt term, as the mouth would remain open from the vowel of the first word, across the minute intervening pause, and on through the vowel of the following word).

B. *Mark off the feet using the slash (/)*. In order to do so, one must, of course, recognize the particular metrical pattern in which the poem is composed; in the *Aeneid* and ancient epic generally the pattern followed is the dactylic hexameter (perhaps familiar to you from Ovid or the longer, hexameter lines of Catullus' and Martial's elegiac couplets).

This so-called "heroic" meter of epic consists of a six-foot line, with a dactyl (¯ ˘ ˘) in the first five feet and a spondee (¯ ¯) in the sixth (the last syllable of the line, even if apparently short, is to be regarded as long due to the natural pause occurring at the end of each verse). In any of the first four feet (rarely in the fifth), a spondee might be substituted for the characteristic dactyl, often slowing down the movement of the line for emphasis or some other special effect. The pattern may be schematized as follows:

$$\bar{}\ \smile\smile/\bar{}\ \smile\smile/\bar{}\ \smile\smile/\bar{}\ \smile\smile/\bar{}\ \smile\smile/\bar{}\ \bar{}$$

The opening line of the *Aeneid* would be marked as follows:

Ārmă vĭrūmquĕ cănō, Trōiae quī prīmŭs ăb ōrīs

A predominantly dactylic line may be used to suggest speed (see 1.45, 116, and 418 and the notes on those lines), while a heavily spondaic verse, as suggested above, often produces some kind of emphasis (1.32, 44, 157, and notes).

C. Mark the principal pause in each line, using a double slash (///). In longer lines of verse such as the dactylic hexameter, the rhythm was usually slowed by one or sometimes two major pauses that generally coincided with the close of some sense unit (i.e., the end of a phrase, a clause, or a sentence) and which, therefore, are often easily noted in a modern text by some mark of punctuation. More often than not the principal pause occurs within a foot, where it is called a "caesura," rather than at the end of a foot, where it is called a "diaeresis"; in fact, in classical Latin poetry, the majority of the word endings in a line are at caesurae, or, to put it another way, most words begin in one foot and continue over into the next, a deliberate device intended to interweave the feet more closely and prevent a choppy, sing-song effect. In Vergil's hexameters the principal pause is most commonly a caesura following the first syllable in the third foot, with the next commonest pattern a pair of such caesurae in the second and fourth feet. Since diaereses are less common, they are occasionally employed for special emphasis (see 1.52, 116, and notes).

Lines 55–57 of *Aeneid* One are fully scanned as follows:

Īl[lī īn]dīgnāntēs magnō cŭm mūrmŭrĕ mōntīs

cīrcūm claūstră frĕmūnt; cēlsā sĕdĕt Aēŏlŭs ārcē,

scēptră tĕnēns, mōllĭt[que a]nĭmōs ĕt tēmpĕrăt īrās.

Note: the common 3rd-foot caesurae in 55 and 56 and the 2nd/4th-foot caesurae in 57, setting off the clause *mollitque animos*.

Once you have worked out the scansion of a passage, you are ready to read it aloud. We know that the Romans, while not ignoring the actual word accent, gave additional stress to the first long syllable of each foot in a verse. It is a peculiarity of Latin poetry that this verse accent, or "ictus" (see PD below), did not always coincide with the normal word accent; "conflict" between ictus and accent (i.e., their occurrence on different syllables) was sometimes used by poets to underscore some physical violence or emotional discordance in the subject described (1.43, 53, and notes), and words were sometimes arranged so that the ictus would accentuate rhyming syllables (1.80, 87, and notes). In reading aloud, you should give at least some stress to the syllable bearing the ictus (i.e., the first syllable of each foot) as well as observe the long and short quantities and the principal pauses (i.e., the ends of phrases, clauses, and sentences). Vergil, like other classical Roman poets, tended to avoid an excess of end-stopped lines in favor of enjambed or "run-on" lines (see PD, "enjambement"); thus the reader should avoid an exaggerated pause at the end of a verse, unless it does in fact coincide with the end of a sense unit.

READING EXPRESSIVELY

The final step, and this is a challenge in reading English aloud as well as Latin, is to read expressively. The ancient poet, as we have noted already, wrote not only for educated readers but also for recitation, to entertain a listening audience: the poetry recitation was a performance and, if successful, an intellectually and emotionally stirring experience (the fourth-century commentator Donatus tells us that Augustus' sister Octavia fainted as Vergil himself dramatically recited a passage from *Aeneid* Six describing her deceased son Marcellus). The opposite could be true as well; Martial complains (in Epigram 1.34) of the infelicitous results when his own poems were recited by an inept reader:

> Quem recitas meus est, o Fidentine, libellus:
> sed male cum recitas, incipit esse tuus!

Poetry was performance, as this little epigram implies, and Vergil would never have recited his poetry in a sing-song monotone, but would have read dramatically, varying the tenor of his voice to suit the mood and giving proper emphasis to key words and phrases, speaking sometimes as narrator *in propria persona*, but often performing the roles of both Aeneas and Dido, of Jupiter and Juno, and of the many other characters who were his *dramatis personae*, just as would an actor in a play. You should approach each passage in this book by first reading it aloud, and as you complete a passage, once you have read and translated and discussed it and considered its every nuance, you should again read the passage aloud, one last time, rhythmically and expressively, in order to approximate as nearly as possible the effect intended by Vergil and, in the true sense of *recitatio*, to excite his verses back to life.

A NOTE TO STUDENTS ON THE USE OF THIS TEXT

Readers of this book are likely to have had at least some previous experience with Latin poetry, Catullus or Ovid or Martial perhaps, though possibly only selections included in a beginning or intermediate text. This volume, however, should serve even the newcomer to Latin verse: peculiarities of grammar, diction, and word-order, many of them surveyed above, are generally explained in the notes, at least at their initial occurrence, and most common poetic devices and figures of speech are defined below, along with references to representative examples in the text; your attention is drawn to grammatical terms and poetic devices by printing them in the notes in SMALL CAPITAL LETTERS LIKE THIS, and the definitions of such terms that you may not be familiar with should be learned at their first occurrence. Latin words likely to be unfamiliar are glossed in the facing notes, with an asterisk marking those that occur more than once in the book and which should therefore be memorized, and all words in the text (except those that appear only once and are glossed at that single occurrence) are listed in the end Vocabulary; lists of the Latin words occurring most frequently in this book follow the Vocabulary and should prove useful for study and review. Words or phrases set in *italics* in the notes indicate possible translations; quotation marks ("…"), on the other hand, generally indicate freer paraphrases, and you should still be prepared to provide a more literal translation, if called upon by your instructor to do so. The notes together with the discussion questions are designed to be complementary and are intended to assist readers with, and provoke your thinking about, matters of both interpretation and style; explanatory notes are more generously provided for the earlier selections and are sparser later on, when you are expected to be more conversant with the manner and matter of Vergil's poetry and where, accordingly, questions are more often asked of you than answered for you. Most place-names mentioned in the Latin text and notes appear on one of the four maps, specially designed to accompany this edition, which appear following this Introduction. Abbreviations employed in the notes and elsewhere in this book are listed at the end of this Introduction, and you should familiarize yourself with them before proceeding; and, finally, tables with paradigms of Latin verbs, nouns, adjectives, and other parts of speech are included at the back of the book for convenient reference.

It is our hope that, with the assistance of this text, you will very quickly become accustomed to Vergil's Latinity and the dynamics of his narrative. A final—and vital—word of advice is to read each assigned passage aloud, aloud and expressively, as Vergil intended them to be read; imagine an opera without music or your favorite film without its soundtrack, and you will have some idea of what is to be missed in only reading silently one of the most intensely dramatic and musical of Latin poets.

"Vergil's tomb" and Crypta Neapolitana:
columbarium and tunnel from Naples to Puteoli
Late Republic

MANTVA ME GENVIT, CALABRI RAPVERE, TENET NVNC
PARTHENOPE; CECINI PASCVA, RVRA, DVCES.

Vergil's "Epitaph"

POETIC, RHETORICAL, AND METRICAL DEVICES
AND FIGURES OF SPEECH

The following figures of speech and poetic and rhetorical devices occur in the selections from Vergil's poetry included in this book; definitions are followed by references to representative examples that appear early in the text, are commented upon in the notes, and should be analyzed as you review these definitions.

Allegory: a prolonged metaphor, i.e., a type of imagery involving the extended use of a person or object to represent some concept outside the literal narrative of a text (e.g., *Fama* or Rumor, *Aeneid* 4.173–97).

Alliteration: deliberate repetition of sounds, especially initial consonant sounds, in successive words, for musical (and occasionally onomatopoetic) effect (1.8, 16–17, 35).

Anaphora: repetition of words or phrases for emphasis (1.9–10, 16, 76); often with asyndeton (see below).

Anastrophe: the reversal of normal word order, as with a preposition following its object or a delayed conjunction, often with the effect of emphasizing the word(s) placed earlier (1.5, 13, 19).

Aposiopesis: a dramatic interruption in mid-sentence (1.135, 2.100).

Apostrophe: address to some person or thing not present, usually for emotional effect (1.97, 2.241–42).

Assonance: repetition of vowel or syllable sounds in successive words, for musical (and sometimes onomatopoetic) effect (1.80, 91, 117).

Asyndeton: omission of conjunctions where one or more would ordinarily be expected in a series of words or phrases; often employed in connection with anaphora (see above) and underscoring the words in the series (1.9–10, 16, 44); cf. polysyndeton below.

Bucolic Diaeresis: an emphatic pause between words between the fourth and fifth feet, relatively uncommon in Vergil and generally employed to emphasize the word immediately preceding or following (1.348, 502); see diaeresis below.

Caesura: a pause between words occurring within a metrical foot; the effect at the principal caesura in a line of verse (very often within the third foot, sometimes in both the second and fourth, in the dactylic hexameter) is sometimes to emphasize the word immediately preceding or following (1.11, 46); cf. diaeresis below.

Chiasmus: arrangement of words or phrases in an oppositional, ABBA order, often to emphasize some contrast or to create a word-picture (1.11, 51).

Dactyl: a metrical foot made up of one long syllable followed by two shorts; a series of dactyls in dactylic hexameter verse is sometimes employed to suggest rapid, abrupt, or violent action (1.45, 116, 418).

Diaeresis: a pause between words coinciding with the end of a metrical foot, less common than caesura and sometimes employed to emphasize the word immediately preceding or following (1.52, 116); see bucolic diaeresis above.

Diastole: lengthening of an ordinarily short vowel (and hence the syllable containing it), usually when it occurs under the ictus and before a caesura; sometimes reflecting an archaic pronunciation (1.8, 30); cf. systole below.

Ecphrasis: a digression from the main narrative but generally connecting to it thematically and sometimes describing a painting or other pictorial representation (1.159–69, 6.20—33).

Elision: suppression or contraction of a vowel (or a vowel plus -*m*) or diphthong at the end of a word before a word beginning with a vowel or a diphthong (or with *h-* plus a vowel or diphthong); the phenomenon generally reflects actual speech patterns, and it is a factor in the metrical scansion of a line of verse, where it is occasionally employed to suggest rapid action or for some other special effect (1.100, 109, 418, 2.172).

Ellipsis: omission of one or more words necessary to the sense of a sentence but easily understood from the context; often a form of the verb *sum* or a speech verb (1.11, 37).

Enjambement: delay of the final word or phrase of a sentence (or clause) to the beginning of the following verse, to emphasize an idea or image or to create suspense (1.4, 11).

Framing: enclosure of a line of verse by placing two closely connected words, often a noun and modifying adjective, at the beginning and end (1.15, 50).

Golden Line: a form of interlocked word order (see below) in which a verb is positioned in the middle of the verse, with adjectives preceding and nouns following in symmetrical arrangement (1.128, 291).

Hendiadys: use of two nouns connected by a conjunction (or occasionally a preposition), often instead of one modified noun expressing a single complex idea; the usual effect is to give equal prominence to an image that would ordinarily be subordinated, especially some quality of a person or thing (1.61, 293).

Hiatus: lack of elision where two syllables would ordinarily be elided, usually employed for emphasis at the end of a clause (1.16, 405).

Hyperbaton: separation of words that logically belong together, such as noun-adjective pairs, often for emphasis or to create a word-picture (1.36, 4.124 and 165, 12.941-42).

Hyperbole: emphatic overstatement of a point or a description (1.233, 2.439); cf. litotes below.

Hypermetric Line: a line of verse with an extra syllable at the end which elides with the first syllable of the following verse (1.332, 2.745).

Hysteron Proteron: description of events in an order reversing their logical sequence (2.259, 353).

Ictus: the verse accent, or beat, occurring on the first syllable of each foot in the dactylic hexameter; when the ictus coincides with the normal word accent, the rhythm flows more smoothly and rapidly, and when the two conflict (i.e., occur on different syllables) there is a more disjointed effect; assonance and other sound effects can be accentuated by carefully arranging words so that selected syllables fall under the ictus (1.7, 8, 16, 43).

Interlocked Word Order (Synchysis): arrangement of related pairs of words in an alternating ABAB pattern (e.g., adj. A / adj. B / noun A / noun B), often emphasizing the close connection between two thoughts or images (1.4, 132).

Irony: the use of language with a meaning opposite that suggested by the context (2.182, 309).

Litotes: a form of deliberate understatement, generally with a softening effect and often achieved through describing one quality by denying its opposite (1.387, 2.91); cf. hyperbole above.

Metaphor: an implied comparison, using one word for another that it suggests, usually with a visual effect (1.301, 2.20).

Metonymy: a type of imagery in which one word, generally a noun, is employed to suggest another with which it is closely related (1.1, 78).

Onomatopoeia: use of words whose sounds suggest their meaning or the general meaning of their immediate context (1.35, 51, 87).

Oxymoron: use of seemingly contradictory words within the same phrase or clause (2.269).

Personification: a type of imagery by which human traits are attributed to plants, animals, inanimate objects, or abstract ideas (1.51, 150).

Pleonasm: a purposefully redundant description, where more words are employed than needed (2.524, 4.276 and 277-78).

Polyptoton: repetition of a key word with changes in form, e.g., a noun with different case endings (1.325, 1.396).

Polysyndeton: use of a greater number of conjunctions than usual or necessary, often to emphasize the elements in a series (1.18, 87); cf. asyndeton above.

Praeteritio: suggesting that one will pass over a topic and then going on to mention it (4.43, 6.122).

Prolepsis: attribution of some characteristic to a person or thing before it is logically appropriate, especially application of a quality to a noun before the action of the verb has resulted in that quality (1.69, 6.181).

Prosopopoeia: representation of an absent or dead person, or even something inanimate (cf. personification above), as speaking or acting (Aeneas does this frequently, in narrating for Dido Troy's fall and his subsequent wanderings, in Books Two and Three; and cf. Vergil's depiction of Rumor in 4.173-97).

Rhetorical Question: a question, often exclamatory or expressing indignation, that is posed by a speaker but in fact expects no answer (1.37, 4.265).

Simile: an explicit comparison (often introduced by *ut, velut, qualis, ceu,* or *similis*) between one person or thing and another, the latter generally something more familiar to the reader (frequently a scene from nature) and thus more easily visualized; some of Vergil's similes are quite brief (1.82, 2.223–24), while others are extended and involve numerous and frequently complex points of comparison (1.148–56, 430–36).

Spondee: a metrical foot made up of two long syllables; a series of these in a dactylic hexameter line is sometimes used for emphasis or to suggest slow or ponderous or solemn action (1.32, 44, 157).

Syncope: omission of a short, unaccented vowel, reflecting contractions common in daily speech and often employed in poetry for metrical convenience (1.26, 249).

Synecdoche: a type of metonymy in which a part is named in place of an entire object, or a material for a thing made of that material, or an individual in place of a class (1.35, 69).

Synizesis: the running together or contraction of two vowels into a single syllable, often treating the vowels *i* and *u* as consonants (1.2, 41).

Systole: shortening of a vowel which was ordinarily long, sometimes reflecting an archaic pronunciation, and not ordinarily occurring when the syllable containing the vowel was under the ictus (1.16, 114); cf. diastole above.

Tmesis: separation of a compound word into its constituent parts, generally for metrical convenience (1.192, 412).

Transferred Epithet: application of an adjective to one noun when it properly applies to another, often involving personification and focusing special attention on the modified noun (1.4, 101).

Tricolon Crescens: a climactic series of three (or more) examples or illustrations, each (or at least the last) more fully developed or more intense than the preceding (1.99–101, 330–32).

Word-Picture: a type of imagery in which the words of a phrase are arranged in an order that visually suggests the image being described (1.52, 128).

Zeugma: use of a single word with a pair of others (e.g., a verb with two objects, an adjective with two nouns), when it logically applies to only one of them or applies to them both, but in two quite different ways (1.264, 315).

ABBREVIATIONS

The following abbreviations are employed in the notes and end Vocabulary:

(1)	regular first conjugation verb, with endings in *-ō, -āre, -āvī, -ātus*	impers.	impersonal
		impf.	imperfect tense
		ind.	indirect
(2)	regular second conjugation verb, with endings in *-eō, -ēre, -uī, -itus*	indecl.	indeclinable
		indef.	indefinite
		indic.	indicative mood
(4)	regular fourth conjugation verb, with endings in *-iō, -īre, -īvī, -ītus*	inf(s).	infinitive(s)
		interj(s).	interjection(s)
		interrog.	interrogative
abl.	ablative case	intrans.	intransitive
abs.	absolute	Lat.	Latin
acc.	accusative case	lit.	literally
act.	active voice	loc.	locative case
A.D.	after Christ (Lat. *anno Domini,* lit., *in the year of the Lord*)	m.	masculine gender
		med.	medieval
adj(s).	adjective(s), adjectival	ms(s).	manuscript(s)
adv(s).	adverb(s), adverbial	n.	neuter gender
anteced(s).	antecedent(s)	nom.	nominative (case)
appos.	appositive, apposition, appositional	obj(s).	object(s), objective
		partic(s).	participle(s)
B.C.	before Christ	pass.	passive voice
ca.	about (Lat. *circa*)	perf.	perfect tense
C.E.	Christian era	pers.	person, personal
cent.	century	pl.	plural
cf.	compare (Lat. *confer*)	plpf.	pluperfect tense
cl(s).	clause(s)	pred.	predicate
class.	classical	prep(s).	preposition(s), prepositional
compar.	comparative	pres.	present tense
compl.	complement, complementary	pron(s).	pronoun(s)
conj(s).	conjunction(s)	quest(s).	question(s)
dat.	dative case	ref.	reference
decl.	declension	reflex.	reflexive
dir.	direct	rel.	relative
eccl.	ecclesiastical	sc.	supply, namely (Lat. *scilicet*)
e.g.	for example (Lat. *exempli gratia*)	sent(s).	sentence(s)
Eng.	English	sg.	singular
esp.	especially	state(s).	statement(s)
etc.	and others (Lat. *et cetera*)	subj(s).	subject(s), subjective
f.	feminine gender; (after numerals) and following	subjunct.	subjunctive mood
		superl.	superlative
fut.	future tense	trans.	transitive
gen.	genitive case	vb(s).	verb(s)
hist.	historical	voc.	vocative case
i.e.	that is (Lat. *id est*)	vs.	as opposed to, in comparison with (Lat. *versus*)
imper.	imperative		

MAPS

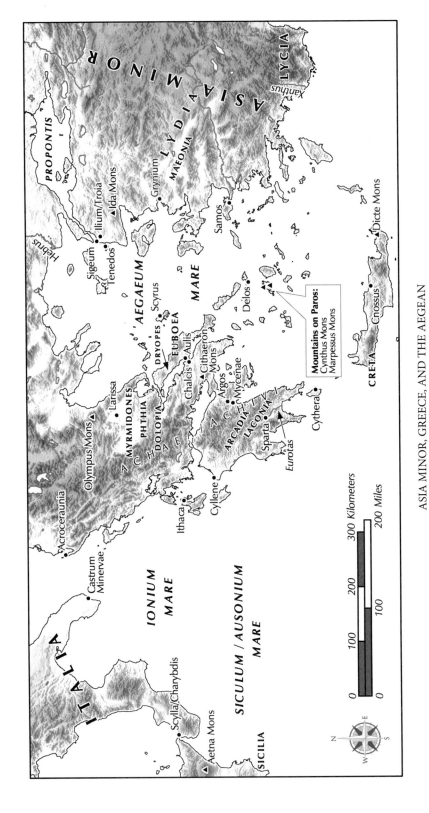

ASIA MINOR, GREECE, AND THE AEGEAN

All maps by Richard A. LaFleur, Rachel Barckhaus, Tom Elliott, and Jeffrey Becker; copyright 2012, Ancient World Mapping Center.
Please visit the AWMC via The University of North Carolina Chapel Hill website for additional information and free downloads.

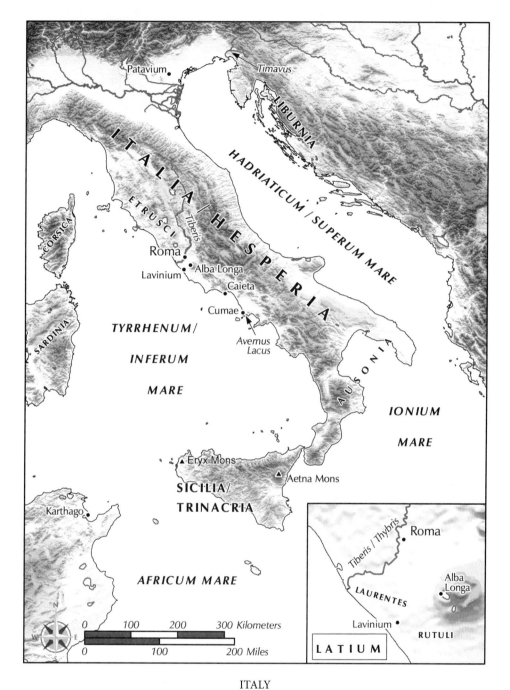

Patavium

Timavus

LIBURNIA

ITALIA / HESPERIA

HADRIATICUM / SUPERUM MARE

ETRUSCI

Tiberis

Roma

Lavinium • Alba Longa

Caieta

CORSICA

Cumae

Avernus
Lacus

TYRRHENUM /

SARDINIA

INFERUM

MARE

AUSONIA

IONIUM

MARE

Eryx Mons

Aetna Mons

SICILIA /
TRINACRIA

Karthago

AFRICUM MARE

0   100   200   300 Kilometers

0   100   200 Miles

N
W   E
S

Inset:

Tiberis / Thybris

Roma

Alba
Longa

LAURENTES

Lavinium

RUTULI

LATIUM

ITALY
*All maps by Richard A. LaFleur, Rachel Barckhaus, Tom Elliott, and Jeffrey Becker; copyright 2012,
Ancient World Mapping Center. Please visit the AWMC via The University of North Carolina Chapel
Hill website for additional information and free downloads.*

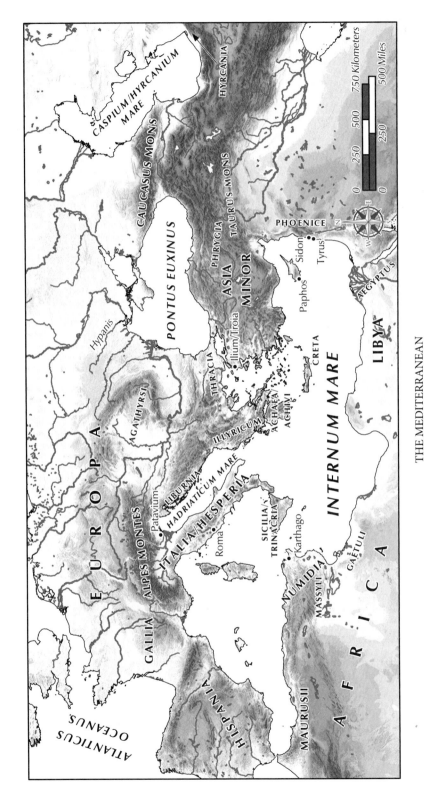

THE MEDITERRANEAN

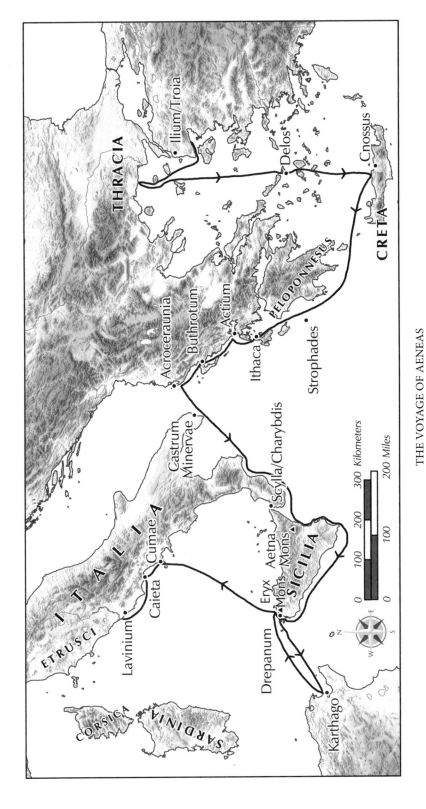

THE VOYAGE OF AENEAS

All maps by Richard A. LaFleur, Rachel Barckhaus, Tom Elliott, and Jeffrey Becker; copyright 2012, Ancient World Mapping Center.
Please visit the AWMC via The University of North Carolina Chapel Hill website for additional information and free downloads.

Aeneid BOOK I

(Verses 1–578)

VERGIL'S proclamation in the opening verse of his prologue to *Aeneid* One that he sings of "arms and the man" signals the content of his epic: his song is of war and a hero, the Trojan Aeneas, whose destiny is to become essentially founder of Rome and, indeed, the first Roman. However, the poet's appeal to his Muse (lines 8–11) also highlights other important themes, the violent nature of men and gods and the question of divine justice and deserved, or undeserved, suffering, the perennial problem of Greek tragedy. Why do bad things happen to good people? Following the prologue, Vergil immediately commences his story and includes a prophecy that anticipates the ultimate consequences of his hero's adventures. Thus we know in advance, in broad outline at least, the outcome of the epic action: our interest and entertainment reside not so much in the externals of the plot, but in the stirring drama that will unfold in the poem's 12 books.

The action begins with a storm at sea, devised by Juno, who is resolutely opposed to the Trojans and means to obstruct Aeneas' destiny, in this instance with the collaboration of Aeolus, lord of the winds. Neptune's intervention calms the storm, just as an exemplary statesman might pacify a civil insurrection, and the surviving Trojans land safely on the central coast of North Africa (modern Tunisia). Aeneas' mother, Venus, confronts Jupiter on her son's behalf to gain reassurances regarding Aeneas' destiny, and later, in disguise, she counsels her son on proper procedures in an alien land where Dido rules the rising city of Carthage. The Trojans are courteously received by the young queen; Venus' son, Cupid ("Desire"), replaces Aeneas' son, Ascanius (known also as Iulus), at a gala banquet; and, upon Dido's request, Aeneas consents to relate his adventures both to enlighten her and to entertain the assembly.

Vergil's epic begins *in medias res* by exploring Juno's hatred of the Trojans for past insults and her readiness to obstruct Aeneas' progress to fated Italy by a storm at sea. Aeolus, ruler of the winds, is seduced into unleashing a hurricane against the Trojan ships; one vessel is lost and the rest are scattered. Neptune, irritated by the trespass against his realm, sends the winds scurrying back to their ruler and calms the sea. Aeneas recovers seven of his ships and comes safely ashore in an unknown, somewhat threatening harbor. While he explores the terrain, he comes upon and kills seven deer to provide a consoling and restorative banquet for his sailors.

Juno's ties with Punic Carthage are underlined in her opposition to the Trojans' destiny. Her recourse to courteous and deferential Aeolus (Greek *aiolos* means "variable, shifty") befits her role as goddess of the air, and her promise of a bride reflects her role as goddess of marriage. Aeneas is first introduced during the storm, terror stricken and regretful that his heroic career will end with his drowning as victim of a massive assault by the elements. So Vergil wins our respect for the hero and our regret for his suffering. The simile of the statesman, which introduces Neptune as peacemaker, contains elements that reflect important facets of the epic: *furor*, which applies to nature and to human nature, the impulse to madness, particularly of civil war and human error, and *pietas*, which is embodied in the unidentified statesman, the fidelity of the ideal leader to family, state, and the gods. The deer hunt staged by Aeneas right after his arrival in Tunisia is token of Aeneas' *pietas* toward his crews and his awareness of their needs, but it also serves to foreshadow "martial" and aggressive aspects of the Dido and Aeneas episode. Love and the hunt are repeatedly accented in the account of their amorous liaison: but which one is the hunter and which one is the quarry? Is Dido the huntress— like Diana in her simile, and like the "uniformed" huntress in Book Four, Venus in disguise—searching for a husband? Or is Aeneas the hunter, in pursuit of a city, romance, and adventure? The shipwreck and the divinely engineered rescue in the preface to the African episode parallel the disastrous fall of Troy and the divinely directed evacuation of Aeneas' family and their fellow refugees by Venus, Jupiter, and a transformed Creusa in Book Two.

The Storm, woodcut from a 1664 French translation of the *Aeneid*

The scene-shift to Olympus, a "cinematic" device that Vergil employs frequently, always marking an important crux in the story and a staple of the epic tradition, confirms Aeneas' mission with an optimistic vision of a new Golden Age where Rome's destiny will be consummated: a promise of conquest, civilization, and peace. We begin to appreciate that world order must rest on suffering and sacrifice, and we are led to anticipate that Aeneas will experience both. The dispatch of Mercury, son of Jupiter and Maia, to ensure that Dido will receive the Trojans hospitably is a reminder that the Carthaginians were xenophobic. Intrusions into their territory were resisted with determination and the force of their celebrated naval resources. The appearance of Venus reminds us that Aeneas has divine associations and so a guaranteed apotheosis some day. Like any nurturing mother, the goddess reassures her son after hearing his complaints. Impersonating a huntress, and wearing boots that are intended to recall the elevated shoes of tragic performers, she provides a prologue to the impending tragedy by relating details of Dido's marriage to Sychaeus, the murder of her husband by her brother, the royal treasure hidden and revealed, her flight with sympathizers from Sidon, the tricky purchase of property (Byrsa), and her constitutional settlement at Carthage. The omen of the swans, sacred to Venus, and so appropriately interpreted by her, forecasts the return of the 12 ships lost in the storm, and is typical of the omens and prodigies that appear frequently in the poem.

Aeneas and his faithful comrade Achates, rendered invisible for safety's sake by Venus, marvel at the grandeur of the rising city, its evident prosperity, its display of engineering prowess and cultural sophistication. Scenes of the Trojan War (technically speaking, an *ecphrasis*, a pictorial digression) displayed in the compound of the Temple of Juno excite wonder and sorrow. The gallery's contents foreshadow comparable situations in the "Iliadic" *Aeneid,* Books Seven–Twelve, where another "Trojan" war must be fought in order to gain Latium. We should remind ourselves that Juno (= the Carthaginian goddess Tanit) occupies the temple, and that her patronage and services extended to Greeks, not Trojans, at Troy. Although Aeneas seems relieved to find that his past history and trials are known and so anticipates sympathy and assistance from Carthage, in fact the temple honors the deity who was Aeneas' most vengeful enemy and depicts her role in the Greek victory at Troy. Aeneas misreads the "message": the sanctuary murals are not designed to highlight Trojan *virtus,* but instead reveal that Dido and her people are naturally hostile toward the Trojans (297–304). Dido's entrance, associated with the dazzling Diana simile, features an interview with Ilioneus, "man of Ilium" (i.e., of Troy), who represents Aeneas' lost but reassembled companions. Aeneas and Achates finally become visible, and formal introductions ensue (520–656). Sympathy, humanity, and mutual understanding are in the foreground of this initial encounter between Trojans and Carthaginians. Mercury's mission to pacify any aggressive reaction by Dido has been successful, and Aeneas plans to introduce his son Ascanius bearing gifts for the queen. Because Venus is distressed to have her own son in Juno's "hostile" city, she substitutes Cupid ("Desire") for Ascanius in order to induce Dido to fall in love with the Prince Charming, and so win security for Aeneas. A palace banquet, entertainment, and libations to the gods are provided by the hospitable and beautiful young queen and her court, including a "scientific" recital by Iopas, the Punic minstrel, whose song may be meant to reflect the Epicurean, pleasure-loving nature of Dido's court (657–747). At the book's close, the ill-fated queen (*infelix Dido* the narrator calls her at verse 749), already infatuated with Aeneas, invites him to provide a recital of his misfortunes and wanderings (Books Two and Three) to her Carthaginian and Trojan guests.

"Aeneas Presents Cupid in the Clothes of Ascanius to Dido"
Giambattista Tiepolo (1696–1770)
Villa Valmarana, Vicenza, Italy

1 ***arma, -ōrum,** n. pl., *weapons, arms;* here, by METONYMY (for this and other
  figures of speech and poetic and rhetorical devices, consult the list of
  definitions in the general Introduction), *war, warfare, violence.* Homer's
  Iliad likewise began with a word for violence, a major theme of that epic as
  of the *Aeneid.*
  virum: Aeneas, who is not actually referred to by name until line 92; Vergil's
   characterization of the Trojan prince in these opening verses deliberately
   recalls Homer's introduction of Odysseus (Ulysses) in the very beginning of
   his *Odyssey,* which similarly opened with the word for "man" or "hero."
  canō: Vergil's use of this verb (vs. **recitō**) again looks back to Homer's epics,
   which originally were sung or chanted to musical accompaniment.
  Trōiae: with **ōrīs;** in Lat. poetry nouns in the gen. case, like adjs. and advs., are
   often separated from the words they modify.
  ***ōra, -ae,** f., *border, edge; coast, shore; region, land.*
2 **Ītaliam:** sc. **ad** here and with **Lāvīnia . . . lītora;** preps. usual in Lat. prose,
   including those indicating PLACE TO WHICH (as here) and other place
   constructions, are often omitted in verse. The word's initial **I-,** ordinarily
   short, is scanned long in epic verse to fit the dactylic meter.
  fātō: ABL. OF CAUSE; destiny is another pervasive theme of the *Aeneid.*
  profugus, -ī, m., *fugitive, refugee.*
  ***Lāvīnius, -a, -um,** *Lavinian, of Lavinium* (a large town south of Rome important
   during the early Republic).
  Lāvīnia: According to tradition, Lavinium was founded by Aeneas near the site
   where he and his followers first landed in Latium and named after the Latin
   princess Lavinia, whom he ultimately made his bride; with SYNIZESIS of
   the **-ia** the word is here scanned as a trisyllable (some mss. and editors read
   Lāvīna here).
3 ***lītus, lītoris,** n., *seashore, coast.*
  multum: with **iactātus,** which itself is neatly FRAMED by the modifying phrases
   et (in) terrīs . . . et (in) altō.
  ille: like **profugus** (2), in appos. with **quī** (1).
  terrīs: Lat. poets often employ pl. for sg. (the so-called "poetic pl.") and
   vice-versa.
  ***iactō (1),** *to throw, cast; to drive back and forth, toss about, torment; to talk/think*
   about; to brag about, show off, flaunt oneself.
  altō: here, as often, *the deep, the sea.*
4 ***superus, -a, -um,** *above, upper, higher;* m. pl. as noun, *gods.*
  vī superum: ENJAMBED for emphasis; **vī** is ABL. OF CAUSE and **superum** is an
   archaic gen. pl. form, common in epic, = **superōrum.**
  saevae . . . īram: INTERLOCKED WORD ORDER (SYNCHYSIS), a favorite device in
   Lat. poetry; Juno's hostility toward the Trojans (the reasons for which are
   related in 12–28) represents a dominant force in the story.
  ***memor, memoris,** *keeping in memory, mindful, unforgetting.*
  memorem: a TRANSFERRED EPITHET, modifying **īram** but logically applying to
   Iūnōnis.
  ***Iūnō, Iūnōnis,** f., *Juno* (queen of the gods, sister and wife of Jupiter; identified
   with the Greek Hera, she was goddess of childbirth and protectress of
   women, and, of course, nemesis of the Trojans).

PROLOGUE: *Vergil announces his subject*

1   Arma virumque canō, Trōiae quī prīmus ab ōrīs
2 Ītaliam fātō profugus Lāvīniaque vēnit
3 lītora—multum ille et terrīs iactātus et altō
4 vī superum, saevae memorem Iūnōnis ob īram,

Vergil and the Muses Calliope and Melpomene, 3rd century C.E.
Roman mosaic Musée National du Bardo, Tunis, Tunisia

5 **et:** delayed here (ANASTROPHE), the conj. properly introduces **multa . . . passus** and links that phrase with the earlier partic. **iactātus.**

*patior, patī, passus sum, to suffer, endure.

*condō, condere, condidī, conditus, to put into, store (up); to hide; to found, establish.

dum conderet: until he could found; **dum** in this sense takes an ANTICIPATORY SUBJUNCT., here with the added force of a PURPOSE CL.

urbem: Lavinium.

6 **deōs:** Aeneas brought with him from Troy the state's tutelary gods, the Penates (line 68 below), entrusted to him by the ghost of the Trojan prince Hector.

genus . . . Rōmae (7): sc. **sunt;** for the delay of **unde,** see note on **et** (5).

7 **Albānus, -a, -um*, Alban, of Alba (Alba Longa, a city south of Rome and east of Lavinium—for these and most of the placenames mentioned in this book, see the maps following the general Introduction).

Albānī . . . patrēs: Vergil means the country's *founding fathers,* and perhaps specifically the traditional ancestors of Rome's patrician families. After Aeneas' death, his son Ascanius founded Alba Longa, where, according to tradition, their descendants ruled for three centuries before establishing a new settlement at Rome.

altae moenia Rōmae: the DIAERESES and coincidence of ictus and accent in the second half of the line add emphasis to the majestic climax of the poet's lengthy opening pronouncement.

8 **Mūsa:** invoking a Muse for inspiration was a convention of ancient verse from Homer onward; Calliope, though unnamed here, was foremost of the nine Muses and the patron deity of epic. ALLITERATION contributes to the line's musicality.

mihī: the short final -**i** in this and other words is often lengthened in verse, esp. in a syllable falling under the ictus (DIASTOLE).

*memorō (1), to speak, say; to speak of as, call, name; to tell about, narrate; to remind, call to mind.

Mūsa . . . memorā: Mnemosyne, mother of the Muses, was goddess of memory.

*nūmen, nūminis, n., divine power, divine will, divine sanction; divinity, godhead; divine presence.

*laedō, laedere, laesī, laesus, to injure, harm; to displease, offend.

quō nūmine laesō: freely, *with what offense to her divinity;* but what is the lit. translation of this ABL. ABS.?

9 **deum:** for the form, see above on **superum** (4).

*volvō, volvere, voluī, volūtus, to move in a curved course, bring/turn around, roll; to unroll (a scroll), spin out (a thread); to turn around in the mind; to undergo.

cāsus, -ūs, m., falling, fall; accident, chance; event; misfortune, disaster, risk.

tot volvere cāsūs / . . . tot adīre labōrēs (10): ANAPHORA, ASYNDETON, and the parallelism of the two similarly positioned inf. phrases (both objs. of **rēgina . . . impulerit** and each with **virum** as subj.) emphasize the gravity of Aeneas' suffering.

5 multa quoque et bellō passus, dum conderet urbem
6 īnferretque deōs Latiō—genus unde Latīnum
7 Albānīque patrēs atque altae moenia Rōmae.

The poet invokes his divine Muse

8   Mūsa, mihī causās memorā, quō nūmine laesō
9 quidve dolēns rēgīna deum tot volvere cāsūs

Quaestiōnēs

1. In addition to the themes of violence and destiny, what several other thematic elements (which, as you will see, are central to the narrative's development) are mentioned or alluded to in lines 1–7? Which might be said to look backward to Homer and Troy and which look forward to Rome?

2. Though some readers view **altae** (7) as a transferred epithet, properly applying to **moenia,** in what ways can the term be seen here as an appropriate characterization of Rome?

"Virgil's Muse"
Jean-Baptiste Corot
(1796–1875)
Louvre, Paris, France

10 ***īnsignis, -is, -e**, *clearly visible, conspicuous; remarkable, noteworthy, outstanding.*
    ***pietās, pietātis**, f., *dutiful respect, devotion* (to the gods, family, country).
      pietāte: ABL. OF SPECIFICATION; Vergil characterizes Aeneas as **pius** throughout
        the poem.

11 ***impellō, impellere, impulī, impulsus**, *to strike (against); to drive, push, impel.*
    impulerit: subjunct. in IND. QUEST. The ENJAMBEMENT both emphasizes
      the preceding statement and, with the strong CAESURA and full stop that
      follow, prepares us for the question posed next by the narrator—a profound
      philosophical question that is central to the epic, i.e., are the gods truly
      susceptible to such human passions as anger and vengefulness?
    Tantaene . . . īrae: SC. **sunt;** ELLIPSIS, esp. of the vb. **esse,** is common in poetry.
      The CHIASMUS delays **īrae** to line's end, both for suspense and to echo the
      identically positioned **īram** in verse 4. The effect of the pl. here is to suggest
      the wide range of the gods' wrathful emotions and actions and their repeated
      outbursts of anger.
    animīs: DAT. OF POSSESSION, *do divine minds have . . ..*
    *****caelestis, -is, -e**, *in the sky, from the sky; celestial, heavenly, divine;* as a noun, *god,*
        goddess.

12 *****Tyrius, -a, -um**, *Tyrian, of Tyre* (a major city on the coast of Phoenicia).
    tenuēre: = **tenuērunt;** this alternate perf. tense form is common in poetry.
    colōnus, -ī, m., *farmer; settler, colonist.*
    Tyriī . . . colōnī: according to tradition, Carthage was settled by Phoenician
      colonists in the 9th cent. B.C., thus producing an anachronism here, since the
      traditional date for the Trojan War was 400 years earlier.

13 *****Karthāgō, Karthāginis**, f., *Carthage* (capital of the Phoenician settlement in
      North Africa, in modern Tunisia).
    Karthāgō, Ītaliam: a deliberately pointed juxtaposition.
    contrā: governs both **Ītaliam** (ANASTROPHE, common in poetry, esp. with
      disyllabic preps.) and **ōstia.**
    Tiberīnus, -a, -um, *of the Tiber river.*

14 *****ōstium, -ī**, n., *door; opening; mouth* (of a river or harbor).
    *****ops, opis**, f., *power, ability; resources, riches* (often pl.); *aid, assistance.*
    opum: GEN. OF SPECIFICATION; Eng. would say *in resources.*
    *****asper, -pera, -perum**, *rough; sharp, thorny; violent, fierce, cruel, savage.*

15   **quam . . . terrīs . . . omnibus ūnam:** obj. of **coluisse;** the arrangement, a
    CHIASMUS with the rel. pron. **quam** and its modifier **ūnam** *(alone)* FRAMING
    the line, underscores the point.
    fertur: *is said,* a frequent sense of the vb. in Vergil.

10   īnsignem pietāte virum, tot adīre labōrēs
11   impulerit. Tantaene animīs caelestibus īrae?

Setting the stage: Carthage and the wrath of Juno

12   Urbs antīqua fuit (Tyriī tenuēre colōnī)
13   Karthāgō, Ītaliam contrā Tiberīnaque longē
14   ōstia, dīves opum studiīsque asperrima bellī,
15   quam Iūnō fertur terrīs magis omnibus ūnam

Quaestiō

Why is the juxtaposition **omnibus ūnam** (15) especially effective?

This book is not about heroes. English poetry is not yet fit to speak of them. Nor is it about deeds, or lands, nor anything about glory, honour, might, majesty, dominion, or power, except war. Above all I am not concerned with Poetry. My subject is War, and the Pity of War. The poetry is in the pity. Yet these elegies are to this generation in no sense consolatory. They may be in the next. All a poet can do today is warn. That is why the true Poets must be truthful.

Wilfred Owen, killed in action in France, November 11, 1918,
from the preface to a planned book of verse,
Disabled and Other Poems

16 **posthabeō (2)**, *to subordinate, esteem less, regard as inferior.*
    coluisse: here *to have cherished;* with **fertur.**
    Samos, -ī, f., *Samos* (an island off the coast of Asia Minor, birthplace of Juno and an important cult center).
    posthabitā . . . Samō: ABL. ABS.
    Samō. Hīc: HIATUS, allowed in particular at a full stop, as here, where the effect is an esp. dramatic pause.
    Hīc . . . / hīc . . . hoc (17): ANAPHORA and ASYNDETON are often employed together; **hoc,** which refers to f. **urbs,** is n. by attraction to **rēgnum.**
    illius: the second -i- is shortened here, and often, when not under the ictus (SYSTOLE).

17 *****currus, -ūs,** m., *chariot.*
    rēgnum: PRED. NOUN with **hoc . . . esse,** the entire phrase being an IND. STATE. depending on **tenditque fovetque.**
    gentibus: DAT. OF REF.

18 *****quā,** adv., *where, by which route; by any chance, in any way.*
    *****tendō, tendere, tetendī, tentus** or **tēnsus,** *to extend (outward, upward), stretch out, spread out; to stretch back, pull tight, draw* (a bow); *to direct, aim (for), make one's way (toward).*
    *****foveō, fovēre, fōvī, fōtus,** *to keep warm; to comfort, soothe; to cherish* (a hope *that,* + acc. + inf.).
    tenditque fovetque: a type of POLYSYNDETON common in epic, used to link closely related words; the pres. is often used with **iam** where in Eng. we would employ a past tense.

19 *****prōgeniēs, -ēī,** f., *offspring, progeny; race, family, lineage.*
    sed: conjs. are often delayed as here, a type of ANASTROPHE.
    *****enim,** conj., *for;* after **sed,** *indeed, in fact.*
    dūcī / . . . / ventūrum (esse) . . . volvere (22): all infs. in IND. STATE. depending on **audierat.**

20 **audierat:** = **audīverat;** such perf. system forms, with loss of intervocalic -v- and loss or shortening of an adjacent vowel, are common in poetry.
    Tyriās . . . arcēs: again, separation of adj. and noun and delay of a connecting word (conj., rel. pron.) are peculiarities of word order common to Lat. verse; the prose order of this cl. would be **quae arcēs Tyriās ōlim verteret.** The allusion, of course, is to Rome's defeat of Carthage in the Punic Wars and the final destruction of the city in 146 B.C.
    verteret: subjunct. in a REL. CL. OF PURPOSE, = **ēverteret,** *would overturn;* poetry often uses a simple vb. form where prose would have a compound.

21 *****hinc,** adv., *from this* (place, person, time, thing—here **Trōiānō ā sanguine**), *hence; next, then.*
    *****lātē,** adv., *over a wide area, widely, far and wide* (here modifying the verbal idea in **rēgem** = **regnantem**).
    rēgem: in appos. with **populum,** *as ruler.*

16 posthabitā coluisse Samō. Hīc illius arma,
17 hīc currus fuit; hoc rēgnum dea gentibus esse,
18 sī quā fāta sinant, iam tum tenditque fovetque.
19 Prōgeniem sed enim Trōiānō ā sanguine dūcī
20 audierat Tyriās ōlim quae verteret arcēs;
21 hinc populum lātē rēgem bellōque superbum

Hera (Juno) Ludovisi
5th cent. B.C.
Museo Nazionale Romano
delle Terme, Rome, Italy

22 *excidium, -ī, n., *(military) destruction* (here DAT. OF PURPOSE).

*Libya, -ae, f., *North Africa, Libya* (here, as often, = Carthage).

Parca, -ae, f., *Parca* (a Roman goddess of birth); pl., *the Fates.*

volvere Parcās: the Fates (Clotho, Lachesis, and Atropos) were often depicted spinning thread for the tapestry of a person's life or of the future in general; or the allusion here may be to unrolling the book (volūmen) of fate.

23 *metuō, metuere, metuī, metūtus, *to fear, be afraid of; to view with alarm.*

veteris . . . bellī: i.e., the Trojan War, which had ended several years earlier (as indicated in 31–32).

memor: a deliberate echo of memorem (4); Juno is unforgetting and unforgiving.

*Sāturnius, -a, -um, *of Saturn* (an ancient Roman god identified with the Greek deity Kronos), *of the Saturnian age* (the first Golden Age); as an epithet of the gods, the m. usually = Jupiter, the f. = Juno.

Sāturnia: subj. of arcēbat (31), following the long intervening parenthesis in 25–28.

24 *Argī, -ōrum, m. pl., *Argives* (citizens of Argos in southern Greece, site of a major temple to Juno), *Greeks.*

prīma . . . Argīs: Juno had supported the Greeks in the Trojan War; prīma here perhaps points to her leading role among the gods who opposed Troy, and it certainly has a temporal sense, suggesting that this opposition was but the initial stage in her ongoing persecution of the Trojans.

25 necdum, conj., *and not (even) yet.*

saevī: the theme of savagery recurs throughout the poem, and this adj. is frequently applied not only to Juno (cf. saevae 4) but also to Aeneas.

26 *excidō, excidere, excidī, *to fall from, fall off, drop out.*

manet: sg. (instead of the unmetrical manent), in agreement with the first of its four subjs.

*mēns, mentis, f., *mind, heart; purpose, design; frame of mind, attitude; will.*

altā mente: sc. in (and for the omitted prep., see note on Ītaliam 2).

*repōnō, repōnere, reposuī, repositus or (by SYNCOPE) repostus, *to put back, replace; to restore; to put/store away; to put/lay down.*

27 iūdicium, -ī, n., *legal proceeding, trial; judgment, decision, verdict.*

*Paris, Paridis, m., *Paris* (a Trojan prince, son of king Priam).

iūdicium Paridis: when the goddess Discord brought to the wedding of Peleus and Thetis (Achilles' parents) a golden apple inscribed "For the loveliest," Paris decided the apple should go, not to the other contestants Juno or Minerva, but to Venus, who had promised him the most beautiful mortal woman as his own bride; Paris later claimed his prize, Helen, wife of the Greek king Menelaus, seducing her from her husband and thus precipitating the Trojan war.

*spernō, spernere, sprēvī, sprētus, *to dissociate* (from); *to reject with scorn, spurn, disregard.*

sprētae . . . fōrmae: APPOSITIONAL GEN.

*iniūria, -ae, f., *unlawful conduct; injustice, a wrong; injury; insult.*

22 ventūrum excidiō Libyae; sīc volvere Parcās.
23 Id metuēns veterisque memor Sāturnia bellī,
24 prīma quod ad Trōiam prō cārīs gesserat Argīs
25 (necdum etiam causae īrārum saevīque dolōrēs
26 exciderant animō: manet altā mente repostum
27 iūdicium Paridis sprētaeque iniūria fōrmae

"The Judgment of Paris"
Triptych, 1885–87
Max Klingner (1857–1920)
Oesterreichische Galerie, Vienna, Austria

28 *invīsus, -a, -um, *hateful, hated, odious, disliked.*
    genus invīsum: an allusion to Dardanus, ancestor of the Trojan kings, who
        was Jupiter's son by Electra (daughter of Atlas) and the most beloved of his
        illegitimate children.
    Ganymēdēs, Ganymēdis, m., *Ganymede* (son of Troy's founder, Tros).
    raptī Ganymēdis: admiring the young man's beauty, Zeus (in the form of an
        eagle in some versions of the tale) had carried him off to Olympus and
        installed him there as cupbearer to the gods, in place of Juno's daughter Hebe;
        in later myth the story takes on homoerotic associations, a further cause for
        Juno's annoyance.

29 **hīs accēnsa:** the phrase parallels **id metuēns** (23) and restores the connection to
    the subj. **Sāturnia,** which had been interrupted by the parenthetical details in
    25–28 (to which **hīs** refers); the vb. **accendere** is used frequently throughout
    the poem of intense and often violent passions.
    *super, adv., *over, above; in addition, besides.*

30 *Trōs, Trōis,** nom. pl. **Trōes,** acc. pl. (a Greek form) **Trōas,** *a Trojan;* specifically
    Troy's eponymous founder, *Tros.*
    reliquiae, -ārum, f. pl., *remnants, remains; survivors; vestiges, traces.*
    rēliquiās: the **-e-** is lengthened here under the ictus (DIASTOLE); the word
        otherwise, with three successive short syllables, could not be used in dactylic
        hexameter verse.
    *Danaī, Danaum** or **Danaōrum,** m. pl., *Danaans* (descendants of Danaus,
        legendary king of Argos, the name was commonly used of the Greeks in the
        Trojan War).
    immītis, -is, -e, *bitter, sour; harsh, merciless.*
    *Achillēs, Achillis** or **Achillī,** m., *Achilles* (son of Peleus and Thetis, Greek
        chieftain in the Trojan War and hero of Homer's *Iliad*).
    Danaum . . . Achillī: SUBJ. GEN.; i.e., with **rēliquiās,** those whom the Greeks and
        Achilles had left (alive).

31 *arceō, arcēre, arcuī,** *to hold in, control, restrain; to keep away, repulse.*
    Latiō: ABL. OF SEPARATION.

32 **errābant . . . fātīs:** the slow opening spondees add gravity to the line.
    maria . . . circum: ANASTROPHE.

33 **Tantae mōlis erat:** characteristic of Lat. poetry is this use of the PRED. GEN. in
    place of a PRED. NOM.; lit., *it was of so great a mass,* but freely, *so massive a
    task it was.*
    Tantae . . . gentem: the one-line sentence, with its heavy coincidence of ictus and
    accent (cf. on line 7), the echo of **conderet urbem** identically positioned in
    5, and the return to the theme of Rome's foundation, all effectively punctuate
    the close of Vergil's prologue.

34 *cōnspectus, -ūs,** m., *sight, view; appearance; contemplation.*
    *Siculus, -a, -um,** *of Sicily, Sicilian.*
    *tellūs, tellūris,** f., *ground, earth; land, country.*

28 et genus invīsum et raptī Ganymēdis honōrēs)—
29 hīs accēnsa super iactātōs aequore tōtō
30 Trōas, rēliquiās Danaüm atque immītis Achillī,
31 arcēbat longē Latiō; multōsque per annōs
32 errābant, āctī fātīs maria omnia circum.
33 Tantae mōlis erat Rōmānam condere gentem.

*The story begins: as the Trojans depart from Sicily en route to
their destined goal of Latium, Juno expresses her outrage*

34   Vix ē cōnspectū Siculae tellūris in altum

Quaestiōnēs

1. What several reasons does the narrator give in lines 12–28 for Juno's hostility
   toward the Trojans?

2. Vergil is fond of tripartite structure. Comment on each of the three parts of
   the prologue (1–33): What are the specific functions of each division? What
   character appears in all three parts? Where are the two most explicit references
   to the founding of the city of Rome and how are they emphatically positioned?

3. Identify the several references to fate in the prologue (1–33) and discuss what
   at this point in the narrative appears to be its power vis-a-vis the actions of men
   and gods.

"The Three Fates"
Pietro della Vecchia
(1608–78)
Galleria Estense,
Modena, Italy

35 *vēlum, -ī, n., *sail; sheet, awning, cloth;* idiom, (**ventīs**) **vēla dare,** *to expose one's sails (to the winds), to sail.*
   dabant laetī: sc. **Trōiānī** as subj.; Lat. often uses an adj. where in Eng. translation one might employ an adv. (here *happily*). With the prologue concluded, the narrative opens abruptly (**in mediās rēs,** as Horace observed was typical of epic) with the Trojans seemingly close to reaching their destined goal of Italy.
   spūma, -ae, f., *foam, froth* (esp. of the sea).
   spūmās salis: Eng. would say "salty foam," but in Lat. verse it is common to modify one noun with another rather than with an adj.; the ALLITERATIVE (and perhaps deliberately ONOMATOPOETIC) phrase here stands for the sea (SYNECDOCHE).
   *aes, aeris,** n., *bronze; a bronze implement* (here another SYNECDOCHE for the bronze prows of the Trojan ships).
   *ruō, ruere, ruī,** *to rush; to rush wildly, charge; to collapse;* trans., *to rush through/over.*
36 *aeternus, -a, -um,** *endless, eternal, everlasting, enduring.*
   aeternum . . . vulnus: HYPERBATON, a variant word order quite common in the *Aeneid.*
   sub: here *deep down in.*
37 **haec sēcum:** sc. **locūta est** in a CUM TEMPORAL CL.; speech vbs. are often omitted in verse (ELLIPSIS). For **sēcum,** the Eng. idiom is *to* (rather than *with*) *herself.*
   *inceptum, -ī,** n., *undertaking, enterprise; attempt, intention.*
   *dēsistō, dēsistere, dēstitī,** *to leave off, desist, cease (from)* (+ abl., dat., or prep.).
   Mēne . . . dēsistere: exclamatory acc. + inf. in a RHETORICAL QUEST., *am I, defeated* (**victam**), *to cease . . .!*
38 *Teucrī, -ōrum,** m. pl., *descendants of Teucer* (father-in-law of Dardanus and ancestor of the Trojan kings), *Trojans.*
39 *quippe,** adv. and conj., *for, indeed, to be sure; of course, naturally* (here, and often, sarcastic).
   *Pallas, Palladis,** f., *Pallas (Athena), Minerva* (originally in Italy Minerva was goddess of the household arts, but through her identification with the Greek Athena a goddess of warfare as well).
   Pallasne . . . Oīleī (41): Ajax had assaulted the Trojan princess Cassandra in the temple of Minerva (see 2.403–15 below), who took revenge by setting fire to the Greek fleet and killing him.
   exūrō, exūrere, exussī, exustus, *to destroy by fire, burn completely, incinerate.*
   *classis, classis,** f., *class* (of citizens); *naval force, fleet.*
40 *Argīvus, -a, -um,** *of Argos, Argive, Greek* (here gen. pl.—see on **superum** 4).
   ipsōs: sc. **Argīvōs.**
   *summergō, summergere, summersī, summersus,** *to (cause to) sink, submerge.*
   *pontus, -ī,** m., *sea.*

35 vēla dabant laetī et spūmās salis aere ruēbant,
36 cum Iūnō, aeternum servāns sub pectore vulnus,
37 haec sēcum: "Mēne inceptō dēsistere victam
38 nec posse Ītaliā Teucrōrum āvertere rēgem—
39 quippe vetor fātīs! Pallasne exūrere classem
40 Argīvum atque ipsōs potuit summergere pontō

Quaestiōnēs

1. What is the rhetorical effect of the hyperbaton seen in **aeternum . . . vulnus** (36)? How does the line's meter further Vergil's intent here?

2. Comment on the word order of **exūrere classem / . . . ipsōs . . . summergere** (39–40).

Athena Promachos
1st cent. B.C. Roman copy of
5th cent. B.C. Greek original
Villa dei Papiri, Herculaneum, Italy
Museo Archeologico, Naples, Italy

41   **ūnius:** i.e., Ajax; for the short -i-, see on **illius** (16).

    noxa, -ae, f., *injurious behavior, wrongdoing.*

    ***furia, -ae,** f., often pl., *avenging rage, fury; goddess of vengeance, Fury.*

    ***Aiax, Aiācis,** m., *Ajax* (a Greek hero in the Trojan War, son of Oileus—the so-called "lesser Ajax," not to be confused with the more renowned Ajax, son of Telamon); the first syllable is scanned long due to the intervocalic -i-.

    Oīleus, -ī, m., *Oileus* (king of the Locrians and one of the Argonauts).

    Oīleī: i.e., *(son) of Oileus;* the gen. -**eī** ending here is scanned as a single syllable (SYNIZESIS).

42   **Ipsa:** Minerva was the only deity permiited to wield Jupiter's thunderbolt.

    ***Iuppiter, Iovis,** m., *Jupiter* (Roman equivalent of Zeus, king of the gods).

    ***rapidus, -a, -um,** *swiftly moving, rapid, quick.*

    ***iaculor, -ārī, -ātus sum,** *to throw a javelin; to shoot at, strike; to hurl, throw.*

43   ***disiciō, disicere, disiēcī, disiectus,** *to break up and scatter, disperse; to dispel.*

    disiēcitque . . . ventīs: conflict of ictus and accent and the harsh **t/q/r** ALLITERATION produce sound effects appropriate to the violent action; for the -**que . . . -que** conjs., cf. on **tenditque . . . fovetque** (18).

    ***ratis, ratis,** f., *raft, boat, ship.*

44   **illum . . . acūtō (45):** the lack of conj. with the preceding cls. (ASYNDETON) is, like the demonstrative pron. itself, deliberately emphatic; the series of spondees in 44 and the opening dactyls in 45 suit the very different actions described in the two lines.

    exspīrō (1), *to breathe out, exhale; to expire, die, perish.*

    trānsfīgō, trānsfīgere, trānsfīxī, trānsfīxus, *to pierce through, puncture.*

45   ***turbō, turbinis,** m., *spinning object, top; whirlwind, tornado; whirlpool.*

    ***corripiō, corripere, corripuī, correptus,** *to seize hold of, snatch up, seize and carry off; to hasten upon, hasten over; to attack, overcome.*

    ***scopulus, -ī,** m., *projecting rock, crag, cliff, peak; boulder* (here DAT. WITH COMPOUNDS).

    ***īnfīgō, īnfīgere, īnfīxī, īnfīxus,** *to drive in, implant; to transfix, impale.*

    ***acūtus, -a, -um,** *pointed, sharp, tapering; high-pitched.*

46   ***ast,** conj. (archaic form of **at**), *but, but if; and if.*

    ego: the pron. subj. is itself emphatic, as are the strong CAESURA and the spondees following.

    ***dīvus, -ī,** m., *god* (**dīvum** here, and often, = **dīvōrum**).

47   **soror:** Jupiter and Juno were children of Saturn (see on **Sāturnia** 23).

48   ***quisquam, quicquam** or **quidquam,** *any person, anyone, anything.*

    ***adōrō (1),** *to plead with, address; to approach as a suppliant, pray to, worship.*

    adōrat . . . impōnet (49): the tense shift suggests both the present and future affronts to Juno's majesty.

49   ***supplex, supplicis,** *making humble entreaty, (as a) suppliant* (often used as a noun).

    honōrem: here *a sacrificial offering.*

50   ***flammō (1),** *to set fire to, burn, inflame.*

    ***volutō (1),** *to roll (forward); to turn over (in the mind), think about.*

    Tālia . . . volutāns: the partic. and its obj. enclose the line (FRAMING), producing an effective CHIASMUS.

41 ūnius ob noxam et furiās Aiācis Oīleī?
42 Ipsa, Iovis rapidum iaculāta ē nūbibus ignem,
43 disiēcitque ratēs ēvertitque aequora ventīs,
44 illum exspīrantem trānsfīxō pectore flammās
45 turbine corripuit scopulōque īnfīxit acūtō;
46 ast ego, quae dīvum incēdō rēgīna Iovisque
47 et soror et coniūnx, ūnā cum gente tot annōs
48 bella gerō. Et quisquam nūmen Iūnōnis adōrat
49 praetereā aut supplex ārīs impōnet honōrem?"

*Juno visits Aeolia, where king Aeolus rules the winds and
keeps them imprisoned in a cave like wild horses*

50   Tālia flammātō sēcum dea corde volūtāns,

Quaestiōnēs

1. What two rhetorical devices are employed in 47 to emphasize Juno's relationship to Jupiter?

2. What may be the intended effect of Juno's use of **Iūnōnis** rather than simply **meum** in 48?

3. Discuss several specific ways in which Juno contrasts her own circumstances with what Pallas had been permitted to do (37–49).

> Could angry Pallas, with revengeful spleen,
> The Grecian navy burn, and drown the men?
> She, for the fault of one offending foe,
> The bolts of Jove himself presum'd to throw:
> With whirlwinds from beneath she toss'd the ship,
> And bare expos'd the bosom of the deep;
> Then, as an eagle gripes the trembling game,
> The wretch, yet hissing with her father's flame,
> She strongly seiz'd, and with a burning wound
> Transfix'd, and naked, on a rock she bound.
> But I, who walk in awful state above,
> The majesty of heav'n, the sister wife of Jove,
> For length of years my fruitless force employ
> Against the thin remains of ruin'd Troy!
> What nations now to Juno's pow'r will pray,
> Or off'rings on my slighted altars lay?

From the translation of John Dryden, 1698

51 *nimbus, -ī, m., *rain-cloud, cloud; downpour, cloudburst, rain-storm.*
   *fētus, -a, -um, *having young offspring; pregnant; teeming, abounding.*
   *furō, furere, *to be mad, be crazed; to rage.*
   *auster, -trī, m., *south wind; south (here = stormy winds in general).*
   loca fēta furentibus Austrīs: a masterfully crafted phrase, with CHIASMUS, a
      vivid PERSONIFICATION (Aeolus' cave, like a womb, is *pregnant* with the
      winds), and an f/s ALLITERATION that is perhaps meant to suggest the sounds
      of the raging winds (ONOMATOPOEIA).

52 Aeolia, -ae, f., *Aeolia (home of Aeolus, in the Aeolian, or Lipari, Islands).*
   venit. Hīc: the DIAERESIS provides a dramatic pause before the description of
      Aeolus' palace.
   *vāstus, -a, -um, *uncivilized, desolate; awe-inspiring; immense, huge.*
   *Aeolus, -ī, m., *Aeolus (mythic king of the winds).*
   *antrum, -ī, n., *cave, cavern.*
   vāstō rēx Aeolus antrō: the CHIASMUS here produces a typical Vergilian WORD-
      PICTURE, with the words for the king actually positioned in the line within
      the two-word phrase describing his immense cavern.

53 *luctor, -ārī, -ātus sum, *to wrestle; to struggle (to escape), resist violently.*
   luctantēs ventōs: the harsh conflict of ictus and accent on these two words
      provides a sound effect appropriate to Vergil's depiction of the struggling
      winds.
   sonōrus, -a, -um, *loud, resounding, sonorous, noisy.*

54 *premō, premere, pressī, pressus, *to press, grip tightly; to press upon (in pursuit);
      to subdue, suppress, hold back; to tread upon, step on.*
   *vinculum or vinclum, -ī, n., *chain, shackle; link, bond (uniting people).*
   *carcer, carceris, m., *jail, prison, dungeon;* sg. or pl., *the barriers at the start of a
      race-course.*
   *frēnō (1), *to control horses with a bridle, rein in.*
   carcere frēnat: Vergil intends us to imagine the winds as racehorses, champing
      at the bit to be released from their stalls; the image is continued through
      line 63.

55 indignāns, indignantis, *full of anger, resentful, indignant.*

56 *claustrum, -ī, n., *bolt, bar (for a door or gate); cage, prison; stalls (on a
      racecourse).*
   *fremō, fremere, fremuī, fremitūrus, *to rumble, roar, growl; to grumble, cry out,
      clamor for.*
   *celsus, -a, -um, *high, lofty, tall.*

57 *scēptrum, -ī, n., *royal staff, sceptre; sovereignty, kingship (here pl. for sg.).*
   molliō (4), *to soften, relax; to soothe, make calm.*
   *temperō (1), *to exercise restraint, restrain oneself; to restrain, moderate, temper; to
      control, regulate.*
   īrās: pl. for sg., with the senses of *bursts of rage* or *fits of anger.*

58 *nī, conj. (= nisi), *unless, if not.*
   *profundus, -a, -um, *deep, bottomless; dense, profound; boundless.*

51 nimbōrum in patriam, loca fēta furentibus Austrīs,
52 Aeoliam venit. Hīc vāstō rēx Aeolus antrō
53 luctantēs ventōs tempestātēsque sonōrās
54 imperiō premit ac vinclīs et carcere frēnat.
55 Illī indignantēs magnō cum murmure montis
56 circum claustra fremunt; celsā sedet Aeolus arce,
57 scēptra tenēns, mollitque animōs et temperat īrās.
58 Nī faciat, maria ac terrās caelumque profundum

Quaestiōnēs

1. What very striking metrical and aural effects, besides conflict of ictus and accent in the first half of the verse, contribute to the poem's "soundtrack" in line 53?

2. Discuss the meter and sound effects in 55; how is the language onomatopoetic?

3. Comment on the word-picture in 56.

59 **rapidī:** for the adj., cf. on **laetī** (35); the line's heavy ALLITERATION of **r** may be
an ONOMATOPOEIA, meant to suggest the roaring of the winds
verrō, verrere, versus, *to sweep clean, sweep away, sweep along.*
aura, -ae, f., air; breeze, wind; atmosphere; breath; pl., the heavens.

60 *omnipotēns, omnipotentis, all-powerful, omnipotent;* with **pater,** often = Jupiter.
*abdō, abdere, abdidī, abditus, to hide, conceal; to hide oneself, go and hide; to
plunge, bury* (a weapon).
abdidit: sc. **ventōs.**
*āter, -tra, -trum, black, dark-colored; devoid of light, dark; dark with blood,
stained; ill-omened, funereal, terrible, gloomy.*

61 **metuēns . . . montēs:** the ALLITERATION aptly echoes that in line 55.
mōlem . . . et montēs . . . altōs: HENDIADYS for *massive, towering mountains.*
īnsuper, adv., on top, above; in addition, as well, besides.

62 **quī . . . scīret (63):** REL. CL. OF CHARACTERISTIC or PURPOSE.
foedus, foederis, n., agreement, treaty, league; compact, condition, bond.

63 *laxus, -a, -um, spacious, room; loose, slack; wide open, gaping.*

64 **quem:** Lat. frequently employs a rel. pron. at the beginning of a sent., where in
Eng. translation we would use a pers. pron. (here *him*).
vōx, vōcis, f., voice; utterance, speech, word.

65 *namque, conj., certainly, to be sure; for* (explanatory and causal).
rēx: the offbeat rhythm caused by the monosyllabic ending is emphatic.

66 *mulceō, mulcēre, to touch lightly, caress; to soothe, pacify, calm.*
mulcēre dedit . . . tollere: **dō** + inf. is a poetic usage.
flūctus, -ūs, m., wave, billow, waters (of the sea).

67 *inimīcus, -a, -um, unfriendly, inimical, hostile; harmful, injurious.*
Tyrrhēnus, -a, -um, *Tyrrhenian, Tuscan, Etruscan.*
Tyrrhēnum . . . aequor: west of Latium, north of Sicily (see map of Italy).

68 *Īlium, -ī, n., Ilium* (another name for the city of Troy).
Penātēs, Penātium, m. pl., Penates (gods who protected the Roman foodstore
and, by extension, the household, the family, and the state).
Īlium . . . Penātēs: Vergil sets the two key words at the line's beginning and end;
the language is brilliantly figurative, picturing the Trojan refugees carrying all
of Troy with them and depicting the Penates themselves as vanquished along
with the nation they were to protect.

69 incutiō, incutere, incussī, incussus, *to strike (on, into); to instil (into).*
obruō, obruere, obruī, obrūtus, to cover up; to overwhelm, overturn, sink.
puppis, puppis, acc. puppim, f., stern of a boat; (by METONYMY) *boat, ship.*
summersās . . . obrue puppēs: an example of PROLEPSIS, as the ships cannot be
submerged until they have first been sunk; as here, Lat. often uses partic. +
vb., where Eng. would employ two vbs. *(sink and overwhelm).*

70 *dīversus, -a, -um, turned in different directions, from different directions; set
apart, separated, distant, remote; different.*
disice: -i- in compounds of **iaciō** represents the sound of the original -ii-
(consonant + vowel), so that the **dis**- syllable here is long.

59 quippe ferant rapidī sēcum verrantque per aurās;
60 sed pater omnipotēns spēluncīs abdidit ātrīs,
61 hoc metuēns, mōlemque et montēs īnsuper altōs
62 imposuit, rēgemque dedit quī foedere certō
63 et premere et laxās scīret dare iussus habēnās.

Juno entreats Aeolus to unleash the winds
and scatter the Trojan fleet

64   Ad quem tum Iūnō supplex hīs vōcibus ūsa est:
65 "Aeole (namque tibī dīvum pater atque hominum rēx
66 et mulcēre dedit flūctūs et tollere ventō),
67 gēns inimīca mihī Tyrrhēnum nāvigat aequor,
68 Īlium in Ītaliam portāns victōsque Penātēs:
69 incute vim ventīs summersāsque obrue puppēs,
70 aut age dīversōs et disice corpora pontō.

Quaestiōnēs

1. How does Vergil match meter to meaning in the opening feet of 59?

2. Compare the meter of 64 to that in 36–37; what is Vergil's purpose in both instances?

71 **mihi**: DAT. OF POSSESSION.

*   ***praestāns, praestantis**, surpassing others, outstanding, excellent.*
    praestantī corpore: ABL. OF DESCRIPTION.

72 **quae . . . pulcherrima**: sc. **eam** as antecedent (and obj. of **iungam** and **dicābō**) and **est** as vb.; Juno here borrows something from Venus' bag of tricks (see above on the judgment of Paris, line 27).

*   **Dēïopēa, -ae**, f., *Deiopeia* (fairest of the Nymphs who attended Juno, elsewhere in Vergil an attendant of Cyrene).

73 ***cōnūbium, -ī**, n., *intermarriage* (between two groups of people); *marriage, wedding* (a technical Roman word; often scanned as trisyllabic with SYNIZESIS of the -i-).

*   **cōnūbiō . . . dicābō**: the words are repeated by Juno verbatim at 4.126, where, as goddess of marriage, she offers Aeneas Dido as his bride.
*   ***stabilis, -is, -e**, standing firm, steady; stable, immovable; lasting, enduring.*
*   ***proprius, -a, -um**, one's own absolutely/in perpetuity; one's own property.*
*   ***dicō** (1), to indicate, show; to give over, assign, devote, designate.*

75 ***exigō, exigere, exēgī, exāctus**, to drive out/forth; to achieve, complete, carry out; to spend (time in); to find out.*

*   ***prōlēs, prōlis**, f., *offspring, progeny; generation, race, breed.*
    pulchrā . . . prōle: ABL. OF DESCRIPTION.

76 **Aeolus haec**: for ELLIPSIS of the speech vb., see on line 37.

*   **Tuus . . . labor (77)**: sc. **est**, *it is your task* (to).
*   **Tuus . . . mihi . . . / Tū mihi (78)**: ANAPHORA and ASYNDETON emphasize Aeolus' characterization of his relationship to Juno.

77 ***explōrō** (1), to reconnoitre, inspect; to inquire into, ascertain.*

*   ***capessō, capessere, capessīvī**, to take hold of, grasp; to head for, go towards; to take charge of, undertake.*
*   ***fās**, indecl. n., *right, ordained* (by divine law); *morally right, fitting, proper.*

78 ***quīcumque, quaecumque, quodcumque**, whoever, whatever; no matter of what kind* (often depreciatory, as here, *however small, inadequate*).

*   **rēgnī**: idiomatic GEN. OF THE WHOLE with **quodcumque hoc**, *this* (bit of) *kingdom, however meager.*
*   **scēptra Iovemque**: HENDIADYS; by METONYMY **scēptra**, again poetic pl. as in 57, represents Jupiter's divine authority.

79 **conciliō** (1), to join, unite; to win over, make favorable, gain the favor of.

*   **dās**: sc. **mihi** from the preceding line (and see note on 66).

80 **nimbōrum . . . tempestātum**: placement of the -**um** syllables under the ictus accentuates the booming ASSONANCE of this highly ALLITERATIVE verse; the four-word line is unusual.

*   ***potēns, potentis**, able, capable; strong, powerful*
    facis . . . potentem: sc. **mē**; i.e., "you give me power (over)."

81 **dicta**: sc. **sunt** (and remember that forms of **esse** are often in ELLIPSIS).

*   ***cavus, -a, -um**, having a depression on the surface, concave; hollow; full of caves, cavernous, porous.*
*   ***cuspis, cuspidis**, f., *sharp point, tip* (of a spear); *spear, lance.*
    Haec . . . cuspide: the harsh ALLITERATION of **c** is appropriate to the violent action being described.

71 Sunt mihi bis septem praestantī corpore Nymphae,
72 quārum quae fōrmā pulcherrima, Dēïopēa,
73 cōnūbiō iungam stabilī propriamque dicābō,
74 omnēs ut tēcum meritīs prō tālibus annōs
75 exigat et pulchrā faciat tē prōle parentem."

The lord of the winds agrees to Juno's request

76 Aeolus haec contrā: "Tuus, ō rēgīna, quid optēs
77 explōrāre labor; mihi iussa capessere fās est.
78 Tū mihi quodcumque hoc rēgnī, tū scēptra Iovemque
79 conciliās, tū dās epulīs accumbere dīvum
80 nimbōrumque facis tempestātumque potentem."

The winds rush forth and overwhelm the Trojans in a tumultuous thunderstorm, threatening their destruction

81 Haec ubi dicta, cavum conversā cuspide montem

Quaestiōnēs

1. How do the word order in 71 and the meter in 72 add emphasis to Juno's offer?

2. What is the poet's intent in framing verse 74 with the paired words **omnēs . . . annōs**?

3. Describe the various strategies Juno employs in 64–75 to persuade Aeolus to carry out her request.

4. Comment on the anaphora and asyndeton in 78–79; why are these devices used here and how are they effective?

5. Comment on the multiple sound effects in 80 and explain how they may be regarded as onomatopoetic.

82 *latus, lateris, n., *side* (of a body or an object); *flank* (of an army).
    impulit in latus: the ENJAMBEMENT and dactylic rhythm help suggest the
        rapidity of Aeolus' movement.
    *agmen, agminis, n., *stream, current* (of water); *multitude, throng; series,*
        succession, line; line (of troops), *army, march; herd, team* (of horses).
    velut . . . factō: the brief SIMILE compares the winds to a band of soldiers, or, if
        Vergil means to resume the imagery first introduced in 53–54, to a team of
        horses.

83 **perflō** (1), *to blow across/over, sweep through.*
    data . . . perflant: a highly ALLITERATIVE line, with the harsh, clattering **t**'s and
        the roaring **r**'s providing an apt sound effect; to make his narration more
        vivid, Vergil employs here, as often, the HIST. PRES.

84 *incubō, incubāre, incubuī, incubitūrus, *to lie/recline* (on); *to brood* (over); *to*
        swoop down (on).
    Incubuēre: for the ending, see on **tenuēre** (12).
    tōtum: sc. **id** = **mare** (obj. of **ruunt**, here trans.).
    *īmus, -a, -um, *lowest, bottommost; lowest part of, bottom of; deepest, innermost.*

85 *Eurus, -ī, m., *east (southeast) wind.*
    *Notus, -ī, m., *south wind.*
    *crēber, -bra, -brum, *at frequent intervals, closely spaced; frequent, repeated,*
        constant; numerous, abundant; + abl., *crowded/packed* (with), *full* (of).
    *procella, -ae, f., *violent wind, storm, gale, squall.*

86 Āfricus, -ī, m., *southwest wind.*
    vāstōs volvunt: ALLITERATION of **v** produces an airy, whooshing sound that
        suggests the rush of the winds.

87 *īnsequor, īnsequī, īnsecūtus sum, *to follow closely, pursue, chase; to assault.*
    Īnsequitur: Vergil likes to place this word at the beginning of its cl., aptly
        connecting the preceding action with what follows (cf. 1.105, 4.161).
    *strīdor, strīdōris, m., *high-pitched sound* (depending on context, *squeak, creak,*
        grating, screech; whistling, whirring, hissing; shriek, squeal).
    clāmorque . . . strīdorque: coincidence of ictus and accent picks out the internal
        rhyme and thus strengthens the ONOMATOPOEIA; for the epic POLYSYNDETON,
        cf. 85 and 88, and see the note on line 18.
    **rudēns, rudentis, m., *rope* (esp. ropes used on a ship).

90 *intonō, intonāre, intonuī, *to thunder.*
    *polus, -ī, m., (north and south) *pole; heaven, sky.*
    *aethēr, aetheris, acc. aethera, m., *(upper) air, heaven, sky.*

91 **praesēns, praesentis,** *present, face to face; immediate, instant.*
    praesentem . . . mortem: a somberly musical line, with extensive ALLITERATION
        and ASSONANCE; and for the coincidence of ictus and accent in the line's
        second half, a metrical effect Vergil often uses to close out a dramatic scene,
        see on line 7 and cf. line 33.
    intentō (1), *to hold out* (toward), *point* (at); *to make threats of, threaten.*

82 impulit in latus; ac ventī, velut agmine factō,

83 quā data porta ruunt et terrās turbine perflant.

84 Incubuēre marī tōtumque ā sēdibus īmīs

85 ūnā Eurusque Notusque ruunt crēberque procellīs

86 Āfricus, et vāstōs volvunt ad lītora flūctūs.

87 Īnsequitur clāmorque virum strīdorque rudentum;

88 ēripiunt subitō nūbēs caelumque diemque

89 Teucrōrum ex oculīs; pontō nox incubat ātra;

90 intonuēre polī et crēbrīs micat ignibus aethēr

91 praesentemque virīs intentant omnia mortem.

Quaestiōnēs

1. Vergil's application of the word **imperiō** to Aeolus (line 54) prompts the audience to think of his leadership in Roman terms; discuss in detail Vergil's characterization of this king in 52–82 and how Romans would respond to him as a leader.

2. How is the word order in 91 especially emphatic?

He said, and hurl'd against the mountain side
His quiv'ring spear, and all the god applied.
The raging winds rush thro' the hollow wound,
And dance aloft in air, and skim along the ground;
Then, settling on the sea, the surges sweep,
Raise liquid mountains, and disclose the deep.
South, East, and West with mix'd confusion roar,
And roll the foaming billows to the shore.
The cables crack; the sailors' fearful cries
Ascend; and sable night involves the skies;
And heav'n itself is ravish'd from their eyes.
Loud peals of thunder from the poles ensue;
Then flashing fires the transient light renew;
The face of things a frightful image bears,
And present death in various forms appears.

From the translation of John Dryden, 1698

92 ***extemplō**, adv., *without delay, at once, immediately.*

*Aenēās, Aenēae, acc. **Aenēan**, voc. **Aenēā**, m., *Aeneas* (Trojan prince, son of Venus and Anchises, and legendary ancestor of the Romans).

*frīgus, frīgoris, n., *cold, cold weather; chill* (of the body, old age, death, fear); *weakness, numbness, torpor* (here ABL. OF MEANS or ABL. OF CAUSE).

*membrum, -ī, n., *part/organ of the body, limb, member;* pl., *body.*

solvuntur frīgore membra: the identical phrase is applied by Vergil to Aeneas' arch-enemy, Turnus, at the moment of his death (12.951, below).

93 ***ingemō, ingemere, ingemuī**, *to utter a cry of pain/anguish, moan, groan.*

duplex, duplicis, *(folded) double; two together, both.*

*sīdus, sīderis, n., *heavenly body, star, planet;* usually pl., *the heavens, stars.*

*palma, -ae, f., *palm* (of the hand).

tendēns palmās: in a gesture of prayer.

94 ***quater**, adv., *on four occasions, four times; four times* (in degree).

beātus, -a, -um, *happy, fortunate, blessed.*

95 **quīs:** = **quibus**, an archaic form common in epic, here dat. with **contigit** (96)

96 ***contingō, contingere, contigī, contāctus**, *to be in contact with, touch;* **contigit**, impers. + dat. + inf., *to fall to one's lot, to grant to someone* (to do something), *happen.*

quīs . . . (95) / contigit: lit., *to whom it fell* (to); freely, *whose lot it was* (to).

oppetō, oppetere, oppetīvī, oppetītus, *to encounter, meet; to meet one's death, perish.*

97 ***Tȳdīdēs, Tȳdīdae**, voc. **Tȳdīdē**, m., *son of Tydeus* (the **-īdēs** suffix is patronymic), *Diomedes* (one of the foremost Greek leaders in the Trojan War; Aeneas was nearly slain by him in hand-to-hand combat in *Iliad* 5.297f., before being rescued by Venus).

Ō . . . Tȳdīdē: APOSTROPHE.

Mēne . . . potuisse (98): for the exclamatory acc. + inf. construction, cf. **mēne . . . dēsistere (37).**

*Īliacus, -a, -um, *of Ilium, Trojan.*

*occumbō, occumbere, occubuī, *to be laid low, meet with* (death); *to fall, die.*

98 **dextrā:** use of **dextra** for **manus dextra** is common in Vergil.

99 **ubi:** remember that in poetry conjs., rel. prons., and other words that ordinarily introduce a cl. are often delayed (ANASTROPHE); the ANAPHORA and TRICOLON CRESCENS are meant to reflect Aeneas' agitated state and his indignation.

Aeacidēs, Aeacidae, m., *son/descendant of Aeacus; Achilles* (grandson of Aeacus).

*tēlum, -ī, n., *weapon, spear* (here ABL. OF CAUSE or MEANS).

*Hector, Hectoris, acc. **Hectora**, m., *Hector* (oldest son of Priam and Hecuba, and Troy's most renowned hero in the Trojan War).

100 ***Sarpēdōn, Sarpēdonis**, m., *Sarpedon* (son of Jupiter and Laodamia, a Lycian king and ally of the Trojans, slain by Patroclus in the Trojan War).

ubi ingēns (99) / Sarpēdōn: the irregular CAESURA and ELISION at the end of 99 and the ENJAMBEMENT add special weight to the name of this valiant warrior, who fell in battle despite his father Jupiter's wishes.

*Simoīs, Simoentis, m., *Simois* (a tributary of the Trojan river Scamander).

Overcome with fear, Aeneas laments that he may be lost at sea rather than having died with honor on Troy's battlefields

92   Extemplō Aenēae solvuntur frīgore membra;
93 ingemit et, duplicēs tendēns ad sīdera palmās,
94 tālia vōce refert: "Ō terque quaterque beātī,
95 quīs ante ōra patrum Trōiae sub moenibus altīs
96 contigit oppetere! Ō Danaüm fortissime gentis
87 Tȳdīdē! Mēne Īliacīs occumbere campīs
98 nōn potuisse tuāque animam hanc effundere dextrā,
99 saevus ubi Aeacidae tēlō iacet Hector, ubi ingēns
100 Sarpēdōn, ubi tot Simoīs correpta sub undīs

Quaestiō

What is remarkable about the meter in 92 and how is it effective?

Death and Sleep carrying the
body of Sarpedon
Black-figure amphora,
5th–4th cent. B.C.
Louvre, Paris, France

101 **virum:** for the form, see on **superum** (4).

    fortia: a TRANSFERRED EPITHET, more logically applying to **virum.**

102 **iactantī:** here *wildly speaking, shouting;* sc. **eī** (Aeneas), DAT. OF REF.

    *****strīdō, strīdere, strīdī,** *to creak, squeak, grate; to whistle, shriek, howl.*

    *****Aquilō, Aquilōnis,** m., *north wind, northeast wind.*

103 *****adversus, -a, -um,** *opposite, in/from the opposite direction, facing, opposing, in front of.*

104 *****rēmus, -ī,** m., *oar.*

    *****prōra, -ae,** f., *prow;* (METONYMY) *ship.*

    āvertit: here intrans.

105 *****cumulus, -ī,** m., *heap, pile, mound; mass* (of water), *wave* (here ABL. OF MANNER).

    praeruptus, -a, -um, *broken off, precipitous, sheer.*

    praeruptus aquae mōns: the movement from trisyllable to disyllable to the relatively infrequent monosyllabic ending produces an irregular rhythm meant to suggest the sudden crash of the mountainous wave.

106 **Hī . . . hīs:** *some (sailors) . . . others;* men and ships are now scattered on the sea.

    *****dehīscō, dehīscere,** *to split open, gape.*

107 **terram . . . harēnīs:** the r/f/s ALLITERATION is perhaps meant to suggest the ocean's seething.

    *****aestus, -ūs,** m., *heat, hot weather; stormy sea, surge, swell.*

108 **Trēs . . . abreptās:** sc. **nāvēs.**

    *****saxum, -ī,** n., *rock, boulder, stone.*

    *****lateō, latēre, latuī,** *to hide, lie hidden, be concealed; to escape the notice of.*

    *****torqueō, torquēre, torsī, tortus,** *to twist tightly; to turn, roll; to hurl.*

109 **saxa . . . Ārās:** the line is regarded by some editors as an interpolation, but it provides just the sort of detail that Vergil often liked to include; we do not know for certain either the location of these rocks or why they were called *the Altars,* but clearly Vergil had some specific landmark in mind.

    *****Italus, -a, -um,** gen. pl. m. **Italum,** *Italian;* m. as noun, *an Italian.*

    quae in: such ELISION of two monosyllables is relatively uncommon in Vergil.

110 **dorsum, -ī,** n., *back; ridge, reef.*

    *****immānis, -is, -e,** *savage, brutal; frightful; of enormous size, huge.*

111 **brevia:** here, as often, *shallow (water), shallows, shoals.*

    *****Syrtis, Syrtis,** f., *Syrtis* (a sandy coastal region east of Carthage); often, as here, generalized in pl., *sandbanks, shoals.*

    miserābile vīsū: *pitiful to behold;* n. adj. + the abl. supine (ABL. OF SPECIFICATION), often employed by Vergil, as here, for dramatic effect.

112 **inlīdō, inlīdere, inlīsī, inlīsus,** *to injure by crushing; to dash (on/into).*

    *****vadum, -ī,** n., *shallow, shoal; bottom* (of the sea).

    *****agger, aggeris,** m., *mound, heap, pile; earthwork, rampart; bank* (of a river).

    *****cingō, cingere, cīnxī, cīnctus,** *to surround, encircle; to gird up one's dress* (for action); *to gird, equip.*

113 *****Lycius, -a, -um,** *of Lycia* (a country in southern Asia Minor, an ally of Troy in the Trojan War), *Lycian;* m. pl. as noun, *Lycians.*

    *****fīdus, -a, -um,** *faithful, loyal, devoted; trustworthy, reliable.*

    *****Orontēs, Orontī,** acc. **Orontēn,** m., *Orontes* (a Lycian warrior).

101 scūta virum galeāsque et fortia corpora volvit!"

The storm rages and mountainous waves overwhelm the fleet

102   Tālia iactantī strīdēns Aquilōne procella
103 vēlum adversa ferit, flūctūsque ad sīdera tollit.
104 Franguntur rēmī, tum prōra āvertit et undīs
105 dat latus, īnsequitur cumulō praeruptus aquae mōns.
106 Hī summō in flūctū pendent; hīs unda dehīscēns
107 terram inter flūctūs aperit, furit aestus harēnīs.
108 Trēs Notus abreptās in saxa latentia torquet
109 (saxa vocant Italī, mediīs quae in flūctibus, Ārās,
110 dorsum immāne marī summō), trēs Eurus ab altō
111 in brevia et syrtēs urget—miserābile vīsū!—
112 inlīditque vadīs atque aggere cingit harēnae.
113 Ūnam, quae Lyciōs fīdumque vehēbat Orontēn,

Quaestiōnēs

1. Aeneas is first introduced by name in 92 and speaks for the first time in 94–101; what insights into his character are revealed here? How do his actions and words suit what might be expected of a Homeric hero? Evaluate his behavior in light of the fact that he is at this point fully aware (as becomes clear later on in the narrative) that his mission is to found a new settlement in Italy.

2. Comment on the metrics in the second half of verse 101.

3. Contrast the meter of 104 with that in 105; how do the shifting rhythms suit the actions described?

114 ipsius: i.e., Aeneas; **ipse** is regularly used for the principal character in a
    narrative sequence, even if not the character most recently mention. Here the
    second -i- is shortened, as often, by SYSTOLE.

    *vertex, verticis, m., *whirlpool, eddy; whirlwind; crown of the head; summit,*
    peak, top.

    ā vertice: *from high up,* i.e., *crashing down.*

    pontus: here a poetic amplification for **unda.**

115 *excutiō, excutere, excussī, excussus, *to shake off/out, knock off/out; to throw out,*
    expel.

    magister: i.e., the helmsman; subj. of both **excutitur** and **volvitur.**

116 volvitur in caput: ENJAMBEMENT, the quick dactyls, and the strong DIAERESIS
    (like that in the preceding line) help convey the sudden violence of the
    action.

    illam: the ship of Orontes.

    ibīdem, adv., *in that very place, in the same place.*

117 circum: here, as often, used as an adv.

    voro (1), *to swallow ravenously, devour; to engulf.*

    torquet . . . vertex: a highly ONOMATOPOETIC line, with ASSONANCE of the **or/ir/**
    er syllables effectively suggesting the roaring of the whirlpool.

118 *rārus, -a, -um, *loose, loosely woven; widely spaced, scattered, here and there.*

    nō, nāre, nāvī, *to swim.*

    *gurges, gurgitis, m., *eddy, whirlpool; stream, flood.*

119 virum: = **virōrum;** and cf. the line's arrangement with 101 above.

    tabula, -ae, f., *flat piece of wood, board, plank.*

    *Trōius, -a, -um, *of Troy, Trojan* (here, as often, trisyllabic).

    *gaza, -ae, f., *treasure.*

120 Iam . . . iam . . . / et quā . . . et quā (121): the ANAPHORA serves to focus our
    attention on the four warriors and their ships, thus making the description
    less general and more personal.

    *validus, -a, -um, *powerful, strong, robust; tough, sturdy.*

    *Īlioneus, -ī, m., *Ilioneus* (a Trojan warrior; for scansion of the -eī here, see note
    on Oīleī 41).

    *Achātēs, Achātae, voc. Achātē, m., *Achates* (Trojan warrior and close companion
    of Aeneas, often described in the poem, as in 188 below, with the epithet
    fīdus).

121 quā: **nāvem** is antecedent.

    Abās, Abantis, m., *Abas* (another Trojan warrior).

    grandaevus, -a, -um, *of great old age, aged.*

    Alētēs, Alētī, m., *Aletes* (another Trojan).

122 *hiems, hiemis, f., *winter, wintry weather; rough weather, storm.*

    *compāgēs, compāgis, f., *binding, bond, tie; joint, seam.*

123 imbrem: here *sea-water;* with **inimīcum,** a PERSONIFICATION.

    fatīscō, fatīscere, *to split open, crack, gape.*

124 Intereā: a conj. frequently used by Vergil to introduce a scene change.

    magnō . . . murmure: ABL. OF ATTENDANT CIRCUMSTANCE.

125 *Neptūnus, -ī, m., *Neptune* (brother of Jupiter, Juno, and Pluto, and god of the
    sea, horses, and earthquakes).

114 ipsius ante oculōs ingēns ā vertice pontus
115 in puppim ferit: excutitur prōnusque magister
116 volvitur, in caput, ast illam ter flūctus ibīdem
117 torquet, agēns circum, et rapidus vorat aequore vertex.
118 Appārent rārī nantēs in gurgite vāstō,
119 arma virum tabulaeque et Trōïa gaza per undās.
120 Iam validam Īlioneī nāvem, iam fortis Achātae,
121 et quā vectus Abās, et quā grandaevus Alētēs,
122 vīcit hiems; laxīs laterum compāgibus omnēs
123 accipiunt inimīcum imbrem rīmīsque fatīscunt.

Neptune, god of the sea, is aroused by the tumult
and chastises the winds for their insolence

124 Intereā magnō miscērī murmure pontum
125 ēmissamque hiemem sēnsit Neptūnus et īmīs

Quaestiōnēs

1. Comment on the increasing detail Vergil provides in his description of the wrecked ships in 108–17.

2. Some editors prefer the reading **vortex** (an archaic form) in 117; what is one stylistic argument in favor of this variant?

3. What are the most striking metrical features of verse 118? How does meter suit meaning in the line?

4. Comment on the sound effects in 124 and compare with line 55.

126 *stāgnum, -ī, n., *standing water, still water, pool, lagoon.*
 *refūsus, -a, -um, *poured back, churned up, overflowed.*
 *graviter, adv., *heavily; gravely, grievously, seriously; intensely.*
 graviter commōtus: Neptune is so described not only because he is angry but also, as Austin remarks, because "he was himself the sea."
 altō: sc. **in,** ABL. OF PLACE WHERE.

127 *prōspiciō, prōspicere, prōspexī, prōspectus, *to see before one, see in front; to watch; to look forth/ahead (at).*
 *placidus, -a, -um, *kindly, indulgent; calm, tranquil, peaceful; calming.*

128 **Disiectam . . . classem:** nearly a GOLDEN LINE, the scattered arrangement matches the scene Vergil is describing, creating a sort of WORD-PICTURE.

129 **caelī:** SUBJ. GEN.

131 *Zephyrus, -ī, m., *west wind.*
 Eurum . . . Zephyrum: imagined earlier (85–86) as horses, the winds here are depicted as persons or divinities (PERSONIFICATION).
 *dehinc, adv., *thereupon, then* (scanned as a monosyllable here by SYNIZESIS).
 *for, fārī, fātus sum, *to speak, talk; to speak prophetically; to say, tell.*

132 **Tanta . . . vestrī:** INTERLOCKED WORD ORDER.
 *fīdūcia, -ae, f., often + gen., *trust (in), reliance (on), confidence (in).*
 generis . . . fīdūcia: the winds were offspring of Eos or Aurora, the goddess of dawn, and the Titan Astraeus, both regarded as minor deities by the Olympian Neptune.

134 **mōlēs:** here *massive upheaval.*

135 **Quōs ego:** Neptune suddenly breaks off in the middle of his reprimand, as he is about to threaten the winds (**quōs**) with some punishment (APOSIOPESIS); the quick dactylic beginning, the strong DIAERESIS and emphatic spondees following, and the end-stopped line all intensify the dramatic moment.
 *praestō, praestāre, praestitī, praestātus, *to excel, surpass; + inf., to be preferable, be better, be more important.*

136 **nōn similī poenā:** i.e., with more than just a stern reprimand.
 **commissum, -ī, n., *undertaking, enterprise, deed; misdeed, offense.*
 **luō, luere, luī, *to atone for, make amends for, expiate, pay for.*

137 **mātūrō (1), *to bring to maturity; to hasten, hurry.*
 *fuga, -ae, f., *running away, flight.*

138 **illī . . . ille (139) . . . illā (140):** Neptune effectively makes his point by repeating the demonstrative (ANAPHORA) and carefully positioning **mihi** in 139 to contrast with **illī** in the preceding line.
 *pelagus, -ī, n., *sea, ocean* (here OBJ. GEN.).

139 *sors, sortis, f., *lot (as used in divination); destiny, fortune.*
 sorte datum: the heavens, the oceans, and the Underworld were distributed *by lot* to Jupiter, Neptune, and Pluto, respectively.

140 **vestrās, Eure:** Neptune refers to all the winds, while addressing one specifically.
 *aula, -ae, f., *courtyard; royal residence, palace.*
 illā . . . aulā / Aeolus (141): the soundplay and ENJAMBEMENT underscore Neptune's contemptuous tone.

126 stāgna refūsa vadīs, graviter commōtus, et, altō
127 prōspiciēns, summā placidum caput extulit undā.
128 Disiectam Aenēae tōtō videt aequore classem,
129 flūctibus oppressōs Trōas caelīque ruīnā;
130 nec latuēre dolī frātrem Iūnōnis et īrae.
131 Eurum ad sē Zephyrumque vocat, dehinc tālia fātur:
132 "Tantane vōs generis tenuit fidūcia vestrī?
133 Iam caelum terramque, meō sine nūmine, ventī,
134 miscēre et tantās audētis tollere mōlēs?
135 Quōs ego—sed mōtōs praestat compōnere flūctūs.
136 post mihi nōn similī poenā commissa luētis.
137 Mātūrāte fugam rēgīque haec dīcite vestrō:
138 nōn illī imperium pelagī saevumque tridentem,
139 sed mihi sorte datum. Tenet ille immānia saxa,
140 vestrās, Eure, domōs; illā sē iactet in aulā
141 Aeolus et clausō ventōrum carcere rēgnet."

Quaestiōnēs

1. How does the arrangement in 129 produce a word-picture?

2. Characterize Neptune's tone in 132–41, referring to specific aspects of his style and diction (including his use of personal and demonstrative pronouns and possessives).

The Fountain of Neptune
Marble and bronze, 1559–75
Bartolomeo Ammannati (1511–92)
Piazza della Signoria, Florence, Italy

142 **Sīc ait:** like **tālia fātur** in 131, such formulae were regularly employed by Vergil
to punctuate the beginnings and endings of speeches.
*__dictum__, -ī, n., *utterance, word, speech.*
cito, compar. **citius**, adv., *quickly, swiftly, fast.*
*__tumidus__, -a, -um, *swollen, distended.*
*__plācō__ (1), *to placate, conciliate; to calm; to appease.*

143 *__colligō__, **colligere**, **collēgī**, **collēctus**, *to gather together, collect, pick up.*
*__fugō__ (1), *to cause to flee, drive away, dispel.*

144 **Cȳmothoē**, **Cȳmothoēs**, f., *Cymothoe* (one of the Nereids, sea-nymphs who were
daughters of the ocean god Nereus and the Oceanid Doris).
*__Trītōn__. **Trītōnis**, m., *Triton* (an ocean divinity, son and attendant of Neptune).
*__adnītor__, **adnītī**, **adnīxus sum**, *to rest on, lean on, support oneself on; to exert
oneself, make an effort.*

145 **dētrūdō**, **dētrūdere**, **dētrūsī**, **dētrūsus**, *to push away, push off.*
dētrūdunt nāvēs: the spondaic rhythm is perhaps meant to suggest the immense
effort involved.
*__levō__ (1), *to lift (up), raise; to support; to lift off, remove; to relieve, lighten.*
ipse: i.e., Neptune (see the note on **ipsius** 114).

147 **summās . . . undās:** a common sort of internal rhyme, achieved by setting adj. +
modified noun (or vice versa) at the CAESURA and line's end, respectively.
perlābor, **perlābī**, **perlāpsus sum**, *to move smoothly through, glide over, skim.*

148 **velutī:** = **velut**, commonly used in introducing the first element of a SIMILE;
often, as here (154), with **sīc** introducing the second element; here with **cum
saepe**, *just as often (happens) when . . .*; the simile here describes a natural
(albeit divinely precipitated) phenomenon by comparing it with an incident
in human society, reversing the pattern usual in Homer and in epic generally,
where human actions are more often compared with events in nature.
magnō in populō: probably *in a huge throng* rather than *in a great nation.*

149 *__saeviō__, **saevīre**, **saeviī**, **saevītūrus**, *to behave ferociously, rage; to be violent.*
animīs: *in their hearts*, or perhaps ABL. OF CAUSE, *because of their anger.*
ignōbilis, -is, -e, *unknown; of low birth, common; ignoble, base.*
*__vulgus__, -ī, n., *common people, public; crowd, throng, mob; flock, herd;* **in vulgus
(vulgum)**, idiom, *to the public, publicly.*

150 *__fax__, **facis**, f., *torch* (used for light); *torch* (for setting fires), *firebrand; light.*
*__volō__ (1), *to fly, move through the air; to move quickly, hurry, speed.*
*__ministrō__ (1), + dat., *to act as a servant (to), attend to;* + acc., *to provide; to
manage, look after, regulate.*
furor arma ministrat: rage, here personified, transforms whatever implements
are at hand into weapons; **furor** (like **saevitia**—cf. **saevit** in the preceding
line and see note on 25) is an important recurring theme in the poem (cf. the
more elaborate PERSONIFICATION in 294).

151 **pietāte . . . ac meritīs:** ABL. OF CAUSE or perhaps SPECIFICATION.
gravem: here *of great authority, revered.*
sī: for delay of the conj., which here should precede **pietāte**, see on **sed** (19); with
sī, **quem** here is an indef. adj. modifying **virum**.

*Like a powerful speaker subduing a violent mob, Neptune
drives away the clouds and calms the sea*

142   Sīc ait, et dictō citius tumida aequora plācat
143 collēctāsque fugat nūbēs sōlemque redūcit.
144 Cȳmothoē simul et Trītōn adnīxus acūtō
145 dētrūdunt nāvēs scopulō; levat ipse tridentī
146 et vāstās aperit syrtēs et temperat aequor
147 atque rotīs summās levibus perlābitur undās.
148 Ac velutī magnō in populō cum saepe coorta est
149 sēditiō saevitque animīs ignōbile vulgus
150 iamque facēs et saxa volant, furor arma ministrat;
151 tum, pietāte gravem ac meritīs sī forte virum quem

Quaestiō

What aspect of the poet's characterization of the great man in verse 151 prompts us
to compare him with Aeneas himself?

Neptune in his chariot, Roman mosaic, 4th cent. C.E.
Museum, Sousse, Tunisia

152 **cōnspexēre:** = **cōnspexērunt**, pl. because referring to the individuals making up the mob.

    sileō, silēre, siluī, *to make no sound, be silent; to stop speaking, grow silent.*

    arrēctus, -a, -um, *raised up, erect; upright, standing on end;* with **aurēs**, idiom, *attentive.*

    auris, auris, f., *ear.*

    astō, astāre. astitī, *to stand by/nearby; to stand at/on/in; to stand still.*

153 **regit . . . mulcet:** CHIASMUS; for **mulcet** of calming the sea, cf. line 66.

154 **sīc:** correlative with **velutī** (see on 148).

    sīc . . . fragor: the harsh c/g ALLITERATION and repeated clash of ictus and accent, all recalling the violence of the storm, end suddenly, like the storm itself, with the abrupt DIAERESIS following **fragor.**

155 **prōspiciēns:** set in the same position as in 127, the word deliberately recalls Neptune's initial appearance; the repeated image (**altō / prōspiciēns** 126–27, **aequora . . . / prōspiciēns** 154–55) neatly FRAMES the scene.

    genitor, genitōris, m., *father; creator* (often applied to Jupiter and Neptune).

    invehō, invehere, invexī, invectus, *to carry, transport;* pass., *to ride, drive.*

156 *flectō, flectere, flexī, flexus*, *to bend, curve; to turn, redirect; to influence.*

    currū: = **curruī**, dat.

    lōrum, -ī, n., *leather strap, thong;* pl., *(a horse's) reins.*

    secundus, -a, -um, *following; moving, coursing; compliant, favorable, propitious.*

157 **Aeneadēs, Aeneadae**, m., esp. pl., *companions of Aeneas, Trojans.*

    quae proxima lītora: = **lītora quae sunt proxima.**

    cursus, -ūs, m., *running, rushing; journey, course;* **cursū**, *at a run, quickly.*

    Dēfessī . . . cursū: metrical and other sound effects add a fine musicality to the scene shift, first with the opening spondees (slow to suit **dēfessī**), then with the striking ASSONANCE of **Aeneadae quae** (with **ae** twice under the ictus), and finally with the dactylic rhythms and coincidence of ictus and accent in the line's second half (quick to suit **cursū / contendunt** 158).

158 *contendō, contendere, contendī, contentus*, *to draw tight, stretch; to exert, strive; to hasten; to compete, contend.*

    vertuntur: here as often this vb. has a reflex. sense, and Eng. would use an act.; lit., *are turned = turn themselves* or, simply, *turn.*

159 **Est . . . locus:** beginning with a series of slow spondees, Vergil proceeds to a detailed but imaginary description (based in part on Homer) of the harbor at Carthage (159–69); this sort of digression, usually to describe some important scene, is known as an ECPHRASIS.

    sēcessus, -ūs, m., *withdrawal, seclusion; secluded place* (here *inlet*).

    portus, -ūs, m., *harbor, port.*

160 **efficiō, efficere, effēcī, effectus**, *to construct, make; to make naturally, form.*

    obiectus, -ūs, m., *interposition; barrier.*

    omnis: with **unda**, identically positioned in the next verse; the disjuncture here and in the phrase **sinūs . . . reductōs** (161) aptly suggests the breaking of the waves described in the strong vbs. **frangitur** and **scindit**, thus producing a kind of WORD-PICTURE.

152 cōnspexēre, silent arrēctīsque auribus astant;
153 ille regit dictīs animōs et pectora mulcet—
154 sīc cūnctus pelagī cecidit fragor, aequora postquam
155 prōspiciēns genitor caelōque invectus apertō
156 flectit equōs currūque volāns dat lōra secundō.

Aeneas and the men from seven of his ships land on the coast
of North Africa and make preparations for a meal

157   Dēfessī Aeneadae quae proxima lītora cursū
158 contendunt petere et Libyae vertuntur ad ōrās.
159 Est in sēcessū longō locus: īnsula portum
160 efficit obiectū laterum, quibus omnis ab altō

Quaestiōnēs

1. Lines 148–56 contain the first and one of the most famous of numerous elaborate similes employed in the *Aeneid*. Comment on the several correspondences between the storm, a phenomenon of nature first precipitated and then dispelled by the gods, and the human action described here; in view of the politics of Vergil's day, explain how this comparison would be especially meaningful for his audience.

2. How does this man's leadership, as depicted in 151–53, contrast with that of Aeolus in 52–63?

3. Comment on the verb tenses in 156 and their effect.

4. Compare the storm scene in 82–156 with that in *Odyssey* 5.291–387.

5. How does Vergil manipulate the meter in 159 to focus our attention?

Knowledge and refinement were the pearls of great price, not soft exposures leaving the poem perpetually out of focus, its value and significance forever indeterminate. Students were invited inside the poem . . . . Vergil described how a statesman might stand before a riotous crowd and, "with virtue and high service crowned," alleviate their distemper: "His words their minds control, their passions soothe." There was no divorce of the public and private. Sentiments like these children took in almost with their mother's milk. Their earliest lessons contained moral admonitions couched in precise, elegant language, examples of moral virtue matched to the finest expressions.

Tracy Simmons, Climbing Parnassus, *on the teaching and*
value of poetry in ancient Rome

161 *sinus, -ūs, m., *fold* (of a garment), pl., *clothes; chest, breast, bosom; embrace; innermost part, heart* (of a place); *curve, bend* (here *ripple*); *bay, gulf.*
    sēsē: a common alternate for sē.
    reductōs: here *receding.*
162 Hinc atque hinc: i.e., on both sides.
    *rūpēs, rūpis, f., *steep rocky cliff, crag.*
    *minor, -ārī, -ātus sum, *to threaten, menace* (here *rise menacingly*).
164 *tūtus, -a, -um, *protected, secure, safe; free of danger, without risk.*
    tum: here *in addition/besides* or *further on.*
    *scaena, -ae, f., *background* (before which a play is performed), (natural) *scenery; stage.*
    *coruscus, -a, -um, *trembling, quivering; flashing, gleaming, glistening.*
    silvīs . . . coruscīs: ABL. OF DESCRIPTION.
165 *dēsuper, adv., *from above, up above.*
    *horreō, horrēre, horruī, *to stand up, bristle, be rigid; to be unsightly, dreadful, gloomy; to shudder (at), shiver, be fearful.*
    *nemus, nemoris, n., *woodland, forest; thicket; sacred grove.*
    *immineō, imminēre, *to rise up, project, overhang, overlook, be overhead.*
166 Fronte: here the *face (of the cliff)* looking out toward the island and the bay.
167 *intus, adv., *within, inside.*
    *dulcis, -is, -e, *sweet* (in taste, smell); *not salty, fresh; delightful, dear.*
    vīvō . . . saxō: i.e., the formations are natural and not carved by human hands.
    sedīle, sedīlis, n., *seat, bench, chair.*
168 Hīc . . . / Hūc (170): the two locative advs. bring Vergil's panorama of the harbor to an end; for the strong DIAERESIS in 168, cf. line 52.
    *fessus, -a, -um, *tired, weary, exhausted.*
    *vinculum, -ī, n., *chain, bond, shackle.*
169 uncus, -a, -um, *curved at the end, hooked.*
    alligō (1), *to tie, bind, fasten.*
    *ancora, -ae, f., *anchor.*
    *morsus, -ūs, m., *biting, bite; grip, hook.*
170 Hūc: the adv. marks the close of the ECPHRASIS.
    septem . . . nāvibus: ABL. ABS.
    omnī / ex numerō (171): originally there were 20 ships (line 381).
171 *subeō, subīre, subiī, subitus, often + dat., *to go underneath; to move/rise up; to come up to, approach; to come up with assistance.*
173 tābeō, tābēre, *to waste away, rot, decay; to melt, drip.*
    *artus, -ūs, m., *joint* (in the body); *arm, leg, limb.*
174 Ac . . . Achātēs: the harsh ALLITERATION of c in this line and the next provides a sound effect suited to the action.
    *silex, silicis, m., *hard rock, stone, flint.*
    scintilla, -ae, f., *spark* (of fire).
    *excūdō, excūdere, excūdī, excūsus, *to hammer out, forge, fashion; to cause to be emitted by striking, strike out.*

161 frangitur inque sinūs scindit sēsē unda reductōs.

162 Hinc atque hinc vāstae rūpēs geminīque minantur

163 in caelum scopulī, quōrum sub vertice lātē

164 aequora tūta silent; tum silvīs scaena coruscīs

165 dēsuper, horrentīque ātrum nemus imminet umbrā.

166 Fronte sub adversā scopulīs pendentibus antrum;

167 intus aquae dulcēs vīvōque sedīlia saxō,

168 Nymphārum domus. Hīc fessās nōn vincula nāvēs

169 ūlla tenent, uncō nōn alligat ancora morsū.

170 Hūc septem Aenēās collēctīs nāvibus omnī

171 ex numerō subit ac, magnō tellūris amōre

172 ēgressī, optātā potiuntur Trōes harēnā

173 et sale tābentēs artūs in lītore pōnunt.

174 Ac prīmum silicī scintillam excūdit Achātēs

Quaestiōnēs

1. What details of Vergil's description of the harbor in 159–69 invest the scene with a mysterious and ominous character? Compare this scene with Homer's description of the harbor at Ithaca (*Odyssey* 13.96f.).

2. Identify three stylistic devices that help make the sentence **Hīc . . . morsū** (168–69) an effective closure for the harbor scene.

3. Comment on the effect of the meter in 170.

175 *suscipiō, suscipere, suscēpī, susceptus, *to catch from below, save (from falling); to support, hold up; to take up, have* (a child).

suscēpit . . . ignem: freely, *ignited the fire;* cf. the Eng. idiom "to catch fire."

folium, -ī, n., *leaf.*

āridus, -a, -um, *devoid of moisture, dry.*

176 nūtrīmentum, -ī, n., *nourishment, sustenance* (here *fuel*).

rapuit: here *waved, fanned* or perhaps *kindled.*

fōmes, fōmitis, m., *wood chips, kindling.*

177 *Cerēs, Cereris, f., *Ceres* (goddess of grain and fruit, identified with the Greek Demeter, mother of Persephone/Proserpina); (by METONYMY) *wheat, bread, food.*

corruptus, -a, -um, *rotten, decayed; impure, adulterated; spoiled, damaged.*

Cereālis, -is, -e, *of Ceres.*

Cererem . . . Cereālia: the repeated references to Ceres and the detailed description give the action in 174–79 a ritualistic character.

arma: here *tools, utensils.*

178 *expediō (4), *to untie, unwrap; to make ready, prepare;* pass., *to be prepared, ready, make one's way.*

rērum: gen. (in the sense of cause or specification) with the adj. fessī, . . . *of their lot, with their circumstances.*

*frūx, frūgis, f., *produce, fruit;* esp. pl., *grain.*

receptās: here *rescued, saved.*

179 torreō, torrēre, torruī, tostus, *to heat, dry out.*

180 *cōnscendō, cōnscendere, cōnscendī, cōnscēnsus, *to go on board* (a ship), *set out on* (the sea); *to climb to* (the top of), *ascend.*

omnem: *complete = unimpeded.*

181 prōspectus, -ūs, m., *vista, view.*

pelagō: for the abl. with prōspectum, see note on altō (126).

*Antheus, -ī, acc. Anthea, m., *Antheus* (a Trojan warrior and companion of Aeneas).

Anthea sī quem / . . . videat (182): quem is indef. after sī, *in case he might see anything of Antheus.*

182 *Phrygius, -a, -um, *Phrygian, of Phrygia* (in western Asia Minor); *Trojan.*

birēmis, birēmis, f., *ship with two rows of oars, bireme* (an anachronism, as such ships, used by the Romans, had not yet been invented by Trojan War times).

183 *Capys, Capyis, acc. Capyn, m., *Capys* (another companion of Aeneas).

in puppibus arma: a decorated shield or other armor was hung on the stern to identify the ship's captain.

Caīcus, -ī, m., *Caicus* (another Trojan warrior).

184 *cervus, -ī, m., *stag, deer.*

Nāvem . . . nūllam, trēs . . . cervōs: the line's opening spondees focus our attention on the absence of any of his ships from Aeneas' view, while the CHIASMUS and ASYNDETON then abruptly shift our attention to the stags on the shore.

185 *armentum, -ī, n., *herd* (often, as here, collective pl.).

175 suscēpitque ignem foliīs atque ārida circum
176 nūtrīmenta dedit rapuitque in fōmite flammam.
177 Tum Cererem corruptam undīs Cereāliaque arma
178 expediunt fessī rērum, frūgēsque receptās
179 et torrēre parant flammīs et frangere saxō.

Climbing a nearby hill to look for their lost ships, Aeneas and
Achates spot a herd of deer; Aeneas shoots seven of them
and the two men take the carcasses back to camp

180   Aenēās scopulum intereā cōnscendit, et omnem
181 prōspectum lātē pelagō petit, Anthea sī quem
182 iactātum ventō videat Phrygiāsque birēmēs
183 aut Capyn aut celsīs in puppibus arma Caīcī.
184 Nāvem in cōnspectū nūllam, trēs lītore cervōs
185 prōspicit errantēs; hōs tōta armenta sequuntur

Quaestiōnēs

1. What are the most striking sound effects in 177–79?

2. Compare 181–83 with 120–22; what is the effect of Vergil's use of individual names in these passages?

186 *vallēs, vallis, f., *valley* (here poetic pl.).

*pāscō, pāscere, pāvī, pāstus, *to feed, pasture* (domestic animals); pass., *to feed (on), graze (on).*

187 *cōnstō, cōnstāre, cōnstitī, *to stand together, take up a position, stand (up).*

*arcus, -ūs, m., *bow* (for shooting arrows).

*sagitta, -ae, f., *arrow.*

188 tēla: in appos. with **arcum . . . sagittās** (187); the prose order would be **tēla quae Achātēs fīdus gerēbat.**

189 *ductor, ductōris, m., *military commander, leader* (poetic for **dux**).

alta: OBJ. COMPL.

190 *cornū, -ūs, n., *horn, antler.*

*arboreus, -a, -um, *of/belonging to trees; treelike* (here *branching*).

cornibus arboreīs: ABL. OF DESCRIPTION.

*sternō, sternere, strāvī, strātus, *to lay out on the ground, spread; to scatter, strew; to strike down, lay low, slay.*

191 miscet: here *scatters.*

frondeus, -a, -um, *abounding in foliage, leafy.*

192 *priusquam, conj. + indic. or, introducing a cl. of purpose or anticipation, subjunct., *before, until* (often, as here, separated into two words by TMESIS, with one or more other words intervening).

*absistō, absistere, abstitī, *to stand back, withdraw; to stop, cease.*

victor: *as victor;* Eng. would more commonly use an adv., *victoriously.*

193 *fundō, fundere, fūdī, fūsus, *to pour (out); to emit; to give birth to; to pour forth* (sounds), *utter freely; to rout, drive out; to lay low, slay; to spread (out), stretch (out).*

*humus, -ī, f., *earth, ground.*

*aequō (1), *to make level; to make equal, equalize, equate; to match.*

194 *socius, -ī, m., *companion, comrade; partner, colleague; ally.*

partior, partīrī, partītus sum, *to share, distribute, divide out, apportion* (here sc. **corpora** as obj.).

in: here *among.*

195 Vīna . . . dīvidit (197): the prose order might be **vīna quae hērōs, Acestēs bonus, (in) cadīs (in) lītore Trīnacriō onerārat et (Trōiānīs) abeuntibus dederat, (Aenēās) deinde dīvidit.**

cadus, -ī, m., *jug, jar* (a large container for wine).

onerārat: = onerāverat; for the SYNCOPATED form, see note on **audierat** (20).

*Acestēs, Acestae, acc. Acestēn, m., *Acestes* (a Sicilian king and friend of Aeneas).

196 Trīnacrius, -a, -um, *of Sicily, Sicilian* (from an old Greek name for the island meaning "three-cornered," so-called for its triangular shape).

*hērōs, hērōos, m., *hero* (a legendary hero or a man with heroic qualities); often used as an appos. with adj. force, *heroic.*

197 *maereō, maerēre, *to be sad, mourn, grieve.*

198 neque enim: often used by Vergil to introduce a parenthetical remark, with **neque**, as here, essentially equivalent to **nōn**; with **sumus** the parenthesis is elliptical, = (*I say this to you, for we are not . . .*).

*ignārus, -a, -um, often + gen., *ignorant, unaware (of), unacquainted (with).*

ante: adv. with **malōrum**, = *earlier.*

186 ā tergō et longum per vallēs pāscitur agmen.
187 Cōnstitit hīc arcumque manū celerēsque sagittās
188 corripuit, fīdus quae tēla gerēbat Achātēs,
189 ductōrēsque ipsōs prīmum capita alta ferentēs
190 cornibus arboreīs sternit, tum vulgus et omnem
191 miscet agēns tēlīs nemora inter frondea turbam;
192 nec prius absistit quam septem ingentia victor
193 corpora fundat humī et numerum cum nāvibus aequet;
194 hinc portum petit et sociōs partītur in omnēs.

As his comrades share the wine brought on their ships from Troy,
Aeneas encourages them and reminds them of their destiny

195   Vīna bonus quae deinde cadīs onerārat Acestēs
196 lītore Trīnacriō dederatque abeuntibus hērōs
197 dīvidit, et dictīs maerentia pectora mulcet:
198 "Ō sociī (neque enim ignārī sumus ante malōrum),

Quaestiō

How is the wide separation of **omnem** from **turbam** appropriate to the scene
described in 190–91?

Deer hunt
Detail of "Alexander
Sarcophagus"
Late 4th cent. B.C.
Sidon
Archaeological Museum,
Istanbul, Turkey

199 **passī:** Eng. would more typically employ a rel. cl., "men who have endured."

200 **Vōs et . . . vōs et (201):** ANAPHORA, rendered even more effective by both the careful positioning and the use of ASYNDETON; **et** here, as often, = **etiam.**

Scyllaeus, -a, -um, *of Scylla* (a half-human mermaid creature that, along with the monster Charybdis, haunted the Straits of Messina, between the eastern end of Sicily and the toe of Italy, seizing sailors from their ships and devouring them).

*__rabiēs, -ēī,__ f., *savageness, ferocity* (of animals); *frenzy, madness.*

*__penitus,__ adv., *from within; far within, deep down; far (away).*

*__sonō, sonāre, sonuī, sonitus,__ *to make a (loud) noise, sound; to echo, resound; to sound like, produce the sound* (of something).

201 *__accēdō, accēdere, accessī, accessus,__ *to draw near, approach, reach.*

accestis: = **accessistis,** another common SYNCOPATED perf. form.

Cyclōpius, -a, -um, *of/belonging to the Cyclopes* (mythical one-eyed giants who lived near Mt. Aetna on the island of Sicily; the Trojans' escape from these monsters, and from Scylla and Charybdis, is described in the third book of the *Aeneid*).

202 **expertī:** sc. **estis.**

revocāte: here *restore, summon back;* the CHIASMUS in **revocāte . . . mittite** accentuates the contrasting ideas, a common intent in the use of this device.

*__maestus, -a, -um,__ *unhappy, sad, mournful; gloomy, stern, grim.*

203 **mittite:** = **dīmittite** (see note on **verteret 20**).

*__forsan,__ adv., *perhaps.*

*__iuvō, iuvāre, iūvī, iūtus,__ *to help, assist;* impers. + inf., *it helps, profits, avails* (to do something).

204 *__discrīmen, discrīminis,__ n., *dividing point; critical point, crisis; danger; difference, distinction; discrimination, decision.*

discrīmina rērum: Lat. often uses two nouns (here lit., *dangers of situations*) where Eng. would use adj. + noun (*dangerous situations*); the effect is to focus more attention on the "adjectival" noun.

205 **in Latium:** while Aeneas has been made aware through a series of prophecies that a new home awaits him and his followers in the west, we are not told elsewhere in the poem that he already knew the name Latium; some scholars thus regard the mention of Latium here as a slip on Vergil's part, one of a few marks of imperfection that the poet would likely have corrected had he not died before polishing his final version of the poem.

*__quiētus, -a, -um,__ *at rest, asleep; restful, quiet, peaceful.*

206 *__illīc,__ adv., *there.*

fās: sc. **est,** impers. with **rēgna resurgere** as subj., *it is divinely ordained for . . . .*

resurgō, resurgere, resurrēxī, resurrectus, *to rise again, get up again; to be restored.*

207 **dūrō (1),** *to harden; to become hard; to harden oneself, endure.*

-met, particle suffixed to certain prons. for emphasis.

208 **vōce:** i.e., *aloud,* vs. **corde (209).**

209 *__spēs, -eī,__ f., *hope.*

spem . . . dolōrem: a highly effective use of CHIASMUS and adversative ASYNDETON serving to emphasize the disparity between Aeneas' outward appearance and his inner thoughts.

altum: OBJ. COMPL. with adv. force.

199 Ō passī graviōra, dabit deus hīs quoque fīnem.

200 Vōs et Scyllaeam rabiem penitusque sonantēs

201 accestis scopulōs, vōs et Cyclōpia saxa

202 expertī: revocāte animōs maestumque timōrem

203 mittite; forsan et haec ōlim meminisse iuvābit.

204 Per variōs cāsūs, per tot discrīmina rērum

205 tendimus in Latium, sēdēs ubi fāta quiētās

206 ostendunt; illīc fās rēgna resurgere Trōiae.

207 Dūrāte, et vōsmet rēbus servāte secundīs."

Concealing his own anxieties, Aeneas dines with his men
and joins with them afterward in lamenting the
uncertain fate of their missing comrades

208   Tālia vōce refert cūrīsque ingentibus aeger

209 spem vultū simulat, premit altum corde dolōrem.

Quaestiōnēs

1. What is the effect of the anaphora in 198–99?

2. What rhetorical devices are employed in 204?

3. How does meter suit meaning in 207?

4. Compare the scene in 180–209 with Homer *Odyssey* 10.144f.

5. Contrast Vergil's characterization of Aeneas in his second speech in the poem (198–209) with that in his first speech (92–101); in what ways might the first speech be viewed as retrospective and "Trojan" and the second forward-looking and "Roman." Cite specific references in both speeches to illustrate your points.

6. Compare this speech (198–209) with that of Odysseus in Homer *Odyssey* 12.208f.; what are the most striking similarities and differences?

7. Vergil routinely employs the device of the "omniscient narrator"; how is this apparent in 208–09?

210 *praeda, -ae, f., *booty, plunder, spoil, loot; prey* (of a hunter, animal, etc.).
  *accingō, accingere, accīnxī, accīnctus, *to gird, surround; to equip, arm; to prepare, get ready* (for).
  daps, dapis, f., often pl. with sg. meaning, *sacrificial meal; feast, banquet.*

211 tergus, tergoris, n., *back* (of an animal, esp. the meat or the hide).
  *dīripiō, dīripere, dīripuī, dīreptus, *to tear away, pull off; to plunder, rob.*
  *costa, -ae, f., *rib; flank, back* (of a body).
  *nūdō (1), *to strip bare, strip off; to uncover, expose (to view), reveal.*

212 pars: i.e., of the Trojans; collective pl., hence pl. secant and figunt.
  *secō, secāre, secuī, sectus, *to sever, cut* (with a knife, etc.); *to cut into pieces; to cut through, move rapidly through, cleave a path through.*
  verū, verūs, n., *spit, skewer.*
  trementia: sc. viscera, with both secant and figunt.
  *fīgō, fīgere, fīxī, fīxus, *to drive in, fix in, insert; to pierce, shoot* (with a weapon); *to set down, place firmly, plant.*

213 aēnum, -ī, n., *bronze vessel; pot, cauldron* (here for cooking or cleaning up).

214 *victus, -ūs, m., *sustenance, nourishment, food; way of life.*
  *herba, -ae, f., *small plant, herb;* sg. or pl., *grass.*

215 *impleō, implēre, implēvī, implētus, + abl. or gen., *to fill* (often used reflexively, as here; i.e., *they are filled with = they fill themselves with*).
  *Bacchus, -ī, m., *Bacchus* (the god of vegetation, the grapevine, and wine); by METONYMY, *wine.*
  ferīna, -ae, f., *flesh of wild animals, meat.*

216 exēmpta . . . sermōne (217): an elegant variation, with CHIASMUS in 216 followed by INTERLOCKED WORD ORDER in the next verse; as usual, forms of esse must be supplied (ELLIPSIS), est with exēmpta and sunt with remōtae.
  mēnsae . . . remōtae: traditionally the dining tables were removed after a Roman meal, but here the meaning is simply that the meal was concluded; mēnsa often refers to a course or an entire meal, rather than specifically to a table (which obviously the shipwrecked Trojans did not have here).

217 *āmittō, āmittere, āmīsī, āmissus, *to send away; to lose.*
  āmissōs . . . sermōne: by positioning the long ō syllables under the ictus Vergil accentuates the ASSONANCE, which here is perhaps meant to have a mournful effect.

218 spemque metumque inter: the POLYSYNDETON and ANASTROPHE help suggest the ambivalence of the Trojans' emotions.
  *dubius, -a, -um, *uncertain, undecided, hestitant, wavering.*
  dubiī: the adj. here looks back to spem . . . inter (*wavering between . . .*) and forward to seu . . . crēdant (*uncertain whether . . .*).
  *seu or sīve, conj., *whether, or if;* as correlatives, *whether . . . or.*
  vīvere: sc. Trōiānōs; this inf. expresses the Trojans' spem, those in the next line their metum.
  crēdant: subjunct. in an IND. QUEST. introduced by dubiī seu.

210 Illī sē praedae accingunt dapibusque futūrīs:
211 tergora dīripiunt costīs et viscera nūdant;
212 pars in frūsta secant veribusque trementia fīgunt,
213 lītore aēna locant aliī flammāsque ministrant.
214 Tum victū revocant vīrēs, fūsīque per herbam
215 implentur veteris Bacchī pinguisque ferīnae.
216 Postquam exēmpta famēs epulīs mēnsaeque remōtae,
217 āmissōs longō sociōs sermōne requīrunt,
218 spemque metumque inter dubiī, seu vīvere crēdant

Quaestiō

What may be the intended effect of the quick series of verbs in 211–13?

Kylix (wine cup) with eyes and mask of Bacchus
Greek, ca. 540 B.C.
Louvre, Paris, France

219 *extrēmus, -a, -um, *situated at the end, the end of; the rear of; last (part of); final; end (of life); extreme.*

    patī: use of the pres. tense rather than the perf. adds vividness and poignancy.

    exaudiō (4), *to hear.*

    exaudīre vocātōs: possibly a ref. to the Roman custom of shouting out the name of the deceased at funerals, known as **conclāmātiō.**

220 *praecipuē, adv., *particularly, especially.*

    pius: the epithet, applied to Aeneas throughout the poem, connotes devotion to the gods, country, and family and a determination to place their interests before one's own (see note on **pietās** 10).

221 **Amycus, -ī, m.,** *Amycus* (a Trojan warrior).

222 **Lycus, -ī, m.,** *Lycus* (another Trojan).

    Gyās, Gyae, acc. **Gyān,** m., *Gyas* (a Trojan).

    *Cloanthus, -ī, m., *Cloanthus* (a Trojan).

    Orontī (220) / . . . Cloanthum: of these five men, only Orontes had died; Gyas and Cloanthus appear later in Book One, and Amycus and Lycus in Book Nine.

223 **Et . . . erat:** a striking transition, abruptly shifting the scene from earth and the Trojans' lamentations for their lost colleagues to heaven and the gods.

224 *dēspiciō, dēspicere, dēspexī, dēspectus, *to look down on/at; to look down upon, despise, scorn.*

    vēlivolus, -a, -um, *speeding along with sails; with swift sails.*

    vēlivolum: a TRANSFERRED EPITHET, logically applying to the ships that dot the sea below but imaginatively employed by Vergil to describe the sea itself as viewed from Jupiter's lofty vantage point.

    iacentēs: here *widespread, scattered.*

225 *lātus, -a, -um, *broad, wide; wide-open, gaping; extensive, widespread.*

226 *dēfīgō, dēfīgere, dēfīxī, dēfīxus, *to fix by thrusting down, imbed; to keep (one's eyes, thoughts, etc.) fixed on, focus; to keep (one's eyes, etc.) rigidly fixed.*

    *lūmen, lūminis, n., *light, radiance; eye,* esp. pl.; *glance, gaze, sight, vision.*

227 **tālēs . . . cūrās:** i.e., his concerns over what he saw happening in Libya.

228 **trīstior:** in comparison with her customary cheerfulness.

    suffundō, suffundere, suffūdī, suffūsus, *to fill (from beneath); to pour on, cover.*

    oculōs suffūsa: lit., *filled with respect to her eyes* = *with her eyes filled;* in a common poetic usage, the partic. has a reflex. force (the so-called Greek MIDDLE VOICE) and the noun is ACC. OF SPECIFICATION (or RESPECT), another Greek construction.

    *nitēns, nitentis, *shining, bright, radiant.*

229 *adloquor, adloquī, adlocūtus sum, *to speak to, address.*

    *Venus, Veneris, f., *Venus* (goddess of love and generation, identified with the Greek Aphrodite, mother of Aeneas).

    deum: for the form, see note on line 9.

230 *fulmen, fulminis, n., *lightning* (that strikes), *thunderbolt.*

219 sīve extrēma patī nec iam exaudīre vocātōs.

220 Praecipuē pius Aenēās nunc ācris Orontī,

221 nunc Amycī cāsum gemit et crūdēlia sēcum

222 fāta Lycī fortemque Gyān fortemque Cloanthum.

Jupiter surveys the earth from heaven, and Venus
complains to him of Aeneas' suffering

223   Et iam fīnis erat, cum Iuppiter, aethere summō

224 dēspiciēns mare vēlivolum terrāsque iacentēs

225 lītoraque et lātōs populōs, sīc vertice caelī

226 cōnstitit et Libyae dēfīxit lūmina rēgnīs.

227 Atque illum, tālēs iactantem pectore cūrās,

228 trīstior et lacrimīs oculōs suffūsa nitentēs

229 adloquitur Venus: "Ō quī rēs hominumque deumque

230 aeternīs regis imperiīs et fulmine terrēs,

Quaestiō

What is Vergil's purpose in specifically naming several of Aeneas' comrades in 220–22? Comment on the use of anaphora in these lines.

Colossal head of Zeus
Otricoli, Italy, 3rd cent. C.E.
Museo Pio Clementino,
Vatican Museums, Vatican State

231 **quid . . . / quid (232)**: the ANAPHORA and ASYNDETON here, and in 234–36
(**hinc . . . hinc** and **quī . . . quī**), help to convey the intense emotion of Venus'
entreaty.

meus: the word signals the protective role toward her son that Venus will play
throughout the poem.

committere . . . potuēre (232): both **Aenēās** and **Trōes** are subjs.

tantum: adj. with **quid**, *what (offense) so great.*

232 **quibus**: DAT. OF REF.

233 **cūnctus . . . orbis**: HYPERBOLE.

ob Ītaliam: i.e., because their destination is Italy, a country that is fated one day
to overwhelm Juno's beloved Carthage.

234 **hinc**: i.e., from the Trojans.

Rōmānōs: like **ductōrēs**, subj. or pred. noun with **fore** (= **futūrōs esse**), *the
Romans would arise/there would be Romans;* the line's spondaic rhythm helps
emphasize the point.

235 **revocātō**: here *restored, reborn.*

***Teucer, -crī**, m., *Teucer* (father-in-law of Dardanus and ancestor of the
Trojan kings).

236 **quī . . . tenērent**: subjunct. in a SUBORDINATE CL. IN IND. STATE. or perhaps with
the force of a REL. CL. OF PURPOSE.

diciō, diciōnis, f., *dominion, sovereignty; power, authority, sway.*

237 **pollicitus**: sc. **es.**

***sententia, -ae**, f., *thinking, opinion, sentiment; purpose, intention; thought, idea.*

vertit: i.e., from the earlier plan.

238 **Hōc**: i.e., the promise of Troy's rebirth as the Roman empire.

***equidem**, adv., *for my part, personally speaking* (esp. with 1st pers.); *indeed,
in truth.*

***occāsus, -ūs**, m., *opportunity, chance; downfall, destruction.*

239 ***sōlor, -ārī, -ātus sum**, *to give solace, comfort, console; to provide solace for.*

sōlābar: reflex., *I was consoling myself for;* possibly with CONATIVE force, *I tried
to console myself for.*

fātīs . . . fāta: i.e., one possible destiny against another.

***contrārius, -a, -um**, often + dat., *opposite, opposing; opposed, hostile.*

***rependō, rependere, rependī, repēnsus**, *to weigh, balance; to pay/give (in
return).*

240 **eadem**: i.e., the same as for the past several years since Troy's fall.

241 **īnsequitur . . . labōrum**: the emphatic ENJAMBEMENT and the question following
repeat the dynamics of verse 237.

242 **Antēnor, Antēnōris**, m., *Antenor* (a Trojan prince who had escaped the city's
destruction and, according to legend, founded a new settlement in Cisalpine
Gaul at Patavium, modern Padua).

***ēlābor, ēlābī, ēlāpsus**, *to slip out/away from; to escape.*

***Achīvus, -a, -um**, *Achaean, Greek* (referring esp. to those who fought at Troy).

231 quid meus Aenēās in tē committere tantum,
232 quid Trōes potuēre, quibus tot fūnera passīs
233 cūnctus ob Ītaliam terrārum clauditur orbis?
234 Certē hinc Rōmānōs ōlim volventibus annīs,
235 hinc fore ductōrēs, revocātō ā sanguine Teucrī,
236 quī mare, quī terrās omnēs diciōne tenērent,
237 pollicitus—quae tē, genitor, sententia vertit?
238 Hōc equidem occāsum Trōiae trīstēsque ruīnās
239 sōlābar, fātīs contrāria fāta rependēns;
240 nunc eadem fortūna virōs tot cāsibus āctōs
241 īnsequitur. Quem dās fīnem, rēx magne, labōrum?
242 Antēnor potuit, mediīs ēlāpsus Achīvīs,

Quaestiōnēs

1. Explain how the framing of line 233 is appropriate to what Vergil is describing.

2. What several thematic elements from lines 1–11 of the poem's prologue are recalled in the opening lines of Venus' speech (231–41)?—note the several specific verbal echoes. What do you see as the purpose, or the effect, of this repetition?

Roman bronze helmet
of the Thracian type
with scenes of the sack of Troy
Herculaneum, 1st cent. B.C.
Museo Archeologico, Naples, Italy

243 **Illyricus, -a, -um,** *of Illyria* (a region on the eastern coast of the Adriatic, a sea known for its treacherous sailing conditions).

penetrō (1), *to penetrate; to cross, pass by.*

intimus, -a, -um, *innermost, most remote.*

tūtus: Eng. would more likely employ an adv. (see note on **laetī** 35).

244 **Liburnus, -ī,** *Liburnian* (a resident of Liburnia, a district in Illyria; the Liburnians were known for their savagery).

*****fōns, fontis,** m., *spring, fountain, source;* often pl., *water* (from a spring), *waters* (of a sea, river).

superāre: here *to pass,* i.e., sail past.

Timāvus, -ī, m., *Timavus* (a river flowing from the Alps, much of the way underground, into the Gulf of Trieste at the north of the Adriatic sea).

Timāvī / . . . montis / . . . sonantī / . . . locāvit (247): Vergil plays here with end-line rhyme, along with the more common internal rhyme in **Patavī . . . locāvit;** these sound effects, as well as the ALLITERATION in **novem vāstō** and **murmure montis** (cf. **murmure montēs** 55) and **prōruptum et pelagō premit,** are esp. apt in view of the point of **sonantī.**

245 **per ōra novem:** the river courses through several underground channels, emerging into the sea through a number of openings near the coast.

246 **mare . . . pelagō:** an epicism for the massive rush of the river's waters.

prōruptum: Eng. would use a pres. act. partic., *bursting forth.*

*****arvum, -ī,** n., *(plowed) field;* often pl., *lands, countryside.*

247 **Patavium, -ī,** n., *Patavium* (a city in eastern Cisalpine Gaul, near the Adriatic coast, modern Padua; here APPOS. GEN.).

Hīc . . . Patavī: the adv. here means *in this region* rather than *at this very spot,* as Padua is actually some distance from the Timavus; from Venus' perspective on Olympus, however, the two sites would appear relatively close.

248 **arma . . . fīxit:** a triumphant leader might dedicate his weapons to the gods and hang them up in a temple.

249 **placidā . . . quiēscit:** an allusion to Antenor's peaceful retirement (not, as some commentators suppose, to his death).

compostus: = **compositus** (SYNCOPE).

250 **nōs, tua:** both words are emphatic, stressing Venus' indignation and her identification with her son's, and the Trojans', cause.

*****adnuō, adnuere, adnuī, adnūtus,** *to beckon, nod; to nod assent; to grant, concede, promise; to approve.*

251 **īnfandum:** ACC. OF EXCLAMATION.

ūnīus ob īram: cf. the identically positioned **Iūnōnis ob īram** in 4; here Venus refrains from accusing Juno by name.

252 *****prōdō, prōdere, prōdidī, prōditus,** *to put forward, project; to give birth to, produce; to give up, betray, reveal.*

disiungō, disiungere, disiūnxī, disiūnctus, *to unyoke; to separate, keep apart.*

243 Illyricōs penetrāre sinūs atque intima tūtus
244 rēgna Liburnōrum et fontem superāre Timāvī,
245 unde per ōra novem vāstō cum murmure montis
246 it mare prōruptum et pelagō premit arva sonantī.
247 Hīc tamen ille urbem Patavī sēdēsque locāvit
248 Teucrōrum et gentī nōmen dedit armaque fīxit
249 Trōïa, nunc placidā compostus pāce quiēscit:
250 nōs, tua prōgeniēs, caelī quibus adnuis arcem,
251 nāvibus (īnfandum!) āmissīs ūnīus ob īram,
252 prōdimur atque Italīs longē disiungimur ōrīs.

Quaestiōnēs

In what several respects are Antenor's circumstances, as described by Venus in 242–49, aptly contrasted with Aeneas'? What is the point of the many details Vergil includes here?

"Jupiter and Thetis"
Jean Auguste Dominique Ingres
(1780–1867)
Musée Granet,
Aix-en-Provence, France

253 **honōs . . . nōs:** the sound effect is accentuated through placement of the
rhyming syllables under the ictus; by *us* Venus means her son and the
Trojans.

    in scēptra: pl. for sg. and a common METONYMY, *to power.*

    ***repōnō, repōnere, reposuī, repositus,** *to put back, replace; to restore; to lay back,
lay to rest.*

254 **Ollī:** an archaism for **illī;** DAT. WITH COMPOUND VERBS.

    ***subrīdeō, subrīdēre, subrīsī, subrīsus,** *to smile (at).*

    sator, satōris, m., *sower, planter; progenitor, creator.*

255 **serēnō (1),** *to clear up, brighten, lighten.*

256 ***lībō (1),** *to pour a libation of, make an offering of; to touch lightly;* with **ōscula,** *to
kiss gently.*

    ***nāta, -ae,** f., *daughter.*

    dehinc: for the scansion, see on 131, where the same formula (**dehinc tālia
fātur**) is used of Neptune addressing the winds.

257 **metū:** for the dat. form, cf. **currū** (156).

    ***Cytherēa, -ae,** f., *the Cytherean, Venus* (the goddess was so called after the
Aegean island of Cythera, which was sacred to her and in some accounts
her birthplace).

    ***immōtus, -a, -um,** *unmoved, motionless; undisturbed; unchanged, unaltered.*

    immōta: PRED. ADJ.

258 **tibī:** DAT. OF REF., *I tell you, I assure you;* the final -ī is lengthened under the ictus
(DIASTOLE).

    ***cernō, cernere, crēvī, crētus,** *to sift; to distinguish, separate; to see, perceive.*

    ***Lavīnium, -ī,** n., *Lavinium* (see note on line 2).

259 ***sublīmis, -is, -e,** *high up, aloft.*

    sublīmem . . . caelī: i.e., Aeneas will become a god.

260 **magnanimus, -a, -um,** *great-hearted, great-spirited; noble, brave, bold.*

    magnanimum Aenēān: a highly effective and sonorous ENJAMBEMENT.

    neque mē sententia vertit: a direct and emphatic response to Venus' question in
237, deliberately echoing her words **quae tē . . . sententia vertit.**

261 **fābor . . . fātōrum (262):** exhibiting his characteristic fondness for
etymologizing, Vergil here plays on the connection between **fārī** *(to utter
prophetically)* and **fātum** *(a prophetic utterance, fate).*

    ***quandō,** adv. and conj., *when; since.*

    remordeō, remordēre, remordī, remorsus, *to bite back; to gnaw, vex, bother.*

262 **volvēns:** for the image, see note on **volvere Parcās** (22).

    arcānum, -ī, n., *secret, mystery* (here obj. of both **volvēns** and **movēbō**).

    movēbō: *set into motion = depict, disclose.*

264 **contundō, contundere, contudī, contūsus,** *to pound to pieces, crush; to subdue,
quell, suppress.*

    pōnet: ZEUGMA, as the vb. has two different senses with its ALLITERATIVE pair of
objs., *establish* with **mōrēs** (here political *institutions*) and *build* with **moenia.**

265 **rēgnantem:** sc. **eum,** i.e., Aeneas; Vergil often uses partics. in this way, with the
noun or pron. referent to be supplied (cf. **iactantī** 102).

    vīderit . . . trānsierint (266): dum, *until,* often takes the fut. or fut. perf. indic.,
as here (and cf. **dōnec . . . dabit** 273–74); if suspense or purpose is implied,
however, the subjunct. is used.

253　Hic pietātis honōs? Sīc nōs in scēptra repōnis?"

*Jupiter assures Venus that Aeneas' destiny,
and Rome's, will be fulfilled*

254　　Ollī subrīdēns hominum sator atque deōrum
255　vultū, quō caelum tempestātēsque serēnat,
256　ōscula lībāvit nātae, dehinc tālia fatur:
257　"Parce metū, Cytherēa; manent immōta tuōrum
258　fāta tibī; cernēs urbem et prōmissa Lavīnī
259　moenia, sublīmemque ferēs ad sīdera caelī
260　magnanimum Aenēān; neque mē sententia vertit.
261　Hic tibi (fābor enim, quandō haec tē cūra remordet,
262　longius et volvēns fātōrum arcāna movēbō)
263　bellum ingēns geret Ītaliā populōsque ferōcēs
264　contundet mōrēsque virīs et moenia pōnet,
265　tertia dum Latiō rēgnantem vīderit aestās

Quaestiōnēs

1. With specific reference to the text, identify several rhetorical devices that Venus employs in 229–53 in order to enlist her father's aid.

2. How does meter suit meaning in 255?

"The Birth of Venus"
Sandro Botticelli
(1444–1510)
Uffizi, Florence, Italy

266   **ternī, -ae, -a,** *three, three at a time, three in a row, three successive.*

     ***Rutulus, -a, -um,** often m. as a noun, *Rutulian, of the Rutuli* (the first mention in the poem of this ancient Latin tribe who, under the leadership of their prince Turnus, would prove fierce in their opposition to the Trojan incursion).

     hiberna, -ōrum, n. pl., (time spent in) *winter encampment* (here simply *winters*).

     tertia . . . aestās (265) / terna . . . hiberna: the parallel positioning accentuates the ASSONANCE and ANAPHORA, and the wide separation of adj. and noun (with FRAMING in 265 and INTERLOCKED WORD ORDER in 266) helps underscore the duration of Aeneas' reign in Latium before his death.

     ***subigō, subigere, subēgī, subāctus,** to drive (from below); to tame, subdue.*

267   ***Ascanius, -ī,** m., *Ascanius* (son of Aeneas and his wife Creusa, also called Ilus and Iulus; legendary founder of the Latin town of Alba Longa).

     ***Ĭūlus, -ī** (trisyllabic), m., *Iulus* (Ascanius' cognomen, connecting him to the Julian gens, the family of Julius Caesar and Augustus).

     Ĭūlō: dat. by attraction to the case of **cui,** instead of the nom. that might be expected in appos. to **cognōmen.**

268   **Īlus, -ī,** m., *Ilus* (another name of Ascanius).

     rēs: sc. **pūblica,** *state.*

     Īlius, -a, -um, *of Ilium, of Troy, Trojan.*

     Ĭūlō (267) / . . . Īlia: the point of this etymologizing is to connect the family of Julius Caesar through Iulus/Ilus to Ilium/Troy, the Trojan royal house, and ultimately to Venus, mother of Aeneas—an ancestry claimed by both Caesar and Augustus.

     rēgnō: ABL. OF SPECIFICATION, *in power.*

269   **trīgintā,** indecl. adj., *thirty.*

     volvendīs mēnsibus: *of revolving months* (ABL. OF DESCRIPTION); cf. **volventibus annīs** (234).

     orbēs: *circuits (of the earth),* i.e., *years.*

270   ***expleō, explēre, explēvī, explētus,** to fill (up/out); to complete, reach the end of.*

271   ***trānsferō, trānsferre, trānstulī, trānslātus,** to transport, transfer.*

     Alba Longa, -ae, f., *Alba Longa* (a town in Latium, about 12 miles southeast of Rome, founded by Ascanius; see note on **Albānī** 7).

     mūniō (4), *to provide with walls, fortify.*

272   **Hīc . . . annōs:** the halting monosyllables, the slow spondaic rhythms, the ALLITERATION of **t,** and the internal rhyme in **tōtōs . . . annōs,** all make this a particularly sonorous verse. The progression from three years, to 30, to 300 is deliberate, three being regarded as a mystical number; reckoning backward from Rome's traditional founding by Romulus and Remus in 753 B.C. yields a date of ca. 1100 B.C. for the action of the *Aeneid,* a century later than the legendary date of the Trojan War—but Vergil was more interested in the magical symmetry of 333 than in chronological niceties.

     rēgnābitur: impers. pass., *it will be reigned,* but more freely, *kings* (the legendary descendants and successors of Ascanius at Alba) *will rule.*

266 ternaque trānsierint Rutulīs hiberna subāctīs.
267 At puer Ascanius, cui nunc cognōmen Ïūlō
268 additur (Īlus erat, dum rēs stetit Īlia rēgnō),
269 trīgintā magnōs volvendīs mēnsibus orbēs
270 imperiō explēbit, rēgnumque ab sēde Lavīnī
271 trānsferet, et Longam multā vī mūniet Albam.
272 Hīc iam ter centum tōtōs rēgnābitur annōs

Quaestiō

Comment on the suitability of the meter in 269.

"Romulus and Remus"
Peter Paul Rubens (1577–1640)
Musei Capitolini, Rome, Italy

273 *Hectoreus, -a, -um, *of Hector* (the foremost Trojan prince, eldest son of Priam and Hecuba); *Trojan.*

    gente . . . Hectoreā: = gente Hectoris; Vergil (and Lat. poetry in general) frequently employs an adj. where prose would use a proper noun in the gen.

    *sacerdōs, sacerdōtis, m./f., *priest, priestess.*

274 *Mārs, Mārtis, m., *Mars* (Italian god of agriculture and war, counterpart of the Greek Ares); *warfare, fighting* (here ABL. OF AGENT without a prep.).

    gravis: here *pregnant.*

    partus, -ūs, m., *(the action of) giving birth.*

    Īlia, -ae, f., *Ilia* (another name—again chosen to connect Rome to Ilium/Troy—for king Numitor's daughter Rhea Silvia, a Vestal virgin, descendant of Aeneas, and mother of Romulus and Remus, the twin founders of Rome).

275 *fulvus, -a, -um, *brown, tawny, sandy, yellow.*

    nūtrīx, nūtrīcis, *(a child's) nurse, wet-nurse.*

    lupae . . . nūtrīcis: according to the famous legend, Romulus and Remus, the rightful successors to the throne at Alba, were exposed as infants on the flooded banks of the Tiber river by their great-uncle Amulius, who had seized control of the government from his older brother Numitor; when the flood-waters receded, the boys were found and nursed by a she-wolf, and then subsequently rescued and raised by a local shepherd (Faustulus) and his wife (Acca Larentia), with whom they lived until discovering their true identity, overthrowing Amulius, and founding the city of Rome on the banks of the Tiber, where they had years earlier been left to die. Note the line's INTERLOCKED WORD ORDER.

    *tegmen, tegminis, n., *cover, covering; armor, shield; skin, hide.*

    tegmine laetus: Romulus wore the wolf-skin in proud recognition of the she-wolf that had saved him.

276 Rōmulus, -ī, m., *Romulus* (twin brother of Remus and legendary eponymous founder of Rome; the brothers were children of Numitor's daughter, Rhea Silvia, and the god Mars).

    Māvortius, -a, -um, *of Mars* (also called Mavors—see 6.872 below).

    Māvortia . . . / moenia (277): so called since Romulus was a son of Mars.

278 rērum: here *of space;* Vergil's audience doubtless applauded this scene of Jupiter predicting that their empire would know limits of neither time nor space.

279 imperium sine fīne dedī: the brief, ALLITERATIVE clause, with its quick dactylic rhythms and the emphatic use of the perf. tense, recapitulates the point of the preceding verse in its pronouncement of the Augustan conception of Rome as the eternal city.

    *quīn, adv., *indeed, in fact; moreover, furthermore; why not.*

280 metū: either ABL. OF MEANS or, perhaps more likely, ABL. OF CAUSE.

    *fatīgō (1), *to tire out, weary, exhaust; to harass, assail.*

282 rērum: here *of the world.*

    togātus, -a, -um, *toga-clad, wearing the toga* (the formal outer garment worn by free Roman men, and a symbol of Roman nationality and civil authority).

    Iūnō (279) / . . . togātam: Jupiter's prediction here is only finally realized in Book 12 (807–42 below).

273 gente sub Hectoreā, dōnec rēgīna sacerdōs
274 Mārte gravis geminam partū dabit Īlia prōlem.
275 Inde, lupae fulvō nūtrīcis tegmine laetus,
276 Rōmulus excipiet gentem et Māvortia condet
277 moenia Rōmānōsque suō dē nōmine dīcet.
278 Hīs ego nec mētās rērum nec tempora pōnō:
279 imperium sine fīne dedī. Quīn aspera Iūnō,
280 quae mare nunc terrāsque metū caelumque fatīgat,
281 cōnsilia in melius referet, mēcumque fovēbit
282 Rōmānōs, rērum dominōs gentemque togātam.

Quaestiōnēs

1. What are the most striking sound effects in 277?

2. Explain how **rērum ... togātam** (282) may allude to Romans in both their military and civilian roles; comment also on the sound effects in this line.

Capitoline She-Wolf
Etruscan bronze, 5th century B.C.
Twins later added by Antonio Pollaiuolo
Musei Capitolini, Rome, Italy

283 **Sīc placitum:** sc. **est mihi,** idiom, *thus it has pleased me* = *thus it has been decreed by me;* the point, as Austin remarks, is "crisp and authoritative."

Veniet . . . Argīs (285): i.e., the conquest and annexation of Greece as a Roman province will avenge the Trojans for the sack of Troy.

lūstrum, -ī, n., *long period of time, age, generation.*

*****aetās, aetātis,** f., *(one's) age; (period of) time, age; old age.*

284 **Assaracus, -ī,** m., *Assaracus* (a Trojan king, grandfather of Anchises, and thus ancestor of the Romans).

Pthīa, -ae, f., *Pthia* (a town in Thessaly, birthplace of Achilles).

*****Mycēnae, -ārum,** f. pl., *Mycenae* (a city in the Argolid in southern Greece, home of king Agamemnon, leader of the Greek forces in the Trojan War).

285 **servitium, -ī,** n., *slavery, servitude.*

*****dominor, -ārī, -ātus sum,** *to rule, be in control, dominate.*

Argīs: a ref. not only to the Greeks in general but to Argos, home of the hero Diomedes.

286 *****orīgō, orīginis,** f., *first appearance, beginning; birth; starting point.*

pulchrā . . . orīgine: ABL. OF ORIGIN; **pulchrā** here = *noble.*

Caesar, Caesaris, m., *Caesar* (here likely a reference to Gaius Julius Caesar, rather than to Augustus, who, as his adoptive son, had taken his name—but there is perhaps a deliberate, and characteristically Vergilian, ambiguity).

Nāscētur . . . Caesar: a majestic line, with its resounding spondees and suspenseful INTERLOCKED WORD ORDER, vb. first, epithets following, and the subj. **Caesar** reserved to the end.

287 **terminō (1),** *to mark the boundaries of, limit.*

*****astrum, -ī,** n., usually pl., *star;* pl., *sky, heavens; heaven* (home of the gods).

quī terminet astrīs: REL. CL. OF PURPOSE; the prose order would be **quī imperium Ōceanō (et) fāmam astrīs terminet.**

288 **Iūlius, -ī,** m., *Julius* (here Julius Caesar—see note on 286).

Iūlius . . . Ĭūlō: FRAMING the line with the two names helps underscore the etymological connection (see on 268)

289 **caelō . . . / accipiēs (290):** i.e., he will become a god in heaven; Caesar was officially deified in 42 B.C.

*****spolium, -ī,** n., *skin, hide* (of an animal); usually pl., *arms, weapons* (stripped from a fallen soldier), *spoils, booty.*

onustus, -a, -um, *having a load, loaded, (heavily) laden.*

spoliīs . . . onustum: a reference to Julius Caesar's successful campaigns in Asia Minor and Egypt during the early 40's B.C. (though there is perhaps also a secondary allusion to Augustus' victory over Cleopatra and Marc Antony at the battle of Actium in 31 B.C. and possibly also to his defeat of the Parthians in 20).

290 *****vōtum, -ī,** n., *vow* (made to a god to do something in return for a granted prayer); *votive offering; prayer.*

291 **Aspera . . . bellīs:** except for the intrusion of the adv. **tum,** a perfect GOLDEN LINE (adj.[a]/adj.[b]/vb./noun[a]/noun[b]).

mītēscō, mītēscere, *to soften, become less tough; to become less fierce.*

283 Sīc placitum. Veniet lūstrīs lābentibus aetās
284 cum domus Assaracī Pthīam clārāsque Mycēnās
285 servitiō premet ac victīs dominābitur Argīs.
286 Nāscētur pulchrā Trōiānus orīgine Caesar,
287 imperium Ōceanō, fāmam quī terminet astrīs,
288 Iūlius, ā magnō dēmissum nōmen Ïūlō.
289 Hunc tū ōlim caelō spoliīs Orientis onustum
290 accipiēs sēcūra; vocābitur hic quoque vōtīs.
291 Aspera tum positīs mītēscent saecula bellīs:

Julius Caesar
1st cent. B.C.
Museo Pio Clementino,
Vatican Museums,
Vatican State

292 **cānus, -a, -um,** *white; white-/grey-haired.*
> **Fidēs:** *Good Faith,* personified and worshipped as a goddess, was from earliest times (hence **cāna**) venerated as one of the prime Roman virtues.
> ***Vesta, -ae,** f., *Vesta* (goddess of the domestic hearth and protectress of families).
> **Remus, -ī,** m., *Remus* (legendary twin brother of Romulus).
> ***Quirīnus, -ī,** m., *Quirinus* (a god worshipped on Rome's Quirinal hill, associated with Mars and identified with the deified Romulus).

293 ***iūs, iūris,** n., *law; right, justice; privilege.*
> ***dīrus, -a, -um,** *awful, dire, dreadful* (here a TRANSFERRED EPITHET).
> ***ferrum, -ī,** n., *iron; iron tool; sword; armed might.*
> ***artus, -a, -um,** *tight, tightly fastened.*
> **ferrō et compāgibus artīs:** HENDIADYS for *tightly fastened iron chains.*

294 **Bellī:** personified, like **Fidēs** (292), *War* here is associated with the god Janus, whose temple doors were closed only when Rome was at peace; this had occurred only three times in Rome's history, most recently under Augustus (in 29 and 25 B.C.). The line's opening spondees suit the notion of the temple doors held fast.
> **Furor:** the madness of civil war in particular, another vivid PERSONIFICATION; cf. **furor arma ministrat** (150).
> ***impius, -a, -um,** *wicked, immoral, impious* (esp. apt here because of the allusion to civil strife).

295 **saeva sedēns super:** ALLITERATION, perhaps even ONOMATOPOEIA suggesting the creature's angry hissing.
> ***vinciō, vincīre, vīnxī, vīnctus,** *to fasten (with bonds), tie (up).*
> ***aēnus, -a, -um,** *(made of) bronze, brazen.*

296 ***nōdus, -ī,** m., *knot* (formed by tying); *knot, node* (of a tree); *knotty problem, difficulty.*
> ***horridus, -a, -um,** *rough, bristly; wild, rugged; unkempt; grim, dreadful.*
> **fremet horridus:** the adj. here has adv. force, as often in Lat. verse.
> ***cruentus, -a, -um,** *stained with blood, bloody, bleeding.*

297 **Haec ait:** Vergil commonly uses such phrases to mark the close of speeches, an esp. important device for listening audiences.
> **Māia, -ae,** f., *Maia* (eldest of the seven Pleiades, mother of Mercury by Jupiter; here ABL. OF ORIGIN).
> ***gignō, gignere, genuī, genitus,** *to bring into being, create; to give birth to.*
> **Māiā genitum:** the partic. here essentially = **fīlium,** i.e., Mercury (the Greek Hermes), Jupiter's messenger.

298 **novae:** with **Karthāginis** not **arcēs** (cf. line 366 below); the 4th-cent. commentator Servius remarks that **Karthāgō** was Punic for **nova cīvitās,** so Vergil may be etymologizing here.
> ***pateō, patēre, patuī,** *to open up, be open, lie open; to be visible, be revealed.*
> **pateant:** in primary sequence as part of Jupiter's command to Mercury, vs. **arcēret,** which is in secondary sequence (after the HIST. PRES. main vb. **dēmittit** 297) to indicate the overall purpose of the mission.

292 cāna Fidēs et Vesta, Remō cum frātre Quirīnus
293 iūra dabunt; dīrae ferrō et compāgibus artīs
294 claudentur Bellī portae; Furor impius intus,
295 saeva sedēns super arma et centum vīnctus aēnīs
296 post tergum nōdīs, fremet horridus ōre cruentō.”

*Jupiter dispatches Mercury to Carthage to insure
that Dido and her people welcome the Trojans*

297   Haec ait et Māiā genitum dēmittit ab altō,
298 ut terrae utque novae pateant Karthāginis arcēs

Quaestiōnēs

1. How is meter appropriate to meaning in the first half of 294?

2. Lines 291–96 allude to the **Pāx Rōmāna** established by Augustus; with specific reference to the Latin, comment on the several images of peace evoked in these lines. What is the point of the reference to Remus in this context?

3. Compare in detail Vergil's description in 293–96 of Furor's imprisonment with his description of the winds' imprisonment in 52–57. What specific verbal correspondences do you detect? What traits do Aeolus' winds and Furor have in common? Do you think Vergil deliberately connects the two, and, if so, what may his purpose be?

4. Contrast the scene in 223–96 with those in *Iliad* 1.495f. and *Odyssey* 5.5f., which were important sources for Vergil; how is Jupiter's response here a very significant amplification of those in Homer?

"Flying Mercury"
Bronze, after 1565
Giambologna
(1529–1608)
Louvre, Paris, France

299 *hospitium, -ī, n., *entertainment of guests, hospitality; guest-host relationship; welcome, reception.*

hospitiō: ABL. OF ATTENDANT CIRCUMSTANCE or MANNER or possibly DAT. OF PURPOSE.

*nescius, -a, -um, *not knowing, unaware, ignorant* (of).

*Dīdō, Dīdōnis, acc. Dīdō, f., *Dido* (queen of Carthage and daughter of the Tyrian king Belus, first named here and of course a major player throughout *Aeneid* 1–4).

300 arcēret: sc. eōs (the Trojans).

*āēr, āeris, acc. sg. āera, m., *air; heaven, sky; mist, cloud.*

301 *rēmigium, -ī, n., *set of oars, oarage; oarsmen.*

*āla, -ae, f., *wing; wing* (of an army), *squadron.*

rēmigiō ālārum: the same METAPHOR is used of Daedalus' wings in 6.19 below.

citus, -a, -um, *swift, quick* (here with adv. force; cf. on **horridus** 296).

302 pōnunt: = dēpōnunt; use of a simple vb. in place of an associated compound is common in Lat. verse (cf. positīs . . . bellīs 291).

*Poenus, -ī, m., *Carthaginian.*

303 in prīmīs, idiom, *especially, particularly, above all.*

304 benignus, -a, -um, *kind, beneficent, generous.*

quiētum (303) / . . . benignam: CHIASMUS, with each adj. emphatically positioned at line's end.

306 *ut prīmum, idiom, *as soon as.*

*almus, -a, -um, *nurturing, fostering, life-giving;* as applied esp. to goddesses and priestesses, *gracious, kindly, benevolent.*

exīre: this and the several infs. following depend on **cōnstituit** (309).

307 *accēdō, accēdere, accessī, accessus, *to go to, come to, draw near, approach.*

quās . . . accesserit: like **quī teneant** (308), IND. QUEST. depending on **quaerere** (309).

308 *incultus, -a, -um, *uncultivated, wild.*

inculta videt: sc. ea esse, n. to refer to antecedents of different genders, **locōs, ōrās**); the final syllable of the vb. here, occurring at the CAESURA and under the ictus, is scanned long.

*fera, -ae, f., *wild animal, beast.*

-ne . . . -ne: here *whether . . . or.*

309 exācta: partic. from **exigō**, used here as a substantive, *what he had found out.*

310 convexum, -ī, n., *curve, hollow; arch, dome, vault.*

convexō nemorum: i.e., in a cove on the wooded shore, or perhaps beneath the over-arching trees of the grove; the entire scene in 310–11 looks back to the description in 162–65.

cavātus, -a, -um, *hollow; hollowed out, cavelike.*

311 circum: here adv.

312 occulō, occulere, occuluī, occultus, *to hide from view, conceal.*

*gradior, gradī, gressus sum, *to proceed, step, walk.*

313 bīnī, -ae, -a, *two each; two, a set* (of), *a pair* (of).

lātō . . . ferrō: i.e., with broad blades; ABL. OF DESCRIPTION.

crīspō (1), *to curl; to shake, brandish; to balance* (something that is shaking).

hastīle, hastīlis, n., *shaft of a spear; spear.*

299 hospitiō Teucrīs, nē fātī nescia Dīdō
300 fīnibus arcēret. Volat ille per āera magnum
301 rēmigiō ālārum ac Libyae citus astitit ōrīs.
302 Et iam iussa facit, pōnuntque ferōcia Poenī
303 corda, volente deō; in prīmīs rēgīna quiētum
304 accipit in Teucrōs animum mentemque benignam.

Aeneas and Achates explore the area and encounter
Venus in the guise of a young huntress

305   At pius Aenēās per noctem plūrima volvēns,
306 ut prīmum lūx alma data est, exīre locōsque
307 explōrāre novōs, quās ventō accesserit ōrās,
308 quī teneant (nam inculta videt), hominēsne feraene,
309 quaerere cōnstituit sociīsque exācta referre.
310 Classem in convexō nemorum sub rūpe cavātā
311 arboribus clausam circum atque horrentibus umbrīs
312 occulit; ipse ūnō graditur comitātus Achātē,
313 bīna manū lātō crīspāns hastīlia ferrō.

Quaestiōnēs

1. Comment specifically on the ways in which Vergil marks the scene shift at 305–06.

2. What descriptive details are shared between the scenes in 162–65 and 310–11?

3. How has Vergil created a word-picture in 311?

314 **Cui:** = **eī** (Aeneas), dat. with the compound **obvia**; Lat. often uses a rel. pron. at
the beginning of a sent., where Eng. would employ a pers. pron.

obvius, -a, -um, in the path of, in front of; idiom with **sē ferre,** to encounter.

315 **habitus, -ūs,** m., *condition; appearance, dress.*

gerēns: ZEUGMA, as the vb. has varying senses with each of its three objs.

316 **Spartānus, -a, -um,** *of Sparta* (a city of southern Greece noted for its militarism
and the hardiness of its athletic young women), *Spartan.*

quālis, -is, -e, interrog., *of what sort, what kind;* rel., *of which sort/kind, (such) as,
(just) as* (someone) *when she/he* (often, with or without the correlative **tālis,**
introducing a SIMILE).

Thrēissus, -a, -um, *of Thrace* (a district in northern Greece whose people were
regarded as warlike), *Thracian.*

317 **Harpalycē, Harpalycēs,** f., *Harpalyce* (daughter of the Thracian king Harpalycus,
who raised her as a warrior; after his death she lived in the wild and became a
legendarily fast runner, swifter than horses and even the wind).

quālis (316) . . . / **Harpalycē:** *such as Harpalyce (when she . . .).*

volucer, -cris, -cre, flying; winged, swift.

praevertor, praevertī, praeversus sum, *to urge on; to outstrip, outrun.*

Hebrus, -ī, m., *Hebrus* (a river in Thrace).

318 *umerus, -ī,* m., *shoulder.*

dē mōre, idiom, *according to custom, in the usual manner.*

habilis, -is, -e, *easy to handle; ready (for use).*

319 **vēnātrīx, vēnātrīcis,** f., *huntress.*

coma, -ae, f., often pl., *hair (of the head).*

diffundō, diffundere, diffūdī, diffūsus, to spread widely, scatter.

dederat . . . diffundere: for **dare** + inf., cf. line 66 above.

320 *nūdus, -a, -um,* naked, nude; empty, deserted.

genū, -ūs, n., *knee* (here ACC. OF SPECIFICATION or RESPECT—see on 228 above).

genū nōdō: the CAESURA accentuates the internal rhyme in **nūda . . . nōdō.**

collēcta: the partic. has act. force, with **sinūs . . . fluentēs** as obj.; see note on
oculōs suffūsa (228).

fluō, fluere, flūxī, flūxus, to flow, stream.

321 **heus,** interj., *hey (there), hello* (used to attract someone's attention).

mōnstrāte: sc. **mihi.**

meārum / . . . **sorōrum** (322): the prose order would be **sī quam sorōrum
meārum hīc errantem forte vīdistis.**

322 **quam:** indef. after **sī,** *any.*

323 **succīnctus, -a, -um,** *bound up, girded;* + abl., *equipped* (with).

pharetra, -ae, f., *quiver.*

maculōsus, -a, -um, *stained, blotted; variegated, spotted, striped.*

lynx, lyncis, f., *lynx.*

324 *spūmō* (1), *to foam, froth, be covered with foam; to foam with saliva.*

aper, -prī, m., *wild boar.*

325 **Venus . . . Veneris:** POLYPTOTON (remember to regularly consult the general
Introduction's list of "Poetic, Rhetorical, and Metrical Devices and Figures of
Speech," which includes definitions and references to other examples).

ōrsus: sc. **est** (likewise with **audīta** and **vīsa** in the next line).

326 **mihi:** DAT. OF AGENT; the second **-ī** is lengthened under the ictus (DIASTOLE).

314 Cui māter mediā sēsē tulit obvia silvā,

315 virginis ōs habitumque gerēns et virginis arma

316 Spartānae, vel quālis equōs Thrēissa fatīgat

317 Harpalycē volucremque fugā praevertitur Hebrum.

318 Namque umerīs dē mōre habilem suspenderat arcum

319 vēnātrīx dederatque comam diffundere ventīs,

320 nūda genū nōdōque sinūs collēcta fluentēs.

321 Ac prior "Heus," inquit, "iuvenēs, mōnstrāte, meārum

322 vīdistis sī quam hīc errantem forte sorōrum,

323 succīnctam pharetrā et maculōsae tegmine lyncis,

324 aut spūmantis aprī cursum clāmōre prementem."

325   Sīc Venus et Veneris contrā sīc fīlius ōrsus:

326 "Nūlla tuārum audīta mihī neque vīsa sorōrum,

Quaestiōnēs

1. Comment on the word order in lines 313 and 314.

2. How does meter suit meaning in 317?

327 **memorem:** DELIBERATIVE SUBJUNCT., *should I call.*
    tibi: DAT. OF POSSESSION with **est** understood.
329 **an . . . an:** here *either . . . or.*
    *Phoebus, -ī, m., *Phoebus Apollo* (god of the sun, civilization, and the arts,
        brother of Diana).
    sanguinis: i.e., the bloodline or family; GEN. OF THE WHOLE.
330 **sīs . . . levēs . . . doceās (332):** the series of JUSSIVE SUBJUNCT. cls. form a
        dramatic TRICOLON CRESCENS.
    fēlīx: here *propitious, favorable.*
    quaecumque: sc. **es.**
331 **quō . . . / iactēmur (332):** IND. QUEST. with **doceās.**
    orbis: sc. **terrārum.**
332 **locōrumque:** the word produces a rare HYPERMETRIC LINE, a syllable too long,
        with the **-que** eliding with **errāmus** at the beginning of the next verse.
333 **errāmus . . . āctī:** with the ASSONANCE of **ā** and **hūc . . . flūctibus,** the
        ALLITERATION in **ventō . . . vāstīs,** and the slow, labored spondees, the line
        is especially sonorous and well-suited to Aeneas' description of his men's
        suffering.
    vāstīs et flūctibus: cf. **vāstōs . . . flūctūs (86);** for the word order, see note on
        sed (19).
334 **Multa . . . dextrā:** for **dextrā** see note on 98 above; nearly a GOLDEN LINE, the
        single verse aptly closes Aeneas' speech with a majestic offer of sacrifice to the
        goddess.
    nostrā: = **meā.**
    *hostia, -ae, f., *sacrificial animal, sacrificial victim.*
    Multa . . . hostia: collective sg., *many a . . . .*
335 *dignor, -ārī, -ātus sum, *to consider* (someone/acc.) *worthy* (of something/abl.).
336 *gestō (1), *to carry with one, carry about; to wear; to carry* (in one's mind), *harbor*
        (thoughts, etc.).
337 *purpureus, -a, -um, *purple, crimson* (Tyre was well known for exporting
        purple dye).
    *altē, adv., *high, in a high position.*
    sūra, -ae, f., *calf* (of the leg).
    coturnus, -ī, m., *(high) boot* (worn by hunters and tragic actors).
338 *Pūnicus, -a, -um, *Punic, Carthaginian.*
    Agēnor, Agēnoris, m., *Agenor* (brother of Belus and legendary founder of Tyre).
339 *Libycus, -a, -um, *Libyan, of Libya* (a region of North Africa); *(North) African.*
    fīnēs Libycī: sc. **sunt.**
    intractābilis, -is, -e, *unmanageable, unconquerable.*
341 *germānus, -ī, m., *brother* (here Dido's brother Pygmalion—see 346f.).
    Longa . . . longae: i.e., it would take long to tell the whole complicated story.
342 *ambāgēs, ambāgum, f. pl., *roundabout course, twists and turns; enigmas.*
    *fastīgium, -ī, n., *sharp point, tip; rooftop, top; high point.*
343 *Sȳchaeus, -ī, m., *Sychaeus* (deceased husband of Dido).
    dīs, dītis, *wealthy, rich.*
    aurī: GEN. OF SPECIFICATION with **dītissimus;** Eng. would say *in gold.* **Aurī** is a
        widely accepted EMENDATION; the mss. have **agrī,** which may be the correct
        reading.

327 ō—quam tē memorem, virgō? Namque haud tibi vultus
328 mortālis, nec vōx hominem sonat; ō, dea certē
329 (an Phoebī soror? an Nymphārum sanguinis ūna?),
330 sīs fēlīx nostrumque levēs, quaecumque, labōrem,
331 et quō sub caelō tandem, quibus orbis in ōrīs
332 iactēmur doceās: ignārī hominumque locōrumque
333 errāmus ventō hūc vāstīs et flūctibus āctī.
334 Multa tibi ante ārās nostrā cadet hostia dextrā."

Venus, still in disguise, tells Aeneas and Achates where
they are and relates to them the story of Dido's
flight from Tyre and her founding of Carthage

335   Tum Venus: "Haud equidem tālī mē dignor honōre;
336 virginibus Tyriīs mōs est gestāre pharetram
337 purpureōque altē sūrās vincīre coturnō.
338 Pūnica rēgna vidēs, Tyriōs, et Agēnoris urbem;
339 sed fīnēs Libycī, genus intractābile bellō.
340 Imperium Dīdō Tyriā regit urbe profecta,
341 germānum fugiēns. Longa est iniūria, longae
342 ambāgēs; sed summa sequar fastīgia rērum.
343 Huic coniūnx Sȳchaeus erat, dītissimus aurī

Quaestiōnēs

1. How is the enjambement in 328 especially effective?

2. Based on what you know of Diana (the Greek Artemis), why is it not surprising that Aeneas in 329 mistakes the huntress for her?

3. Comment on the word-picture in 337.

4. What is the effect of the anaphora and asyndeton in 341?

5. What is the most striking sound effect in 342?

344 **Phoenīx, Phoenīcis**, m., *Phoenician, of Phoenicia* (country along the eastern
Mediterranean coast, former home of Dido; here GEN. OF THE WHOLE).
miserae: i.e., Dido; DAT. OF AGENT.

345 **cui**: the antecedent is **Sȳchaeus** (343) not **miserae** (344).
*****intāctus, -a, -um**, *untouched; undamaged; unharmed, unscathed; virgin* (here
sc. **eam**).
iugō (1), *to bind; to join in marriage* (for the SYNCOPE, see on **audierat** 20).

346 **ōminibus**: i.e., the auspices ritually taken at the wedding.
*****Tyros, -ī**, f., *Tyre* (capital of Phoenicia).

347 *****Pygmaliōn, Pygmaliōnis**, m., *Pygmalion* (brother of Dido and co-heir of the
throne at Tyre).

348 **Quōs inter**: = **inter eōs** (i.e., the family); ANASTROPHE.
medius: in the pred. with **quōs inter**, i.e., *into their midst*.
furor. Ille: the strong DIAERESIS following the fourth foot (the so-called BUCOLIC
DIAERESIS) is unusual and focuses extra attention on both words.
Sychaeum: the **y** is shortened to suit the meter (SYSTOLE).

349 **impius**: used earlier in connection with **furor** at 294.
*****caecus, -a, -um**, *blind, blinded; dark, black, gloomy; unseen, hidden.*
amōre / . . . amōrum (350): Vergil's emphatic placement of these two words (and
cf. **amantem** 352) underscores the two very different passions he describes.
Amōre is ABL. OF CAUSE; use of the pl. **amōrēs** in referring to a specific
relationship is common in Lat. prose and verse.

350 *****incautus, -a, -um**, *incautious, unwary, unsuspecting.*

351 *****germāna, -ae**, f., *sister.*
*****factum, -ī**, n., *deed, act, action.*
aegram: here, with **amantem** (352), *lovesick.*

352 **multa malus simulāns**: an elegantly musical phrase; for **malus** Eng. would
employ an adv., *wickedly.*
*****vānus, -a, -um**, *empty, insubstantial; illusory, meaningless; useless, (in) vain.*
*****spēs, speī**, f., *hope, exspectation.*
lūsit: here *deceived.*
*****amāns, amantis**, m./f., *sweetheart, lover.*

353 **Ipsa . . . imāgō**: FRAMING the line with these key related words, delaying **imāgō**
to the end, and ENJAMBEMENT of **coniugis** (354) all create suspense, and the
ALLITERATION in **ipsa sed in somnīs** adds an appropriately eerie sound effect.
in somnīs: i.e., as often, = *in a dream.*
*****inhumātus, -a, -um**, *unburied* (here a further insult dealt by Pygmalion to
Sychaeus).

354 *****attollō, attollere**, *to raise, lift up, elevate.*
*****pallidus, -a, -um**, *pale, colorless, pallid.*
modīs . . . mīrīs: the expression is commonly used of a mystical or uncanny
occurrence.

355 **crūdēlēs . . . pectora**: a sonorous line, opening with slow, somber spondees and
then accelerating in the violently ALLITERATIVE dactyls -**iectaque pectora**.
*****trāiciō, trāicere, trāiēcī, trāiectus**, *to throw across; to transfix, pierce.*

356 *****retegō, retegere, retēxī, retēctus**, *to uncover, lay bare; to make visible, reveal.*

344 Phoenīcum et magnō miserae dīlēctus amōre,
345 cui pater intāctam dederat prīmīsque iugārat
346 ōminibus. Sed rēgna Tyrī germānus habēbat
347 Pygmaliōn, scelere ante aliōs immānior omnēs.
348 Quōs inter medius vēnit furor. Ille Sychaeum
349 impius ante ārās atque aurī caecus amōre
350 clam ferrō incautum superat, sēcūrus amōrum
351 germānae; factumque diū cēlāvit et aegram,
352 multa malus simulāns, vānā spē lūsit amantem.
353 Ipsa sed in somnīs inhumātī vēnit imāgō
354 coniugis, ōra modīs attollēns pallida mīrīs:
355 crūdēlēs ārās trāiectaque pectora ferrō
356 nūdāvit, caecumque domūs scelus omne retēxit.

Quaestiōnēs

1. How does Vergil use word order effectively in 347?

2. What several actions detailed by Vergil in 349–52 justify his characterization of Pygmalion as **impius?**

"Portrait of Dido"
Dosso Dossi
(ca. 1479–1542)
Galleria Doria Pamphili,
Rome, Italy

357 **celerō** (1), *to hasten, hurry, rush.*
   *****suādeō, suādēre, suāsī, suāsus,** *to suggest, urge, advise* (often + inf. in poetry vs. the **ut** cl. common in prose).
358 **auxilium:** in appos. to **veterēs . . . thēsaurōs** (359), *as an aid.*
   *****reclūdō, reclūdere, reclūsī, reclūsus,** *to open (up), lay open; to dig up; to reveal, uncover; to draw* (a sword).
359 **thēsaurus, -ī,** m., *treasure-chamber, vault; treasure.*
   *****ignōtus, -a, -um,** *unknown, unfamiliar, strange;* as a substantive, *stranger.*
   ignōtum: i.e., no one but Sychaeus knew of its existence.
   argentum, -ī, n., *silver.*
   *****pondus, ponderis,** n., *weight, mass.*
361 **quibus:** DAT. OF POSSESSION; sc. **eī,** subj. of **conveniunt,** as antecedent.
   *****odium, -ī,** n., *dislike, hatred.*
   *****tyrannus, -ī,** m., *tyrant, despot.*
364 *****ops, opis,** f., *power, ability; resources, wealth.*
   dux . . . factī: sc. **est;** an often quoted epigram.
365 *****dēveniō, dēvenīre, dēvēnī, dēventūrus,** *to come to, arrive at.*
366 **novae Karthāginis arcem:** cf. 298 above.
367 *****mercor, -ārī, -ātus sum,** *to buy, purchase* (here sc. **sunt**).
   *****solum, -ī,** n., *base, bottom* (of a structure); *soil, ground, land, property.*
   Byrsa, -ae, f., *Byrsa* (legendary name of the citadel of Carthage and Greek for "bull's hide"—confused with the Phoenician word for "citadel," which was **bosra**).
   **factī . . . `Byrsam':** in appos. with **solum,** *(called) `Byrsa' from the name of their deed* (which is alluded to in the following verse).
368 **taurīnus, -a, -um,** *of a bull.*
   taurīnō . . . tergō: According to legend the Tyrian settlers purchased from the natives at a set price as much property as they could surround with a bull's hide; shrewdly, they cut the hide into very narrow strips and plotted out a large expanse of land. By FRAMING the line with adj. and noun Vergil produces a clever WORD-PICTURE.
   possent: subjunct. subordinate cl. in an implied IND. STATE., referring to the agreement made between the natives and the settlers ("they said that the Tyrians could purchase as much land as . . .").
369 **vōs quī:** = **quī (estis) vōs.**
370 **tālibus:** sc. **verbīs respondet.**
371 **suspīrō** (1), *to sigh, speak with a sigh.*
372 **Ō dea:** despite her denial in 335–37, Aeneas knows she must be a goddess.
   sī . . . compōnet (374): a MIXED FUT. CONDITION (unless the ms. variant **compōnat** is correct, as some editors assume).
   *****pergō, pergere, perrēxī, perrēctūrus,** *to make one's way, move on, proceed.*
373 **vacō** (1), *to be empty;* impers. + inf., *there is time/opportunity* (to).
   annālis, annālis, m., *book of annals;* pl., *annals, records, history.*

357 Tum celerāre fugam patriāque excēdere suādet
358 auxiliumque viae veterēs tellūre reclūdit
359 thēsaurōs, ignōtum argentī pondus et aurī.
360 Hīs commōta, fugam Dīdō sociōsque parābat.
361 Conveniunt quibus aut odium crūdēle tyrannī
362 aut metus ācer erat; nāvēs, quae forte parātae,
363 corripiunt onerantque aurō. Portantur avārī
364 Pygmaliōnis opēs pelagō; dux fēmina factī.
365 Dēvēnēre locōs ubi nunc ingentia cernēs
366 moenia surgentemque novae Karthāginis arcem,
367 mercātīque solum, factī dē nōmine 'Byrsam,'
368 taurīnō quantum possent circumdare tergō.
369 Sed vōs quī tandem? Quibus aut vēnistis ab ōrīs?
370 Quōve tenētis iter?"

Aeneas replies, identifying himself and briefly chronicling
his travails and his fated mission

Quaerentī tālibus ille
371 suspīrāns īmōque trahēns ā pectore vōcem:
372 "Ō dea, sī prīmā repetēns ab orīgine pergam
373 et vacet annālēs nostrōrum audīre labōrum,

Quaestiōnēs

1. How does meter suit meaning in 357? Comment on the word order in the same line.

2. Venus' narrative of Dido's travails and her eventual founding of Carthage in 338–68 constitute a story within a story, a sort of miniature epic known as an "epyllion"; what are the essential dramatic actions in this mini-epic? In what several respects does Dido's story parallel Aeneas'?

3. At what several points in Venus' narrative (338–68) are there details to support the emendation of **agrī** to **aurī** in 343?

374 **ante:** here adv., *beforehand, sooner*, i.e., before the whole tale can be told.
compōnet: here *lay to rest*.
vesper, -perī, m., *evening* (here PERSONIFIED).
*Olympus, -ī, m., *Mt. Olympus* (mythical home of the gods on the border
between Thessaly and Macedonia); *sky, heaven(s)*.

377 *fors, fortis,** f., *chance, luck; destiny; chance happening, accident.*
forte suā: i.e., *capriciously, in a random act of nature;* **forte** is deliberately
repeated from 375 in a different sense, a type of wordplay Vergil enjoyed.
appellō, appellere, appulī, appulsus, *to drive* (something) *to, bring to.*

380 **Ītaliam . . . patriam:** according to tradition, Troy's founder, Dardanus, had
migrated to Troy from Etruria, so Italy was in fact the Trojans' fatherland.
genus ab Iove summō: Dardanus was son of Jupiter and Electra; **genus** is acc.,
in parallel with **patriam** as obj. of **quaerō** (Aeneas seeks out his native Italian
kinsmen), not nom. with **est** understood, as some editors assume.

381 **Bis . . . aequor:** a GOLDEN LINE.
dēnī, -ae, -a, *ten each; a group of ten; ten.*

382 **mātre deā:** ironic, as Aeneas remains unaware that he is speaking with his
mother.

383 *convellō, convellere, convulsī, convulsus,** *to tug at, pull violently; to pull up, tear
up; to undermine, tear down; to shake, batter.*
*supersum, superesse, superfuī,** *to be above; to survive, remain.*

384 *egeō, egēre, eguī** + gen. or abl., *to need, want; to be needy, indigent.*
egēns: here functioning simply as an adj.; the Romans took pride in their
humble origins, contrasted here with Phoenician wealth.
*dēsertus, -a, -um,** *empty of people, deserted; left alone, lonely;* n. pl. as noun,
unfrequented places, wilderness.
*peragrō (1),** *to travel over, wander throughout.*

385 **Eurōpa, -ae,** f., *Europe.*
*Asia, -ae,** f., *Asia.*
*pellō, pellere, pepulī, pulsus,** *to beat against, push; to drive away; to dispel.*
*queror, querī, questus sum,** *to complain (of), protest* (here sc. **eum**).

386 **interfor, -ārī, -ātus sum,** *to speak while another is speaking, interrupt, interpose.*

387 *quisquis, quidquid,** *whoever, whatever.*
Quisquis es: with continued deceit, and looking back to **sī . . . iit** (375–76),
Venus pretends not to know of Aeneas' fame.
haud . . . invīsus: LITOTES.

388 **vītālis, -is, -e,** *of/pertaining to life, necessary to life.*
*carpō, carpere, carpsī, carptus,** *to pluck, gather, harvest; to seize; to eat away,
erode, consume;* idiom, with **aurās,** *to draw breath.*
advēneris: perf. subjunct. with the **i** shortened (as was common in verse); REL.
CAUSAL CL., i.e., "since you have arrived safely at Carthage."

389 *perferō, perferre, pertulī, perlātus,** *to carry to* (a place), *carry* (oneself) *to = go
to* (a place); *to tolerate, endure.*

390 *redux, reducis,** *bringing/leading back (home); returning, restored.*
reducēs . . . relātam: SC. esse; CHIASMUS.

374 ante diem clausō compōnet Vesper Olympō.
375 Nōs Trōiā antīquā, sī vestrās forte per aurēs
376 Trōiae nōmen iit, dīversa per aequora vectōs
377 forte suā Libycīs tempestās appulit ōrīs.
378 Sum pius Aenēās, raptōs quī ex hoste Penātēs
379 classe vehō mēcum, fāmā super aethera nōtus;
380 Ītaliam quaerō patriam et genus ab Iove summō.
381 Bis dēnīs Phrygium cōnscendī nāvibus aequor,
382 mātre deā mōnstrante viam, data fāta secūtus;
383 vix septem, convulsae undīs Eurōque, supersunt.
384 Ipse ignōtus, egēns, Libyae dēserta peragrō,
385 Eurōpā atque Asiā pulsus."

*The goddess encourages Aeneas and Achates to enter the city,
and she interprets twelve swans flying overhead as a sign
that twelve more of their ships have survived the storm*

Nec plūra querentem
386 passa, Venus mediō sīc interfāta dolōre est:
387 "Quisquis es, haud, crēdō, invīsus caelestibus aurās
388 vītālēs carpis, Tyriam quī advēneris urbem;
389 perge modo atque hinc tē rēgīnae ad līmina perfer.
390 Namque tibī reducēs sociōs classemque relātam

Quaestiōnēs

1. Do Aeneas' remarks in identifying himself in 378–79 strike you as arrogant, as some readers have felt, or do they reflect his indignation over the misfortunes fate has dealt him?

2. Compare Aeneas' speech and his demeanor in 370–85 with his two earlier speeches at 92–101 and 198–209. What are the specific correspondences, and how does Vergil employ these scenes to build up a consistent characterization of the Trojan prince?

3. How is the interlocked word order in 386 appropriate to the context?

391 **nūntiō** (1), *to bring word of, announce, report.*
　　in tūtum: sc. **locum.**
392 ***augurium, -ī,** n., *(the art of) augury; omen, portent, sign.*
393 ***aspiciō, aspicere, aspexī, aspectus,** *to look at, observe, behold.*
　　sēnī, -ae, -a, *six each; a group of six; six.*
　　bis sēnōs: the 12 swans represent the 12 ships that had been unaccounted for;
　　　　Aeneas set sail with 20 (381) and has seven with him (383), hence only one,
　　　　that of Orontes (113f.), had actually been lost in the storm.
　　***laetor, -ārī, -ātus sum,** *to rejoice, be glad, be delighted.*
　　cycnus, -ī, m., *swan* (a bird sacred to Venus and a favorable omen in augury).
394 ***aetherius, -a, -um,** *of/relating to the upper air, of the sky, of heaven.*
　　***plaga, -ae,** f., *open expanse, tract; region; net, trap* (used by hunters).
　　āles, ālitis, m./f., *large bird, fowl, bird of prey;* **āles Iovis,** *eagle.*
395 ***turbō** (1), *to agitate, stir up, disturb; to harass, attack; to confuse, alarm.*
　　terrās . . . capere (396): cf. our idiom "to land"; thus **captās** (sc. **terrās**) in 396 =
　　　　the places where others have already landed.
　　***ōrdō, ōrdinis,** m., *row, line, order, rank;* idiom, **ex ōrdine,** *in order.*
396 **capere . . . captās:** POLYPTOTON.
　　dēspectō (1), *to look down at, survey.*
　　videntur: here *are seen* not *seem.*
397 **strīdentibus:** here *rustling.*
398 **coetus, -ūs,** m., *meeting, encounter; group, band, circle.*
　　***cantus, -ūs,** m., *singing, song; music* (of instruments), *blast* (of a horn).
399 **haud aliter:** LITOTES.
　　***pūbēs, pūbis,** f., *adult population, company, band* (of able-bodied men); *youth,*
　　　　young men.
　　puppēsque . . . pūbēsque: for the POLYSYNDETON, see note on 18.
401 **Perge modo:** Venus repeats the command of 389, neatly concluding her speech.
　　***dērigō, dērigere, dērēxī, dērēctus,** *to direct, aim, guide, steer.*
　　***gressus, -ūs,** m., *step, walk, course.*
402 **āvertēns:** for this intrans. usage, cf. **āvertit** (104).
　　***roseus, -a, -um,** *made of roses; rose-colored.*
　　***cervīx, cervīcis,** f., *neck, back of the neck.*
　　***refulgeō, refulgēre, refulsī,** *to radiate light, shine brightly, gleam.*
403 **ambrosius, -a, -um,** *like ambrosia* (the food of the gods), *ambrosial, divine.*
　　odor, odōris, m., *smell, odor; pleasant scent, fragrance.*
404 ***spīrō** (1), *to breathe; to pulse, throb; to live.*
　　dēfluō, dēfluere, dēflūxī, dēflūxus, *to flow down, stream down, cascade.*
405 **incessus, -ūs,** m., *walk, manner of walking.*
　　et vēra incessū: the slow spondees help suggest the majesty of Venus' gait; the
　　　　vb. **incēdō** is similarly used of Juno in line 46.
　　dea. Ille: the abrupt HIATUS and the juxtaposition of the delayed subj. **dea** and
　　　　the demonstrative **ille** dramatically mark the highly visual shift from the
　　　　goddess' apocalypse to Aeneas' shocked recognition of her as his mother.
406 **fugientem:** sc. **eam** (see note on **rēgnantem** 265).

391 nūntiō et in tūtum versīs Aquilōnibus āctam,
392 nī frūstrā augurium vānī docuēre parentēs.
393 Aspice bis sēnōs laetantēs agmine cycnōs,
394 aetheriā quōs lapsa plagā Iovis āles apertō
395 turbābat caelō; nunc terrās ōrdine longō
396 aut capere aut captās iam dēspectāre videntur:
397 ut reducēs illī lūdunt strīdentibus ālīs
398 et coetū cīnxēre polum cantūsque dedēre,
399 haud aliter puppēsque tuae pūbēsque tuōrum
400 aut portum tenet aut plēnō subit ōstia vēlō.
401 Perge modo et, quā tē dūcit via, dērige gressum."

*Aeneas recognizes his mother and reproaches her for the deceit;
as she departs, the goddess veils her son and Achates in
an obscuring mist so they can approach the city unseen*

402   Dīxit et āvertēns roseā cervīce refulsit,
403 ambrosiaeque comae dīvīnum vertice odōrem
404 spīrāvēre; pedēs vestis dēflūxit ad īmōs,
405 et vēra incessū patuit dea. Ille ubi mātrem
406 agnōvit, tālī fugientem est vōce secūtus:

Quaestiōnēs

1. In what respects is the image of the swans especially appropriate as an omen of the Trojan ships? Comment on the visual and verbal correspondences between the descriptions in 393–98 (the swans) and 390–91/399–400 (the ships).

2. Comment on the multiple sound effects in 399–400.

3. How do the goddess' dress and hair in 403–04 contrast with her appearance in 319–20? What are the specific verbal correspondences?

4. How does Vergil's use of the bucolic diaeresis in 405 compare with that in 348?

407 *quid, adv., *why.*

 *totiēns, adv., *as often; so often.*

 quoque: i.e., like the other gods and men who have caused him misfortune.

 *falsus, -a, -um, *false, deceitful.*

410 Tālibus: sc. verbīs.

 *incūsō (1), *to blame, reproach; to complain of, condemn* (here sc. eam as obj.).

411 *obscūrus, -a, -um, *dim, dark, obscure; hidden, not visible; incomprehensible.*

 obscūrō gradientēs āere: WORD-PICTURE.

 *saepiō, saepīre, saepsī, saeptus, *to surround, enclose; to envelop, cover.*

412 *nebula, -ae, f., *mist, fog; cloud* (of dust, smoke, etc.).

 *circumfundō, circumfundere, circumfūdī, circumfūsus, *to pour around; to surround.*

 circum . . . fūdit: TMESIS.

 *amictus, -ūs, m., *mantle, cloak; covering.*

 multō . . . amictū: a typically Vergilian elaboration of obscūrō . . . saepsit in the preceding verse.

413 cernere nē quis: ANASTROPHE produces the CHIASMUS cernere . . . quis . . . quis contingere.

 quis . . . quis: indef. after nē/neu, *anyone.*

 *neu, conj., *nor, or not; and (that) . . . not.*

414 *mōlior, mōlīrī, mōlītus sum, *to work to bring about, work at, engineer, undertake, contrive; to build, construct.*

 *mora, -ae, f., *loss of time, delay.*

415 Paphus, -ī, f., *Paphos* (a town in southeast Cyprus, sacred to Venus).

 *revīsō, revīsere, *to go and see again, revisit, return to.*

416 templum illī: sc. est.

 Sabaeus, -a, -um, *Sabaean, of the Sabaeans* (a tribe in southwest Arabia known for their production of frankincense).

417 tūs, tūris, n., *frankincense.*

 caleō, calēre, caluī, *to be hot, be warm.*

 *serta, -ae, f., *garland.*

 *recēns, recentis, *of recent origin/occurrence; fresh, recently gathered.*

 hālō (1), *to emit* (a scent, etc.); *to be fragrant.*

418 Corripuēre viam intereā: both the dactyls and the ELISION help convey how quickly the men make their way toward the city.

 *sēmita, -ae, f., *path, track, trail.*

419 plūrimus: again Vergil uses an adj. where Eng. would employ an adv.

 urbī: with imminet (420, DAT. WITH COMPOUNDS).

420 *aspectō (1), *to gaze upon, look at, observe, watch.*

421 mōlem: here *the massive buildings.*

 *māgālia, māgālium, n. pl. (a Punic word), *huts, tents.*

 *quondam, adv., *formerly; in ancient times; in the future, in time to come; on occasion, at times* (common in SIMILES).

422 mīrātur . . . viārum: the extensive m/r/t ALLITERATION suggests the noisy scene.

 *strātum, -ī, n., *coverlet, blanket, bedding; bed, couch* (esp. in pl.); idiom, strāta viārum, *paved roads.*

407 "Quid nātum totiēns, crūdēlis tū quoque, falsīs
408 lūdis imāginibus? Cūr dextrae iungere dextram
409 nōn datur ac vērās audīre et reddere vōcēs?"
410 Tālibus incūsat gressumque ad moenia tendit.
411 At Venus obscūrō gradientēs āere saepsit
412 et multō nebulae circum dea fūdit amictū,
413 cernere nē quis eōs neu quis contingere posset
414 mōlīrīve moram aut veniendī poscere causās.
415 Ipsa Paphum sublīmis abit sēdēsque revīsit
416 laeta suās, ubi templum illī, centumque Sabaeō
417 tūre calent ārae sertīsque recentibus hālant.

Climbing a hill that overlooked Carthage, Aeneas and Achates
marvel at the buildings and the flurry of activity,
and then, still invisible, they descend into the city

418 Corripuēre viam intereā, quā sēmita mōnstrat,
419 iamque ascendēbant collem, quī plūrimus urbī
420 imminet adversāsque aspectat dēsuper arcēs.
421 Mīrātur mōlem Aenēās, māgālia quondam,
422 mīrātur portās strepitumque et strāta viārum.

Quaestiōnēs

1. Comment on the word order in **dextrae . . . dextram** and **vērās . . . vōcēs**
   (408–09) and explain how it is appropriate to the complaint Aeneas is making.

2. Compare the scene at 314–417 with the encounter between Athena and
   Odysseus at Homer *Odyssey* 7.19f.

3. How does meter suit meaning in 419?

4. Comment on the metrical and other sound effects in 421.

423 *īnstō, īnstāre, īnstitī, *to set foot on; to press on; to loom, threaten;* + dat., *to apply oneself* (to), *press on* (with).

　dūcere: *are constructing;* this and the four infs. following are all HIST. INFS., which are typically employed, as here, in quick, lively narration (and with nom. subjs.).

424 subvolvō, subvolvere, *to roll uphill.*

425 *tēctum, -ī, n., *roof, ceiling; roofed building, house, dwelling; shelter* (here DAT. OF PURPOSE).

　conclūdō, conclūdere, conclūsī, conclūsus, *to enclose, surround.*

　*sulcus, -ī, m., *furrow, trench.*

　conclūdere sulcō: for foundations or marking a boundary.

426 magistrātus, -ūs, m., *state office, magistracy; state official, magistrate.*

　*legō, legere, lēgī, lēctus, *to gather; to select, choose; to travel over; to read.*

　legunt: the vb. has varying meanings with each of its three objs. (ZEUGMA).

　sānctumque senātum: i.e., a place for the senate house; an impressively sonorous phrase, Romanizing Vergil's conception of Carthaginian society.

427 *effodiō, effodere, effōdī, effossus, *to dig up, dig out; to hollow out by digging.*

　theātrum, -ī, n., *theater* (some mss. and editors read here theātrīs, dat. pl.)

428 *fundāmentum, -ī, n., *substructure for a building, foundation.*

　columna, -ae, f., *column, pillar.*

429 excīdō, excīdere, excīdī, excīsus, *to cut out/down; to hollow out, excavate; to cut/ break through.*

　*decus, decoris, n., *honor, glory; something that adorns, ornament, decoration; grace, beauty.*

430 quālis . . . labor (431): *such labor as this, work like this;* quālis, often with tālis understood as here, introduces a complex SIMILE extending through verse 436.

　apis, apis, f., *bee.*

　flōreus, -a, -um, *adorned with flowers, flowery, flowering.*

431 adultus, -a, -um, *full-grown, mature.*

432 *fētus, -ūs, m., *birth; offspring; fruit.*

　līquēns, līquentis, *liquid, flowing.*

　*mel, mellis, n., *honey.*

　līquentia mella / . . . cellās (433) / . . . fragrantia mella (436): end-line rhyme this extensive is relatively uncommon in class. Lat. verse.

433 *stīpō (1), *to compress, pack tight; to crowd* (around), *surround.*

　distendō, distendere, distendī, distentus, *to stretch out; to fill up, distend.*

　nectar, nectaris, n., *nectar* (the drink of the gods); *honey.*

　cella, -ae, f., *larder, cellar; small room, chamber; cell.*

434 venientum: for the more usual venientium.

　agmine factō: a military METAPHOR.

435 fūcus, -ī, m., *drone* (here in appos. with ignāvum . . . pecus).

　praesēpe, praesēpis, n., *stall* (for cattle or horses; here, with pecus, a METAPHOR for the bees and their hive).

423 Īnstant ārdentēs Tyriī: pars dūcere mūrōs
424 mōlīrīque arcem et manibus subvolvere saxa,
425 pars optāre locum tēctō et conclūdere sulcō;
426 iūra magistrātūsque legunt sānctumque senātum.
427 Hīc portūs aliī effodiunt; hīc alta theātrī
428 fundāmenta locant aliī, immānēsque columnās
429 rūpibus excīdunt, scaenīs decora apta futūrīs:
430 quālis apēs aestāte novā per flōrea rūra
431 exercet sub sōle labor, cum gentis adultōs
432 ēdūcunt fētūs, aut cum līquentia mella
433 stīpant et dulcī distendunt nectare cellās,
434 aut onera accipiunt venientum, aut agmine factō
435 ignāvum fūcōs pecus ā praesēpibus arcent;

Quaestiō

Identify the several instances of anaphora and asyndeton in 421–28; how do these
devices contribute to both the visual aspects of the passage and its emotionality?

Roman theatre
2nd/3rd century C.E.
Timgad, Algeria

436 *ferveō, fervēre, ferbuī, *to be intensely hot, to boil; to be active/busy, to seethe with activity.*

    redoleō, redolēre, *to give off a smell;* + abl., *to be fragrant* (with).

    thymum, -ī, n., *thyme* (a plant variety noted for its nectar).

    fragrāns, fragrantis, *sweet-smelling, fragrant* (some mss. have the alternative form **fraglantia** here).

437 Ō . . . surgunt: a brief but intensely emotional response, which receives added emphasis in the conflict of ictus and accent throughout the four opening spondees.

    fortūnātus, -a, -um, *lucky, fortunate.*

438 suspiciō, suspicere, suspexī, suspectus, *to look up at; to regard with mistrust, be suspicious of.*

    fastīgia suspicit: Aeneas and Achates have now approached the city and look up in wonder at the rooftops of the buildings.

439 mīrābile dictū: *marvelous to recount;* ABL. OF SPECIFICATION of the supine, used with a n. adj., a favorite construction of Vergil's.

440 mediōs: sc. virōs.

    ūllī: DAT. OF AGENT.

441 *lūcus, -ī, m., *(sacred) grove, woodland.*

    umbrae: for the gen. cf. dītissimus aurī (343); with laetissimus Eng. would say "pleasantly shady" or simply "abundantly shady."

442 quō: with locō (443), *in which place, where.*

443 *rēgius, -a, -um, *royal, regal.*

444 mōnstrārat: for the SYNCOPATED form, cf. iugārat (345).

    caput . . . equī: the horse's head, found often on coins from Carthage, was a symbol of the city's prosperity and military might. In their flight from Tyre, Juno had given the Phoenicians an oracle guiding them to the general location of their new city; after first digging up an ox's head, an unfavorable sign, they excavated at another location a horse's head, a favorable sign, and on that site they established their new home.

    fore . . . gentem (445): IND. STATE. with a speech vb. understood from mōnstrārat and signum ("for Juno had ordained that . . . ").

445 *ēgregius, -a, -um, *outstanding, excellent, splendid.*

    vīctū: *to sustain,* abl. supine with facilem, i.e., a place well-suited to making a living, an allusion to Carthage's success in commerce.

446 *Sīdōnius, -a, -um, *Sidonian, of Sidon* (an important coastal city of Phoenicia).

447 opulentus, -a, -um, *rich (in resources), wealthy.*

    *dīva, -ae, f., *goddess.*

448 aereus, -a, -um, *(made) of bronze.*

    cui: = cuius.

    *gradus, -ūs, m., *step, pace; step* (of a building), *stair, rung* (of a ladder).

    *nectō, nectere, nexī, nexus, *to weave, interweave; to bind; to join together, connect* (here sc. sunt).

436 fervet opus redolentque thymō fragrantia mella.
437 "Ō fortūnātī, quōrum iam moenia surgunt!"
438 Aenēās ait et fastīgia suspicit urbis.
439 Īnfert sē saeptus nebulā (mīrābile dictū)
440 per mediōs, miscetque virīs neque cernitur ūllī.

*The two heroes discover a temple to Juno and on its
walls murals depicting the Trojan War*

441   Lūcus in urbe fuit mediā, laetissimus umbrae,
442 quō prīmum iactātī undīs et turbine Poenī
443 effōdēre locō signum, quod rēgia Iūnō
444 mōnstrārat, caput ācris equī; sīc nam fore bellō
445 ēgregiam et facilem vīctū per saecula gentem.
446 Hīc templum Iūnōnī ingēns Sīdōnia Dīdō
447 condēbat, dōnīs opulentum et nūmine dīvae,
448 aerea cui gradibus surgēbant līmina nexaeque

Quaestiōnēs

1. What numerous activities does Aeneas see from the hilltop overlooking Carthage in 421–36, and what important features of a civilized society do they represent?

2. What are the several points of comparison in the bee simile at 430–36, and what makes the simile particularly appropriate to describing the activities going on in Carthage? How else is the simile especially apt, given that Aeneas was viewing the city from a hilltop a good distance away?

3. What does Vergil's simile in 430–36 tell you about the Romans' knowledge of the activities of bees, and why would they have known so much about this particular insect?

4. Compare Vergil's description of the activities of bees at their hive in 430–36 with his description in *Georgics* 4.162–69.

5. Compare Aeneas' emotional outburst in 437 with his brief speech in 94–101; what insights into his character do the two speeches provide?

6. Comment on the word order in **bellō** / . . . **vīctū** (444–45) and its intended effect; compare the characterization of Carthage in verse 14.

7. Comment on the zeugma in 447.

8. What is most unusual in the meter of line 448? How does this metrical peculiarity actually suit the context?

449 *trabs, trabis, f., *trunk* (of a tree); *length of timber, beam.*

    nexaeque (448) / aere trabēs: *its beams were bound together with bronze* (rivets or plates); the trabēs were the doorposts and frames or perhaps the crossbeams overhead supporting the roof.

    *foris, foris, f., *door* (of a building); pl., *double-doors.*

    *cardō, cardinis, m., *pivot, axis; hinge, socket* (of a door).

450 Hōc prīmum . . . hīc prīmum (451): ANAPHORA and ASYNDETON help to dramatize the moment.

    oblāta: sc. eī; lit., *presented,* but freely *appearing* (to him); the vb. is often used technically of unexpected omens.

451 *lēniō, lēnīre, lēniī, lēnītus, *to moderate; to calm, comfort.*

    *salūs, salūtis, f., *safety; salvation, refuge.*

452 *adflīctus, -a, -um, *battered, harassed; shattered, ruined.*

453 *lūstrō (1), *to move around* (a place); *to look around, see, survey;* with lūce etc., *to illuminate, light up.*

    *singulī, -ae, -a, *one each; every (single); individual.*

454 opperior, opperīrī, oppertus sum, *to wait for, await.*

455 *artifex, artificis, m., *artisan, artist, craftsman; contriver, perpetrator.*

    manūs: here *handicraft, handiwork.*

    inter sē: here an idiom, *working in concert,* or possibly *competing with each other.*

456 Īliacās . . . pugnās: the Trojan War was a favorite subject of ancient art and is here depicted in a series (ex ōrdine) of murals, whose detailed description constitutes an elaborate ECPHRASIS.

457 vulgātus, -a, -um, *common, popular; well-known, celebrated.*

458 *Atrīdēs, -ae, m., *son/descendant of Atreus* (pl. = Menelaus, king of Sparta, and Agamemnon, king of Mycenae and commander of the Greek forces at Troy).

    *Priamus, -ī, m., *Priam* (king of Troy).

459 Quis: here, as often in Vergil, an adj. (the distinction between the interrog. pron. and adj., quis and quī, was not always maintained, with both words sometimes serving either function).

460 *regiō, regiōnis, f., *direction, line; region, locality, district.*

    labōris: here *suffering, sorrow.*

461 ēn, interj., *behold, observe, see.*

    *praemium, -ī, n., *payment; reward, prize.*

    *laus, laudis, f., *praise, commendation.*

    laudī: DAT. OF POSSESSION.

462 sunt . . . tangunt: a poignant, ALLITERATIVE, and frequently quoted epigram.

    rērum: here *for* (rather than *of*) *misfortune* (OBJ. GEN.); rēs can be translated in a great many ways, depending on context.

    mortālia: again, not just *mortal affairs* but *man's mortality* or *sorrows.*

449 aere trabēs, foribus cardō strīdēbat aēnīs.
450 Hōc prīmum in lūcō nova rēs oblāta timōrem
451 lēniit, hīc prīmum Aenēās spērāre salūtem
452 ausus et adflīctīs melius cōnfīdere rēbus.
453 Namque sub ingentī lūstrat dum singula templō,
454 rēgīnam opperiēns, dum quae fortūna sit urbī
455 artificumque manūs inter sē operumque labōrem
456 mīrātur, videt Īliacās ex ōrdine pugnās
457 bellaque iam fāmā tōtum vulgāta per orbem,
458 Atrīdās Priamumque et saevum ambōbus Achillem.
459 Cōnstitit et, lacrimāns, "Quis iam locus," inquit, "Achātē,
460 quae regiō in terrīs nostrī nōn plēna labōris?
461 Ēn Priamus. Sunt hīc etiam sua praemia laudī,
462 sunt lacrimae rērum et mentem mortālia tangunt.

Quaestiō

How does Vergil employ word order in 448–49 to emphasize an important element in the construction and appearance of Juno's temple?

Funeral mask of "Agamenmon"
ca. 1500 B.C., Mycenae, Greece
National Archaeological Museum, Athens, Greece

463 **Solve . . . salūtem:** as is characteristic of his style, Vergil concludes the speech and the scene with a pointed, single-line sentence and with an echo of a key word from earlier in the scene (**salūtem** here and in 451); cf. note on 401. With **solve metūs** cf. Jupiter's consolatory remark to Venus, **parce metū,** in identical metrical position at 257.

    haec . . . fāma: i.e., the renowned story of the Trojan war depicted on the temple's walls; note the INTERLOCKED WORD ORDER.

    tibi: for this sense of the dat., cf. 258 and note above.

    *****aliquī, aliquae, aliquod,** *some; any.*

464 *****inānis, -is, -e,** *empty; unoccupied, idle; meaningless, unimportant; vain, futile.*

465 *****largus, -a, -um,** *generous, bountiful; plentiful, copious.*

    ūmectō (1), *to make wet, moisten.*

    *****flūmen, flūminis,** n., *river, stream.*

466 **utī:** = **ut;** here *how* (+ IND. QUEST.).

    bellō (1), *to wage war, fight* (here modifying **Grāī** 467).

    *****Pergama, -ōrum,** n. pl., *Pergama (the citadel of Troy), Troy.*

467 *****hāc,** adv., *this way, in this direction;* **hāc . . . hāc,** *in this direction . . . in that, on this side . . . on that.*

    *****Grāius, -a, -um,** *Greek;* nom. pl. sometimes **Grāī,** often as a noun, *the Greeks.*

    Grāī . . . Achillēs (468): note the CHIASTIC arrangement (Greeks, Trojans, Trojans, Greek).

    *****iuventūs, iuventūtis,** f., *(group of) young men, the youth.*

468 *****Phryx, Phrygis,** *Phrygian, of Phrygia* (in western Asia Minor), *Trojan.*

    Phryges: in view of the parallel with **Grāī** (467), sc. **fugerent;** the **e** is short in imitation of the Greek form.

    cristātus, -a, -um, *crested, wearing a crested helmet.*

    currū cristātus Achillēs: an aptly harsh, violent ALLITERATION.

469 **Rhēsus, -ī,** m., *Rhesus* (king of Thrace and a Trojan ally, slain in his camp on his first night at Troy by Diomedes and Ulysses).

    niveus, -a, -um, *snowy, snow-white.*

    tentōrium, -ī, n., *tent* (referring here to Rhesus' entire camp).

470 **lacrimāns:** in the same metrical position in 459, and cf. **lacrimae** (462), **ūmectat . . . vultum** (465), and **ingentem gemitum dat** (485); revealing his own humanity (and in keeping with a convention of ancient epic), Aeneas weeps throughout the scene over the suffering of his countrymen and the devastation of Troy.

471 **Tȳdīdēs . . . cruentus:** a powerful line, symmetrically arranged, opening with heavy spondees, and closing with a harsh ALLITERATION that suits the violent image.

    vāstō (1), *to leave desolate; to devastate, destroy.*

473 **pābulum, -ī,** n., *fodder; pasture.*

    pābula . . . bibissent: it had been foretold that the Greeks could not win the war if ever the horses of Rhesus pastured in Troy or drank from the Xanthus, hence the immediate assault on his camp.

    gustō (1), *to taste; to partake of* (food or drink).

    *****Xanthus, -ī,** m., *Xanthus* (a river of Troy).

463 Solve metūs; feret haec aliquam tibi fāma salūtem."

The murals portray countless heroes from
the war, even Aeneas himself

464   Sīc ait atque animum pictūrā pāscit inānī,
465 multa gemēns, largōque ūmectat flūmine vultum.
466 Namque vidēbat utī bellantēs Pergama circum
467 hāc fugerent Grāī, premeret Trōiāna iuventūs;
468 hāc Phryges, īnstāret currū cristātus Achillēs.
469 Nec procul hinc Rhēsī niveīs tentōria vēlīs
470 agnōscit, lacrimāns, prīmō quae prōdita somnō
471 Tȳdīdēs multā vāstābat caede cruentus,
472 ārdentēsque āvertit equōs in castra priusquam
473 pābula gustāssent Trōiae Xanthumque bibissent.

Quaestiōnēs

1. Discuss Aeneas' initial reaction to the gallery of paintings in 450–63, and especially his brief speech in 459–63. How are we as readers meant to respond, knowing Juno's feelings toward the Trojans?

2. Comment on the two very striking metaphors in 464–65.

Achilles in combat
Black-figure tripod, 6th cent. B.C., Athens, Greece
Musée des Beaux-Arts, Lille, France

474 **Parte aliā:** i.e., of the mural.

    āmissīs: here *let go, dropped.*

    Trōilus, -ī, m., *Troilus* (the youngest son of Priam, ambushed in his chariot and slain by Achilles; there was a prophecy that Troy could not be sacked if Troilus lived to his 20th year).

475 ***īnfēlīx, īnfēlīcis,** unproductive; inauspicious, disastrous; unfortunate, unlucky.*

    ***impār, imparis,** unequal* (to, + dat.); *unevenly matched.*

    congressus, -ūs, m., *encounter, meeting; engagement, contest.*

476 **haeret:** *is caught in,* + abl. (though **currū** is perhaps dat.—see note on 156).

    resupīnus, -a, -um, *lying face upwards, on one's back.*

477 **cervīxque comaeque:** ALLITERATION and the epic POLYSYNDETON add intensity.

478 **pulvīs:** the vowel and syllable are lengthened through DIASTOLE.

    īnscrībitur: here simply *marked, scored* (by the inverted spear, which Troilus holds onto as he is dragged along the ground).

479 ***aequus, -a, -um,** level, flat; fair, just, right; favorable, kind; equal, matched.*

    nōn aequae: i.e., *hostile.*

480 ***crīnis, crīnis,** m., lock of hair, tress;* pl., *hair* (of the head).

    ***Īlias, Īliadis,** f., Trojan woman* (for the short **e** here, see on **Phryges** 468).

    ***passus, -a, -um,** extended, spread out, streaming, flowing.*

    peplus, -ī, m., *peplus* (a long woman's robe of the sort ritually offered by the Greeks at the Panathenaic festival, and here by the Trojans, to Athena).

481 **suppliciter,** adv., *in a suppliant manner.*

    ***tundō, tundere, tutudī, tūnsus,** to strike with repeated blows, beat.*

    tūnsae pectora: *beating their breasts,* a sign of mourning; the perf. partic. of deponent vbs. often has pres. force, and for the reflex. construction, see note on **oculōs suffūsa** (228).

482 ***fīxus, -a, -um,** firmly established, unwavering, fixed.*

483 **Ter . . . mūrōs:** Vergil uses **parte aliā** (474) and **intereā** (479) to turn our attention to the two preceding vignettes but employs no such transitional device to mark the scene shift here; the effect is to suggest that Aeneas moves his eyes abruptly to this grisly image. In *Iliad* 24 Achilles dragged Hector's body three times, not around Troy's walls, but around the tomb of his dear friend Patroclus, whom Hector had slain.

    ***raptō (1),** to carry away forcibly, drag violently (off).*

484 ***exanimis, -is, -e,** and **exanimus, -a, -um,** lifeless, dead.*

    aurō: ABL. OF PRICE; in Book 24 of the *Iliad* Achilles offered the mutilated corpse of Hector to his father for a ransom.

485 **Tum . . . gemitum:** the opening spondees, the resounding ASSONANCE in **Tum/tem/-tum** (each syllable under the ictus), and the delayed CAESURA in the fourth foot all help suggest the sound of Aeneas' groan (ONOMATOPOEIA).

    ***gemitus, -ūs,** m., pained/sorrowful sound, groan, moan.*

    dat: sc. **Aenēās;** our attention is abruptly shifted away from the murals to Aeneas himself and the emotions the scenes are stirring in him.

487 ***inermis, -is, -e,** and **inermus, -a, -um,** unarmed, defenseless.*

488 **permixtus, -a, -um,** *indiscriminately mixed* (with); *embroiled, engaged* (with).

474 Parte aliā fugiēns āmissīs Trōilus armīs,
475 īnfēlīx puer atque impār congressus Achillī,
476 fertur equīs currūque haeret resupīnus inānī,
477 lōra tenēns tamen; huic cervīxque comaeque trahuntur
478 per terram, et versā pulvīs īnscrībitur hastā.
479 Intereā ad templum nōn aequae Palladis ībant
480 crīnibus Īliades passīs peplumque ferēbant
481 suppliciter, trīstēs et tūnsae pectora palmīs;
482 dīva solō fīxōs oculōs, āversa, tenēbat.
483 Ter circum Īliacōs raptāverat Hectora mūrōs
484 exanimumque aurō corpus vēndēbat Achillēs.
485 Tum vērō ingentem gemitum dat pectore ab īmō,
486 ut spolia, ut currūs, utque ipsum corpus amīcī
487 tendentemque manūs Priamum cōnspexit inermēs.
488 Sē quoque prīncipibus permixtum agnōvit Achīvīs,

Quaestiōnēs

1. What is the predominant sound effect in 481 and what is its purpose?

2. What rhetorical device does Vergil employ in 486 and what is its intended effect? How many elisions are in the line and how do they contribute to this effect?

"Achilles Dragging the Body of Hector around the Walls of Troy"
Etching in black ink with surface tone on ivory
laid paper, 11 x 6 3/4 inches, ca. 1648
Pietro Testa (1611–50)

489 *Ēōus/Eōus, -a, -um, *of/relating to the dawn; eastern, oriental.*

    *aciēs, -ēī, f., *sharp edge* (of a weapon); *line of sight, glance, eye; army, battle, battle-line, pl., ranks.*

    Memnōn, Memnonis, m., *Memnon* (king of Ethiopia and an ally of Troy, son of Tithonus and the goddess of the dawn, Aurora or Eos).

490 Amāzonis, Amāzonidis, f., *Amazon* (a member of the mythic northern tribe of female warriors, allies of the Trojans who came to their aid after the death of Hector).

    lūnātus, -a, -um, *crescent-shaped.*

    pelta, -ae, f., *(light) shield.*

491 Penthesilēa, -ae, f., *Penthesilea* (queen of the Amazons, slain by Achilles, who at the moment of her death fell in love with her).

    mīlibus: i.e., her fellow Amazons.

492 *subnectō, subnectere, subnexī, subnexus, *to bind* (one thing under another); *to bind up, tie up, fasten.*

    exsertus, -a, -um, *protruding, exposed.*

    *cingulum, -ī, n., *belt, sword-belt* (often ornately embossed or plated).

    mamma, -ae, f., *breast.*

    exsertae . . . mammae: the Amazons fought with one breast exposed; according to a Greek legend based on the false etymology **a** + **mazon** = "lacking a breast," they cut off and cauterized their right breasts to facilitate their use of the bow.

493 bellātrīx, bellātrīcis, f., *female warrior* (here in appos. to **virgō**).

    virīs . . . virgō: typical Vergilian wordplay, perhaps with an eye to the false etymology **virgō** < **vir.**

494 dum . . . / dum (495): again ANAPHORA and ASYNDETON are employed to intensify the emotional effect.

    *Dardanius, -a, -um, *Dardanian, of Dardanus* (son of Zeus and Electra, founder of Dardania in the Troad, and ancestor of Priam), *Trojan.*

    mīrandus, -a, -um, *remarkable, wondrous, amazing.*

    videntur: here a true pass., *are seen/being viewed* (not *seem*).

495 obtūtus, -ūs, m., *gaze.*

497 incessit: Dido's gait is as majestic as that of Venus or Juno; see note on **incessus** 405 and cf. **rēgīna . . . / incessit** here with **incēdō rēgīna** (46). The image anticipates the SIMILE in the following lines, comparing Dido to Diana.

498 Quālis . . . / exercet (499): the same words, identically positioned, introduce the bee simile in 430–31; Vergil's intent is perhaps to suggest that the Diana-like Dido is, indeed, queen of the busy "hive" that is Carthage.

    Eurōtās, -ae, m., *Eurotas* (the river on whose banks stood Sparta, where there was a shrine to Diana/Artemis).

    *iugum, -ī, n., *yoke* (of a plow); *ridge, cliff; bench.*

    *Cynthus, -ī, m., *Cynthus* (a mountain on the Aegean island of Delos, birthplace of Diana and Apollo).

489 Ēōāsque aciēs et nigrī Memnonis arma.
490 Dūcit Amāzonidum lūnātīs agmina peltīs
491 Penthesilēa furēns mediīsque in mīlibus ārdet,
492 aurea subnectēns exsertae cingula mammae,
493 bellātrīx audetque virīs concurrere virgō.

Still unseen, Aeneas and Achates witness first Dido's arrival
at the temple and then the approach of their Trojan
comrades whose safety Venus had foretold

494 Haec dum Dardaniō Aenēae mīranda videntur,
495 dum stupet obtūtūque haeret dēfixus in ūnō,
496 rēgīna ad templum, fōrmā pulcherrima Dīdō,
497 incessit, magnā iuvenum stīpante catervā.
498 Quālis in Eurōtae rīpīs aut per iuga Cynthī

Quaestiōnēs

1. Discuss the several scenes depicted in the murals at 466–93. How many
   are there and how are they arranged? What is Vergil's intent in including
   Penthesilea in the closing vignette? What do you see as the overall function of
   the elaborate ecphrasis?

2. What is Vergil's purpose in applying the epithet **Dardanius** to Aeneas in 494?

Eos (Aurora) with the
body of her son Memnon,
slain by Achilles
Interior of red-figure
kylix, ca. 490–480 B.C.
Capua, Italy
Louvre, Paris, France

499 **exercet:** here *leads, guides.*
> **Dīāna, -ae,** f., *Diana* (the Roman counterpart of Artemis, sister of Apollo and virgin goddess of woodlands, archery, and hunting).
> *****chorus, -ī,** m., *chorus of singing and dancing; performers of a chorus; band of nymphs, worshippers, revelers* (here woodland nymphs in Diana's retinue).
> **mīlle:** in the same metrical position as **mīlibus** (491), the word and the image it evokes of a vast troupe of followers is meant to connect the two scenes— Dido possesses the qualities and the following of both Penthesilea and Diana. Textual interconnections of this sort, sometimes subtle, sometimes quite elaborate, are characteristic of Vergil's artistry.

500 **hinc atque hinc:** see note on 162.
> *****glomerō (1),** *to form into a ball; to collect together into a mass, to accumulate; to collect into a crowd, mass together* (often pass. in a reflex. sense).
> **Orēas, Orēadis,** f., *Oread* (a mountain nymph).
> **Orēades; illa:** BUCOLIC DIAERESIS (cf. 348 and 405).

501 *****superēmineō, superēminēre,** *to stand out above, tower over.*

502 **Lātōna, -ae,** f., *Latona, Leto* (mother by Jupiter of Diana and Apollo).
> *****tacitus, -a, -um,** *not speaking, silent, quiet.*
> **pertemptō (1),** *to probe, feel; to stir* (emotionally).

504 **operī . . . futūrīs:** possibly HENDIADYS, *the work of her future kingdom.*

505 **foribus:** the doors to the shrine within the temple, which would contain the cult statue and be covered by a vaulted roof.
> *****testūdō, testūdinis,** f., *tortoise, turtle; shell of a tortoise; vaulted roof; tortoise formation* (a military formation made by a line of soldiers with their shields locked above their heads), *tortoise* (a siege machine with a sloping roof).

506 **armīs:** by METONYMY for **armātīs,** i.e., the **caterva iuvenum** of 497.
> *****solium, -ī,** n., *high-backed chair; royal chair, throne.*
> **subnīxus, -a, -um,** + abl., *propped up* (by), *resting* (on).
> *****resīdō, resīdere, resēdī,** *to take one's seat, be seated; to settle down, subside, grow calm.*

507 *****lēx, lēgis,** f., *law, statute.*

508 *****iūstus, -a, -um,** *just, fair.*
> **trahēbat:** here *was assigning.*

509 *****concursus, -ūs,** m., *gathering, crowd, assembly.*

510 *****Sergestus, -ī,** m., *Sergestus* (a Trojan warrior).
> **Anthea . . . Cloanthum:** of these three heroes, from the ships that had been scattered by the storm, Antheus was mentioned in 181, Cloanthus in 221 (with the same formula at line's end, **fortemque Cloanthum**); Sergestus first appears here but turns up again below at 4.288.

512 *****dispellō, dispellere, dispulī, dispulsus,** *to drive apart, scatter, disperse.*
> *****āvehō, āvehere, āvexī, āvectus,** *to carry off; pass., to go away, depart.*

513 *****obstipēscō, obstipēscere, obstipuī,** *to be dumbstruck, stunned, astounded.*

514 **laetitia, -ae,** f., *joy, happiness.*
> **laetitiāque metūque:** POLYSYNDETON highlights the two conflicting emotions, which are explained in order by **avidī . . . / ārdēbant** (515) and **rēs . . . turbat.**
> *****avidus, -a, -um,** *greedy; eager, ardent.*

499 exercet Dīāna chorōs, quam mīlle secūtae
500 hinc atque hinc glomerantur Oreades; illa pharetram
501 fert umerō gradiēnsque deās superēminet omnēs
502 (Lātōnae tacitum pertemptant gaudia pectus):
503 tālis erat Dīdō, tālem sē laeta ferēbat
504 per mediōs, īnstāns operī rēgnīsque futūrīs.
505 Tum foribus dīvae, mediā testūdine templī,
506 saepta armīs soliōque altē subnīxa, resēdit.
507 Iūra dabat lēgēsque virīs, operumque labōrem
508 partibus aequābat iūstīs aut sorte trahēbat—
509 cum subitō Aenēās concursū accēdere magnō
510 Anthea Sergestumque videt fortemque Cloanthum
511 Teucrōrumque aliōs, āter quōs aequore turbō
512 dispulerat penitusque aliās āvexerat ōrās.
513 Obstipuit simul ipse, simul percussus Achātēs
514 laetitiāque metūque; avidī coniungere dextrās

Quaestiōnēs

1. Comment on both the word order and the sound effects in 502.

2. When Venus first appears to Aeneas in 314–24, she is disguised as a huntress in search of her female companions, and Vergil compares her first to an armed Spartan maiden and then, in a simile, to the Thracian warrior Harpalyce. Here, in 496–504, immediately following the scene of the warrior Penthesilea, Vergil introduces Dido, depicting her as godlike in her beauty and her bearing, and then comparing her, in a simile, to Diana, goddess of the hunt. What other specific verbal and visual correspondences do you detect between the two passages, and what can you say of Vergil's purposes in making these connections?

3. Compare Vergil's description of Dido and his use of the simile in 496–504 with Homer's description of Nausicaa in *Odyssey* 6.102f.

4. As remarked in the notes, the repetition of **quālis . . . exercet** in 498–99 suggests the possibility of a deliberate link between Vergil's depiction of Dido here and the bee simile in 430–36. What several additional correspondences, both general and specific, do you find between the descriptions of Carthage in 421–36 and of Dido and her countrymen in 496–508?

515   **incognitus, -a, -um,** *unknown, unfamiliar, strange, unexplained.*
      rēs . . . incognita: Aeneas and Achates are astounded that their countrymen have come to the same temple at which they had themselves just arrived, and they are uncertain of how they and their comrades will be received.

516   ***dissimulō (1),** *to conceal, disguise; to pretend* (that something is not what it is).
      dissimulant: here intrans., *they remain concealed* (or, possible though less likely, *they conceal their feelings*).
      cavā: here *encircling, protecting.*
      speculor, -ārī, -ātus sum, *to see, look into, investigate.*
      amiciō, amicīre, amicuī, amictus, *to cover, clothe; to surround.*

517   **quae . . . virīs:** sc. **sit;** IND. QUEST.

519   **veniam:** here *favor, assistance* (from the queen).

520   **intrōgredior, intrōgredī, intrōgressus sum,** *to go in, enter.*
      intrōgressī: sc. **sunt.**
      ***cōram,** adv., *face to face, in one's presence, with/before one's own eyes.*
      data: what form of **sum** should be supplied?–such ELLIPSIS after **postquam** was common.
      ***cōpia, -ae,** f., *supply, abundance; body of men, band, (military) force; opportunity, freedom.*

521   **maximus:** i.e., in age, *eldest.*
      Īlioneus: as the senior member of this group of Trojan refugees, Ilioneus addresses the queen first.

522   **novam cui . . . urbem:** for the word order, see note on **Tyriās . . . arcēs,** above line 20.

523   **iūstitia, -ae,** f., *justice, fairness, equity.*
      gentēs: i.e., the hostile tribes neighboring Carthage.

524   **maria omnia:** ACC. OF EXTENT OF SPACE, common with verbs of traveling; the phrase is FRAMED by the ALLITERATIVE **ventīs . . . vectī.**

525   ***prohibeō (2),** *to keep at a distance (from), keep away, exclude; to forbid the use/ enjoyment of.*

526   **propius:** compar. of **prope,** *more closely/protectively,* i.e., paying careful attention.

527   **Nōn . . . ferrō:** The slow spondaic opening of this sentence lends force to Ilioneus' point.
      ***populō (1),** *to ravage, plunder.*
      populāre . . . vertere (528): both indicate purpose, a use of the inf. relatively common in poetry.
      Penātēs: ordinarily the household gods, but here, by METONYMY, for the *homes* themselves.

529   **ea:** *this (sort of), such.*
      superbia, -ae, f., *pride, disdain;* with both **vīs** and **superbia,** sc. **est.**
      victīs: DAT. OF POSSESSION.

530   ***Hesperia, -ae,** f., *Hesperia* (= *the land to the west,* i.e., Italy).
      cognōmine (or **nōmine**) **dīcere,** idiom, *to (call by) name.*

531   ***ūber, ūberis,** n., *woman's breast; animal's udder; fertile soil; abundant produce.*
      armīs . . . ūbere: both are ABL. OF SPECIFICATION.
      glaeba, -ae, f., *lump of earth; cultivated soil.*

515 ārdēbant, sed rēs animōs incognita turbat.

516 Dissimulant et nūbe cavā speculantur amictī

517 quae fortūna virīs, classem quō lītore linquant,

518 quid veniant; cūnctīs nam lēctī nāvibus ībant,

519 ōrantēs veniam, et templum clāmōre petēbant.

Ilioneus, leader of the emissaries from the Trojan ships,
introduces himself and his countrymen to Dido,
and seeks permission to beach and repair their fleet

520   Postquam intrōgressī et cōram data cōpia fandī,

521 maximus Īlioneus placidō sīc pectore coepit:

522 "Ō rēgīna, novam cui condere Iuppiter urbem

523 iūstitiāque dedit gentēs frēnāre superbās,

524 Trōes tē miserī, ventīs maria omnia vectī,

525 ōrāmus: prohibē īnfandōs ā nāvibus ignēs,

526 parce piō generī, et propius rēs aspice nostrās.

527 Nōn nōs aut ferrō Libycōs populāre Penātēs

528 vēnimus aut raptās ad lītora vertere praedās;

529 nōn ea vīs animō nec tanta superbia victīs.

530 Est locus–"Hesperiam" Grāī cognōmine dīcunt–

531 terra antīqua, potēns armīs atque ūbere glaebae;

Quaestiōnēs

1. Identify the enjambement in 524-25 and comment on its emotional effect.

2. What device of sound effect do you hear in 526?–and remember ALWAYS to read aloud, in order to appreciate the poem's musicality!

3. Identify the two instances of anaphora in 527-29 and explain how word order intensifies its effect and the point Ilioneus is trying to emphasize.

532 **Oenōtrius, -a, -um,** *of the Oenotri* (legendary early inhabitants of Italy), *Oenotrian;* **Oenōtrī = Oenōtriī.**

coluēre: for the form, see note on **tenuēre** (12).

fāma: sc. **est,** *the story is (that)* . . ., a common construction introducing IND. STATE., here (532-33) = **fāma (est) minōrēs dīxisse gentem "Ītaliam" dē nōmine ducis.**

minōrēs: here, as often, not *smaller,* but *younger,* i.e., *descendants* (cf. **māiōrēs** in the sense of *elders, ancestors*).

533 **ducis:** Italus, Italy's eponymous legendary king.

534 **Hic . . . fuit:** i.e., their destination was Italy; the verse is the first of over 50 short lines in the poem (another occurs at 560 below), a sign of the work's incomplete revision at the time of Vergil's death.

535 *****adsurgō, adsurgere, adsurrēxī, adsurrēctus,** *to rise up, be built up.*

nimbōsus, -a, -um, *full of rain clouds, stormy.*

*****Orīōn, Orīōnis,** m., *Orion,* a huntsman slain by the goddess Diana and transformed into a constellation whose rising and setting were associated with stormy weather; used here, by METONYMY, for the storm that scattered the Trojan fleet.

536 **tulit:** sc. **nōs.**

procāx, procācis, *insolent, demanding; uncontrollable.*

procācibus Austrīs: PERSONIFICATION, as the adj. is regularly applied to persons.

537 *****salum, -ī,** n., *sea* (in motion), *swell, billow; open sea, deep.*

*****invius, -a, -um,** *pathless, trackless, that cannot be traveled, untraveled.*

538 **adnō (1),** *to swim toward; to sail/drift toward.*

539 **hoc:** the word was originally spelled **hocc** (from **hod + ce**) and was often in verse pronounced with the double consonant and thus scanned as a long syllable.

barbarus, -a, -um, *foreign; uncivilized; cruel, savage.*

540 *****permittō, permittere, permīsī, permissus,** *to send forth; to hand over, relinquish; to allow, permit.*

harēnae: delaying this noun to the end of the clause further suggests Ilioneus' indignation; the Trojans are not only denied the conventional hospitality of being offered lodging, but are even prevented from resting on the beach. ALLITERATION of the harsh **p/t** and the aspirate **h** adds a sound effect suited to the angry tone.

541 *****cieō, ciēre, cīvī, citus,** *to move, set in motion, stir up.*

prīmā: with **terrā,** *on the border of* . . ..

*****cōnsistō, cōnsistere, cōnstitī,** *to halt, stop, stand (at/on/in).*

542 **hūmānus, -a, -um,** *human.*

mortālia . . . arma: i.e., **arma mortālium,** by contrast with **deōs** in the following line.

temnō, temnere, *to scorn, despise.*

cient . . . vetant . . . (541) . . . temnitis: the shift from 3rd pers. to 2nd, in condemning the (potential) hostility, personalizes and thus intensifies the accusatory tone.

532	Oenōtrī coluēre virī; nunc fāma minōrēs
533	"Ītaliam" dīxisse ducis dē nōmine gentem.
534	Hic cursus fuit,
535	cum, subitō adsurgēns flūctū, nimbōsus Orīōn
536	in vada caeca tulit penitusque procācibus Austrīs
537	perque undās superante salō perque invia saxa
538	dispulit; hūc paucī vestrīs adnāvimus ōrīs.
539	Quod genus hoc hominum? Quaeve hunc tam barbara mōrem
540	permittit patria? Hospitiō prohibēmur harēnae;
541	bella cient prīmāque vetant cōnsistere terrā.
542	Sī genus hūmānum et mortālia temnitis arma,

Quaestiōnēs

1. What is unusual in the meter of 536, and how is it, along with the alliterative **caec-/-cāc-,** appropriate to the action described?

2. How might the alliteration of **s** in 537 be regarded as onomatopoetic?

3. What rhetorical devices add intensity to the indignant tone of Ilioneus' two questions in 539-40?

543   **spērāte**: not *hope*, but *expect*.

      fandus, -a, -um (gerundive of **for, fārī, fātus sum**, *to speak*), *what may be spoken of/said, speakable; proper, lawful.*

      *⁎**nefandus, -a, -um**, *unspeakable, wicked, impious.*

      fandī atque nefandī: Vergil means us to think of the religious terms **fās**, *divine right*, and **nefās**, *sacrilege.*

544   **erat . . . nōbīs**: if you do not recognize the construction, see note on **sunt mihi** (71).

      quō: ABL. OF COMPARISON with **iūstior**; the prose order would be **quō alter fuit nec iūstior pietāte nec maior bellō et armīs**, *than whom no other was either . . . .*

545   **pietāte . . . bellō . . . armīs**: for the abl. usage, cf. **pietāte** (10) and note on 531.

546   **quem**: = **hunc**; Lat. often employs a rel. to refer to someone or something in the preceding sent., where we would use a pers. pron. or, as here, a demonstrative; cf. note on **quem** in 64 above.

      vēscor, vēscī + abl., *to use, enjoy; to feed upon.*

547   **occubō, occubāre**, *to lie against/on top of; to lie dead.*

548   **nōn metus**: sc. **est nōbīs**, i.e., **nōn metuimus**.

      officium, -ī, n., *beneficial act, service; courtesy, civility; obligation, duty.*

      *⁎**certō (1)**, *to contend (for superiority), compete; to contend in battle, fight; to struggle, labor.*

      certāsse: = **certāvisse**; for the contracted form, see note on **audierat**, line 20 above, and cf. **onerārat**, 195.

      priōrem: modifies **tē**, but with adv. force, *you first.*

549   **paeniteō, paenitēre, paenituī**, *to cause dissatisfaction, give reason for regret*; idiom, **paenitet**, impers., with inf. as subj. + acc. of the person affected, (to do something) *causes* (one) *to regret* = (one) *regrets* (to do something).

      paeniteat: POTENTIAL SUBJUNCT. with **officiō . . . priōrem**, *nor would you regret to have contended (to be) first in an act of kindness* (or, more freely, with R. D. Williams, *taking the initiative in a contest of kindness*).

      Sunt . . . Acestēs (550): Ilioneus' point is that, even if Aeneas is dead, his friend Acestes, a powerful king in Sicily (line 195), will repay the queen's kindness.

      et: as often (cf. line 200 above), = **etiam**.

551   *⁎**quassō (1)**, *to shake repeatedly/violently; to batter, damage.*

      *⁎**subdūcō, subdūcere, subdūxī, subductus**, *to draw up, raise; to haul up, beach.*

552   **silvīs**: sc. **in**; recall that preps. usual in Lat. prose are frequently omitted in verse.

      aptāre: here, *to form, fashion, shape.*

      stringere: with **rēmōs**, *to trim (branches into) oars.*

553   **receptō**: modifies both **sociīs** and **rēge**, but, as is common in Lat., it agrees with the nearer of the two nouns.

      sī . . . tendere (554): the condition logically belongs within the following PURPOSE CL., *so that, if . . . .*

      dātur: i.e., by fate.

554   **laetī**: for this very common use of an adj. with the force of an adv., see note on **dabant laetī**, line 35 above.

543 at spērāte deōs memorēs fandī atque nefandī.
544 Rēx erat Aenēās nōbīs, quō iūstior alter
545 nec pietāte fuit, nec bellō maior et armīs.
546 Quem sī fāta virum servant, sī vēscitur aurā
547 aetheriā neque adhūc crūdēlibus occubat umbrīs,
548 nōn metus, officiō nec tē certāsse priōrem
549 paeniteat. Sunt et Siculīs regiōnibus urbēs
550 armaque, Trōiānōque ā sanguine clārus Acestēs.
551 Quassātam ventīs liceat subdūcere classem
552 et silvīs aptāre trabēs et stringere rēmōs,
553 sī datur Ītaliam sociīs et rēge receptō
554 tendere, ut Ītaliam laetī Latiumque petāmus;

Ship mosaic from Carthage, 2nd cent. A.D.
Bardo Museum, Tunis, Tunisia

555 *sīn, conj., *but if.*
　　absūmō, absūmere, absūmpsī, absūmptus, *to use up, spend; to destroy, consume;*
　　　　with absūmpta sc. est.
　　Teucrum: = Teucrōrum.
　　pater . . . Teucrum: in an emotional APOSTROPHE, Ilioneus addresses his
　　　　countrymen's absent leader, Aeneas.

556 *restō, restāre, restitī, *to remain, linger; to be left, remain* (to be done).

557 *fretum, -ī, n., *strait, channel.*
　　Sīcania, -ae, f., *Sicania,* an archaic name for Sicily.
　　*saltem, adv., *at least.*

558 advehō, advehere, advexī, advectus, *to convey, bring* (to a place); passive, *to
　　　　arrive by travel, sail.*
　　advectī: sc. sumus.

559 Tālibus: sc. both verbīs (cf. line 410 above) and dīxit; such phrases, often
　　　　elliptical in this way, commonly punctuate the end of speeches.

560 *Dardanidēs, -ae, m., *descendant of Dardanus* (see note on Dardaniō 1.494),
　　　　Trojan; for the incomplete line, see note on 534 above.

561 vultum dēmissa: ACC. OF RESPECT with a MIDDLE VOICE partic. (see note on
　　　　oculōs suffūsa, 228 above); lit., *lowered with respect to her face,* but in natural
　　　　Eng. idiom, *with her face* (i.e., her eyes) *lowered*–a gesture of humility.
　　*profor, profārī, profātus sum, *to speak out, hold forth.*

562 sēclūdō, sēclūdere, sēclūsī, sēclūsus, *to separate, keep at a distance; to put away*
　　　　(from oneself).

563 *dūrus, -a, -um, *hard, solid; hardy, strong, enduring; harsh, pitiless.*
　　novitās, novitātis, f., *newness.*

564 custōde: COLLECTIVE SG.
　　*tueor, tuērī, tuitus sum, *to look at; to watch over, protect.*

565 nesciat: POTENTIAL SUBJUNCT. (see above note on 549); with quis, *who could . . . .*

566 virtūtēsque virōsque: not only do the ASSONANCE and POLYSYNDETON add to
　　　　the line's musicality but the phrase also, through HENDIADYS, accentuates
　　　　the connection between vir and virtūs, another example of the sort of
　　　　etymologizing wordplay Vergil was so fond of (see note on fābor . . .
　　　　fātōrum, 261-62 above, and cf. notes on 268, 288, 298, and 493).
　　incendia: used for devastation generally.

567 obtūnsus (also obtūsus), -a, -um, (of a weapon or tool) *blunt, dull;* (of the
　　　　senses, intellect) *dull, obtuse.*

568 *āversus, -a, -um, *turned away; distant, remote.*
　　Sōl: here the sun-god, pictured as yoking the horses of his chariot, which daily
　　　　pulls the sun across the heavens; Carthage, Dido avers, is not so remote
　　　　and uncivilized a country as to be "in the dark" regarding such major world
　　　　events as the Trojan War.

569 Seu . . . sīve (570): the correlative conjs. are positioned at the beginning of
　　　　these successive verses to emphasize Dido's response to the two different
　　　　destinations Acestes has mentioned.
　　Sāturnia: i.e., Italian; Saturn (Saturnus), who ushered in and reigned as king
　　　　during Italy's Golden Age, was an agricultural deity, and hence the epithet is
　　　　aptly applied to arva.

555 sīn absūmpta salūs, et tē, pater optime Teucrum,
556 pontus habet Libyae nec spēs iam restat Ïūlī,
557 at freta Sīcaniae saltem sēdēsque parātās,
558 unde hūc advectī, rēgemque petāmus Acestēn."
559 Tālibus Īlioneus; cūnctī simul ōre fremēbant
560 Dardanidae.

Dido replies, not only offering assistance but even inviting
the Trojans to settle in Carthage on equal terms with her citizens

561   Tum breviter Dīdō, vultum dēmissa, profātur:
562 "Solvite corde metum, Teucrī; sēclūdite cūrās.
563 Rēs dūra et rēgnī novitās mē tālia cōgunt
564 mōlīrī et lātē fīnēs custōde tuērī.
565 Quis genus Aeneadum, quis Trōiae nesciat urbem,
566 virtūtēsque virōsque aut tantī incendia bellī?
567 Nōn obtūnsa adeō gestāmus pectora Poenī,
568 nec tam āversus equōs Tyriā Sōl iungit ab urbe.
569 Seu vōs Hesperiam magnam Sāturniaque arva

Quaestiōnēs

1. Analyze Ilioneus' speech in 522-58, particularly in terms of the speaker's objectives and his rhetorical strategies; in what different ways, e.g., does he attempt to gain Dido's sympathy? What specifically does he hope to gain from her? As always, support your answers with specific references to the text.

2. What is exceptional in the meter of 564 and what does it add to Dido's defensive statement in 563-64?

3. Anaphora and asyndeton are commonly employed together (see notes on lines 9-10 and 16 above); what is the effect in verse 565?

4. From what major scene earlier in the book did we already learn of the acute awareness of the Trojan War and its heroic action that Dido declares here in 567-68?

570   **Eryx, Erycis,** m., *Eryx,* name of a town and a mountain in northwest Sicily, so called for the eponymous hero Eryx, a son of Venus and thus half-brother of Aeneas.

571   **auxiliō:** with **tūtōs** the word may imply an armed cohort.

    tūtōs: sc. **vōs.**

572   **et hīs . . . rēgnīs:** the adv. (**et = etiam**), the wide separation of the demonstrative adj. and modified noun, and the suspenseful delay of that noun to the very end of the verse, all lend special impact to this third, extraordinary offer of support.

    *****pariter,** adv., *together, side by side; equally; in the same manner, alike; at the same time, simultaneously.*

573   **Urbem:** the noun, which logically should be nom. and subj. of **est,** is attracted into the case of the rel. pron. directly following–a rare and deliberate archaism.

    *****statuō, statuere, statuī, statūtus,** *to set upright; to put up, erect, build.*

    subdūcite: Dido's use of the word in the same metrical position as **subdūcere** (551) echoes and directly responds to Ilioneus' request.

574   **mihi:** DAT. OF AGENT (cf. **ūllī,** 440) or possibly DAT. OF REF., something like "as far as my actions" or "in my thinking."

    agētur: *handled, treated, dealt with;* the sg. verb adds to the point that both peoples will be treated as one.

575   *****utinam,** adv., used with subjunct. to express wishes, *if only, would that, I wish that.*

    compellō, compellere, compulī, compulsus, *to drive together; to drive, force.*

576   **adforet:** essentially an alternative form for **adesset,** employed in a pres. tense wish comparable to a pres. contrary to fact condition, *would that he were here.*

    certōs: i.e., *reliable, trustworthy.*

577   **extrēma:** cf. Eng. idiom, "the far reaches."

578   **quibus . . . silvīs aut urbibus:** you are now accustomed in reading poetry to supplying preps. usual in prose, here **in;** but do also recall that forms of **quis** are indef., = *any,* after **sī, nisi, nē,** and **num.**

570 sīve Erycīs fīnēs rēgemque optātis Acestēn,
571 auxiliō tūtōs dīmittam opibusque iuvābō.
572 Vultis et hīs mēcum pariter cōnsīdere rēgnīs?
573 Urbem quam statuō vestra est; subdūcite nāvēs;
574 Trōs Tyriusque mihī nūllō discrīmine agētur;
575 atque utinam rēx ipse, Notō compulsus eōdem,
576 adforet–Aenēās! Equidem per lītora certōs
577 dīmittam et Libyae lūstrāre extrēma iubēbō,
578 sī quibus ēiectus silvīs aut urbibus errat."

Quaestiōnēs

1. What is exceptional in the word order of 575-76, and what seems to be the dramatic effect?

2. In what specific ways does Dido, in her speech at 562-78, allay Ilioneus' concerns, and how does she offer to help? What one offer seems most extraordinary and unexpected, and how would you explain the queen's motivations?

Dido welcomes Aeneas
In the background is Troy, in ruins;
on the left: Aeneas and companions see the omen of the flying swans
Bartolomeo da S.Vito, illuminated manuscript (Ms.Kings 24, fol. 59), ca. 1497-99

Aeneid BOOK II

BOOK Two of the *Aeneid,* one of the epic's most powerful episodes, deals with Troy's doomsday, with the Greeks' strategy of the wooden horse that towers over their deserted camp, with the suspicion and seeming impiety of the Trojan priest, Laocoön, who distrusts Greeks on every count and who dies agonizingly with his two sons by the attack of twin sea serpents, and with the devious rhetoric of Sinon, a Greek captive, allegedly a deserter, who persuades the credulous Trojans to accept the "gift"—a *fatalis machina feta armis*—that will presently release its deadly brood of Greek warriors and so bring down the city. The Trojans are taken by surprise during the night, and the city succumbs to murderous onslaught. King Priam is butchered and decapitated in his palace compound. Aeneas witnesses the slaughter and joins a counter-offensive where Trojans are disguised as Greeks, but to no avail. Venus counsels her son against killing Helen, instigator of the war. Aeneas withdraws from the action to return home, where he tries, vainly at first, to persuade his crippled father Anchises to join in the family's departure. Omens involving Ascanius-Iulus and celestial signals finally induce Anchises to join the refugees. During the evacuation, Creusa, Aeneas' royal wife, mother of Ascanius-Iulus, becomes separated from the group and, her fate unclear, has to be left behind as votary of the goddess Cybele, one of Troy's protective deities.

Vergil's Book Two is often called "The Tragedy of Troy." How "tragic" is Aeneas' (and Vergil's) account of the fall of Troy? Should we regard Greek tragedy as a primary model for the account, or assume that Vergil's own experience of war was a primary ingredient? R.G. Austin in his commentary (Oxford, 1964, p. ix) was convinced that Vergil's personal experience was indeed central to the issue:

> Virgil has lived through the last hours of Troy, knowing how the minds of men (civilians and military alike) work in war-time, familiar with the personal tragedies that war brings, sharing in the destruction of a city whose stones he has known and loved; he has seen men shot down in ignorance by their own side, old men murdered in their homes, women and children lined up for prison camps; he has endured the incomprehensible injustice of what must be interpreted as the will of heaven.

Vergil's personal involvement in a world turned upside down in the civil wars that bloodied Rome throughout his lifetime, must have left indelible memories of oppression and killing, of eviction and humiliation; his response was an epic with a grippingly tragic universality.

Greek tragedy, nevertheless, did exert a profound influence on his work. The triadic structure of Book Two is transparent: Part I, Sinon, Laocoön, and the Wooden Horse (1–249); Part II, The Fall of Troy (250–558); and Part III, The Departure of Aeneas (559–804). The entire narrative is an eyewitness report to Dido by Aeneas and is comparable, though on a larger scale, to messengers' accounts of disasters in Greek tragedy.

Because Aeneas offers a narrative of personal involvement, he expresses some reluctance to recount the painful memories of Troy's final hours. He begins by telling how happy the Trojans are to emerge from their 10-year siege and to visit the deserted Greek quarters. But the wooden horse on the shore is a source of controversy: some favor hauling it into the city, while others call for its destruction. Laocoön, priest of Neptune, shows his contempt for its alleged sanctity by hurling a spear into the horse's side. A Greek captive, Sinon, whose name suggestively connotes a serpent's sinuosity, is dragged before Priam and, by his skillful, devious rhetoric, is able to excite the pity and win the confidence of his captors. The horse, according to Sinon, is meant to compensate for the protective wooden image of Pallas (Athena) which had been stolen by the Greeks to damage the Trojan fortunes; its size will prevent its entry into the city and so prevent its becoming a protector of the city. Suddenly two large serpents emerge from the sea to attack and kill Laocoön and his innocent sons. The Trojans interpret the priest's death as retaliation for his sacrilege against the Horse, and the creature with its deadly cargo of warriors is dragged into the city through a breach in the walls.

The episode is a masterpiece of Vergilian creativity, cinematic art and ingenuity, and rhetorical display. Sinon is Vergil's creation, although the character mirrors Odysseus in several respects. Generally speaking, he behaves like a Greek tragic messenger, except that tragic messengers generally tell the truth; Sinon's revelations, well articulated and convincingly circumstantial, are mostly lies. Ironically, the Greek whom Sinon claims to detest, Odysseus, is in reality a model for the deceitful, insinuating Sinon. Why are the Trojans deceived? After all, Sinon is far from being a patriot and, by his own admission, he was meant to be sacrificed for alleged treasonable behavior after the death of his protector, Palamedes. If the Trojans had followed suit and regarded him as an appropriate sacrificial victim, as a scapegoat for Greek barbarities, and if they had taken advantage of his being prepared earlier for sacrifice, Troy might have been saved. But Trojan humanity and credulity rejected murder, and the sequel was disaster. Sinon also portrays himself as endowed with virtues that would appeal to the Trojans (and later to Romans): steadfast in misfortune, a man of inviolable truth, loyal to a friend (Palamedes), with none of the pretense of Odysseus, and pious towards his homeland, children, and gods (57–198). Sinon's characterization is a tour de force. And Laocoön's story accents both Trojan piety and tragic necessity: engaged in sacrificing a bull on the shore, he and his sons, unable to save their father, die terribly; visual and aural features of the simile comparing Laocoön's cries of anguish to the bellowing of a sacrificial bull parallel and extend the action.

Vergil's account of Troy's final night is intensely dramatic, and rich in cinematographic effects. Aeneas' dream vision of the mutilated Hector is another masterpiece, as unforgettable as Hamlet's scene and dialogue with the ghost of his murdered father at Elsinore. Aeneas' dream address to the apparition is a valid intrusion; it heightens the effect of the ghostly warning to leave. The episode of Panthus, priest of Apollo, with his son is a preview of Aeneas' own departure with Ascanius, but carries the tragic suggestion that Panthus and his son will both be lost in the battle. The Coroebus episode is remarkable, since it involves Trojan (rather than Greek) duplicity. Coroebus came to Troy to marry Cassandra, prophetess daughter of Priam, but war intervened. When the Trojans, with Aeneas, follow his advice to make themselves indistinguishable from Greeks by impersonation— by putting on Greek armor—and the strategy is questioned, Coroebus responds: "trickery or courage? When it is a question of an enemy, who will ask?" (390). That deliberate erasure of differences is a reflection of civil war, which permeates so much of the epic's military action. The Helen episode (567–88) remains problematic; is it truly Vergilian, awaiting completion and proper insertion into the holocaust narrative, or is it a later interpolation? It seems genuinely Vergilian to most critics, who assume that it was removed for some compelling reason from the posthumously edited copy. Can you find a reason?

The assault on Priam's palace is filled with sound and fury, with desperate measures of defense, sacrificial engagements, and Greek barbarity. The scene of the royal couple Priam and Hecuba, huddled with their children at the palace altar, normally a place of sanctuary, the death of Polites ("Citizen") before his parents' eyes, the murderous onslaught of Achilles' son Pyrrhus (Neoptolemus), and the brutal sacrifice of Priam feebly resisting are heartbreaking. Although Priam apparently dies at the palace altar, Vergil redirects his camera to show us the aged king's beheaded corpse exposed on the shore, *sine nomine corpus* . . ..

The final act, Aeneas' departure, features another Venus-Aeneas episode, the second in Book Two, a *dea ex machina* scene that might derive from a Euripidean tragedy, with pertinent dialogue, sound, and light. A reading of Euripides' *The Trojan Women* will enrich your appreciation of the second and third "acts" of this dramatic book. The detailed account of Anchises' refusal to leave the city, the pitiful appeals of family and household, and Aeneas' decision to face death at Troy, must have caused Dido considerable anguish as she listened to the tale. Heavenly intervention, in the diadem of fire on Ascanius' head, and the fall of the star (or comet) to mark their departure route towards Mount Ida, persuade Anchises to agree to retreat. The family set off together, with the familiar icon of Aeneas carrying on his shoulder crippled Anchises with the Vestal fire and Penates, Ascanius-Iulus trying to match his father's stride, and Creusa following. Because Creusa is missing at the reunion point, Aeneas feels compelled to return to the burning city, like Orpheus in search of his lost Eurydice.

Vergil's portrait of Creusa is a marvel of characterization—a remarkable vignette of marital love, devotion to family, and reverence for the divine will (virtues that serve in part, as we shall see, to intensify our perception of Dido's faults in Book Four). Creusa's is a personal testimony to *pietas* and to love, to the wisdom born of suffering, and to the triumph of the human spirit over adversity.

Eneidos

Que secũdo gneidos libro cõtineãt. ouidi⁹.
℘Coticuere omnes: tũc sic fortissimus heros
Fata recensebat troie, casusᶜᵍ suorum:
Fallaces graios: simulatacᶜᵍ dona minerue
Lacontis pœnã, et l axantem clauſtra sinonẽ
Somnũ quo monit⁹ acc eperat hectoris atrũ:
Iam flãmas cœli: troum patrieᶜᵍ ruinas.
Et regis priami fatum miserabile semper:
Impoſituᶜᵍ patrẽ collo: dextracᶜᵍ prehenſũ
Aſcanium: fruſtra tergum comitante creuſa,
Ereptã hanc fato, socioſcᶜᵍ in monte reptos,

"The Trojan Horse," woodcut by Sebastian Brant (1457–1521)
From an edition of Vergil's "Opera" by L. Junta (Venice 1537)

1 *conticēscō, conticēscere, conticuī, *to cease to talk, become silent; to be silent about* (the prefix here has intensive force; for the form, see note on **tenuēre** 1.12).

    intentī: the adj. here, as often, has adv. force.

    ōra tenēbant: i.e., they held their gaze; the line's heavily spondaic rhythms suit the rapt attention Vergil describes, and the tense shift from perf. to impf. suggests how the banqueters immediately fell silent and then remained so.

2 *torus, -ī, m., *bed, couch* (for reclining at a meal).

    torō . . . altō: the phrase suggests Aeneas' position as guest of honor.

    ōrsus: sc. **est**; cf. 1.325 above.

3 **iubēs**: sc. **mē**.

4 **ut . . . / ēruerint (5)**: **ut** here = *how*; IND. QUEST. dependent on **renovāre** (3), *to renew (by telling)*.

    lāmentābilis, -is, -e, *pitiable, deplorable, lamentable*.

    Trōiānās . . . lāmentābile: the repeated long ā's (ASSONANCE), three of them under the ictus add a plaintive sound.

5 *ēruō, ēruere, ēruī, ērūtus, *to dig up, uproot; to lay low, destroy*.

    -que . . . / et (6): an epic archaism for **et . . . et**, *both . . . and*.

    miserrima: sc. **ea**, in appos. with the **ut** cl. and anteced. of **quae** and **quōrum** (6).

6 **pars magna**: Aeneas is not boasting here but suggesting how deeply involved he was in the catastrophe.

    Quis: used as a pron. here and as an adj. with **mīles** in 7 (see note on 1.459)

    fandō: GERUND of **fārī**, *in telling/speaking*, by contrast with **īnfandum** (3).

7 *Myrmidones (-ēs), Myrmidonum, m. pl., *Myrmidons* (a tribe in Thessaly, led by Achilles in the Trojan War).

    *Dolopes (-ēs), Dolopum, m. pl., *Dolopians* (another Thessalian tribe, connected with Achilles' son Pyrrhus).

    Myrmidonum Dolopumve: GEN. OF THE WHOLE with **quis** (6); **-ve** is used here, vs. **aut**, to juxtapose the two closely related words, whose ASSONANCE is accentuated by the ictus on the **-um** syllables.

    *Ulixēs, -ī, m., *Ulysses* (Roman name for the Greek hero Odysseus, who was noted as much for his guile as for his valor).

8 **temperet**: POTENTIAL SUBJUNCT., *would (be able to) . . .*.

    *ūmidus, -a, -um, *wet, moist, damp*.

9 *praecipitō (1), *to cause to fall headlong, hurl down*; intrans., *to fall headlong, plunge downward*.

    praecipitat . . . somnōs: a marvelously symphonic line, with the dactyls and harsh c/t/d ALLITERATION sounding out the downward crash of night and the falling stars, the internal rhyme underscored by the ictus in **-dentque cadentia**, and the sibilants in **suādent . . . sīdera somnōs** suggesting the hush of sleep; even Vergil delighted in the sound effects, which he repeated in 4.81 below.

10 **amor**: sc. **tibi est**; with **cognōscere**, a use of the inf. common in verse.

11 *suprēmus, -a, -um, *highest; farthest; last, final*.

    suprēmum . . . labōrem: i.e., death.

*Dido and her court listen in rapt attention as Aeneas reluctantly
agrees to relate to them the horrific tale of Troy's final day*

1   Conticuēre omnēs intentīque ōra tenēbant;
2 inde torō pater Aenēās sīc ōrsus ab altō:
3 "Īnfandum, rēgīna, iubēs renovāre dolōrem,
4 Trōiānās ut opēs et lāmentābile rēgnum
5 ēruerint Danaī, quaeque ipse miserrima vīdī
6 et quōrum pars magna fuī. Quis tālia fandō
7 Myrmidonum Dolopumve aut dūrī mīles Ulixī
8 temperet ā lacrimīs? Et iam nox ūmida caelō
9 praecipitat suādentque cadentia sīdera somnōs.
10 Sed sī tantus amor cāsūs cognōscere nostrōs
11 et breviter Trōiae suprēmum audīre labōrem,

Quaestiōnēs

1. Comment on the word order in line 1.

2. In what respects is Aeneas aptly called **pater** in line 2?

3. What device of word order does Vergil employ in line 3 and how is it effective?

"Aeneas Telling Dido of His Misfortunes at Troy"
Pierre Narcisse Guerin (1778–1833), Louvre, Paris, France

12 **lūctū:** ABL. OF CAUSE.

13 **incipiam:** ENJAMBEMENT and the abrupt CAESURA in the second foot effectively punctuate Aeneas' opening remarks and prepare us for the story to come.

14 **Danaum:** for this very common gen. pl. form, see note on **superum** (1.4).
   tot . . . annīs: the war was now in its 10th year.

15 ***īnstar,*** in acc. and nom. only, n., often + gen., *the equal, equivalent* (of/to, in size, effect, moral worth—here in appos. to **equum**).
   Palladis arte: the role of the virgin goddess Athena/Minerva in Troy's destruction figures prominently in this book; see line 31 and passim. Homer tells us in *Odyssey* 8.493 that the Greek Epeos built the horse (see 264 below) with the guidance of Minerva, who was goddess of craftsmen.

16 **intexō, intexere, intexuī, intextus,** *to weave (into), make by weaving.*
   abies, abietis, f., *silver fir; fir-wood.*
   abiete: regularly trisyllabic in verse, with the **i** consonantal.

17 **vōtum:** sc. **equum esse.**
   reditū: i.e., their safe passage back to Greece.
   vagor, -ārī, -ātus sum, *to wander, roam; to spread freely/unchecked.*

18 ***dēlēctus, -a, -um,*** *chosen for excellence, hand-picked, select.*
   virum: for the form cf. 1.119.
   sortior, sortīrī, sortītus sum, *to draw lots; to choose by lot, select.*

19 ***inclūdō, inclūdere, inclūsī, inclūsus,*** *to insert, enclose.*
   inclūdunt . . . complent (20): the two vbs. aptly enclose the highly ALLITERATIVE couplet in a CHIASTIC arrangement.
   caverna, -ae, f., *hollow cavity in the earth, cave, cavern; cavernous space.*

20 ***uterus, -ī,*** m., *abdomen, belly; womb* (often with ref. to its contents, an unborn child).
   uterum: Vergil consistently uses this term for the horse's belly (at verses 38, 52, 243, and 258), and it becomes increasingly clear as the narrative progresses that he intends us to imagine the beast's womb as, METAPHORICALLY, pregnant with violence and war.
   armō (1), *to fit with weapons, arm, equip.*
   mīlite: here collective sg., *band of soldiers, soldiery.*

21 **in cōnspectū:** i.e., of Troy.
   Tenedos, -ī, f., *Tenedos* (modern Bozcaada, an island a few miles off the coast of Troy, associated in Homer's *Iliad,* 1.38 and 452, with Apollo).

22 **dīves opum:** Vergil applies the same description, in the same metrical position, to Carthage at 1.14; though perhaps coincidental, it may have been his intent to link the two locations, as both represent threats to the future of Troy and Rome.
   Priamī: with **rēgna** not **opum,** another example of the sort of ANASTROPHE common in Vergil and in Lat. verse generally.

23 **statiō, statiōnis,** f., *standing place; anchorage.*
   male, adv., *unpleasantly; badly, poorly; hardly, not at all.*
   carīna, -ae, f., *keel, hull* (of a ship); poetic (by METONYMY or SYNECDOCHE), *boat, ship.*

12 quamquam animus meminisse horret lūctūque refūgit,
13 incipiam.

> *Frustrated by their failure to sack Troy after 10 years of war, the*
> *Greeks build a colossal wooden horse, fill it with troops, and,*
> *leaving it outside Troy's gates, sail off to a nearby island*

    "Frāctī bellō fātīsque repulsī,
14 ductōrēs Danaum, tot iam lābentibus annīs,
15 īnstar montis equum dīvīnā Palladis arte
16 aedificant sectāque intexunt abiete costās;
17 vōtum prō reditū simulant; ea fāma vagātur.
18 Hūc, dēlēcta virum sortītī corpora, fūrtim
19 inclūdunt caecō laterī penitusque cavernās
20 ingentēs uterumque armātō mīlite complent.
21 Est in cōnspectū Tenedos, nōtissima fāmā
22 īnsula, dīves opum Priamī dum rēgna manēbant,
23 nunc tantum sinus et statiō male fīda carīnīs:

Quaestiōnēs

1. What reasons does Aeneas give in 3–12 for his reluctance to tell his Carthaginian hosts of Troy's destruction? List the several words he uses that suggest his grief over his country's loss. Cf. Odysseus' speech to Alcinous in *Odyssey* 9.12f.

2. What correspondences do you find, in form, function, and content, between 2.1–13 and 1.1–11?

3. Comment on the word order in verse 13 (**frāctī . . . repulsī**).

4. What is the effect of enjambing **ingentēs** in 20?

> There is an yle in sight of Troy and Tenedos it hight,
> A welthy land while Priams state and kingdome stood vpright,
> But now a bay, and harber bad for ships to lie at roade,
> To that they went, and hid them close that none was seene abroade.
> Wee thought them gon, and with the winde to Greece to haue been fled.
>
> *From the translation of Thomas Phaer and Thomas Twyne, 1573*

24 **hūc**: similarly positioned in 18; Greeks are hidden both in the horse and on the island, poised to assault Troy. The line's slow spondees heighten the tension.
  prōvehō, prōvehere, prōvexī, prōvectus, *to carry forth;* pass. in middle sense, *to go forth, sail forth.*

25 ***reor, rērī, ratus sum**, *to believe, think, imagine, suppose* (here sc. **sumus** and, also a common ELLIPSIS, **eōs = Danaōs** as subj. of the infs.).

26 ***ergō**, conj./adv., *therefore.*
  Ergō . . . lūctū: a remarkable transitional line, with its grave spondees, the **o**'s and **s**'s perhaps meant to imitate Troy's long (but unjustified) sigh of relief, and the INTERLOCKED WORD ORDER yielding the pathetically ironic climax in **Teucria lūctū**.
  solvit sē: i.e., *frees itself, relaxes.*
  Teucria, -ae, f., *Troy* (see on **Teucrī** 1.38).

27 ***pandō, pandere, passus**, *to spread out, open out; to open (up); to reveal.*
  īre: = **exīre**, i.e., **ex urbe** (on the use of simple vbs. in place of compounds, see on **verteret** 1.20); sc. **nōs** as subj.
  ***Dōricus, -a, -um**, *Doric, of Doris* (a region in northern Greece), *Greek.*

28 **dēsertōs . . . relictum**: CHIASMUS, and an esp. sonorous line, with the ALLITERATIVE **l**'s and the internal rhyme in **dē** and **ōs** accentuated in each case by the ictus.

29 **hīc . . . hīc . . . hīc . . . hīc (30)**: ANAPHORA of the demonstrative (together with ASYNDETON) and the use of quite abrupt DIAERESES instead of CAESURAE for the principal pauses very effectively point our attention now in one direction, now in another, as Aeneas' eye, via the poet's highly cinematographic technique, surveys the deserted strand.
  tendēbat: here, in a common idiom, *pitched his tents, encamped.*

31 **stupet . . . mīrantur (32)**: the shift from collective sg. to pl. is a natural one.
  ***innūptus, -a, -um**, *unmarried, maiden, virgin.*
  exitiālis, -is, -e, *destructive, fatal, deadly.*
  ***Minerva, -ae**, f., *Minerva* (Roman goddess of crafts, wisdom, and warfare, associated with Pallas Athen).
  dōnum . . . Minervae: Aeneas has in mind Sinon's story that the horse was *an offering to Minerva* (183–94 below, esp. **dōna Minervae** 189); but since Sinon's story was a fabrication, and the goddess has already been identified as aiding in the horse's contruction (15), there is likely an ironic double entendre here, with **Minervae** construed as GEN. OF POSSESSION: the doomsday machine is her "gift" to Troy.

32 **mōlem mīrantur**: ALLITERATION of **m** is often intended to produce a somber or grim effect, as here. Use of the noun **mōlem** plus gen. **equī** rather than **equum** and some adj. focusses attention on the massiveness of the creature; Servius reports the tradition that it was 120 feet long and 30 wide and had moving parts, including tail, knees, and eyes.
  Thymoetēs, -ae, m., *Thymoetes* (a Trojan citizen).

33 **dūcī . . . locārī**: prose would have an **ut** cl. with **hortātur** instead of an inf.

24 hūc sē prōvectī dēsertō in lītore condunt;
25 nōs abiisse ratī et ventō petiisse Mycēnās.

The city's gates are opened, and the Trojans survey the deserted
Greek camp and debate what to do with the wooden horse

26   "Ergō omnis longō solvit sē Teucria lūctū.
27 Panduntur portae; iuvat īre et Dōrica castra
28 dēsertōsque vidēre locōs lītusque relictum:
29 hīc Dolopum manus, hīc saevus tendēbat Achillēs;
30 classibus hīc locus, hīc aciē certāre solēbant.
31 Pars stupet innūptae dōnum exitiāle Minervae
32 et mōlem mīrantur equī; prīmusque Thymoetēs
33 dūcī intrā mūrōs hortātur et arce locārī,

Quaestiōnēs

1. Comment on the sound effects in verse 25.

2. How is the phrase **panduntur portae** (27) especially effective?

3. What, besides the anaphora, produces the most striking sound effect in line 30?

4. Characterize the Trojans' initial response to seeing the deserted shore in 26–30; how is their response quite understandable psychologically, in view of the circumstances?

5. Comment on the word order in verse 33.

Athena (Minerva)
constructing the
Trojan horse
Red-figure kylix
5th cent. B.C.
Museo Archeologico
Florence, Italy

34 **dolō:** Servius reports that Thymoetes' wife and son had been executed by Priam, hence the allusion here to his possible connivance with the Greeks.

35 **Capys:** Capys escaped from Troy with Aeneas and is mentioned in 1.183 above.

quōrum . . . mentī: sc. **eī** as anteced. of **quōrum** and **est** with the collective sg. **mentī** (DAT. OF POSSESSION); freely, *those whose judgment was . . .*.

36 *__**īnsidiae, -ārum,**__ f. pl., *ambush; treachery, plot, trick.*

37 *__**subiciō, subicere, subiēcī, subiectus,**__ *to throw from below; to place underneath/ below; to place (someone/something)* under the control of.

-que: here, as occasionally in both prose and verse, = **-ve.**

ūrō, ūrere, ussī, ustus, *to destroy by fire, burn.*

38 **terebrō (1),** *to drill a hole in, bore through* (with a tool known as a **terebra,** which was also the word for both a surgical instrument and a siege machine used for drilling through walls).

terebrāre . . . uterī: in view of the sexual imagery used elsewhere of the **uterus** in this book (see note on 2.20 above), some readers suppose that Vergil here means to evoke an image of abortion.

*__**latebra, -ae,**__ f., *hiding place; hole, lair* (of an animal).

terebrāre cavās . . . temptāre latebrās: INTERLOCKED WORD ORDER, with both infs. sharing the single dir. obj.

39 *__**incertus, -a, -um,**__ *not fixed, subject to chance; uncertain, unsure;* (of a weapon) *not firmly held.*

studia: here *factions.*

40 **Prīmus:** adv. in sense, like **prīmus** in 32 above.

41 *__**Lāocoōn, Lāocoontis,**__ m., *Laocoön* (Laocoön, one of Priam's sons, a priest of Apollo who had offended that god by making love to his wife in the god's temple; his story was the subject of a lost tragedy by Sophocles, which was likely a source for Vergil).

*__**dēcurrō, dēcurrere, dēcurrī, dēcursus,**__ *to run down (from), hurry down.*

42 **et procul:** i.e., even as he was rushing toward the crowd; sc. **inquit.**

īnsānia, -ae, f., *insanity, madness.*

43 **āvectōs:** sc. **esse.**

44 **Sīc . . . Ulixēs:** Laocoön assumes that the wily Ulysses is somehow involved.

45 **Aut . . . Achīvī:** in this regard Laocoön's intuition was perfect.

lignum, -ī, n., *wood* (often applied disparagingly, as here, to an object made of wood).

occultō (1), *to hide, conceal.*

46 **aut haec in:** the soundplay with **aut hōc in-** in the preceding line underscores the alternative functions that Laocoön assumes the horse serves; similarly **aut** is positioned first in 48.

fabricō (1), *to fashion, design; to build, construct.*

*__**māchina, -ae,**__ f., *machine; crane; siege-engine* (for breaking down or scaling city walls).

47 **īnspectūra . . . ventūra . . . urbī:** the rhyming syllables are positioned under the ictus for added emphasis; as often, the fut. partics. here indicate purpose.

urbī: the DAT. OF DIRECTION was common in poetry, where prose would use a prep. + acc. construction.

34 sīve dolō seu iam Trōiae sīc fāta ferēbant.

35 At Capys, et quōrum melior sententia mentī,

36 aut pelagō Danaum īnsidiās suspectaque dōna

37 praecipitāre iubent subiectīsque ūrere flammīs,

38 aut terebrāre cavās uterī et temptāre latebrās.

39 Scinditur incertum studia in contrāria vulgus.

The Trojan priest Laocoön warns his countrymen that the horse
must be a trick and then hurls his spear into its womb

40   "Prīmus ibi ante omnēs, magnā comitante catervā,

41 Lāocoön ārdēns summā dēcurrit ab arce

42 et procul, 'ō miserī, quae tanta īnsānia, cīvēs?

43 Crēditis āvectōs hostēs? Aut ūlla putātis

44 dōna carēre dolīs Danaum? Sīc nōtus Ulixēs?

45 Aut hōc inclūsī lignō occultantur Achīvī,

46 aut haec in nostrōs fabricāta est māchina mūrōs,

47 īnspectūra domōs ventūraque dēsuper urbī,

Quaestiōnēs

1. Explain how Vergil creates a word-picture in line 39. In what other ways does the verse effectively close out this scene?

2. Compare Vergil's description of the debate over the horse in 31–39 with that of Homer in *Odyssey* 8.505f.

3. Compare **magnā . . . catervā** (40) with 1.497; what does the detail here add to Vergil's characterization of Laocoön?

4. In what several respects does Laocoön's language in 42–44 reveal his agitated state of mind?

5. Explain how Vergil employs meter, sound effects, and word order in 45 to dramatize Laocoön's point.

48   **aliquis:** here used as an adj. rather than a pron. (cf. note on **quis** 1.459).

    *****error, errōris,** m., *wandering, roaming; maze, deception, trick; confusion, mistake.*

    nē crēdite: nē + imper. is an archaism common in verse for **nōlī** + inf.

49   **Quidquid . . . ferentēs:** a frequently quoted line, as memorable for its
      ALLITERATION and lively dactylic rhythms as for its succinctness.

    et: as often, = **etiam.**

    dōna: here, as in 31 and 36, the word is used ironically.

50   **fātus:** here with the sense of speaking prophetically.

51   *****curvus, -a, -um,** *curved; having many bends/turns, winding.*

    *****alvus, -ī,** f., *belly; womb; hollow cavity.*

52   **contorqueō, contorquēre, contorsī, contortus,** *to twist, rotate; to hurl* (a
      spinning weapon).

    recutiō, recutere, recussī, recussus, *to strike* (something, causing it to recoil or
      vibrate).

    in latus (51) . . . recussō: Vergil uses meter to good effect in these lines, with
      the dactyls suggesting, in 51, the speed of Laocoön's huge spear and, in 52,
      its quivering motion as it stuck in the horse's womb, and the ENJAMBEMENT
      of **contorsit,** with its three long syllables and the abrupt CAESURA following,
      suggesting the powerful force of his throw.

53   **īnsonō, īnsonāre, īnsonuī,** *to make a loud noise, resound.*

    īnsonuēre . . . cavernae: like the horse's womb, the line itself reverberates with its
      rapid dactyls; and, by placing **-tum** under the ictus and just at the midpoint
      of the verse, Vergil lets us hear the groaning of the horse's timbers—or is
      it the creature moaning in labor, as the time nears for her to give birth to
      her deadly offspring? The line's internal rhyme and its intricate structure
      deliberately recall the sound effects and structure of verse 38, where Capys
      had urged the sort of assault on the horse that Laocoön has here commenced.

    cavae . . . cavernae: a play on the words' etymologies as well as their ASSONANCE;
      cf. **cavernās** (19) and **cavās** (38).

54   **sī . . . fuisset, / impulerat . . . (55) / stāret . . . manērēs (56):** a MIXED PAST/
      PRESENT CONTRARY-TO-FACT CONDITION with a shift first to the more vivid
      plpf. indic. (with Laocoön as subj.) and then to the impf. subjunct. for added
      poignancy; the ANAPHORA and ASYNDETON in 54 likewise lend intensity to
      Aeneas' sorrowful lament.

    mēns: though some would understand **nostra,** supposing that Aeneas refers to
      the Trojans' failure to heed Laocoön's warning, the word is better taken, like
      fāta, with **deum (deōrum);** cf. **deae mēns** (170).

    *****laevus, -a, -um,** *(on the) left; ill-omened, unfavorable, unpropitious.*

55   *****Argolicus, -a, -um,** *Argive* (see note on 1.24), *Greek.*

    *****foedō (1),** *to make filthy, defile, pollute; to wound, mangle, mutilate.*

    foedāre latebrās: like line 53, an intentional echo of 38 (**temptāre latebrās,**
      identically positioned at line's end); Laocoön's spear has penetrated the horse,
      but the Trojans will not probe and defile its inner recesses.

48 aut aliquis latet error; equō nē crēdite, Teucrī.
49 Quidquid id est, timeō Danaōs et dōna ferentēs.'
50 Sīc fātus, validīs ingentem vīribus hastam
51 in latus inque ferī curvam compāgibus alvum
52 contorsit. Stetit illa tremēns, uterōque recussō
53 īnsonuēre cavae gemitumque dedēre cavernae.
54 Et, sī fāta deum, sī mēns nōn laeva fuisset,
55 impulerat ferrō Argolicās foedāre latebrās,

Quaestiō

Analyze the several arguments Laocoön makes, both explicitly and implicitly, in his brief speech in 42–49 and comment on their effectiveness.

The Trojan horse, fresco from Pompeii, 1st cent. C.E.
Museo Archeologico Nazionale, Naples, Italy

56 **stāret . . . manērēs:** some mss. read **stārēs** and some **manēret**, but the shift from third to second pers. is especially effective and most likely what Vergil wrote; Aeneas first laments Troy's fall and then, in a poignant APOSTROPHE, addresses her citadel as if it were alive and towering still over the city.

57 **revinciō, revincīre, revīnxī, revīnctus,** *to restrain with bonds, tie up.*

manūs . . . revīnctum: ACC. OF SPECIFICATION (RESPECT) with reflex. partic.; for the construction, see note on **oculōs suffūsa** (1.228).

58 **pāstōrēs . . . trahēbant:** the spondees and conflict of ictus and accent are perhaps meant to suggest the force with which the shepherds were dragging their captive.

59 **Dardanidae:** with **pāstōrēs** (58).

quī: the anteced. is **iuvenem** (57).

***ultrō,** adv., *in addition, besides, even; of one's own accord, on one's own initiative.*

60 **hoc ipsum:** i.e., his capture and the betrayal of Troy; for the scansion, see note on **hoc** (1.539).

***struō, struere, strūxī, strūctus,** *to set in place, arrange; to construct, build; to plan, contrive.*

61 **fīdēns, fīdentis** + gen., *confident* (in).

utrumque: i.e., for either of the two outcomes mentioned in the next line.

62 ***versō (1),** *to turn (around); to turn over in the mind, ponder; to implement.*

63 **vīsō, vīsere, vīsī,** *to go and look (at).*

64 ***circumfundō, circumfundere, circumfūdī, circumfūsus,** *to pour around;* pass., *to spread around/out, surround.*

ruit certantque: Vergil first uses the sg. vb. of the group, then switches to the pl. to focus on the individuals as they mock their prisoner.

inlūdō, inlūdere, inlūsī, inlūsus, *to make sport of, mock.*

65 **Accipe:** here *listen to, hear;* like **disce** (identically positioned in the next line), addressed at once by Aeneas to Dido, and by Vergil to his reader.

***crīmen, crīminis,** n., *charge, accusation; misdeed, crime.*

66 **disce omnēs:** sc. **Danaōs** (though some readers understand **īnsidiās**); an emphatic ENJAMBEMENT and another of the 55 incomplete lines in the poem, 10 of them in Book Two alone (see note on 1.534).

67 **inermis:** ironic, as Sinon's lies proved to be the most powerful weapon of all against Troy's defenses.

68 **circumspexit:** the word looks back to **circumfūsa** (64); as the young men had surrounded him, so Sinon now looks all around at them. The fifth-foot spondee produces a rare SPONDAIC LINE, one of only about three dozen in the *Aeneid;* the abrupt rhythm is perhaps intended to suggest the halting of Sinon's gaze as he slowly looks about at his captors. The spondees and clipped monosyllables in the next line continue the effect.

69 ***heu,** interj., indicating dismay or sorrow, *alas.*

70 ***dēnique,** adv., *at last, finally.*

***restō, restāre, restitī,** *to remain, linger; to be left, remain* (to be done).

56 Trōiaque nunc stāret, Priamīque arx alta manērēs.

The Greek Sinon allows himself to be captured
and is interrogated by the Trojans

57   "Ecce, manūs iuvenem intereā post terga revīnctum
58 pāstōrēs magnō ad rēgem clāmōre trahēbant
59 Dardanidae, quī sē ignōtum venientibus ultrō,
60 hoc ipsum ut strueret Trōiamque aperīret Achīvīs,
61 obtulerat, fīdēns animī atque in utrumque parātus,
62 seu versāre dolōs seu certae occumbere mortī.
63 Undique vīsendī studiō Trōiāna iuventūs
64 circumfūsa ruit certantque inlūdere captō.
65 Accipe nunc Danaum īnsidiās et crīmine ab ūnō
66 disce omnēs.
67 Namque ut cōnspectū in mediō turbātus, inermis
68 cōnstitit atque oculīs Phrygia agmina circumspexit,
69 'Heu, quae nunc tellūs,' inquit, 'quae mē aequora possunt
70 accipere? Aut quid iam miserō mihi dēnique restat,

Quaestiō

How does Vergil's word-choice in 63–64 emphasize the Trojans' excited curiosity about Sinon?

About the captive, tides of Trojans flow;
All press to see, and some insult the foe.
Now hear how well the Greeks their wiles disguis'd;
Behold a nation in a man compris'd.
Trembling the miscreant stood, unarm'd and bound;
He star'd, and roll'd his haggard eyes around,
Then said: 'Alas! what earth remains, what sea
Is open to receive unhappy me?'

From the translation of John Dryden, 1698

71 **cui**: with both **neque . . . locus** (sc. **est**) and **poenās . . . poscunt** (72).
    neque: here = **nōn**.
    ***usquam**, adv., *in any place, anywhere.*
    super: here adv., *besides, furthermore.*

72 ***īnfēnsus, -a, -um**, *bitterly hostile; angry, furious.*

73 **Quō**: = **hōc**; use of the rel. in place of a demonstrative is common in Lat.
    ***comprimō, comprimere, compressī, compressus**, *to restrain, hold back, check.*
    conversī . . . compressus: sc. **sunt** and **est**, respectively; the intensifying prefixes
        underscore the Trojans' rush of sympathy in response, ironically, to Sinon's
        lies.

74 ***crēscō, crēscere, crēvī, crētus**, *to be born* (+ abl., *from, of*); *to grow, increase* (here
        sc. **sit**).

76 [**Ille . . . fātur**:]: the line (repeated in 3.612 and lacking here in some mss.) is
        clearly an interpolation, as **inquit** in 78 makes **fātur** redundant.
    ***formīdō, formīdinis**, f., *fear, terror, alarm.*

77 **fuerit quodcumque**: i.e., *no matter what happens.*
    ***fateor, fatērī, fassus sum**, *to acknowledge, accept; to admit guilt, confess.*

79 **Fortūna**: a common PERSONIFICATION.
    ***Sinōn, Sinōnis**, m., *Sinon* (a Greek warrior).

80 ***fingō, fingere, fīnxī, fictus**, *to make, form, fashion, create; to make up, pretend*
        (Vergil neatly FRAMES the line with two forms of the vb.).
    mendāx, mendācis, *false, lying, deceitful* (here OBJ. COMPL., like **miserum** 79 and
        vānum).
    ***improbus, -a, -um**, *morally unsound; shameless, wicked.*

81 **aliquod**: with **nōmen** (82), *some mention of . . . .*

82 **Bēlīdēs, -ae**, m., *descendant of Belus* (legendary Egyptian king, son of Poseidon
        and ancestor of several Greek royal families, including that of Palamedes).
    Palamēdēs, Palamēdis, m., *Palamedes* (son of the Euboean king Nauplius, hated
        by Odysseus for revealing his attempts to escape service in Troy).
    ***inclutus, -a, -um**, *famous, renowned, celebrated.*

83 **prōditiō, prōditiōnis**, f., *treacherous abandonment, betrayal.*
    ***Pelasgus, -a, -um**, *Pelasgian, of the Pelasgians* (an ancient Aegean tribe); m. pl. as
        noun, *Pelasgians, Greeks.*

84 ***īnsōns, īnsontis**, *innocent, guiltless.*
    indicium, -ī, n., *evidence, charge.*
    ***quia**, conj., *since, because.*
    vetābat: a good example of the CONATIVE IMPF., *was trying to . . . .*

85 ***nex, necis**, f., *murder, slaughter* (here DAT. OF DIRECTION).
    cassus, -a, -um, + abl., *devoid of, lacking, bereft of.*
    cassum lūmine: i.e., *dead.*
    lūgeō, lūgēre, lūxī, lūctus, *to mourn, grieve (over), bewail.*

86 **illī**: DAT. OF REF. with **comitem**.
    cōnsanguinitās, cōnsanguinitātis, f., *blood-relationship, kinship.*

88 ***vigeō, vigēre, viguī**, *to be strong; to be influential/powerful; to flourish.*
    stābat . . . vigēbat: sc. **Palamēdēs**.

71 cui neque apud Danaōs usquam locus, et super ipsī
72 Dardanidae īnfēnsī poenās cum sanguine poscunt?'
73 Quō gemitū conversī animī, compressus et omnis
74 impetus. Hortāmur fārī quō sanguine crētus,
75 quidve ferat; memoret quae sit fīdūcia captō.

Vowing to speak the truth, Sinon contrives a story
about a fierce enmity between himself and Ulysses

76 ["Ille haec, dēpositā tandem formīdine, fātur:]
77 'Cūncta equidem tibi, rēx, fuerit quodcumque, fatēbor
78 vēra,' inquit; 'neque mē Argolicā dē gente negābō.
79 Hoc prīmum; nec, sī miserum Fortūna Sinōnem
80 fīnxit, vānum etiam mendācemque improba finget.
81 Fandō aliquod sī forte tuās pervēnit ad aurēs
82 Bēlīdae nōmen Palamēdis et incluta fāmā
83 glōria, quem falsā sub prōditiōne Pelasgī
84 īnsontem īnfandō indiciō, quia bella vetābat,
85 dēmīsēre necī, nunc cassum lūmine lūgent:
86 illī mē comitem et cōnsanguinitāte propinquum
87 pauper in arma pater prīmīs hūc mīsit ab annīs.
88 Dum stābat rēgnō incolumis rēgumque vigēbat

Quaestiōnēs

1. What is the effect of Vergil's positioning of **cūncta** and **vēra** in 77–78?

2. What is most remarkable in the sound effects and metrics of verse 84?

89 **concilium, -ī,** n., *council, assembly.*
  et: = **etiam.**
90 *__**invidia, -ae,**__ f., *ill will, envy, jealousy; dislike, hatred.*
  pellāx, pellācis, *seductive, deceitful.*
91 **haud ignōta:** LITOTES.
  superīs . . . ōrīs: a poignant euphemism for dying.
  *__**concēdō, concēdere, concessī, concessus,**__ *to go, go away, withdraw.*
92 **tenebrae, -ārum,** f. pl., *darkness (of night); obscurity, concealment.*
93 **mēcum:** *in my heart.*
  *__**indignor, -ārī, -ātus sum,**__ *to regard with indignation, resent.*
94 *__**dēmēns, dēmentis,**__ *out of one's mind, insane, mad, frenzied.*
  fors . . . tulisset: = **sī quae fors tulisset,** *if any chance might have brought it about,*
    i.e., *if the opportunity arose;* the plpf. subjunct. is used within an IND. STATE.
    in place of the fut. perf. in dir. speech.
95 *__**patrius, -a, -um,**__ *of a father, a father's; ancestral; of one's birthplace, native.*
  remeō (1), *to go/come back, return* (**remeāssem** = **remeāvissem**).
96 **ultor, ultōris,** m., *one who exacts retribution, avenger.*
  mē (94) . . . / prōmīsī ultōrem: sc. **fore** (= **futūrum esse**), i.e., of Palamedes.
97 **lābēs, lābis,** f., *fall, collapse; defect, blemish, taint.*
  malī lābēs: possibly *taint of evil,* something like our expression, "a bad mark"
    (against someone); but some editors, influenced by the interpretation of the
    ancient commentator Servius, take **malī** as a sort of OBJ. GEN., *a slip into*
    misfortune.
98 *__**spargō, spargere, sparsī, sparsus,**__ *to scatter, sprinkle, spatter; to spread.*
  terrēre . . . spargere . . . quaerere (99): HIST. INFS., often used in describing
    quick, dramatic actions, an effect intensified here by the ANAPHORA of **hinc.**
99 **ambiguus, -a, -um,** *uncertain, doubtful; suspicious, devious, treacherous.*
  *__**cōnscius, -a, -um,**__ *sharing knowledge; inwardly aware, conscious; with a guilty*
    conscience, guilty; confederate, allied; as m. or f. noun, *accomplice, accessory.*
  arma: effectively delayed to line's end; Ulysses' weapons, like Sinon's, were his
    lies.
100 **requiēscō, requiēscere, requiēvī, requiētūrus,** *to rest; to desist, cease.*
  *__**Calchās, Calchantis,**__ acc. **Calchanta,** m., *Calchas* (the leading Greek soothsayer
    in the Trojan War).
  *__**minister, -trī,**__ m., *servant, assistant; agent, accomplice.*
  Nec . . . ministrō: APOSIOPESIS.
101 **ingrātus, -a, -um,** *ungrateful, thankless; unwelcome, unpleasant.*
  *__**revolvō, revolvere, revoluī, revolūtus,**__ *to roll back; to go over again.*
103 **id:** i.e., the simple fact that he is a Greek; dir. obj. of **audīre.**
  *__**sat**__ (= **satis**), adv. and indecl. adj./noun, *enough, sufficient(ly).*
  *__**iamdūdum,**__ adv., *some time ago; for a long time, long since; now after all this time.*

89 conciliīs, et nōs aliquod nōmenque decusque
90 gessimus. Invidiā postquam pellācis Ulixī
91 (haud ignōta loquor) superīs concessit ab ōrīs,
92 adflīctus vītam in tenebrīs lūctūque trahēbam
93 et cāsum īnsontis mēcum indignābar amīcī.
94 Nec tacuī dēmēns et mē, fors sī qua tulisset,
95 sī patriōs umquam remeāssem victor ad Argōs,
96 prōmīsī ultōrem et verbīs odia aspera mōvī.
97 Hinc mihi prīma malī lābēs, hinc semper Ulixēs
98 crīminibus terrēre novīs, hinc spargere vōcēs
99 in vulgum ambiguās et quaerere cōnscius arma.
100 Nec requiēvit enim, dōnec Calchante ministrō—
101 sed quid ego haec autem nēquīquam ingrāta revolvō,
102 quidve moror? Sī omnēs ūnō ōrdine habētis Achīvōs,
103 idque audīre sat est, iamdūdum sūmite poenās:

Quaestiōnēs

1. How do meter and sound effects add to the sense of pathos in 93?

2. What rhetorical devices, besides the use of historical infinitives, lend intensity to Sinon's remarks in 97–99?

Calchas
Stone figure from
east pediment,
temple of Zeus
480 B.C.
Archaeological Museum
Olympia, Greece

104   **hoc:** for the syllable quantity, see the note on line 60.

      ***Ithacus, -a, -um,** *Ithacan, from Ithaca* (a small island off the west coast of Greece, legendary home of Ulysses); as a noun, *the Ithacan* (used disparagingly here and below by Sinon, who chooses not to call his alleged persecutor by his proper name).

      velit . . . mercentur: POTENTIAL SUBJUNCT.

      magnō: sc. **pretiō,** ABL. OF PRICE.

105   ***scītor, -ārī, -ātus sum,** *to seek to know, inquire about; to question* (someone).

107   ***prōsequor, prōsequī, prōsecūtus sum,** *to follow, escort; to continue, proceed.*

      pavitō, -āre, *to be fearful; to fear, be in dread of.*

      pectore: here = *emotions.*

108   **cupiēre:** = **cupīvērunt** (for the form, see on **tenuēre** 1.12 and **audierat** 1.20).

110   **fēcissent:** a contrary-to-fact wish, sometimes called the OPTATIVE SUBJUNCT.

111   **interclūdō, interclūdere, interclūsī, interclūsus,** *to block, cut off.*

112   **contextus, -a, -um,** *joined by weaving, interwoven.*

      acernus, -a, -um, *(made of) maple-wood.*

      hic . . . acernīs: the INTERLOCKED ORDER produces a kind of WORD-PICTURE, suggesting the interwoven planks of the horse. In line 16 Aeneas says the horse was made of fir (and cf. **pīneā . . . claustra** 258–59), and later (186, 230, and 260) it is said to be of oak; some see this as an inaccuracy, but Vergil may simply be generalizing or he may mean that a variety of materials were employed.

114   **Suspēnsī:** i.e., by the uncertainty.

      Eurypylus, -ī, m., *Eurypylus* (a Greek warrior mentioned in *Iliad* 2.736).

      scītātum: acc. supine, regularly used after vbs. of motion (here **mittimus** 115) to indicate purpose.

      ōrāculum, -ī, n., *divine utterance, oracle.*

      ōrācula Phoebī: there were several shrines to Apollo where priestesses might be consulted for oracles, the most famous at Delphi.

115   ***adytum, -ī,** n., *shrine, sanctuary.*

116   **plācāstis:** for the form, see note on **audierat** (1.20).

      ***caedō, caedere, cecīdī, caesus,** *to strike, beat; to kill, murder, slay.*

      Sanguine . . . caesā: perhaps a HENDIADYS for **sanguine virginis caesae;** Agamemnon had sacrificed his daughter Iphigenia at the outset of the war in order to gain the gods' support and assure fair winds for the launching of the Greek fleet.

118   **quaerendī:** sc. **sunt.**

      animā: here *life.*

      ***litō (1),** *to gain favor/atone by sacrifice* (often + ABL. OF MEANS); *to offer (in propitiation).*

      litandum: sc. **est;** impers., *it must be atoned by sacrifice* = *you must atone by sacrifice.*

119   **Vulgī . . . aurēs:** = **Ut haec vōx ad aurēs vulgī vēnit.**

120   ***gelidus, -a, -um,** *cold, icy.*

104 hoc Ithacus velit et magnō mercentur Atrīdae.'

*Sinon continues with his lie, telling his captors that the Greeks had
planned to sacrifice him to the gods in order to insure their
safe return home after leaving behind the wooden horse*

105 "Tum vērō ārdēmus scītārī et quaerere causās,
106 ignārī scelerum tantōrum artisque Pelasgae.
107 Prōsequitur pavitāns et fictō pectore fātur:
108 'Saepe fugam Danaī Trōiā cupiēre relictā
109 mōlīrī et longō fessī discēdere bellō;
110 fēcissentque utinam! Saepe illōs aspera pontī
111 interclūsit hiems et terruit Auster euntēs.
112 Praecipuē cum iam hic trabibus contextus acernīs
113 stāret equus, tōtō sonuērunt aethere nimbī.
114 Suspēnsī Eurypylum scītātum ōrācula Phoebī
115 mittimus, isque adytīs haec trīstia dicta reportat:
116 "Sanguine plācāstis ventōs et virgine caesā,
117 cum prīmum Īliacās, Danaī, vēnistis ad ōrās;
118 sanguine quaerendī reditūs animāque litandum
119 Argolicā." Vulgī quae vōx ut vēnit ad aurēs,
120 obstipuēre animī gelidusque per īma cucurrit

Quaestiōnēs

1. What several details of Sinon's story in 69–72 and 77–104 are particularly
    effective in evoking the Trojans' sympathy and trust?

2. Comment on the word order and the multiple sound effects in 107.

3. In what several ways is the language of the oracle in 116–19 especially emphatic?

121 **parent . . . poscat:** subjunct. in IND. QUEST., dependent on the verbal idea
 implied in **tremor,** *(wondering fearfully) for whom they would prepare death*
 and whom . . . (Servius' interpretation—or possibly **fāta** is subj. rather than
 obj., *for whom the fates are preparing and whom . . .*).

 Apollō, Apollinis, m., *Phoebus Apollo* (god of the sun, civilization, prophecy,
 and the arts, brother of Diana).

 ossa . . . Apollō: the strong CAESURAE, the clipped phrases, the ASYNDETON, and
 the noisy **t/p** ALLITERATION all suggest the Trojans' anxious chatter about the
 import of Apollo's oracle.

122 *vātēs, vātis,* m., *prophet, seer, soothsayer; poet, bard.*

 vātem . . . tumultū: again sound effects, meter (esp. the conflict of ictus and
 accent), and the INTERLOCKED WORD ORDER help suggest the commotion
 Vergil is describing.

123 **prōtrahō, prōtrahere, prōtrāxī, prōtractus,** *to drag forward/out.*

 mediōs: sc. **nōs** or **Graecōs.**

 dīvum: for the form, see note on 1.46.

124 **flāgitō (1),** *to demand (to know); to ask repeatedly.*

 mihi: sc. **esse,** *was for me.*

 multī crūdēle canēbant . . . tacitī ventūra vidēbant (125): a nice example of the
 sort of rhyming couplet occasionally found in the poem.

 canēbant: here *were predicting.*

125 **ventūra:** Eng. would employ a rel. cl., *what was to come.*

126 **quīnī, -ae, -a,** *five each; five.*

 Bis quīnōs: the circumlocution produces a mystical effect.

 ille: the seer Calchas.

 tēctus: i.e., in his tent.

 recūsō (1), *to object, protest; to decline, refuse.*

127 **oppōnō, oppōnere, opposuī, oppositus,** *to put in the way of, expose to.*

128 **Vix:** here *reluctantly.*

129 **(ex) compositō,** idiom, *by pre-arrangement, as agreed.*

 rumpit: here, in a common idiom, *bursts forth into.*

 dēstinō (1), *to fix in position; to designate, destine; to mark out, target.*

130 **adsentiō, adsentīre, adsēnsī, adsēnsus,** *to agree, approve, assent.*

 quae: sc. **ea,** with **conversa,** as anteced.

 quisque, quaeque, quidque, *each (person/thing).*

132 **īnfanda: diēs** is f. when referring to a specific day (and also here, as elsewhere in
 Vergil, for metrical convenience).

 sacrum, -ī, n. (often pl. with sg. meaning), *sacred object; sacrificial victim,*
 offering; religious ceremony, rite.

133 *salsus, -a, -um,* *salted, salty.*

 salsae frūgēs: a common ritual offering to accompany the sacrifice.

 tempus, temporis, n., *side of the forehead, temple.*

 vittae: ribbons were traditionally tied around the head of a sacrificial victim.

134 **Ēripuī . . . rūpī:** by FRAMING the line with these two vbs., Vergil highlights both
 their ASSONANCE and the violence of Sinon's escape.

 lētum, -ī, n., *death; destruction.*

121 ossa tremor, cui fāta parent, quem poscat Apollō.
122 Hīc Ithacus vātem magnō Calchanta tumultū
123 prōtrahit in mediōs; quae sint ea nūmina dīvum
124 flāgitat. Et mihi iam multī crūdēle canēbant
125 artificis scelus et tacitī ventūra vidēbant.
126 Bis quīnōs silet ille diēs tēctusque recūsat
127 prōdere vōce suā quemquam aut oppōnere mortī.
128 Vix tandem, magnīs Ithacī clāmōribus āctus,
129 compositō rumpit vōcem et mē dēstinat ārae.
130 Adsēnsēre omnēs et, quae sibi quisque timēbat,
131 ūnius in miserī exitium conversa tulēre.
132 Iamque diēs īnfanda aderat; mihi sacra parārī
133 et salsae frūgēs et circum tempora vittae.
134 Ēripuī, fateor, lētō mē et vincula rūpī,

Quaestiōnēs

1. What traits of Ulysses' character are briefly glimpsed in 122–25?

2. How do lines 130–31 reflect Vergil's insight into the darker side of human nature?

The sack of Troy, woodcut from a 1664 French translation of the *Aeneid*

135 **līmōsus, -a, -um,** *muddy, slimy.*
    *lacus, -ūs, m., *lake, pond, pool; waters* (of the Underworld).
    *ulva, -ae, f., *sedge, rush* (or other similar aquatic plants).
136 **dēlitēscō, dēlitēscere, dēlituī,** *to go into hiding, conceal oneself.*
    vēla darent: ANTICIPATORY SUBJUNCT.; for the idiom, here and in (**vēla**)
        dedissent, see on 1.35.
    sī . . . dedissent: *if they would have . . .* (for the subjunct., see note on **tulisset** 94).
137 **mihi:** DAT. OF POSSESSION; sc. **est.**
138 **dulcēs nātōs:** generally assumed to be yet another of Sinon's lies, aimed at
      winning the Trojans' sympathy, since he claimed in line 87 that his father had
      sent him to the war in his youth.
    *exoptātus, -a, -um, *hoped for, much desired.*
139 **illī:** Sinon's countrymen.
    fors, adv., *perhaps, maybe.*
    et: = etiam.
    reposcō, reposcere, *to demand* (something, acc., here **poenās**) *from* (someone,
      acc., here **quōs,** Sinon's family).
140 **effugium, -ī,** n., *flight, escape.*
    *piō (1), *to cleanse by expiation, expiate.*
141 **Quod:** here *but.*
    tē: obj. of **ōrō** (143).
142 **sī qua est:** with **fidēs** (143); the entire cl. is obj. of **per,** *by whatever faith*
      there is . . .. For indef. **qua** = **quae,** cf. 94 above.
    quae restet: REL. CL. OF CHARACTERISTIC with the indef. anteced. **qua.**
143 **intemerātus, -a, -um,** *undefiled, pure.*
144 ***dignus, -a, -um,** *appropriate, suitable, worthy; deserving; deserved.*
145 **Hīs . . . ultrō:** the pointed, essentially CHIASTIC single-line sent. effectively marks
      the end of Sinon's long speech and anticipates its fateful consequences.
    miserēscō, miserēscere, *to have compassion* (toward someone); *to feel pity.*
146 **Ipse . . . Priamus (147):** Vergil aptly employs INTERLOCKED WORD ORDER to
      describe the removal of Sinon's bonds; **prīmus** and **Priamus** are set in
      the same metrical position to underscore both their connection and the
      ASSONANCE.
    manicae, -ārum, f. pl., *handcuffs, manacles.*
147 ***amīcus, -a, -um,** *friendly, well disposed; favorable, supportive.*
148 **Quisquis es . . . / noster eris (149):** i.e., even though an enemy, we will take you
      in—according to Servius, a formulaic phrase for accepting a fugitive from the
      enemy camp.
    *oblīvīscor, oblīvīscī, oblītus sum, + acc. or gen., *to lose remembrance of, forget*
      (about).
149 **ēdisserō, ēdisserere, ēdisseruī, ēdissertus,** *to set forth in words, relate.*
150 **quō:** *for what purpose;* the series of rapid-fire quests. in this verse and the next
      suggests Priam's agitated state of mind.
    mōlem . . . immānis: the two words together suggest the immensity of the horse.
    *auctor, auctōris, m., *creator, originator, proposer; ancestor, father.*

135 līmōsōque lacū per noctem obscūrus in ulvā
136 dēlituī, dum vēla darent, sī forte dedissent.
137 Nec mihi iam patriam antīquam spēs ūlla videndī
138 nec dulcēs nātōs exoptātumque parentem,
139 quōs illī fors et poenās ob nostra reposcent
140 effugia, et culpam hanc miserōrum morte piābunt.
141 Quod tē per superōs et cōnscia nūmina vērī,
142 per sī qua est quae restet adhūc mortālibus usquam
143 intemerāta fidēs, ōrō, miserēre labōrum
144 tantōrum, miserēre animī nōn digna ferentis.'

Taken in by Sinon's lies, the Trojans pity him, and Priam
asks him to explain the purpose of the wooden horse

145 "Hīs lacrimīs vītam damus et miserēscimus ultrō.
146 Ipse virō prīmus manicās atque arta levārī
147 vincla iubet Priamus dictīsque ita fātur amīcīs:
148 'Quisquis es, āmissōs hinc iam oblīvīscere Grāiōs—
149 noster eris—mihique haec ēdissere vēra rogantī:
150 quō mōlem hanc immānis equī statuēre? Quis auctor?

Quaestiōnēs

1. Comment on the sound effects in 136.

2. What is the intended effect of the spondaic rhythms and the conflict of ictus and accent in 138?

3. Analyze the speech in 107–44 and comment specifically on the numerous devices by which Sinon continues to build up sympathy for himself; how are his language and argumentation particularly effective in his summation at 141–44?

4. How does Priam's, and his fellow Trojans', behavior in 145–47 contrast with Sinon's?

5. Comment on the arrangement of **mihi . . . rogantī** (149) and its effect.

151 *rēligiō, rēligiōnis, f., *religious feeling, religion; religious act/ritual/offering.*

152 Dīxerat: in the absence of punctuation marks in ancient texts, and also with the listening audience in mind, such speech words were regularly employed to mark the end of a speech; cf. note on sīc ait (1.142).

    *īnstruō, īnstruere, īnstrūxī, īnstrūctus, *to build; to equip, fit out; to provide.*

    arte Pelasgā: cf. 106 above.

153 *sufferō, sufferre, sustulī, sublātus, *to lift up; to offer; to withstand, resist.*

    *exuō, exuere, exuī, exūtus, *to take off, set aside; to strip* (something, acc.) *from* (something, abl.).

    ad sīdera palmās: in identical metrical position in 1.93 for this same gesture of prayer; sīdera in both passages = *the heavens.*

154 aeternī ignēs: i.e., the sun, moon, stars, and planets, and the gods associated with them.

    violābilis, -is, -e, *subject to violation* (with nōn, *inviolable*).

155 *testor, -ārī, -ātus sum, *to call* (someone, a deity) *to witness; to swear by.*

    *ēnsis, ēnsis, m., *sword.*

157 fās . . . / fās (158): sc. est.

    *sacrō (1), *to make sacred, sanctify, consecrate.*

    *resolvō, resolvere, resoluī, resolūtus, *to loosen, undo, relax; to unravel, solve; to break, violate.*

158 *ōdī, ōdisse, ōsus, defective vb. with chiefly perf. system forms, *to hate.*

    omnia ferre (= efferre) sub aurās: cf. the Eng. idiom, "to bring everything out into the open."

159 teneor . . . nec: = nec . . . teneor (ANASTROPHE).

160 Tū: = Trōia (161, with servāta); Sinon dramatically addresses the city itself.

    manēas: here *abide by.*

161 sī . . . sī: ANAPHORA and ASYNDETON help underscore the intense irony.

162 *coepī, coepisse, coeptus, defective vb. with chiefly perf. system forms, *to begin, commence, initiate.*

163 semper stetit: ALLITERATION and esp. the strong DIAERESIS emphasize Sinon's point.

    Impius . . . enim (164): = Sed enim ex quō (tempore) Tȳdīdēs impius.

164 inventor, inventōris, m., *discoverer, inventor.*

165 *fātālis, -is, -e, *fateful; destined, fated; deadly, fatal.*

    *adgredior, adgredī, adgressus sum, *to proceed toward, approach; to assault, attack;* + inf., *to proceed* (to do something).

    *āvellō, āvellere, āvulsī, āvulsus, *to pluck off, tear/wrench away; to take away.*

166 *Palladium, -ī, n., *Palladium, statue of Pallas* (Athena/Minerva).

    fātāle (165) . . . / Palladium: it had been foretold that Troy could never be taken so long as the Palladium was safe in its temple on the citadel, hence the determination of Ulysses and Diomedes to steal it.

167 *sacer, -cra, -crum, *sacred, hallowed, holy.*

    *effigiēs, -ēī, f., *statue, image.*

168 virgineus, -a, -um, *of a young girl/virgin, virginal, chaste.*

    virgineās: with vittās, a TRANSFERRED EPITHET.

151 Quidve petunt? Quae rēligiō? Aut quae māchina bellī?'
152 Dīxerat.

> *Sinon continues his story, telling the Trojans that Ulysses' and*
> *Diomedes' theft of the statue of Minerva from her temple had*
> *angered the goddess and obliged the Greeks to return home*
> *in order to seek new omens and regain divine favor*

    "Ille, dolīs īnstrūctus et arte Pelasgā,
153 sustulit exūtās vinclīs ad sīdera palmās;
154 'Vōs, aeternī ignēs, et nōn violābile vestrum
155 testor nūmen,' ait, 'vōs ārae ēnsēsque nefandī,
156 quōs fūgī, vittaeque deum, quās hostia gessī:
157 fās mihi Grāiōrum sacrāta resolvere iūra,
158 fās ōdisse virōs atque omnia ferre sub aurās,
159 sī qua tegunt, teneor patriae nec lēgibus ūllīs.
160 Tū modo prōmissīs maneās servātaque servēs
161 Trōia fidem, sī vēra feram, sī magna rependam.
162 Omnis spēs Danaum et coeptī fidūcia bellī
163 Palladis auxiliīs semper stetit. Impius ex quō
164 Tȳdīdēs sed enim scelerumque inventor Ulixēs,
165 fātāle adgressī sacrātō āvellere templō
166 Palladium caesīs summae custōdibus arcis,
167 corripuēre sacram effigiem manibusque cruentīs
168 virgineās ausī dīvae contingere vittās,

Quaestiōnēs

1. In what specific ways do Priam's questions in 150–51 recall Laocoön's warnings about the horse in 42–49?

2. What is the point of Sinon's wordplay in **servātaque servēs** (160)?

3. How does Vergil use meter to emphasize meaning in 165?

4. How does the meter in 167 suit the action described?

5. Comment on the sound effects and structure of line 168.

169 **ex illō**: the phrase connects back to **ex quō** (163), just as **spēs Danaum** in the next verse deliberately repeats the same phrase in 162.

fluere . . . referrī: the HIST. INFS. help suggest how quickly the Greeks' fortunes were reversed.

*__retrō__, adv., *toward the rear, backwards; back again.*

sublābor, sublābī, sublāpsus sum, *to fall to the ground, collapse; to sink, ebb.*

170 **frāctae vīrēs**: the spondaic rhythm and the strong CAESURAE preceding and following underscore this point.

āversa deae mēns: Vergil employs the progression from trisyllable to disyllable to the relatively rare monosyllabic ending and the resultant offbeat rhythm to dramatize the abrupt change of heart Sinon ascribes to Minerva.

171 **Nec**: with **dubiīs**, i.e., *unambiguous.*

ea signa: *indications of this fact* (i.e., her anger).

*__Trītōnius, -a, -um__, *of lake Tritonis* (in north Africa, near the birthplace of Athena/Minerva and sacred to her); as a noun, *the Tritonian, Athena/Minerva.*

*__mōnstrum, -ī__, n., *omen, sign, portent; monstrous event/thing/act; monster.*

172 *__simulācrum -ī__, n., *likeness; image, statue; phantom, spectre.*

positum (erat) . . . ārsēre: an example of PARATAXIS, the juxtaposition of two independent cls., where one is logically dependent and would ordinarily be introduced by a subordinating conj. (. . . *had hardly been set up, when . . .*); the effect is intensified by the ELISION in **simulacrum: ārsēre.**

174 **sūdor, sūdōris**, m., *sweat.*

ter: here, and elsewhere in the poem, a mystical number.

175 *__ēmicō, ēmicāre, ēmicuī, ēmicātūrus__, *to dart forth, dash out, spring up.*

parma, -ae, f., *(small round) shield.*

parmamque . . . hastamque: coincidence of ictus and accent highlights the internal rhyme.

176 **Extemplō temptanda**: juxtaposition of the words accentuates their ASSONANCE.

177 **posse . . . Pergama**: like **temptanda (esse) . . . aequora** (176), IND. STATE. with **canit** (176).

*__exscindō, exscindere, exscidī, exscissus__, *to cut off; to demolish, destroy.*

178 **nūmen**: Minerva's statue, or her divine grace, or both.

180 **quod**: here *as to the fact that.*

ventō petiēre Mycēnās: cf. **ventō petiisse Mycēnās** (25); through this intentional verbal echo, Vergil means us to see Sinon cunningly playing on the Trojans' own mistaken theory of the Greeks' disappearance.

petiēre: for the form, cf. **cupiēre** (108 above).

181 **remētior, remētīrī, remēnsus sum**, *to travel back over, re-traverse.*

182 *__imprōvīsus, -a, -um__, *unforeseen, unexpected.*

imprōvīsī aderunt: ENJAMBED to underscore the irony, as the Greeks will indeed return unexpectedly—but even sooner than Sinon suggests.

dīgerō, dīgerere, dīgessī, dīgestus, *to disseminate; to classify, interpret.*

183 **Hanc**: with **effigiem** (184); Vergil often sets such noun-adj. pairs at the beginning of consecutive lines (cf. **cūncta . . .** / **vēra** 2.77–78).

prō . . . prō: here *in atonement for.*

nūmine laesō: the same expression is used of Juno in 1.8.

169 ex illō fluere ac retrō sublāpsa referrī
170 spēs Danaum, frāctae vīrēs, āversa deae mēns.
171 Nec dubiīs ea signa dedit Trītōnia mōnstrīs.
172 Vix positum castrīs simulācrum: ārsēre coruscae
173 lūminibus flammae arrēctīs, salsusque per artūs
174 sūdor iit, terque ipsa solō—mīrābile dictū!—
175 ēmicuit parmamque ferēns hastamque trementem.
176 Extemplō temptanda fugā canit aequora Calchās
177 nec posse Argolicīs exscindī Pergama tēlīs
178 ōmina nī repetant Argīs nūmenque redūcant
179 (quod pelagō et curvīs sēcum āvexēre carīnīs—
180 et nunc quod patriās ventō petiēre Mycēnās,
181 arma deōsque parant comitēs, pelagōque remēnsō
182 imprōvīsī aderunt); ita dīgerit ōmina Calchās.

The horse was built, Sinon concludes, to atone for the stolen
Palladium, and its size was meant to keep the Trojans from
bringing it into Troy and regaining Minerva's favor

183 "'Hanc prō Palladiō, monitī, prō nūmine laesō

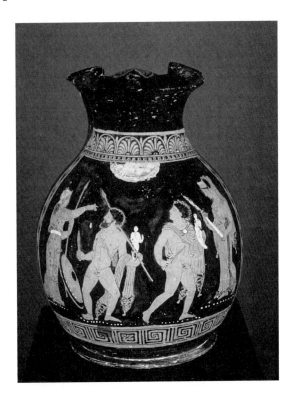

Ulysses and Diomedes
stealing the Palladium
Oinochoe (wine jug)
4th cent. B.C. Apulia, Italy
Louvre
Paris, France

184 *nefās, n., indecl., *impious act, sacrilege; crime; portent, horror.*
    quae . . . piāret: REL. CL. OF PURPOSE.

185 *immēnsus, -a, -um, *immeasurable, boundless; huge, immense.*
    hanc . . . immēnsam . . . mōlem: the expansive arrangement of the phrase helps
        suggest the vast size of the horse.

186 *rōbur, rōboris, n., *oak-tree; oak-wood* (or any hard wood); *firmness, strength.*
    texō, texere, texuī, textus, *to weave; to construct; to fit together.*
    rōboribus textīs: see note on 112.
    caelō: DAT. OF DIRECTION.

188 antīquā sub rēligiōne: i.e., in place of the stolen Palladium.

190 magnum exitium . . . futūrum (191): sc. esse, inf. (like ventūram [esse]
        and manēre 194) in IND. STATE., dependent on the speech vb. implied in
        Calchās . . . iussit (185–86).
    quod: with ōmen, *which omen* = *this omen.*
    ipsum: i.e., Calchas.

192 sīn manibus vestrīs: the CHIASMUS with sī vestra manus (189) helps emphasize
        the contrasting scenarios, and the juxtaposition vestrīs vestram adds further
        point.
    ascendisset: sc. dōnum/equus as subj.; for the plpf. subjunct. (here and in
        violāsset 189), see note on tulisset (94).

193 Asiam . . . / ventūram (194): this part of Calchas' supposed prophecy was
        realized when Rome subjugated Greece in the 2nd cent. B.C.
    Pelopēus, -a, -um, *of Pelops* (legendary king of Mycenae, father of Atreus and
        Thyestes).

194 ea fāta: i.e., the magnum exitium foretold in 190.

195 īnsidiīs . . . arte: ABL. OF CAUSE.
    periūrus, -a, -um, *perjured, lying, treacherous.*

196 captī: sc. sumus.

197 Lārīsaeus, -a, -um, *of Laris(s)a* (the chief city of Thessaly, Achilles' homeland),
    Laris(s)aean.

198 *domō, domāre, domuī, domitus, *to tame, subdue.*
    mīlle carīnae: in Homer's catalog in *Iliad* Book Two the number of ships in the
        Greek fleet that assaulted Troy was 1,186—not as elegant a fit for Vergil's
        hexameter as, simply, mīlle.

199 miserīs: sc. nōbīs, with obicitur (200) = DAT. WITH COMPOUND VBS.;
        ALLITERATION of m here, as often, is meant to produce an effect of
        foreboding.
    multō: ABL. OF DEGREE OF DIFFERENCE with magis (200).

200 *obiciō, obicere, obiēcī, obiectus, *to throw (in the way), put before; to present to.*
    obicitur: the first syllable is long since the i following represents an original ii
        (obiicitur from ob + iacitur).
    imprōvidus, -a, -um, *not seeing into the future, improvident.*
    imprōvida pectora turbat: ALLITERATION and coincidence of ictus and accent
        lend emphasis to this phrase.

184 effigiem statuēre, nefās quae trīste piāret.

185 Hanc tamen immēnsam Calchās attollere mōlem

186 rōboribus textīs caelōque ēdūcere iussit,

187 nē recipī portīs aut dūcī in moenia posset,

188 neu populum antīquā sub rēligiōne tuērī.

189 Nam sī vestra manus violāsset dōna Minervae,

190 tum magnum exitium (quod dī prius ōmen in ipsum

191 convertant!) Priamī imperiō Phrygibusque futūrum;

192 sīn manibus vestrīs vestram ascendisset in urbem,

193 ultrō Asiam magnō Pelopēa ad moenia bellō

194 ventūram et nostrōs ea fāta manēre nepōtēs.'

195   "Tālibus īnsidiīs periūrīque arte Sinōnis

196 crēdita rēs, captīque dolīs lacrimīsque coāctīs,

197 quōs neque Tȳdīdēs nec Lārīsaeus Achillēs,

198 nōn annī domuēre decem, nōn mīlle carīnae.

Suddenly two huge serpents appear out of the sea, assault Laocoön
and his two sons, and glide to Minerva's shrine on the citadel

199   "Hīc aliud maius miserīs multōque tremendum

200 obicitur magis atque imprōvida pectora turbat.

Quaestiōnēs

1. Comment on the varying effects of the three instances of chiasmus in 192–94 (**manibus . . . urbem**, **Asiam . . . ventūram**, and **nostrōs . . . nepōtēs**).

2. What several stylistic features make lines 195–98 an especially poignant closure to the Sinon episode?

201 **ductus:** here *chosen.* The selection of Laocoön by lot as priest to Neptune, to
offer sacrifice to the god on the occasion of the Greeks' presumed departure
by sea, was ill-fated for two reasons. First, Laocoön, formerly priest of Apollo,
had earlier committed a sacrilege by making love to his wife in the god's
temple. Second, his selection was a reminder to Neptune of a prior affront
to his divinity: 10 years earlier, the Trojans had, in a fit of rage, murdered
Neptune's priest—whose name had also been Laocoön—for his failure to
insure the god's destruction of the Greek fleet as it was enroute to Troy.
Thus Apollo was outraged at Laocoön for the sacrilege in his temple, and
Neptune can only have taken offense at the Trojans' last-minute choice of
this man, namesake of his slain priest, to suddenly reinstitute his cult after a
decade of neglect in an effort to doom the Greek armada. Vergil's audience
would have been aware of all these details and thus more clearly understood
than modern readers the context and implications of Laocoön's destruction;
the entire *Aeneid,* in fact, is grounded upon and enriched by this sort of
hypertext, so much of which, unfortunately, is lost to us.

202 **sollemnis, -is, -e,** *ceremonial, solemn; usual, customary, traditional.*
   *****taurus, -ī,** m., *bull.*
   *****mactō (1),** *to slay sacrificially, sacrifice.*

203 **geminī:** with **anguēs** (204).
   Tenedō: the serpents come from the very island where the Greek army is in
   hiding, thus anticipating the return of the Greek fleet that very night.
   tranquillus, -a, -um, *calm, tranquil.*

204 **horrēscō, horrēscere,** *to shake with fear, tremble, shudder.*
   immēnsīs: the adj., applied also to the horse in 185, recurs in the same metrical
   position in 208; the colossal size of both horse and serpents suggests the
   enormity of the peril with which Troy was faced.
   orbibus: here *coils.*
   *****anguis, anguis,** m./f., *snake, serpent.*

205 *****incumbō, incumbere, incubuī,** *to bend towards, lean on; to lie down upon; to
   press upon; to press on* (with an activity), *exert oneself.*

206 **quōrum:** = **eōrum** (here, as often, the rel. is used for the pers. pron.).
   *****iuba, -ae,** f., *mane; crest, plume.*

207 **superant undās:** the snakes tower over the sea just as the horse towers over the
   city (**dēsuper urbī** 47).
   pars cētera: i.e., the rest of their bodies, trailing behind their upraised heads and
   breasts.

208 *****pōne,** adv., *in the rear, behind.*
   legit: here *skims over.*
   sinuō (1), *to bend, curve; to move in a curved course, wind.*
   volūmen, volūminis, n., *roll, coil.*

210 **ārdentēs . . . oculōs:** for the construction, see note on **oculōs suffūsa** (1.228).
   *****sufficiō, sufficere, suffēcī, suffectus,** *to supply, provide; to imbue, stain.*

201 Lāocoön, ductus Neptūnō sorte sacerdōs,
202 sollemnēs taurum ingentem mactābat ad ārās.
203 Ecce autem geminī ā Tenedō tranquilla per alta—
204 horrēscō referēns!—immēnsīs orbibus anguēs
205 incumbunt pelagō pariterque ad lītora tendunt;
206 pectora quōrum inter flūctūs arrēcta iubaeque
207 sanguineae superant undās, pars cētera pontum
208 pōne legit sinuatque immēnsa volūmine terga.
209 Fit sonitus spūmante salō; iamque arva tenēbant
210 ārdentēsque oculōs suffectī sanguine et ignī

Quaestiōnēs

1. What are the most striking metrical and sound effects in 202 and how are they appropriate to the scene described?

2. Comment on Vergil's use of **ecce** in 203 and above in 57; how do the two scenes introduced by this word serve a similar dramatic function in the Laocoön episode?

3. What is the intended effect of the wide separation of **geminī** from **anguēs** in 203–04?

4. What device of word order is employed in 205, and how is it appropriate to the image being described?

Laocoön group, marble
Roman copy, perhaps after
Hagesander, Athenodorus,
and Polydorus of Rhodes
1st cent. C.E.
Vatican Museums
Vatican State

211 **sībilus, -a, -um,** *hissing.*

    sībila . . . ōra: the phrase effectively FRAMES the line.

    *****vibrō (1),** *to move quickly back and forth; to dart out; to flicker.*

212 *****diffugiō, diffugere, diffūgī,** *to run away in different directions, scatter.*

    *****vīsus, -ūs,** m., *power of seeing, vision; gaze; a thing seen, a sight.*

    *****exsanguis, -is, -e,** *bloodless; pale* (here an echo of **sanguine** 210).

    agmine certō: a military term, again anticipating the forthcoming Greek assault (see note on **Tenedō** 203).

214 **Lāocoonta petunt:** following the emphatic epithet **certō,** the ENJAMBEMENT here underscores the conscious, divinely guided determination of the assault.

    serpēns, serpentis, m., *snake, serpent.*

215 *****implicō, implicāre, implicāvī/implicuī, implicātus/implicitus,** *to fold; to enfold, wrap around.*

    dēpāscor, dēpāscī, dēpastus sum, *to eat up, devour.*

216 **post:** here adv.

    ipsum: here, as often, Vergil uses the intensive pron. in referring to the principal character in a scene.

    auxiliō: DAT. OF PURPOSE.

217 **spīra, -ae,** f., *coil.*

    et iam: the monosyllables at line's end and the DIAERESIS preceding prepare us suspensefully for the next image in the serpents' ferocious attack.

218 **medium, -ī,** n., *middle, center.*

    *****collum, -ī,** n., often pl. for sg. in poetry, *neck.*

    squāmeus, -a, -um, *covered with scales, scaly.*

    circum / . . . datī (219): TMESIS for **circumdatī,** here act. with **terga** (219) as dir. obj. and **collō** DAT. WITH COMPOUNDS.

219 **superant:** here *tower above* (him); cf. **superant undās** (207).

    capite: sg. for pl., *with their heads.*

220 *****dīvellō, dīvellere, dīvellī, dīvulsus,** *to tear open/apart.*

221 **perfundō, perfundere, perfūdī, perfūsus,** *to pour through/over; to soak, drench.*

    saniēs, -ēī, f., *bloody gore* (from a wound).

    vittās: a priest's sacred headbands, but here, drenched in blood, they anticipate Laocoön's depiction as a sacrificial victim in 223–24 (see note on **vittae** 133).

    venēnum, -ī, n., *poison, venom.*

222 *****horrendus, -a, -um,** *terrible, fearful, horrendous.*

223 **quālēs . . . cum:** *such . . . as when.*

    mūgītus, -ūs, m., *bellowing; wailing.*

    mūgītūs, fūgit: the noun is itself ONOMATOPOETIC, and the long **ū** sound is continued in the verb.

    *****saucius, -a, -um,** *wounded; suffering.*

211 sībila lambēbant linguīs vibrantibus ōra.
212 Diffugimus vīsū exsanguēs. Illī agmine certō
213 Lāocoonta petunt; et prīmum parva duōrum
214 corpora nātōrum serpēns amplexus uterque
215 implicat et miserōs morsū dēpāscitur artūs;
216 post ipsum auxiliō subeuntem ac tēla ferentem
217 corripiunt spīrīsque ligant ingentibus; et iam
218 bis medium amplexī, bis collō squāmea circum
219 terga datī, superant capite et cervīcibus altīs.
220 Ille simul manibus tendit dīvellere nōdōs,
221 perfūsus saniē vittās ātrōque venēnō,
222 clāmōrēs simul horrendōs ad sīdera tollit—
223 quālēs mūgītūs, fūgit cum saucius āram

Quaestiōnēs

1. What several visual elements are employed in 203–11?

2. What is the most striking extended sound effect in 209–11? Compare the similar though more abbreviated effect in line 207.

3. What device of word order is employed in **parva . . . nātōrum** (213–14) and how is it suited to the image described?

4. How is the clause **miserōs . . . artūs** (215) especially visual? Consider even the effect of the verb's prefix.

"Laocoön" (detail)
Black and white chalk
on gray-toned paper
ca. 1815–25
Albert Bertel Thorvaldsen
(Danish, 1770–1844)
Ceseri Collection
Georgia Museum of Art
University of Georgia

224 **taurus:** an extremely effective ENJAMBEMENT, momentarily delaying the identity of the creature with which Laocoön is being compared; the SIMILE suggests a tragic reversal, as the priest, who had himself at the beginning of this scene been sacrificing a bull at the altar (201–02), now becomes himself the sacrificial beast.

*securis, securis, acc. securim, f., *axe.*

incertam excussit cervice securim: the harsh ALLITERATION of c and conflict of ictus and accent are meant to suggest the violent crashing blow of the ill-aimed sacrificial axe.

225 *lapsus, -us, m., *slipping, falling; gliding, sliding, slithering.*

*delubrum, -i, n., *temple, shrine.*

draco, draconis, m., *snake, serpent.*

226 **petunt . . . arcem:** the vb. clearly suggests that, as with **agmine certo / Laocoonta petunt** in 212–13, the serpents' movement here is deliberate and divinely guided, not accidental.

Tritonis, Tritonidis, f., *the goddess of Tritonis, Athena/Minerva* (see note on **Tritonius** 171).

227 **sub . . . orbe:** the symmetry of these two phrases, and the ANAPHORA and POLYSYNDETON, lend majesty to the line, and the dactyls bring the scene quickly to its close.

*clipeus, -i, m., *shield* (usually round, as here, and made of bronze).

228 *tremefactus, -a, -um, *trembling* (with fear).

229 **insinuo (1),** *to wind one's way in, get in.*

*pavor, pavoris, m., *sudden fear, terror, fright.*

tremefacta (228) . . . pavor: the INTERLOCKED WORD ORDER suits Vergil's depiction of the terror winding its way into the Trojans' hearts—like a snake in fact, as **insinuat** here is likely intended to recall **sinuat** in 208.

expendo, expendere, expendi, expensus, *to weigh; to pay out; to pay the penalty for* (a crime).

*mereo (2) and **mereor, mereri, meritus sum,** *to receive as one's wage, earn; to merit, deserve.*

merentem: Eng. would use an adv., *deservedly.*

230 **sacrum:** with **robur;** the ANASTROPHE in **sacrum qui** helps underscore the sudden shift in the Trojans' perception of the horse as a sacred object.

The reputation of some, distinguished as their work may be, has been obscured by the number of artists engaged with them on a single task, because no individual monopolizes the credit nor again can several of them be named on equal terms. This is the case with the Laocoön in the palace of General Titus, a work superior to any painting and any bronze. Laocoön, his children and the wonderful clasping coils of the snakes were carved from a single block in accordance with an agreed plan by those eminent craftsmen Hagesander, Polydorus, and Athenodorus, all of Rhodes.

Pliny the Elder, "Natural History," 36.4.37, translated by D.E. Eichholz

224 taurus et incertam excussit cervīce secūrim.
225 At geminī lāpsū dēlūbra ad summa dracōnēs
226 effugiunt saevaeque petunt Trītōnidis arcem,
227 sub pedibusque deae clipeīque sub orbe teguntur.

The Trojans, terror-stricken and assuming Laocoön had been punished for desecrating the horse and offending Minerva, throw open their gates and admit the doomsday machine— pregnant with war—into the very heart of the city

228 "Tum vērō tremefacta novus per pectora cūnctīs
229 īnsinuat pavor, et scelus expendisse merentem
230 Lāocoonta ferunt, sacrum quī cuspide rōbur

Quaestiōnēs

1. Comment specifically on the several devices Vergil employs in 216–24 to depict in vivid detail both the sights and the sounds he is describing.

2. How does Laocoön's reversal of fortune, from sacrificer to sacrificial victim in 223–24, prefigure Troy's own circumstances? Think in part of the relationship of both Laocoön and Troy to the god Neptune, who will appear later in Book Two playing an active role in the physical destruction of the city. In what several respects then is Laocoön an apt symbol for Troy itself, in terms of their virtues, their failings, and their ultimate fate?

3. Compare lines 225–27 with 203–05, considering word order, diction, and the details of the serpents' movements; how do the interconnections between the two passages effectively frame the scene? Where are the two references to a sacrificial bull positioned relative to these two passages, and how does this positioning also contribute to the overall structure of the episode?

4. The twin serpents are clearly a symbol of the human agency in Troy's forthcoming destruction; in what ways is their carefully detailed movement from Tenedos, across the becalmed sea, and finally (in 225–27) to the sanctuary of Minerva on Troy's citadel symbolic also of the divine agency in the city's fall? (Think of the three deities specifically associated with these three sites.)

231 *scelerātus, -a, -um, *accursed; criminal; sinful, atrocious.*

    scelerātam: the adj. echoes and emphasizes the point in the identically positioned **scelus** (229).

    *intorqueō, intorquēre, intorsī, intortus, *to bend back; to hurl.*

    quī (230) . . . / **laeserit et** . . . **intorserit:** *since he* . . .; REL. CAUSAL CL.

232 **sēdēs:** i.e., Minerva's temple, where the **simulacrum** of the horse would replace the **simulacrum** (172) of the stolen Palladium—an action playing into Sinon's hands (see note on 188).

233 **conclāmō** (1), *to shout loudly, cry out, exclaim.*

    nūmina conclāmant: for the incomplete line, see note on line 66 above.

234 **Dīvidimus . . . pandimus:** an elegant and pointed line, ALLITERATIVE, emphatically end-stopped, and with a CHIASTIC arrangement that suggests the opening up of the city's fortification walls (**mūrōs**) and massive double gates, thus exposing the walls of the buildings within (**moenia**); we are likely meant to imagine the Trojans dismantling the gates' lintel and superstructure in order to admit the towering horse.

235 **pedibus:** sc. **equī.**

    rotārum / . . . lāpsūs (236): lit., *the glidings of wheels,* but how would this be rendered in idiomatic Eng.? Cf. **lāpsū** in identical metrical position in 225; the serpents and the horse, though "immense" (see note on 204), glide easily, mysteriously on their missions of destruction.

236 **stuppeus, -a, -um,** *made of flax/hemp.*

    stuppea vincula: the phrase is used by other authors of the rigging of ships— Vergil here again perhaps foreshadows the coming assault by the Greek fleet which the horse's admission into the city anticipates.

237 **intendō, intendere, intendī, intentus,** *to stretch (across/around).*

    intendunt . . . fātālis: following the quick, excited actions of 235–36, the spondees here effectively slow the pace as the poet directs his camera and our eyes to the deadly horse itself.

    *scandō, scandere, *to climb to the top of; to climb into; to tower over.*

    māchina mūrōs: a deliberate echo of line 46.

238 **fēta armīs:** for the METAPHOR, cf. **fēta furentibus Austrīs** (1.51). ENJAMBEMENT and the wordplay in **fātālis (237)/fēta** produce the stunningly paradoxical image of a *doomsday machine pregnant with war.* The irony in this vision of pregnancy and new life is further intensified in the next moment, as we see the children of Troy rushing joyfully to touch the creature that will soon wreak destruction on their world.

    innūptae: cf. **innūptae dōnum exitiāle Minervae** (2.31); the young Trojan girls here, like Minerva herself, are virginal and unwed—and, as Vergil poignantly implies, never to be wed.

239 **sacra:** dir. obj. of **canunt,** i.e., *sacred songs;* or possibly obj. of **circum** (238), functioning as a prep. rather than as an adv.

    *fūnis, fūnis, m., *rope, cable.*

231 laeserit et tergō scelerātam intorserit hastam.
232 Dūcendum ad sēdēs simulācrum ōrandaque dīvae
233 nūmina conclāmant.
234 Dīvidimus mūrōs et moenia pandimus urbis.
235 Accingunt omnēs operī pedibusque rotārum
236 subiciunt lāpsūs et stuppea vincula collō
237 intendunt; scandit fātālis māchina mūrōs,
238 fēta armīs. Puerī circum innūptaeque puellae
239 sacra canunt fūnemque manū contingere gaudent;

Quaestiō

How does the crowd's behavior in 228–33 compare with that in 130–31?

The Trojan horse
Relief from neck
of amphora
640 B.C.
Archaeological
Museum
Mykonos, Greece

240 **inlābor, inlābī, inlāpsus sum,** *to move smoothly, glide (into).*
    illa . . . inlābitur urbī: the dactylic rhythms (interrupted only by the ominous **mināns**) and the liquid consonants help suggest the creature's smoothly gliding, snake-like passage into the city.

242 **Dardanidum:** an alternative form for **Dardanidārum.**

243 ***subsistō, subsistere, substitī,** *to stand firm; to halt (in one's path), stop short.*
    Quater . . . (242) / substitit: it was considered bad luck to stumble at a threshold, a point emphasized by the ENJAMBEMENT of **substitit** and the abrupt DIAERESIS following.

245 **īnfēlīx:** the word certainly means *inauspicious* or even *calamitous,* but in view of its proximity to **uterō** (243), Vergil clearly has in mind also its root meaning of *infertile, unproductive;* the horse is pregnant but will beget only death and destruction.
    ***sistō, sistere, stetī, status,** *to cause to stand, set (up); to halt, stop; to steady, stabilize.*

246 **tunc,** adv., *then.*
    fātīs . . . futūrīs: either ABL. OF MANNER or DAT. OF PURPOSE.
    ***Cassandra, -ae,** f., *Cassandra* (daughter of Priam and Hecuba, she was given prophetic powers by Apollo but, scorning his amorous advances, was then cursed by the god with always prophesying the truth but never being believed).

247 **iussus, -ūs,** m., *order, command.*

248 ***ultimus, -a, -um,** *farthest; last, final.*
    esset: subjunct. in a REL. CAUSAL CL., explaining **miserī.**

249 **vēlō (1),** *to cover; to decorate (ritually).*
    ***frōns, frondis,** f., *leafy part of a tree, foliage* (sometimes, as here, for wreathes or garlands).

250 **ruit . . . nox:** Vergil imagines the turning of the heavens around the earth and, in contrast to lines 8–9 and our own metaphor of "nightfall," pictures the darkness of night rising up out of the Ocean; the line's dactyls, the abrupt ELISION in **caelum et,** and the offbeat rhythm resulting from the monosyllabic ending, all help suggest, along with the vb. **ruit** itself, the suddenness of the action.

251 ***involvō, involvere, involvī, involūtus,** *to enclose in a cover, wrap up, cover.*
    involvēns . . . polumque: following the quick dactylic rhythms of the preceding verse, this line's spondees and the POLYSYNDETON (which continues over into the next verse) emphasize the total envelopment of the earth in darkness, an effect enhanced by the somber ASSONANCE of **um/am/um.**

252 **fūsī:** i.e., in sleep.

240 illa subit mediaeque mināns inlābitur urbī.
241 ō patria, ō dīvum domus Īlium et incluta bellō
242 moenia Dardanidum! Quater ipsō in līmine portae
243 substitit atque uterō sonitum quater arma dedēre;
244 īnstāmus tamen immemorēs caecīque furōre
245 et mōnstrum īnfēlīx sacrātā sistimus arce.
246 Tunc etiam fātīs aperit Cassandra futūrīs
247 ōra, deī iussū nōn umquam crēdita Teucrīs.
248 Nōs dēlūbra deum miserī, quibus ultimus esset
249 ille diēs, fēstā vēlāmus fronde per urbem.

After celebrating what they mistakenly assume to be their good
fortune, the Trojans fall into a deep sleep and the Greek
invaders, under cover of night, assault the city

250 "Vertitur intereā caelum et ruit Ōceanō nox,
251 involvēns umbrā magnā terramque polumque
252 Myrmidonumque dolōs; fūsī per moenia, Teucrī

Quaestiōnēs

1. What is the emotional effect of the apostrophe in 241–42? How does it compare with the apostrophe in line 56?

2. The word **līmen** occurs numerous times in Book Two. In view of Vergil's frequent use of symbolism elsewhere, what larger significance might the image of the **līmen** have in 242–43?

3. Explain how the action in 244–45 again demonstrates Vergil's insight into human psychology.

4. How does Vergil use meter to reinforce meaning in 245? What are the line's other most noteworthy effects of sound and structure?

5. Discuss specifically the several ways in which Vergil evokes pity for the Trojans in 235–49 by infusing the scene with irony and pathos.

6. Lines 250f. are the beginning of the book's second "act"; in what ways does Vergil very effectively mark the scene shift?

7. What is the effect of the enjambement in 252?

253 **conticuēre:** the word appears in the same metrical position in the book's
opening verse; here ENJAMBEMENT emphasizes the utter silence, as did the
word's initial position as the book's first word in line 1.

sopor, sopōris, m., *(deep/overpowering) sleep* (often applied to a drunken stupor
or to the sleep of death).

sopor . . . artūs: cf. **serpēns amplexus uterque / implicat et miserōs morsū
dēpāscitur artūs** (214–15); in the first of a series of images connecting the
action here to that of the serpents in the preceding scene, Vergil depicts
sleep enfolding the Trojans' limbs in a way that recalls the snakes' assault on
Laocoön and his sons.

*****complector, complectī, complexus sum,** *to embrace; to surround, enfold.*

254 **phalānx, phalāngis,** f., *phalanx (a body of armed infantry); army.*

255 **tacitae . . . lūnae:** the PERSONIFICATION in both this phrase and **amīca silentia**
suggests that all of nature is conspiring with the Greeks to implement Troy's
doom, just as the night in 250–52 conceals their treachery.

256 **flammās:** as a signal to Sinon.

rēgia puppis: i.e., the ship carrying Agamemnon and Menelaus.

257 **fātīsque deum:** cf. **fāta deum** (54).

*****inīquus, -a, -um,** *uneven, unequal; unjust, unfair.*

258 **pīneus, -a, -um,** *(made of) pine.*

pīnea . . . rōbore (260): for the wood used in the horse's construction, see note
on 112.

259 *****laxō (1),** *to open up, clear (out); to undo, loosen; to free, let go.*

laxat: Vergil's use of the vb. involves both ZEUGMA, since the dir. objs. require
two different senses, and HYSTERON PROTERON, since logically the second
action precedes the first; i.e., first Sinon loosens the fastenings and then frees
the Greeks hiding inside.

Sinōn: Vergil suspensefully delays Sinon's name to the very end of his lengthy
sent.

patefaciō, patefacere, patefēcī, patefactus, *to reveal, uncover; to open up* (often
in a medical context, i.e., surgically).

260 **cavō sē rōbore:** WORD-PICTURE.

prōmō, prōmere, prōmpsī, prōmptus, *to bring forth;* reflex., *to emerge from
hiding.*

261 **Thessandrus, -ī,** m., *Thessandrus (a Greek warrior, known, like those
subsequently named here, from Homer and other accounts of the Trojan
War).*

Thessandrus . . . Epēos (264): Vergil has nine men in the horse (three groups of
three), while other ancient sources tell of up to 3,000.

Sthenelus, -ī, m., *Sthenelus (another Greek soldier).*

253 conticuēre; sopor fessōs complectitur artūs.
254 Et iam Argīva phalānx, īnstrūctīs nāvibus, ībat
255 ā Tenedō tacitae per amīca silentia lūnae,
256 lītora nōta petēns, flammās cum rēgia puppis
257 extulerat, fātīsque deum dēfēnsus inīquīs
258 inclūsōs uterō Danaōs et pīnea fūrtim
259 laxat claustra Sinōn. Illōs patefactus ad aurās
260 reddit equus laetīque cavō sē rōbore prōmunt
261 Thessandrus Sthenelusque ducēs et dīrus Ulixēs,

Quaestiōnēs

What several specific correspondences are there between the appearance and movements of the Greek fleet in 255–57 and of the serpents in 203–13? What was the intended effect of these correspondences?

Cassone panel: the Trojan horse
Painting on wood, 15th cent.
Musée de la Renaissance, Ecouen, France

262　lāpsī: the Greek invaders, like the serpents that anticipated their assault and the horse itself (see note on **rotārum / . . . lāpsūs** 235–36), slip quietly toward their fateful mission.

　　fūnem: in view of the repeated image of the womb in 258 (**uterō,** and see note on 20), we are meant to imagine the horse as giving birth to its deadly brood of Greek warriors; and some scholars have even suggested that the **fūnem** here is intended to evoke the image of an umbilical cord.

　　Acamās, Acamantis, m., *Acamas (a Greek warrior).*

　　Thoās, Thoantis, m., *Thoas (another Greek warrior).*

263　*Pēlīdēs, -ae,** m., *son of Peleus* (king of Phthia and husband of Thetis), *Achilles; descendant of Peleus.*

　　*Neoptolemus, -ī,** m., *Neoptolemus (known also as Pyrrhus, son of Achilles).*

　　prīmus: here = **dux** (cf. **ducēs** 261).

　　Machāōn, Machāonos, m., *Machaon (a Greek physician and warrior).*

264　**Menelāus, -ī,** m., *Menelaus* (king of Sparta, brother of Agamemnon and husband of Helen).

　　fabricātor, fabricātōris, m., *designer, builder.*

　　Epēōs, -ī, m., *Epeos* (the Greek who built the Trojan horse; see note on **Palladis arte** 15).

265　*invādō, invādere, invāsī, invāsus,** *to assault, attack, invade.*

　　Invādunt . . . sepultam: the grave spondees, conflict of ictus and accent, the mournful ASSONANCE of **nō/nō,** and the CHIASTIC arrangement culminating in the shocking epithet **sepultam,** all lend weight to the poignant end-stopped line and its stark, ominous metaphor (an image adapted by Vergil from the early epic poet Ennius).

　　somnō vīnōque: HENDIADYS for *a drunken sleep;* the Trojans have celebrated the Greeks' presumed departure with wine and feasting late into the night.

266　*vigil, vigilis,** m., *guard, watchman, sentry.*

269　**dōnō:** ABL. OF MEANS.

　　serpō, serpere, serpsī, *to crawl, creep, glide, slither* (like a snake).

　　grātissima serpit: Vergil's choice of this particular vb., from which the noun **serpēns** derives, and the hissing ALLITERATION of this phrase and the following verse (where **maestissimus** is deliberately positioned to echo **grātissima**) are meant to suggest that sleep, ordinarily so pleasant to weary mortals (**mortālibus** 268, another aptly chosen word), here–in a vivid OXYMORON–"creeps most pleasingly snakelike" over the Trojans with deadly purpose.

270　**ecce:** with **ante oculōs** (sc. **meōs**) the word compels our visualization of Aeneas' dream; Aeneas here first introduces himself into his narrative, asleep after the night's celebration and visited by a horrific nightmare.

271　**largōsque effundere flētūs:** cf. **largōque ūmectat flūmine vultum** (1.465), a description of Aeneas' weeping over the murals at Juno's temple in Carthage, among them (at 1.483–87) a scene of Hector's corpse which Vergil may intend us here to recall (cf. also **raptātus** in the next verse with **raptāverat Hectora . . . Achillēs** 1.483–84).

272　**bīgae, -ārum,** f. pl., *pair of horses; (two-horse) chariot.*

　　ut quondam: sc. (Hector) **erat.**

262 dēmissum lāpsī per fūnem, Acamāsque Thoāsque
263 Pēlīdēsque Neoptolemus prīmusque Machāōn
264 et Menelāus et ipse dolī fabricātor Epēos.
265 Invādunt urbem somnō vīnōque sepultam;
266 caeduntur vigilēs, portīsque patentibus omnēs
267 accipiunt sociōs atque agmina cōnscia iungunt.

The ghost of Hector appears to Aeneas in a dream, warning him
that Troy is lost and that flight is his only recourse

268   "Tempus erat quō prīma quiēs mortālibus aegrīs
269 incipit et dōnō dīvum grātissima serpit.
270 In somnīs, ecce, ante oculōs maestissimus Hector
271 vīsus adesse mihī largōsque effundere flētūs,
272 raptātus bīgīs ut quondam, āterque cruentō

Quaestiōnēs

Comment on the series of names in 261–64. Why does Vergil name so many of the warriors? What special use does he make of conjunctions? Which names does he position most emphatically? How does he effectively employ meter to close out the series?

273 per . . . pedēs trāiectus lōra: the partic. here has act. force, lit., *having pierced thongs through his feet*, but freely, *with his feet pierced by thongs.*

*tumeō, tumēre, tumuī, *to be distended, swell, be swollen.*

pulvere . . . tumentēs: a sonorous line with ALLITERATION of both **p** and **t** and the internal rhyme of **pedēs/tumentēs**, accentuated by placing the words at the CAESURA and line's end (a common device of elegiac verse). The detail of Hector's swollen feet is perhaps meant to suggest that he was still alive as Achilles dragged him behind his chariot.

274 ei, interj. expressing anguish, + dat., *woe, alas.*

*mūtō (1), *to change; to exchange.*

275 redit: the HIST. PRES. suggests how vividly Aeneas envisions his comrade when still alive and triumphant.

*exuviae, -ārum, f. pl., *armor stripped from an enemy, spoils; mementos.*

exuviās . . . Achillī: i.e., the armor that Achilles had given his friend Patroclus and which Hector stripped from Patroclus when he killed him in battle.

indūtus: here reflex. + acc., *having put on, attired in.*

276 Danaum . . . ignēs: INTERLOCKED WORD ORDER; in one battle Hector had led the Trojans in assaulting the Greek camp and setting fire to their ships.

277 squāleō, squālēre, squāluī, *to be covered with dirt, be dirty.*

squālentem . . . crīnēs: the slow spondees and conflict of ictus and accent focus our attention on the grisly details.

*barba, -ae, f., *beard.*

*concrēscō, concrēscere, concrēvī, concrētus, *to harden, become stiff.*

278 gerēns: modifying **Hector** (270) and in parallel with **raptātus** (272) and **trāiectus** (273), following the lengthy parenthesis in 274–76.

279 Ultrō: with **compellāre** (280) not **flēns** (cf. **ultrō . . . compellat** 2.372, **compellat . . . ultrō** 4.304); i.e., Aeneas spoke first.

flēns ipse: Aeneas himself wept, just as Hector did (271).

280 *compellō (1), *to address, speak to, call out to.*

exprōmō, exprōmere, exprōmpsī, exprōmptus, *to bring out; to express, speak.*

281 Ō lūx . . . spēs ō: the ANAPHORA and CHIASMUS together lend a tone of urgency to Aeneas' invocation.

*Dardania, -ae, f., *Dardania, Troy.*

282 tenuēre: sc. **tē.**

Hector . . . / exspectāte (283): voc.

ab ōrīs / . . . tuōrum (283) / . . . labōrēs (284): an elegant end-line rhyme.

283 Ut: i.e., *how (happily)*; with **aspicimus** (285).

post . . . labōrēs (284): ANAPHORA (**post . . . post**) and POLYSYNDETON (-**que . . . -que**) serve to intensify the pathos.

285 *indignus, -a, -um, *undeserving, unworthy; undeserved, unmerited.*

287 Ille nihil: sc. **respondet.**

morātur: here *delays over, pays attention to.*

288 gemitūs . . . dūcēns: cf. **gemitum dat pectore ab imo** (1.485), of Aeneas sighing over the depiction of Hector's corpse in Juno's temple (and see note on 271 above).

289 deā: ABL. OF ORIGIN.

273 pulvere perque pedēs trāiectus lōra tumentēs—
274 ei mihi, quālis erat, quantum mūtātus ab illō
275 Hectore quī redit exuviās indūtus Achillī
276 vel Danaum Phrygiōs iaculātus puppibus ignēs!—
277 squālentem barbam et concrētōs sanguine crīnēs
278 vulneraque illa gerēns, quae circum plūrima mūrōs
279 accēpit patriōs. Ultrō flēns ipse vidēbar
280 compellāre virum et maestās exprōmere vōcēs:
281 'ō lūx Dardaniae, spēs ō fīdissima Teucrum,
282 quae tantae tenuēre morae? Quibus Hector ab ōrīs
283 exspectāte venīs? Ut tē post multa tuōrum
284 fūnera, post variōs hominumque urbisque labōrēs
285 dēfessī aspicimus! Quae causa indigna serēnōs
286 foedāvit vultūs? Aut cūr haec vulnera cernō?'
287 Ille nihil, nec mē quaerentem vāna morātur,
288 sed graviter gemitūs īmō dē pectore dūcēns,
289 'Heu fuge, nāte deā, tēque hīs,' ait, 'ēripe flammīs.

Quaestiōnēs

1. Comment on the sound effects in 282.

2. In what ways do Aeneas' remarks to Hector in 281–86 convey the agitation and confusion so typical of dreams?

3. Identify the most striking metrical and sound effects in 286.

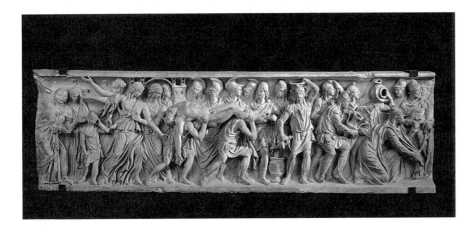

Sarcophagus with burial of Hector's body
Marble, ca. 190–200 C.E., Louvre, Paris, France

290 *culmen, culminis, n., *summit of a building, roof, rooftop; height, zenith.*

292 hāc: sc. dextrā, i.e., by Hector's own hand in battle.

293 *commendō (1), *to commit, entrust.*

294 moenia . . . / magna (295): i.e., the walls of a mighty new city; moenia in 298 has the same sense.

295 *pererrō (1), *to wander through/over; to look over, think over/about.*
  pererrātō . . . pontō: = quae, pontō pererrātō, dēnique statuēs.

296 vittās: here the sacred headbands of the virgin priestesses who tended Vesta's cult; or perhaps a HENDIADYS for (a statue of) *Vesta in her ribbons.* These objects and the embers from the goddess' shrine are the sacra of 293.

297 aeternum . . . ignem: Vergil solemnly concludes his description of Aeneas' dream and Vesta's holy shrine with a GOLDEN LINE; fire is a recurring image in this book, and the flame which was tended in Vesta's temple and could never be extinguished represents here the survival of Troy, whose gods Aeneas will carry into Italy (īnferret . . . deōs Latiō 1.6).
  penetrālis, -is, -e, *penetrating; inner, innermost (part of).*

298 Dīversō: i.e., throughout the city.

299 *sēcrētus, -a, -um, *set apart, separate; withdrawn, remote, secluded.*
  secrēta: with domus (300); sc. est.

300 *Anchīsēs, -ae, abl. Anchīsā, acc. Anchīsēn, m., *Anchises (a member of the Trojan royal house and father of Aeneas by Venus).*
  obtegō, obtegere, obtēxī, obtēctus, *to cover, protect; to hide, conceal, screen.*
  *recēdō, recēdere, recessī, recessus, *to draw back, retire, withdraw; to be set back, be secluded.*

301 clārēscō, clārēscere, clārēscuī, *to grow loud, become clear/distinct.*
  ingruō, ingruere, ingruī, *to advance threateningly; to threaten.*
  *horror, horrōris, m., *standing on end, bristling (of hair); horror, dread.*

303 ascēnsus, -ūs, m., *climbing, ascent.*
  superō: here *I go up to.*
  arrēctīs auribus astō: cf. arrēctīs . . . auribus astant (1.152).

304 seges, segetis, f., *field of wheat.*
  flamma furentibus Austrīs: cf. fēta furentibus Austrīs (1.51) of the winds in Aeolia; the ALLITERATION in both instances is ONOMATOPOETIC.

305 rapidus: here in its most basic sense (cf. the vb. rapere) of rushing violently along and carrying away everything in its path.
  montānus, -a, -um, *of/belonging to the mountains, (of a) mountain.*
  torrēns, torrentis, m., *rushing stream, torrent.*

306 sternit . . . sternit: ANAPHORA, ASYNDETON, and conflict of ictus and accent all suggest the swift violence of the destruction.
  sata, -ōrum, n. pl., *cultivated plants, crops.*
  laeta: here *rich, fruitful.*
  boum: = bovum.

290 Hostis habet mūrōs; ruit altō ā culmine Trōia.
291 Sat patriae Priamōque datum: sī Pergama dextrā
292 dēfendī possent, etiam hāc dēfēnsa fuissent.
293 Sacra suōsque tibī commendat Trōia Penātēs;
294 hōs cape fātōrum comitēs, hīs moenia quaere
295 magna pererrātō statuēs quae dēnique pontō.'
296 Sīc ait et manibus vittās Vestamque potentem
297 aeternumque adytīs effert penetrālibus ignem.

Aeneas awakens from his nightmare and, discovering
Troy in flames, arms himself for battle

298 "Dīversō intereā miscentur moenia lūctū,
299 et magis atque magis, quamquam sēcrēta parentis
300 Anchīsae domus arboribusque obtēcta recessit,
301 clārēscunt sonitūs armōrumque ingruit horror.
302 Excutior somnō et summī fastīgia tēctī
303 ascēnsū superō atque arrēctīs auribus astō:
304 in segetem velutī cum flamma furentibus Austrīs
305 incidit, aut rapidus montānō flūmine torrēns
306 sternit agrōs, sternit sata laeta boumque labōrēs

Quaestiōnēs

1. How does Hector's speech in 289–95 differ in tone from Aeneas' in 281–86?
   What is the effect of the short, rapid-fire clauses? How does Hector's counsel
   justify Aeneas' ultimate flight from Troy?

2. What central thematic elements of the *Aeneid* does Hector touch upon in
   289–95? Compare his speech in this regard with lines 1–11 of Book One, and
   detail the specific connections between the two passages.

3. Compare Hector's appearance to Aeneas in 270–95 with the appearance of
   Sychaeus to Dido in 1.353–59. What are the specific correspondences, and what
   may Vergil's intent have been in linking the two passages?

4. In what way is the framing of verse 298 with the phrase **dīversō . . . lūctū**
   appropriate to the sense?

307 *praeceps, praecipitis, *rushing/falling headlong, rushing forward.*

308 sonitum: a deliberate echo of sonitūs in the same metrical position in 301.

309 *manifestus, -a, -um, *detected in the act, flagrant* (of crimes); *evident, obvious; clearly visible.*

    manifesta fidēs: the hissing ALLITERATION underscores the phrase's irony.

    *patēscō, patēscere, patēscuī, *to open (out); to be open to view; to be evident.*

310 Dēiphobus, -ī, m., *Deiphobus* (a Trojan prince who married Helen after Paris' death and whose shade Aeneas encounters in the Underworld in Book Six).

    dedit . . . ruīnam: = ruit, i.e., *collapsed.*

    *amplus, -a, -um, *large, spacious; splendid, magnificent.*

311 Volcānus, -ī, m., *Vulcan* (god of fire and the forge); by METONYMY, *fire.*

    proximus: i.e., in the neighboring house.

312 Ūcalegōn, Ūcalegontis, m., *Ucalegon* (in Homer an advisor to Priam).

    ārdet (311) / Ūcalegōn: METONYMY for domus Ūcalegontis ārdet.

    Sīgēus, -a, -um, *of Sigeum* (a coastal town near Troy).

    relūceō, relūcēre, relūxī, *to shine (out),* here with reflected light.

313 *exorior, exorīrī, exortus sum, *to emerge, appear; to rise up, arise.*

    clangor, clangōris, m., *crying, clamor; blare, blast.*

    tuba, -ae, f., *trumpet.*

314 Arma . . . in armīs / . . . in armīs (317): Beginning with the brilliant juxtaposition arma āmēns, Vergil neatly FRAMES this entire four-line vignette of Aeneas rushing into battle with one of the poem's chief thematic words; **in arcem** and **mentem** at line's end in 315 and 316 enhance the sound effects.

    *āmēns, āmentis, *out of one's mind, insane; excited, frantic.*

    *ratiō, ratiōnis, f., *reasoning, reason; justification, purpose; manner, means.*

315 bellō: DAT. OF PURPOSE.

316 ārdent animī: pl. for sg., with the COMPL. INFS. glomerāre and concurrere (315).

317 praecipitat: a deliberate echo of the identically positioned **praecipitēs** in 307, and cf. **furentibus** (304)/**furor** (316); Vergil's point is to associate Aeneas' frenzy with the elemental violence of nature.

    *succurrō, succurrere, succurrī, succursus, *to run quickly; to rush to the rescue (of); to come to mind, occur;* impers., *the thought occurs (that).*

    pulchrum . . . morī: sc. esse (dependent on succurrit), *that it is a glorious thing to . . ..*

307 praecipitēsque trahit silvās; stupet īnscius altō,
308 accipiēns sonitum, saxī dē vertice pāstor.
309 Tum vērō manifesta fidēs, Danaumque patēscunt
310 īnsidiae. Iam Dēiphobī dedit ampla ruīnam
311 Volcānō superante domus, iam proximus ārdet
312 Ūcalegōn; Sīgēa ignī freta lāta relūcent.
313 Exoritur clāmorque virum clangorque tubārum.
314 Arma āmēns capiō; nec sat ratiōnis in armīs,
315 sed glomerāre manum bellō et concurrere in arcem
316 cum sociīs ārdent animī; furor īraque mentem
317 praecipitat, pulchrumque morī succurrit in armīs.

Quaestiōnēs

1. Referring to specific words and phrases, comment on the several points of correspondence between the scene in 298–303 and the simile employed to describe it in 304–08. What in particular is the significance of comparing Aeneas with a shepherd?

2. In view of the echo of **arrēctīs . . . auribus astant** (1.152) in **arrēctīs auribus astō** (303), Vergil may be inviting our comparison of the two similes in which the phrases appear (1.148–53 and here at 304–08). In what respects are the similes alike, and in what fundamental way (think of the natural forces and human actions compared in each instance) do they differ in function?

3. Compare the simile in 304–08 with Homer's simile in *Iliad* 4.452f.

4. Comment on the placement of **īnsidiae** (310) and its effect.

5. What is the intended effect of the anaphora in 310–11?

6. Comment on the several poetic and rhetorical devices employed in 313, and compare this line with 1.87; what does the remarkable similarity between these two verses tell you about Vergil's method of composition?

7. Discuss the several ways in which Vergil provides us insight into Aeneas' state of mind in 314–17.

Dulce et decōrum est prō patriā morī.
Horace, Carmina *3.2.13*

318 **Ecce autem:** the phrase is similarly employed in 203, in the same metrical
position (and cf. 57), to introduce a startling interruption in the action.
 *Panthūs, -ī, voc. **Panthū,** m., *Panthus (a priest of Apollo at Troy).*
 ēlapsus Achīvum: cf. **Antenor . . . ēlapsus Achīvīs** (1.242).

319 ***Othryadēs, -ae,** m., *son of Othryas.*
 arcis Phoebīque: HENDIADYS for **Phoebī in arce.**

320 **sacra . . . victōsque deōs:** the same as those Hector's phantom had held in 293,
i.e., ritual objects including small statues of the Penates, protecting deities of
the homeland.

321 **trahit:** ZEUGMA, as the vb. clearly has a different sense with **sacra** and **deōs** (320)
than it has with **nepōtem** (320), to which it most immediately applies.
 āmēns: Panthus' agitated mental state is the same as Aeneas' (**āmēns** 314).

322 **rēs summa:** *the most critical situation* or *the decisive struggle.*
 prēndimus: = **prehendimus,** pres. tense or perhaps perf.
 arcem: here *stronghold, defensive position.*

324 **summa:** here *final;* this echo of **summa** in the same metrical position in 322
deliberately connects Panthus' reply to Aeneas' quest.—the situation is not
merely critical, it is catastrophic.
 diēs: for the gender here, see on line 132 above.
 inēluctābilis, -is, -e, *that one cannot struggle out of, inescapable, unavoidable.*

325 **Fuimus . . . fuit:** i.e., and are no longer.

326 ***ferus, -a, -um,** *untamed, wild; savage, fierce, ferocious.*

328 ***arduus, -a, -um,** *tall, lofty, towering.*

329 **equus:** suspensefully delayed following the two emphatically positioned epithets,
arduus and **astāns,** in the preceding line.
 victor: a bitter, grudging concession, hammered home by the ENJAMBEMENT of
īnsultāns in the following verse; this is Sinon's final appearance in the book,
and here Aeneas learns from Panthus of both his treachery and the trick of
the horse.
 incendia miscet: i.e., he is setting fires all around him.

330 **īnsultō (1),** *to leap up, trample upon; to mock, jeer.*
 bipatēns, bipatentis, *opening in two directions* (of a city's double gates); *wide
open* (cf. 266).

331 **quot:** with **mīlia** and in appos. with **aliī** (332), *as many . . . as.*

332 ***angustus, -a, -um,** *narrow* (here a substantive with **viārum** = **viās angustās;** cf.
strāta viārum 1.422).

333 ***oppositus, -a, -um,** *in front (of), facing, opposite; opposed, hostile.*
 stat . . . necī (334): the Greek squadrons stalking Troy's steets are described, as if
viewed from afar, as a single, vast, gleaming swordblade, drawn and ready to
destroy the city's defenders.
 *mūcrō, mūcrōnis, f., *point* (of a sword or other implement); *sword.*
 mūcrōne coruscō: ABL. OF DESCRIPTION.

334 **prīmī . . . vigilēs** (335): i.e., the watchmen posted at the city's gates and towers
and thus Troy's first line of defense against a night attack (cf. 266).

335 **caecō:** i.e., with rage.
 Mārte: a common METONYMY for *war, battle.*

Panthus, Apollo's priest, rushes to Anchises' palace
and reports to Aeneas details of the Greek assault

318   "Ecce autem tēlīs Panthūs ēlapsus Achīvum,
319   Panthūs Othryadēs, arcis Phoebīque sacerdōs,
320   sacra manū victōsque deōs parvumque nepōtem
321   ipse trahit cursūque āmēns ad līmina tendit.
322   'Quō rēs summa locō, Panthū? Quam prēndimus arcem?'
323   Vix ea fātus eram, gemitū cum tālia reddit:
324   'Vēnit summa diēs et inēluctābile tempus
325   Dardaniae. Fuimus Trōes, fuit Īlium et ingēns
326   glōria Teucrōrum; ferus omnia Iuppiter Argōs
327   trānstulit; incēnsā Danaī dominantur in urbe.
328   Arduus armātōs mediīs in moenibus astāns
329   fundit equus victorque Sinōn incendia miscet
330   īnsultāns. Portīs aliī bipatentibus adsunt,
331   mīlia quot magnīs umquam vēnēre Mycēnis;
332   obsēdēre aliī tēlīs angusta viārum
333   oppositīs; stat ferrī aciēs mūcrōne coruscō
334   stricta, parāta necī; vix prīmī proelia temptant
335   portārum vigilēs et caecō Mārte resistunt.'

Quaestiōnēs

1. What poetic and rhetorical devices does Vergil employ in 324–27 to intensify the pathos of Panthus' opening remarks?

2. Comment on the cinematographic qualities of Panthus' description in 328–35, specifically identifying the several poetic and rhetorical devices Vergil employs to compel our visualization of the terror in the city's streets.

337 *Erīnys, Erīnyos, f., *Erinys, a Fury* (the spirit of revenge and destructive violence); *fury, frenzy.*

338 fremitus, -ūs, m., *rumbling noise, roar, growl.*

339 *Rhīpeus, -ī, m., *Rhipeus (a Trojan warrior).*

340 Ēpytus, -ī, m., *Epytus (another Trojan warrior).*
   oblātī: lit., *offered, presented,* but here, in a common reflex. sense, *presenting themselves, coming up* (to assist Aeneas as volunteers).
   per lūnam: the moon, first mentioned in 255, is still shining here but is no longer visible in 360 as the night progresses.
   *Hypanis, Hypanis, m., *Hypanis (a Trojan).*
   *Dymās, Dymantis, m., *Dymas (a Trojan).*

341 adglomerō (1), *to mass together (at), join forces (with).*
   *Coroebus, -ī, m., *Coroebus (a Trojan hero and suitor of Cassandra).*
   Coroebus: Coroebus, Dymas, Hypanis, Rhipeus, and Panthus all are named again in 424–30 as each is slain in a skirmish with the Greeks.

342 Mygdonidēs, -ae, m., *son of Mygdon* (a Phrygian king, ally of the Trojans).

343 *īnsānus, -a, -um, *of unsound mind, frenzied, mad; crazed, tempestuous.*

344 gener: i.e., *as a son-in-law (to be);* Cassandra had been pledged to him (cf. spōnsae 345).

345 quī nōn . . . / audierit (346): REL. CAUSAL CLAUSE, explaining īnfēlīx, *since he . . . did not heed;* for the incomplete line, see note on 66 above.
   *praeceptum, -ī, n., *order, instruction.*
   furentis: i.e., when she was in an oracular trance.

347 Quōs: as often, rel. for pers. pron., = eōs (subj. of ardēre), i.e., Coroebus, Rhipeus, and the other warriors who had joined Aeneas at Anchises' home.
   cōnferciō, cōnfercīre, cōnfersī, cōnfertus, *to pack closely together.*
   audēre in proelia: *(and that they were) daring for battle;* some editors accept the conjectured reading ārdēre, *were ablaze/eager.*

348 super: here adv., *besides, moreover,* i.e., to inflame them further.
   hīs: sc. dictīs.
   fortissima . . . / pectora (349): in appos. with iuvenēs; cf. Eng. "braveheart."

349 vōbīs: DAT. OF POSSESSION with cupīdō certa; sc. est.
   audentem: sc. mē, obj. of sequī, which in turn depends on cupīdō; in prose the entire cl. might be sī cupis sequī mē extrēma audentem. Some mss., perhaps correctly, read audendī, which would be construed with cupīdō (*a desire to face*); in either case, the word is positioned to echo audēre (347).
   extrēma: here a substantive, *death,* obj. of audentem.
   *cupīdō, cupīdinis, f., *desire, lust.*

350 quae . . . fortūna: i.e., how ill-fated the situation is.

352 quibus: ABL. OF AGENT (with the prep. omitted, as often in verse).

353 Moriāmur . . . ruāmus: often cited as an example of HYSTERON PROTERON.

Shocked by Panthus' report, Aeneas is joined by a
few brave comrades, whom he encourages to rush
with him into battle and certain death

336   "Tālibus Othryadae dictīs et nūmine dīvum
337   in flammās et in arma feror, quō trīstis Erīnys,
338   quō fremitus vocat et sublātus ad aethera clāmor.
339   Addunt sē sociōs Rhīpeus et maximus armīs
340   Ēpytus, oblātī per lūnam Hypanisque Dymāsque
341   et laterī adglomerant nostrō, iuvenisque Coroebus
342   Mygdonidēs—illīs ad Trōiam forte diēbus
343   vēnerat, īnsānō Cassandrae incēnsus amōre,
344   et gener auxilium Priamō Phrygibusque ferēbat,
345   īnfēlīx quī nōn spōnsae praecepta furentis
346   audierit!
347   Quōs ubi cōnfertōs audēre in proelia vīdī,
348   incipiō super hīs:
                              'Iuvenēs, fortissima frūstrā
349   pectora, sī vōbīs audentem extrēma cupīdō
350   certa sequī, quae sit rēbus fortūna vidētis:
351   excessēre omnēs, adytīs ārīsque relictīs,
352   dī quibus imperium hoc steterat; succurritis urbī
353   incēnsae. Moriāmur et in media arma ruāmus.

Quaestiōnēs

1. Comment on the purpose of the enjambement in 353.

2. The hysteron proteron in 353 is not merely an ornamental device: what
   dramatic, psychological effect is it intended to convey? The sentence is rendered
   even more memorable by its multiple sound effects; comment specifically on the
   soundplay.

354 **salūs ... spērāre:** sc. **est;** the verse ending, **spērāre salūtem,** echoes 1.451, perhaps deliberately contrasting the more hopeful situation there with the current, utterly desperate crisis. The line, powerfully concluding Aeneas' brief speech to his fellow warriors, is a brilliant and often quoted epigram, whose most striking features include its symmetrical and elliptical phrasing, the alternation between **salūs** and the suspensefully delayed **salūtem,** and the poignant contrast between **ūna** and **nūllam.**

355 **Sīc ... additus:** the quick dactylic sent., summing up the effect of Aeneas' words on his comrades, closes in an abrupt DIAERESIS, effectively setting up the SIMILE that follows; the SIMILE itself opens dramatically with a jarring offbeat rhythm created by the two CAESURAE and the monosyllabic line ending.

*__ceu,__ conj., introducing SIMILES, *in the same way as, as, like;* + subjunct., *as if.*

356 **raptor, raptōris,** m., *one who ravages, plunderer, marauder, robber* (here with adj. force, *ravaging, ravening*).

venter, ventris, m., *lower abdomen, belly, stomach.*

357 **catulus, -ī,** m., *young dog, pup; whelp, cub.*

catulī ... relictī: an almost subliminal reminder of the Trojan warriors' own children, defenseless in their homes—including Iulus, to whom Aeneas in his blind rage gives no thought at all until much later in the action (563).

358 *__faucēs, faucium,__ f. pl., *throat; jaws.*

359 *__vādō, vādere,__ *to advance, proceed, go.*

mediae ... / urbis (360): with **iter** = **in mediam urbem.**

360 *__circumvolō (1),__ *to fly/hover around; to encircle.*

cavā circumvolat umbrā: the adj. here = *enveloping* (cf. 1.516). The arrangement constitutes an apt WORD-PICTURE, which is made even more effective by the ALLITERATION and ASSONANCE; a variant on this line occurs in 6.866 below.

361 **clādēs, clādis,** f., *calamity, disaster; slaughter, carnage.*

362 **explicet ... possit:** POTENTIAL SUBJUNCTS.

364 *__iners, inertis,__ *lazy, sluggish; powerless, lifeless.*

*__passim,__ adv., *widely scattered, here and there; in every direction.*

365 **rēligiōsus, -a, -um,** *religious; sacred.*

366 **līmina:** a key thematic image in this book (see discussion quest. on 242–43 above), the word is emphasized here through ENJAMBEMENT and the abrupt DIAERESIS.

367 *__praecordia, -ōrum,__ n. pl., *chest, breast; heart* (as seat of the emotions).

*__virtūs, virtūtis,__ f., *manliness, courage; merit, virtue, goodness.*

victīs ... virtūs / victōrēs (368): ALLITERATION and the careful word order help to underscore the contrast Vergil intends between victors and vanquished.

369 **pavor:** the second syllable is lengthened by DIASTOLE.

354 Ūna salūs victīs nūllam spērāre salūtem.'

Like ravening wolves, Aeneas and his men, enraged,
race forth into the terrible black night

355 "Sīc animīs iuvenum furor additus. Inde, lupī ceu
356 raptōrēs ātrā in nebulā, quōs improba ventris
357 exēgit caecōs rabiēs catulīque relictī
358 faucibus exspectant siccīs, per tēla, per hostēs
359 vādimus haud dubiam in mortem mediaeque tenēmus
360 urbis iter; nox ātra cavā circumvolat umbrā.
361 Quis clādem illīus noctis, quis fūnera fandō
362 explicet aut possit lacrimīs aequāre labōrēs?
363 Urbs antīqua ruit, multōs domināta per annōs;
364 plūrima perque viās sternuntur inertia passim
365 corpora perque domōs et rēligiōsa deōrum
366 līmina. Nec sōlī poenās dant sanguine Teucrī;
367 quondam etiam victīs redit in praecordia virtūs
368 victōrēsque cadunt Danaī. Crūdēlis ubīque
369 lūctus, ubīque pavor et plūrima mortis imāgō.

Quaestiōnēs

1. Compare Aeneas' words to his comrades in 348–54 with his similarly brief outburst at 1.94–101; what is his state of mind in each passage and in what ways are the circumstances that evoke his remarks similar?

2. Identify the poetic devices exemplified by both **per tēla, per hostēs** in 358 and **haud dubiam** in 359 and comment on the effect of each.

3. Comment on the effectiveness of the description in 355–60, identifying specifically the several points of comparison involved in the simile.

4. How is the phrase **lacrimīs aequāre labōrēs** (362) especially remarkable, in terms of both arrangement and sound effects?

5. Comment on the purposeful arrangement of the phrase **plūrima . . . inertia . . . / corpora** in 364–65.

6. Explain specifically how Vergil evokes a profound sense of pathos through his choice and placement of words in 361–69.

370 **Prīmus . . . magnā comitante catervā:** Vergil uses this phrase formulaically to introduce a scene change; cf. line 40 above (of Laocoön).

371 ***Androgeōs, -ī,** m., *Androgeos* (a Greek captain).

    ***socius, -a, -um,** *associated, kindred, related; allied, confederate.*

372 **ultrō . . . compellat:** see note on 279 above.

373 **sērus, -a, -um,** *belated, slow, delayed.*

374 **sēgnitiēs, -ēī,** f., *sloth, inertia, inaction.*

    ferunt: i.e., *carry off (booty), plunder.*

377 **dēlabor, dēlābī, dēlāpsus sum,** *to fall (down), slip.*

    dēlāpsus: here, in imitation of a Greek construction, nom. in agreement with the subj., in place of the more usual acc. + inf. **sē dēlāpsum esse.**

378 ***reprimō, reprimere, repressī, repressus,** *to hold in check, hold back.*

    Obstipuit . . . repressit: the abrupt, end-stopped line suits the action; Androgeos immediately halted in his tracks and fell silent, realizing instantly his fatal mistake.

379 **asprīs:** SYNCOPE for **asperīs.**

    sentis, sentis, m., *briar, bramble.*

380 ***nītor, nītī, nīxus** or **nīsus sum,** *to rest one's weight on, lean on, tread upon; to be supported, be held up; to strain, struggle, grapple* (with).

    ***trepidus, -a, -um,** *alarmed, fearful, anxious; agitated; trembling, shaking.*

    ***repente,** adv., *suddenly, in an instant.*

    trepidusque repente refūgit: the dactylic rhythm suits the action and the assonance of **re** adds an aptly harsh sound effect.

381 **attollentem . . . tumentem:** sc. **eum** (= **anguem** 379); though the obj. is **īrās,** the partic. **attollentem** deliberately evokes an image of the angry snake lifting up its head to strike. The position of the two partics. accentuates the internal rhyme.

    ***caerulus (caeruleus), -a, -um,** *blue; greenish-blue* (used esp. of serpents; here ACC. OF SPECIFICATION).

382 ***secus,** adv. (common with **haud** in similes), *otherwise, differently.*

    abībat: CONATIVE IMPF.

383 ***inruō, inruere, inruī,** *to rush in, dash in.*

    ***dēnsus, -a, -um,** *dense, thick; crowded together, massed, closely packed.*

384 **passim:** with **sternimus** (385), which is itself ENJAMBED for dramatic effect.

385 **aspīrō (1),** *to breathe/blow on* (often used to suggest a favorable wind); *to inspire; to favor, aid.*

    Fortūna: here PERSONIFIED, the goddess of fortune.

386 ***successus, -ūs,** m., *success, successful outcome.*

    ***exsultō (1),** *to spring up, leap about; to exult.*

387 **prīma:** here, as often, Lat. employs an adj. where Eng. would have an adv.

388 **dextra:** here *right-minded, favorable, auspicious,* modifying the subj., where we might expect it to be construed with **sē** (cf. note on **dēlāpsus** 377 above).

389 ***īnsigne, īnsignis,** f., *decoration; insignia.*

390 **in hoste:** i.e., *in wartime.*

391 **comāns, comantis,** *having long hair; having horse-hair plumes, plumed.*

The Greek captain Androgeos mistakes Aeneas and his men for
fellow Greeks—in the skirmish that follows, Androgeos'
soldiers are all slain and the Trojans don their armor
as a ruse to trick the other enemy troops they encounter

370   "Prīmus sē, Danaum magnā comitante catervā,

371 Androgeōs offert nōbīs, socia agmina crēdēns

372 īnscius, atque ultrō verbīs compellat amīcīs:

373 'Festīnāte, virī! Nam quae tam sēra morātur

374 sēgnitiēs? Aliī rapiunt incēnsa feruntque

375 Pergama: vōs celsīs nunc prīmum ā nāvibus ītis?'

376 Dīxit, et extemplō (neque enim respōnsa dabantur

377 fīda satis) sēnsit mediōs dēlāpsus in hostēs.

378 Obstipuit retrōque pedem cum vōce repressit.

379 Imprōvīsum asprīs velutī quī sentibus anguem

380 pressit, humī nītēns, trepidusque repente refūgit

381 attollentem īrās et caerula colla tumentem,

382 haud secus Androgeōs vīsū tremefactus abībat.

383 Inruimus dēnsīs et circumfundimur armīs,

384 ignārōsque locī passim et formīdine captōs

385 sternimus: aspīrat prīmō Fortūna labōrī.

386 Atque hīc successū exsultāns animīsque Coroebus

387 'ō sociī, quā prīma,' inquit, 'Fortūna salūtis

388 mōnstrat iter, quāque ostendit sē dextra, sequāmur:

389 mūtēmus clipeōs Danaumque īnsignia nōbīs

390 aptēmus. Dolus an virtūs, quis in hoste requīrat?

391 Arma dabunt ipsī.' Sīc fātus, deinde comantem

Quaestiōnēs

1. In what way is the word order in 379 particularly effective?

2. Discuss the simile in 379–82; how is it especially appropriate in this context and how may the serpent depicted here be compared with those that assaulted Laocoön? Finally, compare Homer's simile in *Iliad* 3.33f.

3. Comment on the word order and its effects in lines 383 and 384.

392 **Androgeī:** some editions have **Androgeō**, a Greek gen., but there is little support in the mss. for this reading.

decōrus, -a, -um, *handsome, beautiful; glorious, honorable, noble.*

clipeī . . . īnsigne decōrum: Vergil's phrasing (*the shield's handsome design*) is highly visual, training his camera on the shield's decoration, whereas standard Eng. would say "the handsomely designed shield"; the device is common in epic, focusing on the attribute rather than the object.

393 **induitur:** for the reflex. force, see note on **indūtus (275).**

accommodō (1), *to fit/fasten on, apply.*

396 **immisceō, immiscēre, immiscuī, immixtus,** *to mix in, mingle* (with).

haud: with **nostrō;** i.e., even the gods were deceived by the ruse.

397 **multa . . . noctem:** the INTERLOCKED WORD ORDER, a nearly symmetrical GOLDEN LINE, suits the confused action of skirmish after skirmish in the moonless night.

caecam: an elegant METAPHOR; in the total darkness, the night itself is unseeing.

398 **cōnserō, cōnserere, cōnseruī, cōnsertus,** *to fasten together;* with **proelium,** *to join battle, engage in battle.*

*Orcus, -ī, m., Orcus, Dis (the god of the Underworld); *the Underworld, Hades* (here DAT. OF DIRECTION).

400 **pars . . . / scandunt . . . conduntur (401):** a collective sg. subj. often takes a pl. vb.; the pass. **conduntur** here has reflex. force (*hide themselves*).

ingentem: with **equum (401),** which is effectively delayed to build suspense; the horse is mentioned for the last time here, as the terrified Greeks seek refuge within its womb.

*turpis, -is, -e, foul, loathsome; ugly, unsightly; shameful, disgraceful.

402 **nihil . . . fās:** = **nōn est fās.**

fīdō, fīdere, fīsus sum + dat., *to have confidence in, trust (in).*

403 **Priamēius, -a, -um,** *of/belonging to Priam.*

405 **ad caelum . . . lūmina . . . / lūmina (406):** to entreat the gods for aid (the usual gesture was **palmās tendere:** see note on 1.93); ANAPHORA focuses attention on the pathos of Cassandra's situation.

406 **tener, -nera, -nerum,** *soft, tender, delicate.*

407 **speciēs, -ēī, f., spectacle, sight; look, appearance; impression.*

*furiātus, -a, -um, maddened, enraged.

410 **dēlūbrī:** i.e., of Minerva.

411 **nostrōrum:** ENJAMBED for emotional effect; the Trojans defending the temple mistake Aeneas' band for Greeks and assault them with what in modern warfare we call "friendly fire."

obruimur: the final syllable, under the ictus and at the CAESURA, is lengthened by DIASTOLE.

392 Androgeī galeam clipeīque īnsigne decōrum
393 induitur laterīque Argīvum accommodat ēnsem.
394 Hoc Rhīpeus, hoc ipse Dymās omnisque iuventūs
395 laeta facit: spoliīs sē quisque recentibus armat.
396 Vādimus, immixtī Danaīs, haud nūmine nostrō,
397 multaque per caecam congressī proelia noctem
398 cōnserimus, multōs Danaum dēmittimus Orcō.
399 Diffugiunt aliī ad nāvēs et lītora cursū
400 fīda petunt; pars ingentem formīdine turpī
401 scandunt rūrsus equum et nōtā conduntur in alvō.

As the Trojans rush to rescue Cassandra, they are attacked, first
by their own countrymen, who mistake them for Greeks, and then
by the enemy soldiers who had seized the Trojan princess

402 "Heu, nihil invītīs fās quemquam fīdere dīvīs!
403 Ecce trahēbātur passīs Priamēia virgō
404 crīnibus ā templō Cassandra adytīsque Minervae,
405 ad caelum tendēns ārdentia lūmina frūstrā,
406 lūmina, nam tenerās arcēbant vincula palmās.
407 Nōn tulit hanc speciem, furiātā mente, Coroebus
408 et sēsē medium iniēcit peritūrus in agmen;
409 cōnsequimur cūnctī et dēnsīs incurrimus armīs.
410 Hīc prīmum ex altō dēlūbrī culmine tēlīs
411 nostrōrum obruimur oriturque miserrima caedēs

Quaestiōnēs

1. Compare Vergil's use of the word **ecce** in 403 with its use in 57, 203, and 318 above; what is the poet's dramatic purpose in each instance?

2. The violence Cassandra suffers in 403f. recalls to some extent the sacrifice of Iphigenia in 116–19, and it certainly anticipates the plight of Priam's wife Hecuba and Aeneas' own Creusa, both detailed later in the book. What can you say at this point about the role of women in Vergil's war narrative? What would the effect be on contemporaries in his audience?

412 *faciēs, -ēī, f., *appearance; sight, scene; form, shape, image; face, countenance.*
faciē . . . errōre: ABL. OF CAUSE.

413 ēreptae virginis: OBJ. GEN., i.e., *over the maiden's rescue.*

414 Āiāx: for the role of Ajax, son of Oileus, in the assault on Cassandra, see note on 1.39.

415 geminī Atrīdae: Agamemnon ultimately took Cassandra back to Greece as his consort, the consequences of which (among the king's other transgressions) are dramatized in the tragedy by Aeschylus that bears his name.

416 ceu: the word should introduce the cl. but is delayed by a type of ANASTROPHE that is very common in Vergil.

417 cōnflīgō, cōnflīgere, cōnflīxī, cōnflīctus, *to strike together, collide, clash.*

418 Eurus . . . saevit: an effective ONOMATOPOEIA, as the hissing ALLITERATION easily suggests the sound of the winds howling through the forests.
saevitque tridentī: cf. saevumque tridentem, of Neptune, in the same metrical position at 1.138; the trident is regularly an attribute of Neptune in literature and art.

419 *spūmeus, -a, -um, *covered with foam, foamy, frothy.*
·Nēreus, -ī, m., *Nereus (a sea-god, father of the Nereids).*
fundus, -ī, m., *bottom, base; the depths (of the sea).*

420 sī quōs: *if any = whatever (men).*

421 *agitō (1), *to set in motion, move; to stir up, drive (forward/out); to distress, vex, harass.*

422 *mentior, mentīrī, mentītus sum, *to lie (about), deceive; to disguise; to assume/put on falsely (as a disguise).*

423 ōra: here *voices, speech.*
*sonus, -ī, m., *sound, noise; pronunciation, accent, tone* (here ABL. OF SPECIFICATION).
discors, discordis, *disagreeing, discordant; different.*
*signō (1), *to mark, inscribe; to mark, notice; to indicate, point out, show.*
ōra . . . signant: the standard convention in ancient epic (as in most modern war films) is that the enemies speak the same language and readily understand one another; but here Vergil takes a more realistic approach to suit his dramatic purposes.

424 *īlicet, adv., *on the spot, immediately, straightaway.*
obruimur: an echo of obruimur in the same metrical position at 411.

425 Pēneleus, -ī, m., *Peneleus (a Greek warrior).*
armipotēns, armipotentis, *powerful in arms, warlike, (of a) warrior.*
dīvae armipotentis: Minerva, at whose temple the action is occurring (404, 410).

426 *prōcumbō, prōcumbere, prōcubuī, prōcubitus, *to bend/lean forward; to fall forward/down.*

427 aequum, -ī, n., *right, justice, fairness.*

412 armōrum faciē et Grāiārum errōre iubārum.
413 Tum Danaī gemitū atque ēreptae virginis īrā
414 undique collēctī invādunt, ācerrimus Āiāx
415 et geminī Atrīdae Dolopumque exercitus omnis:
416 adversī ruptō ceu quondam turbine ventī
417 cōnflīgunt, Zephyrusque Notusque et laetus Eōīs
418 Eurus equīs; strīdunt silvae saevitque tridentī
419 spūmeus atque īmō Nēreus ciet aequora fundō.
420 Illī etiam, sī quōs obscūrā nocte per umbram
421 fūdimus īnsidiīs tōtāque agitāvimus urbe,
422 appārent; prīmī clipeōs mentītaque tēla
423 agnōscunt atque ōra sonō discordia signant.
424 Īlicet obruimur numerō, prīmusque Coroebus
425 Pēneleī dextrā dīvae armipotentis ad āram
426 prōcumbit; cadit et Rhīpeus, iūstissimus ūnus
427 quī fuit in Teucrīs et servantissimus aequī

Quaestiōnēs

1. Comment on both the word order and the sound effects in 412.

2. What is the intended effect of the word order in 416?

3. Discuss the simile in 416–19 and the several points of comparison Vergil makes between the battle scene and the storm; what correspondences do you see with the simile at 1.148–56 and in what fundamental way do the two similes differ in terms of the poet's narrative strategy? Compare Homer's simile in *Iliad* 9.4f.

4. What is the purpose of the enjambement in 422?

5. Discuss in detail Vergil's characterization of Coroebus, from his first introduction at 339–46 and reappearance in 386–93 and 407–08 to his death at 424–26. What are the young man's principal traits, and what dramatic effects does Vergil achieve through his focus on this one relatively minor character? Compare the screen-writer's and director's treatment of similarly minor characters in modern war films you may have seen.

428 **vīsum:** sc. **est;** i.e., the gods thought it better to deal with him in accordance with their own plan, a conception adopted from Stoic philosophy.

Hypanisque Dymāsque: in the same metrical position at 340; one by one the courageous warriors who had joined Aeneas earlier at his father's home (336–41)—Coroebus, Rhipeus, Hypanis, Dymas, and Panthus—all fall in battle either to the Greeks or to "friendly fire" (the scene in 428–29 recalls 410–11).

429 **cōnfīgō, cōnfīgere, cōnfīxī, cōnfīxus,** *to fasten together; to pierce, run through, strike down.*

430 **īnfula, -ae,** f., *(sacred) woolen headband.*

433 **vītāvisse . . . meruisse (434):** sc. **mē** as subj.

vicis (gen.; nom. sg. not attested), f., *returning circumstance, turn (of events); plight, lot; requital, revenge.*

vītāvisse vicēs: the ALLITERATION adds a perhaps deliberate breathless effect, suggesting the high emotion in Aeneas' APOSTROPHE to his fallen countrymen and their city.

Danaum: here *from the Greeks* (SUBJ. GEN.); some editors take **Danaum** with **manū (434),** but more likely it goes with **vicēs,** as it clearly does with the parallel **tēla,** and **manū** means *by my own hand* (i.e., by his own actions against the Greeks in battle).

434 **ut caderem:** RESULT CL.

435 **Īphitus, -ī,** m., *Iphitus* (a Trojan warrior).

Peliās, -ae, m., *Pelias* (another Trojan warrior).

aevum, -ī, n., *time, (one's) age; old age.*

439 **bella:** a dramatic HYPERBOLE for **proelia.**

forent: = **essent,** subjunct. in a CONTRARY-TO-FACT CONDITIONAL construction common with **ceu.**

nūllī tōtā: an emphatic, poignant juxtaposition.

440 *indomitus, -a, -um,* *untamed, unrestrained, wild.*

441 **āctā testūdine:** either an anachronistic ref. (there are others in the *Aeneid*) to the Roman (but not Homeric) siege machine known as a **testūdō,** essentially a wooden screen used to protect armed personnel in their assault on a city— one could think of tanks as a sort of modern analogue—or a more general ref. to a squadron of attackers raising their shields together above their heads for a similar defensive purpose.

442 **parietibus:** quadrisyllabic (SYNIZESIS); treating the first **i** as a consonant allows for scanning **par-** as a long syllable.

scālae, -ārum f. pl., *ladder, scaling ladder* (for military use).

443 *sinistra, -ae,* f., *left hand.*

444 **prōtegō, prōtegere, prōtēxī, prōtēctus,** *to shield, cover, protect.*

prēnsō (1), *to grasp (at), sieze hold of.*

445 **contrā:** here adv., *in turn, at the same time.*

turris, turris, acc. **turrim** or **turrem,** f., *tower* (on a building or a city's walls).

domōrum: i.e., the several structures comprising Priam's palace.

446 **hīs:** with **tēlīs (447);** the suspenseful delay of the noun adds to the powerful sense of desperation that Vergil means to evoke.

ultima: here substantive, *the end, their last hour.*

428 (dīs aliter vīsum); pereunt Hypanisque Dymāsque,
429 cōnfīxī ā sociīs; nec tē tua plūrima, Panthū,
430 lābentem pietās nec Apollinis īnfula tēxit.
431 Īliacī cinerēs et flamma extrēma meōrum,
432 testor, in occāsū vestrō nec tēla nec ūllās
433 vītāvisse vicēs Danaum, et, sī fāta fuissent
434 ut caderem, meruisse manū. Dīvellimur inde,
435 Īphitus et Peliās mēcum (quōrum Īphitus aevō
436 iam gravior, Peliās et vulnere tardus Ulixī),
437 prōtinus ad sēdēs Priamī clāmōre vocātī.

Aeneas and those of his comrades who had escaped death
rush to assist in the defense of Priam's palace

438   "Hīc vērō ingentem pugnam, ceu cētera nusquam
439 bella forent, nūllī tōtā morerentur in urbe,
440 sīc Mārtem indomitum Danaōsque ad tēcta ruentēs
441 cernimus obsessumque āctā testūdine līmen.
442 Haerent parietibus scālae, postēsque sub ipsōs
443 nītuntur gradibus, clipeōsque ad tēla, sinistrīs
444 prōtēctī, obiciunt, prēnsant fastīgia dextrīs.
445 Dardanidae contrā turrēs ac tōta domōrum
446 culmina convellunt; hīs sē, quandō ultima cernunt,

Quaestiōnēs

1. What is the emotional effect of bringing back on stage at 424–30, not just Coroebus, but several of the heroes Vergil had introduced by name in 336–41?

2. What dramatic purpose is served by the extended apostrophe in 429–34? How is it essential to the scene shift in the lines immediately following?

447 **extrēmā . . . in morte:** *at the point of/on the brink of . . . .*

448 **aurātus, -a, -um,** *golden, gilded.*

    parentum: i.e., *forefathers, ancestors.*

449 **dēvolvō, dēvolvere, dēvoluī, dēvolūtus,** *to roll down.*

451 ***īnstaurō (1),** *to repeat, start afresh, renew; to restore, revive.*

    īnstaurātī: sc. **sunt,** construed here with the series of COMPL. INFS. following.

453 **pervius, -a, -um,** *passable, allowing passage (in and out).*

    ***ūsus, -ūs,** m., *use, purpose; utility.*

    pervius ūsus: the lit. translation, something like *a utility allowing passage,* is unidiomatic; the sense is *a well-used/familiar passageway.*

454 **tēctōrum . . . Priamī:** here again the lit. translation is not idiomatic; the meaning is (a passageway) *connecting the parts of Priam's palace.*

    relictī: here *remote.*

455 **ā:** = **in;** the line's slow spondees aptly introduce Andromache, suiting the tone evoked in the epithet **īnfēlīx.**

    manēbant / . . . solēbat (456) / . . . trahēbat (457): a relatively rare instance of end-line rhyme in three successive verses.

456 **Andromachē, Andromachēs,** f., *Andromache* (wife of Hector).

    incomitātus, -a, -um, *unaccompanied, unattended.*

457 **socer, -cerī,** m., *father-in-law;* pl., *father- and mother-in-law.*

    ***avus, -ī,** m., *grandfather.*

    Astyanax, Astyanactis, acc. **Astyanacta,** m., *Astyanax* (only child of Andromache and Hector, later brutally thrown from Troy's walls when the city had fallen).

458 **Ēvādō:** i.e., from the hidden entranceway.

459 **tēla . . . Teucrī:** INTERLOCKED WORD ORDER, nearly a GOLDEN LINE, intensifying the pathos in the epithets **miserī** and **inrita.**

    manū: here *with violence,* a common sense of the word, esp. in the abl.

    inritus, -a, -um, *not valid; ineffectual, useless.*

460 **Turrim:** obj. of the partic. **adgressī (463)** and the vbs. **convellimus** and **impulimus (464–65).**

    praeceps, praecipitis, n., *precipice.*

461 **ēductam:** *rising up;* Lat. often uses a perf. partic. where Eng. would have a pres. partic.

462 **solitae:** sc. **sunt,** with **vidērī (461).**

    Achāicus, -a, -um, *Achaean, Greek.*

463 **circum:** here adv.

    ***labō, labāre, labāvī, labātūrus,** *to stand unsteadily, be shaky, totter, give way.*

464 **iūnctūra, -ae,** f., *join, joint, seam, connection.*

    tabulātum, -ī, n., *story* (of a building), *floor.*

447 extrēmā iam in morte parant dēfendere tēlīs,
448 aurātāsque trabēs, veterum decora alta parentum,
449 dēvolvunt; aliī strictīs mūcrōnibus īmās
450 obsēdēre forēs, hās servant agmine dēnsō.
451 Īnstaurātī animī rēgis succurrere tēctīs
452 auxiliōque levāre virōs vimque addere victīs.

*Aeneas mounts to the rooftop of the royal palace and
helps his countrymen topple one of its defensive
towers onto the assaulting Greeks below*

453 "Līmen erat caecaeque forēs et pervius ūsus
454 tēctōrum inter sē Priamī, postēsque relictī
455 ā tergō, īnfēlīx quā sē, dum rēgna manēbant,
456 saepius Andromachē ferre incomitāta solēbat
457 ad socerōs et avō puerum Astyanacta trahēbat.
458 Ēvādō ad summī fastīgia culminis, unde
459 tēla manū miserī iactābant inrita Teucrī.
460 Turrim in praecipitī stantem summīsque sub astra
461 ēductam tēctīs, unde omnis Trōia vidērī
462 et Danaum solitae nāvēs et Achāica castra,
463 adgressī ferrō circum, quā summa labantēs
464 iūnctūrās tabulāta dabant, convellimus altīs
465 sēdibus impulimusque; ea lāpsa repente ruīnam
466 cum sonitū trahit et Danaum super agmina lātē

Quaestiōnēs

1. The battle scene in 438–52 is particularly detailed; what might Vergil's purpose in this be?

2. How does meter suit meaning in 452? Comment on the line's other sound effects.

3. What is Vergil's purpose in describing in such detail at 453–57 the doorway by which Aeneas entered Priam's palace?

468 **tēlōrum . . . genus:** for the short line, see note on 66 above.

469 **līmine:** Vergil uses the word five times in this scene (here, and at 480, 485, 500, and 508), evoking the image of the horse's entrance into the city at 242–43.

*Pyrrhus, -ī, m., *Pyrrhus* (son of Achilles; the name means "fire" or "fire-red"—used here to play on **lūce . . . aēnā** (470), instead of his other name, "Neoptolemus," which means "New Ptolemy" or "New War"—see line 263).

471 *coluber, -brī, m., *snake, serpent.*

mala: i.e., poisonous.

grāmen, grāminis, n., *grass; plant, herb.*

pāstus: here, as often, deponent.

472 **quem:** here considerably delayed (ANASTROPHE), the rel. pron. should in translation introduce the cl.

brūma, -ae, f., *winter solstice; winter.*

473 **positīs:** = **dēpositīs**, simple for compound form, common in verse.

exuviīs: here the snake's *skin*, shed in molting.

nitidus, -a, -um, *shining, resplendent.*

*iuventa, -ae, f., *youth; youthfulness, youthful vigor.*

474 **convolvō, convolvere, convoluī, convolūtus, *to roll together, coil up.***

convolvit sublātō pectore terga: cf. **pectora . . . arrēcta** (206) and **sinuat . . . terga** (208) of the snakes that assaulted Laocoön and his sons.

475 **arduus:** used of the horse in 475, one of several instances in which similar imagery is applied to both the horse and the various serpents appearing in Book Two (see notes on lines 204, 207, 235, and 262).

trisulcus, -a, -um, *three-forked;* of a snake's tongue, simply *forked.*

arduus . . . trisulcīs: the heavy ALLITERATION of **s** is ONOMATOPOETIC, suggesting the serpent's hissing, as in 211, where **linguīs** appears in the same metrical position.

476 **Periphās, Periphantis, m., *Periphas* (a Greek warrior).**

agitātor, agitātōris, m., *driver, charioteer.*

477 **armiger, -gerī, m., *armor-bearer, squire.***

Automedōn, Automedontis, m., *Automedon* (Achilles' chariot-driver, from the island of Scyros).

Scy–rius, -a, -um, *Scyrian, of Scyros* (an Aegean island east of Euboea, realm of Pyrrhus' grandfather, king Lycomedes).

478 *succēdō, succēdere, successī, successūrus, *to move to a position below, come to the foot of, stoop down to/beneath; to come up to, advance on.*

479 **Ipse:** regularly used of the principal character in a scene, here Pyrrhus.

*bipennis, bipennis, f., *two-edged axe.*

480 **perrumpō, perrumpere, perrūpī, perruptus, *to burst apart, break through.***

vellō, vellere, vellī or vulsī, vulsus, *to pull out/from, tear from.*

481 **aerātus, -a, -um, *bronze covered, bronze-bound.***

trabe: here a *panel* of the door.

*fīrmus, -a, -um, *strong, stout; solid; firm, determined; reliable, sure.*

cavō (1), *to hollow out; to make a hole in, cut through.*

467 incidit. Ast aliī subeunt, nec saxa nec ūllum
468 tēlōrum intereā cessat genus.

Pyrrhus himself, the son of Achilles, bursts
through the doors of Priam's palace

469   "Vēstibulum ante ipsum prīmōque in līmine, Pyrrhus
470 exsultat, tēlīs et lūce coruscus aēnā:
471 quālis ubi in lūcem coluber, mala grāmina pāstus,
472 frīgida sub terrā tumidum quem brūma tegēbat,
473 nunc, positīs novus exuviīs nitidusque iuventā,
474 lūbrica convolvit sublātō pectore terga
475 arduus ad sōlem, et linguīs micat ōre trisulcīs.
476 Ūnā ingēns Periphās et equōrum agitātor Achillis,
477 armiger Automedōn, ūnā omnis Scy-ria pūbēs
478 succēdunt tēctō et flammās ad culmina iactant.
479 Ipse inter prīmōs correptā dūra bipennī
480 līmina perrumpit postēsque ā cardine vellit
481 aerātōs; iamque, excīsā trabe, firma cavāvit

Quaestiōnēs

1. Explain the appropriateness of the meter in 465–66 and the enjambement in 467.

2. What poetic device is exemplified by **tēlīs et lūce . . . aēnā** (470)?

3. What are the several points of comparison in the simile at 469–75? Which is visually most striking?

4. Compare Vergil's snake similes in both 378–82 and 469–75 with his depiction of the serpents that attack Laocoön in 2.201–11. In what specific respects are the descriptions similar, and what do the snakes in these passages symbolize?

482 **ingentem . . . fenestram**: the CHIASTIC arrangement, a kind of WORD-PICTURE, suits the image of this gaping hole, opening outward—an aperture that not only permits the entry of Pyrrhus and his comrades but also opens up the interior of the palace to the view of Aeneas and, therefore, of Vergil's audience.

483 **Appāret . . . / appārent (484)**: a highly effective ANAPHORA that prompts our visualization of the scene through Aeneas' eyes.

484 *__penetrāle, penetrālis__*, n., *inner part, innermost recess; inner shrine; innermost part of a home, inner chamber.*

486 *__interior, interior, interius__*, *interior, inner (part of).*

487 **miscētur**: i.e., *is in an uproar.*
　cavae: here *vaulted.*
　__plangor, plangōris__, m., *beating of the breast* (a sign of grief); *lamentation.*
　__aedēs, aedis__, f., *room, apartment, hall*; pl., *dwelling, house, palace.*
　aedēs / . . . ululant (488): PERSONIFICATION; the halls, echoing the women's shrieks, seem to cry out themselves with lamentation.

488 *__fēmineus, -a, -um__*, *of/relating to a woman/women, female, womanly.*
　aurea sīdera: a lilting ASSONANCE and an image of brightness and calm starkly contrasting with the dark horror below.

489 *__pavidus, -a, -um__*, *terror-stricken, frightened.*

490 **ōscula fīgunt**: a common gesture of grief.

492 **ariēs, arietis**, m., *male sheep, ram; battering ram.*
　ariete: the **i** here is treated as a consonant (SYNIZESIS); cf. **parietibus (442)**.

493 *__ēmoveō, ēmovēre, ēmōvī, ēmōtus__*, *to move out, remove; to dislodge.*

494 **Fit via vī**: the staccato rhythm suggests the sudden violence of the action; the violent **rumpunt** continues the sound effects.
　__aditus, -ūs__, m., *approach, entry; doorway; access* (to a person).
　trucīdō (1), *to butcher, slaughter.*

496 **Nōn sīc**: i.e., *not with such great force.*
　__amnis, amnis__, m., *river, stream.*

497 *__ēvincō, ēvincere, ēvīcī, ēvictus__*, *to overcome, overwhelm.*
　mōlēs: here *barriers, banks.*

498 **fertur**: i.e., *rushes*, a common sense of **ferō** in the pass. (cf. 511).

> Inside the palace, all was confusion, groans, agony.
> The echoing halls resounded through and through with the keening
> Of women, whose wails and shrieks beat at the golden stars.
>
> *From the translation of C. Day Lewis, 1952*

482 rōbora et ingentem lātō dedit ōre fenestram.

483 Appāret domus intus et ātria longa patēscunt;

484 appārent Priamī et veterum penetrālia rēgum,

485 armātōsque vident stantēs in līmine prīmō.

486 At domus interior gemitū miserōque tumultū

487 miscētur, penitusque cavae plangōribus aedēs

488 fēmineīs ululant; ferit aurea sīdera clāmor.

489 Tum pavidae tēctīs mātrēs ingentibus errant

490 amplexaeque tenent postēs atque ōscula fīgunt.

491 Īnstat vī patriā Pyrrhus; nec claustra nec ipsī

492 custōdēs sufferre valent; labat ariete crēbrō

493 iānua, et ēmōtī prōcumbunt cardine postēs.

494 Fit via vī; rumpunt aditūs prīmōsque trucīdant

495 immissī Danaī et lātē loca mīlite complent.

496 Nōn sīc, aggeribus ruptīs cum spūmeus amnis

497 exiit oppositāsque ēvīcit gurgite mōlēs,

498 fertur in arva furēns cumulō campōsque per omnēs

Quaestiōnēs

1. Comment on the word order in 483 and explain how it is appropriate to the image described.

2. What device of word order does Vergil employ in 489 and how does it suit his meaning? Compare the arrangement in 234.

3. The personification in **aedēs . . . ululant** (487–88) has suggested to some readers that Pyrrhus' initial assault on the palace was meant to be seen metaphorically as a rape. What other language in 482–94 could be regarded as personifying and thus as supporting this interpretation? Does Vergil's use of sexual imagery in describing the Trojan horse lend credence to this view?

4. In what other ways are the wooden horse and Priam's palace similarly described?—identify the several verbal correspondences between lines 481–95 and descriptions of the horse, particularly in 19–20 and 50–53.

5. How does meter suit meaning in 498?

499 *stabulum, -ī, n., *shelter for animals, stable, shed; lair, den.*

501 *Hecuba, -ae, f., *Hecuba* (wife of Priam and mother to many of his children, including Hector, Cassandra, and Polites).

　*nurus, -ūs, f., *daughter-in-law; young married woman.*

　centum . . . nurūs: Priam had 50 daughters and 50 sons; each of the sons had wives, hence the generalized number here, *a hundred daughters.*

　per: here *amid, in the midst of.*

503 *thalamus, -ī, m., *chamber, apartment; bedroom* (of a married couple).

　Quīnquāgintā . . . thalamī: those of Priam's sons and their brides.

504 barbaricus, -a, -um, *barbarian, foreign.*

　barbaricō . . . aurō spoliīsque: HENDIADYS.

505 prōcubuēre: ENJAMBEMENT and the irregular CAESURA, following the initial short syllable of the second foot, underscore the pathos of this vb.

　*dēficiō, dēficere, dēfēcī, dēfectus, *to let down, fail, fall short.*

506 forsitan, adv., *it may be, perhaps,* often + POTENTIAL SUBJUNCT.

　et: = etiam, with requīrās; the second pers. vb. serves to remind us of Aeneas' audience, Dido (and her court).

　Priamī . . . fāta: = quae fuerint fāta Priamī, IND. QUEST.; the brief, one-line sent. introduces a slight scene shift, focusing now on the king.

507 Urbis . . . vīdit: the harsh ALLITERATION of **t** and conflict of ictus and accent provide an apt soundtrack for the violent image the poet's words evoke.

　utī: = ut, *when,* introducing the cl.

508 medium: a TRANSFERRED EPITHET, logically applying to penetrālibus.

509 diū: with dēsuēta.

　*senior, senior, (senius), *of a greater age, older;* often m. as substantive, *older man, old man.*

　dēsuētus, -a, -um, *disaccustomed, disused, unused.*

510 *inūtilis, -is, -e, *useless, ineffectual.*

511 cingitur: here reflex. with ferrum as obj., *he girds on . . . .*

　fertur: cf. 498 and note.

　moritūrus: fut. partic. of morior.

512 nūdō: here *open;* the open courtyard in the middle of the palace recalls, anachronistically, Roman architecture and at the same time explains how Aeneas can observe the events taking place there from his rooftop vista.

　axis, axis, m., *axle; axis* (of the earth, of the heavens); *vault* (of heaven), *sky.*

513 *iūxtā, adv. and prep. + acc., *nearby, close by.*

514 incumbēns . . . Penātēs: the line's spondaic rhythm helps focus our attention on the pitiable scene.

515 *altāria, altārium, n. pl., *altar* (for burned offerings).

516 *columba, -ae, f., *pigeon, dove* (contrasted with other birds for their gentleness).

517 condēnsus, -a, -um, *closely packed, crowded together.*

518 iuvenālis, -is, -e, *of a young man, of youth.*

499 cum stabulīs armenta trahit. Vīdī ipse furentem
500 caede Neoptolemum geminōsque in līmine Atrīdās,
501 vīdī Hecubam centumque nurūs Priamumque per ārās
502 sanguine foedantem quōs ipse sacrāverat ignēs.
503 Quīnquāgintā illī thalamī, spēs tanta nepōtum,
504 barbaricō postēs aurō spoliīsque superbī
505 prōcubuēre; tenent Danaī quā dēficit ignis.

The aged Priam rushes to arm himself and defend the palace

506   "Forsitan et Priamī fuerint quae fāta requīrās.
507 Urbis utī captae cāsum convulsaque vīdit
508 līmina tēctōrum et medium in penetrālibus hostem,
509 arma diū senior dēsuēta trementibus aevō
510 circumdat nēquīquam umerīs et inūtile ferrum
511 cingitur, ac dēnsōs fertur moritūrus in hostēs.
512 Aedibus in mediīs nūdōque sub aetheris axe
513 ingēns āra fuit iūxtāque veterrima laurus,
514 incumbēns ārae atque umbrā complexa Penātēs.
515 Hīc Hecuba et nātae nēquīquam altāria circum,
516 praecipitēs ātrā ceu tempestāte columbae,
517 condēnsae et dīvum amplexae simulācra sedēbant.
518 Ipsum autem sūmptīs Priamum iuvenālibus armīs

Quaestiōnēs

1. Considering in particular the image in **cum stabulīs armenta trahit,** comment in detail on the several correspondences between the simile in 496–99 and the action Vergil uses it to describe in 491–95 and 499–500. Compare Homer's simile at *Iliad* 5.87f.

2. What is the intended effect of the anaphora in 499–501?

3. On a symbolic level, how do the references to **līmen** in 469–508 compare with the image in 242–43?

4. How are both the simile and the word order in 516 particularly appropriate to the image of Hecuba and her daughters huddled around the altar?

520 **cingī**: sc. **tē** as subj.

Aut: the conj., introducing a second quest. rather than an alternative to the first, is a common colloquialism.

521 **dēfēnsor, dēfēnsōris**, m., *defender, protector.*

***iste, -a, -ud,** *that (of yours); such (as you speak of/refer to); this.*

522 **adforet**: = **adesset** (see note on 1.576).

523 **tandem**: here, as often, *please.*

524 *****effor, effārī, effātus sum,** *to utter, say, speak.*

Sīc ōre effāta: Aeneas could not have heard these words from his rooftop position, so we must engage here, as often in both ancient and modern fiction, in a "willing suspension of disbelief." The expression **ōre effāta** is a type of PLEONASM common in the *Aeneid* (cf. **tālī . . . ōre locūtus,** 4.276 below)

525 *****longaevus, -a, -um,** *of great age, aged.*

526 **Ecce autem**: for the scene-shift device, like a film director's cue, cf. 203 (appearance of the serpents from Tenedos) and esp. **ecce autem tēlīs Panthūs ēlāpsus Achīvum** (318), which like this line is also spondaic.

Polītēs, -ae, m., *Polites (a son of Hecuba and Priam).*

527 **per tēla, per hostēs**: cf. 358, where the same phrases appear in identical metrical position.

528 *****porticus, -ūs,** f., *portico, colonnade.*

*****vacuus, -a, -um,** *empty, deserted.*

529 *****īnfestus, -a, -um,** *hostile, warlike; threatening.*

vulnere: here, as often in poetry, *a weapon* (that threatens a wound).

530 **iam iamque**: the ANAPHORA suggests the immediacy of the peril, a notion reinforced by the CHIASMUS in **manū tenet et premit hastā.**

534 **abstineō, abstinēre, abstinuī, abstentus,** *to keep from, to hold back.*

vōcī īraeque: perhaps best construed as HENDIADYS, *his angry voice.*

535 **ausīs**: partic. as substantive, *reckless acts.*

536 **pietās**: here *pity, compassion.*

quae . . . cūret: REL. CL. OF PURPOSE.

537 **persolvō, persolvere, persoluī, persolūtus,** *to pay back, give in recompense.*

grātēs, grātium, f. pl., *thanks* (the line's ponderous spondees underscore the grim irony in Priam's call for thanksgiving, an effect enhanced by the line's CHIASTIC arrangement and the caustic ENJAMBEMENT of **dēbita** in 538).

538 **quī**: **tibi** (535) is the anteced.

mē cernere: **faciō** + inf. is not uncommon in verse.

539 **fēcistī . . . foedāstī fūnere**: the ALLITERATION, with its hissing sound, is meant to convey the angry bitterness of the old man's reproach.

540 *****serō, serere, sēvī, satus,** *to plant* (seeds), *sow; to give birth to, beget.*

quō: ABL. OF ORIGIN with **satum (esse).**

Achillēs: though Achilles had slain Hector in battle, he nonetheless dutifully returned the son's corpse to his father Priam.

519 ut vīdit, 'Quae mēns tam dīra, miserrime coniūnx,
520 impulit hīs cingī tēlīs? Aut quō ruis?' inquit.
521 'Nōn tālī auxiliō nec dēfēnsōribus istīs
522 tempus eget; nōn, sī ipse meus nunc adforet Hector.
523 Hūc tandem concēde; haec āra tuēbitur omnēs,
524 aut moriēre simul.' Sīc ōre effāta, recēpit
525 ad sēsē et sacrā longaevum in sēde locāvit.

Pyrrhus slays Polites before the eyes of his parents, Hecuba and
Priam, and then savagely murders and beheads the king himself

526 "Ecce autem ēlāpsus Pyrrhī dē caede Polītēs,
527 ūnus nātōrum Priamī, per tēla, per hostēs
528 porticibus longīs fugit et vacua ātria lūstrat
529 saucius. Illum ārdēns īnfestō vulnere Pyrrhus
530 īnsequitur, iam iamque manū tenet et premit hastā.
531 Ut tandem ante oculōs ēvāsit et ōra parentum,
532 concidit ac multō vītam cum sanguine fūdit.
533 Hīc Priamus, quamquam in mediā iam morte tenētur,
534 nōn tamen abstinuit nec vōcī īraeque pepercit:
535 'At tibi prō scelere,' exclāmat, 'prō tālibus ausīs
536 dī, sī qua est caelō pietās quae tālia cūret,
537 persolvant grātēs dignās et praemia reddant
538 dēbita, quī nātī cōram mē cernere lētum
539 fēcistī et patriōs foedāstī fūnere vultūs.
540 At nōn ille, satum quō tē mentīris, Achillēs
541 tālis in hoste fuit Priamō; sed iūra fidemque

Quaestiōnēs

1. Discuss Vergil's characterization of Priam and Hecuba in 506–25 and identify specifically the several means he uses to evoke a strong sense of pathos in this scene.

2. Comment on the placement of **saucius** in 529 and **concidit** in 532.

542 ērubēscō, ērubēscere, ērubuī, *to blush (at); to feel shame (over), respect.*

543 **Hectoreum:** for use of the adj. instead of a proper noun in the gen., see note on 1.273.

544 **imbellis, -is, -e,** *not suited to war, not ready to fight* (here *feeble*).
   *ictus, -ūs, m., *thrust, blow; wound; force, impact.*

545 *raucus, -a, -um, *hoarse; harsh-sounding, noisy, clanging.*

546 **umbō, umbōnis, m.,** *boss* (of a shield).
   summō . . . umbōne: *from the surface of . . . .*

547 **Referēs . . . ībis:** HYSTERON-PROTERON; the fut. tense vbs. here have virtually the force of an imper.

549 *dēgener, dēgeneris, *base-born; degenerate, contemptible.*
   mementō: imper. of **meminī.**

550 **altāria ad ipsa:** the intensive pron. conveys special emphasis here; for the impiety of the act, cf. 1.348–50 on Pygmalion's murder of Dido's husband Sychaeus.
   trementem: from old age, not fear, as Servius remarks.

551 **lāpsō, lapsāre,** *to lose one's footing, slip.*
   in multō lāpsantem sanguine: WORD-PICTURE.

552 **laevā:** sc. **manū.**

553 **capulus, -ī, m.,** *sword-handle, hilt.*
   tenus, prep. + abl. (regularly postpositive), *right up to, as far as.*

554 **fīnis:** usually m., but often f. in poetry.
   *exitus, -ūs, m., *departure, exit; end, death.*

555 **prōlābor, prōlābī, prōlāpsus sum,** *to slip/fall (forward); to give way, collapse.*

557 *rēgnātor, rēgnātōris, m., *ruler, governor.*
   rēgnātōrem: readers and editors sometimes debate whether this noun is in appos. to **illum** (Priam, 554) or instead to **Pergama** (556); the answer—as often in such instances of poetic ambiguity—is that it refers to each of them, as both king and kingdom are in this single moment dying.
   *truncus, -ī, m., *body* (of a man, excluding his head and limbs), *trunk, torso; trunk* (of a tree).

558 **āvulsumque . . . corpus:** in a powerful, masterful line, the strong and unusually positioned DIAERESIS following **caput** helps suggest the violence that Pyrrhus has wreaked upon Priam's body; the abrupt scene shift to the Trojan beach, with its image of the aged king's head and mutilated body, is a brilliant example of Vergil's cinematography; finally, the ringing ASSONANCE in **et sine nōmine** lends a grim musicality to the scene's closing moment with its fleeting glimpse of Priam's nameless corpse. Some scholars see in this image an allusion to the death of Pompey, who was slain in Egypt following his flight from Pharsalus, beheaded, and left on the shore as carrion.

542 supplicis ērubuit corpusque exsangue sepulcrō
543 reddidit Hectoreum mēque in mea rēgna remīsit.'
544 Sīc fātus senior tēlumque imbelle sine ictū
545 coniēcit, raucō quod prōtinus aere repulsum
546 et summō clipeī nēquīquam umbōne pependit.
547 Cui Pyrrhus: 'Referēs ergō haec et nūntius ībis
548 Pēlīdae genitōrī. Illī mea trīstia facta
549 dēgeneremque Neoptolemum nārrāre mementō.
550 Nunc morere.' Hoc dīcēns, altāria ad ipsa trementem
551 trāxit et in multō lāpsantem sanguine nātī,
552 implicuitque comam laevā, dextrāque coruscum
553 extulit ac laterī capulō tenus abdidit ēnsem.
554 Haec fīnis Priamī fātōrum, hic exitus illum
555 sorte tulit, Trōiam incēnsam et prōlāpsa videntem
556 Pergama, tot quondam populīs terrīsque superbum
557 rēgnātōrem Asiae. Iacet ingēns lītore truncus
558 āvulsumque umerīs caput et sine nōmine corpus.

Quaestiōnēs

1. Comment on the sound effects in 542.

2. Identify the device of word order employed in **implicuit . . . extulit** (552–53) and explain how it well suits the image Vergil is describing.

3. Identify several of the most effective elements Vergil employs in building his characterization of Pyrrhus in 526–53.

4. In what ways do lines 554–58 provide a fitting close to this episode?

Murder of Priam
Black-figure amphora
520–510 B.C.
Vulci, Italy
Louvre
Paris, France

559 **At . . . horror:** a highly effective one-line transition, with its spondaic rhythms, the halting monosyllables at the start, conflict of ictus and accent, the foreboding assonance of the **um** syllables (each of the three under the ictus), and the grim subj. reserved to the end—all suggesting how Aeneas is at last shocked back into his senses.

   circumstō, circumstāre, circumstetī, *to stand around, surround, encompass.*

560 **subiit . . . subiit (562):** the vb., repeated for emphasis, is commonly employed to suggest a mental image.

561 **aequaevus, -a, -um,** *of the same age, of like age.*

   aequaevum . . . vulnere vīdī / vītam (562): the airy ALLITERATION of **v** is perhaps meant to suggest the old man's gasping for his last breath.

562 **exhālō (1),** *to exhale, breathe out;* + **vītam,** *to expire, die.*

   *Creūsa, -ae, f., Creusa (a daughter of Priam and Hecuba, Aeneas' wife and mother of Iulus/Ascanius).

   Creūsa / . . . Iūlī (563): Creusa is mentioned here for the first time in the book; both names are delayed to line's end to build suspense.

564 **cōpia, -ae, f.,** *supply, abundance; body of men, band, (military) force; opportunity, freedom.*

565 *dēserō, dēserere, dēseruī, dēsertus, *to leave (behind), abandon.*

   saltus, -ūs, m., *jump, leap.*

567 **[Iamque . . . ferēbar] (588):** These lines are preserved by the fourth-cent. commentator Servius, who says they were genuine but had been excised by Vergil's first editors (Varius and Tucca), and do not appear in any early mss. of the *Aeneid;* scholars variously regard them as authentic or as an interpolation.

   adeō: here *indeed,* intensifying **iam,** or with **ūnus,** *entirely (alone).*

   super . . . eram: TMESIS.

   Vestae: Vergil likely means us to see the irony in Helen, the quintessential adulteress, taking refuge in the temple of Vesta, goddess of hearth, home, and family.

568 **servantem . . . latentem:** the two partics. FRAME the line, a favorite Vergilian device.

569 *Tyndaris, Tyndaridis,* acc. **Tyndarida,** f., *daughter of Tyndareus (king of Sparta and husband of Leda), Helen.*

   clāra: some editors accept the conjectured reading **clāram.**

570 **errantī . . . ferentī:** sc. **mihi;** for the FRAMING, see note on 568. Aeneas has been moving about on the rooftop (he only comes down at line 632), surveying the palace area.

571 **sibi:** with **īnfestōs** (DAT. WITH ADJS.).

   īnfestōs . . . Teucrōs: cf. the arrangement of **tacitam . . . latentem** (568); Helen's kidnapping by Paris and consort with him in Troy had of course precipitated the Trojan war and enraged parties on both sides, not least her husband Menelaus.

The assault on the royal family reminds Aeneas at last of his own
aged father Anchises, his wife Creusa, and their young son Iulus

559   "At mē tum prīmum saevus circumstetit horror.
560 Obstipuī; subiit cārī genitōris imāgō,
561 ut rēgem aequaevum crūdēlī vulnere vīdī
562 vītam exhālantem; subiit dēserta Creūsa
563 et dīrepta domus et parvī cāsus Iūlī.
564 Respiciō et quae sit mē circum cōpia lūstrō.
565 Dēseruēre omnēs dēfessī, et corpora saltū
566 ad terram mīsēre aut ignibus aegra dedēre.

Aeneas, his comrades gone, suddenly sees Helen and in a fit
of rage considers killing her and avenging his countrymen

567   "[Iamque adeō super ūnus eram, cum līmina Vestae
568 servantem et tacitam sēcrētā in sēde latentem
569 Tyndarida aspiciō; dant clāra incendia lūcem
570 errantī passimque oculōs per cūncta ferentī.
571 Illa sibi īnfestōs ēversa ob Pergama Teucrōs

Quaestiōnēs

1. Comment on the scansion of **domus** (563).

2. Recall that throughout the lengthy narrative of 458–566 Aeneas has been observing the action from a rooftop of Priam's palace complex, standing high above the scene, watching the Greeks' assault, and even somehow witnessing, at an altar deep inside the palace, Pyrrhus' butchery of the Trojan prince Polites before his parents' eyes and then his savage beheading of Priam himself. What is curious about Aeneas' passivity here? Why does Vergil have him play this spectator's role? What dramatic and even cinematographic functions are served? How might you film this scene if you were a motion picture director?

3. Lines 559–66 serve as a transitional passage, marking the end of the book's second act, the destruction of Troy, and an introduction to the third and final act, Aeneas' rescue of his family. How are the lines particularly effective in this regard?

573 **praemetuō, praemetuere, praemetuī,** *to fear beforehand, to be apprehensive over.*

575 **exārdēscō, exārdēscere, exārsī,** *to catch fire, blaze/flare up.*

576 **ulcīscī:** with **īra** (575), *a rage to . . . .*

    scelerātās . . . poenās: the adj. is best viewed as a TRANSFERRED EPITHET, applying logically to Helen herself and meaning, with **poenās,** *penalties for her criminal acts* (cf. **merentēs / . . . poenās** 585–86 and note); some readers take the phrase to mean something like *guilty retribution,* suggesting Aeneas' own recognition that killing a woman, even Helen, would have been a criminal act, but this seems out of balance with **ulcīscī patriam** and a mistaken anticipation of 583–85.

577 ***scīlicet,** adv., *naturally, surely;* often ironic or indignant, *to be sure, doubtless, surely not.*

    Scīlicet . . . meōrum (587): a soliloquy in which Aeneas, as he tells his story to Dido, recalls his thoughts at the moment of seeing Helen.

    haec: i.e., Helen.

    Sparta, -ae, f., *Sparta* (a major city in the Greek Peloponnese, home of Helen and Menelaus).

578 ***pariō, parere, peperī, partus,** *to give birth to; to bring forth, produce; to create, procure, obtain, win.*

    ***triumphus, -ī,** m., *triumphal procession; triumph, victory.*

579 ***coniugium, -ī,** n., *marriage; husband, wife.*

581 ***occidō, occidere, occidī, occāsus,** *to fall, collapse (in the way); to die.*

    Occiderit . . . lītus (582): the three sents. form a dramatic TRICOLON CRESCENS.

582 **sūdō** (1), *to sweat; to become wet, be soaked.*

583 **etsī,** conj., *even if, although.*

584 **nec habet:** this is the reading of several late mss. and is accepted by a number of scholars; the earliest extant reading, preserved in Servius and accepted by some editors, is **habet haec,** which if correct would have to be taken with the unusually delayed **tamen** in the next line. Conceivably Vergil may have written **habet nec,** as in many scripts **nec** and **haec** could be easily confused.

585 ***exstinguō, exstinguere, exstīnxī, exstīnctus,** *to extinguish, put out; to kill; to obliterate, annihilate.*

    exstīnxisse . . . sūmpsisse: with **laudābor** (586), I *shall be praised for having . . .;* the hissing **ss** ALLITERATION here, which continues through **explēsse** in 586 and **satiāsse** in 587, is likely meant to suggest Aeneas' violent hatred of Helen.

    nefās: Helen is viewed as evil incarnate, the very personification of sacrilege.

    sūmpsisse merentēs / . . . poenās (586): for the TRANSFERRED EPITHET and the construction in general, cf. **scelerātās sūmere poenās** (576); some readers take this near repetition as evidence that the passage is not authentic, but this and other infelicities in the Helen episode may simply show the same lack of polish that occasionally turns up elsewhere in what was, after all, an unfinished work.

572 et Danaum poenam et dēsertī coniugis īrās
573 praemetuēns, Trōiae et patriae commūnis Erīnys,
574 abdiderat sēsē atque ārīs invīsa sedēbat.
575 Exārsēre ignēs animō; subit īra cadentem
576 ulcīscī patriam et scelerātās sūmere poenās.
577 'Scīlicet haec Spartam incolumis patriāsque Mycēnās
578 aspiciet, partōque ībit rēgīna triumphō?
579 Coniugiumque domumque patrēs nātōsque vidēbit,
580 Īliadum turbā et Phrygiīs comitāta ministrīs?
581 Occiderit ferrō Priamus? Trōia ārserit ignī?
582 Dardanium totiēns sūdārit sanguine lītus?
583 Nōn ita. Namque etsī nūllum memorābile nōmen
584 fēmineā in poenā est nec habet victōria laudem,
585 exstīnxisse nefās tamen et sūmpsisse merentēs

"Venus Presenting Helen to Paris," Gavin Hamilton (1723–98)
Museo di Roma, Rome, Italy

586 **explēsse:** = **explēvisse**, with **animum . . . iuvābit**, *it will be a pleasure to have filled . . . .*

587 **ultrīx, ultrīcis**, f. adj., *that exacts revenge, avenging.*

   ultrīcis flammae: the gen. is often employed with words indicating fullness or plenty (cf. **implentur . . . Bacchī** 1.215), here with **explēsse**, *to have filled . . . with an avenging . . .*; Servius' reading, **ultrīcis fāmam**, is inexplicable and most editions accept the reading here, found in the same late mss. mentioned above in the note on line 584.

   satiō (1), *to satisfy.*

588 **furiātā mente:** the phrase occurs at the same metrical position in 407 above.

590 **refulsit:** the same vb. is used of Venus at 1.402 above.

591 **cōnfiteor, cōnfitērī, cōnfessus sum,** *to admit, confess; to reveal (oneself as), disclose, reveal by one's appearance.*

   quālis . . . quanta (592): i.e., with the same appearance and stature; in order not to overwhelm them, the gods ordinarily appeared to mortals in a disguised or more muted form than they did in one another's presence.

592 ***caelicola, -ae,** m./f., *inhabitant of heaven, heaven-dweller, god, goddess.*

   prehēnsum: sc. **mē.**

594 **quis:** here, as often., the interrog. pron. functions as an adj.

595 **quōnam,** adv., *to what place, where (on earth/in the world).*

   nostrī: i.e., Venus and Anchises, Aeneas' parents; OBJ. GEN.

597 **līqueris:** subjunct. in an IND. QUEST. (the second **i** is shortened by SYSTOLE).

   superet: here *survives.*

   coniūnxne: **-ne,** *whether,* introduces another IND. QUEST.; in prose the suffix would have been attached to the first word in the cl. (**superet**), but its unusually delayed position here serves to underscore Aeneas' obligation to his wife.

598 **Quōs omnēs:** obj. of **circum** in 599 (ANASTROPHE).

599 **resistat, / . . . tulerint . . . hauserit (600):** the pres. and perf. subjuncts. are employed instead of the impf. and plpf. to add vividness and immediacy to the PRES. CONTRARY-TO-FACT CONDITION; or **tulerint** and **hauserit** are perhaps to be read as fut. perf. in a MIXED FUT. CONDITION.

600 **hauserit:** sc. **sanguinem eōrum.**

601 **tibi:** DAT. OF REF., *I tell you, I assure you.*

   Lacaena, -ae, f. adj., *Laconian, of Laconia* (the district of the Greek Peloponnese where Sparta was located).

602 **culpātus, -a, -um,** *worthy of censure, reprehensible, guilty.*

   inclēmentia, -ae, f., *unkindness, harshness, severity.*

   dīvum inclēmentia, dīvum: sc. **sed** as the connective to **nōn . . . Paris** (601–02); the ASYNDETON further intensifies the highly emotional ANAPHORA in **dīvum . . . dīvum.**

603 **sternit . . . ā culmine Trōiam:** cf. **ruit altō ā culmine Trōia** (290).

586 laudābor poenās, animumque explēsse iuvābit
587 ultrīcis flammae et cinerēs satiāsse meōrum.'

*Venus suddenly appears to Aeneas, reminds him of his
duty to rescue his family, and miraculously reveals to
his vision the gods themselves, directly assisting the
Greeks in Troy's complete and inevitable annihilation*

588 "Tālia iactābam et furiātā mente ferēbar,]
589 cum mihi sē, nōn ante oculīs tam clāra, videndam
590 obtulit et pūrā per noctem in lūce refulsit
591 alma parēns, cōnfessa deam quālisque vidērī
592 caelicolīs et quanta solet, dextrāque prehēnsum
593 continuit roseōque haec īnsuper addidit ōre:
594 "'Nāte, quis indomitās tantus dolor excitat īrās?
595 Quid furis? Aut quōnam nostrī tibi cūra recessit?
596 Nōn prius aspiciēs ubi fessum aetāte parentem
597 līqueris Anchīsēn, superet coniūnxne Creūsa
598 Ascaniusque puer? Quōs omnēs undique Grāiae
599 circum errant aciēs et, nī mea cūra resistat,
600 iam flammae tulerint inimīcus et hauserit ēnsis.
601 Nōn tibi Tyndaridis faciēs invīsa Lacaenae
602 culpātusve Paris, dīvum inclēmentia, dīvum,
603 hās ēvertit opēs sternitque ā culmine Trōiam.

Quaestiōnēs

1. What do you see as the most compelling arguments for, or against, accepting the authenticity of lines 567–88?

2. How are Vergil's descriptions of Venus in 1.402–05 and here at 589–93 comparable?

604 **omnem . . . nūbem (606):** a WORD-PICTURE, for the phrase here lit. surrounds the poet's description of Aeneas' clouded vision; the image is extended in the elaborate ABCCBA CHIASMUS of **obducta tuentī / mortālis . . . vīsūs tibi . . . ūmida.**

obdūcō, obdūcere, obdūxī, obductus, *to lead toward/against; to cover* (with clouds, darkness).

605 **hebetō (1),** *to make blunt; to make dim, weak.*

606 **cālīgō, cālīgāre,** *to be misty/cloudy; to make cloudy.*

608 **disiectās . . . / saxa (609):** conflict of ictus and accent and the juncture **saxīs / saxa** help suggest the violence of the scene Venus describes to her son, an "apocalypse of terror," as R.G. Austin terms it.

609 **undō (1),** *to rise in waves, surge; to billow, eddy.*

610 **mūrōs magnōque ēmōta:** the ALLITERATION is perhaps meant to suggest the rumbling sound of the city's walls as Neptune, in his role as god of earthquakes, tears them from their foundations; the line's heavy spondees and conflict of ictus and accent add to the effect. The god had been cheated of offerings promised him by Troy's founder Laomedon when he had helped Apollo construct its walls, and the more recent offense to his priest Laocoön (see note on 201 above) gave him further cause for his wrath.

611 **quatiō, quatere, quassus,** *to move vigorously back and forth; to shake.*

612 **Scaeus, -a, -um,** *Scaean* (with **portae,** the westward gates of Troy).

616 **īnsideō, īnsidēre, īnsēdī, īnsessus,** *to sit, be seated at, settle on.*

Pallas (615) / īnsēdit: Athena/Minerva, protectress of citadels and revered by the Trojans, here joins the Greeks in besieging Troy's stronghold.

effulgeō, effulgēre, effulsī, *to shine/blaze forth, flash, gleam.*

Gorgō, Gorgonis, f., *Gorgon, Medusa* (a monster with snakes for hair, who could turn mortals to stone with her gaze—her image appeared on Athena's shield).

Gorgone saeva: some editors take **saeva** to be abl. (in this position the final **a** is ANCEPS, i.e., it could be long or short), functioning with **Gorgone** as ABL. OF MEANS, but it is more likely nom., making the abl./nom. phrase parallel to **nimbō effulgēns.**

618 ***Dardanus, -a, -um,** *Dardanian, of Dardanus* (son of Zeus and Electra, founder of Dardania in the Troad, and ancestor of Priam), *Trojan.*

suscitō (1), *to arouse, stir up.*

619 **Ēripe:** here *hasten;* cf. Hector's admonition in 289.

fugam fīnem: the line's CHIASTIC arrangement serves to juxtapose these key ALLITERATIVE nouns.

620 **nusquam aberō:** the double negative lends emphasis to Venus' promise.

līmine: this important thematic word (see discussion quest. on 242–43) appears again emphatically positioned, here closing out Venus' speech, the purpose of which is in fact to encourage Aeneas' passage from one threshold—another act of aggression, against a woman this time, who herself had taken refuge at the **līmina Vestae (567)**—and toward the threshold of his father's home (cf. **līmina 634**), from hostility and violence to rescue of family and flight.

621 **spissus, -a, -um,** *thick, dense.*

604 Aspice—namque omnem, quae nunc obducta tuentī
605 mortālēs hebetat vīsūs tibi et ūmida circum
606 cālīgat, nūbem ēripiam; tū nē qua parentis
607 iussa timē neu praeceptīs pārēre recūsā—
608 hīc, ubi disiectās mōlēs āvulsaque saxīs
609 saxa vidēs, mixtōque undantem pulvere fūmum,
610 Neptūnus mūrōs magnōque ēmōta tridentī
611 fundāmenta quatit totamque ā sēdibus urbem
612 ēruit. Hīc Iūnō Scaeās saevissima portās
613 prīma tenet sociumque furēns ā nāvibus agmen,
614 ferrō accīncta, vocat.
615 Iam summās arcēs Trītōnia, respice, Pallas
616 īnsēdit, nimbō effulgēns et Gorgone saeva.
617 Ipse pater Danaīs animōs vīrēsque secundās
618 sufficit, ipse deōs in Dardana suscitat arma.
619 Ēripe, nāte, fugam fīnemque impōne labōrī;
620 nusquam aberō et tūtum patriō tē līmine sistam.'
621 Dīxerat et spissīs noctis sē condidit umbrīs.

Quaestiōnēs

1. Comment on the word order in **mixtō . . . fūmum** (609).

2. What is the effect of the enjambement of **ēruit** (612) and the diaeresis following?

3. Contrast Neptune's actions in 608–12 with those in 1.124–47. In what ways are the characterizations consistent, and in what ways inconsistent? Why does Vergil present him in one instance taking actions that will ultimately aid the Trojans and in another wreaking destruction upon their city?

4. Discuss the highly cinematographic nature of the narrative in 604–20. In what specific ways does the poet prompt us to visualize the action (consider his choice of verbs, use of anaphora, etc.), and how would you as a film director photograph the scene?

5. Compare Venus' remarks to her son in 1.387–401 with her speech here in lines 594–620; in what respects do the two speeches serve a similar function? Analyze the specific arguments Venus employs here to influence Aeneas' actions.

6. Compare Venus' speech in 594–620 with Hector's warning to Aeneas in 289–95; how are we meant to respond to the fact that Aeneas has to be reminded again of his duty to gods and family and of the necessity of flight?

622 **Appārent . . . deum** (623): Vergil, the consummate dramatist, closes this scene with a haunting, apocalyptic image of the gods, colossal and terror-inspiring, presiding over the once-mighty kingdom's utter ruin; the ALLITERATION in 623 adds a grim musicality to the closing moment.

625 **Neptūnius, -a, -um**, *of Neptune, Neptune's* (applied to Troy here because of the god's role in both the founding, and the destruction, of the city; see note on line 610).

626 *ornus, -ī, f., *flowering ash (tree).*

    summīs . . . ornum: the INTERLOCKED WORD ORDER suspensefully delays the nouns to line's end, building anticipation of the nature of the SIMILE.

627 **cum:** with **velutī** (626), *just as when.*

    accīdō, accīdere, accīdī, accīsus, *to cut nearly through, cut/hack at.*

628 **agricola, -ae,** m., *farmer.*

    certātim, adv., *in competition, with rivalry.*

    usque, adv., *continuously, all the time* (here with **dōnec** 630).

    minātur: i.e., to fall.

629 **comam:** here, of course, the tree's leafy boughs; ACC. OF SPECIFICATION (for this Greek construction, see note on 1.228).

    *concutiō, concutere, concussī, concussus,** *to cause to vibrate, shake, agitate; to strike; to shake (emotionally), distress, upset.*

    nūtō (1), *to nod (one's head); to bend forward/downward, sway.*

630 **suprēmum,** adv., *for the last time, one last time.*

631 **congemō, congemere, congemuī, congemitus,** *to cry out in grief/pain, groan, moan.*

632 **Dēscendō:** Aeneas at last comes down from the palace rooftop, where he has been since the scene change in line 458.

    deō: m. (vs. **deā**) as a ref. to divinity in general, though its specific application is to Venus.

    flammam . . . recēdunt (633): not only is the arrangement of **dant tēla . . . flammaeque recēdunt** CHIASTIC, but so also is **flammam . . . hostēs / . . . tēla . . . flammae.**

634 **perventum:** sc. **erat;** impers. pass., *it had been arrived = I had arrived.*

    līmina: see note on **līmine** (620).

635 **tollere:** Aeneas would have to carry Anchises, since his father was lame (see note on 648–49).

> Yes, there were horrors hinted in that night.
> I thought a veil was parted from my eyes
> And thought I saw our gods, of monstrous size,
> Splash barefoot in our blood, and with delight.
>
>   *From A.E. Stallings, "Crazy to Hear the Tale Again (The Fall of Troy)"*

622 Appārent dīrae faciēs inimīcaque Trōiae

623 nūmina magna deum.

Aeneas pauses, gazing at the city as it collapses into flames—like
the fall of a towering mountain ash—then climbs down from the
palace rooftop and makes his way to his father's house

624   "Tum vērō omne mihī vīsum cōnsīdere in ignēs

625 Īlium et ex īmō vertī Neptūnia Trōia:

626 ac velutī summīs antīquam in montibus ornum

627 cum ferrō accīsam crēbrīsque bipennibus īnstant

628 ēruere agricolae certātim, illa usque minātur

629 et tremefacta comam concussō vertice nūtat,

630 vulneribus dōnec paulātim ēvicta suprēmum

631 congemuit trāxitque iugīs āvulsa ruīnam.

632 Dēscendō ac, dūcente deō, flammam inter et hostēs

633 expedior: dant tēla locum flammaeque recēdunt.

When Aeneas reaches his ancestral home, he finds
his aged father Anchises unwilling to leave

634   "Atque ubi iam patriae perventum ad līmina sēdis

635 antīquāsque domōs, genitor, quem tollere in altōs

Quaestiōnēs

1. What poetic device is seen in **ferrō . . . crēbrīsque bipennibus** (627)?

2. What is the most striking sound effect in 629, and how is it appropriate to the action described?

3. What figure of speech does Vergil employ in 626–31? In what very specific ways is the assault on the tree like the assault on Troy? Identify the several words Vergil has chosen in order to personify the tree; what is the emotional effect of the personification, and in what ways are we prompted to think not only of Troy but of the palace, the royal family, and Priam in particular? Finally, compare the description in Homer *Iliad* 4.482f.; which of the two scenes is more effective?

637 *abnegō (1), *to refuse, decline.*
    prōdūcō, prōdūcere, prōdūxī, prōductus, to lead forth, produce; to prolong,
        extend.
638 *exsilium, -ī,* n., *exile, banishment.*
    quibus: DAT. OF POSSESSION; SC. **est.**
    integer, -gra, -grum, *untouched, fresh.*
    integer aevī: i.e., *young;* **aevī** is GEN. OF SPECIFICATION.
639 *solidus, -a, -um,* *made of the same material throughout, solid; firm, unyielding.*
    solidae . . . vīrēs: the near-perfect symmetry of the phrase (CHIASMUS) suits the
        image of the sturdy strength of youth.
641 **Mē:** subj. of **dūcere,** here = **prōdūcere** (cf. 637).
642 **super:** adv. common with **satis,** *more (than enough).*
    ūna: here a rare pl. with the poetic pl. **excidia** (643); Troy had previously been
        sacked by Hercules, after he, like Neptune, had been cheated by Priam's father
        Laomedon.
643 **superāvimus:** for the sense here, + dat., cf. **superet** (597).
644 **positum:** = **dēpositum,** i.e., *laid out, laid to rest* (like a corpse).
    adfor, adfārī, adfātus sum, to speak to, address.
    adfātī: modifying the voc. **vōs,** understood from 638 and 640; in this context,
        where Anchises pictures himself as already a corpse, the allusion is to the
        words of farewell traditionally rendered to the dead.
645 **manū:** i.e., by taking arms against the enemy, like his son Aeneas and as even the
        aged Priam had attempted to do.
    miserēbitur: i.e., and kill him.
646 **iactūra, -ae,** f., *casting off; loss, deprivation.*
    iactūra sepulcrī: proper burial was of extreme importance in the ancient world,
        but Anchises is willing to sacrifice even this final rite.
647 **prīdem,** adv., *previously, in the past;* with **iam,** *long ago, for a long time now.*
648 **dēmoror, -ārī, -ātus sum,** *to delay, keep waiting.*
    Iam (647) **. . . dēmoror:** with **iam** Lat. regularly uses a pres. where Eng. would
        employ the perf., *for a long time now* I *have been . . . .*
    quō: sc. **tempore.**
    mē . . . ignī (649): Jupiter struck and crippled Anchises with a thunderbolt when
        he was a young man for boasting that he had made love to Venus and that she
        was the mother of his son.
649 *adflō (1),* *to emit air, breathe on/upon; to inspire.*
650 **perstō, perstāre, perstitī, perstātus,** *to remain standing, stand firm.*
651 **effūsī:** here *dissolved* or *drenched.*
652 **nē . . . vellet** (653): JUSSIVE NOUN CL./IND. COMMAND, after the vb. of pleading
        implied in **lacrimīs** (651), *overwhelmed with tears, (begging) that . . . .*
    vertere: = **ēvertere.**
653 **incumbere:** i.e., *to add his own weight to.*

636 optābam prīmum montēs prīmumque petēbam,

637 abnegat excīsā vītam prōdūcere Trōiā

638 exsiliumque patī. 'Vōs ō, quibus integer aevī

639 sanguis,' ait, 'solidaeque suō stant rōbore vīrēs,

640 vōs agitāte fugam.

641 Mē sī caelicolae voluissent dūcere vītam,

642 hās mihi servāssent sēdēs. Satis ūna superque

643 vīdimus excidia et captae superāvimus urbī.

644 Sīc, ō sīc positum adfātī discēdite corpus.

645 Ipse manū mortem inveniam; miserēbitur hostis

646 exuviāsque petet. Facilis iactūra sepulcrī.

647 Iam prīdem invīsus dīvīs et inūtilis annōs

648 dēmoror, ex quō mē dīvum pater atque hominum rēx

649 fulminis adflāvit ventīs et contigit ignī.'

Despite tearful appeals from all the family, Anchises persists
in his refusal to flee, and so Aeneas determines to
rush back into battle against the Greeks

650   "Tālia perstābat memorāns fīxusque manēbat.

651 Nōs contrā effūsī lacrimīs, coniūnxque Creūsa

652 Ascaniusque omnisque domus, nē vertere sēcum

653 cūncta pater fātōque urgentī incumbere vellet.

Quaestiōnēs

1. Identify the several effects of meter, sound, word choice, and arrangement that make verse 636 so remarkable.

2. What is the term for the device exemplified in **vōs ō . . . vōs** (638–40) and **sīc, ō sīc** (644) and what is the intended effect?

3. Compare Vergil's characterization of Anchises through his speech in 638–49 with that of Priam in 506–11 and 533–46. How and why does the poet connect the two scenes? Finally, what traits do father and son, Anchises and Aeneas, appear to have in common?

654 **Abnegat:** in the same metrical position at 637.

inceptō . . . sēdibus: a ZEUGMA with **haeret.**

655 **Rūrsus . . . miserrimus:** the roaring ALLITERATION of **r** (which recurs eight times) helps suggest the violence of Aeneas' emotions at this moment.

659 **nihil . . . relinquī:** acc. + inf. with **placet,** *it is pleasing that . . ..*

660 **sedet:** *is set/settled.*

hoc: for the long syllable, though the vowel is short, see note on 60 and cf. 664 below.

663 **nātum . . . patris, patrem . . . ārās:** the key words, both objs. of **quī obtruncat,** are arranged CHIASTICALLY to help emphasize the savagery of Pyrrhus' acts; note the varied long/short scansion of **pa/tris, pat/rem,** which only rarely occurs within a single line.

obtruncō (1), *to cut down, slay, butcher.*

664 **Hoc erat . . . quod:** freely, *was this (the reason) why.*

alma parēns: an APOSTROPHE to his mother, Venus; cf. 591.

per tēla, per ignēs: cf. **per tēla, per hostēs** (358 and 527).

665 **mediīs . . . penetrālibus:** WORD-PICTURE; cf. the variation in 508 (**medium in penetrālibus hostem**).

667 **alterum . . . mactātōs: alterum,** *the one,* is sg. to ref. each of Aeneas' family members individually, whereas **mactātōs** is pl. to refer to the group.

669 **revīsam:** sc. **ut;** the conj. introducing a JUSSIVE NOUN CL./IND. COMMAND is often omitted in poetry. In prose **sinō** ordinarily takes acc. + inf.

670 **Numquam:** an intensive colloquialism for **nōn.**

*inultus, -a, -um, *without recompense for injury, unavenged.*

671 **accingor:** with **ferrō,** as often, reflex.; freely, *I strap on my sword.*

sinistram: sc. **manum,** obj. of both **īnsertābam** and **aptāns** (672).

672 **īnsertō (1),** *to thrust in, insert.*

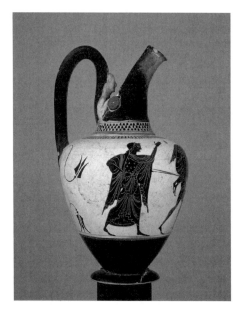

Creusa
Detail from black-figure oinochoe
Southern Italy
520–510 B.C.
Louvre
Paris, France

654 Abnegat inceptōque et sēdibus haeret in īsdem.

655 Rūrsus in arma feror mortemque miserrimus optō.

656 Nam quod cōnsilium aut quae iam fortūna dabātur?

657 'Mēne efferre pedem, genitor, tē posse relictō

658 spērāstī tantumque nefās patriō excidit ōre?

659 Sī nihil ex tantā superīs placet urbe relinquī,

660 et sedet hoc animō, peritūraeque addere Trōiae

661 tēque tuōsque iuvat, patet istī iānua lētō,

662 iamque aderit multō Priamī dē sanguine Pyrrhus,

663 nātum ante ōra patris, patrem quī obtruncat ad ārās.

664 Hoc erat, alma parēns, quod mē per tēla, per ignēs

665 ēripis, ut mediīs hostem in penetrālibus utque

666 Ascanium patremque meum iūxtāque Creūsam

667 alterum in alterius mactātōs sanguine cernam?

668 Arma, virī, ferte arma; vocat lūx ultima victōs.

669 Reddite mē Danaīs; sinite īnstaurāta revīsam

670 proelia. Numquam omnēs hodiē moriēmur inultī.'

As Aeneas takes up his armor, Creusa begs him to take her
and Iulus along with him into battle or else to remain
with them and defend his father's house

671   "Hinc ferrō accingor rūrsus clipeōque sinistram

672   īnsertābam aptāns mēque extrā tēcta ferēbam.

Quaestiōnēs

1. The repetition of **abnegat** from line 637 in the same metrical position at 654 produces a kind of refrain; what is the effect both of this refrain and of the three single verse sentences in 654–56?

2. What is the combined effect of the anaphora and asyndeton in 664 and the enjambement in 665?

3. What stylistic features make line 668 particularly effective?

4. How do you respond—how does Vergil intend us to respond—to Aeneas' impulse once again to rush to arms in 655–70, despite the admonitions he has received from Hector's shade and more recently from his mother?

675 **in omnia:** i.e., to face everything, to risk all perils.

676 **expertus:** i.e., based on his experience.

677 **tūtor, -ārī, -ātus sum,** *to protect, watch over* (here imper.).

678 **quondam:** Creusa poignantly anticipates the loss of her beloved.

    relinquor: 1st pers. sg. to agree with the understood subj. **ego,** though **Iūlus**
        (677) and **pater** are also subjs.

679 **vōciferōr, -ārī, -ātus sum,** *to cry out, shout.*

    ***repleō, replēre, replēvī, replētus,** *to replenish, fill (up).*

682 **levis:** with **apex** (683).

683 **fundere . . . / lambere . . . pāscī (684):** the three infs., all emphatically
        positioned, depend on **vīsus (est)** in 682.

   ***apex, apicis,** m., *crown, diadem; top, peak; point of flame.*

   innoxius, -a, -um, *harmless, innocuous.*

684 **flamma:** subj., along with **apex** (683), of **vīsus (est)** in 682.

685 ***trepidō (1),** *to panic; to rush around; to tremble.*

    flagrō (1), *to be on fire, burn.*

686 **restinguō, restinguere, restīnxī, restīnctus,** *to extinguish, put out, quench.*

    trepidāre . . . (685) / excutere . . . restinguere: HIST. INFS., employed here, as
        regularly, for lively narration of quick, successive actions; the subj. (**nōs**) is
        nom., and the infs. should be translated as impf. indic.

688 **palmās . . . tetendit:** for the gesture of prayer, cf. 1.93.

689 ***prex, precis,** f., *entreaty, prayer.*

690 **hoc tantum:** sc. something like **rogō** or **petō.**

691 **auxilium:** there is some evidence that **augurium,** *an augury,* may be the correct
        reading here; Anchises prays for a second omen (what the Romans called
        technically an **augurium impetrātīvum,** sent as a response to a prayer) to
        confirm the first (an **augurium oblātīvum,** an omen offered spontaneously
        by the gods).

    firmō (1), *to reinforce, strengthen; to confirm.*

Aeneas attended by a doctor,
between Venus and Iulus
Fresco from Casa di Sirico
Pompeii, 1st cent. C.E.
Museo Archeologico Nazionale
Naples, Italy

673 Ecce autem complexa pedēs in līmine coniūnx
674 haerēbat parvumque patrī tendēbat Iūlum:
675 'Sī peritūrus abīs, et nōs rape in omnia tēcum;
676 sīn aliquam expertus sūmptīs spem pōnis in armīs,
677 hanc prīmum tūtāre domum. Cui parvus Iūlus,
678 cui pater et coniūnx quondam tua dicta relinquor?'

Suddenly an omen appears, a fiery light around Iulus' head

679   "Tālia vōciferāns, gemitū tēctum omne replēbat,
680 cum subitum dictūque oritur mīrābile mōnstrum.
681 Namque manūs inter maestōrumque ōra parentum,
682 ecce, levis summō dē vertice vīsus Iūlī
683 fundere lūmen apex, tāctūque innoxia mollēs
684 lambere flamma comās et circum tempora pāscī.
685 Nōs pavidī trepidāre metū crīnemque flagrantem
686 excutere et sānctōs restinguere fontibus ignēs.
687 At pater Anchīsēs oculōs ad sīdera laetus
688 extulit et caelō palmās cum vōce tetendit:
689 'Iuppiter omnipotēns, precibus sī flecteris ūllīs,
690 aspice nōs, hoc tantum, et sī pietāte merēmur,
691 dā deinde auxilium, pater, atque haec ōmina firmā.'

Quaestiō

How is the interlocked word order in 681 appropriate to the scene of Iulus and his parents that Vergil wants us to imagine?

692 **fātus erat . . . / intonuit (693):** for the PARATAXIS, see note on 172 above.

693 **intonuit:** here, as often, impers. + acc., *it thundered on* . . ..
    laevum: i.e., **ad laevum;** thunder and other omens appearing to one's lefthand side were often considered favorable by the Romans (though unfavorable by the Greeks).

694 **stēlla, -ae,** f., *star* (here a meteor or "shooting star").
    facem: here *a fiery tail.*

695 **Illam . . . clāram (696):** subj. of **condere (696).**

696 **Īdaeus, -a, -um,** *of Mt. Ida* (a mountain range southeast of Troy, site of the judgment of Paris and sacred to the goddess Cybele).

697 **signantem . . . viās:** the meteor pointed the way to safety in the forests of Mt. Ida, where at the close of the book (line 804) Aeneas does in fact lead his family and followers.
    *****līmes, līmitis,** m., *strip of land* (marking a boundary), *boundary marker/stone; lane, path, course; line, track, trail* (here the meteor's path, vs. the **sulcus,** its trail).

698 **lātē . . . loca:** cf. 495.
    circum: here adv.
    sulphur, sulphuris, n., *sulphur, brimstone.*
    fūmō (1), *to emit fumes, smoke.*

699 **Hīc:** here, as often, temporal, *hereupon, then.*
    victus: i.e., convinced by the omens.

701 **Iam, iam:** cf. **iam iamque (530).**

703 **nūmine:** here *protection.*

705 **clārior . . . / audītur (706):** i.e., the roar of the fire, and its brilliance, became more intense.

707 **cervīcī:** here *shoulders.*
    impōnere: pass. imper. (not inf.), with reflex. force.

708 **subībō:** sc. **tibi.**
    gravō (1), *to make heavy, load, weigh down.*

709 **quōcumque,** adv., *wherever, in whatever way, however* (here split by TMESIS).
    perīclum: = **perīculum** (SYNCOPE).

711 **servet vēstīgia:** i.e., follow.

712 **famulus, -ī,** m., *servant, attendant.*
    *****advertō, advertere, advertī, adversus,** *to turn (toward); to pay attention, heed.*
    advertite: (ea) **quae dīcam** is the dir. obj. and **animīs** either dat. or abl.

*Jupiter sends another portent, a shooting star, and Anchises is
convinced to join Aeneas and his family in flight from the city*

692   "Vix ea fātus erat senior, subitōque fragōre
693   intonuit laevum, et dē caelō lāpsa per umbrās
694   stēlla, facem dūcēns, multā cum lūce cucurrit.
695   Illam summa super lābentem culmina tēctī
696   cernimus Īdaeā clāram sē condere silvā
697   signantemque viās; tum longō līmite sulcus
698   dat lūcem et lātē circum loca sulphure fūmant.
699   Hīc vērō victus genitor sē tollit ad aurās
700   adfāturque deōs et sānctum sīdus adōrat:
701   'Iam, iam nūlla mora est; sequor et quā dūcitis adsum,
702   dī patriī; servāte domum, servāte nepōtem.
703   Vestrum hoc augurium, vestrōque in nūmine Trōia est.
704   Cēdō equidem nec, nāte, tibī comes īre recūsō.'
705   Dīxerat ille, et iam per moenia clārior ignis
706   audītur, propiusque aestūs incendia volvunt.

*Aeneas takes Anchises on his shoulders, and with Iulus and Creusa
following, the family and attendants flee from the burning city*

707   "'Ergō age, cāre pater, cervīcī impōnere nostrae;
708   ipse subībō umerīs nec mē labor iste gravābit;
709   quō rēs cumque cadent, ūnum et commūne perīclum,
710   ūna salūs ambōbus erit. Mihi parvus Iūlus
711   sit comes, et longē servet vēstīgia coniūnx.
712   Vōs, famulī, quae dīcam animīs advertite vestrīs.

Quaestiōnēs

1. How does meter suit meaning in 692?

2. What device does Vergil employ repeatedly in 701–03 to convey the
   emotionality of Anchises' brief speech?

713 **ēgressīs:** lit., *for those having left,* i.e., *once you have left.*
　　*****tumulus, -ī,** m., *rounded hill, knoll, mound; burial mound, grave.*
　　vetustus, -a, -um, *ancient, old.*

714 **dēsertae:** probably a TRANSFERRED EPITHET, referring to the temple's remote
　　location outside the city (see 741–43 below) or to its abandonment due to the
　　war; or perhaps, as Servius suggests among other possibilities, there may be
　　an allusion to the goddess' "abandonment" by her daughter Proserpina, who
　　had been kidnapped by Pluto and taken to be his bride in the Underworld, an
　　interpretation supported somewhat by Vergil's ref. to the nearby cypress.
　　cupressus, -ī, f., *cypress (tree),* often associated with death and grieving.

716 **dīversō:** i.e., *different directions.*

717 **sacra . . . Penātēs:** the ritual objects and statuettes of the Penates spoken of by
　　Hector's phantom in 293 and brought by Panthus to Aeneas in 320.

718 **dīgredior, dīgredī, dīgressus sum,** *to go away/from, come/depart from, leave.*

719 **attrectō (1),** *to touch, handle.*
　　mē (718) . . . / attrectāre: with **nefās (est);** and sc. **Penātēs** as obj.
　　flūmine vīvō: i.e., fresh, running water, used for ritual cleansing.

720 *****abluō, abluere, abluī, ablūtus,** *to wash off/out; to wash clean, cleanse.*

721 **umerōs . . . colla:** for the construction, see note on **oculōs** (1.228).
　　subiecta: here *bowed.*

722 **īnsternō, īnsternere, īnstrāvī, īnstrātus,** *to spread on/over;* + abl., *to cover* (here
　　reflex.).
　　*****pellis, pellis,** f., *skin, hide.*
　　veste . . . pelle: HENDIADYS.

723 **dextrae sē . . . / implicuit (724):** i.e., he clasped his father's hand; the image
　　of Aeneas with his father on his shoulders, Iulus at his side, and Creusa
　　following behind, was well known in art even before Vergil's time and is
　　most familiar to us today (sans Creusa) in the famous sculpture by Bernini
　　pictured on the cover of this textbook.

724 **nōn:** with **aequīs.**
　　passus, -ūs, m., *step, pace, stride.*
　　nōn passīs aequīs: i.e., with shorter strides; a charming image, as little Iulus (a
　　young child at this point in the story) works hard to keep up with his father.

725 **Ferimur:** for this sense of **ferō** in the pass., see note on 498.
　　*****opācus, -a, -um,** *shady, darkened; dark, dim, gloomy.*
　　opāca locōrum: for **opāca loca;** this common poetic device, employing
　　substantive + gen. noun instead of attributive adj. + noun, focuses the
　　reader's attention visually on the attribute (here the darkness of the night)
　　more than on the obj. itself (cf. **angusta viārum** 332).

726 **dūdum,** adv., *of late, recently.*
　　movēbant: i.e., emotionally.

727 **exāmen, exāminis,** n., *swarm, colony* (of bees); *multitude, throng* (some editors
　　here read **ex agmine**).

713 Est urbe ēgressīs tumulus templumque vetustum
714 dēsertae Cereris, iuxtāque antīqua cupressus,
715 rēligiōne patrum multōs servāta per annōs;
716 hanc ex dīversō sēdem veniēmus in ūnam.
717 Tū, genitor, cape sacra manū patriōsque Penātēs;
718 mē bellō ē tantō dīgressum et caede recentī
719 attrectāre nefās, dōnec mē flūmine vīvō
720 abluerō.'
721   "Haec fātus, lātōs umerōs subiectaque colla
722 veste super fulvīque īnsternor pelle leōnis,
723 succēdōque onerī; dextrae sē parvus Iūlus
724 implicuit sequiturque patrem nōn passibus aequīs;
725 pōne subit coniūnx. Ferimur per opāca locōrum,
726 et mē, quem dūdum nōn ūlla iniecta movēbant
727 tēla neque adversō glomerātī exāmine Grāī,

"Aeneas Fleeing Troy"
Pompeo Batoni (1708–87)
Galleria Sabauda, Turin, Italy

728 **omnēs . . . omnis:** ANAPHORA and the ABCCBA CHIASMUS effectively emphasize Aeneas' anxious emotional state.

729 **suspēnsum . . . timentem:** with **mē** (726).

comitī: i.e., Iulus (see 711).

comitīque onerīque: use of POLYSYNDETON and positioning the two nouns so that the ictus falls on the **tī/rī** syllables accentuates the internal rhyme.

730 *__propinquō (1)__*, often + dat., *to draw near (to), approach*.

731 **ēvāsisse:** *to have gotten through, reached the end of*.

viam: i.e., his escape route from the city.

crēber: with **sonitus** (732); Eng. would more likely use an adv.

734 **aera:** i.e., the Greeks' weapons.

735 **nescio quod:** idiom, here modifying **nūmen,** lit., *I know not what = some (unknown) . . . or other;* the **-o** in **nescio** is shortened by SYSTOLE.

trepidō: with **mihi** (INTERLOCKED WORD ORDER).

male: adv. with **amīcum** = **inimīcum.**

736 **cōnfūsus, -a, -um,** *mixed together; disordered, confused, bewildered*.

āvius, -a, -um, *without roads, unfrequented, out of the way* (here substantive, *byways*).

738 **miserō . . . fātōne ērepta . . . / substitit, errāvitne . . . seu . . . resēdit (739):** the three alternatives Aeneas considers are dependent on **incertum** (740, sc. **est**), *whether she . . . or . . . or . . ., is uncertain;* the loose structure reflects Aeneas' distraught mental state as he recalls the loss of his wife. Some scholars read **miserō** with abl. **fātō,** while others take it as DAT. OF SEPARATION with **mihi** understood.

739 **lassus, -a, -um,** *tired, exhausted* (some mss. here read **lapsa,** *having slipped*).

"Aeneas and Anchises"
Marble statue
Gian Lorenzo Bernini
(1598–1680)
Galleria Borghese
Rome, Italy

728 nunc omnēs terrent aurae, sonus excitat omnis
729 suspēnsum et pariter comitīque onerīque timentem.

As the fugitives near the city's gates and Aeneas
rushes them along to avoid an approaching band
of Greeks, Creusa falls behind and is lost

730 "Iamque propinquābam portīs omnemque vidēbar
731 ēvāsisse viam, subitō cum crēber ad aurēs
732 vīsus adesse pedum sonitus, genitorque per umbram
733 prōspiciēns, 'Nāte,' exclāmat, 'fuge, nāte; propinquant;
734 ārdentēs clipeōs atque aera micantia cernō.'
735 Hīc mihi nescio quod trepidō male nūmen amīcum
736 cōnfūsam ēripuit mentem. Namque āvia cursū
737 dum sequor et nōtā excēdō regiōne viārum,
738 heu, miserō coniūnx fātōne ērepta Creūsa
739 substitit, errāvitne viā seu lassa resēdit,

Quaestiōnēs

1. What symbolic function is served by the image in 707–25 of Aeneas taking his father upon his shoulders and leading his son and wife with them in their flight from the city? Consider the implications of the word **onerī**, which is repeated in 723 and 729.

2. To which of his three family members does Aeneas pay the most attention in 707–29, and to which the least? What may be the poet's purposes in this discrepancy?

3. Comment on Vergil's description of Aeneas' altered state of mind in 725–29 and on the insight it provides into the hero's psychology.

4. Discuss the transformations that occur in the mindsets of both both father and son, Anchises and Aeneas, in lines 671–729.

5. How does meter suit meaning in 732?

6. Explain how the harsh **d/t/c/q** alliteration in 734 adds an onomatopoetic effect.

7. Which of the two interpretations of **miserō** mentioned in the note to 738 seems to you to represent Vergil's intention? Defend your view.

740 **nec . . . reddita:** not strictly true, as Aeneas encounters her phantom at 771–94.

741 **prius:** with **quam** (742).

reflectō, reflectere, reflexī, reflexus, *to bend back; to turn back (to).*

742 **tumulum . . . sacrātam:** the meeting place Aeneas had specified in 713–14.

743 ***dēmum,** adv., *at last, finally.*

744 ***dēsum, dēesse, dēfuī, dēfutūrus,** *to be lacking/missing.*

    omnibus, ūna (743) / **dēfuit:** the juxtaposition, abrupt DIAERESES, and
        ENJAMBEMENT all dramatize Aeneas' sorrowful realization that, of all the
        refugees in his band, only his wife was lost.

    ***fallō, fallere, fefellī, falsus,** *to deceive, trick; to disappoint; to elude, slip away
        from.*

745 **hominumque deōrumque:** with **quem;** for the elided HYPERMETRIC LINE, see
    note on 1.332–33.

748 **recondō, recondere, recondidī, reconditus,** *to put away; to hide away.*

749 ***fulgeō, fulgēre, fulsī,** *to shine brightly, glitter, flash.*

750 **Stat:** here idiom + inf., *it is (my) fixed resolve* (to) = *I am determined* (to).

    revertōr, revertī, reversus sum, *to turn around and go back, return.*

751 **caput:** here, as often, *life.*

    obiectō (1), *to cast before; to expose/subject (to).*

752 ***prīncipiō,** adv., *at first, to start with.*

    portae: the gate through which they had fled the city.

753 **gressum extuleram:** for the idiom cf. **efferre pedem** (657).

754 **observāta sequor:** here, as often, Lat. uses a partic. + vb. where Eng. would
    employ two vbs., *I mark out (keep my eyes on) and follow.*

    lūmine: i.e., *with an intent gaze.*

756 **pedem . . . tulisset:** idiom, = **īsset;** sc. **Creūsa** as subj. For the subjunct., see note
    on 94.

757 **mē . . . tenēbant:** the line's rapid dactylic rhythms and the three ELISIONS help
    convey Aeneas' agitated state.

    referō: inruerant: Vergil employs ASYNDETON here to suggest how sudden was
    Aeneas' realization that his home and hopes were lost.

758 **edāx, edācis,** *devouring, consuming.*

    ventō / volvitur (759): the ALLITERATION is ONOMATOPOETIC, suggesting the rush
    of the winds as they drive on the flames, and the ENJAMBEMENT underscores
    the violence of the fire; the effect is continued in the **f/s** ALLITERATION in 759.

759 **exsuperō** (1), *to rise up/over, tower above.*

    ad aurās: i.e., *up to the sky.*

761 **asy–lum, -ī,** n., *asylum, sanctuary.*

    porticibus vacuīs . . . asȳlō: both nouns are perhaps best construed as ABL. OF
    PLACE WHERE with ASYNDETON, or the first phrase may be descriptive, *in the
    sanctuary with its . . .;* cf. **porticibus longīs . . . et vacua atria** (528 above).

762 **Phoenīx, Phoenīcis,** m., *Phoenix* (a Greek warrior and tutor of Achilles).

    dīrus Ulixēs: one of numerous conventional formulae in Vergil (cf. 261 above).

763 **adservō** (1), *to watch over, guard.*

    Trōia gaza: the phrase occurs also in 1.119 above; in both places Troy's grand
    treasures are imperiled, there by divine agency, here by the Greeks.

740 incertum; nec post oculīs est reddita nostrīs,
741 nec prius āmissam respexī animumve reflexī
742 quam tumulum antīquae Cereris sēdemque sacrātam
743 vēnimus. Hīc dēmum, collēctis omnibus, ūna
744 dēfuit, et comitēs nātumque virumque fefellit.
745 Quem nōn incūsāvī āmēns hominumque deōrumque
746 aut quid in ēversā vīdī crūdēlius urbe?

Aeneas leaves Anchises and Iulus with comrades and
rushes back into the holocaust in search of Creusa

747   "Ascanium Anchīsēnque patrem Teucrōsque Penātēs
748 commendō sociīs et curvā valle recondō;
749 ipse urbem repetō et cingor fulgentibus armīs.
750 Stat cāsūs renovāre omnēs omnemque revertī
751 per Trōiam et rūrsus caput obiectāre perīclīs.
752 Prīncipiō mūrōs obscūraque līmina portae,
753 quā gressum extuleram, repetō et vēstīgia retrō
754 observāta sequor per noctem et lūmine lūstrō:
755 horror ubīque animō, simul ipsa silentia terrent.
756 Inde domum—sī forte pedem, sī forte tulisset!—
757 mē referō: inruerant Danaī et tēctum omne tenēbant.
758 Īlicet ignis edāx summa ad fastīgia ventō
759 volvitur; exsuperant flammae, furit aestus ad aurās.
760 Prōcēdō et Priamī sēdēs arcemque revīsō:
761 et iam porticibus vacuīs Iūnōnis asȳlō
762 custōdēs lēctī, Phoenīx et dīrus Ulixēs,
763 praedam adservābant. Hūc undique Trōïa gaza

Quaestiōnēs

How had Vergil prepared his readers in 710–25 for Creusa's disappearance in 738–46, and what is the effect of this dramatic strategy? In what ways does Vergil show Aeneas' sense of guilt for his beloved wife's loss?

764 **mēnsae . . . deōrum:** i.e., tables from the temples used for ritual.

765 **crātēr, crātēris,** m., *mixing bowl, crater vase* (used esp. for mixing wine and water).

aurō: ABL. OF DESCRIPTION, in prose usually modified by an adj., but the epithet here is transferred to **crātērēs.**

766 *****congerō, congerere, congessī, congestus,** *to bring together, collect, amass; to pile up, heap up* (with).

congeritur: sg. to agree with the nearest subj. and to suit the meter.

Puerī et . . . mātrēs: to be taken back to Greece as slaves, a fate that Creusa will avoid (see 785–87).

768 **umbram:** the shadowy darkness of both night and death.

769 **'Creūsam':** i.e., her name, which is repeated in the same position at the end of verses 772, 778, and 784, in a kind of mournful musical refrain.

770 **nēquīquam . . . vocāvī:** the ELISIONS, ANAPHORA, and the mournful ASSONANCE of the **um** syllables coming each under the ictus, all help suggest the frantic intensity of Aeneas' cries.

ingeminō (1), *to repeat, re-echo.*

771 **Quaerentī et . . . ruentī:** with **mihi** (773); idiomatic Eng. here, as often, would more likely employ a cl. than a partic. phrase, *while I was looking (for her) and . . ..*

772 **īnfēlīx:** the adj. describes Aeneas' response to Creusa's phantom, rather than her own demeanor here, which as seen from her remarks is positive and hopeful for Aeneas' future.

773 **nōtā maior:** i.e., larger than she was in life, as supernatural figures were commonly described in literature.

imāgō. / Obstipuī (774): cf. **obstipuī . . . imāgō** (560), of Aeneas' vision of his father left behind in their home.

774 **Obstipuī . . . haesit:** the identical line is repeated at 3.48 in describing Aeneas' encounter with the ghost of his countryman Polydorus; the following verse too recurs in later books (at 3.153 and 8.35).

steterunt: the second e is shortened for metrical convenience (SYSTOLE).

comae et vōx faucibus: the ELISION, conflict of ictus and accent, and the harsh c/x consonants suggest the sound of Aeneas' words catching in his throat.

775 **dēmō, dēmere, dēmpsī, dēmptus,** *to remove, take away, dispel.*

adfārī . . . dēmere: HIST. INFS.

776 *****indulgeō, indulgēre, indulsī, indultus,** + dat., *to be indulgent/lenient* (to); *to indulge* (in), *give free rein* (to); *to show kindness, be generous* (to).

778 **ēveniō, ēvenīre, ēvēnī, ēventus,** *to come out, come to pass.*

tē . . . portāre: with **fās (est)** in 779, *is it right for you to . . ..*

779 **aut:** = nec.

ille . . . Olympī: the INTERLOCKED WORD ORDER builds suspense and, like the demonstrative **ille,** shows reverence for Jupiter's majesty and his role in the events at Troy.

780 *****arō (1),** *to plow, cultivate; to plow through* (the sea).

781 **Lӯdius, -a, -um,** *Lydian, of Lydia* (a region in western Asia Minor).

764 incēnsīs ērepta adytīs, mēnsaeque deōrum
765 crātērēsque aurō solidī, captīvaque vestis
766 congeritur. Puerī et pavidae longō ōrdine mātrēs
767 stant circum.

Creusa's ghost appears to Aeneas, consoles him in his grief,
and prophesies that he will found a new kingdom
in the west and wed a royal bride

768 "Ausus quīn etiam vōcēs iactāre per umbram,
769 implēvī clāmōre viās, maestusque 'Creūsam'
770 nēquīquam ingemināns iterumque iterumque vocāvī.
771 Quaerentī et tēctīs urbis sine fīne ruentī
772 īnfēlīx simulācrum atque ipsius umbra Creūsae
773 vīsa mihi ante oculōs et nōtā maior imāgō.
774 Obstipuī, steteruntque comae et vōx faucibus haesit.
775 Tum sīc adfārī et cūrās hīs dēmere dictīs:
776 'Quid tantum īnsānō iuvat indulgēre dolōrī,
777 ō dulcis coniūnx? Nōn haec sine nūmine dīvum
778 ēveniunt; nec tē comitem hinc portāre Creūsam
779 fās, aut ille sinit superī rēgnātor Olympī.
780 Longa tibi exsilia et vāstum maris aequor arandum,
781 et terram Hesperiam veniēs, ubi Lȳdius arva

Quaestiōnēs

1. Comment specifically on the several poetic and rhetorical devices and the imagery that Vergil employs in 755–67 to evoke a strong emotional response in his audience.

2. How do diction, meter, and word order contribute to the musicality of verse 771?

3. Comment on the metrical and sound effects in 775; and what is the effect of the two successive end-stopped lines in 774–75?

782 ***opīmus, -a, -um,** *rich, plentiful, abundant;* with **spōlia,** an idiom referring to the spoils taken from an enemy leader by a triumphant Roman commander.

> **virum:** = **virōrum;** not simply a possessive gen. but, with **arva (781) . . . opīma,** a remarkable metaphor suggesting the rich harvest of men who would become Aeneas' allies and heirs and the countless generations of Rome's citizens.

> ***lēnis, -is, -e,** *slowly moving, gentle, light.*

> ***Thȳbris, Thȳbridis,** voc. **Thȳbri,** m., *the river Tiber* (on which Rome was situated); *Tiber* (eponymous god of the river).

> **Lȳdius (781) . . . Thȳbris:** so called because the Etruscans to the north were believed by many to have been immigrants from Asia Minor, just as the Trojans themselves would be.

783 **Illīc . . . coniūnx:** a majestic line with is stately spondees, the **rēs/rēg/rēg** ASSONANCE, and Creusa's poignant revelation that Aeneas will find another bride in his new kingdom.

784 **dīlēctae . . . Creūsae:** OBJ. GEN.

786 **servītum:** the acc. supine of **servīre,** which regularly takes a dat.

787 **Dardanis, Dardanidis,** f., adj., *Dardanian, of Dardanus* (ancestor of Creusa's father Priam and founder of Troy).

> **Dardanis . . . nurus:** the appos. phrase has causal force.

788 ***genetrīx, genetrīcis,** f., *mother, creator.*

> **magna . . . genetrīx:** i.e., the earth goddess Cybele or the **Magna Māter,** identified with Rhea, mother of Jupiter, Neptune, and other major deities. She was goddess of nature in general, and of mountains, and was associated with Mt. Ida, to which Aeneas and his band flee at the end of the book; her orgiastic cult, which held out to followers a chance for immortality, was extremely popular in Phrygia and elsewhere in Asia Minor before spreading to Greece and then to Rome.

790 **Haec ubi dicta dedit . . . / dīcere dēseruit (791):** the c/d/t ALLITERATION and the repeated metrical pattern dactyl/dactyl/**longum** with **-it** under the ictus at the CAESURA together produce a striking musical effect to punctuate the close of Creusa's speech; the dactyls and repeated s's in 791 suggest the quick rush of her apparition as it vanished into the night air. For the formula **haec ubi dicta,** cf. 1.81.

> **lacrimantem . . . volentem:** sc. **mē.**

791 ***tenuis, -is, -e,** *slender, thin.*

792 **Ter . . . / ter (793):** a mystical number, here emphatically repeated; the lines 792–94 (adapted from Homer's *Odyssey* 11.206f.) recur verbatim in Book Six (700–02), where Aeneas reaches out again in vain to embrace the shade of his father Anchises in the Underworld, in each case grasping at figures who are lost and who represent Troy's past as opposed to Rome's future.

> **collō . . . circum:** INTERLOCKED WORD ORDER and TMESIS (of **circumdare**) suit the image of the attempted embrace, and the harsh ALLITERATION of **c** and accentual conflict provide the scene with an apt soundtrack.

793 **comprēndō, comprēndere, comprēndī, comprēnsus,** to take hold of, clasp, grasp (at).

782 inter opīma virum lēnī fluit agmine Thȳbris.
783 Illīc rēs laetae rēgnumque et rēgia coniūnx
784 parta tibī; lacrimās dīlēctae pelle Creūsae.
785 Nōn ego Myrmidonum sēdēs Dolopumve superbās
786 aspiciam aut Grāīs servītum mātribus ībō,
787 Dardanis et dīvae Veneris nurus;
788 sed mē magna deum genetrīx hīs dētinet ōrīs.
789 Iamque valē et nātī servā commūnis amōrem.'
790 Haec ubi dicta dedit, lacrimantem et multa volentem
791 dīcere dēseruit, tenuēsque recessit in aurās.
792 Ter cōnātus ibī collō dare bracchia circum;
793 ter frūstrā comprēnsa manūs effūgit imāgō,

Quaestiōnēs

1. Recall that Aeneas is narrating these events to Dido, who under the influence of Cupid and Venus is already falling in love with her guest; what are the implications of the prophecy in 783–84 for their relationship?

2. Discuss in detail Creusa's speech to Aeneas in 776–89. What does it tell us of her character and of her role as wife and mother? What dramatic functions does the speech serve, both in this immediate context and in moving the story forward? Is she merely a hallucination, a ghost, or some quasi-divine figure (consider verse 788 in this connection)? How does her demeanor contrast with that of Aeneas himself in this scene?

3. Compare in detail Creusa's words to Aeneas in 776–89 with those of Hector in 289–95; in what ways are the two speeches complementary? What more does Aeneas learn from his wife's phantom than he had from Hector?

The Tiber River/Father Tiber
Anonymous
Fontana della Dea Roma
Campidoglio
Rome, Italy

794 *pār, paris, often + dat., *matching, equal; similar* (to), *like.*

    pār . . . somnō: a masterful line whose imagery and musicality are brilliantly captured in the poet C. Day Lewis' translation, *it was like / Grasping a wisp of wind or the wings of a fleeting dream.*

795 Sīc: a word strongly tinged with pathos here, i.e., having seen his wife for the last time and lost her to Cybele and the fates; in other, earlier versions of the story Creusa (Eurydice, as she is called in some accounts) survived the war and escaped with Aeneas, a variant obviously not suited to Vergil's narrative purposes.

    cōnsūmō, cōnsūmere, cōnsūmpsī, cōnsūmptus, *to use up, consume.*

796 adfluō, adfluere, adflūxī, adflūxus, *to flow toward/into, stream together.*

798 exsiliō: DAT. OF PURPOSE with collēctam.

799 parātī: sc. something like īre or prōficīscī.

800 velim: subjunct. in a subordinate cl. within the implied IND. STATE.; i.e., the refugees vowed that they were ready to follow Aeneas' lead wherever he should choose to take them.

    dēdūcere: used here in its common technical sense of leading out a group of settlers to found a new colony; thus Aeneas' and his son's eventual settlements in Italy, and ultimately Rome itself, are viewed as Trojan colonies.

801 Lūcifer, -ferī, m., *Lucifer* ("the light-bringer"), *the morning star* (i.e., the planet Venus; Servius quotes from Varro one tradition in which Venus by the light of her planet directed Aeneas' course all the way from Troy to Latium).

    Īda, -ae, f., *Mt. Ida* (see note on 696 above).

804 Cessī . . . petīvī: the impf. tense vbs. of 801–03 are replaced abruptly with the perf. tense here, suggesting the finality of the action in this closing verse; cessī means at once *I withdrew* and *I yielded/I surrendered*, i.e., to fate. The opening spondees, suggesting the weight upon Aeneas' shoulders, are aptly replaced with dactyls in the line's second half, as the courageous prince, the devoted son and father, moves on with quickened pace toward the new-found destiny shown him by both Hector and Creusa, the ghosts of Troy's past, which he must now and forever leave behind.

    sublātō: sc. umerīs (see 721).

    montēs: Aeneas and his band take temporary refuge from the Greeks in the forests of nearby Mt. Ida (as directed by the omen Jupiter had sent in 695–98), before setting sail on the long and difficult westward journey to be described in Book Three.

Dulcissimum spectāculum vānitātis equus igneus plēnus armātīs, et Trōiae incendium, atque ipsīus umbra Creūsae.

                                     St. Augustine, "Confessions," 1.13

794 pār levibus ventīs, volucrīque simillima somnō.
795 Sīc dēmum sociōs, cōnsūmptā nocte, revīsō.

Discovering that his comrades have been joined by a huge band of
refugees, Aeneas lifts his father onto his shoulders and heads for
the mountains, just as the morning star ushers in the new day

796   "Atque hīc ingentem comitum adflūxisse novōrum
797 inveniō, admīrāns numerum, mātrēsque virōsque,
798 collēctam exsiliō pūbem, miserābile vulgus.
799 Undique convēnēre animīs opibusque parātī
800 in quāscumque velim pelagō dēdūcere terrās.
801 Iamque iugīs summae surgēbat Lūcifer Īdae
802 dūcēbatque diem, Danaīque obsessa tenēbant
803 līmina portārum, nec spēs opis ūlla dabātur.
804 Cessī et sublātō montēs genitōre petīvī."

Quaestiōnēs

1. In what specific respects does C. Day Lewis' translation (quoted in the notes) replicate the artistry of verse 794?

2. Comment on the several ways in which the final scene (796–804) provides a dramatically effective closure to the book; explore fully the symbolism involved in particular in lines 801–04, paying close attention to both key thematic words and the highly visual imagery.

Aeneas and Anchises
Black-figure kylix
ca. 520 B.C.
Louvre
Paris, France

Aeneid BOOK IV

(Verses 1–449, 642–705)

Book Three

BOOK Three, which is not included in our selections but which (like all of the *Aeneid*) you will certainly wish to read in English translation, is meant to recall Odysseus' quest and longing to return to his cherished Ithaca in many respects, except that Aeneas' quest is for an elusive goal in *terra incognita*. Uncertainty, endurance, weariness, and grief characterize his ordeal. His best support in this time of ambiguity and perplexity is *pietas,* his conscientious engagement with Anchises and with his son, Ascanius-Iulus, and a growing awareness, through a series of mostly Apolline revelations, that the glory that is destined will come to pass. You may sense that Book Three has been designed to provide a relaxation of tension after the agony of Book Two, and that, like each of the poem's other odd-numbered books, it helps to diminish the reader's stressful emotional involvement.

Aeneas' journey westward (see the map, "The Voyage of Aeneas," following the general Introduction) covers three spheres: (1) the Aegean, highlighting the ghastly Polydorus episode in Thrace (19–68), followed by Delos, an encouraging, hopeful encounter with Apollo's priest (69–120), and Crete, where the Trojans begin to construct Pergamum but soon depart after pestilence and a vision of the Penates with their promise of Hesperia (121–208); (2) Greece, featuring the Strophades, the Harpies' realm, weird and terrifying (209–77), and Actium, where the refugees celebrate games at Octavian's later victory site (278–93), and finally Buthrotum, where they discover the Trojan prince Helenus and Hector's widow Andromache presiding over a "New Troy" and are encouraged somewhat by Helenus' prophecy (294–505); (3) Italy and Sicily, with the first landfall in Italy at Castrum Minervae (506–47), followed by Mt. Etna, Achaemenides, the abandoned Greek, and the terrifying Cyclops, Polyphemus (548–691); finally the Trojan refugees complete the passage around Sicily, a "tourist" cruise with shipboard views that closes suddenly with the sorrowful loss of Aeneas' father (692–718). What is the overall "message" of this book? Uncertainty (1–293), tempered by the visit with Andromache and the prophecy of Helenus (294–505), followed by a period of desolation with the death of Anchises at Drepanum (506–718).

Where does the poet excel?—particularly in his narrative at Buthrotum, where Andromache, Hector's widow and mother of murdered Astyanax, freed from her Greek master, Neoptolemus, has married Helenus, Priam's prophetic son; her "tragic" story is deeply moving. The encounter with Achaemenides, the castaway Greek, in the shadow of Etna, recalls the Sinon episode in many respects, but the outcome is altogether different: the Trojans' trust in Sinon, their sympathy, and their readiness to credit his detailed account of Greek deceit and cruelty led to the capture and destruction of Troy; their trust in Achaemenides and their readiness to credit the horrendous details of his encounter with Polyphemus led to the Greek's saving role as pilot for the Trojans in Sicilian waters.

Book Four

BOOK Four is Vergil's "Love Story," detailing the rise and fall of the love affair of Dido and Aeneas. Dido's infatuation with Aeneas is complicated by Juno, concerned for her favorite city and its young ruler, and by Venus, anxious about her son's security and the progress of his destiny. Together the goddesses conspire to promote a royal hunt (and another storm), where Dido and Aeneas will celebrate their *coniugium*. Gossip circulates throughout Tunisia. Iarbas, an African prince and a spurned suitor, is jealous and indignant over the romantic development and provokes Jupiter to intervene by dispatching Mercury as messenger of the Olympian's objection to the royal union.

The seeds of dissension are sown, and Dido and Aeneas resort to charges of disloyalty and counter-arguments. Hopes for reconciliation are futile. Finally (450–705), Dido falls back on sorcery, witchcraft, and lamentation. Prompted by Mercury, Aeneas is adamant in his determination to leave. Dido's curses follow after him, with predictions of Hannibal as her avenger. Her final resort is suicide by Aeneas' sword on the "conjugal" couch, which becomes her funeral pyre.

The selections included in this text focus upon the growth and consummation of their love, and upon the breakdown of their relationship. In the opening scenes (1–172) Vergil is careful to highlight how Dido's hero-worship moves toward renewal of love, which she had renounced after the murder of her husband Sychaeus. The queen's sister Anna is her confidante and encourages Dido to renounce her promise never to marry again; that decision constitutes Dido's *culpa* and her tragic error (*hamartia*, as the Greeks called it, a fateful error in judgment).

The involvement of Juno and Venus as champions of Dido's Carthage and of Aeneas' Italian mission respectively lends cosmic proportion to the episode. The *coniugium* that Juno proposes, and Venus apparently accepts, has important political implications. The Royal Hunt is a sensational event, colorful, joyful, competitive, and exciting. The stormy accompaniment to the "marriage" in the cave is a ceremony transformed into a cosmic event by Juno's "aerial" powers.

The second major episode included among our selections from Book Four (173–449) introduces, in a dramatic prosopopoeia, a nightmarish creature, Rumor, timid at first, finally a monster, "frightening and immense." The gossip about the lovers is broadcast and rouses the anger of Iarbas, the African prince who had provided Dido with a meager desert site for her city and with conditions of tenure, but was rejected as her husband. Iarbas questions his trust in Jupiter Hammon and voices his contempt for the effeminate Trojans and his wrath that Aeneas should replay the role of Paris, stealing another Helen. Jupiter's intervention marks the crisis: Mercury is dispatched to remind Aeneas of his destiny and to order him to leave Carthage.

The passage of Mercury to Carthage embodies a graphic picture of Atlas, mountain and giant, Mercury's grandfather—a remarkable instance of celestial *pietas*. Mercury's disgust at Aeneas' role as Dido's architect, luxuriating in an "Eastern" life-style (which for Vergil's audience would recall the liaison between Marc Antony and the Egyptian queen Cleopatra), accentuates Jupiter's message and unsettles Aeneas by his accusation that he lives under a wife's control and is forgetful of his heir Ascanius-Iulus. The conflict between duty and love has to be resolved, and Aeneas decides that passion must surrender to his political mission. The hero's recourse to military language marks his grim determination to separate himself from his generous, loving partner. Dido's realization of what will happen brings her to a Bacchic, Dionysiac frenzy, and her appeal to Aeneas is marked by despondency, reproach, and pathos.

The three speeches that prepare us for the inevitable are superbly crafted and very reminiscent of the arguments in Greek tragedy, particularly those of Medea and Jason in Euripides' *Medea*. Aeneas' reply to Dido's passionate outburst is undeniably cold and formal: he resorts confidently to logic and persuasion in order to defend his position, and his commitment to his destiny compensates for the anguish he experiences in his decision. Dido responds abusively, with anger, hatred, and contempt. She discards Aeneas' arguments, among them that Jupiter's own messenger, Mercury, had ordered him to leave, as mere fabrications and then resorts to curses and a prayer for vengeance: she will assume the role of a Fury in her afterlife.

The sequel to these speeches (not included in our selections) details Dido's resolution to die, and her intention is validated by awful portents and by the recollection of antique prophecies. Her sleep is the occasion for blood-chilling "Freudian" nightmares: she dreams that Aeneas pursues her in a wasteland where no Tyrian companions appear; twin similes identify her with raving Pentheus—who had banished the cult of Dionysus from Thebes, beset by his murderous mother and her Bacchants–and also with Orestes–murderer of his mother to avenge Agamemnon's murder, in flight on stage from his mother's ghost, which is armed with firebrands and black serpents, while avenging fiends crouch at the doorway (450–73).

Dido's readiness to use magic rites (504–21) suggests that Vergil must have associated her with both Homer's Circe and Euripides' Medea (450–552). Without sensing Dido's real purpose, Anna becomes her willing accomplice. Dido says that a pyre must be built to burn all the relics of Aeneas (474–503), but, in fact, she has chosen her own route to death by fire and sword (504–21). The queen's last night is sleepless; she weighs the possibilities of survival, but chooses annihilation as proper atonement for her broken pledge to Sychaeus. When Mercury intervenes again in a vision, stressing the need for Aeneas to leave, the Trojans are prompt to comply. Mercury's outspoken warning to Aeneas includes the contemptuous phrase *varium et mutabile semper / femina*, "a woman is always a fickle and changeable thing." (569–70). How are readers meant to react to that?

Our second selection from Book Four (642–705) highlights the final action: Dido has sent her nurse Barce to bring Anna as witness to the alleged magic rites, rites which will equate with her suicide. Dido's last words, delivered from the funeral pyre, recall her past achievements and reiterate her desire for vengeance on Aeneas (630–62). By now Dido has removed her Medea "mask" and assumed that of Euripides' Alcestis; in her death and in her encounter with Aeneas in Hades (as we shall see in our selections from Book Six) she wears the mask of Sophocles' Ajax. Her dying is cause for lamentation in the palace, comparable with that during the fall of Troy: it was "as though all Carthage or ancient Tyre were collapsing before the inrushing foe, and fierce flames were rolling on over the roofs of men, and over the roofs of the gods" (669–71).

Anna realizes at last that she has been deceived and castigates her sister for her selfish action and neglect of her civic obligations. The final action is subdued and serene. Juno's messenger, the rainbow goddess Iris, comes down to release Dido's struggling spirit. Vergil's comment is precise and instructive: "she was not dying by fate, nor by a death she deserved, but pitifully before her time, set on fire by sudden frenzy" (696–97). As readers we must ask ourselves whether Dido was mad, wicked, or misled, and we must debate carefully whether or not there is a case of willful abandonment against Aeneas, who has left love behind in order to lead his people toward their destiny and the founding of a new kingdom.

Aeneas and Dido
From manuscript of
Servius' commentary
on the *Aeneid*
Ms. 493, folio 74v
1469
Bibliotheque Municipale
Dijon, France

1 **At rēgīna:** the abrupt opening phrase (repeated at 296 below) returns the audience's attention to Dido, who is of course the focus of Book Four.

saucia cūrā / vulnus . . . ignī (2): Vergil combines metaphors conventional in erotic verse, which together here suggest the intensity of Dido's suffering; CHIASMUS (**vulnus alit . . . carpitur ignī**) and the harsh ALLITERATION of **c/g** contribute to the effect.

2 *****vēna, -ae,** f., *blood-vessel, vein; vein, streak* (in stone).

vēnīs: possibly local, *in her veins,* but more likely—and more vividly—instrumental, *with her veins,* i.e., she feeds the wound with her life-blood, keeping it fresh and unhealed.

ignī: a common alternate form in verse for the usual abl. **igne.**

3 **Multa . . . multus:** here with adv. force, *again . . . and again.*

virī virtūs: not merely ASSONANCE but an example of Vergil's fondness for etymologizing (see note on **cavae . . . cavernae** 2.53).

animō: DAT. OF DIRECTION with **recursat.**

*****recursō (1),** *to come racing back, return again and again; to keep recurring* (to the mind).

4 **vultūs:** the poetic pl. here suggests Aeneas' many different expressions.

6 **Postera . . . terrās:** ASSONANCE and ALLITERATION provide the soundtrack to the scene-shift and the coming of dawn.

Phoebēus, -a, -um, *of Phoebus/Apollo* (god of the sun).

lampas, lampadis, f., *torch; lamp, light; sunlight, day.*

7 *****ūmeō, ūmēre,** *to be moist/wet.*

ūmentem . . . umbram: the ASSONANT adj.-noun pair neatly FRAME the line, just as the dewy darkness of night had embraced the heavens, producing an effective WORD-PICTURE.

*****Aurōra, -ae,** f., *Aurora* (goddess of the dawn).

Aurōra: suspensefully delayed and separated from the modifying adj. **postera.**

dīmoveō, dīmovēre, dīmōvī, dīmōtus, *to move apart, scatter, disperse; to move away, remove.*

8 **ūnanimus, -a, -um,** *sharing an attitude/purpose, like-minded, of one heart, loving.*

male: for this sense of the adv., cf. **male fīda** (2.23).

9 *****Anna, -ae,** f., *Anna* (Dido's sister).

suspēnsam: i.e., with anxiety over the dilemma she explains in the following lines.

*****īnsomnium, -ī,** n., *sleeplessness; vision, dream.*

10 **Quis novus hic . . . hospes: quis,** like **quae** (9) and **quam** (11) is exclamatory, not interrog.; Eng. here would use a rel. cl., *what a wondrous stranger this is . . . who has . . ..*

11 **quem . . . ferēns:** lit., *bearing what a self in his face* = *how noble in appearance.*

fortī . . . armīs: ABL. OF DESCRIPTION; with **quam,** *how courageous in . . .. Armīs* here = *weapons,* i.e., in war, or possibly from **armus, -ī,** m., *shoulder.*

12 **genus esse:** = **eum esse genus.**

Listening to Aeneas' tale of heroism and adventure, Dido
is overwhelmed with passion for her Trojan guest

1   At rēgīna, gravī iamdūdum saucia cūrā,
2   vulnus alit vēnīs et caecō carpitur ignī.
3   Multa virī virtūs animō multusque recursat
4   gentis honōs; haerent īnfīxī pectore vultūs
5   verbaque nec placidam membrīs dat cūra quiētem.

At dawn Dido shares her feelings with her
sister Anna and seeks her counsel

6   Postera Phoebēā lūstrābat lampade terrās
7   ūmentemque Aurōra polō dīmōverat umbram,
8   cum sīc ūnanimam adloquitur male sāna sorōrem:
9   "Anna soror, quae mē suspēnsam īnsomnia terrent!
10   Quis novus hic nostrīs successit sēdibus hospes,
11   quem sēsē ōre ferēns, quam fortī pectore et armīs!
12   Crēdō equidem—nec vāna fidēs—genus esse deōrum.

Quaestiōnēs

1. Comment on the word order in line 1.

2. Discuss further the imagery employed in 1–2; how may the "wound" relate to Cupid? What is the point of **caecō?**

The queen, for her part, all that evening ached
With longing that her heart's blood fed, a wound
Or inward fire eating her away.
The manhood of the man, his pride of birth,
Came home to her time and again; his looks,
His words remained with her to haunt her mind,
And desire for him gave her no rest.

From the translation of Robert Fitzgerald, 1983

13 **Dēgenerēs:** an etymologizing wordplay on **genus** (12).
    arguō, arguere, arguī, argūtus, *to show, reveal, prove.*
    Heu . . . canēbat (14): the interj., with the strong DIAERESIS preceding, and the
        spondaic rhythms in 14, all help suggest the intensity of Dido's emotions.

14 **exhauriō, exhaurīre, exhausī, exhaustus,** *to drink up, use up; to see through to the*
    end, complete, undergo, experience.

15 **sedēret:** *it were set* + JUSSIVE NOUN CL./IND. COMMAND, **nē . . . vellem,** *not to . . . .*

16 **cui:** here indef., *anyone.*
    sociō (1), *to join, unite, ally* (to).
    *****iugālis, -is, -e,** *of marriage, matrimonial.*

17 **prīmus amor:** i.e., her deceased husband Sychaeus (see 20–21 below).
    dēcipiō, dēcipere, dēcēpī, dēceptus, *to deceive; to disappoint.*
    dēceptam: sc. **mē.**

18 **pertaedeō, pertaedēre, pertaesus,** often impers. + gen. for the obj. of the
        emotion, *to weary/disgust/sicken* (someone, acc.) *over* (something, gen.).
    pertaesum . . . fuisset: sc. **mē,** *it had wearied me* (of); freely, *I had become*
        sick (of).
    taedae: here the *bridal torch* carried in wedding processions; with **thalamus,**
        METONYMY for marriage.

19 **potuī:** prose would ordinarily employ a subjunct. after **forsan.**
    succumbō, succumbere, succubuī, succubitus, *to sink to the ground; to submit,*
        give in, yield (to).

20 **fāta:** here, as often, *death.*
    Sychaeī: for the quantity of the **y,** see on 1.348.

21 **frāternā:** i.e., *committed by my brother* (for Pygmalion's murder of Sychaeus, see
        1.346f.).

22 **hic:** i.e., Aeneas.
    *****īnflectō, īnflectere, īnflexī, īnflexus,** *to bend; to alter, change.*
    *****sēnsus, -ūs,** m., *sense, feeling.*

24 **optem:** I *would wish* (POTENTIAL SUBJUNCT.).
    dehīscat . . . adigat (25): the conj. **ut,** usual in prose with a JUSSIVE NOUN CL./
        IND. COMMAND, is commonly omitted in poetry.

25 **pater omnipotēns:** Jupiter; cf. 1.60 above.
    adigō, adigere, adēgī, adāctus, *to drive* (someone/something) *to* (a place).

26 *****palleō, pallēre,** *to be pale/bloodless; to have a pale color.*
    *****Erebus, -ī,** m., *Erebus, the Underworld.*

27 **ante . . . quam:** TMESIS; an emphatic repetition of **prius** (24).
    *****pudor, pudōris,** m., *(sense of) shame; conscience.*
    Pudor: the PERSONIFICATION here recalls **Pudīcitia,** a goddess important in
        Augustus' program of moral reform and one sacred to women who had
        married only once and remained faithful to their husbands.

29 **abstulit:** i.e., to his grave; the vb. is further strengthened through ENJAMBEMENT.

13 Dēgenerēs animōs timor arguit. Heu, quibus ille
14 iactātus fātīs! Quae bella exhausta canēbat!
15 Sī mihi nōn animō fīxum immōtumque sedēret
16 nē cui mē vinclō vellem sociāre iugālī,
17 postquam prīmus amor dēceptam morte fefellit,
18 sī nōn pertaesum thalamī taedaeque fuisset,
19 huic ūnī forsan potuī succumbere culpae.
20 Anna (fatēbor enim), miserī post fāta Sychaeī
21 coniugis et sparsōs frāternā caede Penātēs,
22 sōlus hic īnflexit sēnsūs animumque labantem
23 impulit. Agnōscō veteris vēstīgia flammae.
24 Sed mihi vel tellūs optem prius īma dehīscat
25 vel pater omnipotēns adigat mē fulmine ad umbrās,
26 pallentēs umbrās Erebō noctemque profundam,
27 ante, Pudor, quam tē violō aut tua iūra resolvō.
28 Ille meōs, prīmus quī mē sibi iūnxit, amōrēs
29 abstulit; ille habeat sēcum servetque sepulcrō."

Quaestiōnēs

1. Which of Aeneas' qualities appear in 11–14 to be especially important to Dido?

2. How does meter enhance meaning in verse 16?

3. Comment on the positioning of **huic ūnī . . . culpae** in 19 and the effect Vergil likely intended; discuss the implications of the word **culpae** in this context.

4. What action is foreshadowed in 24–27 and what is the dramatic effect?

5. What is the effect of the personification and apostrophe to **Pudor** in 27?

6. What is the most striking sound effect in 28–29?

7. How does anaphora add intensity to Dido's closing declaration in 28–29?

8. Discuss Dido's entire speech in 9–29, referring specifically to the language that provides the clearest insights into the queen's emotional state.

30 **Sīc effāta**: a standard Vergilian formula for marking the close of a speech; cf. 2.524.

  oborior, oborīrī, obortus sum, *to spring/rise up, arise.*

  obortīs: Lat. often employs a perf. pass. partic. where Eng. would have instead a pres. act. partic.

31 **sorōrī**: for the DAT. OF AGENT with the perf. pass. partic. **dīlēcta**, cf. 1.344.

32 **carpēre**: = **carpēris**; for this sense of the vb., cf. **carpitur** (2 above).

33 **Veneris**: with **praemia**.

  nōscō, nōscere, nōvī, nōtus, *to (get to) know, recognize.*

  nōris: = **nōveris**; the fut. perf. often has, as here, the force of a simple fut.

34 **Id**: i.e., her pledge of fidelity to her dead husband.

35 **Estō**: fut. imper. of **esse**; = *be this way, so be it.*

  aegram: sc. **tē**.

  marītī: here *suitors.*

36 **Libyae . . . Tyrō**: in an unusual variation, the first noun is loc., the second abl.

  dēspectus: sc. **est**, sg. to agree with the nearer of the two subjs.

  Ĭarbās, -ae, acc. **Ĭarbān** (trisyllabic), m., *Iarbas* (legendary king of the Gaetulians, a North African tribe).

37 ***Āfrica, -ae***, f., *Africa.*

38 **placitō**: for the act. sense, cf. **placitum** (1.283 above and note); **pugnāre**, here *to resist*, takes the dat. in poetry.

39 **Nec venit in mentem**: the vb. here is impers., with **quōrum . . . (in) arvīs** as subj., *does it not come into/enter your . . . ?*

  cōnsēderis: perf. subjunct. (with the **i** shortened by SYSTOLE) in an IND. QUEST.

40 **Hinc . . . / hinc (42)**: here *on this side . . . on the other side.*

  Gaetūlus, -a, -um, *Gaetulian, of the Gaetulians* (a tribe in northwest Africa).

  īnsuperābilis, -is, -e, *unconquerable, invincible.*

  bellō: ABL. OF SPECIFICATION.

41 ***Numida, -ae***, m., *a Numidian, native of Numidia* (a region of Africa west and south of Carthage: see map of the Mediterranean following the Introduction).

  īnfrēnus, -a, -um, *without reins, unbridled; unrestrained, wild.*

  īnfrēnī: a double-entendre, not only suggesting the Numidians' wildness but also recalling the fact that they were known for their superb horsemanship and rode without bridles.

  inhospitus, -a, -um, *unfriendly, hostile.*

42 ***sitis, sitis***, abl. **sitī**, f., *thirst; arid climate, drought.*

  sitī: ABL. OF CAUSE with **dēserta**.

43 ***Barcaeī, -ōrum***, m. pl., *the people of Barce* (a district of North Africa to the south of Carthage).

  Quid: here, as often, *why.*

  dīcam: *should* I *speak* (DELIBERATIVE SUBJUNCT.); the quest. constitutes a form of PRAETERITIO.

44 ***mina, -ae***, f., *threat, menace.*

45 ***auspex, auspicis***, m., *augur, diviner; patron, supporter.*

  Iūnōne secundā: both as Carthage's patron deity and as goddess of marriage.

47 **Quam . . . urbem . . . hanc**: *What a city . . . here.*

30   Sīc effāta, sinum lacrimīs implēvit obortīs.

*Anna encourages her sister's interest in Aeneas, both for the
sake of love and for the security of their new country*

31   Anna refert: "Ō lūce magis dīlēcta sorōrī,
32   sōlane perpetuā maerēns carpēre iuventā
33   nec dulcēs nātōs Veneris nec praemia nōris?
34   Id cinerem aut mānēs crēdis cūrāre sepultōs?
35   Estō: aegram nūllī quondam flexēre marītī,
36   nōn Libyae, nōn ante Tyrō; dēspectus Ïarbās
37   ductōrēsque aliī, quōs Āfrica, terra triumphīs
38   dīves, alit: placitōne etiam pugnābis amōrī?
39   Nec venit in mentem quōrum cōnsēderis arvīs?
40   Hinc Gaetūlae urbēs, genus īnsuperābile bellō,
41   et Numidae īnfrēnī cingunt et inhospita Syrtis;
42   hinc dēserta sitī regiō lātēque furentēs
43   Barcaeī. Quid bella Tyrō surgentia dīcam
44   germānīque minās?
45   Dīs equidem auspicibus reor et Iūnōne secundā
46   hunc cursum Īliacās ventō tenuisse carīnās.
47   Quam tū urbem, soror, hanc cernēs, quae surgere rēgna

Quaestiōnēs

1. Explore the psychology of Dido's bursting into tears in 30 after her seemingly
   resolute declaration of fidelity to Sychaeus in 24–29.

2. How are Anna's remarks at 45–46 particularly ironic?

Yet must Virgil always appear to us one of the most beautiful and moving
figures in the whole of literature. How sweet must have been that personality
which can still win our affections, across eighteen hundred years of change,
and through the mists of commentaries, and school-books, and traditions!
Does it touch thee at all, oh gentle spirit and serene, that we, who never
knew thee, love thee yet, and revere thee as a saint of heathendom? Have
the dead any delight in the religion they inspire: *id cinerem aut manes credis
curare sepultos?*

Andrew Lang (1844–1912), letter to Lady Violet Lebas

48 **Teucrum:** = **Teucrōrum.**

49 **Pūnica . . . rēbus:** INTERLOCKED WORD ORDER; the standard prose word
order would be **quantīs rēbus glōria Pūnica sē attollet,** *with what great
accomplishments . . ..*

50 **deōs veniam: poscere,** which is commonly employed of prayers, often takes
a double acc., one for the thing requested and the other for the person to
whom the request is being made.

51 **innectō, innectere, innexuī, innexus,** *to fasten/tie on; to weave together; to weave
(plots), devise.*

52 **dēsaeviō, dēsaevīre, dēsaeviī, dēsaevitūrus,** *to work off one's rage; to rage.*
aquōsus, -a, -um, *abounding in water; rainy.*

53 **quassātae . . . ratēs:** i.e., while his ships are still under repair from the damage
incurred in the earlier storm at sea.
*__tractābilis, -is, -e,__ *easy to handle/deal with, manageable; amenable, tractable.*
caelum: i.e., the weather.

54 **incēnsum . . . flammāvit:** some mss. have **impēnsō** here, *immoderate,
uncontrolled;* but **incēnsum** is more likely the correct reading, as Dido was
already ablaze with a passion for Aeneas that her sister's words only further
inflamed.

55 **pudōrem:** here her *conscience;* note the end-line rhyme with **amōre** (54).

56 **pācem:** i.e., the support of the gods.

57 **exquīrō, exquīrere, exquīsīvī, exquīsītus,** *to seek (out), pray for.*
*__bidēns, bidentis,__ m. and f., *sacrificial animal, sheep* (called **bidentēs** because
when young they have two prominent front teeth).

58 **lēgifer, -fera, -ferum,** *law-giving* (applied to Ceres as goddess of agriculture and
hence of civilization).
Lyaeus, -ī, m., *Lyaeus* ("the Liberator," an epithet for the wine god Bacchus, who,
like Ceres and Apollo here, was associated also with marriage).

59 **cui . . . cūrae:** DAT. OF REF. + DAT. OF PURPOSE, the so-called DOUBLE DAT.
vincla iugālia: cf. **vinclō iugālī** (16).

60 **patera, -ae,** f., *shallow bowl* (used in libations).

61 *__candēns; candentis,__ *shining, bright; white.*
vacca, -ae, f., *cow.*
fundit: sc. **vīnum,** in a ritual libation.

62 **ante ōra deum:** i.e., in the presence of their cult statues.
pinguēs: from the sacrificial victims.
spatior, -ārī, -ātus sum, *to walk about slowly, approach* (used often of rituals).

63 **pecus, pecudis,** f., *livestock, animal.*
pecudum . . . exta (64): in a practice known as "haruspicy," the ancients
examined the entrails of sacrificial animals for signs of divine will.

64 **pectoribus:** the final syllable is lengthened under the ictus (DIASTOLE).
inhiō (1), *to open one's mouth; to gape at; to gaze intently at.*

48 coniugiō tālī! Teucrum comitantibus armīs,
49 Pūnica sē quantīs attollet glōria rēbus!
50 Tū modo posce deōs veniam, sacrīsque litātīs
51 indulgē hospitiō causāsque innecte morandī,
52 dum pelagō dēsaevit hiems et aquōsus Orīōn,
53 quassātaeque ratēs, dum nōn tractābile caelum."

Dido propitiates the gods in order to win their favor

54   Hīs dictīs incēnsum animum flammāvit amōre
55 spemque dedit dubiae mentī solvitque pudōrem.
56 Prīncipiō dēlūbra adeunt pācemque per ārās
57 exquīrunt; mactant lēctās dē mōre bidentēs
58 lēgiferae Cererī Phoebōque patrīque Lyaeō,
59 Iūnōnī ante omnēs, cui vincla iugālia cūrae.
60 Ipsa tenēns dextrā pateram pulcherrima Dīdō
61 candentis vaccae media inter cornua fundit,
62 aut ante ōra deum pinguēs spatiātur ad ārās,
63 īnstauratque diem dōnīs, pecudumque reclūsīs
64 pectoribus inhiāns spīrantia cōnsulit exta.

Quaestiōnēs

1. In what several respects does Anna's response to Dido in 31–53 reveal her understanding of her sister's needs and demonstrate that the two truly are **ūnanimae** (as Vergil observes in line 8)? What are her two principal arguments, are they idealistic or pragmatic, and on what different levels were they meant to appeal to Dido?

2. Comment on the echo of line 27 in line 55; what are the dramatic implications? Was Dido's resolve too easily undermined?

65 **Quid . . . / quid (65):** *in what way, how;* here as elsewhere in the poem, Vergil permits his narrator an evaluative comment on the action.

    furentem: sc. **aliquem,** *someone* (i.e., Dido).

66 **Est:** from **edō** (not **sum**).

    Est . . . vulnus (67): the sonorous ALLITERATION in **mollēs flamma medullās** and **vīvit . . . vulnus** and the vivid PERSONIFICATION, which depicts Dido's love as some organism that lives, and feeds, and grows inside her heart, make these two lines particularly effective; and the echo of the similar imagery in lines 1–2 serves as a sort of refrain, effectively introducing the following scene.

    medulla, -ae, f., *marrow* (of the bones); *depths of the mind, heart.*

69 **cerva, -ae,** f., *hind, doe.*

70 **Crēsius, -a, -um,** *of the island of Crete, Cretan* (the Cretans were renowned for their skill as archers, a point Vergil perhaps has in mind here).

71 **agēns:** i.e., *hunting.*

    volātilis, -is, -e, *flying, swift.*

72 **nescius:** a significant correlate to **incautam** (70), underscored through ENJAMBEMENT.

    *****saltus, -ūs,** m., *woodland, grove, glade.*

73 **Dictaeus, -a, -um,** *Dictaean, of Mt. Dicte* (in Crete), *Cretan.*

    lētālis, -is, -e, *deadly, lethal.*

    harundō, harundinis, f., *reed; shaft* (of an arrow), *arrow.*

74 **Nunc . . . / nunc (77):** i.e., during the day and then at night.

75 **ostentō (1),** *to point out, show.*

    parātam: i.e., for him.

77 **eadem . . . convīvia:** i.e., just like the banquet of the previous night.

79 **exposcō, exposcere, expoposcī,** *to ask for, demand, beg.*

    pendet . . . ab ōre: the equivalent Eng. idiom is *hangs on his words.*

80 **vicissim,** adv., *in turn.*

81 **premit:** here *darkens, extinguishes.*

    suādent . . . somnōs: the memorable, highly musical cl. is repeated verbatim from 2.9, deliberately recalling that first banquet, when Dido had called upon her guest to tell of Troy's fall and his subsequent adventures.

82 **relictīs:** by Aeneas at the end of the banquet.

> When day declines, and feasts renew the night,
> Still on his face she feeds her famish'd sight;
> She longs again to hear the prince relate
> His own adventures and the Trojan fate.
> He tells it o'er and o'er; but still in vain,
> For still she begs to hear it once again.
> The hearer on the speaker's mouth depends,
> And thus the tragic story never ends.
>
> *From the translation of John Dryden, 1698*

65 Heu, vātum ignārae mentēs! Quid vōta furentem,

66 quid dēlūbra iuvant?

Dido burns with passion for Aeneas, spends her days
with him, longs for him when they are apart,
and neglects her governance of the city

Est mollēs flamma medullās

67 intereā et tacitum vīvit sub pectore vulnus.

68 Ūritur īnfēlīx Dīdō tōtāque vagātur

69 urbe furēns, quālis coniectā cerva sagittā,

70 quam procul incautam nemora inter Crēsia fīxit

71 pāstor agēns tēlīs līquitque volātile ferrum

72 nescius: illa fugā silvās saltūsque peragrat

73 Dictaeōs; haeret laterī lētālis harundō.

74 Nunc media Aenēān sēcum per moenia dūcit

75 Sīdoniāsque ostentat opēs urbemque parātam,

76 incipit effārī mediāque in vōce resistit;

77 nunc eadem lābente diē convīvia quaerit,

78 Īliacōsque iterum dēmēns audīre labōrēs

79 exposcit pendetque iterum nārrantis ab ōre.

80 Post ubi dīgressī lūmenque obscūra vicissim

81 lūna premit suādentque cadentia sīdera somnōs,

82 sōla domō maeret vacuā strātīsque relictīs

Quaestiōnēs

1. How does meter enhance meaning in line 65? What other stylistic devices add emphasis to 65–66?

2. Discuss the hunting simile in 69–73. How does it evoke sympathy for Dido? In what ways does it foreshadow her ultimate fate? With what character are we meant to associate the **pāstor**, and why is he descibed as **nescius?**

3. Comment on the sound effects in the final clause of the simile (line 73).

4. Explain the effect of the word-picture in 74.

5. Identify the rhetorical device employed in 78–79 and comment on its effect.

83 *absēns, absentis, *not present, absent, although absent.*

84 gremium, -ī, n., *lap, bosom.*

genitōris imāgine: we would say *by his likeness to . . . .*

85 īnfandum: here *beyond words, indescribable,* a powerful word emphasized by its position after the DIAERESIS and before its own cl.

fallere: here *beguile.*

87 exercet . . . parant (88): the shift from sg. to pl. focuses on the Carthaginian youth individually.

prōpugnāculum, -ī, n., *bulwark, rampart, defense.*

bellō: DAT. OF PURPOSE.

88 interrumpō, interrumpere, interrūpī, interruptus, *to break up, interrupt, cut short.*

minae . . . / mūrōrum (89): standard Eng. would use an adj., *threatening walls,* but Vergil uses the noun + gen. construction to lend even greater emphasis to the walls' menacing appearance (see note on mōlem . . . equī 2.32 and cf. rotārum lapsūs 2.235). Some readers, with Servius, take minae to apply more specifically to the walls' *projections,* i.e., its watchtowers.

89 mūrōrum ingentēs: the slow spondees and conflict of ictus and accent help emphasize the enormous scale of the walls.

aequāta . . . caelō: i.e., towering up to the sky; the q/q/c/c ALLITERATION adds a decorative musical effect.

māchina: used at 2.42 of the wooden horse that had towered over Troy's walls; here a crane used in the construction of Carthage's towering fortifications.

90 Quam: = eam, i.e., Dido.

*persentiō, persentīre, persēnsī, persēnsus, *to perceive, realize; to feel deeply.*

pestis, pestis, f., *destruction, death; sickness, disease.*

91 fāmam: i.e., her reputation as a powerful and majestic queen.

*obstō, obstāre, obstitī, obstātus, *to stand in the way of, obstruct, prevent.*

92 Sāturnia: Juno (see note on 1.23).

94 puer . . . tuus: Cupid.

nūmen: in appos. to tū . . . puerque; some late mss. read nōmen, which is accepted by a number of editors as an elaboration of laudem et spolia (83), but nūmen has greater force in intensifying Juno's sarcasm.

95 ūna . . . est: the prose order would be sī ūna fēmina dolō duōrum dīvum victa est; Juno's praise for Venus and Cupid in these opening remarks is intensely ironic, not least in the observation that it has required the powers of the two of them to overcome a single mortal woman.

96 veritam: modifies tē and has moenia nostra as its dir. obj.; Eng. would employ a pres. partic., *fearing.*

tē . . . habuisse (97): with nec . . . fallit, *nor does it escape me that you . . . .*

97 suspectās: OBJ. COMPL. with habuisse domōs.

98 modus: i.e., *the limit/end* (to the struggle of the two goddesses over the ascendancy of the Carthaginians or the Trojans, the future Romans).

quō: *where, to what purpose;* sc. something like contendimus, *do we struggle,* with certāmine tantō (ABL. OF MEANS).

83 incubat. Illum absēns absentem auditque videtque,
84 aut gremiō Ascanium genitōris imāgine capta
85 dētinet, īnfandum sī fallere possit amōrem.
86 Nōn coeptae adsurgunt turrēs, nōn arma iuventūs
87 exercet portūsve aut prōpugnācula bellō
88 tūta parant: pendent opera interrupta minaeque
89 mūrōrum ingentēs aequātaque māchina caelō.

Juno attempts to persuade Venus that the two should join forces
in fostering the love and marriage of Aeneas and Dido

90   Quam simul ac tālī persēnsit peste tenērī
91 cāra Iovis coniūnx nec fāmam obstāre furōrī,
92 tālibus adgreditur Venerem Sāturnia dictīs:
93 "Ēgregiam vērō laudem et spolia ampla refertis
94 tūque puerque tuus (magnum et memorābile nūmen),
95 ūna dolō dīvum sī fēmina victa duōrum est.
96 Nec mē adeō fallit veritam tē moenia nostra
97 suspectās habuisse domōs Karthāginis altae.
98 Sed quis erit modus, aut quō nunc certāmine tantō?

Quaestiōnēs

1. What is the combined effect of the anaphora and polysyndeton in 83?

2. With specific reference to the text, identify the numerous details Vergil employs in 65–85 to build up his image of Dido's agitated mental condition. How realistic a depiction is this of a lover's state of mind?

3. What rhetorical devices and metrical effects emphasize Vergil's point in 86, and what is the special importance of the action in 86–89?

4. What device of word order is employed in line 95 and how does it quite aptly suit the context? How does the word order also serve to underscore the contrast between **ūna** and **duōrum?** Finally, comment on the line's sound effects.

99 **Quīn:** a common colloquialism = *why not?*

pactus, -a, -um, *agreed upon, pledged.*

*****hymenaeus, -ī,** m., usually pl., *marriage, wedding.*

Quīn . . . hymenaeōs: an esp. musical line with ALLITERATION of **p** and the **pāc/pac** and **ae/ae** repetitions.

100 **petīstī:** = **petīvistī.**

102 **Commūnem:** here *in common, jointly.*

103 *****auspicium, -ī,** n., *augury, omen; leadership, authority, auspices; fortune, luck.*

servīre: sc. **eam** (Dido) as subj.

104 **dōtālis, -is, -e,** *as (part of) a dowry.*

dextrae: here a common METONYMY for *power, authority.*

105 **Ollī:** = **illī** (cf. 1.254).

106 **quō:** *by means of which = in order that,* introducing a PURPOSE CL.

107 **contrā:** here *in return, in reply.*

est ingressa: here *began to speak.*

108 **abnuō, abnuere, abnuī,** *to say no, reject, refuse.*

abnuat . . . mālit: DELIBERATIVE SUBJUNCTS.

109 **sī modo:** *if only,* introducing a wish (OPTATIVE SUBJUNCT.)

quod memorās: the anteced. is **factum,** i.e., the marriage of Dido and Aeneas and consequent union of Carthage and Troy.

110 **fātīs:** ABL. OF CAUSE.

incerta . . . sī: *uncertain whether,* introducing an IND. QUEST.

feror: i.e., *carried along, tossed.*

111 **profectīs:** *for those having . . . = for those who have . . . .*

112 *****probō (1),** *to approve (of), commend; to assent to, sanction.*

99 Quīn potius pācem aeternam pactōsque hymenaeōs
100 exercēmus? Habēs tōtā quod mente petīstī:
101 ārdet amāns Dīdō trāxitque per ossa furōrem.
102 Commūnem hunc ergō populum paribusque regāmus
103 auspiciīs; liceat Phrygiō servīre marītō
104 dōtālēsque tuae Tyriōs permittere dextrae."

Venus pretends to agree with Juno,
urging her to consult with Jupiter

105   Ollī (sēnsit enim simulātā mente locūtam,
106 quō rēgnum Ītaliae Libycās āverteret ōrās)
107 sīc contrā est ingressa Venus: "Quis tālia dēmēns
108 abnuat aut tēcum mālit contendere bellō,
109 sī modo quod memorās factum fortūna sequātur?
110 Sed fātīs incerta feror, sī Iuppiter ūnam
111 esse velit Tyriīs urbem Trōiāque profectīs,
112 miscērīve probet populōs aut foedera iungī.

Quaestiōnēs

1. Comment on the word order and the multiple sound effects in 104; how does the word order suit the imagery of marriage and the union of two nations?

2. Identify and analyze the different sorts of arguments, both logical and emotional, that Juno employs in 93–104 in her attempt to enlist the support of her step-daughter Venus; as always, cite specific Latin phrases in the text to support your discussion. Which appeals do you think might potentially have been more persuasive? Compare Juno's rhetorical strategies in her speech to Aeolus at 1.65–75; how is her approach to each god similar, and in what appropriate ways does she vary her approach?

3. Comment on the word order in 112 and its effect.

113 **coniūnx . . . animum:** sc. **Iovis** with each.

    *****precor, -ārī, -ātus sum,** *to pray (for), entreat.*

114 **excēpit:** *took up from there = replied.*

115 **quā ratiōne:** *by what means, how.*

    quod īnstat: *what is pressing = the matter at hand,* subj. of **cōnfierī possit** (116).

116 **cōnfīō, cōnfierī,** *to be done/accomplished, come about, happen.*

    paucīs: sc. **verbīs.**

117 **vēnor, vēnārī, vēnātus sum,** *to go hunting, hunt.*

    Vēnātum: for the form, see note on **scītātum** (2.114).

118 **crāstinus, -a, -um,** *of tomorrow, tomorrow's.*

    ortus, -ūs, m., *rising (of a heavenly body), sunrise.*

119 **Tītān, Tītānis,** m., *Titan* (Vergil alludes to Hyperion, a god of the sun and offspring of one of the giant Titans).

    *****radius, -ī,** m., *ray (of light); pointed rod* (for drawing diagrams).

    orbem: sc. **terrārum.**

120 **nigrō (1),** *to be black.*

    *****commisceō, commiscēre, commiscuī, commixtus,** *to mix together.*

    *****grandō, grandinis,** f., *hail.*

121 **ālae:** here *bands* (of hunters, esp. the attendants who precede the principals in the hunt and flush the animals from the woods, surrounding them with nets).

    indāgō, indāginis, f., *net* (used to trap wild game).

122 *****īnfundō, īnfundere, īnfūdī, īnfūsus,** *to pour in/on/over; to pour down on.*

    tonitrus, -ūs, m., *thunder.*

125 *****voluntās, voluntātis,** f., *will; good will, willingness, pleasure.*

126 **cōnūbiō . . . dicābō:** the line is repeated verbatim from 1.73 above, where Juno promised Aeolus the nymph Deiopeia as his bride; for the scansion of **cōnūbiō,** see note on 1.73.

127 **Hic:** for the quantity of the syllable, see note on **hoc** (2.60).

    adversor, adversārī, adversātus sum, *to act contrary to, oppose, resist.*

128 *****reperiō, reperīre, repperī, repertus,** *to find (out), discover.*

"Aeneas and Dido Hunting"
Jan Miel (1599–1663)
Musée Municipal
Cambrai, France

113 Tū coniūnx, tibi fās animum temptāre precandō.

114 Perge, sequar."

Juno explains to Venus her plan for uniting Dido and Aeneas

Tum sīc excēpit rēgia Iūnō:

115 "Mēcum erit iste labor. Nunc quā ratiōne quod īnstat

116 cōnfierī possit, paucīs (adverte) docēbō.

117 Vēnātum Aenēās ūnāque miserrima Dīdō

118 in nemus īre parant, ubi prīmōs crāstinus ortūs

119 extulerit Tītān radiīsque retēxerit orbem.

120 Hīs ego nigrantem commixtā grandine nimbum,

121 dum trepidant ālae saltūsque indāgine cingunt,

122 dēsuper īnfundam et tonitrū caelum omne ciēbō.

123 Diffugient comitēs et nocte tegentur opācā:

124 spēluncam Dīdō dux et Trōiānus eandem

125 dēvenient. Aderō et, tua sī mihi certa voluntās,

126 cōnūbiō iungam stabilī propriamque dicābō.

127 Hic hymenaeus erit." Nōn adversāta petentī,

128 adnuit atque dolīs rīsit Cytherēa repertīs.

Quaestiōnēs

1. How does Jupiter's prophecy to Venus at 1.257–96 help to explain her seeming approval of Juno's scheme here in 105–14?

2. Compare Venus' reply to Juno in 107–14 with Aeolus' response to the same goddess in 1.76–80; in what ways are the speeches similar in language yet different in intent?

3. What impression of the nature of the gods and their manipulation of humankind are we meant to draw from the exchange between Juno and Venus in 90–114?

4. What devices of word order are employed to especially good effect in line 124?

130 **iubar, iubaris,** n., *first light of day, daylight.*

131 **rēte, rētis,** n., *net* (used for hunting or fishing).

    rāra: with **rētia** = *wide-meshed* (used to cordon off an area of the forest for hunting, vs. the smaller, more tightly meshed **plagae,** which were employed to trap game).

    vēnābulum, -ī, n., *hunting spear.*

    rētia . . . vēnābula: Eng. would more likely say *with their . . .,* but Vergil, for a livelier visual effect, makes the hunters' equipment subj. of **ruunt** along with the hunters themselves.

132 *****Massȳlus, -a, -um,** *Massylian, of the Massyli* (a North African tribe living west of Carthage).

    *****eques, equitis,** m., *horseman, cavalryman, rider.*

    odōrus, -a, -um, *having a smell, scented; of (the faculty of) smelling.*

    odōra canum vīs: Eng. would say "keen-scented dogs"; for the noun + gen. construction, which emphasizes the dogs' powerful sense of smell, see the note on 88–89. The line's unusual off-beat rhythm, created by the three-/two-/one-syllable ending, further intensifies the effect.

133 *****cūnctor, -ārī, -ātus sum,** *to hesitate (over/about), delay; to tarry, linger.*

    prīmī: i.e., *the noblest, the princes.*

134 **ostrum, -ī,** n., *purple dye, purple (color).*

135 **sonipēs, sonipedis,** *making a noise with its feet;* m. substantive, *horse.*

    *****frēnum, -ī,** n., *(a horse's) bridle, harness* (including the reins and bit).

    stat . . . spūmantia: the **s** and **f/r** ALLITERATION is perhaps intended to have an ONOMATOPOETIC effect, suggesting the sound of Dido's horse as it foams and gnashes at its bit; the ASSONANCE in **-mantia mandit** adds further to the line's musicality.

    mandō, mandere, mandī, mānsus, *to chew, bite; (of horses) to champ.*

136 **magnā stīpante catervā:** cf. the similar description of Dido's entourage at 1.497 above, where Vergil goes on to compare the queen with the goddess Diana.

137 *****pictus, -a, -um,** *painted; embroidered* (in color).

    chlamys, chlamydis, f., *cloak, cape.*

    circumdata: here in imitation of the Greek MIDDLE VOICE (see note on **oculōs suffūsa** 1.228) + a dir. obj., *having put on . . . = dressed in . . . .*

    limbus, -ī, m., *(ornamental) border, fringe* (on a garment).

    Sīdoniam . . . limbō: INTERLOCKED WORD ORDER.

138 **cui:** DAT. OF POSSESSION (sc. **est**), = *she had . . . .*

    ex aurō . . . in aurum, / aurea (139): ANAPHORA, with an elegant variation, and the careful positioning at the caesura/line's end/line's beginning, amplify the pictorial effect.

    nōdō (1), *to tie (in knots).*

139 **aurea . . . vestem:** a GOLDEN LINE (quite literally "golden" here!), further elaborating the INTERLOCKED WORD ORDER in 137.

    aurea purpuream: both the queen and her steed (**ostrō . . . et aurō** 134) are richly draped in gold and Tyrian purple (see note on 1.337).

    fībula, -ae, f., *pin, clasp, brooch.*

At dawn Dido and Aeneas, together with their entourage
of both Carthaginians and Trojans, set out on a hunt

129   Ōceanum intereā surgēns Aurōra relīquit.
130 It portīs iubare exortō dēlēcta iuventūs;
131 rētia rāra, plagae, lātō vēnābula ferrō,
132 Massȳlīque ruunt equitēs et odōra canum vīs.
133 Rēgīnam thalamō cūnctantem ad līmina prīmī
134 Poenōrum exspectant, ostrōque īnsignis et aurō
135 stat sonipēs ac frēna ferōx spūmantia mandit.
136 Tandem prōgreditur, magnā stīpante catervā,
137 Sīdoniam pictō chlamydem circumdata limbō;
138 cui pharetra ex aurō, crīnēs nōdantur in aurum,
139 aurea purpuream subnectit fībula vestem.

Aurora, detail from the tomb of Lorenzo de'Medici
Michelangelo
Medici Chapels, S. Lorenzo, Florence, Italy

140   **Nec nōn et:** the effect of the two negatives (LITOTES) is a strong positive, *and then indeed;* the brief sentence and ENJAMBEMENT of **incēdunt** (141) are likewise emphatic.

142   **īnfert sē socium:** = *steps forth to join her.*

143   *hībernus, -a, -um, *of/belonging to/in winter.*

    Lycia, -ae, f., *Lycia* (a country in southern Asia Minor where there was a major temple of Apollo, pictured here as the god's winter abode).

    Xanthus, -ī, m., *Xanthus* (a river in Lycia, not the same as the Trojan Xanthus).

    *fluentum, -ī, n., usually pl., *stream, river.*

144   **Dēlus, -ī,** f., *Delos* (island of the Aegean).

    *māternus, -a, -um, *of/relating to a mother, maternal.*

    Dēlum māternam: Apollo's mother Latona, pregnant by Jupiter, took refuge from Hera on Delos, where she gave birth to both Apollo and Diana.

    invīsō, invīsere, invīsī, invīsus, *to go to see, visit.*

145   **altāria circum:** circum is frequently postpositive, esp. in verse; cf. 1.515 above.

146   **Crēs, Crētis,** m., *Cretan, inhabitant of Crete* (island south of Greece).

    Crētesque: the final syllable is scanned long under the ictus and by separation of the following stop + liquid, an option in verse but unusual when the stop/liquid combination occurs at the beginning of a word. The **e** in the nom. pl. ending here and in **Dryopes** is short because the words are in origin of the Greek third decl., which also has the short vowel.

    Dryopes, Dryopum, m. pl., *the Dryopes* (a tribe in northern Greece).

    Agathyrsī, -ōrum, m. pl., *the Agathyrsi* (a tribe in Scythia).

148   **crīnem . . . implicat aurō:** cf. **crīnēs nōdantur in aurum** (138); while Dido is not in the earlier lines specifically compared to a deity, she is depicted as godlike, just as Aeneas is here likened to Apollo; the connection helps to recall the queen's comparison to Apollo's sister Diana at 1.498–504.

149   **sēgnis, -is, -e,** *sluggish, slow-moving.*

150   **tantum:** i.e., *just so much* as Apollo's.

    ēniteō, ēnitēre, *to shine forth, radiate.*

151   **ventum:** = impers. **ab eīs ventum est** = **vēnērunt.**

    *invius, -a, -um, *pathless, trackless, that cannot be traveled, untraveled.*

    lustrum, -ī, n., *lair, rough/wooded country, wilds.*

152   **dēiectae:** lit., *cast down from, dislodged from,* but Eng. here, as often, would more likely use a pres. act. partic., *slipping down from.*

    capra, -ae, f., *she-goat.*

153   **dēcurrēre:** for the form, see note on **tenuēre** at 1.12.

154   *trānsmittō, trānsmittere, trānsmīsī, trānsmissus, *to send over, pass over; to go across, cross over.*

    trānsmittunt . . . cervī: the spondaic rhythms, conflict of ictus and accent, and the harsh **t/c** ALLITERATION may be meant to suggest how powerfully the deer race across the fields, whereas the next line's opening dactyls perhaps mimic the swiftness of their flight.

155   **pulverulentus, -a, -um,** *dust-covered, dusty.*

157   **hōs . . . illōs:** i.e., the deer and the mountain goats.

158   **darī:** i.e., *would be granted* by the gods.

    inertia: i.e., the more timid, less challenging goats and deer.

140 Nec nōn et Phrygiī comitēs et laetus Ĭūlus
141 incēdunt. Ipse ante aliōs pulcherrimus omnēs
142 īnfert sē socium Aenēās atque agmina iungit.
143 Quālis ubi hībernam Lyciam Xanthīque fluenta
144 dēserit ac Dēlum māternam invīsit Apollō
145 īnstauratque chorōs, mixtīque altāria circum
146 Crētesque Dryopesque fremunt pictīque Agathyrsī;
147 ipse iugīs Cynthī graditur mollīque fluentem
148 fronde premit crīnem fingēns atque implicat aurō,
149 tēla sonant umerīs: haud illō sēgnior ībat
150 Aenēās, tantum ēgregiō decus ēnitet ōre.
151 Postquam altōs ventum in montēs atque invia lustra,
152 ecce ferae saxī dēiectae vertice caprae
153 dēcurrēre iugīs; aliā dē parte patentēs
154 trānsmittunt cursū campōs atque agmina cervī
155 pulverulenta fugā glomerant montēsque relinquunt.
156 At puer Ascanius mediīs in vallibus ācrī
157 gaudet equō iamque hōs cursū, iam praeterit illōs,
158 spūmantemque darī pecora inter inertia vōtīs
159 optat aprum aut fulvum dēscendere monte leōnem.

Quaestiōnēs

1. Discuss in specific detail the several visual techniques Vergil employs in opening
   the hunt scene in 129–42; comment also on the order in which he introduces
   the Africans and Dido and then the Trojans and Aeneas, as well as on other
   strategies of diction and word order he employs to build suspense and bring his
   characters on stage with dramatic flourish.

2. Identify the several detailed correspondences between the description of Aeneas
   and his comparison to Apollo in 141–50 and the description of Dido and her
   comparison to Apollo's sister Diana in 1.494–504 above. Clearly Vergil links the
   two passages deliberately; what were his purposes?

160 **Intereā . . . murmure:** the identical ONOMATOPOETIC phrase is used at 1.124
above, where Vergil describes the storm unleashed by Aeolus also at Juno's
instigation; this image of the heavens contrasts ominously with that at the
beginning of the previous scene (129–30).

163 **Dardanius . . . nepōs Veneris:** i.e., Ascanius, whose father Aeneas was son of
Anchises and Venus.

165 **Spēluncam . . . eandem:** HYPERBATON creates the same striking WORD-PICTURE
seen in 124 above.

166 **Prīma . . . Tellūs:** here the goddess of fertility, *Primal Earth.*
prōnuba Iūnō: Juno, patroness of women and weddings, is present as a *bridal
attendant* when Aeneas and Dido come together as lovers, just as earlier
she had said she would be (**aderō** 125); the signal she gives marks the
commencement of the lovers' mystical "wedding."

167 **fulsēre ignēs:** the lightning flashes recall the torches in a (Roman) wedding.
cōnscius . . . / cōnūbiīs (168): *a witness to their marriage;* the heavens are
PERSONIFIED and, along with the gods of fertility and wedlock and all the
spirits of nature (the Nymphs), attend the mystical union.

168 **ululārunt:** = **ululāvērunt** (see note on **audierat** 1.20), an evocation of the
traditional wedding song and at the same time eerily ominous.

169 **Ille . . . lētī:** a grim irony as the day on which Dido consummated her love for
Aeneas sealed her fate, destining her for eventual suicide and her country for
eternal enmity with Rome (likely the **malōrum** to which Vergil refers).

170 **speciē:** i.e., of impropriety.

171 **furtīvus, -a, -um,** *clandestine, secret, furtive.*
meditor, -ārī, -ātus sum, *to ponder, meditate, contemplate, plan.*

172 **coniugium . . . culpam:** the narrator makes clear that Dido's union with Aeneas
was not a true marriage, though she believes it is (cf. 316 and 324 below);
instead, Juno has perpetrated a cruel hoax, inducing the queen to violate
her oath of fidelity to her deceased husband (see 15f. above and **culpae** 19).
Contributing to the credibility of this plot element is the fact that in Roman
soldiers' unions partners who were not married did nevertheless refer to one
another as **uxor, coniunx,** etc., as attested in funerary inscriptions.
praetexō, praetexere, praetexuī, praetextus, *to border, edge* (with); *to clothe,
cloak, conceal* (with).

173 **Fāma:** in an extended PROSOPOPOEIA, Rumor is presented as an evil, hideous
daughter of mother Earth (**Terra parēns** 178) who grows ever more
monstrous as she moves and spreads her gossip through the world; Vergil's
treatment of the goddess may also be regarded as a form of ALLEGORY.

174 **vēlōx, vēlōcis,** *swift, fast.*
malum . . . ūllum: = **quā nōn ūllum malum (est) vēlōcius;** the rel. pron. **quā** is
ABL. OF COMPARISON.

175 **mōbilitās, mōbilitātis,** f., *movement, (act of) moving.*
adquīrō, adquīrere, adquīsīvī, adquīsītus, *to obtain, acquire, gather.*
vīrēs . . . adquīrit eundō: a frequently quoted **sententia.**

176 **metū:** ABL. OF CAUSE; **prīmō:** here is an adv., not an adj. with **metū.**

During a storm sent by Juno, Dido and Aeneas take shelter in a
cave, become lovers, and the queen calls their union marriage

160   Intereā magnō miscērī murmure caelum
161 incipit, īnsequitur commixtā grandine nimbus,
162 et Tyriī comitēs passim et Trōiāna iuventūs
163 Dardaniusque nepōs Veneris dīversa per agrōs
164 tēcta metū petiēre; ruunt dē montibus amnēs.
165 Spēluncam Dīdō dux et Trōiānus eandem
166 dēveniunt. Prīma et Tellūs et prōnuba Iūnō
167 dant signum; fulsēre ignēs et cōnscius aethēr
168 cōnūbiīs summōque ululārunt vertice Nymphae.
169 Ille diēs prīmus lētī prīmusque malōrum
170 causa fuit; neque enim speciē fāmāve movētur
171 nec iam fūrtīvum Dīdō meditātur amōrem:
172 coniugium vocat, hōc praetexit nōmine culpam.

Swift Rumor rushes over the lands and spreads her tale of Dido's
passion for Aeneas and their neglect of their realms

173   Extemplō Libyae magnās it Fāma per urbēs,
174 Fāma, malum quā nōn aliud vēlōcius ūllum:
175 mōbilitāte viget vīrēsque adquīrit eundō,
176 parva metū prīmō, mox sēsē attollit in aurās

Quaestiōnēs

1. Identify and comment on the detailed correspondences between 161–68 and
   120–27; what do you suppose Vergil's purpose was in these several repetitions?

2. Compare Vergil's sensational account of the "wedding" of Dido and Aeneas in
   160–72 with Apollonius of Rhodes' account of the marriage of Jason and Medea
   in the cave of Macris (*Argonautica* 4.1139–45). What are the most striking
   similarities and differences between the two events? How is Vergil's story
   enlarged through his deliberate allusion and the resonances between the two
   texts and the two pairs of characters?

177   **nūbilum, -ī,** n., *cloud.*

178   **Terra . . . deōrum:** the extensive ALLITERATION of **r** is perhaps meant to suggest the angry roaring of Earth or her demonic daughter.

    inrītō (1), *to move to anger, provoke.*

    deōrum: here OBJ. GEN., i.e., *toward/against the gods;* Earth despised the gods for their destruction of her offspring the Titans and Giants and so gave birth last (**extrēmam** 179) to Rumor, to punish them with her malicious speech.

179   **perhibeō (2),** *to present, give; to say, suppose.*

    perhibent: the subj. *they = people* (in general, and other writers who had told the story before Vergil, Hesiod among them).

    Coeus, -ī, m., *Coeus* (one of the Titans, colossal creatures born from Uranus and Earth).

    Enceladus, -ī, m., *Enceladus* (a Giant who conspired against Jupiter and was destroyed by him along with the other Titans and Giants).

180   **prōgignō, prōgignere, prōgenuī, prōgenitus,** *to produce as offspring, give birth to, bear.*

    pernīx, pernīcis, *swift, agile.*

    prōgenuit . . . ālīs: pedibus is ABL. OF SPECIFICATION with **celerem,** whereas **pernīcibus ālīs** is perhaps best construed as ABL. OF DESCRIPTION. ALLITERATION of **p** and the quick opening dactyls (cf. 177) add suitable sound effects.

181   **mōnstrum horrendum, ingēns:** Vergil had used the same description of the giant cyclops Polyphemus in 3.658; the ELISIONS, slow spondees, and ALLITERATION of **m,** all establish an ominous tone and suggest the creature's unstoppable force.

    cui: DAT. OF POSSESSION.

    plūma, -ae, f., *feather.*

182   *****vigil, vigilis,** *wakeful, watchful, vigilant.*

    subter, adv., *beneath, below, underneath.*

183   *****totidem,** indecl. adj., *the same number (of), (just) as many.*

    subrigō, subrigere, subrēxī, subrēctus, *to raise/lift up, erect.*

184   **mediō:** sc. in, with **caelī . . . terraeque,** = *midway between.*

185   **dēclīnō (1),** *to bend down, lower.*

186   **lūce sedet:** positioned to balance and contrast with **nocte volat** (184).

187   **turribus aut:** ANASTROPHE.

    territō (1), *to frighten repeatedly, scare* (frequentative form of **terreō**).

188   **fictus, -a, -um,** *untrue, made up.*

    prāvus, -a, -um, *crooked, twisted, distorted; corrupt, perverse.*

    fictī prāvīque . . . vērī: all three are employed as SUBSTANTIVES with **tenāx . . . nūntia.**

    *****tenāx, tenācis,** *clinging, gripping; persistent, tenacious.*

    nūntia: = **nūntius** (here f. since referring to **Fāma**).

189   **multiplex, multiplicis,** *having many twists and turns; manifold, multiple; shifting, changeable.*

    replēbat, / . . . canēbat (190): for the end-line rhyme, cf. 54–55 above and 256–57 and 331–32 below.

190   **īnfectus, -a, -um,** *not done/performed.*

177 ingrediturque solō et caput inter nūbila condit.

178 Illam Terra parēns īrā inrītāta deōrum

179 extrēmam, ut perhibent, Coeō Enceladōque sorōrem

180 prōgenuit, pedibus celerem et pernīcibus ālīs,

181 mōnstrum horrendum, ingēns, cui quot sunt corpore plūmae,

182 tot vigilēs oculī subter—mīrābile dictū!—

183 tot linguae, totidem ōra sonant, tot subrigit aurēs.

184 Nocte volat caelī mediō terraeque, per umbram

185 strīdēns, nec dulcī dēclīnat lūmina somnō;

186 lūce sedet custōs aut summī culmine tēctī

187 turribus aut altīs, et magnās territat urbēs,

188 tam fictī prāvīque tenāx quam nūntia vērī.

189 Haec tum multiplicī populōs sermōne replēbat,

190 gaudēns, et pariter facta atque īnfecta canēbat:

Quaestiōnēs

1. What effect does Vergil intend to achieve by his positioning of the words **illam . . . / extrēmam . . . sorōrem / . . . celerem** (179–80)?

2. Identify the rhetorical device employed most prominently in 182–83, and comment on its effect.

3. Comment on the sound effects in both 185 and 187.

Gigantomachy / Battle of Gods and Giants
North frieze of the Siphnian Treasury at Delphi, ca. 525 B.C.
Archaeological Museum, Delphi, Greece

191 **vēnisse Aenēān:** IND. STATE. dependent on **canēbat** (190) and in appos. to **facta atque īnfecta** (190).

  sanguine crētum: cf. 2.74 above.

192 **cui:** with **virō**, *to which man* = *a man to whom.*

193 **lūxus, -ūs,** m., *soft-living, indulgence, extravagance.*

  quam longa: sc. **est,** *as long as it* (the winter) *is.*

  fovēre: with **hiemem** as obj., *while away, enjoy;* sc. **eōs** (Dido and Aeneas) as subj. of the IND. STATE.

194 **immemorēs . . . captōs:** modifying the subj. of **fovēre** (193).

195 **Haec:** acc.; i.e., the gossip in 191–94.

  virum: = **virōrum.**

  in ōra: not merely into their ears but onto their lips, to be passed maliciously along to others.

196 **dētorqueō, dētorquēre, dētorsī, dētortus,** *to turn (away), bend.*

  Ĭarbān: for Iarbas, see line 36 above and note.

197 **aggerō (1),** *to place (at); to heap up (over); to reinforce, intensify.*

198 **Hammō(n), Hammōnis,** m., *Hammon* (an Egyptian god having the form of a ram, often associated by the Romans, as here, with Jupiter).

  Hammōne satus: for the construction, see note on **quō** (2.540).

  Garamantis, Garamantidis, *Garamantian, of the Garamantes* (an African tribe living in the eastern Sahara desert).

200 **vigilem . . . ignem:** i.e., a sacred flame kept perpetually burning, like the fire maintained in temples of Vesta.

201 **excubiae, -ārum,** f. pl., *keeping watch, vigil; guard, sentinel, sentry* (here in appos. with **ignem** 200).

  *****cruor, cruōris,** m., *blood, gore; bloodshed, slaughter.*

202 **pingue solum:** sc. **erat;** for **pingue,** see line 62 and note.

  flōrēns, flōrentis, *flowering, flowery; brilliant, colorful.*

203 **animī:** loc. with **āmēns,** *distraught in his heart;* cf. **fidēns animī** (2.61).

  rūmor, rūmōris, m., *gossip, rumor.*

  amārus, -a, -um, *bitter, harsh.*

205 **multa Iovem:** **ōrāre** can take an acc. for both the person prayed to and the thing prayed for, though **multa** here is nearly equivalent to **saepe.**

  supīnus, -a, -um, *upturned, face up;* (of the hands) *turned palms upward.*

  manibus . . . supīnīs: the usual gesture of prayer; see notes on 1.93, 2.153 and 658.

206 **Maurūsius, -a, -um,** *Moorish, of Mauretania* (a country in North Africa).

207 **epulor, -ārī, -ātus sum,** *to dine sumptuously, feast, banquet.*

  Lēnaeus, -a, -um, *Lenaean, Bacchic, of Bacchus* (the god of wine).

  honōrem: here *offering* (of wine).

208 **haec? An tē, genitor:** the monosyllables and resultant abrupt caesurae help convey Iarbas' agitated state of mind; the series of spondees and the ELISIONS in the next verse similarly underscore his indignation.

209 **caecī:** with **ignēs** (here *thunderbolts*) = *aimless,* i.e., not divinely directed; emphatically positioned, like **nēquīquam** and **inānia** (210).

191 vēnisse Aenēān, Trōiānō sanguine crētum,
192 cui sē pulchra virō dignētur iungere Dīdō;
193 nunc hiemem inter sē lūxū, quam longa, fovēre,
194 rēgnōrum immemorēs turpīque cupīdine captōs.
195 Haec passim dea foeda virum diffundit in ōra.
196 Prōtinus ad rēgem cursūs dētorquet Ïarbān
197 incenditque animum dictīs atque aggerat īrās.

The African king Iarbas, himself rejected as a suitor by
Dido, is enraged by the queen's affair with Aeneas

198   Hic, Hammōne satus raptā Garamantide nymphā,
199 templa Iovī centum lātīs immānia rēgnīs,
200 centum ārās posuit vigilemque sacrāverat ignem,
201 excubiās dīvum aeternās; pecudumque cruōre
202 pingue solum et variīs flōrentia līmina sertīs.
203 Isque āmēns animī et rūmōre accēnsus amārō
204 dīcitur ante ārās media inter nūmina dīvum
205 multa Iovem manibus supplex ōrāsse supīnīs:
206 "Iuppiter omnipotēns, cui nunc Maurūsia pictīs
207 gēns epulāta torīs Lēnaeum lībat honōrem,
208 aspicis haec? An tē, genitor, cum fulmina torquēs,
209 nēquīquam horrēmus, caecīque in nūbibus ignēs

Quaestiōnēs

Comment on the wealth of detail in Vergil's description of the monstrous **Fāma**
(173–97), which is so vivid that some scholars suggest it may have been inspired by a
painting known to the poet and his audience; what are the numerous visual effects?
How might the scene be handled in a modern fantasy or science-fiction film?

210 **terrificō (1)**, *to inspire terror (in), frighten, terrify.*

211 **nostrīs:** the word's displaced position is emphatic.

212 **exiguus, -a, -um,** *small, slight, tiny, puny* (again, positioned for emphasis, underscoring Iarbas' indignation).

    pretiō posuit: Iarbas had sold land to Dido; the harsh ALLITERATION is perhaps intended to suggest the king's anger. On the founding of Carthage, see 1.365–68 above.

213 **locī lēgēs:** i.e., legal terms for maintaining possession of the land *(conditions of tenure).*

215 **ille Paris:** Paris was notorious at once for his amorousness and his effeminacy; calling Aeneas by his name intensifies the insult in this and the following verses.

    sēmivir, -ī, m. and adj., *half-man, effeminate, eunuch.*

    comitātus, -ūs, m., *escort, retinue; throng, attendant crowd.*

216 **Maeonius, -a, -um,** *Maeonian, of Maeonia* (in eastern Lydia).

    *****mentum, -ī,** n., *chin.*

    mitra, -ae, f., *mitra* (an eastern headdress secured with ribbons around the chin).

    madeō, madēre, *to be wet, dripping* (here with oil or perfume, an eastern custom regarded by Romans as a sign of effeminacy).

    Maeoniā . . . madentem: the extensive ALLITERATION (seven **m**'s!) suggests some unmanly sound like moaning or whimpering.

217 **raptō:** *what he has stolen,* i.e., Dido and her kingdom.

218 **ferimus fāmamque fovēmus:** the ALLITERATION is clearly ONOMATOPOETIC, producing an indignant hissing effect; **fāmam** here = *story,* i.e., the misconception that Jupiter responds to men's prayers and sacrifices.

220 **Omnipotēns:** a common epithet of Jupiter (cf. 1.60, 2.689, 4.25 and 206 above), here used in place of his name.

221 **oblītōs:** with **amantēs;** Eng. idiom would more likely employ a rel. cl., *lovers who had . . ..*

    meliōris: i.e., *nobler.*

222 **Mercurius, -ī,** m., *Mercury* (messenger of Jupiter, identified with the Greek messenger god and guide of souls; cf. 1.297–304 above).

    adloquitur: the final syllable is lengthened under the ictus and before the caesura (DIASTOLE).

    *****mandō (1)**, *to hand over, consign; to assign, entrust; to command, order.*

223 **lābere:** imper. of **labor,** here *glide.*

    *****penna, -ae,** f., *wing; feather.*

225 **urbēs:** obj. of **exspectat** as well as **respicit.**

227 **illum . . . tālem:** *such a man.*

228 **Grāium:** = **Grāiōrum.**

    ideō, adv., *for that reason.*

    Nōn (227) . . . ideō: with both **prōmīsit** and **vindicat.**

    bis vindicat: Venus had rescued her son twice in the war at Troy; the pres. tense emphasizes the ongoing consequences of her actions as Aeneas' protectress.

210 terrificant animōs et inānia murmura miscent?
211 Fēmina, quae, nostrīs errāns in fīnibus, urbem
212 exiguam pretiō posuit, cui lītus arandum
213 cuique locī lēgēs dedimus, cōnūbia nostra
214 reppulit ac dominum Aenēān in rēgna recēpit.
215 Et nunc ille Paris cum sēmivirō comitātū,
216 Maeoniā mentum mitrā crīnemque madentem
217 subnexus, raptō potitur: nōs mūnera templīs
218 quippe tuīs ferimus fāmamque fovēmus inānem."

*In response to Iarbas' prayer, Jupiter dispatches his
messenger Mercury to admonish Aeneas and remind
him of his duty to Troy and the future city of Rome*

219   Tālibus ōrantem dictīs ārāsque tenentem
220 audiit Omnipotēns, oculōsque ad moenia torsit
221 rēgia et oblītōs fāmae meliōris amantēs.
222 Tum sīc Mercurium adloquitur ac tālia mandat:
223 "Vāde age, nāte, vocā Zephyrōs et lābere pennīs
224 Dardaniumque ducem, Tyriā Karthāgine quī nunc
225 exspectat fātīsque datās nōn respicit urbēs,
226 adloquere et celerēs dēfer mea dicta per aurās.
227 Nōn illum nōbīs genetrīx pulcherrima tālem
228 prōmīsit Grāiumque ideō bis vindicat armīs,

Quaestiō

Comment on the word order as well as the meter and other sound effects in 210.

229 **fore quī:** = **futūrum esse virum quī**; the whole expression is highly elliptical: from line 227 sc. **illum** as subj. of the IND. STATE. and **prōmīsit** as the speech vb. governing the construction.

    quī . . . regeret (230) . . . / prōderet . . . mitteret (231): REL. CL. OF PURPOSE.

    gravidus, -a, -um, *heavy with young, pregnant; swollen, teeming.*

    gravidam . . . frementem: the CHIASMUS focuses attention on the highly compelling PERSONIFICATION, which depicts the future Italy as a strong, raging beast, *pregnant with power and roaring with warfare.* Vergil employs the same vb. **fremere** in PERSONIFYING the beastlike **Furor** at 1.296.

230 **altō:** here *noble.*

    ā sanguine Teucrī: a deliberate echo from 1.235, in Venus' speech to Jupiter.

231 **orbem:** sc. **terrārum.**

232 **nūlla:** here, as often, essentially = **nōn.**

    accendit: sc. **eum** (Aeneas).

233 **suā . . . laude:** ABL. OF CAUSE.

234 **invidet:** *begrudge;* here, as often, **invidēre** takes a dat. for the person envied and an acc. for the thing.

235 **spē inimīca:** for the HIATUS cf. 1.16 and note.

236 *****Ausonius, -a, -um,** *Ausonian, of the Ausones* (early inhabitants of Campania in south Italy); *Italian, Roman.*

237 **summa, -ae,** f., *sum; full extent, sum-total.*

    estō: fut. imper. of **sum;** the form was often employed in legal or religious documents and has that sort of force here. This entire closing line of Jupiter's speech, with its three abrupt cls., the strong DIAERESIS following **nāviget,** the **haec/hic** ANAPHORA and ASYNDETON, and the final imper., has the power of a divine commandment.

238 **patris . . . pedibus (239):** another extensive ALLITERATIVE sequence, adding a strong musicality to the scene-shift.

239 **tālaria, tālarium,** n. pl., *wings fastened to the ankles, winged sandals.*

240 **quae sublīmem . . . portant (241):** sc. **eum** as dir. obj.; the adj. functions as OBJ. COMPL.

241 **flāmen, flāminis,** n., *blast (of wind), gust; wind, breeze.*

    rapidō pariter cum flāmine: i.e., just as quickly as the wind.

242 **virgam:** the caduceus, a staff entwined with snakes, was associated with Mercury.

    animās . . . / pallentēs (243): cf. **pallentēs umbrās** (line 26 above); like his Greek counterpart Hermes, Mercury escorted the souls of the dead into the Underworld and, reincarnated or as ghostly apparitions, out of the Underworld as well.

    ēvocō (1), *to call out/forth, summon.*

243 *****Tartara, -ōrum,** n. pl., *Tartarus, the Underworld.*

244 **resignō (1),** *to unseal; to loosen, open.*

    lūmina . . . resignat: in Roman custom, family members closed the eyes of their loved ones when they died, then reopened them at their funerals; Mercury is here imagined as presiding over this ritual.

229 sed fore quī gravidam imperiīs bellōque frementem
230 Ītaliam regeret, genus altō ā sanguine Teucrī
231 prōderet, ac tōtum sub lēgēs mitteret orbem.
232 Sī nūlla accendit tantārum glōria rērum
233 nec super ipse suā mōlītur laude labōrem,
234 Ascaniōne pater Rōmānās invidet arcēs?
235 Quid struit? Aut quā spē inimīcā in gente morātur
236 nec prōlem Ausoniam et Lāvīnia respicit arva?
237 Nāviget! Haec summa est; hic nostrī nūntius estō."

Mercury ties on his golden sandals and flies toward the earth

238   Dīxerat. Ille patris magnī pārēre parābat
239 imperiō; et prīmum pedibus tālāria nectit
240 aurea, quae sublīmem ālīs sīve aequora suprā
241 seu terram rapidō pariter cum flāmine portant.
242 Tum virgam capit: hāc animās ille ēvocat Orcō
243 pallentēs, aliās sub Tartara trīstia mittit,
244 dat somnōs adimitque, et lūmina morte resignat.

Quaestiōnēs

Compare Jupiter's speech to Mercury in 223–37 with Venus' speech to Jupiter in 1.229–53; how are the two speeches similarly motivated and what are some of the specific verbal correspondences? Compare also Jupiter's reply to his daughter at 1.257–96 with his speech to Mercury here; what resonances do you find between these two passages?—what actions occur immediately after each speech, and how do they compare? What are Vergil's artistic purposes in making such connections between books?

245 *frētus, -a, -um, + abl., *relying (on), trusting (to), confident (of).*
    agit ventōs: i.e., as if they were a team of horses; cf. the imagery in 1.52–63 and see the note on 1.54.
    *turbidus, -a, -um, *violently agitated, turbulent; troubled, gloomy; confused, disturbed.*
    trānō (1), *to swim across, sail across; to pass through.*
247 *Atlās, Atlantis, m., *Atlas* (a Titan condemned to holding the world upon his shoulders, and a mountain of the same name in northwest Africa).
    fulciō, fulcīre, fulsī, fultus, *to hold up, support.*
248 adsiduē, adv., *continuously, forever.*
    cui: DAT. OF POSSESSION = *whose.*
249 pīniferus, -a, -um, *pine-bearing, pine-covered, pine-wreathed.*
    pulsō (1), *to strike, beat, drive.*
250 nix, nivis, f., *snow.*
    īnfundō, īnfundere, īnfūdī, īnfūsus, *to pour into/over; to clothe.*
251 glaciēs, -ēī, f., *ice.*
    rigeō, rigēre, *to be stiff/rigid; to be cold.*
252 **paribus:** i.e., *balanced, even.*
    nītor, nītī, nīxus sum, *to rest one's weight/lean (on); to balance (oneself), poise.*
    *Cyllēnius, -a, -um, *Cyllenian, of Mt. Cyllene* (a mountain in Arcadia where Mercury was born).
253 **cōnstitit:** Vergil likes to position this vb. at the beginning of the verse and preceding a strong DIAERESIS, aptly, since it implies coming to a firm standstill (cf. 1.226, 1.459, and 2.68 above).
255 piscōsus, -a, -um, *abounding in fish, teeming with fish.*
256 **Haud aliter:** a common LITOTES (cf. 1.399 above), continuing the SIMILE introduced with **avī similis** (254).
    inter: ANASTROPHE of the prep. produces a sort of WORD-PICTURE in **terrās inter caelum;** and note the strong ASSONANCE in **-ter/ter-/-ter,** each syllable bearing either ictus or accent.
257 harēnōsus, -a, -um, *containing sand, sandy.*
258 **māternō . . . avō:** Atlas was father of Maia and hence Mercury's grandfather.
259 ālātus, -a, -um, *having wings, winged.*
    māgālia: the same Carthaginian word employed at 1.421 above.
    planta, -ae, f., *sole of the foot, foot.*
260 *fundō (1), *to lay the foundations of; to found; to give a firm base to, fix.*
    *novō (1), *to make something new, create, build; to change, alter.*
261 **illī:** DAT. OF POSSESSION with **erat** (262).
    stēllātus, -a, -um, *starry, starred, covered/studded with stars.*
    stēllātus . . . / ēnsis (262): either the hilt of the sword or the scabbard might be decorated in this fashion.
    ïaspis, ïaspidis, f., *chalcedony, jasper.*

245 Illā frētus, agit ventōs et turbida trānat
246 nūbila. Iamque volāns, apicem et latera ardua cernit
247 Atlantis dūrī, caelum quī vertice fulcit,
248 Atlantis, cīnctum adsiduē cui nūbibus ātrīs
249 pīniferum caput et ventō pulsātur et imbrī,
250 nix umerōs īnfūsa tegit, tum flūmina mentō
251 praecipitant senis, et glaciē riget horrida barba.
252 Hīc prīmum paribus nītēns Cyllēnius ālīs
253 cōnstitit; hinc tōtō praeceps sē corpore ad undās
254 mīsit avī similis, quae circum lītora, circum
255 piscōsōs scopulōs humilis volat aequora iūxtā.
256 Haud aliter terrās inter caelumque volābat
257 lītus harēnōsum ad Libyae, ventōsque secābat,
258 māternō veniēns ab avō Cyllēnia prōlēs.

Mercury reproaches Aeneas for neglecting his duty
to Troy and Italy and his son Ascanius

259   Ut prīmum ālātīs tetigit māgālia plantīs,
260 Aenēān fundantem arcēs ac tēcta novantem
261 cōnspicit. Atque illī stēllātus ïaspide fulvā

Quaestiōnēs

1. In 246–51 Vergil means us to see at once both Atlas the giant and Atlas the mountain; how does his language contribute to the deliberate ambiguity?

2. Comment on the highly visual effects of the simile in 252–58, including the effect of the anaphora in 254.

3. What similar narrative and cinematographic functions are served by both the Rumor scene in 173–218 and the scene of Mercury's descent to earth in 238–58?

4. Compare Vergil's description of Mercury in 238–58 with Homer's in *Odyssey* 5.43f.; why has Vergil in this instance followed his model so closely?

5. How does meter suit meaning in 260? Comment on the line's other sound effects as well.

262 **mūrex, mūricis**, m., *murex (a shellfish that produced a purple dye, exported esp. from Phoenicia); purple.*

laena, -ae, f., *cloak.*

263 **dēmissa**: Eng. idiom requires a pres. act. partic. (see note on **obortīs** 30 above), *hanging down from.*

264 **tenuī . . . aurō**: i.e., with gold thread.

*discernō, discernere, discrēvī, discrētus, to separate, mark off, divide; to decide, settle, resolve.

discrēverat: in this context = *had interwoven.*

265 **continuō**, adv., *immediately, at once.*

invādit: a strong word for a verbal assault, but well suited to the ferocity of Mercury's attack, which commences with an indignant rhetorical quest. and the abrupt monosyllables, "**Tū nunc . . .?**"

266 **fundāmenta locās**: cf. **fundāmenta locant** in the same metrical position at 1.428; Vergil means to remind us by this echo that Aeneas is now engaged in the same sort of work that he witnessed the Carthaginians performing when he first saw the city.

uxōrius, -a, -um, *of/belonging to a wife; fondly attached to a wife; under a wife's control.*

269 **rēgnātor . . . quī**: the spondaic rhythms lend weight to Mercury's description of Jupiter's majesty, as do the repetition (ANAPHORA) and positioning of **ipse** in 268 and 270.

271 **terō, terere, trīvī, trītus**, *to rub (away), wear (down); to destroy, waste.*

teris . . . terrīs: ASSONANCE underscores the wordplay.

273 **[nec . . . labōrem]**: this verse, which echoes line 233, does not appear in the principal mss. and is generally regarded as an interpolation.

274 **Ascanium . . . Ĭūlī**: Vergil uses the alternate names for Aeneas' son deliberately, "Ascanius" looking to his childhood, and "Iulus" looking toward his future as progenitor of the Julian **gēns.**

surgentem: i.e., as he grows into young manhood.

hērēdis Ĭūlī: with **spēs**, either SUBJ. GEN., *Iulus' hopes as your heir,* or OBJ. GEN., *the expectations of Iulus as your heir.*

278 **in tenuem . . . auram**: a standard formula for the disappearance of a god or a ghost; cf. **tenuēsque recessit in aurās** (2.791 above) of Creusa's phantom.

262 ēnsis erat Tyriōque ārdēbat mūrice laena
263 dēmissa ex umerīs, dīves quae mūnera Dīdō
264 fēcerat et tenuī tēlās discrēverat aurō.
265 Continuō invādit: "Tū nunc Karthāginis altae
266 fundāmenta locās pulchramque uxōrius urbem
267 exstruis? Heu, rēgnī rērumque oblīte tuārum!
268 Ipse deum tibi mē clārō dēmittit Olympō
269 rēgnātor, caelum et terrās quī nūmine torquet,
270 ipse haec ferre iubet celerēs mandāta per aurās:
271 quid struis? Aut quā spē Libycīs teris ōtia terrīs?
272 Sī tē nūlla movet tantārum glōria rērum
273 [nec super ipse tuā mōlīris laude labōrem,]
274 Ascanium surgentem et spēs hērēdis Ĭūlī
275 respice, cui rēgnum Ītaliae Rōmānaque tellūs
276 dēbētur." Tālī Cyllēnius ōre locūtus;
277 mortālēs vīsūs mediō sermōne relīquit
278 et procul in tenuem ex oculīs ēvānuit auram.

Quaestiōnēs

1. What very human emotion does Mercury exhibit in 265–67? How does Vergil employ word order, meter, and other sound effects esp. in 267 to emphasize the god's emotional state?

2. What device of word order is employed in 272, and what is the effect of repositioning the adjectives?

3. Identify the two instances of pleonasm in lines 276-78; how do they differ?

4. Compare Mercury's speech in 265–76 with Jupiter's charge to him in 223–37; identify specifically all the words, phrases, and ideas that are repeated, and comment on the intended effect of these repetitions. What bearing do the resonances between these two speeches have on the question of whether or not line 273 is in fact an interpolation?

5. How can Mercury's visit to Aeneas in 259–78 be taken literally and at the same time be construed as symbolizing the Trojan leader's conscience?

6. How does meter reinforce meaning in verse 278?

279 *aspectus, -ūs, m., *sight, vision.*

    At . . . aspectū: The grave spondees, conflict of ictus and accent, and the gasping -ās/as- ASSONANCE lend a striking musical effect to this horrific moment.

    *obmūtēscō, obmūtēscere, obmūtuī, *to become incapable of speech, be dumbstruck; to become/remain silent.*

280 arrēctae . . . haesit: cf. Aeneas' identical response to the ghost of his wife Creusa in 2.774 (**obstipuī, steteruntque comae et vōx faucibus haesit**).

282 monitus, -ūs, m., *warning, admonition.*

283 agat . . . / audeat . . . sūmat (284): DELIBERATIVE SUBJUNCTS. suggesting the uncertainty in Aeneas' mind.

    Quō: with **adfātū** (284).

    ambiō, ambīre, ambīvī, ambītus, *to visit in rotation; to visit/approach* (in search of support or sympathy).

    furentem: knowing Dido's passion, Aeneas (correctly) anticipates her reaction.

284 adfātus, -ūs, m., *address, speech.*

    exōrdium, -ī, n., *starting point, beginning* (often of a speech).

286 partēs: here *directions.*

287 alternō (1), *to waver, alternate.*

    potior, potior, potius, *stronger, more powerful; more desirable, preferable.*

288 Mnēstheus, -ī, acc. Mnēsthea, m., *Mnestheus* (a Trojan officer).

    Serestus, -ī, m., *Serestus* (another Trojan warrior).

    Mnēsthea . . . Serestum: cf. **Anthea Sergestumque videt fortemque Cloanthum** (1.510 above and note); Vergil typically uses names formulaically in this way and for an individualizing effect.

289 aptent: here *fit out, outfit;* this vb., as well as **cōgant, parent,** and **dissimulent,** are all IND. COMMANDS or JUSSIVE NOUN CLS. dependent on the notion of command in **vocat** (288), *he summons them to outfit . . ..*

    tacitī: Eng. would employ an adv.

290 arma: here probably the ships' *tackle* (as opposed to *weapons* against an attack by the Carthaginians, which Vergil does not otherwise factor into his plot).

291 sēsē . . . / temptātūrum (293): SC. **esse;** IND. STATE., after an implied speech vb. suggested by **sententia** (287), *(he decides that) he will try (to find) . . ..*

    optima: usually taken to be a reflection of Aeneas' own esteem for Dido, and not just the poet-narrator's evaluation.

292 spēret: here *would . . . expect.*

293 mollissima: i.e., *the kindest.*

294 rēbus: i.e., *for the circumstances/for his purpose.*

    dexter: here, as often, *favorable, propitious.*

    ōcius, adv., *quickly, speedily.*

295 facessō, facessere, facessīvī, facessītus, *to carry out quickly, perform eagerly.*

*Persuaded by Mercury's speech but unsure how to explain to Dido
that he must depart, Aeneas orders his men to ready the fleet*

279　　　At vērō Aenēās aspectū obmūtuit āmēns,

280　arrēctaeque horrōre comae et vōx faucibus haesit.

281　Ārdet abīre fugā dulcēsque relinquere terrās,

282　attonitus tantō monitū imperiōque deōrum.

283　Heu, quid agat? Quō nunc rēgīnam ambīre furentem

284　audeat adfātū? Quae prīma exōrdia sūmat?

285　Atque animum nunc hūc celerem nunc dīvidit illūc

286　in partēsque rapit variās perque omnia versat.

287　Haec alternantī potior sententia vīsa est:

288　Mnēsthea Sergestumque vocat fortemque Serestum,

289　classem aptent tacitī sociōsque ad lītora cōgant,

290　arma parent et quae rēbus sit causa novandīs

291　dissimulent; sēsē intereā, quandō optima Dīdō

292　nesciat et tantōs rumpī nōn spēret amōrēs,

293　temptātūrum aditūs et quae mollissima fandī

294　tempora, quis rēbus dexter modus. Ōcius omnēs

295　imperiō laetī pārent et iussa facessunt.

Quaestiōnēs

1. Comment on the sound effects in line 282.

2. Discuss in detail the insights we are given into Aeneas' character by the scene in 279–95; consider the significance of the adjectives **dulcēs** in 281 and **optima** in 291. How do the questions in 283–84 involve us, the audience, in Aeneas' dilemma?

296 **At rēgīna:** the same two words open the book in line 1, focusing attention directly upon the queen.

297 **praesentiō, praesentīre, praesēnsī, praesēnsus,** *to perceive/sense beforehand; to apprehend beforehand, have a presentiment of.*
mōtus, -ūs, m., *movement; change/shift* (of events).
excēpit: here *caught word of, picked up on.*

298 **omnia tūta:** i.e., although everything seemed safe.
Eadem impia Fāma: a deliberate evocation of the scene in 173f.

299 **dētulit:** here *reported* + IND. STATE.

300 *__inops, inopis,__ *lacking wealth, poor; resourceless, helpless;* + gen., *devoid* (of), *deficient* (in).

301 *__bacchor, -ārī, -ātus sum,__ *to celebrate the rites of Bacchus* (god of wine); *to act like a Bacchante* (a Bacchic celebrant), *rage, rave.*
exciō, excīre, excīvī, excitus, *to rouse, startle, stir up, excite.*

302 **Thyias** (disyllabic, with **yi** a diphthong like **ui**), **Thyiadis,** f., *cultist, Bacchante.*
stimulō (1), *to goad, fire up, excite.*
trietēricus, -a, -um, *occurring every third year, in alternate years.*
Bacchō: here *Bacchic cry/shout* (noisy celebrations were part of the orgiastic Bacchic revels).

303 **orgia, -ōrum,** n. pl., *secret rites, mysteries, revels.*
Cithaerōn, Cithaerōnis, m., *Mt. Cithaeron* (a mountain in southern Boeotia associated with the cult of Bacchus).
quālis (301) . . . Cithaerōn: the SIMILE dramatically emphasizes the point that Dido is a woman possessed and not in rational control of her senses.

304 **ultrō:** for the sense employed here, see note on **ultrō . . . compellāre** (2.279–80 above).

305 **spērāstī:** = **spērāvistī;** for the SYNCOPATED form, see note on **audierat** (1.20).
*__perfidus, -a, -um,__ *treacherous, false, deceitful.*

307 **dextera:** = **dextra;** the *right hand* as a pledge of loyalty, esp. in marriage, an allusion to their "wedding" in the cave.

308 **moritūra . . . fūnere:** at the hands of her enemies (cf. 325–26), as Aeneas would interpret this; though the narrator intends an allusion, of course, to the queen's death by her own hand, a course she only later decides upon.

309 **sīdere:** here = *season;* with Dido's angry recriminations here, cf. Anna's contriving in 52–53.

310 *__properō (1),__ *to hurry, hasten.*

311 **aliēnus, -a, -um,** *foreign, alien.*

312 **manēret:** i.e., still standing.

313 **undōsus, -a, -um,** *abounding in waves; stormy.*

314 **tuam tē:** the juxtaposition of these words, reserving **tē** to line's end, and the monosyllabic ending and resultant offbeat rhythm, all add emotional intensity to Dido's appeal; **tē** is obj. of **ōrō,** supplied from 319.

*Dido learns from Rumor of the fleet's preparations and,
in a frenzy, races through the city to find Aeneas*

296   At rēgīna dolōs (quis fallere possit amantem?)
297 praesēnsit, mōtūsque excēpit prīma futūrōs,
298 omnia tūta timēns. Eadem impia Fāma furentī
299 dētulit armārī classem cursumque parārī.
300 Saevit inops animī tōtamque incēnsa per urbem
301 bacchātur, quālis commōtīs excita sacrīs
302 Thyias, ubi audītō stimulant trietērica Bacchō
303 orgia nocturnusque vocat clāmōre Cithaerōn.

*The queen encounters Aeneas, rages at him for planning to
abandon her, and implores him to change his mind*

304   Tandem hīs Aenēān compellat vōcibus ultrō:
305 "Dissimulāre etiam spērāstī, perfide, tantum
306 posse nefās tacitusque meā dēcēdere terrā?
307 Nec tē noster amor, nec tē data dextera quondam,
308 nec moritūra tenet crūdēlī fūnere Dīdō?
309 Quīn etiam hībernō mōlīrī sīdere classem
310 et mediīs properās Aquilōnibus īre per altum,
311 crūdēlis? Quid, sī nōn arva aliēna domōsque
312 ignōtās peterēs, et Trōia antīqua manēret,
313 Trōia per undōsum peterētur classibus aequor?
314 Mēne fugis? Per ego hās lacrimās dextramque tuam tē
315 (quandō aliud mihi iam miserae nihil ipsa relīquī),

Quaestiōnēs

1. Compare Dido's behavior in 296–303 with Aeneas' in the immediately preceding
   scene; what fundamental differences between the two characters is highlighted
   by the juxtaposition of the two scenes?

2. What rhetorical devices are employed in 307–08 and what is the combined
   effect?

317 **fuit . . . meum (318):** = **aut sī quicquam meum fuit tibi dulce.**

318 **istam:** with **mentem (319),** *intention/purpose,* each emphatically placed.

320 **Nomades, Nomadum,** m. pl., *Nomads;* in North Africa, *Numidians.*

321 **ōdēre:** sc. **mē.**

    īnfēnsī Tyriī: sc. **sunt.**

    eundem: lit., *the same (you),* though we might simply say *again* or *also;* the word, emphatically positioned, further intensifies the effect of the ANAPHORA **tē propter . . . tē propter,** as does Vergil's use of ANASTROPHE (metrically he could just as well have written **propter tē**).

323 **moribundus, -a, -um,** *on the point of death, dying* (see note on **moritūra 308**).

    hospes: no longer "husband" or "lover," **hospes** is what Dido had called Aeneas when they first met (see 1.753 above). Servius remarks that Vergil was overcome by emotion as he recited these lines to Augustus.

324 **dē coniuge:** i.e., *from the name of . . ..*

326 ****dēstruō, dēstruere, dēstrūxī, dēstrūctus,** *to demolish, destroy.*

    an . . . (325) / dēstruat: = **an dum Pygmaliōn frāter moenia mea dēstruat,** ANTICIPATORY SUBJUNCT.; for Pygmalion, see note on 1.347 above. The concerns mentioned in 325–26 intentionally echo those expressed by Anna at 36–44.

    captam: sc. **mē.**

327 **sī qua:** with **subolēs (328).**

328 **subolēs, subolis,** f., *offspring, child.*

    parvulus: DIMINUTIVES are rare in epic, belonging instead to the language of elegy; this word, the only diminutive adj. in the *Aeneid,* is thus intended to evoke intense pathos.

329 **tamen:** i.e., in Aeneas' absence.

    quī tē . . . referret: *who would bring you back,* i.e., *remind me of you;* REL. CL. OF CHARACTERISTIC.

330 **omnīnō,** adv., *entirely, altogether, completely, utterly.*

    capta: *taken by force, vanquished;* here and elsewhere in the book Vergil uses military imagery in describing love's assault, a convention adapted from elegiac poetry.

331 **monita, -ōrum,** n. pl., *advice, warnings* (here ABL. OF CAUSE).

    tenēbat / . . . premēbat (332): for the end-line rhyme, see note on 189–90.

332 ****obnīxus, -a, -um,** *straining, exerting great effort; determined, resolute.*

    obnīxus . . . premēbat: Aeneas represses his emotions only with enormous effort; cf. **premit altum corde dolōrem** (1.209).

333 **Ego tē:** an intensely emotional juxtaposition.

    plūrima: obj. of **prōmeritam** (335, sc. **esse**) and anteced. of **quae;** prose order would be **ego numquam negābō tē prōmeritam (esse) plūrima quae fandō ēnumerāre valēs (= potes).**

    fandō: we would simply say "in words."

334 **ēnumerō (1),** *to set forth, list, enumerate.*

316 per cōnūbia nostra, per inceptōs hymenaeōs,
317 sī bene quid dē tē meruī, fuit aut tibi quicquam
318 dulce meum, miserēre domūs lābentis et istam,
319 ōrō, sī quis adhūc precibus locus, exue mentem.
320 Tē propter Libycae gentēs Nomadumque tyrannī
321 ōdēre, īnfēnsī Tyriī; tē propter eundem
322 exstīnctus pudor et, quā sōlā sīdera adībam,
323 fāma prior. Cui mē moribundam dēseris, hospes
324 (hoc sōlum nōmen quoniam dē coniuge restat)?
325 Quid moror?—an mea Pygmaliōn dum moenia frāter
326 dēstruat aut captam dūcat Gaetūlus Ïarbās?
327 Saltem sī qua mihī dē tē suscepta fuisset
328 ante fugam subolēs, sī quis mihi parvulus aulā
329 lūderet Aenēās, quī tē tamen ōre referret,
330 nōn equidem omnīnō capta ac dēserta vidērer."

Concealing the true measure of his love, Aeneas tells Dido that he
does care for her, but that he had not married her and owed his
allegiance instead to his country, his son, and to the gods

331   Dīxerat. Ille Iovis monitīs immōta tenēbat
332 lūmina et obnīxus cūram sub corde premēbat.
333 Tandem pauca refert: "Ego tē, quae plūrima fandō
334 ēnumerāre valēs, numquam, rēgīna, negābō

Quaestiōnēs

1. Compare the military imagery in 330 with the language employed by Juno in
    4.93–95 above; what are Vergil's purposes in employing such imagery?

2. Analyze Dido's speech in 305–30; what specific arguments does she employ,
    and what different types of appeal, and which might potentially have been most
    successful with Aeneas?

3. Compare this same speech (in 305–30) with that of the deserted Ariadne to
    Theseus in Catullus 64.132f., noting the several close verbal correspondences;
    how can such intertextuality serve to enlarge and enrich the meaning of a
    poem?

335 **prōmereor, prōmerērī, prōmeritus sum**, *to deserve, earn, merit.*
    piget, pigēre, piguit, impers. + acc. + inf., *it displeases, irks, causes regret for*
        (someone to do something).
    Elissa, -ae, f., *Elissa* (Dido's Phoenician name; here gen. with **meminisse**).
336 **dum . . . meī**: sc. **sum**; i.e., as long as he has any consciousness at all, as long as
    he lives.
    spīritus, -ūs, m., *breathing, breath; spirit, soul.*
337 **Prō rē**: legalistic, *for my own case, in defense of my conduct.*
    abscondō, abscondere, abscondī, absconditus, *to hide (away), conceal, keep*
        secret (here inf. with **spērāvī 338**).
    fūrtum, -ī, n., *robbery, theft; stealth, deceit, trickery.*
338 **nē finge**: = **nōlī fingere**, *do not imagine* (such a thing).
    nec . . . vēnī (339): Dido, under the influence of Juno, had regarded her
        relationship with Aeneas as a marriage, but Aeneas himself did not; the slow
        spondees and accentual conflict in 339 underscore his point.
339 *****praetendō, praetendere, praetendī, praetentus**, *to hold out; to extend across,*
        stretch forth.
341 *****spōns, spontis**, f., *will, volition.*
343 **Priamī . . . manērent**: because he would have rebuilt what could still be called,
    even after the king's death, Priam's city.
344 **recidīvus, -a, -um**, *falling back* (into the soil); *reborn.*
    posuissem: = **reposuissem**, I *would have restored;* in some versions of the story
        Aeneas did indeed remain behind in Troy and rebuild the city (Vergil often
        alludes to, and expected his educated Roman audience to be aware of, plot
        options from the Trojan saga and related narrative traditions that he chooses
        not to explore or elaborate in his own reinterpretation of the legend).
345 **Ītaliam . . . / Ītaliam (346)**: ANAPHORA, ASYNDETON, and positioning of the
    repeated noun at the beginning of the line in 346 all serve to intensify
    Aeneas' point.
    Grȳnēus, -a, -um, *Grynean, of Grynium* (a town in Aeolia known for its cult of
        Apollo).
346 **Lyciae . . . sortēs**: there was a famous shrine to Apollo at Patara in Lycia; Vergil
    told in Book Three of prophecies that Aeneas had received from Apollo
    (though none from Lycia).
347 **hic**: Italy; m. by attraction to the gender of **amor**.
348 *****Phoenissus, -a, -um**, *Phoenician, of Phoenicia* (country along the eastern
    Mediterranean coast, former home of Dido).
        tē (347) . . . / Phoenissam: *you as a Phoenician.*
    dētinet: sg. to agree with the nearer of the two subjs. (**arcēs** and **aspectus**).
349 **quae . . . / invidia est (350)**: freely, *why do you begrudge (that)* + acc./inf.
350 **fās**: sc. **est**, + acc./inf.
    exter, -tera, -terum, *external; foreign.*
351 **patris Anchīsae**: with **turbida . . . imāgō (353)**; these visions are not mentioned
    elsewhere in the story but are a reminder, like the references to Ascanius and
    the gods in the lines following, of Aeneas' breach of **pietās**.
    *****quotiēns**, adv., *as often (as).*

335 prōmeritam, nec mē meminisse pigēbit Elissae

336 dum memor ipse meī, dum spīritus hōs regit artūs.

337 Prō rē pauca loquar. Neque ego hanc abscondere fūrtō

338 spērāvī (nē finge) fugam, nec coniugis umquam

339 praetendī taedās aut haec in foedera vēnī.

340 Mē sī fāta meīs paterentur dūcere vītam

341 auspiciīs et sponte meā compōnere cūrās,

342 urbem Trōiānam prīmum dulcēsque meōrum

343 rēliquiās colerem, Priamī tēcta alta manērent,

344 et recidīva manū posuissem Pergama victīs.

345 Sed nunc Ītaliam magnam Grȳnēus Apollō,

346 Ītaliam Lyciae iussēre capessere sortēs;

347 hic amor, haec patria est. Sī tē Karthāginis arcēs

348 Phoenissam Libycaeque aspectus dētinet urbis,

349 quae tandem Ausoniā Teucrōs cōnsīdere terrā

350 invidia est? Et nōs fās extera quaerere rēgna.

351 Mē patris Anchīsae, quotiēns ūmentibus umbrīs

Quaestiō

In what way is the meter in 342 especially effective?

352 **igneus, -a, -um,** *of fire, fiery.*

353 **admoneō, admonēre, admonuī, admonitus,** *to warn, admonish.*

354 **mē puer Ascanius:** sc. **admonet** from 353; the phrase is positioned to parallel **mē patris Anchīsae** (351).

    capitis: caput used here, as often, for *person;* OBJ. GEN. with **iniūria,** *the wrong being done to . . ..*

355 **fraudō (1),** *to deprive, cheat;* + abl., *to deprive of, cheat out of.*

356 *****interpres, interpretis,** m., *intermediary, agent; spokesman, messenger.*

357 **utrumque caput:** i.e., by both his own life and Dido's.

    celerēs . . . aurās: cf. Jupiter's own words at 226 (**celerēs . . . mea dicta per aurās**) and Mercury's at 270 (**celerēs mandāta per aurās**).

360 **querēla, -ae,** f., *appeal, complaint.*

361 **sponte:** sc. **meā;** Aeneas closes his speech with a succinct summation of the point made in 340–46 (cf. **sponte** in the same metrical position in 341).

362 **āversa:** i.e., she had turned slightly away from him, watching him only with sidelong glances.

363 **tōtum:** our idiom is "from top to bottom" or "from head to toe."

"Mercury Attaching His Sandals," Jean-Baptiste Pigalle (1714–85)
Louvre, Paris, France

352 nox operit terrās, quotiēns astra ignea surgunt,
353 admonet in somnīs et turbida terret imāgō;
354 mē puer Ascanius capitisque iniūria cārī,
355 quem rēgnō Hesperiae fraudō et fātālibus arvīs.
356 Nunc etiam interpres dīvum Iove, missus ab ipsō
357 (testor utrumque caput), celerēs mandāta per aurās
358 dētulit: ipse deum manifestō in lūmine vīdī
359 intrantem mūrōs vōcemque hīs auribus hausī.
360 Dēsine mēque tuīs incendere tēque querēlis;
361 Ītaliam nōn sponte sequor."

Enraged, Dido rejects Aeneas' excuses and promises vengeance

362   Tālia dīcentem iamdūdum āversa tuētur,
363 hūc illūc volvēns oculōs, tōtumque pererrat

Quaestiōnēs

1. How does Vergil use both diction and meter to emphasize Aeneas' point in 358–59?

2. Comment on the structure of 360.

3. Lines 331–61, positioned at the very center of the book, present us with Aeneas' only direct speech to Dido and the scene is crucial to our interpretation of his action. T.E. Page, a 19th-century editor of the *Aeneid*, remarked of the speech that "Not all Virgil's art can make the figure of Aeneas here appear other than despicable," adding in the introduction to his text that "to an appeal that would move a stone Aeneas replies with the cold and formal rhetoric of an attorney"— but is this a fair assessment? Identify specifically the several different arguments Aeneas employs in these lines in defense of his decision to leave Carthage. Which might indeed seem abrupt, callous, or even legalistic? But how does Vergil intend our response to Aeneas' tone here to be conditioned by the feelings for Carthage and Dido that are attributed to him in his response to Mercury at 279–95 (especially in lines 281 and 291), by the insight the narrator provides in his preface to the speech in 331–32, and by Aeneas' own remarks, especially his final assertion in 361? When viewed from the perspective of Stoic ideals and the Roman conception of **pietās**, why are Aeneas' departure and his response to Dido's entreaties inevitable? On the other hand, when viewed against those same standards of **pietās** and Stoicism and his divine mission, what has been Aeneas' most grievous lapse in the action of this book, and can we forgive him for it?

364 **tacitīs**: i.e., *expressionless*.

365 **Nec . . . tigrēs (367)**: challenging a person's parentage was a common feature of invective, but here Dido's words contrast sharply with her first address to Aeneas in 1.615–18 (and cf. line 12 above).

    tibi: DAT. OF POSSESSION with **parēns** and **Dardanus**; sc. **fuit** with both subjs.

    generis: with **auctor**.

    Dardanus, -ī, m., *Dardanus* (son of Zeus and Electra, founder of Dardania in the Troad, and ancestor of Priam).

366 **perfide**: repeated from 305.

    *****cautēs, cautis**, f., *rock, cliff, crag, reef*.

367 **Caucasus, -ī**, m., *the Caucasus mountains* (in the Caucasus, between the Black Sea and the Caspian Sea, regarded by the ancients as a harsh and intemperate region).

    Hyrcānus, -a, -um, *Hyrcanian, of Hyrcania* (a country to the southeast of the Caspian Sea).

    admōrunt: = **admōvērunt**; sc. **tibi**.

368 **quid**: here, as often, *why*.

    quae . . . maiōra: i.e., *what greater wrongs*.

369 **Num . . . est (370)**: TRICOLON CRESCENS, ANAPHORA, ASYNDETON, and Dido's bitter reference to Aeneas in third pers., all underscore the severity of the queen's indignation. The charge in **num lūmina flexit** deliberately recalls the scene in 331–32.

370 *****miseror, -ārī, -ātus sum**, *to view with compassion, feel sorry for, pity*.

371 **anteferō, anteferre, antetulī, antelātus**, *to put* (something, someone) *before* (another), *give precedence to*.

    Quae . . . anteferam: lit., *what things shall I put before what*; i.e., *what shall I say or do first, what next?*

372 **Sāturnius . . . pater**: Jupiter; cf. **Sāturnia** of Juno in 1.23.

376 **augur, auguris**, m., *augur, interpreter of omens; prophet, seer*.

378 **fert horrida iussa per aurās**: Dido's own sarcastic elaboration of Aeneas' **mandāta per aurās / dētulit** (357–58).

379 **Scīlicet**: here, as often, the word's tone is sarcastic.

    quiētōs: sc. **eōs**; Eng. would say "in their tranquillity."

380 **sollicitō (1)**, *to harass, disturb, worry*.

    refellō, refellere, *to refute, rebut, argue against*.

    Scīlicet (379) . . . refellō: the quick dactylic rhythms of these two lines suit the abrupt tenor of Dido's remarks.

382 **sī quid . . . possunt**: i.e., *if they have any power*; sc. something like **facere**.

383 **supplicium, -ī**, n., *punishment; suffering, torment*.

    hausūrum: i.e., **tē hausūrum esse**; the image is that of Aeneas shipwrecked on the reefs and drowning in the waters of Dido's hatred.

385 **sēdūcō, sēdūcere, sēdūxī, sēductus**, *to draw aside; to separate* (from).

386 **umbra**: *as a ghost*; Dido clearly implies here and in the following line that she will soon be dead, by suicide as we see later in the book.

387 **mānēs . . . sub īmōs**: i.e., *deep in the Underworld*.

364 lūminibus tacitīs et sīc accēnsa profātur:

365 "Nec tibi dīva parēns generis nec Dardanus auctor,

366 perfide, sed dūrīs genuit tē cautibus horrēns

367 Caucasus Hyrcānaeque admōrunt ūbera tigrēs.

368 Nam quid dissimulō aut quae mē ad maiōra reservō?

369 Num flētū ingemuit nostrō? Num lūmina flexit?

370 Num lacrimās victus dedit aut miserātus amantem est?

371 Quae quibus anteferam? Iam iam nec maxima Iūnō

372 nec Sāturnius haec oculīs pater aspicit aequīs.

373 Nusquam tūta fidēs. Ēiectum lītore, egentem

374 excēpī et rēgnī, dēmēns, in parte locāvī.

375 Āmissam classem, sociōs ā morte redūxī

376 (heu furiīs incēnsa feror!): nunc augur Apollō,

377 nunc Lyciae sortēs, nunc et Iove missus ab ipsō

378 interpres dīvum fert horrida iussa per aurās.

379 Scīlicet is superīs labor est, ea cūra quiētōs

380 sollicitat. Neque tē teneō neque dicta refellō:

381 ī, sequere Ītaliam ventīs, pete rēgna per undās.

382 Spērō equidem mediīs, sī quid pia nūmina possunt,

383 supplicia hausūrum scopulīs et nōmine 'Dīdō'

384 saepe vocātūrum. Sequar ātrīs ignibus absēns

385 et, cum frīgida mors animā sēdūxerit artūs,

386 omnibus umbra locīs aderō. Dabis, improbe, poenās.

387 Audiam et haec mānēs veniet mihi fāma sub īmōs."

Quaestiōnēs

1. How specifically do Dido's words in 376–78 echo Aeneas' in 345–58? What is the intended effect?

2. Comment on the emotional effect of the three imperatives and asyndeton in 381.

3. Explain how the phrase **mediīs . . . scopulīs** (382–83) forms a word-picture.

4. Analyze the differences between Dido's earlier speech at 305–30 and her response to Aeneas in 365–87; in what specific ways have her tone and purpose changed?

388 **medium:** *midway, in mid-course.*

abrumpō, abrumpere, abrūpī, abruptus, *to break (apart); to break off, cut short, end.*

389 **aegra:** i.e., *at heart.*

390 **cūnctantem . . . parantem:** sc. **eum;** the pron. modified by a partic. is often omitted (cf. **dolentem** 393). **Cūnctantem et multa parantem / dīcere** seems a deliberate echo of **lacrimantem et multa volentem / dīcere** (2.790–91), again of Aeneas' response as the phantom of Creusa vanishes into thin air.

391 **famula, -ae,** f., *maid-servant, (female) attendant.*

392 **marmoreus, -a, -um,** *(made of) marble.*

393 **pius:** a key thematic word, employed at a critical moment in the drama and indeed for the first time in this book.

395 **labefaciō, labefacere, labefēcī, labefactus,** *to make unsteady, shake.*

animum labefactus: we might say *shaken to the heart;* for the construction, see note on **oculōs suffūsa** (1.228).

396 **exsequor, exsequī, exsecūtus sum,** *to follow, go along with; to carry out, execute, perform.*

398 **ūnctus, -a, -um,** *covered with oil, oiled, greased* (here, with pitch).

carīna: sg. for pl.

399 *****frondēns, frondentis,** *covered with leaves, leafy.*

frondentēs . . . rēmōs: in their eagerness to depart, the Trojan sailors quickly fashion new oars from freshly cut branches still sprouting leaves; **rēmōs et rōbora** = HENDIADYS.

400 **īnfabricātus, -a, -um,** *unfashioned, unwrought, unshaped.*

401 **cernās:** POTENTIAL SUBJUNCT.

402 **formīca, -ae,** f., *ant.*

far, farris, n., *barley, wheat, grain.*

*****acervus, -ī,** m., *pile, heap.*

405 **convectō (1),** *to carry, transport.*

it (404) . . . / convectant: the collective noun **agmen** here takes both sg. and pl. vbs.

callis, callis, m., *rough track, path.*

grandis, -is, -e, *large, huge.*

trūdō, trūdere, trūsī, trūsus, *to push, shove.*

pars . . . trūdunt / obnīxae (406): here and below the collective sg. **pars** is construed with pl. adj. and vbs.

388 Hīs medium dictīs sermōnem abrumpit et aurās
389 aegra fugit sēque ex oculīs āvertit et aufert,
390 linquēns multa metū cūnctantem et multa parantem
391 dīcere. Suscipiunt famulae conlāpsaque membra
392 marmoreō referunt thalamō strātīsque repōnunt.

Though longing to console Dido, Aeneas returns to the harbor,
and the queen watches from her palace as his fleet prepares to sail

393   At pius Aenēās, quamquam lēnīre dolentem
394 sōlandō cupit et dictīs āvertere cūrās,
395 multa gemēns magnōque animum labefactus amōre
396 iussa tamen dīvum exsequitur classemque revīsit.
397 Tum vērō Teucrī incumbunt et lītore celsās
398 dēdūcunt tōtō nāvēs. Natat ūncta carīna,
399 frondentēsque ferunt rēmōs et rōbora silvīs
400 īnfabricāta fugae studiō.
401 Migrantēs cernās tōtāque ex urbe ruentēs:
402 ac velut ingentem formīcae farris acervum
403 cum populant hiemis memorēs tēctōque repōnunt,
404 it nigrum campīs agmen praedamque per herbās
405 convectant calle angustō; pars grandia trūdunt

Quaestiōnēs

1. What device of word order is employed in 388 and how is it appropriate to the action described?

2. What effect does Vergil intend in the echo of 2.790–91 here at 390–91? What are the resonances between the two passages?

3. In what several respects does the narrator's language in 393–96 serve to remind us that Aeneas' decision to leave Carthage was sorrowful and driven by his sense of duty; cf. 331–32, and also consider the previous instances in which the term **pius** is applied to Aeneas, at 1.220 and 305 (with the notes on those passages).

4. How does meter suit meaning in 397–98?

5. Comment on the metrical effects in 404–05.

406 **frūmentum, -ī,** n., *grain, wheat.*
grandia (405) . . . **frūmenta:** the grains are huge from the ants' perspective.

407 **opere . . . fervet:** cf. **fervet opus,** similarly placed at the end of the bee SIMILE in 1.436.

408 **Quis . . . sēnsus:** SC. **est** with **tibi,** DAT. OF POSSESSION; i.e., "how did you feel?" The narrator's APOSTROPHE to Dido, and then to Amor (412), adds intense emotionalism to the passage.

409 **fervō, fervere, fervī,** *to be hot, boil; to be busy, seethe with activity* (a third conjugation alternate to **fervēre,** employed here in unusual collocation with the second conjugation form **fervet** in 407).

412 **Improbe:** Dido uses the same epithet of Aeneas in 386.
quid: i.e., *to what (actions),* here exclamatory.

413 **Īre iterum . . . iterum temptāre:** CHIASMUS, ANAPHORA, and ASYNDETON all intensify the pathos; with **temptāre** SC. **eum** (Aeneas) as dir. obj.; and for the phrase **temptāre precandō** cf. 113 above.

414 **cōgitur:** SC. **Dīdō** as subj.
*__summittō, summittere, summīsī, summissus,__ *to surrender, submit* (to); *to moderate, allay.*

415 **inexpertus, -a, -um,** *untried, unattempted.*
moritūra: i.e., "and go to her death."

416 **properārī:** here impers., with the adv. **circum,** lit., *that things are being rushed all around = that there is bustling activity all around.*

417 **undique convēnēre:** a deliberate echo from 2.799, where the Trojans had similarly gathered on the shore to commence their journey under Aeneas' leadership; the forthcoming departure here represents a new beginning, as Vergil means us to see by recalling that earlier scene on the Trojan coast.
carbasus, -ī, m., *canvas, sail.*

418 **nauta, -ae,** m., *sailor.*
laetī nautae: the sailors' excitement here recalls, perhaps intentionally, their exuberance in setting sail from Sicily before the storm in Book One (**vēla dabant laetī** 1.35).

419 **Hunc . . . tantum . . . dolōrem:** the expansive word order underscores the depth of Dido's misery.
spērāre: here *to anticipate.*

422 **colere . . . crēdere:** HIST. INFS.; Servius reports a version of the story in which Aeneas fell in love with Anna, not Dido, a plot variant to which Vergil may be alluding here.
*__arcānus, -a, -um,__ *secret, hidden.*

423 **mollēs:** *gentle, tactful.*
tempora: i.e., *the best times;* with **mollēs aditūs,** a kind of HENDIADYS, = *the proper time to tactfully approach him.* The language deliberately recalls Aeneas' own attempt at finding the right approach to Dido when telling her of his departure at 293–94 (**temptātūrum aditūs et quae mollissima fandī / tempora**).
nōrās: = **nōveras,** *you had learned = you knew;* Dido's use of the past tense reflects her awareness that Aeneas is lost to her.

406 obnīxae frūmenta umerīs, pars agmina cōgunt
407 castīgantque morās, opere omnis sēmita fervet.
408 Quis tibi tum, Dīdō, cernentī tālia sēnsus,
409 quōsve dabās gemitūs, cum lītora fervere lātē
410 prōspicerēs arce ex summā, tōtumque vidērēs
411 miscērī ante oculōs tantīs clāmōribus aequor!
412 Improbe Amor, quid nōn mortālia pectora cōgis!
413 Īre iterum in lacrimās, iterum temptāre precandō
414 cōgitur et supplex animōs summittere amōrī,
415 nē quid inexpertum frūstrā moritūra relinquat.

Dido asks her sister Anna to plead with Aeneas to remain in
Carthage a while longer and wait for more favorable winds

416   "Anna, vidēs tōtō properārī lītore circum:
417 undique convēnēre; vocat iam carbasus aurās,
418 puppibus et laetī nautae imposuēre corōnās.
419 Hunc ego sī potuī tantum spērāre dolōrem,
420 et perferre, soror, poterō. Miserae hoc tamen ūnum
421 exsequere, Anna, mihī; sōlam nam perfidus ille
422 tē colere, arcānōs etiam tibi crēdere sēnsūs;
423 sōla virī mollēs aditūs et tempora nōrās.

Quaestiōnēs

1. Discuss in detail the ant simile in 402–07. How is it appropriate to the action on the shore as Dido views it from her distant palace? What are the specific correspondences between this imagery and the bee simile in 1.430–36 above? What are the differences? Why might Vergil have meant for us in this passage to recall that earlier scene in Book One?

2. What is the purpose of the wide separation of adj. and noun in **tōtum . . . aequor** (410–11)?

3. Comment on the narrative device employed in 412, and compare lines 65 and 169–70 above; what do you see as the intended effect of such subjective observations on the narrative, and how do they involve the audience? Do you consider the device effective or not, and why?

424 **hostem ... superbum:** Dido's angriest characterization of Aeneas up to this point, a degradation from the more neutral **hospes** of 323; having termed the Trojan an enemy, she proceeds in 425–27 to deny that her own actions have been those of a foe.

426 **Aulis, Aulidis,** f., *Aulis* (the Boeotian port from which the Greeks set sail to invade Troy).

427 **revellō, revellere, revellī, revulsus,** *to tear loose, wrench off; to tear up, uproot.*

patris ... revellī: to disturb someone's grave, esp. the grave of someone's father, was regarded as a most heinous act.

428 **dicta ... dēmittere:** the harsh d/t ALLITERATION suits the indignant tone of the queen's complaint; **dēmittere** here = *admit.*

negat: here *refuse.*

430 **ferentēs:** *carrying,* i.e., *favorable.*

432 **pulchrō ut Latiō:** ANASTROPHE helps underscore the sarcastic tone of Dido's description of Latium.

ut ... careat ... relinquat: **ōrō** (431) is construed with both the acc. obj. **coniugium** and, here, with a JUSSIVE NOUN CL./IND. COMMAND.

433 **tempus ināne:** i.e., a brief span of time that in the end will be meaningless.

requiēs, requiētis, acc. **requiem,** f., *rest* (from labor), *respite.*

*****spatium, -ī,** n., *area, space; time* (i.e., time available for some purpose).

434 **victam:** for the military imagery, see note on **capta** (330).

436 **quam:** obj. of both **dederit** and **remittam,** *which, when he has granted it to me, I shall pay back.*

cumulātus, -a, -um, *heaped up, accumulated; increased, augmented, enhanced.*

cumulātam ... remittam: a METAPHOR from financial transactions, *I shall pay it back with interest.*

morte: Anna would suppose this meant *at my death,* i.e., in the distant future, but Dido likely means *by my death,* i.e., by her soon forthcoming suicide.

439 **aut:** = **nec,** with the negative understood from **nūllīs** in 438.

audit: here *listen to, heed.*

440 **obstruō, obstruere, obstrūxī, obstrūctus,** *to block, obstruct, seal.*

fāta obstant ... deus obstruit: Vergil again makes it abundantly clear that Aeneas' intractability is divinely motivated; the juxtaposition **virī deus** helps make the point.

441 **Ac velut ... cum ... / haud secus (447):** introducing a more completely framed SIMILE than in 402–03 above; cf. **ac veluti ... cum** at 1.148 and 2.626–27.

annōsus, -a, -um, *full of years, aged, old, ancient.*

*****quercus, -ūs,** f., *oak-tree.*

annōsō ... quercum: the INTERLOCKED WORD ORDER is perhaps meant to suggest the sturdiness of the tree.

442 **Alpīnus, -a, -um,** *Alpine, of the Alps* (a mountain chain in northern Italy).

Boreās, -ae, m., *north wind.*

flātus, -ūs, m., *blowing, blast* (of wind), *gust.*

illinc, adv., *from that direction, thence.*

443 **ēruere:** compl. inf. with **certant.**

altae / ... frondēs (444): i.e., *the topmost leaves.*

424 Ī, soror, atque hostem supplex adfāre superbum:
425 nōn ego cum Danaīs Trōiānam exscindere gentem
426 Aulide iūrāvī classemve ad Pergama mīsī,
427 nec patris Anchīsae cinerem mānēsve revellī:
428 cūr mea dicta negat dūrās dēmittere in aurēs?
429 Quō ruit? Extrēmum hoc miserae det mūnus amantī:
430 exspectet facilemque fugam ventōsque ferentēs.
431 Nōn iam coniugium antīquum, quod prōdidit, ōrō,
432 nec pulchrō ut Latiō careat rēgnumque relinquat:
433 tempus ināne petō, requiem spatiumque furōrī,
434 dum mea mē victam doceat fortūna dolēre.
435 Extrēmam hanc ōrō veniam (miserēre sorōris),
436 quam mihi cum dederit cumulātam morte remittam."

Aeneas anguishes over the queen and her sister's pleading, but,
like a massive, deeply rooted oak, he holds firm to his decision

437   Tālibus ōrābat, tālēsque miserrima flētūs
438 fertque refertque soror. Sed nūllīs ille movētur
439 flētibus aut vōcēs ūllās tractābilis audit;
440 fāta obstant placidāsque virī deus obstruit aurēs.
441 Ac velut annōsō validam cum rōbore quercum
442 Alpīnī Boreae nunc hinc nunc flātibus illinc
443 ēruere inter sē certant; it strīdor, et altae

Quaestiōnēs

1. Analyze carefully Dido's speech in 416–36; how does it differ in tone and in specific detail from her earlier speeches at 305–30 and 365–87?

2. What rhetorical device is employed in both 437 and 438, and what is its purpose? Comment too on the repetition **flētus/flētibus** (437 and 439) and its effect.

3. What is the most striking sound effect in 442?

444 cōnsternō, cōnsternere, cōnstrāvī, cōnstrātus, *to cover (by strewing), spread over.*
stīpes, stīpitis, m., *trunk* (of a tree).
concussō stīpite: cf. concussō vertice of the mountain ash in the SIMILE at 2.629.
445 ipsa: the oak.
quantum . . . tantum (446): with tendit (446), *as far as . . . just that far.*
446 rādīx, rādīcis, f., *root* (of a plant or tree).
447 adsiduus, -a, -um, *continuous, ceaseless.*
adsiduīs . . . vōcibus: the symmetrical arrangement (CHIASMUS) suits the image
in hinc atque hinc, which recalls nunc hinc nunc . . . illinc in 442 and means
essentially the same thing, *on this side and on that.*
449 lacrimae: Aeneas' own tears perhaps (as Servius comments), and certainly
Anna's (see flētūs . . . flētibus 437–39).
volvuntur: Eng. would use, rather than the trans. pass. vb. *are rolled,* an intrans.,
roll down, stream down.
642 coeptīs: perf. partic. of coepī, employed here as a substantive, lit., *things begun =
her plans, designs.*
efferus, -a, -um, *wild, savage; frantic, furious.*
643 sanguineam: with aciem (here sg. for pl. *eyes*) = *bloodshot.*
macula, -ae, f., *stain, spot, blemish* (here red blotches).
644 interfūsus, -a, -um, *covered, flecked.*
gena, -ae, f., *cheek* (here ACC. OF SPECIFICATION with interfūsa; cf. oculōs
suffūsa 1.228).
646 furibundus, -a, -um, *full of fury, frenzied, raging.*
rogōs: some mss. have gradūs (*steps*) here, perhaps a scribal alteration
interpolated from gradūs . . . altōs (685) and prompted by hesitation over the
pl. rogōs; but such use of pl. for sg. is common in Vergil (see, e.g., note on
647).
ēnsem . . . / Dardanium . . . quaesītum mūnus (647): it is a fine ironic touch
that Dido will die by a Trojan sword, and one she had sought from Aeneas as
a gift.
647 hōs . . . in ūsūs: pl. for sg., *for this purpose.*
648 cubīle, cubīlis, n., *bed, couch.*
649 lacrimīs et mente: perhaps best construed as a HENDIADYS, *in tearful reflection*
(ABL. OF MANNER or perhaps CAUSE).
morāta: as often, Lat. employs a perf. partic. where Eng. would use the pres.,
pausing.
650 novissima: i.e., *her last.*
651 exuviae: the ēnsem . . . Dardanium (646–47) and the Īliacās vestēs (648).
652 exsolvō, exsolvere, exsoluī, exsolūtus, *to unfasten, undo; to set free, release.*
653 *peragō, peragere, perēgī, perāctus, *to do thoroughly, complete; to go through,
deal with.*
quem . . . perēgī: = cursum perēgī quem Fortūna dederat.
654 magna meī . . . imāgō: a lilting, ALLITERATIVE phrase; ghosts were imagined as
larger than life (cf. nōta maior imāgō 2.773 above, of Creusa's phantom).

444 cōnsternunt terram concussō stīpite frondēs;
445 ipsa haeret scopulīs et quantum vertice ad aurās
446 aetheriās, tantum rādīce in Tartara tendit:
447 haud secus adsiduīs hinc atque hinc vōcibus hērōs
448 tunditur, et magnō persentit pectore cūrās;
449 mēns immōta manet, lacrimae volvuntur inānēs.

*Dido, crazed with grief, rushes to her bed-chamber, draws
a sword, and curses Aeneas with her dying breath*

642   At trepida et coeptīs immānibus effera Dīdō,
643 sanguineam volvēns aciem maculīsque trementēs
644 interfūsa genās et pallida morte futūrā,
645 interiōra domūs inrumpit līmina et altōs
646 cōnscendit furibunda rogōs ēnsemque reclūdit
647 Dardanium, nōn hōs quaesītum mūnus in ūsūs.
648 Hīc, postquam Īliacās vestēs nōtumque cubīle
649 cōnspexit, paulum lacrimīs et mente morāta,
650 incubuitque torō dīxitque novissima verba:
651 "Dulcēs exuviae, dum fāta deusque sinēbat,
652 accipite hanc animam mēque hīs exsolvite cūrīs.
653 Vīxī et quem dederat cursum Fortūna perēgī,
654 et nunc magna meī sub terrās ībit imāgō.
655 Urbem praeclāram statuī; mea moenia vīdī;

Quaestiōnēs

Compare the oak tree simile at 441–49 with the mountain ash simile in 2.626–31;
what are the principal similarities and the principal differences? Does Vergil here
intend us to recall that earlier image and, if so, for what purpose?

656   **virum:** i.e., Dido's husband Sychaeus; see 1.343–64 above for his death and Dido's vengeance against his murderer, her brother Pygmalion.

657   ***nimium,** adv., *too, too much, exceedingly, excessively.*

659   ***imprimō, imprimere, impressī, impressus,** *to apply with pressure, press (on/upon); to imprint, engrave* (with).
      ōs impressa: for the construction, see on 1.228.
      Moriēmur inultae: cf. **moriēmur inultī** (2.670).

660   **Sīc, sīc:** Servius suggests, rightly perhaps, that we are to imagine Dido here stabbing herself twice with the sword Aeneas had given her.

662   **mortis:** quite aptly and poignantly, Dido's last word.

666   **bacchātur . . . per urbem:** cf. **per urbem / bacchātur** (300–01); Rumor rages wildly though the city with the news of Dido's death, just as Dido herself had done when she learned from Rumor of Aeneas' preparations to depart.

667   **lāmenta, -ōrum,** n. pl., *wailing, weeping, lamentation.*
      ululātus, -ūs, m., *howling, shrieking.*
      fēmineō ululātū: the HIATUS helps prolong the final -ō and thus accentuate the ONOMATOPOETIC effect.
      ululātū / tēcta fremunt (668): we see and hear the Carthaginians' houses rather than the Carthaginians themselves; cf. the PERSONIFICATION in **plangōribus aedēs / fēmineis ululant** (2.487–88). The shrieking here, at Dido's death, is perhaps meant ironically, tragically to recall that of the Nymphs (**ululārunt** 168) at her "wedding."

668   **resonō (1),** *to echo, resound, reverberate.*

669   **nōn aliter quam:** for the LITOTES and its formulaic use in a SIMILE, see note above on 256.

671   **volvantur:** here, as often with **volvere** and its compounds, Lat. uses a trans. pass. vb. where Eng. would employ an intrans., *roll* (through/over).

656 ulta virum, poenās inimīcō ā frātre recēpī—
657 fēlīx, heu nimium fēlīx, sī lītora tantum
658 numquam Dardaniae tetigissent nostra carīnae."
659 Dīxit, et ōs impressa torō, "Moriēmur inultae,
660 sed moriāmur," ait. "Sīc, sīc iuvat īre sub umbrās.
661 Hauriat hunc oculīs ignem crudēlis ab altō
662 Dardanus et nostrae sēcum ferat ōmina mortis."

*Even as Dido takes her last breath, lamentation fills the city, and
Anna rushes to embrace her sister in the final moments of her life*

663   Dīxerat, atque illam media inter tālia ferrō
664 conlāpsam aspiciunt comitēs, ēnsemque cruōre
665 spūmantem sparsāsque manūs. It clāmor ad alta
666 ātria: concussam bacchātur Fāma per urbem.
667 Lāmentīs gemitūque et fēmineō ululātū
668 tēcta fremunt, resonat magnīs plangōribus aethēr,
669 nōn aliter quam sī immissīs ruat hostibus omnis
670 Karthāgō aut antīqua Tyros, flammaeque furentēs
671 culmina perque hominum volvantur perque deōrum.

Quaestiōnēs

1. In what specific ways is Dido's death speech in 651–62 a reminder of Aeneas' destiny and his unfulfilled mission?

2. Identify the several specific verbal correspondences between 665–68 and 2.486–88 and the similarities between the events described in the two passages. Do you consider the likenesses accidental or deliberate? If the latter, what effect do you suppose Vergil intended?

3. Discuss the simile in 669–71; compare the military imagery seen in 93–95 and 330 above. What effect does Vergil intend in evoking this metaphor here and there throughout Book Four?

4. Comment on the sound effects and other poetic devices employed in **flammae . . . deōrum** (670–71).

672 **trepidō . . . cursū:** ABL. OF MANNER.

    exterreō (2), *to frighten, terrify.*

673 **unguis, unguis,** m., *fingernail.*

    foedāns: a ZEUGMA, meaning *tearing* or *bloodying* with **unguibus ōra** and *bruising* with **pectora pugnīs.**

    pugnus, -ī, m., *clenched hand, fist.*

675 **Hoc . . . fuit:** *was this what that* (i.e., the pyre: see line 676) *was for/about?*

    fraus, fraudis, f., *harm, danger; deceit, guile.*

    fraude petēbās: i.e., *were you deceiving;* Anna had assisted Dido in erecting the pyre at her sister's request, believing, as Dido told her, that its purpose was to burn all the gifts Aeneas had presented to the queen (lines 474–503).676 **Hoc . . . hoc:** i.e., Dido's suicide and Anna's abandonment.

    mihi: DAT. OF REF.

678 **vocāssēs:** = **vocāvissēs** (for the SYNCOPATED form, see note on **audierat** 1.20); sc. **sī** in a PAST CONTRARY TO FACT CONDITION, though some editors take both **vocāssēs** and **tulisset (679)** as past tense JUSSIVE SUBJUNCTS. = *you should have called . . . the same suffering . . . would have taken away . . . .*

679 **ambās:** SC. **nōs.**

680 **strūxī:** sc. **rogum,** easily understood as it is the pyre that dominates the scene and Anna's mind.

    vocāvī / vōce (681): the etymologizing practically amounts to ANAPHORA, and the effect is to intensify our sense of Anna's anguish over her own unwitting complicity in Dido's suicide.

681 **sīc tē . . . positā:** i.e., when Dido was dead; ABL. OF SEPARATION with **abessem.**

    crūdēlis: surely voc., rather than nom. as some editors suppose.

682 **Exstīnxtī:** = **exstīnxistī** (SYNCOPE).

683 **Date:** *grant (that)* with **(ut) abluam** (684, a JUSSIVE NOUN CL./IND. COMMAND), an entreaty addressed either to the gods or to attendants who have approached the pyre with Anna.

    lympha, -ae, f., *water-nymph; water.*

684 **hālitus, -ūs,** m., *exhalation; breath.*

    extrēmus . . . hālitus: = **sī quis hālitus extrēmus** (ANASTROPHE).

685 **ōre legam:** i.e., she will inhale Dido's final breath in a ritual act meant to rescue the dying person's soul.

    gradūs . . . altōs: i.e., of the pyre.

    ēvāserat: here *had climbed to.*

686 **sēmianimis, -is, -e** (regularly scanned as quadrisyllabic with the first **i** treated as a consonant by SYNIZESIS), *half-alive, barely alive.*

687 **siccō (1),** *to dry; to dry up, staunch.*

    cruōrēs: pl. for sg. here to emphasize the massive loss of blood; the force of **siccābat** is thus perhaps conative, *she tried to . . . .*

688 **Illa:** used here, as often, of the key figure in the scene, i.e., Dido.

672 Audiit, exanimis trepidōque exterrita cursū,
673 unguibus ōra soror foedāns et pectora pugnīs
674 per mediōs ruit ac morientem nōmine clāmat:
675 "Hoc illud, germāna, fuit? Mē fraude petēbās?
676 Hoc rogus iste mihi, hoc ignēs āraeque parābant?
677 Quid prīmum dēserta querar? Comitemne sorōrem
678 sprēvistī moriēns? Eadem mē ad fāta vocāssēs;
679 īdem ambās ferrō dolor atque eadem hōra tulisset.
680 Hīs etiam strūxī manibus patriōsque vocāvī
681 vōce deōs, sīc tē ut positā, crūdēlis, abessem?
682 Exstīnxtī tē mēque, soror, populumque patrēsque
683 Sīdoniōs urbemque tuam. Date, vulnera lymphīs
684 abluam et, extrēmus sī quis super hālitus errat,
685 ōre legam." Sīc fāta, gradūs ēvāserat altōs
686 sēmianimemque sinū germānam amplexa fovēbat
687 cum gemitū atque ātrōs siccābat veste cruōrēs.
688 Illa, gravēs oculōs cōnāta attollere, rūrsus

Quaestiōnēs

1. How does meter suit meaning in 672? Comment on the line's other sound effects as well.

2. What very striking rhetorical device is employed in 682–83 and what is its effect?

3. Discuss the psychology of Anna's response to her sister's suicide in her speech at 675–85; are her anger and accusations a normal reaction?

Funeral of Dido
From manuscript of
Servius' commentary
on the *Aeneid*
Ms. 493, folio 142r
1469
Bibliotheque Municipale
Dijon, France

689 **strīdit:** here *hisses,* with the sound of air moving in and out of her lungs through the puncture wound in her chest.

sub pectore vulnus: the same phrase appears in identical metrical position in line 67, where it describes Dido's passion for Aeneas; the wound that had been only figurative in the earlier passage has here become literal.

690 **Ter . . . / ter (691):** the repetition and positioning of the adv. intensifies the pathos of the scene; likewise the slow spondees and conflict of ictus and accent in **ter sēsē attollēns** suggest how labored Dido's efforts were, and the dactyls in **ter revolūta torō est oculīs** how quickly and abruptly she collapsed. The number three has a mystical quality and is similarly employed, and positioned, in 2.792–93 above, where Aeneas thrice attempts to embrace the wispy ghost of his lost beloved, Creusa.

sēsē: obj. of both **attollēns** and **levāvit.**

cubitum, -ī, n., *elbow.*

691 **revolūta . . . est:** for the pass. usage, see note on **volvantur (671).**

692 **repertā:** sc. **lūce.**

694 **obitus, -ūs,** m., *approach, encounter; act of dying, death.*

***Īris, Īridis,** f., *Iris* (messenger of the gods, Juno in particular, and goddess of the rainbow).

695 **luctantem . . . artūs:** a form of HENDIADYS, since Iris was sent in fact to free Dido's soul *from* her limbs.

696 **nec fātō:** i.e., before her fated time (**ante diem 697**).

698 **flāvus, -a, -um,** *yellow; fair-haired, blonde.*

***Prōserpina, -ae,** f., *Proserpina* (the Greek Persephone, daughter of Ceres/ Demeter and goddess of the Underworld).

Prōserpina . . . Orcō (699): in ancient ritual a lock of the deceased's hair was consecrated to the god of the dead (Orcus or Dis, Proserpina's husband).

699 ***Stygius, -a, -um,** *Stygian, of the Styx* (a mythic river in the Underworld); *of Hades, of the Underworld.*

damnō (1), *to condemn; to deliver, consign, assign.*

700 ***croceus, -a, -um,** *(made) of saffron; saffron-colored, yellow, golden.*

rōscidus, -a, -um, *of dew, covered with dew, dewy.*

701 ***color, colōris,** m., *color, hue.*

702 **dēvolō (1),** *to fly down, descend.*

***Dīs, Dītis,** m., *Dis* (lord of the Underworld in Roman religion).

Hunc . . . / sacrum (703): with **Dītī,** *this object sacred (to),* here a lock of Dido's hair (**crīnem 698**), taken not by Proserpina, but in this instance by Iris as the instrument of Juno's pity.

703 **iussa:** Eng. would employ a cl. rather than a partic., *as I have been commanded to do.*

Flēbam Dīdōnem extīnctam ferrōque extrēma secūtam.

St. Augustine, "Confessions," 1.13

689 dēficit; īnfīxum strīdit sub pectore vulnus.
690 Ter sēsē attollēns cubitōque adnīxa levāvit,
691 ter revolūta torō est oculīsque errantibus altō
692 quaesīvit caelō lūcem ingemuitque repertā.

*Juno sends Iris down from Mt. Olympus to cut a lock of Dido's
hair, thus releasing her soul and consecrating it to Dis*

693   Tum Iūnō omnipotēns, longum miserāta dolōrem
694 difficilēsque obitūs, Īrim dēmīsit Olympō
695 quae luctantem animam nexōsque resolveret artūs.
696 Nam quia nec fātō meritā nec morte perībat,
697 sed misera ante diem subitōque accēnsa furōre,
698 nōndum illī flāvum Prōserpina vertice crīnem
699 abstulerat Stygiōque caput damnāverat Orcō.
700 Ergō Īris croceīs per caelum rōscida pennīs,
701 mīlle trahēns variōs adversō sōle colōrēs,
702 dēvolat et suprā caput astitit. "Hunc ego Dītī
703 sacrum iussa ferō tēque istō corpore solvō";

Quaestiō

How are the enjambement and the diaeresis following **dēficit** in 689 especially
effective?

"Death of Dido"
Giovanni Francesco Guercino (1591–1666)
Galleria Spada, Rome, Italy

704 **ūnā:** here adv.

705 **dīlābor, dīlābī, dīlāpsus sum,** *to flow away; to slip away, escape, disappear.*
in ventōs vīta recessit: cf. **recessit in aurēs** of Creusa's phantom at 2.791 above; and for the **v/s** sound effects, suggestive of the rushing winds, see 2.794 and the accompanying note.

"Dido on the Pyre"
Henry Fuseli (1741–1825)
Collection of Richard L. Feigen, New York, New York

704 sīc ait et dextrā crīnem secat, omnis et ūnā
705 dīlāpsus calor atque in ventōs vīta recessit.

Quaestiōnēs

1. Comment on the effectiveness of 693–705 as Book Four's closing scene. Consider the actions of the gods and the ritual elements, the references to fate and to Dido's **furor,** and the various dramatic and visual, cinematographic effects. How does Vergil's introduction of Iris here compare with his use of Rumor earlier in the poem, especially in 173–88?

2. Compare the close of Book Four with Aeneas' encounter with Creusa toward the end of Book Two. What is the significance of the fact that both books conclude with the deaths of women intimately associated with Aeneas? What other similarities, and what principal differences, do you see between the two episodes in terms of Aeneas' relationships with and eventual loss of these two women? How does his political mission factor into both episodes? How and why might the ancient Romans' response to Aeneas' interactions with Creusa and Dido differ from our own?

Death of Dido
Woodcut from a 1664 French translation of the *Aeneid*

Aeneid BOOK VI

(Verses 1–211, 295–332, 384–425, 450–76, 847–901)

Book Five

R. D. Williams in his commentary on *Aeneid* One–Six argues that Book Five "provides a diminution of tension between the intensity of Book 4 and the majesty of Book 6." Although Book Five is not included among the selections in our text, it does provide an entertaining and instructive narrative of the funeral games for Anchises in Sicily, which you will wish to read in English translation.

As the Trojans leave Carthage they see fire in the city, but they sail on into a storm. Palinurus, the helmsman, urges Aeneas to follow the wind to northwest Sicily, where they land near Anchises' tomb at Eryx and are welcomed by the Trojan Acestes (1–34). Aeneas' "escape" from Dido marks the renewal of his bond with his father. After a ceremony at the grave, the appearance of a huge snake signals Anchises' spiritual presence. To celebrate the anniversary of his death, contests are proclaimed, modeled after the funeral games for Patroclus in *Iliad* 23 and reflecting Roman practice: a ship race (104–285), foot-race (286–361), boxing match (362–484), and archery contest (485–544). These events introduce Trojans who will feature in the invasion of Italy: Mnestheus (the camp defender in 9. 787–814), and Nisus and Euryalus (whose tragic deaths occur in 9.176–502). The contests of boxing and archery, marking an emotional crescendo, attach to Sicilian victors Entellus and Acestes. The ship-race resembles chariot races in Rome's Circus Maximus. The final event (545–603) is an equestrian performance involving Ascanius and other Trojans in a series of intricate cavalry maneuvers—a ceremonial display that was adopted by Rome and called the *lusus Troiae.*

During these events, Juno sends Iris to incite the Trojan women to set fire to the ships (604–63). Ascanius leaves the "cavalry ride" to rebuke the women, but the fire cannot be extinguished. When Aeneas prays to Jupiter *Pluvius* ("Rain God"), a thunderstorm saves all but four ships. Aeneas is persuaded by Nautes ("Sailor") and the ghost of Anchises to leave some of his company in Sicily, where Acestes will rule over a new city, while the rest proceed to Italy. Venus complains to Neptune about Juno's hostility to the Trojans and seeks guarantees for Aeneas' safe passage. Neptune promises to bring the Trojans unharmed to Italy, but one life must be forfeited. *Somnus,* god of sleep, overcomes the dutiful pilot, Palinurus, who falls overboard to meet death soon thereafter at the hands of native Lucanians (827–71). The Palinurus episode, his fall overboard and murder, with Somnus as the divine agent, finds a parallel in the casualties of sailors along the same coastline who were seduced by the prophetic songs of the Sirens, swam ashore, and perished in Homer's *Odyssey* 12.39f.

Book Six

BOOK Six, represented by five selections in our text, highlights the Trojan landing at Cumae, the consultation with the Apolline Sibyl, and the tasks required of Aeneas before entering Hades. The death of Misenus and the discovery of the Golden Bough, which are included with the book's other opening events in our first selection, are prelude to Aeneas' descent by way of Lake Avernus. The Underworld journey, past Charon, the ferryman of dead souls, and Cerberus, the three-headed watchdog (both the Charon and Cerberus passages are included in our book), highlights three persons associated with Aeneas during their lives: Palinurus, Dido, and Deiphobus. In the course of his passage through Hades, led by the Sibyl and the Orphic priest Musaeus, Aeneas learns about Tartarus, the prison for arch sinners, and encounters Elysium's bright acres, where the "blest spirits" dwell, and Lethe, the river of forgetfulness, whose waters condition souls to renewed, altered lives in the upper world.

Anchises, with whom Aeneas was determined to visit in the Underworld, provides his son with a review of heroes in the Julian dynasty to come (756–897), including Romulus and Augustus (788–807), and the kings and heroes of the Roman line. His definition of the Roman imperial mission (847–53), also among the selections included here, is an exhortation to his "Roman" son and his descendants. The apparition of the recently deceased Marcellus (42–23 B.C.), nephew of Augustus, prompts sorrow and a moving obituary. Thereafter, Aeneas and the Sibyl return to the upper world by the Ivory Gate of False Dreams.

When the fleet lands at Cumae, Aeneas follows the advice of Helenus (3.441–62), climbs the promontory with Achates, and seeks Apollo's prophetess and her oracular cave. The setting features "enormous temples" built for Apollo by Daedalus after his escape from the labyrinth of Cnossus (on Crete). Door reliefs depict the death of Androgeus, son of Minos, and Athenians sacrificed to avenge the murder of his offspring, the perverse love of Pasiphaë for the bull and her Minotaur offspring, the labyrinth, the love story of Theseus and Ariadne, the flight of Daedalus and his son Icarus, and (left incomplete) Icarus' death. The overall message of this episode is one of sacrifice and the loss of loved ones.

The Sibyl grants an audience to Aeneas and hears his expressions of gratitude to Apollo and his promise of future offerings to the oracular god. From the interior of her grotto the Sibyl supplies hair-raising oracular *responsa,* promising battles like those at Troy. To gain access to the Underworld and to Anchises, Aeneas must find and obtain the Golden Bough, the mysterious passport for his descent to Hades and his return, and in addition perform burial rites for Misenus, a lost companion. The Sibyl cautions Aeneas: *facilis descensus Averno,* "the descent—by way of Avernus—is easy," but the ascent is difficult indeed.

The descent, or *catabasis,* was a customary requirement for heroes, an essential part of their quest, and a guarantee of their divine or preferred heroic status. With the completion of the formalities, Aeneas and the Sibyl, armed with the Golden Bough, enter the House of Dis ("the rich man"), an alternative name for Pluto or Orcus, and at the outset encounter phantoms and demons, psychological and mythical terrors. Vergil furnishes his account with the traditional rivers, Acheron, Cocytus, and Styx, which resemble volcanic streams, and with Charon, the ferryman of the dead, Cerberus, the three-headed watchdog, Tartarus, where sinners reside forever, and Elysium, where the blessed spirits congregate, including Anchises. The banks of the Styx are crowded with shades *(umbrae)* of the unburied dead who must wait a century for their passage across. Aeneas recognizes Palinurus and hears his tale of woe and request for transport across the Styx. His petition is denied, but the Sibyl consoles him by forecasting that the promontory where he died will display his cenotaph and will bear his name, Cape Palinurus. Charon, persuaded by the Golden Bough, takes Aeneas and Deiphobe aboard; upon landing, the Sibyl throws a drugged cake to Cerberus, whereupon they encounter a region in which the shades of infants, those unjustly condemned to death, suicides, and those who died for love, are wandering. One of this text's selections from Book Six (450–76) details Aeneas' meeting with Dido, where his apology is answered only with silence (just as the ghost of Ajax in Hades chose not to respond to Odysseus' apology in Homer's *Odyssey* 11.563f.).

A neutral region contains Greek and Trojan heroes. The Greeks run at the sight of Aeneas, but Dardanians and Trojans crowd around him, including Deiphobus, Helen's husband at Troy after the death of Paris, murdered by Menelaus with Helen's complicity on the last night. The hero and the prophetess press on, bypassing Tartarus, the "penitentiary" for the worst criminals; the Sibyl provides background on their everlasting torments. She deposits the Golden Bough (dedicated to Persephone/Prosperpina, queen of the Underworld) at the threshold of Elysium, the "philosophical" as opposed to the "mythological" Hades, where the Orphic poet and musician, Musaeus, directs them to Anchises, who is reviewing the unborn souls of his Roman descendants. Aeneas attempts to embrace his father but the shade slips from his grasp. Aeneas is never in the poem able to embrace his parents, neither Venus nor deceased Anchises, and not even his transfigured wife Creusa is accessible.

Anchises shows his son where souls drink the water of Lethe ("Forgetfulness") prior to their return to the upper world, required procedure for the transmigration of souls, according to the dictates of the Orphic "mystery" cult. After Anchises has outlined the purification process attaching to the souls of the dead and their eventual reincarnation, Aeneas is repelled by the procedure: why would anyone want to experience the sadness and bitterness of life a second time? Anchises replies (722–51) that there is no reason for the repeated reincarnations except God's command. The new "Roman" souls have undergone purification for the sins they have committed in a former life, and return to earth to live new lives. So, we are led to assume, although Aeneas is alive, he undergoes symbolic death and purification in order to be reborn as a "Roman" pioneer.

Hercules and Cerberus, stone sculpture, Lorenzo Mattielli (ca. 1678-1748)
Hofburg Imperial Palace, Michaelerplatz / The Michael Wing, Vienna, Austria

Thereafter Anchises identifies the future heroes of Rome (752–892) and so provides his son with the models of conduct and achievement that will enrich Rome's future. The pattern of Vergil's march-past is designed to resemble that of a Roman funeral procession (*pompa funebris*), where members of the deceased person's family wore masks (*imagines*) of his ancestors. From the standpoint of structure, Anchises' speech to his son divides into three sections: in the first, lines 756–807, the pre-Roman rulers are linked with a panegyric of Romulus and of Augustus, Rome's antique and present-day "founders." In the second division of his speech, Anchises surveys heroes after Romulus, men like Brutus of the early Republic, the Scipios, Aemilius Paullus, and Fabius Maximus; major antagonists of the Civil War era, Pompey and Julius Caesar, are identified mid-way through his review (826–33), and then he digresses at 847–53 to accent Rome's mission to the world, "to rule the nations with empire, to add civilization to peace, to show mercy to the defeated and to war down the arrogant" (these lines, and all those following to the end of the book, constitute our text's final selection from *Aeneid* Six). And the closing section of Anchises' speech, the Marcellus passage (854–86), diminishes and saddens the prevailing tone of triumph and exultation: although the elder Marcus Claudius Marcellus will win distinction in campaigns against the Gauls and against Hannibal, the younger Marcellus, Augustus' promising nephew and heir, will die prematurely (23 B.C.). His death exemplifies the human cost of empire and pre-figures the sacrificial deaths of heroes in Books Seven–Twelve, Pallas, Lausus, Nisus and Euryalus, Camilla, and Turnus.

The close of the Underworld episode (893–901), with the departure of Aeneas and the Sibyl through the Ivory Gate of False Dreams, is modeled on Penelope's account of her dream and of dreams in general at *Odyssey* 19.562–69, where the myth of two gates of dreams first appears. But what does Vergil mean to imply by Aeneas' departure through the Ivory Gate rather than through the Gate of Horn, the exit for "true shades"? Although some scholars point to an ancient belief that "true dreams" are those that come prior to midnight and "false dreams" those that come after, thus suggesting that Aeneas and the Sibyl departed Hades after midnight, the evidence is scant and that interpretation seems far-fetched to most critics. Dreams have certainly played an important role in the epic up to this point, and it may be that Vergil meant us to reflect on Aeneas' experience in the Underworld as a dream or a blurred vision, something peculiar to this hero: R.D. Williams suggested that Book Six is "a reenactment of his past and a vision of his future." Perhaps in employing the motif of the Gate of False Dreams Vergil also admits to the uncertainty of religious and philosophical conceptions of the afterlife which were current in his day and were illustrated in Book Six. Other readers note that Aeneas' experience in Hades resembles an "initiation" into a mystery cult, where the past is "dramatically" re-enacted, and where "sermons" of instruction and enlightenment are provided for the initiate, ending with the promise of a blissful new life. Perhaps

Aeneas and the Sibyl leave Hades through the Ivory Gate because it is reserved for those exceptional living persons allowed to enter and return from the Underworld, whereas the Gate of Horn is reserved for the souls of those who have actually died and undergone purification and rebirth. Whatever Vergil's precise intent, the ending of Book Six poses a marvelous enigma, and Aeneas' entire adventure at the close of the poem's Odyssean half makes for an exciting and mysterious narrative.

1 **Sīc fātur:** Book Five concluded with Aeneas' tearful apostrophe to his friend and his ship's helmsman, Palinurus, who had fallen overboard, overwhelmed by Sleep during their last night's sailing toward the Italian coast; the scene here provides a smooth transition to the new book.

classī . . . habēnās: this common METAPHOR pictures the Trojan fleet as a team of horses (like Aeolus' winds in 1.63f. above).

2 ***Euboicus, -a, -um,** Euboean, of Euboea (an Aegean island off the coast of Boeotia).

Cūmae, -ārum, f. pl., Cumae (an ancient city of coastal Campania, founded in the 8th cent. B.C. by colonists from Euboean Chalcis and Kyme).

adlābor, adlābī, adlāpsus sum, to glide toward (sc. **classis** as subj.).

3 **obvertō, obvertere, obvertī, obversus,** to turn (to face) toward.

Obvertunt . . . prōrās: the ships were anchored with their hulls toward the coast, their prows seaward, ready for flight, should that be necessary.

dēns, dentis, m., tooth; (toothlike) hook, prong, spike.

4 **ancora fundābat:** sg. for pl.; the impf., vs. the pres. **obvertunt** and **praetexunt** (5), indicates continuing activity.

5 **ēmicō (1),** to dart forth, dash out.

6 **Hesperius, -a, -um,** Hesperian, of Hesperia (= "the land to the west," the name for Italy given to Aeneas by the phantom of Creusa in her prophecy at 2.781).

sēmen, sēminis, n., seed; element; spark.

sēmina . . . silicis (7): for the use of flint in starting fires, cf. 1.174, where Achates similarly kindles a fire after the Trojans' ships have landed on the coast of Carthage.

7 **abstrūsus, -a, -um,** concealed, hidden.

dēnsa . . . / tēcta (8): in appos. with **silvās** (8).

ferārum . . . flūmina (8): for food and water.

8 **rapit:** here = plunder (cf. **rapiunt . . . Pergama** 2.374–75 above).

9 **altus:** both as god of the sun and because his temple here was situated atop a citadel (**arcēs**).

10 **praesideō, praesidēre, praesēdī,** to sit in charge of, keep watch over, preside.

sēcrēta: here substantive, hidden places, retreat, in appos. with **antrum immāne** (11); remains of not one, but two temples of Apollo and of the Sibyl's cave nearby (**procul**) have been excavated at Cumae.

***Sibylla, -ae,** f., Sibyl (a general name for the oracular priestesses of Apollo, the one at Cumae known as Deiphobe).

11 **cui:** into whom, dat. with **īnspīrat** (12).

12 **Dēlius, -a, -um,** Delian, of Delos (Aegean island that was the legendary birthplace of Apollo and Diana).

īnspīrō (1), to breathe into, inspire.

vātēs: Apollo is so called here for his role as god of prophecy; his prominence in this episode doubtless reflects the importance Augustus gave to Apollo as his patron deity in his program of revitalizing Roman religion. Books of Sibylline oracles were preserved in a splendid marble temple to Apollo on the Palatine, dedicated by Augustus to the god in 28 B.C. as a thank-offering for his victories over Sextus Pompey in 38 B.C. and against Antony and Cleopatra at the battle of Actium in 31.

The Trojans at last reach Italy, disembarking on the coast near
Cumae, and Aeneas seeks out Apollo's priestess, the Sibyl

1 Sīc fātur, lacrimāns, classīque immittit habēnās
2 et tandem Euboicīs Cūmārum adlābitur ōrīs.
3 Obvertunt pelagō prōrās; tum dente tenācī
4 ancora fundābat nāvēs et lītora curvae
5 praetexunt puppēs. Iuvenum manus ēmicat ārdēns
6 lītus in Hesperium; quaerit pars sēmina flammae
7 abstrūsa in vēnīs silicis, pars dēnsa ferārum
8 tēcta rapit silvās inventaque flūmina mōnstrat.
9 At pius Aenēās arcēs quibus altus Apollō
10 praesidet horrendaeque procul sēcrēta Sibyllae,
11 antrum immāne, petit, magnam cui mentem animumque
12 Dēlius īnspīrat vātēs aperitque futūra.

Quaestiō

What is the special point of the epithet **pius** in line 9?

"The Bay of Baiae, with Apollo and the Sibyl"
Joseph Mallord William Turner (1775–1851)
Tate Gallery, London

13 **Iam . . . tēcta:** this verse effectively prepares us for the next scene, where we are
    to see the ornately decorated doors of the golden temple of Apollo.
    subeunt: pl. for Aeneas and his attendants.
    ***Trivia, -ae,** f., *meeting place of three roads, crossroads; Trivia* (epithet of
    Diana, Apollo's sister, in her capacity as goddess of crossroads and of the
    Underworld, which Aeneas is soon to visit).
14 ***Daedalus, -ī,** m., *Daedalus* (Athenian inventor compelled by the Cretan king
    Minos to design the labyrinth at Cnossus; later imprisoned by Minos for
    assisting Theseus in his escape from the maze, Daedalus escaped to Cumae
    on wings he had made for himself and his son Icarus, who fell to his death
    after flying too near the sun and melting the wax that fastened the feathers
    to his wings).
    Mīnōius, -a, -um, *of Minos* (legendary king of Crete).
15 **praepes, praepetis,** *flying straight ahead; fleeting, swift.*
16 **īnsuētus, -a, -um,** *uncustomary, unusual, novel.*
    īnsuētum per iter: i.e., by flying.
    ēnō (1), *to swim forth, fly forth.*
    Arctos, -ī, acc. pl. **Arctōs,** f., *the Great Bear, Little Bear* (constellations near the
    celestial north pole); pl., *lands/peoples of the North.*
17 **Chalcidicus, -a, -um,** *Chalcidic, of Calchis* (city of Euboea which colonized
    Cumae).
    levis: as often, Eng. might here employ an adv. rather than the adj.
18 **Phoebe:** again the narrator intrudes his own persona into the story by
    addressing the god directly.
19 **rēmigium ālārum:** for the same phrase used of Mercury's wings, see 1.301
    above.
20 **In foribus:** on the doors to the temple he erected to Apollo, Daedalus had
    produced relief sculptures in gold (**in aurō** 32) with an elaborate pictorial
    account of the horrendous events in Athens and on the island of Crete in
    which he had played a role and from which he had ultimately escaped.
    Androgeus, -ō (Greek gen.), m., *Androgeus* (son of Minos, whose murder by
    the Athenians prompted Minos to demand that Athens each year send seven
    young men and seven maidens to Crete for sacrifice to the Minotaur).
    lētum Androgeō: sc. **inest** (**in pictūrā**) from 26, with this and the following cl.
    tum: i.e., in another part of the picture on the door.
    pendō, pendere, pependī, pēnsus, *to weigh; to pay;* idiom, with **poenās,** *to pay
    the penalty* (of), *pay as a penalty, pay as recompense.*
21 **Cecropidēs, -ae,** m. pl., *descendants of Cecrops* (legendary first king of Athens),
    Athenians.
    septēnī, -ae, -a, *seven each, seven on each occasion, seven at a time.*
    septēna . . . / corpora nātōrum (22): = **septēnōs nātōs,** in appos. with **poenās**
    (20); Vergil mentions only the young men, in a kind of narrative ellipsis, but
    we are meant to imagine the young women as well (unless the poet has in
    mind a different version of the story).
    quotannīs, adv., *annually, every year.*

13 Iam subeunt Triviae lūcōs atque aurea tēcta.

Aeneas surveys the scenes of Minos' labyrinth and the Minotaur
legend wrought by Daedalus on the doors of Apollo's temple

14   Daedalus, ut fāma est, fugiēns Mīnōia rēgna,
15 praepetibus pennīs ausus sē crēdere caelō,
16 īnsuētum per iter gelidās ēnāvit ad Arctōs,
17 Chalcidicāque levis tandem super astitit arce.
18 Redditus hīs prīmum terrīs, tibi, Phoebe, sacrāvit
19 rēmigium ālārum posuitque immānia templa.
20 In foribus lētum Androgeō; tum pendere poenās
21 Cecropidae iussī (miserum!), septēna quotannīs

"Daedalus and Icarus"
Simone Cantarini (1612–48)
Galleria Doria Pamphili, Rome, Italy

22   **stat:** i.e., in the scene on the door.

    urna, -ae, f., *urn, jar.*

    ductīs . . . urna: the names of the 14 individuals to be sacrificed to the Minotaur each year were drawn by lot from an urn.

23   **Contrā:** here adv., *on the opposite side* (of the picture); we are meant to imagine double-doors, with the scenes from Athens on one door, and those from Crete on the other.

    ēlāta: *lifted out of = rising out of.*

    respondet: i.e., *balances* the scene of Athens.

    Cnōsius, -a, -um, *Cnossian, of Cnossus* (chief city of Crete during the reign of Minos).

24   **suppōnō, suppōnere, supposuī, suppositus,** *to put under, position beneath.*

    supposta: = **supposita** (SYNCOPE).

    fūrtō, adv., *craftily, stealthily, by deception.*

25   **Pāsiphaē, -ēs,** f., *Pasiphaë* (daughter of Helios, wife of Minos, and mother of Phaedra, Ariadne, and the Minotaur).

    supposta . . . (24) / Pāsiphaē: Daedalus had fashioned a bronze cow large enough for Pasiphaë to climb inside and designed to entice the bull for which Venus, angered at the queen (hence **crūdēlis** 24), had driven her to lust (in some versions of the myth it was Neptune who drove Pasiphaë to desire the bull); the product of the union was the Minotaur, half man and half beast.

    bifōrmis, -is, -e, *two-formed, hybrid* (often used of mythological monsters with bodies composed of two different creatures).

26   **Mīnōtaurus, -ī,** m., *the Minotaur* (monstrous offspring of Pasiphaë).

    insum, inesse, īnfuī, īnfutūrus, *to be in/on; to appear in; to be part of.*

    inest: sc. **in pictūrā,** with **amor, Pāsiphaē,** and **Mīnōtaurus** as subjs. and sg., as is usual, to agree only with the nearest of the three nouns.

    *****monimentum, -ī,** n., *memorial, reminder.*

27   **inextrīcābilis, -is, -e,** *impossible to disentangle/sort out, insoluble; inextricable, inescapable.*

    inextrīcābilis: the laborious six-syllable word, with its harsh **x/c** ALLITERATION, and the three long syllables slowing the pace after the three opening dactyls, well suits the challenges posed by the labyrinth to those trapped within it.

    error: used at 2.48 above of the Trojan horse (like **dolōs** in 29—cf. 2.44 and 252); the phrase **labor . . . error,** arranged in CHIASMUS, is essentially a HENDIADYS, *that well-known laborious, inextricable maze . . ..* Vergil's depiction of the labyrinth and the Minotaur on the temple doors is generally taken to be a foreshadowing of Aeneas' journey into the labyrinthine recesses of the Underworld and the horrors he will see there; the poet thus invites us to consider the range of parallels between his hero and Theseus.

22 corpora nātōrum; stat ductīs sortibus urna.
23 Contrā, ēlāta marī, respondet Cnōsia tellūs:
24 hīc crūdēlis amor taurī suppostaque fūrtō
25 Pāsiphaē mixtumque genus prōlēsque bifōrmis
26 Mīnōtaurus inest, Veneris monimenta nefandae,
27 hīc labor ille domūs et inextrīcābilis error;

Quaestiō

Comment on the purpose and placement of **hīc . . . hīc** in 24 and 27; what is this device called?

"Theseus and the Minotaur"
Antoine Louis Barye
(1796–1875)
Musée Bonnat
Bayonne, France

As we approach Book Six of the *Aeneid*, I find myself dreading the visit to the underworld. I remember that even *Domina* Chambers admitted that certain passages were almost untranslatable. It was as if, she told us, the syntax becomes as twisting as the minotaur's maze that is carved on the Sibyl's gates through which Aeneas must pass before his visit to the underworld. ". . . It's like a secret he's not supposed to reveal, so he has to disguise the instructions."

Carol Goodman, The Lake of Dead Languages

28 **rēgīnae:** here *princess,* i.e., Ariadne, daughter of Minos and Pasiphaë. Ariadne had fallen in love with the Athenian hero Theseus, who had voluntarily joined the other Athenian victims with the intent of defeating the Minotaur; with the assistance of Daedalus, the princess helped Theseus escape the labyrinth after slaying the beast, only later to be abandoned by him (just as Aeneas abandoned Dido, whose ghost he will encounter in the Underworld).

    sed enim: *but indeed* (cf. 1.19 above); delaying the conj. (ANASTROPHE) helps emphasize the **magnum . . . amōrem.**

30 **caeca . . . vēstīgia:** i.e., of Theseus; Daedalus told Ariadne to have Theseus unravel a roll of thread behind him as he entered the labyrinth, so he could later escape by following the thread to retrace his steps.

31 **sineret:** sc. **sī;** Vergil's use of the impf. rather than the usual plpf. in a PAST CONTRARY-TO-FACT CONDITION makes the APOSTROPHE to Icarus all the more vivid, as if the young man were alive, and present, and able to hear the narrator's lament.

    dolor: i.e., of Daedalus, who is also subj. of **cōnātus erat** (32).

    Īcarus, -ī, m., *Icarus* (Daedalus' son, who plummeted to his death in his flight from Crete—see note on 14).

32 **cāsūs:** the word is related to the vb. **cadere** and here, rather than meaning simply "disaster," lit. refers to Icarus' *fall.*

    effingō, effingere, effīnxī, effīnctus, *to mold, fashion, shape; to portray, depict.*

33 **cecidēre:** intended perhaps as an etymological play on **cāsūs** (32); the artisan's hands dropped to his sides as abruptly and hopelessly as his son had fallen from the sky. Thus Daedalus did not depict the fate of his son; are we meant to consider any parallel to the father-son pair of Aeneas and Ascanius?—is the Daedalus-Icarus story somehow a warning to the Trojan leader?

    prōtinus: here *one after another.*

    omnia: the other scenes depicted on the temple doors; disyllabic by SYNIZESIS.

34 **perlegerent . . . / adforet (35):** for the construction and tenses, see note on **sineret** (31).

    praemittō, praemittere, praemīsī, praemissus, *to send ahead.*

    praemissus Achātēs: Achates (see note on 1.120) had been dispatched to the Sibyl's nearby cave to announce Aeneas' arrival.

35 **adforet:** if you do not recognize the form, see the note on 1.576 and cf. 2.522.

36 **Dēïphobē, -ēs,** f., *Deïphobe* (name of the Sibyl at Cumae).

    Glaucus, -ī, m., *Glaucus* (father of Deïphobe; with the gen. here, sc. **fīlia**).

37 **hoc . . . tempus:** i.e., *this moment/occasion.*

    ista . . . spectācula: here *your sight-seeing,* i.e., spending time gazing at murals.

    sibī . . . poscit: *call for (itself), warrant.*

38 **grex, gregis,** m., *flock, herd.*

    intāctō: i.e., by the yoke = *never yoked* and hence suitable for sacrifice.

    iuvencus, -ī, m., *young bull/ox, bullock.*

39 **praestiterit:** POTENTIAL SUBJUNCT., *it would be better* + inf.; the perf. indicates completed action and hence urgency.

    lēctās . . . bidentēs: the same ritual is described at 4.57, **mactant lēctās dē mōre bidentēs.**

28 magnum rēgīnae sed enim miserātus amōrem,

29 Daedalus ipse dolōs tēctī ambāgēsque resolvit,

30 caeca regēns fīlō vēstīgia. Tū quoque magnam

31 partem opere in tantō, sineret dolor, Īcare, habērēs:

32 bis cōnātus erat cāsūs effingere in aurō,

33 bis patriae cecidēre manūs.

Achates escorts the Sibyl to Aeneas, whom she commands
to offer sacrifices to Apollo and then enter his temple

Quīn prōtinus omnia

34 perlegerent oculīs, nī iam praemissus Achātēs

35 adforet atque ūnā Phoebī Triviaeque sacerdōs,

36 Dēiphobē Glaucī, fātur quae tālia rēgī:

37 "Nōn hoc ista sibī tempus spectācula poscit;

38 nunc grege dē intāctō septem mactāre iuvencōs

39 praestiterit, totidem lēctās ex mōre bidentēs."

40 Tālibus adfāta Aenēān (nec sacra morantur

41 iussa virī), Teucrōs vocat alta in templa sacerdōs.

Quaestiōnēs

1. Comment on the placement of **magnum** and **amōrem** in 28; what is this arrangement called and what is its intended effect?

2. Comment on the emotional effect of the apostrophe to Icarus in 31; in what ways is the apostrophe in 2.56 similar? Cf. also the address to Apollo in line 18.

3. Compare the elaborate ecphrasis on Minos and the Minotaur in 20–33 with that depicting the murals at Juno's temple at 1.456–93 above; in what specific ways do both "digressions" contribute significantly to Vergil's narrative purposes? What several correspondences do you see between Daedalus, and the events on Crete in which he was involved, and Aeneas himself?

4. How does the purpose of the anaphora in 32–33 differ from that of the repetition of **hīc** in 24 and 27?

42 Excīsum . . . latus ingēns: sc. **est**.

> in antrum: *into a cave,* i.e., *to form a cave.*

44 totidem: repeated in the same metrical position from line 39.

45 Ventum erat: ·impers., essentially = **vēnerant**.

46 Deus: Apollo, whose spirit spoke through the Sibyl.

47 color: here *complexion.*

> ūnus: with both **vultus** and **color**; i.e., her facial expressions and appearance
> kept rapidly changing, as the god's spirit entered and took possession of her.

48 cōmptus, -a, -um, *adorned, decorated; arranged, combed* (here PRED. ADJ. after
> **mānsēre**).

> anhēlus, -a, -um, *gasping, panting, breathing hard, heaving* (sc. **est**).

49 vidērī: with **maior**, *(she is) greater to behold;* the prophetess' appearance changes
> suddenly and violently, as she falls into her oracular trance.

50 mortāle: the n. acc. of the adj. is here employed adverbially.

> adflāta est . . . quandō: the conj. is delayed by ANASTROPHE.

51 propior, propius, *nearer, closer.*

> Cessās in: *are you hesitating over.*

52 Trōs, Trōis, m., *a Trojan* (here in appos. with the voc. **Aenēā**).

> ante: sc. **precēs**; i.e., not until Aeneas has prayed.

53 attonitae: i.e., by the presence of Apollo; in an eerie PERSONIFICATION, the
> hundred openings to the Sibyl's cave are described as mouths and the cave
> itself as *awe-struck.*

> fāta: here, not from the noun **fātum**, but partic. of **for**.

54 Gelidus . . . tremor (55): the elaborate ABCBA CHIASMUS (**Gelidus . . . dūra
> cucurrit / ossa tremor**) creates a kind of WORD-PICTURE, with the chill fear
> moving quickly into the very marrow of the Trojans' bones; for the image, cf.
> 2.120–21 above.

56 semper miserāte: rather than the voc. partic. *(having always pitied)* modifying
> **Phoebe**, idiomatic Eng. would likely employ a rel. cl., *(you) who have always
> taken pity on.*

57 dērēxtī: = **dērēxistī** (SYNCOPE).

> manūs: i.e., his aim.

58 corpus in Aeacidae: assisted by Apollo, in his role as archer god, Paris killed
> Achilles with an arrow shot to the heel, his only vulnerable spot; Aeneas here
> by implication prays for similar success against a new Achilles, Turnus, the
> Rutulian king who will resist the Trojans' settlement in Italy.

> *obeō, obīre, obiī, obitus, *to meet face to face, come up against; to enclose, border,
> surround; to take on, deal with; to die.*

59 repostās: here *hidden away, remote.*

60 Massȳlī, -ōrum, m. pl., *the Massylians* (a tribe of north Africa, an allusion here
> to Aeneas' sojourn in Carthage).

> Syrtibus: dat. with the compound **praetenta**, *extending to the . . .;* for this region
> near Carthage, see 1.111 above and note.

61 fugientis: probably gen. with **Ītaliae** (Vergil has the phrase **Ītaliam . . .
> fugientem** at 5.629) or, less likely, acc. pl. (**fugientīs** = **fugientēs**) modifying
> **ōrās**.

42 Excīsum Euboicae latus ingēns rūpis in antrum,
43 quō lātī dūcunt aditūs centum, ōstia centum,
44 unde ruunt totidem vōcēs, respōnsa Sibyllae.
45 Ventum erat ad līmen, cum virgō, "Poscere fāta
46 tempus," ait; "Deus, ecce, deus!" Cui tālia fantī
47 ante forēs subitō nōn vultus, nōn color ūnus,
48 nōn cōmptae mānsēre comae; sed pectus anhēlum,
49 et rabiē fera corda tument, maiorque vidērī
50 nec mortāle sonāns, adflāta est nūmine quandō
51 iam propiōre deī. "Cessās in vōta precēsque,
52 Trōs," ait, "Aenēā? Cessās? Neque enim ante dehīscent
53 attonitae magna ōra domūs." Et tālia fāta,
54 conticuit.

Aeneas prays to Apollo for the safety of the Trojan people
and implores the Sibyl to prophesy their future in Italy

Gelidus Teucrīs per dūra cucurrit
55 ossa tremor, funditque precēs rēx pectore ab īmō:
56 "Phoebe, gravēs Trōiae semper miserāte labōrēs,
57 Dardana quī Paridis dērēxtī tēla manūsque
58 corpus in Aeacidae, magnās obeuntia terrās
59 tot maria intrāvī, duce tē, penitusque repostās
60 Massȳlum gentēs praetentaque Syrtibus arva:
61 iam tandem Ītaliae fugientis prēndimus ōrās.

Quaestiōnēs

Repostās (59) is a contracted form of what verb? What is the technical term for this
sort of contraction?

62 **hāctenus**, adv., *to this point, thus far* (separated by TMESIS; Vergil means here *thus far and no farther*).

  fuerit . . . secūta: = **sit secūta**, *may it have followed us;* for the force of the perf. subjunct., see note on **praestiterit** (39).

63 **vōs . . . fās est parcere**: *it is right for you to . . . .*

  Pergameus, -a, -um, *Pergamene, of Pergama* (the citadel of Troy), *Trojan*.

64 **dī . . . Dardaniae (65)**: though he does not name them here (which would be unpropitious), Juno, Neptune, and Minerva had all been particularly hostile to Troy.

65 **vātēs**: the Sibyl.

66 **praescius, -a, -um**, *prescient, knowing in advance;* + gen., *with foreknowledge of.*

  ventūrī: fut. partic. used as a substantive, *of what is to come, of the future.*

  indēbitus, -a, -um, *not owed/due; not pledged/promised.*

  nōn indēbita: LITOTES.

67 **cōnsīdere**: inf. with the acc. subjs. **Teucrōs, deōs (68)**, and **nūmina (68)**, dependent on **dā (66)**, *grant that the . . . may . . . .*

68 **errantēs . . . deōs**: the Penates in particular (see note on 1.6 above).

69 **Phoebō . . . templum / . . . diēs . . . Phoebī (70)**: a roughly CHIASTIC arrangement; Vergil meant his audience to think of the marble temple to Apollo most recently established by Augustus in 28 B.C. (see note on **vātēs** 12) and of the **Lūdī Apollinārēs**, games instituted in honor of Apollo during the Second Punic War.

  ***marmor, marmoris**, n., *marble, block of marble.*

71 **Tē**: the Sibyl.

73 **gentī**: with **dicta**, *uttered to.*

  lēctōs . . . virōs (74): lines 71–74 refer to Augustus' transfer of the sacred books containing a collection of Sibylline oracles, consulted during crises in Rome's history and according to tradition first written down during the reign of Tarquinius Superbus, to a shrine within the new Palatine temple to Apollo, where a board of 15 priests (the **quīndecemvirī sacrīs faciundīs**, Vergil's **lēctōs . . . virōs**) were assigned responsibility for them.

74 **Foliīs . . . ōrō (76)**: during the course of Aeneas' westward journey (3.441–60), Helenus, one of Priam's sons who had also escaped from Troy, had advised him, in a speech deliberately recalled here, to seek out the Sibyl at Cumae and to implore her to give him a prophecy in her own words, rather than by using the oracular leaves that she often employed in foretelling the future.

  nē . . . mandā: for the archaic construction, see note on **nē crēdite** (2.48).

  carmen, carminis, n., *chant, spell; oracle, prophecy; poem, song.*

75 **rapidīs**: for the sense employed here, see 2.305 and note; if the leaves were swept away by the wind, the oracle would be forever lost.

  lūdibrium, -ī, n., *plaything, toy* (here with **ventīs**, *as playthings for . . .*).

76 **ipsa canās ōrō**: = **ōro ut tū ipsa canās**; positioning **ōrō** at the strong caesura accentuates the wordplay with **ōre**.

62 Hāc Trōiāna tenus fuerit fortūna secūta;

63 vōs quoque Pergameae iam fās est parcere gentī,

64 dīque deaeque omnēs, quibus obstitit Īlium et ingēns

65 glōria Dardaniae. Tūque, ō sānctissima vātēs,

66 praescia ventūrī, dā (nōn indēbita poscō

67 rēgna meīs fātīs) Latiō cōnsīdere Teucrōs

68 errantēsque deōs agitātaque nūmina Trōiae.

69 Tum Phoebō et Triviae solidō dē marmore templum

70 īnstituam fēstōsque diēs dē nōmine Phoebī.

71 Tē quoque magna manent rēgnīs penetrālia nostrīs:

72 hīc ego namque tuās sortēs arcānaque fāta

73 dicta meae gentī pōnam, lēctōsque sacrābō,

74 alma, virōs. Foliīs tantum nē carmina mandā,

75 nē turbāta volent rapidīs lūdibria ventīs;

76 ipsa canās ōrō." Fīnem dedit ōre loquendī.

Quaestiōnēs

1. Why is the force of the litotes in 66 especially appropriate in the context of Aeneas' prayer to the Sibyl and, through her, to Apollo?

2. Analyze the main points made by Aeneas in his prayer at 56–76: what does he ask for, what justification does he give, what does he promise the gods in return?

The Cumaean Sibyl, detail from Sistine Chapel
Michelangelo (1475–1564)
Vatican Palace, Vatican State

77 **patiēns:** partic. of **patior**; with **Phoebī,** *submissive to.* The prophetess is not yet totally under the spiritual control of the god; the spondaic rhythms and conflict of ictus and accent in the next line help suggest her psychic struggle with the god.

immānis: here *wild(ly).*

78 **sī . . . possit / excussisse (79):** with **bacchātur,** the condition has almost the force of a purpose cl. (cf. **sī . . . videat** 1.181–82 above), *she rages like a Bacchante* (as Dido does in 4.301 and Rumor in 4.666), *if thus she might be able to* = *in order to . . . .*

79 **tantō magis:** i.e., **quantō bacchātur,** "the more she rages, ..."

fatīgat: the same vb. is used at 1.316 of controlling a team of horses; with **ōs rabidum** and **fera corda** in the next line, Vergil clearly means to evoke animal imagery here, but his language is viewed by some readers as suggestive of rape.

80 ***rabidus, -a, -um,** (of wild animals) *ravening, raging; rabid, mad; frenzied, wild.*

fingit: i.e., *he molds her to his will.*

83 ***dēfungor, dēfungī, dēfūnctus sum,** *to bring* (some matter) *to an end;* + abl., *to come to the end of, be done with, complete.*

84 **terrae:** either loc. or gen., like **pelagī (83).**

86 **nōn:** with **vēnisse.**

et: = **etiam;** with **volent.**

87 **et Thybrim . . . cernō:** the line's slow, menacing spondaic rhythms and accentual conflict help intensify the Sibyl's grim vision; Creusa had given Aeneas a far more alluring prophecy of the Tiber at 2.781–82 above.

88 **Simoīs . . . Xanthus:** for these two rivers at Troy, which Vergil here deliberately compares with Italy's Tiber, see above at 1.100 and 473.

Dōrica castra: in the same metrical position at 1.27, where the Trojans had fatally misconstrued the removal of the Greeks' camp overnight as an indication that they had abandoned the war and sailed home.

89 **dēfuerint:** Lat. often employs the fut. perf. where Eng. would have the simple fut.

alius . . . deā (90): the *other Achilles* is the Rutulian king Turnus (see note on line 58), whose goddess mother was the nymph Venilia; the Sibyl's prophecy in essence forecasts a second "Trojan War" and in a sense announces that the coming events of the *Aeneid,* in Books Seven-Twelve, will be a second *Iliad.*

90 **addita:** *present in addition/also present* and, as ever, hostile to the Trojans.

91 **egēnus, -a, -um,** *requiring assistance, needy.*

92 **quās . . . nōn ōrāveris:** *to what peoples . . . will you not appeal* = *you will appeal to all peoples . . . .*

Italum: = **Italōrum.**

93 **hospita, -ae,** f. adj, *foreign, alien.*

coniūnx iterum hospita: the first was Helen, and the second will be king Latinus' daughter Lavinia, the Italian princess for whose hand Aeneas and Turnus will become rivals.

94 **externus, -a, -um,** *coming from abroad, foreign, alien.*

thalamī: lit., *bedrooms* (of married couples); here, by a common METONYMY, *marriage.* Verse 94 is one of only two incomplete lines in Book Six (see note on 2.66).

95 **ītō:** fut. imper. of **īre.**

The Sibyl, raging and possessed by Apollo, proclaims through the
hundred doors of her house the god's response to Aeneas' prayer

77   At Phoebī nōndum patiēns immānis in antrō
78 bacchātur vātēs, magnum sī pectore possit
79 excussisse deum; tantō magis ille fatīgat
80 ōs rabidum, fera corda domāns, fingitque premendō.
81 Ōstia iamque domūs patuēre ingentia centum
82 sponte suā vātisque ferunt respōnsa per aurās:
83 "Ō tandem magnīs pelagī dēfūncte perīclīs,
84 (sed terrae graviōra manent), in rēgna Lavīnī
85 Dardanidae venient (mitte hanc dē pectore cūram),
86 sed nōn et vēnisse volent. Bella, horrida bella,
87 et Thybrim multō spūmantem sanguine cernō.
88 Nōn Simoīs tibi nec Xanthus nec Dōrica castra
89 dēfuerint; alius Latiō iam partus Achillēs,
90 nātus et ipse deā; nec Teucrīs addita Iūnō
91 usquam aberit, cum tū, supplex in rēbus egēnīs,
92 quās gentēs Italum aut quās nōn ōrāveris urbēs!
93 Causa malī tantī coniūnx iterum hospita Teucrīs
94 externīque iterum thalamī.
95 Tū nē cēde malīs, sed contrā audentior ītō,

Quaestiōnēs

What is the effect of the anaphora in verse 88 and the enjambement of the verb in
the following line?

But she has not yet given way to Phoebus:
she rages, savage, in her cavern, tries
to drive the great god from her breast. So much
the more, he tires out her raving mouth;
he tames her wild heart, shapes by crushing force.

From the translation of Allen Mandelbaum, 1981

96   **quā . . . salūtis:** cf. **quā prīma . . . fortūna salūtis / mōnstrat iter** (2.387–88).

97   **quod:** rel., *something that;* the anteced. is the entire cl. **via (96) . . . urbe.**

       Grāiā . . . urbe: Aeneas' major ally in the war in Italy will be the Arcadian Greek Evander, aged king of Pallanteum (a legendary settlement on the future site of Rome).

98   **Cūmaeus, -a, -um,** *Cumaean, of Cumae* (see note above on **Cumae 2**).

99   **ambāgēs:** used earlier in the book (line 29) of the labyrinth.

       remūgiō, remūgīre, to moo in response; to respond with a booming noise, bellow back; to resound.

       remūgit: in view of the horse imagery Vergil employs in describing the Sibyl at 78–80 and 100–02, the vb. is clearly meant to suggest the bellowing of a wild horse or at least some wild animal, amplified by the Sibyl's cave with its many openings; for the priestess' inhuman sound, cf. **nec mortāle sonāns** (50).

100   **furentī:** DAT. OF REF., *(on her) as she rages.*

101   **stimulus, -ī,** m., *goad* (for prodding animals); *spur, goad* (to action, to fury).

       stimulōs: Vergil uses the word figuratively, with **sub pectore** (cf. **pectore 78**), but also again, with **frēna** (and cf. **rabida ōra 102** with **ōs rabidum 80**), he evokes the imagery of controlling a raging horse (see note on **fatīgat** 79).

102   **quiērunt:** = **quiēvērunt.**

104   **mī:** = **mihi,** DAT. WITH ADJS. (**nova . . . inopīnave**).

       faciēs: here *form.*

       inopīnus, -a, -um, *unexpected, unanticipated, unforeseen.*

       nova . . . inopīnave: PRED. ADJS. after **nōn ūlla (103) . . . faciēs . . . surgit.**

105   **praecēpī:** *taken in advance,* i.e., *anticipated;* the language of 103–05 reflects Stoic doctrine—Aeneas is a Stoic hero, mentally prepared for any eventuality—and at the same time reminds readers that many of the challenges facing the Trojans were foretold by Helenus in Book Three (456f.) and Anchises in Book Five (730f.).

106   **hīc . . . / dīcitur (107):** sc. **esse.**

       īnfernus, -a, -um, lower, underground; of the Underworld, infernal.

       īnfernī . . . rēgis: Pluto.

107   **tenebrōsus, -a, -um,** *dark, shadowy; gloomy.*

       palūs, palūdis, f., *fen, swamp* (often applied to the murky waters of the Underworld, and here alluding to Lake Avernus—see 118 and note).

       Acherōn, Acherontis, m., *Acheron* (a river of the Underworld whose floodwaters, according to legend, surfaced as the Acherusian swamp, identified today as Lake Fusaro, south of the Cumaean acropolis).

       Acheronte refūsō: ABL. OF PLACE FROM WHICH.

108   **īre . . . / contingat (109):** *let it fall to me to . . . = let me be allowed to . . . .*

       ad cōnspectum . . . et ōra: i.e., to look upon his face.

109   **sacra:** because it was the entrance to the god Pluto's domain.

110   **Illum . . . recēpī (111):** the rescue described in 2.634f. and 707f. above.

112   **maria omnia:** ACC. OF EXTENT OF SPACE.

96 quā tua tē Fortūna sinet. Via prīma salūtis
97 (quod minimē rēris) Grāiā pandētur ab urbe."

Aeneas responds to the Sibyl's prophecy and asks her to guide
him into the Underworld to visit with the shade of his father

98   Tālibus ex adytō dictīs Cūmaea Sibylla
99 horrendās canit ambāgēs antrōque remūgit,
100 obscūrīs vēra involvēns: ea frēna furentī
101 concutit et stimulōs sub pectore vertit Apollō.
102 Ut prīmum cessit furor et rabida ōra quiērunt,
103 incipit Aenēās hērōs: "Nōn ūlla labōrum,
104 ō virgō, nova mī faciēs inopīnave surgit;
105 omnia praecēpī atque animō mēcum ante perēgī.
106 Ūnum ōrō: quandō hīc īnfernī iānua rēgis
107 dīcitur et tenebrōsa palūs Acheronte refūsō,
108 īre ad cōnspectum cārī genitōris et ōra
109 contingat; doceās iter et sacra ōstia pandās.
110 Illum ego per flammās et mīlle sequentia tēla
111 ēripuī hīs umerīs mediōque ex hoste recēpī;
112 ille meum comitātus iter maria omnia mēcum
113 atque omnēs pelagīque minās caelīque ferēbat,

Quaestiō

Compare the Sibyl's response in 83–97 with Aeneas' prayer in 56–76; detail and
discuss the specific correspondences.

114 **invalidus, -a, -um,** *infirm, weak, feeble.*
   *****ultrā,** adv. and prep. + acc., *further; beyond.*
   *****senecta, -ae,** f., *old age.*
116 *****gnātus, -ī** (alternate form of **nātus, -ī**), m., *son.*
117 **alma:** formulaically applied to the Sibyl, in the same metrical position, at 74 above.

   potes . . . omnia: sc. **facere.**
118 **Hecatē, -ēs,** f., *Hecate* (a goddess of the Underworld, worshipped at crossroads and often associated with Diana—see note above on **Trivia** 13).

   praeficiō, praeficere, praefēcī, praefectus, *to put* (someone, acc.) *in charge of* (something, dat.).

   Avernus, -a, -um, *of Avernus* (lake near Cumae and legendary entrance to the Underworld); *of the Underworld, infernal.*

   lūcīs . . . Avernīs: the forests surrounding the lake.
119 **accersō, accersere, accersīvī, accersītus,** *to send for, fetch, summon* (from the dead).

   Orpheus, -ī, m., *Orpheus* (legendary Thracian singer who journeyed into the Underworld to rescue his deceased wife Eurydice; though he failed to bring Eurydice back from the dead, Orpheus did himself return to the world of the living).
120 **Thrēicius, -a, -um,** *Thracian, of Thrace* (district of northern Greece).

   fidēs, fidium, f. pl., *lyre; strings of a lyre.*

   canōrus, -a, -um, *tuneful, melodious.*
121 **Pollūx, Pollūcis,** m., *Pollux* (son of Tyndareus and Leda, and twin brother of Castor).

   alternus, -a, -um, *alternating, reciprocal, in turn.*

   alternā morte: when Castor died, his brother Pollux arranged to take his place in the Underworld for six months of every year (or, according to other versions of the myth, on alternate days).

   redimō, redimere, redēmī, redēmptus, *to buy back; to ransom; to redeem, rescue, save.*

   redēmit / . . . redit (122): ASSONANCE underscores the wordplay ("he bought back"/"he went back").
122 **viam:** COGNATE ACC. with **it** and **redit,** *he traveled and traveled again the journey.*
   Quid . . . memorem (123): PRAETERITIO.

   Thēseus, -ī, acc. **Thēsea,** m., *Theseus* (Athenian hero who defeated the Minotaur and visited the Underworld in an attempt to carry off Proserpina).

   magnum: some editors argue that the adj. modifies **Alcīdēn** (123) and thus place a comma before **magnum** rather than following, but it seems more natural to take the adj. with **Thēsea,** both because of the juxtaposition of noun + adj. and because a strong DIAERESIS between the two words at the end of the fifth foot would be unusually abrupt.

114 invalidus, vīrēs ultrā sortemque senectae.
115 Quīn, ut tē supplex peterem et tua līmina adīrem,
116 īdem ōrāns mandāta dabat. Gnātīque patrisque,
117 alma, precor, miserēre (potes namque omnia, nec tē
118 nēquīquam lūcīs Hecatē praefēcit Avernīs),
119 sī potuit mānēs accersere coniugis Orpheus,
120 Thrēiciā frētus citharā fidibusque canōrīs,
121 sī frātrem Pollūx alternā morte redēmit
122 itque reditque viam totiēns. Quid Thēsea magnum,

Grotto of the Sibyl
Acropolis of Cumae, 6th/5th cent. B.C.
Cumae, Italy

123 *Alcīdēs, -ae, acc. Alcīdēn, voc. Alcīdē, m., *descendant of Alceus* (father of Amphitryon and grandfather of Hercules), *Hercules* (regularly referred to in epic by his patronymic, since the scansion of his own name does not fit into dactylic hexameter; he visited the Underworld to capture the three-headed guard-dog Cerberus).

    mī: SC. est; DAT. OF POSSESSION. Jupiter was Venus' father and hence Aeneas' grandfather.

125 Sate: voc. of the perf. partic. of serō, *born* (from).

126 Anchīsiadēs, -ae, voc. Anchīsiadē, m., *son of Anchises.*

    dēscēnsus, -ūs, m., *walking downhill, descent.*

    *Avernus, -ī, m., *Avernus* (either the lake itself or, by extension, the Underworld—see note on 118).

    facilis dēscēnsus Avernō: a frequently quoted phrase; Avernō may be construed as DAT. OF DIRECTION, *to Avernus,* or as ABL. OF ROUTE, *by way of (Lake) Avernus.*

128 revocāre: here *to retrace.*

130 ēvehō, ēvehere, ēvexī, ēvectus, *to carry away; to raise up.*

131 media omnia: i.e., of the Underworld.

132 *Cōcȳtus, -ī, m., *Cocytus* (the Underworld's river of "lamentation"; the word itself, which is Greek, means "wailing").

    circumveniō, circumvenīre, circumvēnī, circumventus, *to come/go around, surround.*

133 Quod . . . mentī: cf. sed sī tantus amor at 2.10, where it is applied to Dido's longing to hear Aeneas tell of Troy's last day; for quod = sed, cf. 2.141 above.

134 bis: i.e., both as he enters the Underworld and as he exits, or when he enters now on this mystical journey and again later at his death.

    innō (1), *to swim (in); to sail (upon).*

    innāre: cf. the related vb. ēnāvit, used of Daedalus' flight from Crete in line 16 above.

135 īnsānō . . . labōrī: cf. quid tantum īnsānō iuvat indulgēre dolōrī, a quest. asked of Aeneas by Creusa's ghost at 2.776.

137 aureus . . . rāmus: the noun is suspensefully delayed; as R.D. Williams remarks in his note on this verse, the golden bough, a talisman first appearing in Vergil's *Aeneid,* "is a symbol of mystery, a kind of light in darkness, a kind of life in death."

    lentō: here *pliant, flexible.*

    vīmen, vīminis, n., *branch, stem* (usually of flexible stems used in making wicker baskets).

    foliīs . . . vīmine: ABL. OF SPECIFICATION.

138 Iūnōnī īnfernae: Proserpina (see 142).

139 convallis, convallis, f., *valley, glen.*

140 operta: SC. loca.

123 quid memorem Alcīdēn? Et mī genus ab Iove summō."

The Sibyl agrees to guide Aeneas to the Underworld on two
conditions—that he find and pluck from its mystic tree the
golden bough sacred to Proserpina, and that he see
to the proper burial of a fallen comrade

124   Tālibus ōrābat dictīs ārāsque tenēbat,
125 cum sīc ōrsa loquī vātēs: "Sate sanguine dīvum,
126 Trōs Anchīsiadē, facilis dēscēnsus Avernō:
127 noctēs atque diēs patet ātrī iānua Dītis;
128 sed revocāre gradum superāsque ēvādere ad aurās,
129 hoc opus, hic labor est. Paucī, quōs aequus amāvit
130 Iuppiter aut ārdēns ēvexit ad aethera virtūs,
131 dīs genitī potuēre. Tenent media omnia silvae,
132 Cōcȳtusque sinū lābēns circumvenit ātrō.
133 Quod sī tantus amor mentī, sī tanta cupīdō est
134 bis Stygiōs innāre lacūs, bis nigra vidēre
135 Tartara, et īnsānō iuvat indulgēre labōrī,
136 accipe quae peragenda prius. Latet arbore opācā
137 aureus et foliīs et lentō vīmine rāmus,
138 Iūnōnī īnfernae dictus sacer; hunc tegit omnis
139 lūcus et obscūrīs claudunt convallibus umbrae.
140 Sed nōn ante datur tellūris operta subīre

Quaestiōnēs

1. Carefully analyze the specific arguments Aeneas employs in 103–23 to persuade
   the Sibyl to lead him into the Underworld; how do the types of arguments differ,
   and which might be expected to carry greater force?

2. What rhetorical device is employed in both 133 and 134, and what is its effect?

3. Is the echo of 2.776 here in line 135 merely incidental, or is Vergil making some
   deliberate connection?

141 **auricomus, -a, -um,** *golden-haired, golden-tressed.*
    auricomōs . . . fētūs: the arrangement intentionally replicates that of **aureus . . . rāmus** in 137; the phrase should be translated quite literally here, as we are intended by the PERSONIFICATION to imagine the golden bough as something almost human, like a fetus full-term in its mother's womb, ready to be plucked radiant and newly alive from the darkness into the sunlight.
    quis: indef., = *someone, one.*
    dēcerpō, dēcerpere, dēcerpsī, dēcerptus, *to pluck, pull (down from).*

142 **Hoc . . . suum ferrī . . . mūnus:** with **īnstituit** (143), *that this be brought as . . . .*

143 **Prīmō:** SC. **rāmō.**

144 **frondēscō, frondēscere,** *to bear leaves, sprout foliage.*
    virga: here *branch, sprig.*
    metallum, -ī, n., *mine, quarry; metal, ore.*

145 **vēstīgō (1),** *to follow the trail of, track down, search for.*
    rīte: with **carpe manū** (146); Aeneas must properly pluck the bough from its tree with his hands alone, not with his sword (**ferrō** 148).

149 **tibi:** DAT. OF REF., *I must tell you.*

150 **incestō (1),** *to pollute, defile* (ceremonially).
    incestat fūnere: failure to bury a corpse resulted in the ritual pollution of the entire community of those responsible.

151 **cōnsulta:** here *oracles.*
    pendēs: here *linger* (cf. the Eng. colloquialism "to hang around").

152 **Sēdibus . . . suīs:** i.e., *his final abode, his resting-place.*

153 **nigrās:** appropriate as an offering to the dark gods of the Underworld (cf. **ātrī . . . Dītis** 127 above).
    piāculum, -ī, n., *peace offering, expiatory offering.*
    suntō: third pers. pl. fut. imper. of **esse;** the fut. imper. is commonly used in legal or, as here, ritual contexts.

154 **Styx, Stygis,** f., *Styx* (the principal river of the Underworld).

156 **dēfīxus lūmina:** cf. **dēfīxit lūmina** (1.226 above).

157 **volūtat / . . . animō sēcum** (158): cf. **sēcum . . . corde volūtāns** (above 1.50).

158 **ēventus, -ūs,** m., *outcome; fulfilment* (of a dream, prophecy, prayer).
    Cui: = **eī;** as you have seen before, Lat. often employs a rel. pron. where Eng. would use a pers. pron.
    fīdus: on Vergil's frequent use of this epithet for Aeneas' comrade Achates, see note on 1.120 and cf. 1.188 above.

160 **serō, serere, seruī, sertus,** *to link together, join in a series; to discuss.*
    sermōne serēbant: the two words are perhaps connected etymologically and were so considered by the Romans; Vergil at the very least plays on their ASSONANCE.

161 **quem . . . / dīceret** (162): IND. QUEST., with **vātēs** as subj., dependent on **multa . . . serēbant** (160); the Trojans were aware that Palinurus had recently been lost (see note on line 1), and so, in view of the Sibyl's remark **heu nescīs** (150), Aeneas and Achates must wonder which of their other comrades has died without their knowledge.
    *****humō (1),** *to bury, inter.*

141 auricomōs quam quis dēcerpserit arbore fētūs.

142 Hoc sibi pulchra suum ferrī Prōserpina mūnus

143 īnstituit. Prīmō āvulsō, nōn dēficit alter

144 aureus, et similī frondēscit virga metallō.

145 Ergō altē vēstīgā oculīs et rīte repertum

146 carpe manū; namque ipse volēns facilisque sequētur,

147 sī tē fāta vocant; aliter nōn vīribus ūllīs

148 vincere nec dūrō poteris convellere ferrō.

149 Praetereā iacet exanimum tibi corpus amīcī

150 (heu nescīs) tōtamque incestat fūnere classem,

151 dum cōnsulta petis nostrōque in līmine pendēs.

152 Sēdibus hunc refer ante suīs et conde sepulcrō.

153 Dūc nigrās pecudēs; ea prīma piācula suntō.

154 Sīc dēmum lūcōs Stygis et rēgna invia vīvīs

155 aspiciēs." Dīxit, pressōque obmūtuit ōre.

After leaving the Sibyl's grotto, Aeneas and Achates discover the
body of their comrade Misenus and erect for him a worthy tomb

156   Aenēās, maestō dēfīxus lūmina vultū,

157 ingreditur, linquēns antrum, caecōsque volūtat

158 ēventūs animō sēcum. Cui fīdus Achātēs

159 it comes et paribus cūrīs vēstīgia fīgit.

160 Multa inter sēsē variō sermōne serēbant,

161 quem socium exanimum vātēs, quod corpus humandum

Quaestiōnēs

1. What is the technical term for the splitting of **ante . . . quam** in 140–41?

2. Identify the several color words Vergil employs in 127–44; into what two contrasting categories may they be divided, and in which lines has Vergil used word order to emphasize the contrast?

162 **Atque**: used here to signal a sudden transition.

    illī: Aeneas and Achates; the word is somewhat superfluous here and some editors accept the conjectured emendation **illīc**.

    *****Mīsēnus, -ī**, m., *Misenus* (son of Aeolus, god of the winds, or perhaps of the Trojan Aeolus mentioned in *Aeneid* Book Twelve; a famed trumpeter, and close comrade first of Hector, then of Aeneas).

163 **perimō, perimere, perēmī, perēmptus**, *to destroy, annihilate; to kill.*

164 **Aeolis, Aeolidis**, acc. **Aeolidēn**, m., *son of Aeolus* (see note on 162).

    quō: ABL. OF COMPARISON.

165 **aere**: Vergil's audience would recognize this as a METONYMY or SYNECDOCHE for Misenus' trumpet.

    aere . . . cantū: a remarkable ABCCBA CHIASMUS, and the ALLITERATION of the c adds an ONOMATOPOETIC effect suggesting the harsh sound of Misenus' war trumpet.

    ciēre . . . accendere: both infs. explain **praestantior** (164, sc. **est**), *is more outstanding in/at summoning . . ..*

166 **circum**: here *at the side of.*

167 **lituus, -ī**, m., (an augur's) *staff; war-trumpet.*

    et lituō . . . et hastā: the balanced pair of nouns, both ABL. OF SPECIFICATION with **īnsignis**, produce a neatly symmetrical line.

168 **illum**: Hector, slain by Achilles in battle, a scene depicted in the murals at Juno's temple at Carthage (1.483–84).

    *****spoliō (1)**, *to strip; to rob, despoil, deprive* (someone, acc.) *of* (something, abl.).

    vītā victor spoliāvit: an elegant ALLITERATIVE sequence.

170 **addiderat**: for this sense of the vb., cf. **Teucrīs addita Iūnō** (90).

    īnferior, īnferius, *lower, lesser, inferior* (here n. pl. as substantive, *lesser cause, inferior course*).

171 **Sed tum . . . / dēmēns (172)**: these opening spondees and the abrupt DIAERESES following help punctuate the dramatic scene shift.

    *****personō (1)**, *to resound, ring; to make resound.*

    concha, -ae, f., *shellfish; seashell; conch* (a horn made from a shell, in myth an instrument played by the sea-god Triton, who is therefore offended here by Misenus' challenge).

173 **aemulus, -a, -um**, *striving to equal/excel, emulous; jealous, envious.*

174 **spūmōsus, -a, -um**, *foaming, frothy.*

    immergō, immergere, immersī, immersus, *to plunge into, immerse, sink.*

    exceptum (173) . . . virum . . . immerserat: as often, Lat. employs a partic. where Eng. would use a finite vb. in a separate cl., *had caught the man and plunged him.*

175 **Ergō . . . clāmōre**: the line's spondaic rhythm and the repeated long ō sounds suggest the solemn, woeful lamentation described by the poet; cf. the opening of 2.26 above (**ergō omnis longō . . .**) and the note on that line.

    circum: sc. **corpus Misēnī.**

177 **haud mora**: sc. **est**; the phrase essentially = **sine morā.**

    festīnant: here trans., with the substantive partic. **iussa** (176) as dir. obj.

    āram . . . sepulcrī: the pyre to be prepared for Misenus.

162 dīceret. Atque illī Mīsēnum in lītore siccō,
163 ut vēnēre, vident indignā morte perēmptum,
164 Mīsēnum Aeolidēn, quō nōn praestantior alter
165 aere ciēre virōs Mārtemque accendere cantū.
166 Hectoris hic magnī fuerat comes, Hectora circum
167 et lituō pugnās īnsignis obībat et hastā.
168 Postquam illum vītā victor spoliāvit Achillēs,
169 Dardaniō Aenēae sēsē fortissimus hērōs
170 addiderat socium, nōn īnferiōra secūtus.
171 Sed tum, forte cavā dum personat aequora conchā,
172 dēmēns, et cantū vocat in certāmina dīvōs,
173 aemulus exceptum Trītōn, sī crēdere dignum est,
174 inter saxa virum spūmōsā immerserat undā.
175 Ergō omnēs magnō circum clāmōre fremēbant,
176 praecipuē pius Aenēās. Tum iussa Sibyllae
177 (haud mora) festīnant, flentēs, āramque sepulcrī

Quaestiōnēs

1. What is the combined effect of the repetition of **Mīsēnum** from 162 and its placement in 164?

2. What precise verbal echo from 1.220–22 above appears in 175–76? How are the contexts similar? Do you suppose the echo is deliberate or accidental, and what does this suggest about Vergil's method of composition?

View toward Cape Misenum, legendary burial place of Misenus

178 **caelōque ēdūcere:** the same phrase appears identically positioned in 2.186; for the case usage, see the note on that line.

179 **Ītur:** an impers. pass. of **īre,** lit., *it is gone,* but essentially = **eunt;** see note on **ventum erat** (45).

 alta: with **stabula** = *deep,* i.e., in the midst of the forest; cf. **dēnsa ferārum tēcta** (7–8).

180 **picea, -ae,** f., *spruce, pine.*

 *īciō, īcere, īcī, ictus, *to strike* (with a weapon, missile, etc.).

 *īlex, īlicis, f., *holm-oak, ilex.*

181 **fraxineus, -a, -um,** *of ash, of an ash (tree).*

 cuneus, -ī, m., *wedge* (used as a splitting tool).

 fissilis, -is, -e, *easily split, splintering* (with **scinditur** in 182 perhaps an example of PROLEPSIS).

182 **scinditur:** sg. to agree with the nearer of its two subjs. (**trabēs** and **rōbur** 181).

 advolvō, advolvere, advoluī, advolūtus, *to roll toward* (here *down from the mountains,* **montibus,** and *toward* the pyre being constructed for Misenus).

 montibus ornōs: cf. **montibus ornum,** similarly at line's end in 2.626 above.

183 **Nec nōn:** *and no less, and indeed;* see note on 4.140.

185 **Atque:** for the force of the conj. here, see note on 162.

186 **aspectāns . . . sīc:** the spondees suggest the slow, deliberate movement of Aeneas' gaze through the dense forest.

187 **Sī:** here introducing a wish, *if only.*

188 **quandō . . . locūta est (189):** the construction is somewhat PARATACTIC, but the causal cl. explains the basis for Aeneas' optimism over his prospects for finding the golden bough.

 vērē, adv., *truly.*

"Aeneas, the Sibyl, and Charon," Giuseppe Maria Crespi (1665–1747)
Kunsthistorisches Museum, Vienna, Austria

178 congerere arboribus caelōque ēdūcere certant.
179 Ītur in antīquam silvam, stabula alta ferārum;
180 prōcumbunt piceae, sonat icta secūribus īlex,
181 fraxineaeque trabēs cuneīs et fissile rōbur
182 scinditur, advolvunt ingentēs montibus ornōs.

Led by twin doves sent from his mother Venus, Aeneas
discovers the golden bough in a grove near Avernus,
breaks it off, and carries it back to the Sibyl's cave

183   Nec nōn Aenēās opera inter tālia prīmus
184 hortātur sociōs paribusque accingitur armīs.
185 Atque haec ipse suō trīstī cum corde volūtat,
186 aspectāns silvam immēnsam, et sīc forte precātur:
187 "Sī nunc sē nōbīs ille aureus arbore rāmus
188 ostendat nemore in tantō—quandō omnia vērē

Quaestiōnēs

1. The episode of Misenus' death and burial in 162–82 is paralleled by that of Palinurus at the end of Book Five (see note on 6.1 above); both subsequently have the coastal promontories where they were buried named after them, according to the etiological legends to which Vergil refers. Palinurus' death is clearly intended as a kind of sacrifice intended to insure the Trojans' safe arrival on Italy's coast. What do you see as the purpose of the Misenus episode? In discussing the matter, consider these points: What did Misenus do to merit his death and how is this relevant to Aeneas himself? Why does his death occur at this point in the story, just after the Trojans' arrival in Italy? Why does the Sibyl compel Aeneas to bury his comrade's corpse before entering the Underworld?—i.e., what narrative function is served by connecting the two actions?

2. At first glance the considerable detail in 179–82 (which Vergil has adapted from the early epic poet Ennius) might seem superfluous; but in looking ahead to the next scene at 183f., what do you see as the purpose of the detail?

189 **heu nimium:** with **vērē** (188); cf. **fēlīx, heu nimium fēlīx** (4.657 above).

190 **forte:** cf. 171 and 186 (Aeneas' prayer, which is here answered); the events all seem accidental but are in fact divinely directed.

    columbae: doves were sacred to Venus (see **māternās . . . avēs** 193), who has sent them here to guide Aeneas' way (despite the ancient legend that the district was deadly for birds, based on the false but popular etymology, **Avernus** < Greek **a + ornis** = "birdless").

191 **ipsa . . . volantēs:** the line's opening disyllabic and monosyllabic words and dactylic rhythms suit the quickness of the birds' flight, and the ALLITERATION of **v** (continued in **viridī** 192) is perhaps intended to suggest ONOMATOPOETICALLY the whirring of their wings.

192 *****viridis, -is, -e,** *green; covered with vegetation, verdant, grassy.*

    *****sīdō, sīdere, sīdī** or **sēdī,** *to sit down; to come to rest, settle, land.*

194 **Este:** second pers. pl. pres. imper. of **esse.**

195 **opācō (1),** *to shade.*

    opācat / rāmus (196): cf. **arbore opācā** (136) and **opācā īlice** (208–09); the entire episode is painted in chiaroscuro, with the golden bough of immortality gleaming forth from deep within the vast dark forest of death (see discussion quest. above on lines 127–44).

197 **pressit:** here *checked.*

198 **ferant . . . pergant:** sc. **avēs** as subj.

199 **Pāscentēs:** i.e., as they frequently alight to eat, then take to the air again.

    tantum . . . / quantum (200): *only so far as.*

    prōdīre: HIST. INF.

    volandō: we would say *in their flight.*

200 **aciē:** here *in (their range of) sight.*

    possent: subjunct. probably due to the notion of purpose in the birds' actions (they flew deeper into the forest only short distances at a time so that Aeneas could keep them in sight).

    sequentum: = **sequentium,** i.e., Aeneas and Achates; with **oculī.**

201 **oleō, olēre, oluī,** *to (emit a) smell.*

    grave olentis Avernī: volcanic fumes in the nearby **Campī Phlegraeī** *(Flaming Fields)* were associated in popular superstition with the streams of the Underworld; **grave** here is ADV. ACC.

202 **liquidus, -a, -um,** *flowing, liquid, yielding; clear, unclouded.*

203 **sēdibus:** in appos. with **arbore;** in positioning **sēdibus** and **sīdunt** to FRAME the verse, Vergil is likely playing on the etymological connection between the two words.

    gemina: *of double nature,* because it produced both ordinary green foliage and the extraordinary, mystical golden bough; some mss. read **geminae** (cf. **geminae . . . columbae** 190).

189 heu nimium dē tē vātēs, Mīsēne, locūta est."
190 Vix ea fātus erat, geminae cum forte columbae
191 ipsa sub ōra virī caelō vēnēre volantēs,
192 et viridī sēdēre solō. Tum maximus hērōs
193 māternās agnōvit avēs laetusque precātur:
194 "Este ducēs, ō, sī qua via est, cursumque per aurās
195 dērigite in lūcōs ubi pinguem dīves opācat
196 rāmus humum. Tūque, ō, dubiīs nē dēfice rēbus,
197 dīva parēns." Sīc effātus, vēstīgia pressit,
198 observāns quae signa ferant, quō tendere pergant.
199 Pāscentēs, illae tantum prōdīre volandō
200 quantum aciē possent oculī servāre sequentum.
201 Inde, ubi vēnēre ad faucēs grave olentis Avernī,
202 tollunt sē celerēs liquidumque per āera lāpsae
203 sēdibus optātīs geminā super arbore sīdunt,

Quaestiōnēs

1. What is the intended effect of the apostrophe in 189?

2. What are some arguments for and against the ms. variant **geminae** in 203?

Lake Avernus, with view toward Baiae and Cape Misenum

204 **discolor, discolōris,** *differing in color, contrasting (in color).*
   discolor . . . aurī . . . aura: = discolor aura aurī; note both the wordplay on
      the marvelously resonant, if etymologically distinct, **aura/aurī** and the
      purposefully disjointed word order, which seems intended to suggest the
      sheen (**aura**) of the golden bough as it gleams forth in a burst of rays through
      and around the tree's other branches.

205 **Quāle . . . / tālis (208):** the correlatives setting up the SIMILE are carefully
      positioned at the beginning of their respective verses.
   brūmālis, -is, -e, *in/of winter, wintry.*
   viscum, -ī, n., *mistletoe* (a parasitic plant, with evergreen leaves and shiny
      berries, that grows on trees and and is esp. visible in winter when the host
      tree has shed its own leaves).

206 **vireō, virēre, viruī,** *to show green growth, be green/verdant.*
   novā: here *strange, novel, alien.*
   sēminō (1), *to sow, plant; to give birth to, beget, create.*

207 **croceō:** while the mistletoe most familiar in the United States has waxy
      white berries, varieties known in the Mediterranean, including *Loranthus
      europaeus,* has clusters of yellow berries that might easily have prompted
      Vergil's comparison with his golden bough.
   teres, teretis, *round(ed), smooth; polished, elegant.*
   truncōs: here *branches, stems.*

209 **īlice:** one of the sorts of trees used for Misenus' funeral pyre (180); Vergil
      may mean to emphasize the point via the ENJAMBEMENT and the abrupt
      DIAERESIS.
   crepitō (1), *to rattle, rustle.*
   brattea, -ae, f., *thin sheet of metal, (metal) foil.*

210 **refringō, refringere, refrēgī, refrāctus,** *to break back/off.*

211 **cūnctantem:** used most commonly of persons rather than objects (cf. 4.133 and
      390, both times of Dido, 12.919 of Turnus, and 12.940 of Aeneas); the word
      here, emphatically ENJAMBED, is variously interpreted: was the branch merely
      clinging and slow to break off because it was pliant (**lentō vīmine rāmus** 137),
      as any live branch would be, despite the Sibyl's assurance at 146 that **ipse
      volēns facilisque sequētur?** Is there a hint of something imperfect in Aeneas'
      action?—**corripit, extemplō, avidus,** and **refringit** are all strong, emotionally
      charged words. Or is the pause merely suspenseful and for dramatic effect?

295 **Hinc via:** sc. **est.**
   *****Tartareus, -a, -um,** *of Tartarus* (the Underworld), *Tartarean.*
   fert: here, *leads.*

296 **caenum, -ī,** n., *mud, filth, slime.*
   vorāgō, vorāginis, f., *deep hole, chasm, quagmire, watery hollow.*

297 **aestuō (1),** *to burn fiercely, blaze; to boil; to be in violent motion, seethe.*
   ērūctō (1), *to disgorge, belch; to throw up, discharge violently.*

204 discolor unde aurī per rāmōs aura refulsit.
205 Quāle solet silvīs brūmālī frīgore viscum
206 fronde virēre novā, quod nōn sua sēminat arbōs,
207 et croceō fētū teretēs circumdare truncōs,
208 tālis erat speciēs aurī frondentis opācā
209 īlice, sīc lēnī crepitābat brattea ventō.
210 Corripit Aenēās extemplō avidusque refringit
211 cūnctantem, et vātis portat sub tēcta Sibyllae.

The Sibyl leads Aeneas to the River Styx,
where they see the grim boatman Charon
and countless souls longing to be ferried across

295   Hinc via Tartareī quae fert Acherontis ad undās.
296 Turbidus hīc caenō vāstāque vorāgine gurges
297 aestuat atque omnem Cōcȳtō ēructat harēnam.

Quaestiōnēs

1. How should we interpret the imagery in **fētū** (207), and in **sēminat** (206) as well, in view of the golden bough's function as a symbol of immortality, of life in the midst of death, or of life out of death, i.e., rebirth? Compare **auricomōs . . . fētūs** (141) and refer to the accompanying note.

2. The death and initial preparations for Misenus' funeral (162–82) precede the golden bough episode in 183–211, and then the actual funeral immediately follows (212f., not included in this text), so that the Misenus episode literally frames that of the golden bough; what does Vergil intend us to see as the logical connection between the two episodes and in what ways are they complementary?

298 *portitor, portitōris, m, *toll-collector, customs officer; ferryman.*
　　portitor hās horrendus aquās: the INTERLOCKED WORD ORDER suits the
　　　　circumstance that Charon, as harbor-master, held tight control over the river;
　　　　the ALLITERATION of h- adds an airy sound effect, and positioning of the -ās
　　　　syllables under the ictus accentuates the internal rhyme.

299 squālor, squālōris, m., *roughness* (of surface); *dirtiness, filth.*
　　*Charōn, Charōnis, m., *Charon,* mythic ferryman of the Underworld, who
　　　　conveyed the souls of the buried dead across the river Styx (here identified
　　　　with the Acheron).
　　cui: DAT. OF POSSESSION, = cuius, with (in) mentō.

300 cānitiēs, -ēī, f., *white, grey coloring; white/grey hair.*
　　stant: *stand fixed,* i.e., *stare.*

301 dēpendeō, dēpendēre, dēpendī, *to hang down (from).*

302 contus, -ī, m., *pole* (esp. one used on a boat or ship).

303 ferrūgineus, -a, -um, *rust-colored, purplish, dark red; somber-colored, murky.*
　　subvectō (1), *to convey (laboriously) upward/away.*
　　*cumba (cymba), -ae, f., *small boat, skiff.*

304 crūdus, -a, -um, *uncooked, raw; unripe; unimpaired by age, youthful, vigorous.*
　　senectūs, senectūtis, f., *old age.*

307 magnanimum: = magnanimōrum; for the archaic gen. pl. form, see note on vī
　　　　superum (1.4) and cf. virum for virōrum at 1.119.

309 quam multa: with fōlia (310); this and the parallel SIMILE in aut . . . quam
　　　　multae . . . avēs are employed to evoke an image of the number of souls
　　　　rushing to the hellish river's banks, *as many . . .* (as these souls).
　　autumnus, -ī, m., *autumn, fall.*

312 fugat: sc. eās.
　　aprīcus, -a, -um, *sunny; warmed by sunshine, warm.*

313 prīmī: with trānsmittere, *(to be the) first to . . .;* use of the inf. after ōrantēs,
　　　　where one might expect a subjunct. JUSSIVE NOUN CL., imitates a Greek
　　　　construction. The line's heavy spondaic rhythm underscores the steady
　　　　persistence of the ghosts' entreaties.

314 ulterior, ulterius, compar. adj., *situated farther away, more distant.*
　　ulteriōris amōre: the mournful ASSONANCE of -ōr-/-ōr- focuses attention on the
　　　　pathos of the line's final, unexpected word.

315 *nāvita, -ae, m., archaic and poetic form of class. nauta, *sailor.*
　　nunc hōs nunc . . . illōs: ANAPHORA and ASYNDETON accentuate the visual effect
　　　　of the demonstratives.

316 summoveō, summovēre, summōvī, summōtus, *to move* (a person/thing) *away,
　　　　remove.*

317 mīrātus . . . tumultū: the clattering ALLITERATIVE t's and muffled m's are
　　　　perhaps meant to suggest the noisy but indistinct clamor of the throng
　　　　Aeneas hears.

318 virgō: the Sibyl.
　　vult: here *means,* a frequent sense of the verb; indic. here, not the subjunct. one
　　　　might expect, and thus not strictly dependent on dīc.

298 Portitor hās horrendus aquās et flūmina servat

299 terribilī squālōre–Charōn, cui plūrima mentō

300 cānitiēs inculta iacet, stant lūmina flammā,

301 sordidus ex umerīs nōdō dēpendet amictus.

302 Ipse ratem contō subigit vēlīsque ministrat

303 et ferrūgineā subvectat corpora cumbā,

304 iam senior, sed crūda deō viridisque senectūs.

305 Hūc omnis turba ad rīpās effūsa ruēbat,

306 mātrēs atque virī dēfūnctaque corpora vītā

307 magnanimum hērōum, puerī innūptaeque puellae,

308 impositīque rogīs iuvenēs ante ōra parentum:

309 quam multa in silvīs autumnī frīgore prīmō

310 lapsa cadunt folia, aut ad terram gurgite ab altō

311 quam multae glomerantur avēs, ubi frīgidus annus

312 trāns pontum fugat et terrīs immittit aprīcīs.

313 Stābant ōrantēs prīmī trānsmittere cursum

314 tendēbantque manūs rīpae ulteriōris amōre.

315 Nāvita sed trīstis nunc hōs nunc accipit illōs,

316 ast aliōs longē summōtōs arcet harēnā.

317　　Aenēās, mīrātus enim mōtusque tumultū,

318 "Dīc," ait, "ō virgō, quid vult concursus ad amnem?

319 Quidve petunt animae? Vel quō discrīmine rīpās

Quaestiōnēs

1. Vergil paints a vivid picture of the hideous Charon in 298-304; list all the nouns, adjectives, phrases that constitute this image–could you draw a sketch of Charon based on these details?

2. Comment on the rare double simile in 309-12: how do anaphora and word order help link the two; in what multiple ways are the images appropriate to the ghostly vision Vergil describes; in what ways are the two similes alike, and in what ways do they differ?–as always, support your discussion with specific references to the Latin text.

320 **līvidus, -a, -um,** *of a dull, grayish blue color; spiteful, envious, malicious;* Vergil intends the first sense, but likely with a hint at the second.

321 **Ollī:** archaic for **illī;** cf. 1.254.

322 **Anchīsā:** ABL. OF ORIGIN (cf. **ōrīgine,** 1.286 and note, and **nāte deā,** 2.289).
generō (1), *to beget, father.*
deum: if you do not recognize the form (not acc.), see note on **superum** at 1.4.

324 **dī . . . nūmen:** the prose order would be **cuius nūmen dī iūrāre et fallere timent;** the arrangement, with **dī** and **nūmen** in the line's first and last positions, emphasizes that even the gods fear the powers of the Underworld.

327 **dātur:** *is it granted* (to Charon), + infinitive.

328 **trānsportō (1),** *to carry/convey across, ship across;* often with a double acc., one for the person transported (here sc. **eās,** i.e., **animās**) and another for the body of water across which he is being conveyed.
sēdibus: i.e., their final resting place, the grave.
quiērunt: = **quiēvērunt;** you have seen several other examples of contracted perf. tense forms involving the loss of intervocalic -**v**- and sometimes an adjacent vowel, e.g., **audierat** for **audīverat** (1.20 and note) and **nōris** for **nōveris** (4.33).

329 **volitō (1),** frequentative form of **volō (1),** *to fly about; to move swiftly through the air, flutter, flit about.*
lītora circum: if you do not recall the technical term for this device of word order, see note on **contrā,** 1.13.

330 **admittō, admittere, admīsī, admissus,** *to admit, receive, allow to enter.*

331 **Anchīsā satus:** i.e., Aeneas; for the construction, see note on **Hammōne satus,** 4.198, and cf. line 125 above.

385 **Nāvita . . . prōspexit:** the prose order would be **Ut nāvita quōs** (= **eōs,** subj. of **īre** and **advertere,** 386) . . . **prōspexit.**
inde: i.e., from his station on the boat he was ferrying across the Styx.

386 **pedem:** use of sg. for pl. is a common poetic device you have seen before, e.g., **capite,** 2.219.

387 **increpō, increpāre, increpuī, increpitus,** *to made a loud noise, snap, roar; to reproach, shout at angrily.*
ultrō: i.e., Charon was the first to speak, or rather to shout out.

388 **Quisquis es:** the ferryman initially addresses only Aeneas.

389 **istinc,** adv., *from that place you are in, from over there.*
iam istinc: a deliberate echo of **iam inde** in 385; Charon has kept his distance and wants these strangers to do likewise.

390 **sopōrus, -a, -um,** *full of sleep, sleepy, drowsy.*

391 **nefās:** sc. **est.**
vectō (1), *to transport, carry.*

320 hae linquunt, illae rēmīs vada līvida verrunt?"
321 Ollī sīc breviter fāta est longaeva sacerdōs:
322 "Anchīsā generāte, deum certissima prōlēs,
323 Cōcȳtī stagna alta vidēs Stygiamque palūdem,
324 dī cuius iūrāre timent et fallere nūmen.
325 Haec omnis, quam cernis, inops inhumātaque turba est;
326 portitor ille Charōn; hī, quōs vehit unda, sepultī,
327 nec rīpās datur horrendās et rauca fluenta
328 trānsportāre priusquam sēdibus ossa quiērunt.
329 Centum errant annōs volitantque haec lītora circum;
330 tum, dēmum admissī, stagna exoptāta revīsunt."
331 Cōnstitit Anchīsā satus et vēstīgia pressit,
332 multa putāns, sortemque animō miserātus inīquam.

After encountering the ghosts of some fallen Trojan comrades,
Aeneas and the Sibyl press on, but Charon denies them passage
until the prophetess shows him the golden bough

384   Ergo iter inceptum peragunt fluviōque propinquant.
385 Nāvita quōs iam inde ut Stygiā prōspexit ab undā
386 per tacitum nemus īre pedemque advertere rīpae,
387 sīc prior adgreditur dictīs atque increpat ultrō:
388 "Quisquis es, armātus quī nostra ad flūmina tendis,
389 fāre, age, quid veniās, iam istinc, et comprime gressum.
390 Umbrārum hic locus est, somnī noctisque sopōrae:
391 corpora vīva nefas Stygiā vectāre carīnā,

Quaestiōnēs

1. Identify the sound effect in **vada līvida verrunt** (320); does it seem to you in any way onomatopoetic?

2. What effect does Vergil intend in his use of demonstratives in 325-26 (and cf. 320)?

3. What exactly is the fate of the souls of the unburied and what vivid images of their actions are evoked by the two verbs in 329?

4. What is exceptional in the meter of 330, and how does it suit the context?

392 **nec . . . sum laetātus:** an example of LITOTES, as Charon's response to the events described was quite the opposite of joyful.

    Alcīdēn . . . euntem: for Hercules' descent into the Underworld to capture the three-headed dog Cerberus, see note on 123 above; Charon granted him passage, as he did Theseus and Pirithous, and had cause to regret doing so.

393 **Pīrithous, -ī,** m., *Pirithous,* son of Ixion, king of the Lapiths; aided by his comrade Theseus (see above, 27-30 and 122, and notes), Pirithous entered Hades in an attempt to kidnap Proserpina, wife of Pluto and queen of the Underworld, and make her his own bride.

394 ***invictus, -a, -um,** *unconquered, undefeated; unconquerable, invincible.*

    vīribus: ABL. OF RESPECT with **invictī.**

    essent: typically **quamquam** introduces an indic. vb., but the subjunct. is often used in verse, just as it is with concessive cls. introduced by **cum** and **quamvīs.**

395 **Tartareum . . . custōdem:** Cerberus guarded the gates of Tartarus to prevent souls from escaping back to the upper world; in the last of the 12 labors assigned to him by Eurystheus, king of Tiryns, Hercules captured the monstrous hound and dragged him alive to the king's court.

    in vincla: with **petere,** the prep. **in** + acc. indicates the aim of seeking out someone for specific treatment, here *(to put him) into chains.*

396 **rēgis:** i.e., Pluto or Dis, lord of the Underworld, named in the next line; one wonders if Vergil intended the ALLITERATIVE **rēgis traxitque trementem** to suggest the hell-dog's snarling as he was being dragged away from his master–the Romans called the letter **r** the **littera canīna,** *the dog letter,* as its trill suggested to them a dog's growl.

    trementem: not what we would expect of the fearsome canine and so perhaps deliberately comical, a sign of Charon's contempt for the dog that let Hercules man-handle him and steal him from his master–and one wonders, too, why he was lounging at Pluto's throne and not standing guard at the gates of hell!

397 **dominam . . . adortī:** the extensive ALLITERATION of the harsh dentals **d** and **t** suits the anger and indignation of Charon's closing words.

    Dītis: may be taken with both **dominam** and **thalamō.**

    adorior, adorīrī, adortus sum, *to assault, attack;* + inf., *to set to work, attempt.*

398 **Quae contrā:** = **contrā ea (verba);** for the ANASTROPHE, see note on **contrā** in 1.13.

    Amphrȳsius, -a, -um, *Amphrysian, of Amphrysis,* a river in Thessaly associated with the god Apollo and thus, here, with his priestess.

400 **licet:** here, as often, with subjunct., = *(one) is permitted (to), one may.*

401 **aeternum:** here adverbial.

392 nec vērō Alcīdēn mē sum laetātus euntem
393 accēpisse lacū, nec Thēsea Pīrithoumque,
394 dīs quamquam genitī atque invictī vīribus essent.
395 Tartareum ille manū custōdem in vincla petīvit
396 ipsius ā soliō rēgis traxitque trementem;
397 hī dominam Dītis thalamō dēdūcere adortī.”
398 Quae contrā breviter fāta est Amphrȳsia vātēs:
399 “Nūllae hīc īnsidiae tālēs–absiste movērī–
400 nec vim tēla ferunt; licet ingēns iānitor, antrō
401 aeternum lātrāns, exsanguēs terreat umbrās;

Quaestiō

What several specific reasons for Charon's alarm are seen in his speech at 388-97?

Hercules Abducts Cerberus from Hades
Attic black figure amphora
The Lysippides or Andokides Painter
Ca. 530 B.C.
Pushkin State Fine Arts Museum
Moscow, Russia

402 **castus, -a, -um,** *untouched, inviolate; moral; holy, pure; chaste.*
    patruī: Proserpina's husband, Pluto, was brother of her father, Jupiter; such
        unions were okay in myth!
403 **Trōïus:** here, as often, trisyllabic.
    pietāte īnsignis et armīs: pietās (repeated below in 405) was of course Aeneas'
        hallmark; and the phrase here echoes both 1.10, **īnsignem pietāte,** and 1.545,
        nec pietāte fuit, nec bellō maior et armīs.
405 **nūlla:** = an emphatic **nōn,** *in no way, not at all;* for the usage, cf. 4.232 above.
407 **Tumida:** though the quantity of the **-a** is obscured by ELISION, the adj. almost
        certainly modifies **corda** (here poetic pl.), not **īrā.**
    ex īrā: the phrase may be taken with **tumida** or **resīdunt,** or with both.
408 **plūra hīs:** sc. **dicta sunt;** no further words were spoken either by Charon or the
        Sibyl.
    venerābilis, -is, -e, *worthy of respect, venerable, august.*
409 **fātālis virgae:** APPOS. GEN.; for other examples of this construction, see **sprētae**
        fōrmae. (1.27) and **Patavī** (1.247).
    longō post tempore: post is adv., lit. = *afterward by a long time,* but more natural
        Eng. idiom would be simply *after a long time;* Charon had seen the golden
        bough before, in the distant past.
410 **caeruleam:** at 303 Vergil describes Charon's boat as **ferrūginea,** *rust-colored,*
        purplish, dark red–a discrepancy, or does the ghostly craft's color shift as it
        cruises through the varying shadows of the Underworld?
412 **dēturbō (1),** *to bring tumbling down; to dislodge, drive out.*
    forus, -ī, m., *deck, gangway* (esp. for boarding or exiting a boat).
    alveus, -ī, m., *trough, bath-tub; hull/hold of a boat, boat.*
    alveō: pronounced here as a disyllable by SYNIZESIS.
414 **sūtilis, -is, -e,** *made by sewing, stitched together.*
    rīmōsa: as the boat's hull was covered with animal hides, stitched together,
        its seams were gaping open here and there under the huge hero's weight
        (underscored by the ENJAMBEMENT and ELISION of **ingentem Aenēan** in the
        preceding line); the vessel's usual passengers were weightless ghosts.
    palūdem: = **aquam palūdis,** but Vergil amplifies the scale to further enlarge our
        vision of Aeneas' massive body.
415 **vātemque virumque:** the Loeb translation nicely replicates the ALLITERATION
        and ASSONANCE with *(both) seer and soldier.*
416 **īnfōrmis, -is, -e,** *formless; ugly, unsightly.*
    līmus, -ī, m., *mud, mire, slime.*
    glaucus, -a, -um, *blue-grey;* (of vegetation) *grey-green.*
    expōnō, expōnere, exposuī, expositus, *to put out, set out.*
417 **lātrātus, -ūs, m.,** *barking, baying, howling.*
    trifaucis, -is, -e, *having three throats; issuing from three throats.*
418 **recubō, recubāre,** *to lie at ease, recline, rest.*

402 casta licet patruī servet Prōserpina līmen.
403 Trōius Aenēās, pietāte īnsignis et armīs,
404 ad genitōrem īmās Erebī dēscendit ad umbrās.
405 Sī tē nūlla movet tantae pietātis imāgō,
406 at rāmum hunc" (aperit rāmum quī veste latēbat)
407 "agnōscās." Tumida ex īrā tum corda resīdunt;
408 nec plūra hīs. Ille, admīrāns venerābile dōnum
409 fātālis virgae longō post tempore vīsum,
410 caeruleam advertit puppim rīpaeque propinquat.
411 Inde aliās animās, quae per iuga longa sedēbant,
412 dēturbat laxatque forōs; simul accipit alveō
413 ingentem Aenēān. Gemuit sub pondere cumba
414 sūtilis et multam accēpit rīmōsa palūdem.
415 Tandem trāns fluvium incolumēs vātemque virumque
416 īnfōrmī līmō glaucāque expōnit in ulvā.

The Sibyl drugs Cerberus so she and Aeneas may pass
unharmed into the depths of the Underworld

417 Cerberus haec ingēns lātrātū rēgna trifaucī
418 personat, adversō recubāns immānis in antrō.

Quaestiōnēs

1. Identify three arguments the Sibyl employs in 399-407 to allay Charon's concerns.

2. What device of poetic word order is seen in 407, and what is its dramatic effect?

3. If you were to paint accurately the scene Vergil sketches for us in words in 410-14, what several details would you include?

4. Comment specifically on the word order, and its effects, first in 417 and then, comparing **vāstō rēx Aeolus antrō** (1.52), in 418.

"The Inferno," Canto 4
Detail of Charon from one
of 18 marble panels
Benedetto Robazza (1934-)
Sant Angelo, Rome, Italy

419 **horrēre . . . colubrīs:** in a stunning cinematographic moment, the snakes around the hell-hound's three necks seem to be alarmed, even before Cerberus himself, at the strangers' approach; the ASSONANCE in **colla colubrīs** adds a harsh tone and a closing hiss to the soundtrack.

420 **sopōrō (1),** *to send to sleep, render unconscious; to infuse with sleep-inducing qualities.*

medicātus, -a, -um, *medicated, drugged; imbued with a magical/potent substance.*
offa, -ae, f., *lump of food,* esp. a *flour cake* (think dog biscuit!).

421 **guttur, gutturis,** n., *throat.*

422 **obiectam:** sc. **offam;** the immediate echo of **obicit** from the preceding verse helps suggest how quickly the ravenous hound snatched up and devoured the drugged pastry.

immānia terga: pl. for sg.–common enough in verse, but esp. apt here, along with the echo of **immānis** from 418, in describing the immensity of this monster with his three heads, three necks, and correspondingly massive shoulders and back; the effect is continued straight through to the close of the scene in 423, with the repetitions of **ingēns** and **antrō** and the expansive **fūsus** and **tōtō** and **extenditur.**

424 **occupō (1),** *to seize to oneself, take possession of.*
sepultō: i.e., **in somnō.**

425 **inremeābilis, -is, -e,** *by which one cannot return, that allows no return.*

450 **Inter quas:** *among these women.* Descending into the world of the dead, Aeneas encounters ghosts from his past, including Palinurus, who remains unburied, and then, in the midst of several other heroines who died for love, his own beloved Dido; like a drowning man, whose life passes before his eyes in a matter of seconds, Aeneas here, as R. D. Williams has remarked, is traveling through "the sorrows and regrets of his past life."

vulnere: for Dido's **vulnus,** both lit. and figurative, see 4.1–2, 67, and 689 and the notes on those lines.

451 **quam . . . / obscūram (453):** = **ut prīmum Trōïus hērōs iūxtā eam stetit et eam obscūram per umbrās agnōvit.**

452 **ut prīmum:** for this idiom, see 1.306 above and note.

419 Cui vātēs, horrēre vidēns iam colla colubrīs,
420 melle sopōrātam et medicātīs frūgibus offam
421 obicit; ille, famē rabidā tria guttura pandēns,
422 corripit obiectam, atque immānia terga resolvit,
423 fūsus humī, tōtōque ingēns extenditur antrō.
424 Occupat Aenēās aditum, custōde sepultō,
425 ēvāditque celer rīpam inremeābilis undae.

In the Underworld Aeneas encounters the ghost of Dido

450   Inter quās Phoenissa, recēns ā vulnere, Dīdō
451 errābat silvā in magnā; quam Trōïus hērōs
452 ut prīmum iūxtā stetit agnōvitque per umbrās

Quaestiō

What is especially striking in Vergil's positioning of the verbs in 421-25 and what effect does this have as he narrates the action in this closing scene?

Not far from these Phoenician Dido stood,
Fresh from her wound, her bosom bath'd in blood;
Whom when the Trojan hero hardly knew,
Obscure in shades, and with a doubtful view,
(Doubtful as he who sees, thro' dusky night,
Or thinks he sees, the moon's uncertain light,)
With tears he first approach'd the sullen shade.

From the translation of John Dryden, 1698

453   **obscūram:** because she is a ghost.

      quālem . . . quī . . . videt . . . lūnam (454): the highly elliptical expression = *like the moon which one sees* (lit., *like the moon [one sees] who sees it . . .*).

      prīmō: with **mēnse**, *at the beginning of . . .*; i.e., a new moon.

455   **dēmīsit . . . est:** Vergil very deliberately reminds us this one last time of the intensity of Aeneas' love for Dido.

456   **Īnfēlīx Dīdō:** Vergil applies this epithet to the queen (cf. 4.68 above) most appropriately, of course, in this final scene.

457   **exstīnctam . . . secūtam:** sc. **esse** + **tē** as subj.; IND. STATE. with **nūntius vēnerat**. We are not elsewhere in the poem told how Aeneas had heard of Dido's death, or how he could have, but the Trojans' suspicion that she might have taken some extreme course of action (**extrēma secūtam**) is mentioned at the opening of Book Five.

      extrēma: = **mortem;** for the word in this sense, cf. 1.219 above.

461   **iussa:** subj. of **ēgēre** (463) = **ēgērunt;** cf. **iussa tamen dīvum exsequitur** (4.396, and see also 4.378).

462   **sentus, -a, -um,** *rough, rugged.*

      situs, -ūs, m., *decay, neglect, disuse, abandonment.*

463   **queō, quīre, quīvī,** *to be able* (to).

464   **discessus, -ūs,** m., *departure, going away, leaving.*

465   **subtrahō, subtrahere, subtrāxī, subtractus,** *to drag down/away, withdraw.*

466   **Quem fugis:** probably a deliberate echo of Dido's quest. to Aeneas when she realized he was leaving her, **mēne fugis?**, identically positioned at 4.314.

      Extrēmum . . . hoc est: sc. **verbum;** the unusual monosyllables at the end of the verse effectively punctuate Aeneas' final remarks to his lost queen.

467   **ārdentem . . . tuentem:** the words refer to Dido, of course, but are applied more particularly and, esp. in the case of the latter, quite strikingly, to her **animum** (468).

      torvus, -a, -um, *grim, pitiless; fierce, stern.*

      torva: an ADV. ACC. with **tuentem,** *looking* (at him) *fiercely* = *fierce-eyed;* for the construction, cf. **mortāle sonāns** (50).

468   **lēnībat:** archaic for **lēniēbat;** CONATIVE IMPF.

      lacrimās: usually taken, and more logically, to mean his own, not Dido's.

469   **Illa . . . tenēbat:** cf. Vergil's nearly identical description of Minerva/Pallas Athena at 1.482 above, **dīva solō fīxōs oculōs āversa tenēbat.**

470   **inceptō . . . sermōne:** Eng. would use a cl., *when he began to speak.*

      vultum: ACC. OF SPECIFICATION with **movētur;** i.e., her face showed no emotion.

471   **sī . . . stet:** *if she should stand there* (as), a more vivid substitution for *if she were.*

      Marpēsius, -a, -um, *Marpessian, of Mt. Marpessus* (on Paros, one of the Cyclades islands famous for its marble, to which Vergil alludes here—Dido is as cold and immoveable as marble).

473   **umbriferus, -a, -um,** *shade-bearing, shady, shadowy* (here alluding not only to the darkness of Hades, but also to the ghosts that inhabit it).

      prīstinus, -a, -um, *former, previous.*

453 obscūram, quālem prīmō quī surgere mēnse
454 aut videt aut vīdisse putat per nūbila lūnam,
455 dēmīsit lacrimās dulcīque adfātus amōre est:
456 "Īnfēlīx Dīdō, vērus mihi nūntius ergō
457 vēnerat exstīnctam ferrōque extrēma secūtam?
458 Fūneris heu tibi causa fuī? Per sīdera iūrō,
459 per superōs et sī qua fidēs tellūre sub īmā est,
460 invītus, rēgīna, tuō dē lītore cessī.
461 Sed mē iussa deum, quae nunc hās īre per umbrās,
462 per loca senta sitū cōgunt noctemque profundam,
463 imperiīs ēgēre suīs; nec crēdere quīvī
464 hunc tantum tibi mē discessū ferre dolōrem.
465 Siste gradum tēque aspectū nē subtrahe nostrō.
466 Quem fugis? Extrēmum fātō quod tē adloquor hoc est."
467 Tālibus Aenēās ārdentem et torva tuentem
468 lēnībat dictīs animum lacrimāsque ciēbat.
469 Illa solō fīxōs oculōs āversa tenēbat
470 nec magis inceptō vultum sermōne movētur
471 quam sī dūra silex aut stet Marpēsia cautēs.
472 Tandem corripuit sēsē atque inimīca refūgit
473 in nemus umbriferum, coniūnx ubi prīstinus illī

Quaestiōnēs

1. Discuss in detail Aeneas' remarks to Dido's phantom in 456–66. Are you persuaded by his defense of his actions in leaving her? Why or why not?

2. Is the echo of 1.482 here at line 469 accidental or deliberate? Make a case for the latter interpretation—i.e., what are the parallels?

3. Comment on the psychology of Dido's response to Aeneas in 469–71. What does her silence mean? Is her response justified?

4. Compare the narrator's description of Dido in 470–71 to Dido's characterization of Aeneas in 4.366–67 above, as well as the depiction of the queen in the lines preceding each of these couplets (4.362–64 and 6.467–69). What are the several specific correspondences? What do you see as Vergil's intent in making the connection between these two passages?

475 **Nec minus:** i.e., despite Dido's stony response.

476 **euntem:** *as she . . . .*

847 **aliī:** other nations, in particular the Greeks; having traveled through the rest of the Underworld, Aeneas meets in the Elysian Fields with his father Anchises, who here counsels him and at the same time foretells the mission of the vast and powerful empire that Rome shall become.

    spīrantia: the statuary crafted by the Greeks and other fine artists is so lifelike that it seems to be alive and breathing; one thinks of the female statue so lovingly carved by the sculptor Pygmalion in Ovid's tale, which Venus miraculously brought to life.

    mollius, compar. adv., *more softly, softer, more gracefully/delicately* (construed here either with **excūdent** or **spīrantia,** or both).

    aera: *bronzes,* i.e., bronze statues.

849 **ōrābunt . . . melius:** i.e., will be better lawyers and public speakers; Cicero, doubtless, would have disagreed, and Vergil likely exaggerates the point in order to emphasize all the more the mission of the Romans to govern. The adv. **melius** can be understood with the two vbs. following as well as with **ōrābunt.**

    caelī . . . dīcent (850): i.e., others will be better astronomers.

    meātus, -ūs, m., *movement, course, path.*

850 **dēscrībō, dēscrībere, dēscrīpsī, dēscrīptus,** *to mark out, trace, describe.*

    radiō: here an instrument used in geometry and astronomy.

    dīcent: here *predict.*

851 **Rōmāne:** at this pivotal moment in the poem, Aeneas is for the first time addressed as a Roman; as R.D. Williams observes in his introduction to Book Six, it is in this final section of the book that Aeneas "leaves behind the history of Troy in order to start the history of Rome." The word "Roman" is here generalized as well, and addressed to every Roman, or the ideal Roman; the mandate given Aeneas by his father in 851–53 is in a broader sense a mandate to the empire, and the measure of Aeneas' success or failure in this poem, as well as the moral success or failure of the empire, is the extent to which it may appear that Anchises' sage and humane counsel is followed.

    mementō: fut. imper. of **meminī.**

852 **hae . . . artēs:** government, politics, and empire-building, that is, vs. the traditional arts and sciences.

    pācī . . . mōrem: the phrase has been variously interpreted; possibly *to impose a settled pattern upon peace,* i.e., to make peace a way of life, or more likely *to add civilized custom* (i.e., order and justice, cf. 1.264 above) *to peace.*

853 **subiectīs:** perf. partic. of **subicere** used substantively, *the defeated, subjects.*

854 **mīrantibus:** i.e., Aeneas and the Sibyl.

855 **Aspice ut:** *see how;* construction of the phrase with the indic. **ingreditur,** vs. the subjunct. that might be expected, is somewhat PARATACTIC and essentially equivalent to **ecce.**

    Mārcellus, -ī, m., *Marcellus* (hero of the Second Punic War, Marcus Claudius Marcellus, winner of the **spolia opīma** for his defeat of a Gallic general during his consulship in 222 B.C. and renowned as one of the Roman Republic's greatest military commanders).

474 respondet cūrīs aequatque Sychaeus amōrem.
475 Nec minus Aenēās cāsū percussus inīquō
476 prōsequitur lacrimīs longē et miserātur euntem.

Aeneas at last finds the shade of his father Anchises, who counsels
him on the proper mission of what will become the Roman Empire

847 "Excūdent aliī spīrantia mollius aera
848 (crēdō equidem), vīvōs dūcent dē marmore vultūs,
849 ōrābunt causās melius, caelīque meātūs
850 dēscrībent radiō et surgentia sīdera dīcent:
851 tū regere imperiō populōs, Rōmāne, mementō
852 (hae tibi erunt artēs), pācīque impōnere mōrem,
853 parcere subiectīs et dēbellāre superbōs."

Anchises shows Aeneas the soul of the Republican hero Marcellus
and, accompanying him, the young Marcellus, nephew of Augustus

854 Sīc pater Anchīsēs, atque haec mīrantibus addit:
855 "Aspice ut īnsignis spoliīs Mārcellus opīmīs

Quaestiōnēs

1. We see Aeneas weep three times in this scene, at 455, 468, and 476. What are some of the many different factors that may compel his tears, factors both specific to his relationship with Dido and others more generally related to the human condition?

2. Compare Vergil's account of Aeneas' Underworld encounter with Dido in 450–76 to Homer's description of Odysseus' encounter with the Telamonian Ajax in *Odyssey* 542f. What does Vergil specifically draw from Homer? What are the most striking differences between the two episodes?

3. Compare Anchises' prophecy of Rome's destiny in 847–53 with the longer and more detailed prophecy given to Venus by Jupiter at 1.257–96; what major themes are common to both, and what are the principal differences?

856 **ingreditur . . . omnēs:** cf. the description of Diana in the SIMILE employed to describe the majesty of queen Dido at 1.501, **gradiēnsque deās superēminet omnēs;** like Dido in the midst of her royal retinue at Carthage, the general Marcellus here towers over all the other yet to be born shades of Roman heroes that Anchises has pointed out to his son (at 752–846).

857 **rem:** i.e., **rem pūblicam;** obj. perhaps of **turbante** as well as **sistet** (858).

858 **eques:** Marcellus' victory was won in a cavalry engagement.

Gallus, -ī, m., *a Gaul, inhabitant of Gaul* (a vast region to the north of Italy, including modern Belgium and France).

rebellis, -is, -e, *rebellious, rebel.*

Gallum . . . Quirīnō (859): for slaying Viridomarus, the chieftain of the Insubrian Gauls, at the battle of Clastidium in 222 B.C., Marcellus won (or, from Aeneas' perspective, would win) the **spolia opīma** for the third time in Rome's history; the only Romans to receive the same honor previously were (would be) Romulus (identified with the war god *father Quirinus*—see note on 1.292) and Cossus (who had appeared among the spirits Anchises pointed out to Aeneas earlier, at line 841).

859 **suspendet:** the spoils would be hung in the temple of Quirinus for public display.

860 **Atque . . . vidēbat:** spondees slow the pace as Aeneas' gaze turns to the youth accompanying the older Marcellus.

861 **fulgentibus armīs:** cf. 2.749 above (of Aeneas' own arms).

862 **parum,** adv., *little, slightly; not very, not at all.*

lūmina: ACC. OF SPECIFICATION with **dēiectō . . . vultū,** *his expression marked by downcast . . . .*

863 **virum . . . euntem:** the elder Marcellus; for the partic., cf. 476 and note.

864 **stirps, stirpis,** f., *stem, twig; branch* (of a family), *line of descendants.*

865 **circā:** here adv., *all around him,* i.e., in his crowded entourage, a reminder of the young man's popularity.

īnstar: here *presence, majesty.*

866 **nox . . . umbrā:** Aeneas himself had similarly described the darkness of Troy's last night, as he and his men plunged into the death-filled gloom to face the Greek invaders, at 2.360 above (**nox atra cavā circumvolat umbrā**); Vergil thus suggests how Aeneas could readily sense the horror of death hovering over the handsome youth whose phantom moved before him.

867 **lacrimīs . . . obortīs:** for the formula, cf. 4.30 (of Dido).

868 **tuōrum:** i.e., his descendants, the future citizens of Rome.

869 **ostendent . . . fāta:** i.e., they will permit the world only (**tantum**) a glimpse of the young man, Augustus' nephew and intended successor, Marcellus (see note on 883).

870 **esse:** = **vīvere.**

*propāgō, propāginis,** f., *seedling, shoot* (of a plant); *offspring, progeny; race.*

871 **vīsa:** sc. **esset.**

haec . . . dōna: i.e., the gift of a long and eminent life for the young man.

856 ingreditur victorque virōs superēminet omnēs.
857 Hic rem Rōmānam, magnō turbante tumultū,
858 sistet eques, sternet Poenōs Gallumque rebellem,
859 tertiaque arma patrī suspendet capta Quirīnō."
860 Atque hīc Aenēās (ūnā namque īre vidēbat
861 ēgregium fōrmā iuvenem et fulgentibus armīs,
862 sed frōns laeta parum et dēiectō lūmina vultū),
863 "Quis, pater, ille, virum quī sīc comitātur euntem?
864 Fīlius, anne aliquis magnā dē stirpe nepōtum?
865 Quī strepitus circā comitum! Quantum īnstar in ipsō!
866 Sed nox ātra caput trīstī circumvolat umbrā."
867 Tum pater Anchīsēs lacrimīs ingressus obortīs:
868 "Ō gnāte, ingentem lūctum nē quaere tuōrum;
869 ostendent terrīs hunc tantum fāta nec ultrā
870 esse sinent. Nimium vōbīs Rōmāna propāgō
871 vīsa potēns, superī, propria haec sī dōna fuissent.

Quaestiō

Comment on the meter in 868–69.

Marcus Claudius Marcellus
Posthumous statue
1st cent. B.C.
Louvre
Paris, France

872 **virum:** = **virōrum**, with **quantōs . . . gemitūs** (873).
 Māvors, Māvortis, m., *Mavors, Mars* (the Roman god of war; for the variant
  name, cf. 1.276 above).
 Māvortis: with both **urbem** (Rome) and **campus** (873, the Campus Martius,
  which was originally employed for military and political gatherings but
  by Vergil's day had largely become a sort of memorial park and the site of
  numerous temples and victory monuments).

873 **Tiberīnus, -ī,** m., *Tiberinus* (god of the Tiber river).
 quae . . . / fūnera (874): Vergil was himself doubtless present at the young man's
  spectacular funeral.

874 **praeterlābor, praeterlābī, praeterlāpsus sum,** *to glide by, flow past.*
 praeterlābēre: the spirit of the river god is seen in the river itself, as it glides
  (slowly, like this long, spondaic vb.) past the young man's burial place—
  Augustus' own mausoleum, which had been erected for the imperial family
  in 28 B.C. on the Campus Martius, near the banks of the Tiber.
 recentem: *recent* for Vergil's audience; the young Marcellus' death preceded
  Vergil's own by just four years.

875 **quisquam:** here adj. with **puer.**

876 **in tantum,** idiom, *so much, so high.*
 Rōmulus, -a, -um, *of Romulus.*

877 **alumnus, -ī,** f., *nursling, (young) offspring.*

879 **illī . . . armātō** (880): dat. with **sē . . . tulisset / obvius** (for the idiom, see gloss on
  1.314).
 quisquam: emphatically repeated from 875.
 impūne, adv., *unpunished, with impunity, unscathed.*

880 **cum:** here *when* with **īret** (CUM CIRCUMSTANTIAL CL.).
 ***pedes, peditis,** m., *one who goes on foot; footsoldier, infantryman;* idiom, **pedes**
  īre, *to go on foot.*

881 **fodiō, fodere, fōdī, fossus,** *to pierce, prod, jab.*
 calcar, calcāris, n., *spur.*
 armus, -ī, m., *shoulder; side, flank* (esp. of an animal).

882 **sī . . . rumpās:** cf. **sī quā fāta sinant** (1.18 above); here more a hope than a
  condition, *if only somehow you could . . .* (for the construction, cf. 187 above).

883 **Mārcellus, -ī,** m., *Marcellus* (here a descendant of the Marcellus he accompanies,
  son of Augustus' sister Octavia, husband of his daughter Julia, and heir
  apparent to the emperor until his premature and much lamented death in 23
  B.C. at the age of 19).
 tū Mārcellus eris: again, not conditional, but a prophecy of the young man's
  birth. Vergil suspensefully delays naming the youth for over 20 lines, from his
  first introduction in 861; Servius tells us that Marcellus' mother Octavia burst
  into tears as she first listened to Vergil reciting this passage for the imperial
  family).
 date . . . spargam (884) **. . . accumulem . . . fungar** (885): sc. **ut** (for the
  construction, cf. 4.683 above); in this entreaty to the gods, Anchises imagines
  himself as a participant in Marcellus' funeral rites.
 līlium, -ī, n., *lily.*

872 Quantōs ille virum magnam Māvortis ad urbem
873 campus aget gemitūs! Vel quae, Tiberīne, vidēbis
874 fūnera, cum tumulum praeterlābēre recentem!
875 Nec puer Īliacā quisquam dē gente Latīnōs
876 in tantum spē tollet avōs, nec Rōmula quondam
877 ūllō sē tantum tellūs iactābit alumnō.
878 Heu pietās, heu prīsca fidēs invictaque bellō
879 dextera! Nōn illī sē quisquam impūne tulisset
880 obvius armātō, seu cum pedes īret in hostem
881 seu spūmantis equī foderet calcāribus armōs.
882 Heu, miserande puer, sī quā fāta aspera rumpās—
883 tū Mārcellus eris! Manibus date līlia plēnīs

Quaestiōnēs

What effect does Vergil intend by the wide separation of **quantōs . . . gemitūs** in 872–73? Comment on the other effects of word order in this sentence.

"Tu Marcellus eris" or "Vergil Reading the Aeneid to Augustus, Octavia, and Livia"
Jean Auguste Dominique Ingres (1780–1867)
Musée des Augustins, Toulouse, France

884 **flōrēs:** in appos. with **līlia** (883).

885 **accumulō (1),** *to heap up, pile; to load* (with).
    fungor, fungī, fūnctus sum, + abl., *to perform, carry out.*

886 **vagantur:** sc. Aeneas and the Sibyl as subjs.

888 **Quae . . . dūxit:** = **Postquam Anchīsēs nātum per omnia haec loca dūxit;** cf.
    lūstrat dum singula (1.453) of Aeneas examining the temple of Juno at
    Carthage.

890 **exim** (= **exinde**), adv., *thereupon, then, next.*

891 **Laurēns, Laurentis,** *of Laurentum* (town on the coast of Latium).
    Latīnus, -ī, m., *Latinus* (legendary king of Laurentum).

892 **quō . . . modō:** TMESIS, producing INTERLOCKED WORD ORDER with **quemque
    . . . labōrem;** the arrangement accentuates the extensive internal rhyme and
    ASSONANCE in the three long ō's, the three **-que**'s, **-at-/-at-,** and **quem/-rem.**

893 **Somnī:** here generally regarded as a PERSONIFICATION; in Greco-Roman myth,
    Sleep (in Greek **Hypnos**) was a son of Night (**Nox/Nyx**), the twin brother of
    Death (**Mors/Thanatos**), and the father of Dreams (**Somnia/Oneiroi**).

894 **corneus, -a, -um,** *(made) of horn.*

895 **perfectus, -a, -um,** *(thoroughly/completely) made, complete, perfect.*
    elephantus, -ī, m., *elephant;* poetic, *ivory.*

896 **sed . . . mittunt:** i.e., through the Gate of Ivory.
    mānēs: here representing all the spiritual *powers of the Underworld.*

897 **Hīs . . . dictīs** (898): i.e., with all the prophecies Anchises has given his son,
    including doubtless his explanation of these twin Gates of Sleep.

884 purpureōs spargam flōrēs animamque nepōtis
885 hīs saltem accumulem dōnīs et fungar inānī
886 mūnere."

Anchises leads Aeneas through all the fields of Elysium, then tells
him of the wars to be fought and the glory to be won in Italy

Sīc tōtā passim regiōne vagantur
887 āeris in campīs lātīs atque omnia lūstrant.
888 Quae postquam Anchīsēs nātum per singula dūxit
889 incenditque animum fāmae venientis amōre,
890 exim bella virō memorat quae deinde gerenda,
891 Laurentēsque docet populōs urbemque Latīnī,
892 et quō quemque modō fugiatque feratque labōrem.

Anchises reveals to his son the twin Gates of Sleep, and Aeneas,
exiting Hades with the Sibyl through the mystical Ivory Gate,
rejoins his comrades, sails north, and anchors at Caieta

893 Sunt geminae Somnī portae, quārum altera fertur
894 cornea, quā vērīs facilis datur exitus umbrīs,
895 altera candentī perfecta nitēns elephantō,
896 sed falsa ad caelum mittunt īnsomnia mānēs.
897 Hīs ibi tum nātum Anchīsēs ūnāque Sibyllam

Quaestiōnēs

1. What do you see as Vergil's several purposes in bringing together the two Marcelli, one from the early Republic and one from his own day, in 855–86?

2. Comment on the effect Vergil achieves in juxtaposing Anchises' very positive and uplifting prophecy in lines 847–53 with the tragic scene of the younger Marcellus in 860–86.

3. Comment on the arrangement of the clause **vērīs facilis datur exitus umbrīs** (894).

898 **eburnus, -a, -um,** *(made) of ivory.*

portā . . . ēmittit eburnā: why Anchises dispatches Aeneas and the Sibyl back to the Upperworld through the Gate of Ivory, through which the forces of the Underworld send "false dreams," has been a quest. much discussed, though clearly a major reason is that Aeneas and the Sibyl are not **umbrae vērae** (894). The matter was undoubtedly an important one to Vergil, or he would not have closed this book and indeed the first, Odyssean half of his epic in this way; it may be that the answer was clearer to the poet's audience than it is to us, or perhaps Vergil meant to present even his contemporaries with an enigma, just as Book Twelve, at the close of the poem's Iliadic half, also ends on a troubling, enigmatic note.

899 **Ille . . . puppēs (901):** the three successive end-stopped verses and the ASYNDETON, along with the abrupt narration, effectively punctuate the close of the book and of Aeneas' personal "Odyssey."

viam secat: "makes his way" would be too weak, as the idiom implies a quick, even violent passage, as befits Vergil's sudden and abbreviated description of Aeneas' ascent from Hades and return to his men and their ships; perhaps *cuts his way through* (to). The same phrase is used in Book Twelve (line 368) of the Rutulian prince Turnus, rushing through the enemy lines like a wild north wind.

sociōs . . revīsit: an echo, and a quite deliberate one I would suggest, of **sociōs . . . revīsō** at the end of Book Two (line 795), where Aeneas' return to his comrades from the encounter with Creusa's phantom is depicted with the same bold, rapid strokes as his return here from the world of phantoms.

900 **Cāiēta, -ae,** f., *Caieta* (a seaport on the coast near the border of Latium and Campania, according to legend named for Aeneas' nurse, just as coastal sites were also said to be named for Aeneas' helmsman Palinurus and his comrade Misenus; Book Seven opens in fact with a four-line memorial to Caieta's death, thus linking the poem's Iliadic and Odyssean halves via the themes of death and eternal fame).

rēctus, -a, -um, *straight, direct.*

rēctō . . . līmite: *in/by a straight course.* Some editors read **lītore,** *straight along the coast,* and there is good ms. support for that reading; but **līmite** also appears in a number of mss., and the repetition with **lītore** in the next line, which would serve no apparent purpose, is probably an early scribal error of the sort known as "dittography" (accidental recopying of a word from an adjacent line).

901 **Ancora . . . puppēs:** though some editors suspect that this line (repeated from 3.277) is an interpolation, it actually provides a splendid cinematographic moment; we see first a single anchor cast, then the Trojan ships, their long journey ended, standing just off the coast of Latium (so close and yet, in terms of the struggles that lie ahead, so far from the future site of Rome), and then, very slowly, the camera fades.

898 prōsequitur dictīs portāque ēmittit eburnā.
899 Ille viam secat ad nāvēs sociōsque revīsit;
900 tum sē ad Cāiētae rēctō fert līmite portum.
901 Ancora dē prōrā iacitur; stant lītore puppēs.

Quaestiōnēs

Compare Vergil's handling of the motif of the twin Gates of Sleep in 893–98 with
the Homeric original that was his inspiration (*Odyssey* 19.562f.): there Homer has
Penelope assign her dream about Odysseus' return to the Gate of Ivory, suggesting
that her hopes are unrealistic and unattainable; how might Vergil have intended
this intertextual resonance to influence his readers' interpretation of his adaptation?
In view of the emphasis in this brief passage on **Somnus** and **īnsomnia,** what is
one way, beyond that of the surface narrative, that Vergil may have intended us to
interpret Aeneas' magical journey to the land of the dead?

Aeneid BOOK X

(Verses 420–509)

Books Seven–Nine

ALTHOUGH Books Seven, Eight, and Nine are not included in this text, they are briefly summarized here and you will most certainly wish to read them in English translation in their entirety. Book Seven begins with the burial of Caieta, Aeneas' nurse, on a commanding headland near Formiae, and thereafter a successful passage past Circe's domain, and a landing at the Tiber mouth. After an invocation to Erato, we learn that king Latinus' only child Lavinia is sought in marriage by Turnus, the Rutulian prince, but omens have indicated that a foreigner will be her eventual husband (1–106). During a riverside meal (107–47), the harpy Celaeno's prophecy (3.250–54) that the Trojans would one day be reduced to "eating their tables" is humorously fulfilled: Ascanius joyfully equates the ominous *mensae* with the thin bread slices or platters which they consume with their picnic fare. The Trojans have reached their appointed goal and Jupiter endorses that fact. Aeneas dispatches a legation to Latinus, led by Ilioneus, familiar to us from Carthage; the embassy is cordially received (170–285), and Latinus realizes that Aeneas will be his future son-in-law. Juno, angered by the Trojan arrival in Italy, is determined to obstruct the marriage. She sends Allecto, an underworld demon, to harass Latinus' wife Amata, to terrify and incite Turnus to act against Aeneas, and to madden the hounds of Ascanius. During the chase, Ascanius excitedly and without malice kills a pet stag cherished by Silvia, young sister of Tyrrhus, the manager of the royal herds of Latinus (323–539). The peasants on Latinus' estates are enraged and take up arms against the Trojans (540–640). Unable to veto the demands for war, Latinus abdicates his authority to Turnus. Juno bursts open the Gates of War, and the Latins assemble for conflict. Vergil supplies a catalogue of the Italian commanders, including Etruscan Mezentius and his son Lausus (647–54), Messapus (691–705), and finally Turnus, the Rutulian commander-in-chief, and Camilla, the Volscian warrior maiden (783–817).

Book Eight marks the beginning of the war. After being counseled by Father Tiber in a dream and encountering a great white sow, which he sacrifices to Juno (1–107), Aeneas sets about making an alliance with the Arcadian (Greek) ruler, the elderly Evander, at Tiber-side Pallanteum, which is destined to be the site of Rome (102–83). A festival of Hercules provides the background (184–305). Evander, once associated with Priam and Anchises, offers hospitality and military support. Vergil highlights Evander's account of how Hercules throttled the fire-demon Cacus ("the evil one"), who had rustled the oxen that Hercules brought from Spain. Evander discourses on early Italian history and the "Golden" Age of Saturn (a favorite theme of Augustan propaganda) and guides Aeneas around the future site of Rome.

Venus visits Vulcan, her husband, and seduces him into fashioning a set of armor for her (not his) son. Vulcan's Cyclopean foundrymen, lodged at volcanic

"Venus Asks Vulcan for the Armor of Aeneas"
Anthony van Dyck (1599–1641)
Louvre, Paris, France

Lipari and Vulcano in the Aeolian Islands, set to work (370–453). After a night's sleep, Evander urges Aeneas to ally the Trojan-Arcadian forces with the Etruscans; their deposed tyrant, Mezentius, has already fled to join Turnus' camp. Aeneas sets out to enlist the assistance of the Etruscan Tarchon, taking Evander's son Pallas and his Arcadian force with him. Evander is apprehensive about his young son, but entrusts him to Aeneas' surveillance (454–596). Tarchon's camp is located at Caere (modern Cerveteri), where Venus presents her son with the armor forged by Vulcan (597–625). Vergil highlights the shield in an extended *ecphrasis,* a digression devoted to the description of art works and locales, detailing the contents of three concentric circles on its convex surface, a panoramic vision of Rome's experience during the Regal Period, during Republican history through the Battle of Actium, and with a central boss depicting Octavian's triumphal parades of 29 B.C., and the newly dedicated Temple of Apollo (28 B.C.) on Rome's Palatine Hill (626–728).

Book Nine portrays the war in Italy in earnest. Juno sends Iris to advise Turnus to attack the Trojans while Aeneas is absent. The Trojans resolutely defend their camp (1–76). Turnus tries to set fire to the Trojan ships, but they are metamorphosed into nymphs through the intervention of Cybele, Troy's and Creusa's patroness (77–122). That night two young Trojans, Nisus and Euryalus, who featured in the foot race in Sicily (5.315–61), undertake to gain help from Aeneas (176–313), but the objective of their night expedition is forgotten when they enter the enemy's camp and butcher a number of the sleeping troops (314–66). They seize shiny metallic spoils that later reveal their presence in the moonlight. Nisus leaves safely but returns to find that his beloved Euryalus is a prisoner. In the ensuing fight (367–445), Nisus tries but fails to save his younger friend from death and is killed himself by the angry enemy troops. Vergil provides a personal invocation of the two young warriors, vivid testimony of his sensitivity to the appalling waste of war (446–49): "Happy pair! If my poetry has any power, no day shall ever blot you from the memory of time, so long as the house of Aeneas dwells on the Capitol's unshaken rock, and the Father of Rome holds sovereign sway!"

The Trojans realize that the mission to recall Aeneas has failed, when they see the heads of both warriors impaled on spears and paraded before their walls. Euryalus' mother utters a remorseful lament for her lost son (481–97). Vergil invokes the Muse to recall Turnus' bloody success during the battle at the walls, and the casualties mount on both sides. Italian Numanus Remulus comments that the Trojans are effeminate and decadent (590–620) in contrast to the tough vigor and military *virtus* of the Italians. Ascanius kills the arrogant critic. Apollo intervenes to prophesy greatness for Troy and, in mortal form, to warn Ascanius to end his participation in battle (638–58). During the prolonged engagement (672–818), Turnus bursts into the Trojan camp and is confined there when the gates are shut. He slaughters many of the defenders until the Trojans rally under Mnestheus, whereupon Turnus dives into the Tiber and escapes to rejoin his army.

Book Ten

BOOK 10 is devoted largely to violent scenes of battle, with *furor* and *ira* on all sides and with Turnus and Aeneas brought repeatedly to the foreground. Jupiter convenes a council of the gods (1–117), where Venus complains again about Juno's actions in Italy and pleads that Ascanius be permitted to survive and reside in Cyprus or Cythera; Carthage could then easily overwhelm Italy (18–62). Juno in turn blames the war on the Trojans and pleads in her defense that she favors Turnus after the pattern of Venus' earlier support for the adulterous Paris (62–95). Jupiter closes the discussion with an important statement on fate and free will: "Each one's effort *(labor)* shall bring him suffering or success. Jupiter is the same king for all; the fates shall find their way *(fata viam invenient)*" (111–13). R. D. Williams, in his commentary on Books Seven–Twelve understands that "Aeneas and the Trojans receive help from Jupiter when most in need, but they must themselves achieve their destiny."

While the Trojans desperately defend their camp, Aeneas returns by night with his Etruscan and Arcadian allies. The nymphs who were once his ships report what has happened and steer his fleet to shore (118–255). The Rutulians are alarmed by the force and glitter of the Trojan and allied divisions. Aeneas kills a number of Rutulians; Pallas, Evander's young son, rallies his Arcadian troops, fights gamely himself, and engages Etruscan Mezentius' son Lausus in a duel. The selection from Book Ten included in our text (420–509) highlights this action. Juturna, Turnus' divine sister, induces her brother to intervene to save Lausus. Pallas appeals to Hercules for assistance, but Jupiter rejects Hercules' desire to intervene. Although he wounds Turnus slightly, Pallas himself is slain and despoiled of the ornately decorated sword-belt, technically a baldric, across his chest. Vergil once again comments on the action (501–05) and observes, foreshadowing events to come in Book Twelve, that Turnus will one day bitterly regret his impious act, his neglect of the gods, when he retained this war trophy for himself.

Aeneas, despondent and crazed by Pallas' death, runs amok among the enemy. Turnus is his target for revenge, but Juno, who gains Jupiter's permission to delay but not to alter Turnus' destiny, draws him away from the battlefield by substituting a phantom Aeneas (606–88). While Turnus chases the phantom, Mezentius emerges as demonic slayer of the Trojans and their allies. Finally, Mezentius and Aeneas meet in a duel: Aeneas' spear wounds Mezentius and he prepares to kill him. In an effort to save his father, Lausus intercepts and dies by Aeneas' blow (747–832). The grieving victor allows the enemy to retrieve Lausus' corpse. Wounded, Mezentius calls for his horse, mounts, and attacks Aeneas. After Aeneas kills the horse, Mezentius, grounded, meets his death courageously, voicing a dying appeal to share his son's tomb (833–908).

420 **Quem:** Halaesus.

    sīc: with **precātus.**

    *****Pallās, Pallantis,** acc. **Pallanta,** m., *Pallas* (son of the Greek king Evander, who had migrated from Arcadia and established a settlement on one of the hills at Rome, naming it Pallanteum, the future Palatine; Evander had welcomed Aeneas to Italy, and his young son Pallas became one of Aeneas' closest friends and leader of an army allied with the Trojans against Turnus and the Rutulians).

421 **Thȳbri:** Greek voc.; see note on 2.782.

    ferrō: i.e., the spear which he is brandishing; ind. obj. of **dā.**

    missilis, -is, -e, *to be sent forth, to be thrown.*

    missile: with **quod . . . lībrō,** *which* I . . . *and am about to throw.*

    *****lībrō (1),** *to balance, poise; to aim, brandish.*

422 *****Halaesus, -ī,** m., *Halaesus* (one of the Italian leaders opposing the Trojans' settlement in Latium).

423 **Haec . . . habēbit:** in a common votive ritual, Pallas will hang the arms he strips from Halaesus on an oak tree sacred to the river god, father Tiber, as a victory trophy or **tropaeum.**

424 **tēxit:** here *protected.*

    Imāon, Imāonis, acc. **Imāona,** m., *Imaon* (another Italian warrior).

425 **Arcadius, -a, -um,** *Arcadian, of Arcadia* (the district of Greece in the central Peloponnese from which Pallas' father Evander had migrated into Italy).

    dat: here *exposes;* though strikingly inexplicit, Halaesus' death is indicated in this line and in **caede** in the following verse.

426 **nōn . . . sinit (427):** with **perterrita . . . agmina (427),** *he does not desert the . . . .*

    caede virī: with **perterrita;** i.e., the slaughter wreaked by Pallas against Halaesus and countless other Italians in the preceding scene.

    *****Lausus, -ī,** m., *Lausus* (young and handsome son of the exiled Etruscan chieftain Mezentius, an ally of Turnus and the Rutulians; though an opponent of the Trojans, he is characterized in the poem as a noble and courageous warrior).

427 **pars ingēns bellī:** i.e., he bore a huge share of the fighting; for the construction, cf. **quōrum pars magna fuī** of Aeneas (2.6).

    Abās, Abantis, m., *Abas* (an important Etruscan ally of Aeneas; not the same as the Trojan warrior Abas at 1.121 above).

428 **oppositum:** i.e., *who faced him.*

    interimō, interimere, interēmī, interēmptus, *to cut off from life, kill.*

    nōdum: lit., *a knot,* but here *a knotty problem = a difficult obstacle;* Servius comments on the unusual metaphor.

429 **Arcadia, -ae,** f., *Arcadia* (see note on 425 above).

    Etruscī, -ōrum, m. pl., *Etruscans, inhabitants of Etruria* (district of Italy north of Rome; most of the Etruscans had allied themselves with Aeneas and the Trojans).

430 **Grāīs:** DAT. OF AGENT with **imperdita.**

    imperditus, -a, -um, *not killed, unharmed.*

    Grāīs imperdita corpora: i.e., those who had survived the Trojan War; cf. **rēliquiās Danaum atque immītis Achillī** (1.30 above).

    corpora: a common METONYMY or SYNECDOCHE for **virī.**

The young prince Pallas, Aeneas' friend and ally, slays
Halaesus, who had rallied the Italians against him

420 Quem sīc Pallās petit ante precātus:
421 "Dā nunc, Thȳbri pater, ferrō, quod missile lībrō,
422 fortūnam atque viam dūrī per pectus Halaesī.
423 Haec arma exuviāsque virī tua quercus habēbit."
424 Audiit illa deus; dum tēxit Imāona Halaesus,
425 Arcadiō īnfēlīx tēlō dat pectus inermum.

Pallas and Lausus, son of Mezentius, nearly meet in combat,
but Jupiter keeps them apart, saving each for a mightier foe

426   At nōn caede virī tantā perterrita Lausus,
427 pars ingēns bellī, sinit agmina: prīmus Abantem
428 oppositum interimit, pugnae nōdumque moramque.
429 Sternitur Arcadiae prōlēs, sternuntur Etruscī,
430 et vōs, ō Grāis imperdita corpora, Teucrī.

Quaestiōnēs

1. Explain how **fortūnam atque viam** in 422 may be construed as a hendiadys.

2. What three poetic and rhetorical devices are employed in 429–30, and what is the combined effect?

432 **extrēmī:** *those at the rear = the rear-guard.*
addēnseō, addēnsēre, *to make dense/thickly packed; to close up* (the ranks).
nec . . . sinit (433): the ranks of warriors are so densely packed they can hardly move or use their weapons.

433 **sinit:** the second syllable is lengthened under the ictus and before the caesura (DIASTOLE).
Hinc . . . / hinc (434): cf. 4.40.

434 **discrepō (1),** *to differ, be different.*

435 **quīs:** = quibus, *(they were men) to whom.*

437 **magnī rēgnātor Olympī:** cf. **superī rēgnātor Olympī** (2.779).

438 **maiōre sub hoste:** Pallas will die at the hands of Turnus (in the episode at 441f. below), and Lausus at the hands of Aeneas (also in this book, at 809f.).

439 **soror alma:** Turnus' sister was the river nymph Juturna, a favorite of Juno's; in Book Twelve she unsuccessfully attempts to rescue her brother.

440 *****Turnus, -ī, m.,** *Turnus* (son of Venilia and the Rutulian king Daunus, prince of the Rutulians, and—for numerous reasons, including his rivalry with Aeneas for the hand of the Latin princess Lavinia—leader of the resistance to the Trojans' settlement in Italy).
quī: here = **et is deinde.**
secat: see note on 6.899.

441 **pugnae:** DAT. OF SEPARATION (a largely poetic construction) with the compound vb. **dēsistere.**

442 **sōlus . . . Pallās:** the triple ABCABC ANAPHORA serves to dramatize Turnus' arrogance and his bloodlust.
feror: for the passive of **ferō** in this sense, to convey rapid action, cf. **in flammās et in arma feror** of Aeneas (2.337, and also 2.655).

443 **cuperem:** POTENTIAL SUBJUNCT., I *could wish.*
ipse . . . adesset: sc. **ut,** JUSSIVE SUBJUNCT. in the impf., implying a wish that cannot be realized. Servius compared Turnus' cruelty here with Pyrrhus' actual slaying of Polites before the eyes of his aged father, king Priam, in 2.526f.

444 **aequore iussō:** *from the level space* (for the duel) *that had been ordered;* the partic. is a TRANSFERRED EPITHET, logically applying to **sociī.**

445 **Rutulum:** = **Rutulōrum.**
abscessus, -ūs, m., *departure, withdrawal.*

447 **obit:** here *goes over, surveys,* with his eyes.
trux, trucis, *savage, fierce.*

449 **spoliīs . . . raptīs . . . opīmīs:** ABL. OF CAUSE; for the **spolia opīma,** see note on 6.855 and 858 above.

450 **aequus:** *equal* (to) = *(equally) prepared* (for); a response to Turnus' hateful remark in 443.

451 **Tolle:** here *stop, dispense with.*
aequor: for this sense of the word, cf. line 444.

452 *****Arcas, Arcadis, m.,** *an Arcadian, inhabitant of Arcadia* (see note above on 425).
coeō, coīre, coiī, coitus, *to go/come together, meet; to clot, curdle, congeal.*

453 **biiugī, -ōrum, m. pl.,** *(two-horse) chariot.*
apparō (1), *to prepare (for), make ready (to).*

431 Agmina concurrunt ducibusque et vīribus aequīs;
432 extrēmī addēnsent aciēs nec turba movērī
433 tēla manūsque sinit. Hinc Pallās īnstat et urget,
434 hinc contrā Lausus, nec multum discrepat aetās,
435 ēgregiī fōrmā, sed quīs Fortūna negārat
436 in patriam reditūs. Ipsōs concurrere passus
437 haud tamen inter sē magnī rēgnātor Olympī;
438 mox illōs sua fāta manent maiōre sub hoste.

Juturna urges her brother, the Rutulian prince Turnus, to
rescue Lausus, and Turnus vows to face Pallas in a duel

439 Intereā soror alma monet succēdere Lausō
440 Turnum, quī volucrī currū medium secat agmen.
441 Ut vīdit sociōs: "Tempus dēsistere pugnae;
442 sōlus ego in Pallanta feror, sōlī mihi Pallās
443 dēbētur; cuperem ipse parēns spectātor adesset."
444 Haec ait, et sociī cessērunt aequore iussō.
445 At Rutulum abscessū iuvenis tum, iussa superba
446 mīrātus, stupet in Turnō corpusque per ingēns
447 lūmina volvit obitque trucī procul omnia vīsū,
448 tālibus et dictīs it contrā dicta tyrannī:
449 "Aut spoliīs ego iam raptīs laudābor opīmīs
450 aut lētō īnsignī: sortī pater aequus utrīque est.
451 Tolle minās." Fātus, medium prōcēdit in aequor;
452 frīgidus Arcadibus coit in praecordia sanguis.
453 Dēsiluit Turnus biiugīs, pedes apparat īre

Quaestiōnēs

1. Refer specifically to the text in demonstrating how Vergil builds up respect and sympathy for both young heroes, Pallas and Lausus, in 420–38.

2. What is the technical term for the word-ending device seen in **Pallanta . . . Pallās** (442), and what is its effect here?

454 *comminus, adv., *face to face, at close quarters.*
   specula, -ae, f., *look-out post, vantage-point.*
455 meditantem in: *practicing/rehearsing for.*
456 advolō (1), *to fly at/forth; to rush to attack.*
457 contiguus, -a, -um, + dat., *in contact with, close to, in range of.*
   fore: = futūrum esse.
458 īre: HIST. INF.
   ausum: sc. eum, *him daring* (to take the initiative in the fight).
460 Per . . . mēnsās: *by my father's . . .,* a common meaning of per in oaths and
      prayers; Pallas' father Evander had welcomed Hercules into his home in the
      course of one of his adventures and thus earned the hero's gratitude.
   advena, -ae, m., *stranger, traveller.*
461 coeptīs ingentibus: for this use of the partic. coeptum as a substantive, cf.
      coeptīs immānibus (4.642 above).
   adsīs: i.e., to lend assistance.
462 (sēminex), sēminecis (the nom. sg. and a few other case forms are unattested),
      half-dead.
   sēminecī sibi: DAT. OF SEPARATION; cf. 441 above.
463 victōrem: sc. mē from the preceding line, *me as . . . .*
   ferant: here *endure.*
465 inānēs: Hercules anticipated, and rightly, as seen in the following lines, that his
      father Jupiter would not, indeed could not, assist him in rescuing Pallas.
466 genitor: Jupiter, who was father of Hercules by the mortal woman Alcmena.
467 Stat: i.e., is fixed.
   sua: not strictly reflex. in force but referring emphatically to the key figure in the
      cl. (cuique, *every man*); cf. the similar usage in 471.
   inreparābilis, -is, -e, *unable to be regained, irretrievable.*
469 hoc . . . opus: sc. est; in appos. with extendere, *to extend . . ., this is the task . . . .*
471 Sarpēdōn: see note on 1.100.

Hercules and Cacus
Baccio Bandinelli (1488–1560)
Piazza della Signoria, Florence, Italy

454 comminus; utque leō, speculā cum vīdit ab altā
455 stāre procul campīs meditantem in proelia taurum,
456 advolat, haud alia est Turnī venientis imāgō.

Pallas prays to Hercules, then steps forth and casts his spear
against the mighty Turnus, managing only to graze him

457   Hunc ubi contiguum missae fore crēdidit hastae,
458 īre prior Pallās, sī quā fors adiuvet ausum
459 vīribus imparibus, magnumque ita ad aethera fātur:
460 "Per patris hospitium et mēnsās, quās advena adīstī,
461 tē precor, Alcīdē, coeptīs ingentibus adsīs.
462 Cernat sēminecī sibi mē rapere arma cruenta
463 victōremque ferant morientia lūmina Turnī."
464 Audiit Alcīdēs iuvenem magnumque sub īmō
465 corde premit gemitum lacrimāsque effundit inānēs.
466 Tum genitor nātum dictīs adfātur amīcīs:
467 "Stat sua cuique diēs, breve et inreparābile tempus
468 omnibus est vītae; sed fāmam extendere factīs,
469 hoc virtūtis opus. Trōiae sub moenibus altīs
470 tot gnātī cecidēre deum, quīn occidit ūnā
471 Sarpēdōn, mea prōgeniēs; etiam sua Turnum

Quaestiōnēs

1. Comment in detail on Vergil's characterization of Turnus in 440–56, including both positive and negative traits; how does the simile in 454–56 contribute to the characterization? Compare Vergil's simile to Homer's at *Iliad* 16.823f.; how are the two passages connected, and how does this resonance with the Homeric epic enrich our appreciation and understanding of the scene in Vergil?

2. Analyze the structure of Pallas' brief prayer to Hercules in 460–63; what formal elements does it contain?

3. Compare 469–71 with 1.94–101 above; what echoes of the earlier passage do you detect, and are they coincidental or purposeful? In either case, what do you see as the effect of the echoes, and what do they tell you about Vergil's method of composition?

472   **mētās:** the metaphor is drawn from chariot-racing; Turnus has reached the turning-point in his own life, and while he will win this day against Pallas, his own end is in sight.

473   **reiciō, reicere, reiēcī, reiectus,** *to throw back, cast away; to turn back, avert, turn away* (**reicit** here is scanned as a dactyl).

475   **vāgīna, -ae,** f., *sheath* (of a sword).
    dēripiō, dēripere, dēripuī, dēreptus, *to tear off, pull out.*

476   **Illa:** sc. **hasta.**
    umerī . . . summa: = **quā tegmina summa umerī** (i.e., the top of his breastplate) **surgunt.**

477   **incidit:** *struck;* the word is here effectively ENJAMBED.
    viam . . . mōlīta: *forcing its way.*
    ōrās: here *layers* (of bronze and hide), or perhaps *borders* = *rim.*

478   **strīnxit dē:** idiom, = *grazed.*

479   **praefīxus, -a, -um,** *fitted/equipped at the tip* (with), *tipped* (with).
    rōbur: here *the oak shaft* (of his spear).

480   **iacit atque ita fātur:** the harsh ALLITERATION of **t** and conflict of ictus and accent add a violent sound effect well suited to the action Vergil is describing.

481   **num,** interrog. conj. introducing IND. QUESTS., *whether.*
    mage: archaic form of **magis.**
    penetrābilis, -is, -e, *able to be pierced; able to pierce/penetrate.*
    mage . . . penetrābile: i.e., than yours (Pallas').

482   **at . . . ingēns (485):** the complex arrangement is designed to help suggest the great number of layers of iron and bronze and leather Turnus' spear had to penetrate before fatally tearing into Pallas' chest; rearranged into standard prose word order the text would read **at cuspis medium clipeum—tot ferrī terga, tot aeris (terga), quem pellis taurī circumdata totiēns obeat—ictū vibrantī trānsverberat, loricaeque morās et ingēns pectus perforat.**
    tot . . . aeris: in appos. with and describing the composition of **clipeum; terga** here, by a rather striking metaphor (lit., *hides of iron,* etc.), = *layers.*

483   **quem . . . obeat:** a REL. ADVERSATIVE CL., *although a hide . . . surrounded it.*
    circumdata: here reflex. = *encircling.*

484   **vibrantī:** with **ictū** = *shuddering.*
    trānsverberō (1), *to pierce (through), transfix.*

485   ***lōrīca, -ae,** f., *breastplate, cuirass.*
    morās: lit., *delays,* but with **lōrīcae** = *barrier.*
    perforō (1), *to make an opening in/through, bore, pierce, puncture, perforate.*
    pectus perforat: the ALLITERATION in **pec/per,** although not extensive, is amplified through coincidence of ictus and accent and effectively suggests the sound of Turnus' spear striking and piercing Pallas' chest.

486   **Ille:** Pallas.

472 fāta vocant mētāsque datī pervēnit ad aevī."

473 Sīc ait, atque oculōs Rutulōrum reicit arvīs.

474 At Pallās magnīs ēmittit vīribus hastam

475 vāgīnāque cavā fulgentem dēripit ēnsem.

476 Illa volāns umerī surgunt quā tegmina summa

477 incidit atque, viam clipeī mōlīta per ōrās,

478 tandem etiam magnō strīnxit dē corpore Turnī.

Turnus taunts the young warrior, and his own spear, hurled with
deadly force, tears through Pallas' armor and into his breast

479   Hīc Turnus ferrō praefīxum rōbur acūtō

480 in Pallanta, diū lībrāns, iacit atque ita fātur:

481 "Aspice num mage sit nostrum penetrābile tēlum."

482 Dīxerat; at clipeum, tot ferrī terga, tot aeris,

483 quem pellis totiēns obeat circumdata taurī,

484 vibrantī cuspis medium trānsverberat ictū

485 lōrīcaeque morās et pectus perforat ingēns.

486 Ille rapit calidum frūstrā de vulnere tēlum:

Quaestiōnēs

1. Hercules' tears in 465 might seem puzzling to readers, until one realizes Vergil's intention was to recall the scene from Homer's *Iliad* (16.431–61) in which Zeus himself weeps over the death of his own son Sarpedon (mentioned below in 471), whom he was unable to rescue from the inexorable power of Fate. Compare the Homeric passage and comment upon the ways in which Vergil has adapted it to his own purposes in this scene at 464–72. Consider possible implications of the fact that Sarpedon was slain by Patroclus, whose counterpart in the *Aeneid* is Pallas.

2. Discuss the conception of the relative authority of the gods vs. Fate reflected in the scene at 457–73; compare the Homeric conception as seen in *Iliad* 16.431–61.

3. Comment on the effectiveness of 473 as a transitional line.

4. How does meter suit meaning in 474?

5. Comment on the word order in 484; how is it appropriate to the action described?

487 **eādem:** a disyllable with SYNIZESIS of the **e-**, pronounced "yah-dem."

    sequuntur: sc. **tēlum**; i.e., they slip from Pallas' body even as he pulls out the spear.

488 **corruō, corruere, corruī,** *to fall down, collapse.*

    super: sc. **eum** or **corpus.**

489 **hostīlis, -is, -e,** *(of an) enemy, hostile.*

    petit: here *falls to, hits.*

490 **adsistō, adsistere, adstitī,** *to stand by/next to.*

491 **memorēs:** rather than an adj., Eng. idiom would more likely employ a second imper. to balance **referte,** *remember and . . . .*

492 **Euander, -drī,** m., *Evander* (father of Pallas and legendary founder of Pallanteum on the Palatine Hill; see notes on 420, 425, and 460).

    quālem: referring to **Pallanta,** *just as.*

    meruit: explained by **Aenēia . . . / hospitia** (494–95).

493 **sōlāmen, sōlāminis,** n., *consolation, comfort.*

    quidquid . . . humandī est: Eng. would say *whatever . . . there is in* (rather than *of*) *. . . .*

494 **largior, largīrī, largītus sum,** *to give/bestow generously* (ENJAMBEMENT here intensifies the irony and arrogance of Turnus' taunting remark).

    Haud: with **parvō,** ABL. OF PRICE.

    illī stābunt: idiom, *will cost him.*

    Aenēius, -a, -um, *of/for/relating to Aeneas* (the form here, as often, is pronounced and scanned as a quadrisyllable; cf. **Trōïa** 1.119).

496 ***balteus, -ī,** m., *shoulder-band, belt, baldric* (for a sword or other weapon).

    pondera balteī / . . . nefās (497): for the construction, see note on **minae . . . mūrōrum** (4.88–89); for the scansion of **balteī,** see note on **Oīleī** (1.41).

497 **impressum . . . nefās:** Pallas' baldric was engraved with a scene of the slaughter on their wedding night of all but one of the 50 sons of Aegyptus by their 50 brides, the Danaids, daughters of Aegyptus' brother Danaus, who had instigated the murders because of a prophecy that he would be slain by a son-in-law.

    sub: *under cover of.*

498 **foedē,** adv., *foully, wickedly* (with **caesa**).

499 **quae:** n. acc. pl., referring to the entire scene.

    Clonus, -ī, m., *Clonus* (an artist and engraver not otherwise known).

    Eurytidēs, Eurytidae, m., *son of Eurytus* (otherwise unknown).

    caelō (1), *to emboss, engrave, chase.*

500 **quō . . . spoliō:** = **hōc spoliō** (the **balteus**), ABL. WITH SPECIAL DEPONENT VBS. (**potītus**) as well as ABL. OF CAUSE with both **ovat** and **gaudet.**

    ovō (1), *to celebrate (a triumph); to exult, rejoice* (+ abl., *in/over*).

501 **Nescia:** construed both with the gens. **fātī** and **sortis** and with the inf. **servāre** (502), *ignorant of . . . and (of how) to . . . .*

487 ūnā eādemque viā sanguis animusque sequuntur.

488 Corruit in vulnus (sonitum super arma dedēre)

489 et terram hostīlem moriēns petit ōre cruentō.

Turnus stands over the mortally wounded youth, cursing his father
Evander, and then rips from the corpse his richly engraved baldric

490   Quem Turnus super adsistēns:

491 "Arcades, haec," inquit, "memorēs mea dicta referte

492 Euandrō: quālem meruit, Pallanta remittō.

493 Quisquis honōs tumulī, quidquid sōlāmen humandī est,

494 largior. Haud illī stābunt Aenēïa parvō

495 hospitia." Et laevō pressit pede, tālia fātus,

496 exanimem, rapiēns immānia pondera balteī

497 impressumque nefās: ūnā sub nocte iugālī

498 caesa manus iuvenum foedē thalamīque cruentī,

499 quae Clonus Eurytidēs multō caelāverat aurō;

500 quō nunc Turnus ovat spoliō gaudetque potītus.

Turnus shall one day regret his arrogance and despise these
spoils, but for now Pallas' comrades must bear his corpse
to his father, bringing him at once great sorrow and glory

501   Nescia mēns hominum fātī sortisque futūrae

Quaestiōnēs

1. Comment on the quantity of the second syllable of **sanguis** in 487; what is the technical term for this metrical effect?

2. The swordbelt described in 496–500 will prove important in the closing events of Book Twelve, and some scholars connect the scene on the belt to the role of Cleopatra and Egypt in the civil war between Octavian and Marc Antony (sculptures of the Danaids were displayed in the portico of Octavian's temple of Apollo Palatinus, dedicated in 28 B.C.); beyond that, however, in what ways may the scene be regarded as relevant to the action in the Pallas-Turnus episode itself?

502 **rēbus . . . secundīs:** cf. the identically positioned phrase in 1.207 above.

503 **magnō . . . Pallanta (504):** lit., *when he will have wished (that) Pallas (had been) untouched (could have been) bought at a high price* (**magnō** = ABL. OF PRICE); freely, *when he will wish that Pallas had been spared at any price.*

506 **frequēns, frequentis,** *densely packed, crowded, in a crowd/throng, thronging together.*

507 **reditūre:** voc. to agree with **tū** (Pallas) understood and in apposition to **dolor atque decus magnum,** *(you who are) about to return* (to) . . . *as* (a source of) *grief and . . . .*

508 **tē . . . dedit:** the point reminds of us of just how young Pallas was, as this was his very first day on the field of battle.

509 **cum . . . linquis:** the indic., in a CUM TEMPORAL CL. vs. a subjunct. CUM ADVERSATIVE CL., adds vividness to the APOSTROPHE, = (on this very day) *when you are leaving behind.*

Achilles binding the wounds of Patroclus
Interior of red-figure kylix, Sosias, 5th cent. B.C.
Antikenmuseum, Staatliche Museen, Berlin, Germany

502 et servāre modum, rēbus sublāta secundīs!
503 Turnō tempus erit magnō cum optāverit ēmptum
504 intāctum Pallanta et cum spolia ista diemque
505 ōderit. At sociī multō gemitū lacrimīsque
506 impositum scūtō referunt Pallanta frequentēs.
507 ō dolor atque decus magnum reditūre parentī,
508 haec tē prīma diēs bellō dedit, haec eadem aufert,
509 cum tamen ingentēs Rutulōrum linquis acervōs!

Quaestiōnēs

1. What multiple narrative functions are served by Vergil's reflective and even sermonizing aside in 501–05? Briefly compare this passage with the function and emotional tone of 4.65–66 above.

2. Explain the wide separation of **at sociī** from **frequentēs** and how the entire sentence in 505–06 forms a word-picture.

In an ill hour insulting Turnus tore
Those golden spoils, and in a worse he wore.
O mortals, blind in fate, who never know
To bear high fortune, or endure the low!
The time shall come, when Turnus, but in vain,
Shall wish untouch'd the trophies of the slain;
Shall wish the fatal belt were far away;
And curse the dire remembrance of the day.

From the translation of John Dryden, 1698

Aeneid BOOK XII

(Verses 791–842, 887–952)

Book Eleven

BOOK Eleven, which you should read in English translation before going on to the Latin from Book Twelve in this final unit, opens with Aeneas rendering thanks to Mars and erecting a trophy composed of Mezentius' weapons. Burial is the order of the day. Aeneas joins in the lamentation over Pallas' body, which lies in state, and a funeral procession is organized (1–99). An embassy arrives from Laurentum, Latinus' capital. Drances, their spokesman, requests a truce of 12 days to permit the burial of their war dead and promises to advance the cause of peace by reinstating the treaty between Aeneas and Latinus (100–38). Because Rumor had reported Pallas' death, Evander and his people greet the arrival of the cortege in abject grief. Evander asks Aeneas to avenge his son's death (139–81). Funeral rites continue on both sides.

Drances returns to Laurentum to promote condemnation of Turnus' policy, and indicates that Aeneas will rely on a single combat with Turnus to determine the ultimate victory. Amata and others defend Turnus' policy and actions (182–224). Meanwhile, Latinus' embassy to Diomedes in South Italy, aimed at winning his assistance, is reported as a failure. From his own experience with the Trojans at Troy, Diomedes counsels peace with them (225–95). The Council of the Latins reviews alternatives to continuing the hostilities, either to incorporate the Trojans in the state or to furnish them with ships to sail elsewhere (296–335). Drances issues Aeneas' challenge to a duel, and Turnus accepts (336–444). The report that Aeneas' forces are advancing on Laurentum ends the council meeting and spurs Turnus to action.

The Rutulian prince's strategy dictates that Camilla's cavalry will meet Aeneas' forces on the plain, while Turnus himself arranges an ambush in the hills above (498–531). Diana's speech to Opis, her nymph, reviews Camilla's life story and regrets that she will die in the ensuing action (532–96). The cavalry engagement is an exciting, bloody affair. Camilla fights valiantly and claims eight victims, but is finally struck down by Arruns and dies in the arms of a devoted "Amazonian" companion (648–867). Opis avenges her death by killing the runaway Arruns. The Volscian cavalry retreat to the city in confusion, pursued by the enemy; the gates are so hastily closed that Latins are led outside, straining to enter (868–95). The casualties mount, as friend slays friend, and the women prepare to defend their city. Turnus learns that Camilla's cavalry force has been defeated and abandons the ambush just before Aeneas' troops arrive. Both groups press towards the same city in view of each other, but nightfall prevents an engagement.

Book Twelve

BOOK Twelve, which provides Turnus with his moment of truth and concludes hostilities in Italy, should be read in its entirety in English. The build-up to the final duel offers a galaxy of characters and a succession of absorbing, exciting, and delaying incidents. Once again, and for the last time, Vergil's epic merges with tragedy, highlighting the motivations and psychology of the participants, their emotions, their dilemmas, and inner conflicts. We need to be aware that the secret of Vergil's art lies not only in the architecture of the whole epic and in its separate books, but above all in the emotional appeal of his characters, heroes and heroines, human and divine, which is essentially a dramatic appeal.

When Book Twelve opens, Vergil accents the fact that Turnus' recent experience of defeat gives him the reason and the courage to come to grips with himself and to face the inevitable duel (1–80). Latinus tries to deter him, and Amata begs him not to yield to the encounter. Turnus shows an innate willingness to display his heroic courage (in the Homeric mode) by facing his adversary. Vergil has repeatedly stressed Turnus' irrational nature as well as his courage, and his violent passions and self-absorption. While Turnus steels himself for the final battle and his personal contest with Aeneas, the Trojan hero likewise prepares for the action with courage and determination.

Vergil introduces a brief scene on Olympus where Juno deters Juturna from any more intrusive action on her brother's behalf, whereupon the preliminaries for the duel are formally initiated: solemn oaths are sworn, first by Aeneas, then by Latinus on Turnus' behalf. The Trojans seem confident; the Rutulians are anxious about the outcome (81–215). Juturna, in disguise, urges the Rutulians to break the truce, and an omen involving an eagle and a swan is interpreted to mean that the Rutulians should try to save their champion (216–310). When the treaty seems endangered, Aeneas tries to keep his side free from fault, but is shot by an arrow from an unidentified source. Turnus sees his advantage and leads his troops into battle. When Aeneas' physician cannot remove the tormenting arrow, Venus appears; the arrow is released and the goddess heals the wound with her "miracle" herb, dittany (383–440).

When Aeneas rearms and returns to the field, his sole objective is Turnus. Juturna intervenes again disguised as Turnus' charioteer Metiscus, and keeps him out of range. When Aeneas realizes that Turnus will not face him, he gives

"Venus Pouring Dittany on the Wounds of Aeneas"
Giovanni Francesco Romanelli (1610–62)
Louvre, Paris, France

way to battle frenzy and merciless slaughter, and Turnus follows suit (441–553). Venus suggests that Aeneas should lay siege to the Latin capital (554–92). When Amata sees the Trojans advancing and wrongly supposes that Turnus has fallen, she convinces herself that she is the cause of the inevitable disaster, and, like Jocasta, the queen in Sophocles' *Oedipus Rex,* commits suicide by hanging herself (593–613). Turnus is ready to face Aeneas, but when he hears that the city is under siege and that Amata has died, he is at a loss and in a state of shock; nevertheless he asks his friends and allies to cease fighting and to witness his decisive duel with Aeneas (614–96).

When the contest finally begins, spears are ineffective, so the two adversaries resort to close combat. Turnus tries to bring Aeneas down with his sword, but it shatters like an icicle because Turnus has mistakenly armed himself with Metiscus' weapon. Aeneas pursues Turnus and tries unsuccessfully to regain his own spear that clings to the stump of a tree sacred to Faunus. When Juturna regains Turnus' sword and Venus restores her son's spear, the contest is renewed (697–790).

Our initial selection from Book Twelve (791–842) is concerned with the resolution of conflict at the cosmic level. Juno concedes her "failure" but on her own terms. Her enmity yields to the prospect of her supplying protection and advancement for the Italians. Romans and Italians, not Trojans, will be the civilizers of the world to come. "Troy has fallen, and let her stay fallen, name and all" (828). Jupiter intervenes, not by sending Mercury but by dispatching a fiend, a Dira, from Olympus to terrify Turnus by flying in front of his face and to induce Juturna to withdraw once and for all.

In our closing selection (887–952), Turnus attempts to throw a huge rock at Aeneas but his strength is not equal to the task, and Vergil compares his actions to those of a man in a dream. Aeneas hurls his spear and wounds the Rutulian in the thigh. When Turnus, like a fallen gladiator, begs for mercy, Aeneas pauses for humanity's sake, but when he sees Pallas' baldric over Turnus' shoulder, overwhelmingly furious and enraged, he proclaims that it is Pallas himself who is the sacrificer and he kills his suppliant enemy, burying his sword deep in his chest.

What should our reaction be to vengeance killing? Certainly the imagery of sacrificial offering has been an undercurrent from the outset of the epic, and it recurs in this final scene. Turnus is sacrificed, we must suppose, to end the cycle of killings and to gain a lasting peace. Vergil side-steps a reconciliation on earth when Jupiter sends his agent of terror in order to end the action and to fulfill his own promise and purpose. Juno had done the same in Book Seven when she sent the Fury Allecto to incite war in Italy. When the hero assigns the final act of sacrifice to Pallas, the "Italo-Arcadian" offensive hero meets and kills the Italian enemy, the defensive hero Turnus. The epic engagement is thus, in the final reckoning, an episode of civil war, which we know will be Italy's century-long ordeal. Is that why Vergil ends his epic with a disturbing scene of revenge and sacrifice? Was Aeneas right to refuse Turnus' supplication? The abrupt ending with Turnus' defeat and "execution" must be designed to shock the reader. But should we be left in a state of uncertainty? Does Vergil at the end mean to raise doubts about the *imperium sine fine* (1.279) granted by Jupiter? How can we reconcile the callous sacrifice of Turnus by the goddess who originally provoked him to fight? And how do we reconcile ourselves with *pius* Aeneas in the end "burning with fury and terrible in his rage"? What has become of Anchises' instruction *parcere subiectis* (6.853) to his "Roman" son? The epic ends with violence and discord. Should the poem have ended differently, with a spirit of compromise, with mercy and forgiveness? Should Turnus have been spared? Or would you argue that Vergil's epic in fact offers remarkable insight into the realities of history and humanity, and inhumanity? Vergil's "Song of War" has become a classic for a great many reasons: for its dramatic power and its poetic beauty, to be sure, and also, not because it provides us with all the answers, but because of the profound and enduring questions that it raises and compels us to consider.

791 **intereā:** here Vergil turns his camera away from the battlefield, where Turnus and Aeneas are poised for combat, toward Mt. Olympus, where the long struggle between Juno and Jupiter over the destiny of the Trojans must be resolved before the duel can continue to its fateful conclusion.

omnipotentis: TRANSFERRED EPITHET, properly applying to **rēx** = Jupiter; see note on 4.220.

793 **Quae . . . fīnis:** for the gender, see note on 2.554.

794 **indiges, indigetis,** m., *native god, patron deity, native hero* (Aeneas was worshipped under the title of **Iuppiter Indiges**).

scīre: sc. **tē** as subj.

795 **dēbērī:** with **caelō,** *is owed to = has a right to;* i.e., Aeneas is destined for immortality and a place among the gods.

796 **Quid . . . haerēs:** cf. 4.235 and 271 above.

797 **Mortālīn:** = **mortālīne;** modifying **vulnere,** but positioned at the beginning of the verse to underscore the contrast with **dīvum** at the end. The divine Aeneas, son of Venus and thus grandson of Jupiter himself, had been wounded by an enemy warrior's arrow earlier in this episode (10.318–23).

violārī . . . dīvum: subj. (like the inf. phrases **ēnsem . . . reddī** and **vim crēscere** in 798–99) of the impers. vb. **decuit,** *was it fitting for a . . . to be . . . .*

798 *****Iūturna, -ae,** f., *Juturna* (river nymph, favorite of Juno, and sister of Turnus; see note on 10.439).

ēnsem . . . victīs (799): in an earlier scene (731–41) Turnus had left behind his own sword, *snatched from him* (**ēreptum** 799) by a random act of chance, and his sister had restored it to him, thus rescuing him temporarily from certain death (785).

800 **īnflectere:** pass. imper.

801 **nē . . . edit . . . et . . . recursent (802):** a JUSSIVE NOUN CL./IND. COMMAND dependent on **precibus** (800), *my prayers that . . . not . . .;* **edit** is an archaic form of the pres. subjunct., = **edat.** The staccato effect of the line's opening monosyllables and disyllables and the extensive **t/d** ALLITERATION lend a tone of intensity to Jupiter's command, which truly is an order more than an entreaty.

tantus . . . dolor: a dominant facet of Juno's characterization from the outset of the poem (see, e.g., **dolēns** 1.1 and **saevī . . . dolōrēs** 1.25).

802 **tuō dulcī . . . ex ōre:** in a light, very human moment, Jupiter softens the demands he imposes upon his wife with a touch of flattery.

803 **Ventum . . . est:** the brief, abrupt **sententia,** the grave spondees, and even Jupiter's use of the impers. pass., all add a tone of finality to his assertion.

Terrīs . . . bellum (804): the lines recall only generally, but perhaps deliberately, 1.3–4, **et terrīs iactātus et altō / vī superum, saevae memorem Iūnōnis ob īram.**

805 **dēfōrmō (1),** *to spoil the appearance of, disfigure, mar.*

dēfōrmāre . . . hymenaeōs: the allusion is to the grief suffered earlier in the story by the house of king Latinus; the king's wife Amata had committed suicide by hanging (12.593–611) after mistakenly supposing that Turnus, whom she strongly favored over Aeneas for the hand of her daughter Lavinia, had died in battle.

As Aeneas and Turnus at last face each other on the battlefield,
Jupiter commands Juno to cease her hostility against the Trojans

791   Iūnōnem intereā rēx omnipotentis Olympī
792   adloquitur, fulvā pugnās dē nūbe tuentem:
793   "Quae iam fīnis erit, coniūnx? Quid dēnique restat?
794   Indigetem Aenēān scīs ipsa et scīre fatēris
795   dēbērī caelō fātīsque ad sīdera tollī.
796   Quid struis? Aut quā spē gelidīs in nūbibus haerēs?
797   Mortālīn decuit violārī vulnere dīvum?—
798   aut ēnsem (quid enim sine tē Iūturna valēret?)
799   ēreptum reddī Turnō et vim crēscere victīs?
800   Dēsine iam tandem precibusque īnflectere nostrīs
801   nē tē tantus edit tacitam dolor et mihi cūrae
802   saepe tuō dulcī trīstēs ex ōre recursent.
803   Ventum ad suprēmum est. Terrīs agitāre vel undīs
804   Trōiānōs potuistī, īnfandum accendere bellum,
805   dēfōrmāre domum et lūctū miscēre hymenaeōs:

Quaestiōnēs

1. Take careful note of the verbal echo in 796 of Jupiter's words to Mercury in 4.235 and Mercury's to Aeneas in 4.271. Does Vergil mean for us here to recall the earlier scenes from Book Four, and if so, why? Even if the language is only formulaic, what is the effect of the connection among the three passages?

2. What rhetorical device does Jupiter employ repeatedly in 796–99, and what is the intended effect?

> Therwhiles th'almighty king to Iuno speaking thus he told,
> That from a yellow cloud aboue, the battell did behold.
> What shall the end herof be wife? what now remaineth? say.
> Aeneas is a god thou knowest, thy selfe canst not denay,
> And that to heauen he longs, and to the starres to be extold,
> What dost thou worke? or in what hope abidste in clouds so cold?
>
> *From the translation of Thomas Phaer and Thomas Twyne, 1573*

806 ***ulterius,** adv., *(any) further/longer.*

807 **Sāturnia:** for this epithet of Juno, see 1.23 and note.

808 **Ista . . . nōta . . . tua . . . voluntās:** the disjointed word order helps suggest Juno's grudging (**invīta** 809) hesitancy to accommodate her husband's wishes, while the repetition **ista/tua** underscores her total awareness of his superior power.

810 **nec . . . vidērēs:** POTENTIAL SUBJUNCT., with the force of a contrary-to-fact condition, *not (otherwise,* i.e., if not compelled by your authority) *would you . . . .*

   mē . . . sōlam: subj. of **patī** (811).

   āerius, -a, -um, *of/in the air, airy; in the sky, heavenly.*

811 **digna indigna:** sc. **et,** i.e., every consequence of her actions, whether merited or not.

   sub: with **aciē** (812), *close to, right by the . . . .*

814 **suāsī:** here with both an acc. + inf. construction (**Iūturnam . . . succurrere** 813), which is common in poetry, and a JUSSIVE NOUN CL./IND. COMMAND (**ut . . . contenderet** 815), which is usual in prose (some editors take the **ut** cl. to indicate result, *but not so boldly as to . . . ,* which is also a possibility).

   vītā: sc. **frātris.**

   audēre: sc. **eam** (Juturna) as subj., with **probāvī,** *I approved that she . . . .*

815 **contenderet:** an example of ZEUGMA, as the vb. has one meaning with **tēla** *(to cast/throw)* and another with **arcum** *(to pull back/draw tight).*

816 **adiūrō (1),** *to swear by/on.*

   caput . . . fontis: *fountainhead, source.*

   implācābilis, -is, -e, *implacable, inexorable.*

817 **superstitiō, superstitiōnis,** f., *religious awe; religious/superstitious belief/practice.*

   ūna superstitiō: in appos. with the preceding cl.; an oath sworn by the powers of the river Styx was the only oath sanctioned by the gods.

818 **exōsus, -a, -um,** *full of hate, in loathing.*

819 **Illud:** the request that follows in 821–28; the line's slow, spondaic movement and the series of halting monosyllables and disyllables help prepare us for the gravity of Juno's entreaty.

   tenētur: = **retinētur,** *held back,* i.e., *prohibited, forbidden.*

820 **obtestor, -ārī, -ātus sum,** *to beseech, implore, ask for* (something, acc.) *from/of* (someone, acc.).

   maiestās, maiestātis, f., *greatness, dignity, majesty.*

   tuōrum: i.e., his descendants, through both his grandson Aeneas and Latinus, a great-grandson of Jupiter's own father Saturnus.

821 **cōnūbiīs:** for the scansion, see note on 1.73.

   estō: for the form, see 4.35 and note.

823 **indigena, -ae,** m., *native inhabitant;* often used as an adj., esp. with m. pl. nouns, for the original inhabitants of a region, *native, indigenous* (cf. note on **indiges** 794).

824 **Trōas:** acc. pl. (for the form, see note on 1.30), pred. noun after **fierī.**

825 **vōcem:** i.e., their language.

826 **Albānī . . . rēgēs:** the series of kings who would reign at Alba Longa after Ascanius and down to the time of Romulus and the founding of Rome (cf. 1.267–74 above).

806 ulterius temptāre vetō."

Juno relents but prays that the new Roman nation be permitted
to retain the language and culture of her beloved Latins

Sīc Iuppiter orsus;
807 sīc dea summissō contrā Sāturnia vultū:
808 "Ista quidem quia nōta mihī tua, magne, voluntās,
809 Iuppiter, et Turnum et terrās invīta relīquī;
810 nec tū mē āeriā sōlam nunc sēde vidērēs
811 digna indigna patī, sed flammīs cīncta sub ipsā
812 stārem aciē traheremque inimīca in proelia Teucrōs.
813 Iūturnam miserō (fateor) succurrere frātrī
814 suāsī et prō vītā maiora audēre probāvī,
815 nōn ut tēla tamen, nōn ut contenderet arcum;
816 adiūrō Stygiī caput implācābile fontis,
817 ūna superstitiō superīs quae reddita dīvīs.
818 Et nunc cēdō equidem pugnāsque exōsa relinquō.
819 Illud tē, nūllā fātī quod lēge tenētur,
820 prō Latiō obtestor, prō maiestāte tuōrum:
821 cum iam cōnūbiīs pācem fēlīcibus (estō)
822 compōnent, cum iam lēgēs et foedera iungent,
823 nē vetus indigenās nōmen mūtāre Latīnōs
824 neu Trōas fierī iubeās Teucrōsque vocārī
825 aut vōcem mūtāre virōs aut vertere vestem.
826 Sit Latium, sint Albānī per saecula rēgēs,

Quaestiōnēs

1. Compare Jupiter's assertion in 795 with his prophecy at 1.259–60 above. Read again Jupiter's entire speech to Venus at 1.257–96; what other details of the Olympian's prophecy appear to be approaching fulfillment here in 791–806?

2. Comment on the word order and sound effects in 825.

827 **Rōmāna potēns . . . propāgō:** an echo of Anchises' prophecy, **Rōmāna propāgō vīsa potēns** (6.870–71 above).

828 **occiderit:** sc. **ut**; perf. subjunct. after **sinās**.

Trōia: subj. of both **occidit** and **occiderit**, suspensefully delayed to the end of the line and of Juno's bold entreaty.

829 **rērum:** *(all) things,* i.e., *the world.*

repertor, repertōris, m., *discoverer, originator.*

Ollī . . . repertor: cf. **ollī subrīdēns hominum sator atque deōrum,** at the beginning of Jupiter's reply to Venus in Book One (line 254).

830 **Sāturnus, -ī,** m., *Saturn* (Italic deity associated with the Greek Cronus, father of Jupiter and Juno, who are elsewhere in the poem called **Sāturnius** and **Sāturnia,** e.g., 1.23 and 4.372 above).

831 **īrārum . . . flūctūs:** a reminder of Vergil's characterization of Juno in the question he poses at the very beginning of his epic (1.11), **tantaene animīs caelestibus īrae?** And is the phrase **tantōs volvis sub pectore flūctūs** an intentional echo of **vāstōs volvunt ad lītora flūctūs** in Vergil's description of the storm unleashed by Juno in her opening act of malevolence against the Trojans at 1.86?

832 **vērum,** adv., *but (at the same time), however.*

833 **remittō:** here *give in, yield in turn*; the vb. is meant to respond to the related compound **summitte** in the preceding verse, i.e., if Juno will relent, then Jupiter will offer her concessions in return.

834 **Sermōnem:** i.e., their (Latin) language; the verse responds to Juno's request in 825.

835 **commixtī corpore tantum:** probably *mingling in stock only,* though some read **tantum** with **subsīdent** (836) and take **commixtī corpore** to mean *integrated with the mass* (of native Italians).

836 **subsīdō, subsīdere, subsēdī,** *to crouch down, settle; to sink to a lower level, subside, decline.*

rītus, -ūs, m., *rite, ritual.*

Mōrem rītūsque sacrōrum: i.e., the whole body of religious custom and ritual; native Italian religion will be commingled with Trojan beliefs and practices as represented by the Penates that had been dutifully brought by Aeneas to his new country (**īnferret . . . deōs Latiō** 1.6 above and passim).

837 **adiciō, adicere, adiēcī, adiectus,** *to throw at/toward; to insert, attach, add.*

adiciam: for the scansion, see note on **obicitur** (2.200); the internal rhyme with **faciam** is accentuated by positioning the final syllables under the ictus.

838 **genus:** subj. of **īre** (839).

839 **suprā īre deōs pietāte:** an extraordinary concession.

840 **nec . . . honōrēs:** Augustus restored the temple to Juno Regina on the Aventine, and the goddess was worshipped as well in temples on the Esquiline (to Juno Lucina) and the Capitoline (in the sanctuary of Juno Moneta and the ancient temple to the Capitoline Triad, where she was honored along with Jupiter and Minerva).

aequē, adv., *equally, to the same extent.*

celebrō (1), *to crowd around, attend in large numbers; honor, celebrate.*

827 sit Rōmāna potēns Italā virtūte propāgō:
828 occidit, occideritque sinās cum nōmine Trōia."

*Jupiter grants Juno's wishes and proclaims that her Latins shall
subsume the Trojans and create a nation that will surpass all
others in power and in their reverence for her majesty*

829   Ollī subrīdēns hominum rērumque repertor:
830 "Es germāna Iovis Sāturnīque altera prōlēs,
831 īrārum tantōs volvis sub pectore flūctūs.
832 Vērum age et inceptum frūstrā summitte furōrem:
833 dō quod vīs, et mē victusque volēnsque remittō.
834 Sermōnem Ausoniī patrium mōrēsque tenēbunt,
835 utque est nōmen erit; commixtī corpore tantum,
836 subsīdent Teucrī. Mōrem rītūsque sacrōrum
837 adiciam faciamque omnēs ūnō ōre Latīnōs.
838 Hinc genus Ausoniō mixtum quod sanguine surget,
839 suprā hominēs, suprā īre deōs pietāte vidēbis,
840 nec gēns ūlla tuōs aequē celebrābit honōrēs."

Quaestiōnēs

1. What are the most striking rhetorical features of 826–28 and what is their effect?

2. Compare Juno's speech in 808–28 with her speech to the council of gods in Horace *Odes* 3.3, which was composed at about the same time as the *Aeneid;* what are the most striking similarities?

3. Comment on the effectiveness of the meter and other sound effects in 833.

Call them not Trojans: perish the renown
And name of Troy, with that detested town.
Latium be Latium still; let Alba reign.
And Rome's immortal majesty remain.

From the translation of John Dryden, 1698

841 **retorqueō, retorquēre, retorsī, retortus,** *to twist back around; to reverse the course of; to reverse, change, alter.*

retorsit: Vergil means us to think of the word's root meaning, which here suggests the immense force of the goddess' will.

887 ***coruscō (1),*** *to shake, brandish; to quiver, tremble; to glitter, flash, gleam.*

889 **retractō (1),** *to draw back, hang back, retreat.*

890 **Nōn . . . armīs:** the grave spondees, conflict of ictus and accent, the harsh **c**'s and hissing, disdainful **s**'s all suit the violence and reproachfulness of Aeneas' challenge.

891 **faciēs:** here *forms, shapes;* Aeneas taunts his enemy by challenging him to transform himself into a bird (**optā ardua pennīs / astra sequī** 892–93) or some other creature as a means of escape, an allusion perhaps to the mythic shape-changer Proteus.

contrahō, contrahere, contrāxī, contractus, *to draw together; to assemble, collect, muster.*

892 **valēs:** = **potes;** sc. **contrahere.**

893 **astra . . . terrā:** the nouns are positioned to FRAME the line and emphasize Aeneas' point, i.e., that there is no place for Turnus to escape to, not from the very heights of heaven to the bowels of the earth; the WORD-PICTURE in **cavā tē condere terrā** contributes to the image, and the **q/c** ALLITERATION adds a deliberately harsh sound effect.

894 ***fervidus, -a, -um,*** *intensely hot, boiling, burning; seething, blazing (with anger).*

terrent / dicta . . . dī . . . terrent (895): the contrast is underscored by CHIASMUS, ANAPHORA, and ASSONANCE.

Duel of Aeneas and Turnus
Woodcut from a 1664 French translation of the *Aeneid*

841 Adnuit hīs Iūnō et mentem laetāta retorsit;

842 intereā excēdit caelō nūbemque relinquit.

> *Unaware that the conflict on Olympus has now been resolved and*
> *the future union of Italians and Trojans determined, Aeneas*
> *challenges Turnus to face him in a battle to the death*

887 Aenēās īnstat contrā tēlumque coruscat

888 ingēns arboreum, et saevō sīc pectore fātur:

889 "Quae nunc deinde mora est? Aut quid iam, Turne, retractās?

890 Nōn cursū, saevīs certandum est comminus armīs.

891 Verte omnēs tētē in faciēs et contrahe quidquid

892 sīve animīs sīve arte valēs; optā ardua pennīs

893 astra sequī clausumque cavā tē condere terrā."

> *Turnus replies and attempts to hurl a huge stone at Aeneas,*
> *but his strength fails him and the throw falls short*

894 Ille, caput quassāns: "Nōn mē tua fervida terrent

Quaestiōnēs

1. Compare the entire encounter between Jupiter and Juno in 791–842, the final divine dialogue in the poem and a denouement to the story's celestial action, with the poem's first such scene, the dialogue between Venus and Jupiter at 1.223–96 above. What functions do the two passages serve? In what specific ways are they complementary? Vergil invites us to compare in particular Jupiter's speeches of concession to the two goddesses, his daughter and his sister/wife, by introducing each speech (1.254f. and 12.829f.) with strikingly similar formulae (see note on line 829); what similarities are there between the two speeches, and are the concessions contradictory or complementary?

2. What consistencies are there in the characterization of Jupiter in the scenes at 1.223–96 and 12.791–842? What similarities are there in the roles played by Venus and Juno in these episodes? Evaluate the goddesses' interactions with Jupiter from the perspective of gender.

898 **līs, lītis,** f., *disagreement, dispute, quarreling.*

899 **illum:** m., to agree with **līmes (898),** though some mss. have **illud,** agreeing with **saxum (897).**

lēctī: *(carefully) chosen men.*

bis sex: a necessary poetic circumlocution, as **duodecim** with its series of consecutive short syllables does not fit into dactylic hexameter verse; the notion that the heroes of old were far more powerful than modern men is, like much else in the closing scenes of this book, Homeric (cf. *Iliad* 12.445f., of Hector).

900 **quālia . . . hominum . . . corpora:** *such bodies of men as = men of such physique as;* in appos. to **lēctī (899).**

901 **raptum:** sc. **saxum;** Eng. would use a vb., rather than the partic., *he caught it up and . . ..*

torquēbat: CONATIVE, *was attempting to . . ..*

902 **īnsurgō, īnsurgere, īnsurrēxī,** *to get up, rise* (here *to stretch*).

*concieō, conciēre, concīvī, concitus, *to stir up, rouse, set in motion.*

concitus: here *moving rapidly, speeding along;* Turnus runs forward and stretches out his arms as he attempts to throw the huge rock with all his might.

hērōs: with **ille (901),** and delayed to the end of the sent. in order to focus our attention on the man in this heroic posture one last time, before we see him in the following verses faltering, and fearful, and struck down by his mightier foe.

903 **neque . . . sē . . . cognōscit:** *he does not recognize himself,* i.e., he does not have his usual strength.

neque . . . nec . . . -ve . . . -ve (904): POLYSYNDETON enhances the cinematographic effect by prompting us to focus on each individual action; the rhyming of the four carefully positioned partics., **currentem . . . euntem / tollentem . . . moventem (904),** reinforces this effect, suggesting that Turnus attempted to act, but ineffectually, again and again and again.

904 **moventem:** here *throwing.*

905 **genua:** SYNIZESIS of the **u** here not only allows the word to be scanned as a disyllable, but also has the effect of lengthening the first syllable as a consequence of the **nu = nv** consonant cluster.

906 **lapis ipse virī:** the point is that not only does Turnus' usual strength fail him, but the stone he has hurled also seems somehow mystically to lack force; a cinematographer would film Turnus' actions and the rock itself, as it moves through the air towards its intended target, using slow-motion photography.

ināne: here substantive, *space.*

volūtus: lit., *turned,* i.e., thrown with a turning motion, = *whirling.*

907 **pertulit:** *carried the . . . all the way through* (to its target).

908 **velut in somnīs . . . / sīc (913):** in the Homeric SIMILE (*Iliad* 22.199f.) that inspired Vergil's image here, Achilles is in pursuit of Hector and cannot catch up to him, nor can Hector escape; Vergil makes the analogy even more vivid for his audience through his use of the first pers. pl. vbs. **vidēmur (910)** and **succidimus (911).**

895 dicta, feröx; dī mē terrent et Iuppiter hostis.”

896 Nec plūra effātus, saxum circumspicit ingēns,

897 saxum antīquum ingēns, campō quod forte iacēbat,

898 līmes agrō positus lītem ut discerneret arvīs.

899 Vix illum lēctī bis sex cervīce subīrent,

900 quālia nunc hominum prōdūcit corpora tellūs;

901 ille manū raptum trepidā torquēbat in hostem,

902 altior īnsurgēns et cursū concitus, hērōs.

903 Sed neque currentem sē nec cognōscit euntem

904 tollentemve manū saxumve immāne moventem;

905 genua labant; gelidus concrēvit frīgore sanguis.

906 Tum lapis ipse virī, vacuum per ināne volūtus,

907 nec spatium ēvāsit tōtum neque pertulit ictum.

Like a man in the midst of a nightmare, Turnus seems unable
to move or to speak and, panicked, he sees no escape

908   Ac velut in somnīs, oculōs ubi languida pressit

Quaestiōnēs

1. How does Vergil employ meter and other poetic effects in 896–97 to focus our attention on the size of the rock that Turnus sees?

2. What ironic point does Vergil intend to make with the detail provided in 898?

And as, when heavy sleep has clos'd the sight,
The sickly fancy labors in the night;
We seem to run; and, destitute of force,
Our sinking limbs forsake us in the course:
In vain we heave for breath; in vain we cry;
The nerves, unbrac'd, their usual strength deny;
And on the tongue the falt'ring accents die:
So Turnus far'd; whatever means he tried,
All force of arms and points of art employ'd,
The Fury flew athwart, and made th' endeavor void.

From the translation of John Dryden, 1698

910 **velle vidēmur:** the extensive ALLITERATION of **v** in this passage, continued esp. in 912–13, is possibly meant to lend an airy, dreamlike effect; at the very least it adds a delicate musicality to the dream sequence.

cōnātus, -ūs, m., *effort, attempt.*

aegrī: here *weak, faint.*

911 **succidō, succidere, succidī,** *to give way under one* (esp. of the knees); *to collapse, fall down.*

succidimus: this detail looks back to **genua labant** (905), just as **nōn . . . vīrēs** (911–12) recalls 903–04.

913 **quācumque,** adv., *wherever* (more likely than the view that the form is abl. of the adj. **quaecumque,** modifying **virtūte**).

914 **dea dīra:** the ALLITERATIVE phrase refers to the Furies, called **Dīrae** by Vergil in a lengthy description at 12.845–86, where Jupiter dispatches one of them to assail Turnus and and drive off his sister Juturna.

916 **lētum . . . īnstāre:** IND. STATE. with **tremēscit;** Aeneas has not yet cast his spear, and the threat Turnus feels is more general, so **lētum** is more likely the correct reading than **tēlum,** which appears in some of the mss. and is accepted by some editors.

tremēscō, tremēscere, *to tremble, quiver; to tremble at, dread.*

917 **quō . . . ēripiat, . . . quā . . . tendat:** IND. QUESTS. dependent on **videt;** Turnus feels helpless either to escape or to attack.

918 **aurīgam . . . sorōrem:** Juturna, who had courageously fought at Turnus' side, had been compelled to withdraw from the battle by one of the Furies (see above on 914).

919 **Cūnctantī:** the word echoes the identically positioned **cūnctātur** (916).

tēlum Aenēās . . . coruscat: the camera turns back to Aeneas, in slow spondaic rhythm, and we see him again just as we had at the opening of his previous scene—**Aenēās īnstat contrā tēlumque coruscat** (887)—poised to hurl his spear; but Vergil in this instance adds one crucial detail to his description of the Trojan's weapon, **fātāle,** which here means both *fated* and *fatal,* thus unambiguously foreshadowing the events soon to follow.

920 **sortītus fortūnam oculīs:** i.e., seeing, as Turnus faltered, a favorable opportunity to attack.

921 **ēminus,** adv., *from a great distance, at longe range.*

mūrālis, -is, -e, *of/relating to a city's wall/fortifications; for the assault of city-walls.*

numquam: with **sīc** (922); for the negative SIMILE, cf. 2.496–99.

922 **tormentum, -ī,** n., *rope; machine, catapult.*

Mūrālī concita . . . / tormentō . . . saxa (922): INTERLOCKED WORD ORDER; **mūrālī . . . tormentō,** freely, *from a siege-machine* (a catapult designed to hurl rocks against a city's fortification walls).

923 **dissultō, -āre,** *to leap forth from; to burst/flash forth.*

crepitus, -ūs, m., *loud noise, cracking/crashing sound, crack, crash.*

īnstar: here *like.*

924 **ōrās:** here *edge(s), rim.*

909 nocte quiēs, nēquīquam avidōs extendere cursūs
910 velle vidēmur et in mediīs cōnātibus aegrī
911 succidimus; nōn lingua valet, nōn corpore nōtae
912 sufficiunt vīrēs nec vōx aut verba sequuntur:
913 sīc Turnō, quācumque viam virtūte petīvit,
914 successum dea dīra negat. Tum pectore sēnsūs
915 vertuntur variī; Rutulōs aspectat et urbem
916 cūnctāturque metū lētumque īnstāre tremēscit,
917 nec quō sē ēripiat, nec quā vī tendat in hostem,
918 nec currūs usquam videt aurīgamve sorōrem.

*Aeneas casts his spear, which flies like a black tornado
and pierces Turnus' thigh, bringing him to bended knee*

919 Cūnctantī tēlum Aenēās fātāle coruscat,
920 sortītus fortūnam oculīs, et corpore tōtō
921 ēminus intorquet. Mūrālī concita numquam
922 tormentō sīc saxa fremunt nec fulmine tantī
923 dissultant crepitūs. Volat ātrī turbinis īnstar
924 exitium dīrum hasta ferēns ōrāsque reclūdit

Quaestiō

What significant differences do you see between Vergil's simile in 908–14 and the
Homeric original that inspired it in *Iliad* 22.199f.?

The hero measur'd first, with narrow view,
The destin'd mark; and, rising as he threw,
With its full swing the fatal weapon flew.
Not with less rage the rattling thunder falls,
Or stones from batt'ring-engines break the walls:
Swift as a whirlwind, from an arm so strong,
The lance drove on, and bore the death along.

From the translation of John Dryden, 1698

925 **extrēmōs:** here *at the bottom,* as the spear passes through Turnus' shield into his thigh (926).

septemplex, septemplicis, *sevenfold, seven-layered.*

clipeī . . . septemplicis: Bronze-Age shields, as Homer and Vergil described them and archaeology confirms, were made of multiple layers of bronze and animal hide; cf. the description of Pallas' shield at 10.482–85 above.

926 **femur, femoris,** n., *upper leg, thigh.*

Incidit, ictus, / ingēns (927): in the abrupt DIAERESES and harsh **c/g/d/t** ALLITERATION we hear the sudden violence of the spear's impact and mighty Turnus' fall to the ground.

927 **duplicātus, -a, -um,** *doubled (over), bent.*

poples, poplitis, m., *knee-joint, knee.*

duplicātō poplite: the buckling of Turnus' knee here recalls his earlier collapse at 905 (**genua labant**).

928 **cōnsurgō, cōnsurgere, cōnsurrēxī, consurrēctus,** *to rise up together, rise all at once.*

Cōnsurgunt . . . remittunt (929): Vergil's camera draws back from Turnus and pans the Rutulian army and the surrounding countryside; the army, and even the mountains and forests, groan in dismay.

930 **supplex:** here, as often, a substantive.

931 **prōtendō, prōtendere, prōtendī, prōtentus,** *to stretch forth, extend; to lift, raise.*

oculōs . . . (930) / prōtendēns: ZEUGMA, as the vb. has one sense with **oculōs** and another with **dextram.**

dēprecor, -ārī, -ātus sum, *to try to avert by prayer; to seek pardon, beg for mercy* (the word here plays on **precantem** in the preceding verse).

932 **sorte:** *opportunity,* an echo of **sortītus** in 920.

934 **Daunus, -ī,** m., *Daunus* (king of the Rutulians and aged father of Turnus and Juturna).

935 **seu corpus . . . māvīs:** = **vel corpus . . . sī māvīs.**

lūmine: here *life.*

936 **victum:** sc. **mē,** subj. of **tendere;** the wordplay with **vīcistī** effectively underscores Turnus' point.

tendere palmās: for the gesture, see note on 1.93.

937 **Lāvīnia, -ae,** f., *Lavinia* (only child of Amata and king Latinus, princess of Laurentum; see note on 805 above).

938 **ulterius:** though the point should not be pressed, it is tempting to suppose that Vergil may have intended an echo here of line 806 above, where the adv. is identically positioned in Jupiter's mandate to his queen not to press her hatred of the Trojans any further, **ulterius temptāre vetō;** Vergil certainly intends for us to see that, whereas Juno manages at last to control her **īra** and her **furor** and her **saevus dolor,** Aeneas in the end is utterly incapable of doing so (see below, esp. note on **saevī . . . dolōris 945**).

925 lōrīcae et clipeī extrēmōs septemplicis orbēs;
926 per medium strīdēns trānsit femur. Incidit, ictus,
927 ingēns ad terram duplicātō poplite Turnus.
928 Cōnsurgunt gemitū Rutulī tōtusque remūgit
929 mōns circum et vōcem lātē nemora alta remittunt.

> *The Rutulian prince concedes defeat and, as a suppliant, begs*
> *Aeneas to return him, or at least his corpse, to his aged father*

930   Ille humilis supplex oculōs dextramque precantem
931 prōtendēns, "Equidem meruī nec dēprecor," inquit;
932 "ūtere sorte tuā. Miserī tē sī qua parentis
933 tangere cūra potest, ōrō (fuit et tibi tālis
934 Anchīsēs genitor), Daunī miserēre senectae
935 et mē, seu corpus spoliātum lūmine māvīs,
936 redde meīs. Vīcistī et victum tendere palmās
937 Ausoniī vīdēre; tua est Lāvīnia coniūnx;
938 ulterius nē tende odiīs."

Quaestiōnēs

1. What is the term for the word order seen in **clipeī . . . orbēs** (925), and how is it here appropriate to the image Vergil is describing?

2. What device of word order is employed in 927, and what is its effect?

3. How might the extensive assonance of long and short **u** sounds in 928 be regarded as onomatopoetic, particularly in view of the action described in the emphatically positioned verbs, **remūgit** and **remittunt** (929)?

4. Analyze in detail Turnus' last, crucial speech in 930–38. What posture does he take in addressing Aeneas? What aspect of his character is reflected in the entreaty on behalf of his father? Consider not only what reasons Turnus may have for mentioning Aeneas' father, but also what Vergil's purposes may be in focusing on the relationship each man had to his own father. What victories does Turnus concede that Aeneas has won? And finally, what general appeal does Turnus make to Aeneas at the end of his speech, and why is this especially important here at the close of the poem?

939 **oculōs dextramque:** is this only an inadvertent echo of **oculōs dextramque** in identical position just nine lines earlier (930), or another allusion to the connection between these two men, who, although the bitterest of adversaries, have so many traits in common, not least of all their rage? Or perhaps, in yet another brilliant cinematographic touch, Vergil means to focus our attention first on Turnus' eyes and his right hand, in gestures of supplication and entreaty, and moments later on Aeneas' eyes, as he surveys his victim, and his right hand, which he holds back for an instant, hesitating on the brink of slaughter.

940 **cūnctantem:** applied to Aeneas here, to Turnus at 919 (**cūnctantī**).

941 **īnfēlīx . . . / balteus (942):** the cl. is very effectively FRAMED by displacement (ANASTROPHE) of the epithet, which gives it special prominence, and ENJAMBEMENT of the noun, which creates suspense. In fact, the entire ABCBA arrangement of the cl. (nom.-abl.-vb.-abl.-nom.) is at once highly visual and suspenseful: following the strong DIAERESIS at **coeperat** comes a hint of foreboding (**īnfēlīx**), then, as if through Aeneas' eyes (**volvēns oculōs** 939), we see Turnus' shoulder (**umerō**), where there appears (**cum appāruit**), high up on that shoulder (**altō**), the ill-fated belt (**balteus**), that fateful swordbelt stripped from Aeneas' young friend Pallas by Turnus (at 10.496–505 above) in his own moment of vengeful rage.

942 **bulla, -ae,** f., *bulla* (a magical charm); *stud, boss* (on engraved metalwork).

943 **puerī:** the detail serves as a reminder of how young Pallas was when he was slain by Turnus.

victum: a deliberate echo of **victum** in 936—Pallas had been at the mercy of Turnus, who could have spared him, just as Turnus is now at the mercy of Aeneas.

945 **oculīs:** purposely repeated from 939; the camera turns back to Aeneas' eyes, as through them he *drinks in* (**hausit** 946) this reminder of his young friend's death and is filled with terrible rage. For the metaphor **oculīs haurīre,** cf. 4.661–62, where it is also used in the context of death.

saevī . . . dolōris: the same phrase had been applied to Juno at the very outset of the poem, where Vergil attributed to the goddess a propensity for rage and vengefulness that he repeatedly suggests is shared by Aeneas himself; with **saevī monimenta dolōris** here and **furiīs accēnsus et īrā / terribilis** in 946–47, cf. **necdum etiam causae īrārum saevīque dolōrēs / exciderant animō** of Juno at 1.25–26 and **hīs accēnsa** at 1.29 (and see 801 and note above).

monimenta: used elsewhere of the Minotaur, **Veneris monimenta nefandae** (6.26).

948 **ēripiāre:** DELIBERATIVE SUBJUNCT., *are you to be . . . .*

949 **immolō (1),** *to offer* (a victim) *in sacrifice; to kill* (like a sacrificial victim), *sacrifice* (the word here deliberately suggests a ritual slaying).

poenam . . . sūmit: cf. **scelerātās sūmere poenās** (2.576), of Aeneas' desire to slay Helen.

950 **adversō . . . pectore:** as the action of lines 938–49 has taken only a matter of seconds, we should picture Turnus still down on his knee, with his right hand still extended in entreaty, his eyes upturned in supplication to Aeneas, and his chest therefore turned towards his enemy, exposed to his sword.

*Aeneas considers sparing Turnus, when, enraged by the sight of
Pallas' swordbelt on his enemy's shoulder, he buries his sword in
the Rutulian's chest and sends his soul fleeting to the shades*

Stetit ācer in armīs

939 Aenēās, volvēns oculōs, dextramque repressit;
940 et iam iamque magis cūnctantem flectere sermō
941 coeperat, īnfēlīx umerō cum appāruit altō
942 balteus et nōtīs fulsērunt cingula bullīs
943 Pallantis puerī, victum quem vulnere Turnus
944 strāverat atque umerīs inimīcum īnsigne gerēbat.
945 Ille, oculīs postquam saevī monimenta dolōris
946 exuviāsque hausit, furiīs accēnsus et īrā
947 terribilis: "Tūne hinc, spoliīs indūte meōrum,
948 ēripiāre mihī? Pallās tē hōc vulnere, Pallās
949 immolat et poenam scelerātō ex sanguine sūmit."
950 Hoc dīcēns, ferrum adversō sub pectore condit,

Quaestiōnēs

1. Servius' view is that in 938–39 Aeneas stands forth in all his glory, and doubly so, as his **pietās** is evidenced first when he considers showing Turnus mercy, and second when he slays his foe out of respect for Pallas' father Evander, who had (in 11.177f.) implored Aeneas to seek revenge against his son's murderer; is this a reasonable interpretation?

2. Comment on the dramatic effect of the anaphora and polysyndeton in 940 and the multiple instances of enjambement and hyperbaton in 941–44.

3. What is the point of the echo in **vulnere Pallās** (948) of **vulnere Turnus** (943)? How does the anaphora in 948 add to the effect?

4. Compare 941–49 with 10.496–505 above and discuss how Vergil had prepared us in that earlier episode for this last scene of the poem.

In deep suspense the Trojan seem'd to stand,
And, just prepar'd to strike, repress'd his hand.
He roll'd his eyes, and ev'ry moment felt
His manly soul with more compassion melt.

From the translation of John Dryden, 1698

951 **fervidus:** of Aeneas also in 894 above. The forcefully ENJAMBED epithet has great point: it is ASSONANT with **ferrum** (950), connecting Aeneas' violence with his wrath; it contrasts with **frīgore** (the heat of anger, the chill of death); it punctuates the sent. with a quick dactyl and an abrupt DIAERESIS, which is then followed by a series of spondees marking the cold spreading slowly through Turnus' collapsing limbs.

solvuntur frīgore membra: the same phrase, identically positioned, is used to describe Aeneas himself at his first appearance in the epic, just as he is about to express his dismay over the violent storm Aeolus had unleashed at Juno's instigation.

952 **vīta . . . umbrās:** the epic's final line (adapted from Homer and repeated from 11.831, where it had been used of the death of Turnus' ally, the Volscian warrior princess Camilla) begins with the word for life and ends in death and darkness; the flight of Turnus' soul is scored in quick dactyls to the line's midpoint, where the strong and unusually positioned DIAERESIS—a split second of thunderous silence—is followed by the sluggish, reluctant **indignāta.**

"The Death of Turnus"
Niccolo dell'Abate (1509/16–1571)
Galleria Estense, Modena, Italy

951 fervidus; ast illī solvuntur frīgore membra,
952 vītaque cum gemitū fugit, indignāta, sub umbrās.

Quaestiōnēs

1. What significance do you see in the fact that Vergil employs the very same phrase, **solvuntur frīgore membra,** in describing both Aeneas at his first appearance (1.92, above) and Turnus here in his final moment at the poem's close (951)?

2. Compare line 952 with Homer *Iliad* 16.856–57 and 22.362–63; why does Vergil end his poem with this deliberate recollection of Homer, and how does this resonance between the two epics enrich our understanding of this final scene of the *Aeneid?*

3. As you contemplate the poem's closing action, particularly in 930–52, consider again the issue raised earlier (in the discussion question on lines 791–842) of the hierarchy of power among gods, men, and fate. Does Aeneas follow the mandate given him by Anchises during their encounter at 6.851–53 above? Would the gods have wanted Aeneas to slay Turnus? Was the action fated?—and, if so, does Vergil conceive of fate as some external force beyond all control or rather is the human suffering in this final scene, and the suffering depicted throughout the poem, ultimately the consequence of man's own character? If Aeneas is responsible for his actions in this last moment of vengeance and rage, does he ultimately succeed as the poem's hero and emerge as victor, or does he fail, as the powerless victim of his own **saevus dolor, furia,** and **īra?**

"Vergil"
Joos (Justus) van Ghent
(ca. 1435–ca. 1480)
Oil on wood
Louvre
Paris, France

Summary of Forms

I. Nouns

Number Case	1st Declension Fem.	2nd Declension Masc.	Masc.	Masc.	Neut.
Singular					
Nominative	puell**a**	servus	puer	ager	bacul**um**
Genitive	puell**ae**	serv**ī**	puer**ī**	agr**ī**	bacul**ī**
Dative	puell**ae**	serv**ō**	puer**ō**	agr**ō**	bacul**ō**
Accusative	puell**am**	serv**um**	puer**um**	agr**um**	bacul**um**
Ablative	puell**ā**	serv**ō**	puer**ō**	agr**ō**	bacul**ō**
Vocative	puell**a**	serv**e**	puer	ager	bacul**um**
Plural					
Nominative	puell**ae**	serv**ī**	puer**ī**	agr**ī**	bacul**a**
Genitive	puell**ārum**	serv**ōrum**	puer**ōrum**	agr**ōrum**	bacul**ōrum**
Dative	puell**īs**	serv**īs**	puer**īs**	agr**īs**	bacul**īs**
Accusative	puell**ās**	serv**ōs**	puer**ōs**	agr**ōs**	bacul**a**
Ablative	puell**īs**	serv**īs**	puer**īs**	agr**īs**	bacul**īs**
Vocative	puell**ae**	serv**ī**	puer**ī**	agr**ī**	bacul**a**

N.B.: In 2nd decl. nouns that end -**ius**, the voc. sing. is -ī (e.g., **nūntī**, voc. of **nūntius**).

Number Case	3rd Declension M./F.	Neut.	M./F.	Neut.	4th Declension Masc.	Neut.	5th Declension Masc.	Fem.
Singular								
Nominative	dux	nōmen	cīv**is**	mare	arc**us**	gen**ū**	di**ēs**	r**ēs**
Genitive	duc**is**	nōmin**is**	cīv**is**	mar**is**	arc**ūs**	gen**ūs**	di**ēī**	re**ī**
Dative	duc**ī**	nōmin**ī**	cīv**ī**	mar**ī**	arc**uī**	gen**ū**	di**ēī**	re**ī**
Accusative	duc**em**	nōmen	cīv**em**	mare	arc**um**	gen**ū**	di**em**	r**em**
Ablative	duc**e**	nōmin**e**	cīv**e**	mar**ī**	arc**ū**	gen**ū**	di**ē**	r**ē**
Vocative	dux	nōmen	cīv**is**	mar**e**	arc**us**	gen**ū**	di**ēs**	r**ēs**
Plural								
Nominative	duc**ēs**	nōmin**a**	cīv**ēs**	mar**ia**	arc**ūs**	gen**ua**	di**ēs**	r**ēs**
Genitive	duc**um**	nōmin**um**	cīv**ium**	mar**ium**	arc**uum**	gen**uum**	di**ērum**	r**ērum**
Dative	duc**ibus**	nōmin**ibus**	cīv**ibus**	mar**ibus**	arc**ibus**	gen**ibus**	di**ēbus**	r**ēbus**
Accusative	duc**ēs**	nōmin**a**	cīv**ēs**	mar**ia**	arc**ūs**	gen**ua**	di**ēs**	r**ēs**
Ablative	duc**ibus**	nōmin**ibus**	cīv**ibus**	mar**ibus**	arc**ibus**	gen**ibus**	di**ēbus**	r**ēbus**
Vocative	duc**ēs**	nōmin**a**	cīv**ēs**	mar**ia**	arc**ūs**	gen**ua**	di**ēs**	r**ēs**

N.B.: **cīvis** and **mare** are typical of 3rd decl. **i**-stem nouns.
5th decl. nouns have gen. & dat. sing. in -**ēī** if the stem ends -**i**-; otherwise -**eī**.

II. Adjectives

Number Case	1st and 2nd Declensions			3rd Declension		
	Masc.	Fem.	Neut.	Masc.	Fem.	Neut.
Singular						
Nominative	magn**us**	magn**a**	magn**um**	omn**is**	omn**is**	omn**e**
Genitive	magn**ī**	magn**ae**	magn**ī**	omn**is**	omn**is**	omn**is**
Dative	magn**ō**	magn**ae**	magn**ō**	omn**ī**	omn**ī**	omn**ī**
Accusative	magn**um**	magn**am**	magn**um**	omn**em**	omn**em**	omn**e**
Ablative	magn**ō**	magn**ā**	magn**ō**	omn**ī**	omn**ī**	omn**ī**
Vocative	magn**e**	magn**a**	magn**um**	omn**is**	omn**is**	omn**e**
Plural						
Nominative	magn**ī**	magn**ae**	magn**a**	omn**ēs**	omn**ēs**	omn**ia**
Genitive	magn**ōrum**	magn**ārum**	magn**ōrum**	omn**ium**	omn**ium**	omn**ium**
Dative	magn**īs**	magn**īs**	magn**īs**	omn**ibus**	omn**ibus**	omn**ibus**
Accusative	magn**ōs**	magn**ās**	magn**a**	omn**ēs**	omn**ēs**	omn**ia**
Ablative	magn**īs**	magn**īs**	magn**īs**	omn**ibus**	omn**ibus**	omn**ibus**
Vocative	magn**ī**	magn**ae**	magn**a**	omn**ēs**	omn**ēs**	omn**ia**

III. Comparative Adjectives

Number Case	Masc.	Fem.	Neut.
Singular			
Nominative	laetior	laetior	laetius
Genitive	laetiōr**is**	laetiōr**is**	laetiōr**is**
Dative	laetiōr**ī**	laetiōr**ī**	laetiōr**ī**
Accusative	laetiōr**em**	laetiōr**em**	laetius
Ablative	laetiōr**e**	laetiōr**e**	laetiōr**e**
Plural			
Nominative	laetiōr**ēs**	laetiōr**ēs**	laetiōr**a**
Genitive	laetiōr**um**	laetiōr**um**	laetiōr**um**
Dative	laetiōr**ibus**	laetiōr**ibus**	laetiōr**ibus**
Accusative	laetiōr**ēs**	laetiōr**ēs**	laetiōr**a**
Ablative	laetiōr**ibus**	laetiōr**ibus**	laetiōr**ibus**

Adjectives have positive, comparative, and superlative forms. You can usually recognize the comparative by the letters *-ior(-)* and the superlative by *-issimus, -errimus,* or *-illimus*:

Positive	Comparative	Superlative
ignāvus, -a, -um, *lazy*	ignāvior, ignāvius	ignāvissimus, -a, -um
pulcher, pulchra, pulchrum, *beautiful*	pulchrior, pulchrius	pulcherrimus, -a, -um
facilis, -is, -e, *easy*	facilior, facilius	facillimus, -a, -um

Some very common adjectives are irregular in the comparative and superlative:

Positive	Comparative	Superlative
bonus, -a, -um, *good*	**melior, melius,** *better*	**optimus, -a, -um,** *best*
malus, -a, -um, *bad*	**peior, peius,** *worse*	**pessimus, -a, -um,** *worst*
magnus, -a, -um, *big*	**maior, maius,** *bigger*	**maximus, -a, -um,** *biggest*
parvus, -a, -um, *small*	**minor, minus,** *smaller*	**minimus, -a, -um,** *smallest*
multus, -a, -um, *much*	**plūs,** *more*	**plūrimus, -a, -um,** *most, very much*
multī, -ae, -a, *many*	**plūrēs, plūra,** *more*	**plūrimī, -ae, -a,** *most, very many*

N.B.: The singular **plūs** is not an adjective but a neuter substantive, usually found with a partitive genitive, e.g., **Titus plūs vīnī bibit.** *Titus drank **more (of the) wine**.*

IV. Present Participles

Number Case	Masc.	Fem.	Neut.
Singular			
Nominative	portāns	portāns	portāns
Genitive	portant**is**	portant**is**	portant**is**
Dative	portant**ī**	portant**ī**	portant**ī**
Accusative	portant**em**	portant**em**	portāns
Ablative	portant**ī/e**	portant**ī/e**	portant**ī/e**
Plural			
Nominative	portant**ēs**	portant**ēs**	portant**ia**
Genitive	portant**ium**	portant**ium**	portant**ium**
Dative	portant**ibus**	portant**ibus**	portant**ibus**
Accusative	portant**ēs**	portant**ēs**	portant**ia**
Ablative	portant**ibus**	portant**ibus**	portant**ibus**

V. Numbers

Case	Masc.	Fem.	Neut.	Masc.	Fem.	Neut.	Masc.	Fem.	Neut.
Nom.	ūn*us*	ūn*a*	ūn*um*	duo	du*ae*	duo	tr*ēs*	tr*ēs*	tr*ia*
Gen.	ūn*īus*	ūn*īus*	ūn*īus*	du*ōrum*	du*ārum*	du*ōrum*	tr*ium*	tr*ium*	tr*ium*
Dat.	ūn*ī*	ūn*ī*	ūn*ī*	du*ōbus*	du*ābus*	du*ōbus*	tr*ibus*	tr*ibus*	tr*ibus*
Acc.	ūn*um*	ūn*am*	ūn*um*	du*ōs*	du*ās*	duo	tr*ēs*	tr*ēs*	tr*ia*
Abl.	ūn*ō*	ūn*ā*	ūn*ō*	du*ōbus*	du*ābus*	du*ōbus*	tr*ibus*	tr*ibus*	tr*ibus*

	Cardinal	**Ordinal**
I	ūnus, -a, -um, *one*	prīmus, -a, -um, *first*
II	duo, -ae, -o, *two*	secundus, -a, -um, *second*
III	trēs, trēs, tria, *three*	tertius, -a, -um, *third*
IV	quattuor, *four*	quārtus, -a, -um, *fourth*
V	quīnque, *five*	quīntus, -a, -um, *fifth*
VI	sex, *six*	sextus, -a, -um, *sixth*
VII	septem, *seven*	septimus, -a, -um, *seventh*
VIII	octō, *eight*	octāvus, -a, -um, *eighth*
IX	novem, *nine*	nōnus, -a, -um, *ninth*
X	decem, *ten*	decimus, -a, -um, *tenth*
XI	ūndecim, *eleven*	ūndecimus, -a, -um, *eleventh*
XII	duodecim, *twelve*	duodecimus, -a, -um, *twelfth*
XIII	trēdecim, *thirteen*	tertius decimus, -a, -um, *thirteenth*
XIV	quattuordecim, *fourteen*	quārtus decimus, -a, -um, *fourteenth*
XV	quīndecim, *fifteen*	quīntus decimus, -a, -um, *fifteenth*
XVI	sēdecim, *sixteen*	sextus decimus, -a, -um, *sixteenth*
XVII	septendecim, *seventeen*	septimus decimus, -a, -um, *seventeenth*
XVIII	duodēvīgintī, *eighteen*	duodēvīcēsimus, -a, -um, *eighteenth*
XIX	ūndēvīgintī, *nineteen*	ūndēvīcēsimus, -a, -um, *nineteenth*
XX	vīgintī, *twenty*	vīcēsimus, -a, -um, *twentieth*
L	quīnquāgintā, *fifty*	quīnquāgēsimus, -a, -um, *fiftieth*
C	centum, *a hundred*	centēsimus, -a, -um, *hundredth*
D	quīngentī, -ae, -a, *five hundred*	quīngentēsimus, -a, -um, *five hundredth*
M	mīlle, *a thousand;* mīlia, *thousands*	mīllēsimus, -a, -um, *thousandth*

N.B.: The cardinal numbers from **quattuor** to **centum** do not change their form to indicate case and gender. Mīlle is also indeclinable in the singular, but the plural declines as a neuter and takes a partititve genitive: e.g., **mīlle virī**, *a thousand men;* **duo mīlia virōrum**, *two thousand(s of) men.*

The following adjectives have -īus in the gen. sing. and -ī in the dat. sing., just as does ūnus above: **alius, -a, -ud**, *other;* **alter, altera, alterum**, *another;* **ūllus, -a, -um**, *any;* **nūllus, -a, -um**, *no;* **sōlus, -a, -um**, *alone;* **tōtus, -a, -um**, *all;* **uter, utra, utrum**, *which (of two);* **neuter, neutra, neutrum**, *neither;* and **uterque, utraque, utrumque**, *both.*

VI. Personal Pronouns

Number Case	1st Person	2nd Person	3rd Person		
			Masc.	Fem.	Neut.
Singular					
Nominative	ego	tū	is	ea	id
Genitive	meī	tuī	eius	eius	eius
Dative	mihi	tibi	eī	eī	eī
Accusative	mē	tē	eum	eam	id
Ablative	mē	tē	eō	eā	eō
Plural					
Nominative	nōs	vōs	eī	eae	ea
Genitive	nostrī	vestrī	eōrum	eārum	eōrum
	nostrum	vestrum			
Dative	nōbīs	vōbīs	eīs	eīs	eīs
Accusative	nōs	vōs	eōs	eās	ea
Ablative	nōbīs	vōbīs	eīs	eīs	eīs

N.B.: The forms of **is, ea, id** may also serve as demonstrative adjectives, meaning either *this* or *that*.

VII. Reflexive Pronoun

Number Case	Singular	Plural
Singular		
Nominative	—	—
Genitive	suī	suī
Dative	sibi	sibi
Accusative	sē	sē
Ablative	sē	sē

VIII. Relative Pronoun

Number Case	Masc.	Fem.	Neut.
Singular			
Nominative	quī	quae	quod
Genitive	cuius	cuius	cuius
Dative	cui	cui	cui
Accusative	quem	quam	quod
Ablative	quō	quā	quō
Plural			
Nominative	quī	quae	quae
Genitive	quōrum	quārum	quōrum
Dative	quibus	quibus	quibus
Accusative	quōs	quās	quae
Ablative	quibus	quibus	quibus

IX. Interrogative Pronoun

Number Case	Masc.	Fem.	Neut.
Singular			
Nominative	quis	quis	quid
Genitive	cuius	cuius	cuius
Dative	cui	cui	cui
Accusative	quem	quem	quid
Ablative	quō	quō	quō
Plural	Same as the plural of the relative pronoun in chart VIII above.		

X. Indefinite Adjectives and Pronouns

Number Case	Masc.	Fem.	Neut.	Masc.	Fem.	Neut.
Singular						
Nominative	quīdam	quaedam	quoddam	aliquī	aliqua	aliquod
Genitive	cuiusdam	cuiusdam	cuiusdam	alicuius	alicuius	alicuius
Dative	cuidam	cuidam	cuidam	alicui	alicui	alicui
Accusative	quendam	quandam	quoddam	aliquem	aliquam	aliquod
Ablative	quōdam	quādam	quōdam	aliquō	aliquā	aliquō
Plural						
Nominative	quīdam	quaedam	quaedam	aliquī	aliquae	aliqua
Genitive	quōrundam	quārundam	quōrundam	aliquōrum	aliquārum	aliquōrum
Dative	quibusdam	quibusdam	quibusdam	aliquibus	aliquibus	aliquibus
Accusative	quōsdam	quāsdam	quaedam	aliquōs	aliquās	aliqua
Ablative	quibusdam	quibusdam	quibusdam	aliquibus	aliquibus	aliquibus

N.B.: The indefinite pronoun **quīdam, quaedam, quiddam**, *a certain*, pl., *certain, some*, has the same forms as the indefinite adjective, except for **quiddam** in the neuter nominative and accusative singular.

The indefinite pronoun **aliquis, aliquis, aliquid**, *someone, anyone*, has the regular forms of the interrogative pronoun **quis, quis, quid**, as do the indefinite pronouns **quisque, quisque, quidque**, *each one, every one*, **quispiam, quaepiam, quodpiam**, *someone, anyone*, and **quisquam, quisquam, quidquam** (**quicquam**), *someone, anyone*.

Quisque and **quispiam** are used as adjectives as well as pronouns. When they are adjectives, they decline like the relative pronoun **quī, quae, quod** (i.e., **quī** rather than **quis** in the masc. nom. sing., and **quod** rather than **quid** in the neuter sing.).

The indefinite pronoun **quisquis, quisquis, quidquid**, *whoever*, also has the same forms as **quis, quis, quid**, but note that both halves of this word are declined.

XI. Demonstrative Adjectives and Pronouns

Number Case	Masc.	Fem.	Neut.	Masc.	Fem.	Neut.
Singular						
Nominative	hic	haec	hoc	ille	illa	illud
Genitive	huius	huius	huius	illīus	illīus	illīus
Dative	huic	huic	huic	illī	illī	illī
Accusative	hunc	hanc	hoc	illum	illam	illud
Ablative	hōc	hāc	hōc	illō	illā	illō
Plural						
Nominative	hī	hae	haec	illī	illae	illa
Genitive	hōrum	hārum	hōrum	illōrum	illārum	illōrum
Dative	hīs	hīs	hīs	illīs	illīs	illīs
Accusative	hōs	hās	haec	illōs	illās	illa
Ablative	hīs	hīs	hīs	illīs	illīs	illīs

Number Case	Masc.	Fem.	Neut.
Singular			
Nominative	ipse	ipsa	ipsum
Genitive	ipsīus	ipsīus	ipsīus
Dative	ipsī	ipsī	ipsī
Accusative	ipsum	ipsam	ipsum
Ablative	ipsō	ipsā	ipsō
Plural			
Nominative	ipsī	ipsae	ipsa
Genitive	ipsōrum	ipsārum	ipsōrum
Dative	ipsīs	ipsīs	ipsīs
Accusative	ipsōs	ipsās	ipsa
Ablative	ipsīs	ipsīs	ipsīs

Number Case	Masc.	Fem.	Neut.	Masc.	Fem.	Neut.
Singular						
Nominative	is	ea	id	īdem	eadem	idem
Genitive	eius	eius	eius	eiusdem	eiusdem	eiusdem
Dative	eī	eī	eī	eīdem	eīdem	eīdem
Accusative	eum	eam	id	eundem	eandem	idem
Ablative	eō	eā	eō	eōdem	eādem	eōdem
Plural						
Nominative	eī	eae	ea	eīdem	eaedem	eadem
Genitive	eōrum	eārum	eōrum	eōrundem	eārundem	eōrundem
Dative	eīs	eīs	eīs	eīsdem	eīsdem	eīsdem
Accusative	eōs	eās	ea	eōsdem	eāsdem	eadem
Ablative	eīs	eīs	eīs	eīsdem	eīsdem	eīsdem

N.B.: Nom. pl. **iī** is sometimes found instead of **eī**, and dat./abl. pl. **iīs** instead of **eīs**.

XII. Adverbs

Latin adverbs may be formed from adjectives of the 1st and 2nd declensions by adding -*ē* to the base of the adjective, e.g., **strēnuē**, *strenuously*, from **strēnuus, -a, -um**. To form an adverb from a 3rd declension adjective, add -*(i)ter* to the base of the adjective or -*er* to bases ending in -**nt**-, e.g., <u>brev**iter**</u>, *briefly*, from **brevis, -is, -e**, and <u>prūdent**er**</u>, *wisely*, from **prūdēns, prūdentis**.

laet**ē**, *happily*	laet**ius**	laet**issimē**
audāc**ter**, *boldly*	audāc**ius**	audāc**issimē**
fēlīc**iter**, *luckily*	fēlīc**ius**	fēlīc**issimē**
celer**iter**, *quickly*	celer**ius**	celer**rimē**
prūdent**er**, *wisely*	prūdent**ius**	prūdent**issimē**

Note the following as well:

diū, *for a long time*	diūt**ius**	diūt**issimē**
saepe, *often*	saep**ius**	saep**issimē**
sērō, *late*	sēr**ius**	sēr**issimē**

Some adverbs are irregular:

bene, *well*	**melius**, *better*	**optimē**, *best*
male, *badly*	**peius**, *worse*	**pessimē**, *worst*
facile, *easily*	**facilius**, *more easily*	**facillimē**, *most easily*
magnopere, *greatly*	**magis**, *more*	**maximē**, *most*
paulum, *little*	**minus**, *less*	**minimē**, *least*
multum, *much*	**plūs**, *more*	**plūrimum**, *most*

XIII. Regular Verbs Active: Infinitive, Imperative, Indicative

			1st Conjugation	2nd Conjugation	3rd Conjugation		4th Conjugation
	Infinitive		port**āre**	mov**ēre**	mitt**ere**	iac**ere** (-iō)	aud**īre**
	Imperative		port**ā**	mov**ē**	mitt**e**	iac**e**	aud**ī**
			port**āte**	mov**ēte**	mitt**ite**	iac**ite**	aud**īte**
Present	Sing.	1	port**ō**	move**ō**	mitt**ō**	iaci**ō**	audi**ō**
		2	port**ās**	move**s**	mitti**s**	iaci**s**	aud**īs**
		3	porta**t**	move**t**	mitti**t**	iaci**t**	audi**t**
	Pl.	1	port**āmus**	mov**ēmus**	mitt**imus**	iac**imus**	aud**īmus**
		2	port**ātis**	mov**ētis**	mitt**itis**	iac**itis**	aud**ītis**
		3	porta**nt**	move**nt**	mitt**unt**	iaci**unt**	audi**unt**
Imperfect	Sing.	1	port**ābam**	mov**ēbam**	mitt**ēbam**	iaci**ēbam**	audi**ēbam**
		2	port**ābās**	mov**ēbās**	mitt**ēbās**	iaci**ēbās**	audi**ēbās**
		3	port**ābat**	mov**ēbat**	mitt**ēbat**	iaci**ēbat**	audi**ēbat**
	Pl.	1	port**ābāmus**	mov**ēbāmus**	mitt**ēbāmus**	iaci**ēbāmus**	audi**ēbāmus**
		2	port**ābātis**	mov**ēbātis**	mitt**ēbātis**	iaci**ēbātis**	audi**ēbātis**
		3	port**ābant**	mov**ēbant**	mitt**ēbant**	iaci**ēbant**	audi**ēbant**
Future	Sing.	1	port**ābō**	mov**ēbō**	mitt**am**	iaci**am**	audi**am**
		2	port**ābis**	mov**ēbis**	mitt**ēs**	iaci**ēs**	audi**ēs**
		3	port**ābit**	mov**ēbit**	mitt**et**	iaci**et**	audi**et**
	Pl.	1	port**ābimus**	mov**ēbimus**	mitt**ēmus**	iaci**ēmus**	audi**ēmus**
		2	port**ābitis**	mov**ēbitis**	mitt**ētis**	iaci**ētis**	audi**ētis**
		3	port**ābunt**	mov**ēbunt**	mitt**ent**	iaci**ent**	audi**ent**
Perfect	Sing.	1	port**āvī**	mōv**ī**	mīs**ī**	iēc**ī**	aud**īvī**
		2	port**āvistī**	mōv**istī**	mīs**istī**	iēc**istī**	aud**īvistī**
		3	port**āvit**	mōv**it**	mīs**it**	iēc**it**	aud**īvit**
	Pl.	1	port**āvimus**	mōv**imus**	mīs**imus**	iēc**imus**	aud**īvimus**
		2	port**āvistis**	mōv**istis**	mīs**istis**	iēc**istis**	aud**īvistis**
		3	port**āvērunt**	mōv**ērunt**	mīs**ērunt**	iēc**ērunt**	aud**īvērunt**
Pluperfect	Sing.	1	port**āveram**	mōv**eram**	mīs**eram**	iēc**eram**	aud**īveram**
		2	port**āverās**	mōv**erās**	mīs**erās**	iēc**erās**	aud**īverās**
		3	port**āverat**	mōv**erat**	mīs**erat**	iēc**erat**	aud**īverat**
	Pl.	1	port**āverāmus**	mōv**erāmus**	mīs**erāmus**	iēc**erāmus**	aud**īverāmus**
		2	port**āverātis**	mōv**erātis**	mīs**erātis**	iēc**erātis**	aud**īverātis**
		3	port**āverant**	mōv**erant**	mīs**erant**	iēc**erant**	aud**īverant**
Future Perfect	Sing.	1	port**āverō**	mōv**erō**	mīs**erō**	iēc**erō**	aud**īverō**
		2	port**āveris**	mōv**eris**	mīs**eris**	iēc**eris**	aud**īveris**
		3	port**āverit**	mōv**erit**	mīs**erit**	iēc**erit**	aud**īverit**
	Pl.	1	port**āverimus**	mōv**erimus**	mīs**erimus**	iēc**erimus**	aud**īverimus**
		2	port**āveritis**	mōv**eritis**	mīs**eritis**	iēc**eritis**	aud**īveritis**
		3	port**āverint**	mōv**erint**	mīs**erint**	iēc**erint**	aud**īverint**

XIV. Regular Verbs Passive: Infinitive, Imperative, Indicative

			1st Conjugation	2nd Conjugation	3rd Conjugation		4th Conjugation
	Infinitive		port*ārī*	mov*ērī*	mitt*ī*	iac*ī* (-iō)	aud*īrī*
	Imperative		port*āre*	mov*ēre*	mitt*ere*	iac*ere*	aud*īre*
			port*āminī*	mov*ēminī*	mitt*iminī*	iac*iminī*	aud*īminī*
Present	Sing.	1	port*or*	move*or*	mitt*or*	iaci*or*	audi*or*
		2	port*āris*	mov*ēris*	mitt*eris*	iac*eris*	aud*īris*
		3	port*ātur*	mov*ētur*	mitti*tur*	iaci*tur*	aud*ītur*
	Pl.	1	port*āmur*	mov*ēmur*	mitti*mur*	iaci*mur*	aud*īmur*
		2	port*āminī*	mov*ēminī*	mitt*iminī*	iac*iminī*	aud*īminī*
		3	porta*ntur*	move*ntur*	mittu*ntur*	iaciu*ntur*	audiu*ntur*
Imperfect	Sing.	1	portā*bar*	movē*bar*	mittē*bar*	iaciē*bar*	audiē*bar*
		2	portā*bāris*	movē*bāris*	mittē*bāris*	iaciē*bāris*	audiē*bāris*
		3	portā*bātur*	movē*bātur*	mittē*bātur*	iaciē*bātur*	audiē*bātur*
	Pl.	1	portā*bāmur*	movē*bāmur*	mittē*bāmur*	iaciē*bāmur*	audiē*bāmur*
		2	portā*bāminī*	movē*bāminī*	mittē*bāminī*	iaciē*bāminī*	audiē*bāminī*
		3	portā*bantur*	movē*bantur*	mittē*bantur*	iaciē*bantur*	audiē*bantur*
Future	Sing.	1	portā*bor*	movē*bor*	mitt*ar*	iaci*ar*	audi*ar*
		2	portā*beris*	movē*beris*	mitt*ēris*	iaci*ēris*	audi*ēris*
		3	portā*bitur*	movē*bitur*	mitt*ētur*	iaci*ētur*	audi*ētur*
	Pl.	1	portā*bimur*	movē*bimur*	mitt*ēmur*	iaci*ēmur*	audi*ēmur*
		2	portā*biminī*	movē*biminī*	mitt*ēminī*	iaci*ēminī*	audi*ēminī*
		3	portā*buntur*	movē*buntur*	mitt*entur*	iaci*entur*	audi*entur*

		Perfect Passive		Pluperfect Passive		Future Perfect Passive	
Sing.	1	portātus, -a	sum	portātus, -a	eram	portātus, -a	erō
	2	portātus, -a	es	portātus, -a	erās	portātus, -a	eris
	3	portātus, -a, -um	est	portātus, -a, -um	erat	portātus, -a, -um	erit
Pl.	1	portātī, -ae	sumus	portātī, -ae	erāmus	portātī, -ae	erimus
	2	portātī, -ae	estis	portātī, -ae	erātis	portātī, -ae	eritis
	3	portātī, -ae, -a	sunt	portātī, -ae, -a	erant	portātī, -ae, -a	erunt

N.B.: The perfect passive, pluperfect passive, and future perfect passive are formed the same way for all conjugations (fourth principal part with a form of **esse**).

XV. Deponent Verbs

Deponent verbs are conjugated in the same way as passive verbs of the same conjugation; e.g., **cōnārī** is conjugated like the passive of **portāre** (**cōnor** ≈ portor, **cōnāris** ≈ portāris, etc.).

XVI. Regular Verbs Active: Subjunctive

			1st Conjugation	2nd Conjugation	3rd Conjugation		4th Conjugation
Present	Sing.	1	port*em*	move*am*	mitt*am*	iaci*am*	audi*am*
		2	port*ēs*	move*ās*	mitt*ās*	iaci*ās*	audi*ās*
		3	port*et*	move*at*	mitt*at*	iaci*at*	audi*at*
	Pl.	1	port*ēmus*	move*āmus*	mitt*āmus*	iaci*āmus*	audi*āmus*
		2	port*ētis*	move*ātis*	mitt*ātis*	iaci*ātis*	audi*ātis*
		3	port*ent*	move*ant*	mitt*ant*	iaci*ant*	audi*ant*
Imperfect	Sing.	1	portāre*m*	movēre*m*	mittere*m*	iacere*m*	audīre*m*
		2	portāre*s*	movērē*s*	mitterē*s*	iacerē*s*	audīrē*s*
		3	portāre*t*	movēre*t*	mittere*t*	iacere*t*	audīre*t*
	Pl.	1	portārē*mus*	movērē*mus*	mitterē*mus*	iacerē*mus*	audīrē*mus*
		2	portārē*tis*	movērē*tis*	mitterē*tis*	iacerē*tis*	audīrē*tis*
		3	portāre*nt*	movēre*nt*	mittere*nt*	iacere*nt*	audīre*nt*
Perfect	Sing.	1	portāv*erim*	mōv*erim*	mīs*erim*	iēc*erim*	audīv*erim*
		2	portāv*eris*	mōv*eris*	mīs*eris*	iēc*eris*	audīv*eris*
		3	portāv*erit*	mōv*erit*	mīs*erit*	iēc*erit*	audīv*erit*
	Pl.	1	portāv*erimus*	mōv*erimus*	mīs*erimus*	iēc*erimus*	audīv*erimus*
		2	portāv*eritis*	mōv*eritis*	mīs*eritis*	iēc*eritis*	audīv*eritis*
		3	portāv*erint*	mōv*erint*	mīs*erint*	iēc*erint*	audīv*erint*
Pluperfect	Sing.	1	portāviss*em*	mōviss*em*	mīsiss*em*	iēciss*em*	audīviss*em*
		2	portavissē*s*	mōvissē*s*	mīsissē*s*	iēcissē*s*	audīvissē*s*
		3	portāvisse*t*	mōvisse*t*	mīsisse*t*	iēcisse*t*	audīvisse*t*
	Pl.	1	portāvissē*mus*	mōvissē*mus*	mīsissē*mus*	iēcissē*mus*	audīvissē*mus*
		2	portāvissē*tis*	mōvissē*tis*	mīsissē*tis*	iēcissē*tis*	audīvissē*tis*
		3	portāvisse*nt*	mōvisse*nt*	mīsisse*nt*	iēcisse*nt*	audīvisse*nt*

N.B.: The **-i-** in the 2nd pers. sg. and pl. and 1st pers. pl. perf. subjunct. may be long or short.

XVII. Regular Verbs Passive: Subjunctive

			1st Conjugation	2nd Conjugation	3rd Conjugation		4th Conjugation
Present	Sing.	1	port*er*	move*ar*	mitt*ar*	iaci*ar*	audi*ar*
		2	port*ēris*	move*āris*	mitt*āris*	iaci*āris*	audi*āris*
		3	port*ētur*	move*ātur*	mitt*ātur*	iaci*ātur*	audi*ātur*
	Sing.	1	port*ēmur*	move*āmur*	mitt*āmur*	iaci*āmur*	audi*āmur*
		2	port*ēminī*	move*āminī*	mitt*āminī*	iaci*āminī*	audi*āminī*
		3	port*entur*	move*antur*	mitt*antur*	iaci*antur*	audi*antur*
Imperfect	Sing.	1	portāre*r*	movēre*r*	mittere*r*	iacere*r*	audīre*r*
		2	portārē*ris*	movērē*ris*	mitterē*ris*	iacerē*ris*	audīrē*ris*
		3	portārē*tur*	movērē*tur*	mitterē*tur*	iacerē*tur*	audīrē*tur*
	Sing.	1	portārē*mur*	movērē*mur*	mitterē*mur*	iacerē*mur*	audīrē*mur*
		2	portārē*minī*	movērē*minī*	mitterē*minī*	iacerē*minī*	audīrē*minī*
		3	portāre*ntur*	movēre*ntur*	mittere*ntur*	iacere*ntur*	audīre*ntur*
Perfect		1	portātus sim etc.	mōtus sim etc.	missus sim etc.	iactus sim etc.	audītus sim etc.
Pluperfect		1	portātus essem etc.	mōtus essem etc.	missus essem etc.	iactus essem etc.	audītus essem etc.

XVIII. Irregular Verbs: Infinitive, Imperative, Indicative

	Infinitive	esse	posse	velle	nōlle	mālle
	Imperative	es este	— —	— —	nōlī nōlīte	— —
Present	Sing. 1	sum	possum	volō	nōlō	mālō
	2	es	potes	vīs	nōn vīs	māvīs
	3	est	potest	vult	nōn vult	māvult
	Pl. 1	sumus	possumus	volumus	nōlumus	mālumus
	2	estis	potestis	vultis	nōn vultis	māvultis
	3	sunt	possunt	volunt	nōlunt	mālunt
Imperfect	Sing. 1	eram	poteram	volēbam	nōlēbam	mālēbam
	2	erās	poterās	volēbās	nōlēbās	mālēbās
	3	erat	poterat	volēbat	nōlēbat	mālēbat
	Pl. 1	erāmus	poterāmus	volēbāmus	nōlēbāmus	mālēbāmus
	2	erātis	poterātis	volēbātis	nōlēbātis	mālēbātis
	3	erant	poterant	volēbant	nōlēbant	mālēbant
Future	Sing. 1	erō	poterō	volam	nōlam	mālam
	2	eris	poteris	volēs	nōlēs	mālēs
	3	erit	poterit	volet	nōlet	mālet
	Pl. 1	erimus	poterimus	volēmus	nōlēmus	mālēmus
	2	eritis	poteritis	volētis	nōlētis	mālētis
	3	erunt	poterunt	volent	nōlent	mālent
Perfect	Sing. 1	fuī	potuī	voluī	nōluī	māluī
	2	fuistī	potuistī	voluistī	nōluistī	māluistī
	3	fuit	potuit	voluit	nōluit	māluit
	Pl. 1	fuimus	potuimus	voluimus	nōluimus	māluimus
	2	fuistis	potuistis	voluistis	nōluistis	māluistis
	3	fuērunt	potuērunt	voluērunt	nōluērunt	māluērunt
Pluperfect	Sing. 1	fueram	potueram	volueram	nōlueram	mālueram
	2	fuerās	potuerās	voluerās	nōluerās	māluerās
	3	fuerat	potuerat	voluerat	nōluerat	māluerat
	Pl. 1	fuerāmus	potuerāmus	voluerāmus	nōluerāmus	māluerāmus
	2	fuerātis	potuerātis	voluerātis	nōluerātis	māluerātis
	3	fuerant	potuerant	voluerant	nōluerant	māluerant
Future Perfect	Sing. 1	fuerō	potuerō	voluerō	nōluerō	māluerō
	2	fueris	potueris	volueris	nōlueris	mālueris
	3	fuerit	potuerit	voluerit	nōluerit	māluerit
	Pl. 1	fuerimus	potuerimus	voluerimus	nōluerimus	māluerimus
	2	fueritis	potueritis	volueritis	nōlueritis	mālueritis
	3	fuerint	potuerint	voluerint	nōluerint	māluerint

XVIII. Irregular Verbs: Infinitive, Imperative, Indicative (cont.)

			ferre	ferrī	fierī	īre	
	Infinitive		**ferre**	**ferrī**	**fierī**	**īre**	
	Imperative		fer	fer**re**	—	ī	
			fer**te**	feri**minī**	—	ī**te**	
Present	Sing.	1	fer**ō**	feror	fīō	e**ō**	
		2	fers	fer**ris**	fīs	ī**s**	
		3	fert	fer**tur**	fit	i**t**	
	Pl.	1	feri**mus**	feri**mur**	fīmus	ī**mus**	
		2	fer**tis**	feri**minī**	fītis	ī**tis**	
		3	feru**nt**	feru**ntur**	fīunt	eunt	
Imperfect	Sing.	1	ferēba**m**	ferēbar	fīēbam	ībam	
		2	ferēbā**s**	ferēbā**ris**	fīēbās	ībās	
		3	ferēba**t**	ferēbā**tur**	fīēbat	ībat	
	Pl.	1	ferēbā**mus**	ferēbā**mur**	fīēbāmus	ībāmus	
		2	ferēbā**tis**	ferēbā**minī**	fīēbātis	ībātis	
		3	ferēba**nt**	ferēba**ntur**	fīēbant	ībant	
Future	Sing.	1	fera**m**	ferar	fīam	ībō	
		2	fer**ēs**	fer**ēris**	fīēs	ībis	
		3	fere**t**	fer**ētur**	fiet	ībit	
	Pl.	1	fer**ēmus**	fer**ēmur**	fīēmus	ībimus	
		2	fer**ētis**	fer**ēminī**	fīētis	ībitis	
		3	fere**nt**	fere**ntur**	fient	ībunt	
							or, more usually
Perfect	Sing.	1	tul**ī**	lātus sum	factus sum	īv**ī**	i**ī**
		2	tul**istī**	lātus es	factus es	īv**istī**	iistī > īstī
		3	tul**it**	lātus est	factus sit	īv**it**	iit
	Pl.	1	tul**imus**	lātī sumus	factī sumus	īv**imus**	iimus
		2	tul**istis**	lātī estis	factī estis	īv**istis**	iistis > īstis
		3	tul**ērunt**	lātī sunt	factī sunt	īv**ērunt**	i**ērunt**
Pluperfect	Sing.	1	tul**eram**	lātus eram	factus eram	īv**eram**	ieram
		2	tul**erās**	lātus erās	factus erās	īv**erās**	ierās
		3	tul**erat**	lātus erat	factus erat	īv**erat**	ierat
	Pl.	1	tul**erāmus**	lātī erāmus	factī erāmus	īv**erāmus**	ierāmus
		2	tul**erātis**	lātī erātis	factī erātis	īv**erātis**	ierātis
		3	tul**erant**	lātī erant	factī erant	īv**erant**	ierant
Future Perfect	Sing.	1	tul**erō**	lātus erō	factus erō	īv**erō**	ierō
		2	tul**eris**	lātus eris	factus eris	īv**eris**	ieris
		3	tul**erit**	lātus erit	factus erit	īv**erit**	ierit
	Pl.	1	tul**erimus**	lātī erimus	factī erimus	īv**erimus**	ierimus
		2	tul**eritis**	lātī eritis	factī eritis	īv**eritis**	ieritis
		3	tul**erint**	lātī erunt	factī erunt	īv**erint**	ierint

XIX. Irregular Verbs: Subjunctive

Present	Sing.	1	sim	possim	velim	nōlim	mālim
		2	sīs	possīs	velīs	nōlīs	mālīs
		3	sit	possit	velit	nōlit	mālit
	Pl.	1	sīmus	possīmus	velīmus	nōlīmus	mālīmus
		2	sītis	possītis	velītis	nōlītis	mālītis
		3	sint	possint	velint	nōlint	mālint
Imperfect	Sing.	1	essem	possem	vellem	nōllem	māllem
		2	essēs	possēs	vellēs	nōllēs	māllēs
		3	esset	posset	vellet	nōllet	māllet
	Pl.	1	essēmus	possēmus	vellēmus	nōllēmus	māllēmus
		2	essētis	possētis	vellētis	nōllētis	māllētis
		3	essent	possent	vellent	nōllent	māllent
Perfect	Sing.	1	fuerim	potuerim	voluerim	nōluerim	māluerim
		2	fueris	potueris	volueris	nōlueris	mālueris
		3	fuerit	potuerit	voluerit	nōluerit	māluerit
	Pl.	1	fuerimus	potuerimus	voluerimus	nōluerimus	māluerimus
		2	fueritis	potueritis	volueritis	nōlueritis	mālueritis
		3	fuerint	potuerint	voluerint	nōluerint	māluerint
Pluperfect	Sing.	1	fuissem	potuissem	voluissem	nōluissem	māluissem
		2	fuissēs	potuissēs	voluissēs	nōluissēs	māluissēs
		3	fuisset	potuisset	voluisset	nōluisset	māluisset
	Pl.	1	fuissēmus	potuissēmus	voluissēmus	nōluissēmus	māluissēmus
		2	fuissētis	potuissētis	voluissētis	nōluissētis	māluissētis
		3	fuissent	potuissent	voluissent	nōluissent	māluissent

Present	Sing.	1	feram	ferar	fiam	eam
		2	ferās	ferāris	fiās	eās
		3	ferat	ferātur	fiat	eat
	Pl.	1	ferāmus	ferāmur	fiāmus	eāmus
		2	ferātis	ferāminī	fiātis	eātis
		3	ferant	ferantur	fiant	eant
Imperfect	Sing.	1	ferrem	ferrer	fierem	īrem
		2	ferrēs	ferrēris	fierēs	īrēs
		3	ferret	ferrētur	fieret	īret
	Pl.	1	ferrēmus	ferrēmur	fierēmus	īrēmus
		2	ferrētis	ferrēminī	fierētis	īrētis
		3	ferrent	ferrentur	fierent	īrent
Perfect	Sing.	1	tulerim	lātus sim	factus sim	ierim
		2	tuleris	lātus sīs	factus sīs	ieris
		3	tulerit	lātus sit	factus sit	ierit
	Pl.	1	tulerimus	lātī sīmus	factī sīmus	ierimus
		2	tuleritis	lātī sītis	factī sītis	ieritis
		3	tulerint	lātī sint	factī sint	ierint
Pluperfect	Sing.	1	tulissem	lātus essem	factus essem	īssem
		2	tulissēs	lātus essēs	factus essēs	īssēs
		3	tulisset	lātus esset	factus esset	īsset
	Pl.	1	tulissēmus	lātī essēmus	factī essēmus	īssēmus
		2	tulissētis	lātī essētis	factī essētis	īssētis
		3	tulissent	lātī essent	factī essent	īssent

N.B.: The perfect subjunctive of **eō** may be **ierim**, etc., as shown in the chart, or **īverim**.

The pluperfect subjunctive of **eō** may be **īssem**, as shown in the chart, or **īvissem**.

XX. Participles

		Active	Passive
Present	1	portāns, portantis	
	2	movēns, moventis	
	3	mittēns, mittentis	
	-iō	iaciēns, iacientis	
	4	audiēns, audientis	
Perfect	1		portātus, -a, -um
	2		mōtus, -a, -um
	3		missus, -a, -um
	-iō		iactus, -a, -um
	4		audītus, -a, -um
Future	1	portātūrus, -a, -um	portandus, -a, -um
	2	mōtūrus, -a, -um	movendus, -a, -um
	3	missūrus, -a, -um	mittendus, -a, -um
	-iō	iactūrus, -a, -um	iaciendus, -a, -um
	4	audītūrus, -a, -um	audiendus, -a, -um

N.B.: The perfect participles of deponent verbs have active, not passive, meanings: e.g., **portātus** = *having been carried*, vs. **ēgressus** (deponent) = *having gone out*.

N.B.: The future passive participle is also known as the gerundive.

XXI. Infinitives

		Active	Passive
Present	1	portāre	portārī
	2	movēre	movērī
	3	mittere	mittī
	-iō	iacere	iacī
	4	audīre	audīrī
Perfect	1	portāvisse	portātus, -a, -um esse
	2	mōvisse	mōtus, -a, -um esse
	3	mīsisse	missus, -a, -um esse
	-iō	iēcisse	iactus, -a, -um esse
	4	audīvisse	audītus, -a, -um esse
Future	1	portātūrus, -a, -um esse	portātum īrī
	2	mōtūrus, -a, -um esse	mōtum īrī
	3	missūrus, -a, -um esse	missum īrī
	-iō	iactūrus, -a, -um esse	iactum īrī
	4	audītūrus, -a, -um esse	audītum īrī

N.B.: The present and perfect infinitives of deponent verbs have passive forms with active meanings: e.g., **cōnārī** = *to try*, **cōnātus esse, -a, -um** = *to have tried*. The future active infinitive of deponents is the same as for non-deponent verbs, e.g., **cōnātūrus, -a, -um esse**.

N.B.: the future passive infinitive is extremely rare.

XXII. Gerunds

Case Singular	1st Conjugation	2nd Conjugation	3rd Conjugation	3rd -iō Conjugation	4th Conjugation
Genitive	port**andī**	mov**endī**	mitt**endī**	iaci**endī**	audi**endī**
Dative	port**andō**	mov**endō**	mitt**endō**	iaci**endō**	audi**endō**
Accusative	port**andum**	mov**endum**	mitt**endum**	iaci**endum**	audi**endum**
Ablative	port**andō**	mov**endō**	mitt**endō**	iaci**endō**	audi**endō**

N.B.: Gerunds have only singular forms and have no nominative case.

VOCABULARY

This vocabulary lists all words that are not glossed in the running vocabularies (these are relatively common items that most students will be familiar with from prior study), as well as those that are glossed and marked with an asterisk at their initial occurrence; vocabulary items that are asterisked in the notes occur more than once in the text, and so students should memorize such entries when they are first encountered.

A

ā or **ab**, prep. + abl., *from, by*

abdō, abdere, abdidī, abditus, *to hide, conceal; to hide oneself, go and hide; to plunge, bury* (a weapon)

abeō, abīre, abiī or **abīvī, abitūrus,** irreg., *to go away*

abluō, abluere, abluī, ablūtus, *to wash off/ out; to wash clean, cleanse*

abnegō (1), *to refuse, decline*

abripiō, abripere, abripuī, abreptus, *to snatch away*

absēns, absentis, *not present, absent, although absent*

absistō, absistere, abstitī, *to stand back, withdraw; to stop, cease*

absum, abesse, āfuī, āfutūrus, irreg., *to be away, be absent, be distant*

ac, conj., *and*

accēdō, accēdere, accessī, accessus, *to come/go to, draw near, approach, reach*

accendō, accendere, accendī, accēnsus, *to set on fire*

accingō, accingere, accīnxī, accīnctus, *to gird, surround; to equip, arm; to prepare, get ready* (for)

accipiō, accipere, accēpī, acceptus, *to accept, get, receive, welcome*

accumbō, accumbere, accubuī, accubitūrus, *to recline* (at table)

ācer, ācris, ācre, *keen; savage, fierce*

acervus, -ī, m., *pile, heap*

Acestēs, Acestae, acc. **Acestēn,** m., *Acestes* (a Sicilian king and friend of Aeneas)

Achātēs, Achātae, voc. **Achātē,** m., *Achates* (Trojan warrior and close companion of Aeneas)

Acherōn, Acherontis, m., *Acheron* (a river of the Underworld whose floodwaters, according to legend, surfaced as the Acherusian swamp, identified today as Lake Fusaro, south of the Cumaean acropolis)

Achillēs, Achillis or **Achillī,** m., *Achilles* (son of Peleus and Thetis, Greek chieftain in the Trojan War and hero of Homer's *Iliad*)

Achīvus, -a, -um, *Achaean, Greek* (referring esp. to those who fought at Troy)

aciēs, -ēī, f., *sharp edge* (of a weapon); *line of sight, glance, eye; army, battle, battle-line,* pl., *ranks*

acūtus, -a, -um, *pointed, sharp, tapering; high-pitched*

ad, prep. + acc., *to, toward, at, near*

addō, addere, addidī, additus, *to add*

adeō, adv., *so much, to such an extent*

adeō, adīre, adiī, aditus, irreg., *to come to, approach*

adflīctus, -a, -um, *battered, harassed; shattered, ruined*

adflō (1), *to emit air, breathe on/ upon; to inspire*

adfor, adfārī, adfātus sum, *to speak to, address*

adgredior, adgredī, adgressus sum, *to proceed toward, approach; to assault, attack; + inf., to proceed* (to do something)

adhūc, adv., *still, as yet*

adimō, adimere, adēmī, adēmptus, + dat.
to take away (from)

aditus, -ūs, m., *approach, entry; doorway; access* (to a person)

adiuvō, adiuvāre, adiūvī, adiūtus, *to help, assist*

adloquor, adloquī, adlocūtus sum, *to speak to, address*

admīror, -ārī, -ātus sum, *to wonder* (at)

admoveō, admovēre, admōvī, admōtus, *to move toward*

adnītor, adnītī, adnīxus sum, *to rest on, lean on, support oneself on; to exert oneself, make an effort*

adnuō, adnuere, adnuī, adnūtus, *to beckon, nod; to nod assent; to grant, concede, promise; to approve*

adōrō (1), *to plead with, address; to approach as a suppliant, pray to, worship*

adsum, adesse, adfuī, adfutūrus, *to be present, be near*

adsurgō, adsurgere, adsurrēxī, adsurrēctus, *to rise up, be built up*

adveniō, advenīre, advēnī, adventūrus, *to reach, arrive* (at)

adversus, -a, -um, *opposite, in/from the opposite direction, facing, opposing, in front of*

advertō, advertere, advertī, adversus, *to turn (toward); to pay attention, heed*

adytum, -ī, n., *shrine, sanctuary*

Aeacidēs, Aeacidae, m., *son/descendant of Aeacus; Achilles* (grandson of Aeacus)

aedēs, aedis, f., *room, apartment, hall;* pl., *dwelling, house, palace*

aedificō (1), *to build*

aeger, aegra, aegrum, *ill*

Aenēās, Aenēae, acc. **Aenēān,** voc. **Aenēā,** m., *Aeneas* (Trojan prince, son of Venus and Anchises, and legendary ancestor of the Romans)

aēnus, -a, -um, *(made of) bronze, brazen*

Aeolus, -ī, m., *Aeolus* (mythic king of the winds)

aequō (1), *to make level; to make equal, equalize, equate; to match*

aequor, aequoris, n., *expanse; sea*

aequus, -a, -um, *level, flat; fair, just, right; favorable, kind; equal, matched*

āēr, āeris, acc. sg. **āera,** m., *air; heaven, sky; mist, cloud*

aes, aeris, n., *bronze; a bronze implement*

aestās, aestātis, f., *summer*

aestus, -ūs, m., *heat, hot weather; stormy sea, surge, swell*

aetās, aetātis, f., *(one's) age; (period of) time, age; old age*

aeternus, -a, -um, *endless, eternal, everlasting, enduring*

aethēr, aetheris, acc. **aethera,** m., *(upper) air, heaven, sky*

aetherius, -a, -um, *of/relating to the upper air, of the sky, of heaven*

aevum, -ī, n., *time, (one's) age; old age*

Āfrica, -ae, f., *Africa*

ager, agrī, m., *field, territory, land*

agger, aggeris, m., *mound, heap, pile; earthwork, rampart; bank* (of a river)

agitō (1), *to set in motion, move; to stir up, drive (forward/out); to distress, vex, harass*

agmen, agminis, n., *stream, current* (of water); *multitude, throng; series, succession, line; line* (of troops), *army, march; herd, team* (of horses)

agnōscō, agnōscere, agnōvī, agnitus, *to recognize*

agō, agere, ēgī, āctus, *to do, drive; to discuss, debate.* **agō!/agite!** *come on!*

Aiax, Aiācis, m., *Ajax* (a Greek hero in the Trojan War, son of Oileus—the so-called "lesser Ajax")

ait, *he/she says, said*

āla, -ae, f., *wing; wing* (of an army), *squadron*

Albānus, -a, -um, *Alban, of Alba* (Alba Longa, a city south of Rome and east of Lavinium)

Alcīdēs, -ae, acc. **Alcīdēn,** voc. **Alcīdē,** m., *descendant of Alceus* (father of Amphitryon and grandfather of Hercules), *Hercules* (regularly referred to by his patronymic)

aliquī, aliquae, aliquod, *some; any*

aliquis, aliquid, *someone, something*

aliter, adv., *otherwise, differently*

alius, alia, aliud, *another, other;* **aliī . . . aliī,** *some . . . others*

almus, -a, -um, *nurturing, fostering, life-giving* (as applied especially to goddesses and priestesses, *gracious, kindly, benevolent*)

alō, alere, aluī, altus, *to feed, nourish, rear*

altāria, altārium, n. pl., *altar* (for burned offerings)

altē, adv., *high, in a high position*

alter, -tera, -terum, *a/the secund, one (of two), the other (of two), another*

altus, -a, -um, *tall, high; deep.* **altum, -ī,** n., *the deep, the sea*

alvus, -ī, f., *belly; womb; hollow cavity*

amāns, amantis, m./f., *sweetheart, lover*

ambāgēs, ambāgum, f. pl., *roundabout course, twists and turns; enigmas*

ambō, -ae, -ō, *both*

āmēns, āmentis, *out of one's mind, insane; excited, frantic*

amictus, -ūs, m., *mantle, cloak; covering*

amīcus, -a, -um, *friendly, well disposed; favorable, supportive*

amīcus, -ī, m., *friend*

āmittō, āmittere, āmīsī, āmissus, *to send away; to lose*

amnis, amnis, m., *river, stream*

amō (1), *to love, like*

amor, amōris, m., *love*

amplector, amplectī, amplexus sum, *to embrace*

amplus, -a, -um, *large, spacious; splendid, magnificent*

an, conj., *or;* **an . . . an,** *either . . . or*

Anchīsēs, -ae, abl. **Anchīsā,** acc. **Anchīsēn,** m., *Anchises* (a member of the Trojan royal house and father of Aeneas by Venus)

ancora, -ae, f., *anchor*

Androgeōs, -ī, m., *Androgeos* (a Greek captain)

anguis, anguis, m./f., *snake, serpent*

angustus, -a, -um, *narrow*

anima, -ae, f., *soul, heart*

animus, -ī, m., *mind;* pl., *courage, pride*

Anna, -ae, f., *Anna* (Dido's sister)

annus, -ī, m., *year*

ante, adv., *in front; previously, before*

ante, prep. + acc., *before, in front of*

Antheus, -ī, acc. **Anthea,** m., *Antheus* (a Trojan warrior and companion of Aeneas)

antīquus, -a, -um, *ancient*

antrum, -ī, n., *cave, cavern*

aper, -prī, m., *wild boar*

aperiō, aperīre, aperuī, apertus, *to open, open up, reveal*

apex, apicis, m., *crown, diadem; top, peak; point of flame*

Apollō, Apollinis, m., *Phoebus Apollo* (god of the sun, civilization, prophecy, and the arts, brother of Diana)

appāreō, -ēre, -uī, -itūrus, *to appear*

aptō (1), *to place, fit*

aptus, -a, -um, *suitable* (for), *favorable* (to)

apud, prep. + acc., *with, among, at the house of, in front of, before*

aqua, -ae, f., *water*

Aquilō, Aquilōnis, m., *north wind, northeast wind*

āra, -ae, f., *altar*

arbor, arboris, f., *tree*

arboreus, -a, -um, *of/belonging to trees; treelike*

Arcades, Arcadum, m. pl., *Arcadians, inhabitants of Arcadia*

arcānus, -a, -um, *secret, hidden*

Arcas, Arcadis, m., *an Arcadian, inhabitant of Arcadia*

arceō, arcēre, arcuī, *to hold in, control, restrain; to keep away, repulse*

arcus, -ūs, m., *bow* (for shooting arrows)

ārdeō, ārdēre, ārsī, arsūrus, *to burn, blaze; to be eager* (for)

arduus, -a, -um, *tall, lofty, towering*

Argī, -ōrum, m. pl., *Argives* (citizens of Argos in southern Greece, site of a major temple to Juno), *Greeks*

Argīvus, -a, -um, *of Argos, Argive, Greek*

Argolicus, -a, -um, *Argive, Greek*

arma, -ōrum, n. pl., *weapons, arms*

armentum, -ī, n., *herd* (often collective pl.)

armō (1), *to fit with weapons, arm, equip*

arō (1), *to plow, cultivate; to plow through* (the sea)

arrēctus, -a, -um, *raised up, erect; upright, standing on end;* with **aurēs**, idiom, *attentive*

ars, artis, f., *skill*

artifex, artificis, m., *artisan, artist, craftsman; contriver, perpetrator*

artus, -a, -um, *tight, tightly fastened*

artus, -ūs, m., *joint* (in the body); *arm, leg, limb*

arvum, -ī, n., *(plowed) field;* often pl., *lands, countryside*

arx, arcis, f., *citadel, fortress*

Ascanius, -ī, m., *Ascanius* (son of Aeneas and his wife Creusa, also called Ilus and Iulus; legendary founder of the Latin town of Alba Longa)

ascendō, ascendere, ascendī, ascēnsus, *to climb, climb into* (a carriage)

Asia, -ae, f., *Asia*

aspectō (1), *to gaze upon, look at, observe, watch*

aspectus, -ūs, m., *sight, vision*

asper, -pera, -perum, *rough; sharp, thorny; violent, fierce, cruel, savage*

aspiciō, aspicere, aspexī, aspectus, *to look at, observe, behold*

ast, conj. (archaic form of **at**), *but, but if; and if*

astō, astāre, astitī, *to stand by/nearby; to stand at/on/in; to stand still*

astrum, -ī, n., usually pl., *star;* pl., *sky, heavens; heaven* (home of the gods)

at, conj., *but, nevertheless*

āter, -tra, -trum, *black, dark-colored; devoid of light, dark; dark with blood, stained; ill-omened, funereal, terrible, gloomy*

Atlās, Atlantis, m., *Atlas* (a Titan condemned to holding the world upon his shoulders, and a mountain of the same name in northwest Africa)

atque, conj., *and, and also, and in fact*

Atrīdēs, -ae, m., *son/descendant of Atreus* (pl. = Menelaus, king of Sparta, and Agamemnon, king of Mycenae and commander of the Greek forces at Troy)

ātrium, -ī, n., *atrium, main room; hall*

attollō, attollere, *to raise, lift up, elevate*

attonitus, -a, -um, *astonished, astounded*

auctor, auctōris, m., *creator, originator, proposer; ancestor, father*

audeō, audēre, ausus sum, semi-deponent + inf., *to dare* (to)

audiō (4), *to hear, listen to*

auferō, auferre, abstulī, ablātus, irreg., *to carry away, take away*

augurium, -ī, n., *(the art of) augury; omen, portent, sign*

aula, -ae, f., *courtyard; royal residence, palace*

aura, -ae, f., *air; breeze, wind; atmosphere; breath;* pl., *the heavens*

aureus, -a, -um, *golden*

aurīga, -ae, m., *charioteer*

auris, auris, f., *ear*

Aurōra, -ae, f., *Aurora* (goddess of the dawn)

aurum, -ī, n., *gold*

Ausonius, -a, -um, *Ausonian, of the Ausones* (early inhabitants of Campania in south Italy); *Italian, Roman*

auspicium, -ī, n., *augury, omen; leadership, authority, auspices; fortune, luck*

auster, -trī, m., *south wind; south*

aut, conj., *or;* **aut . . . aut**, *either . . . or*

autem, conj., *however, but, moreover*

auxilium, -ī, n., *help*

āvehō, āvehere, āvexī, āvectus, *to carry off;* pass., *to go away, depart*

āvellō, āvellere, āvulsī, āvulsus, *to pluck off, tear/wrench away; to take away*

Avernus, -ī, m., *Avernus* (either the lake itself or, by extension, the Underworld)

āversus, -a, -um, *turned away, distant, remote*

āvertō, āvertere, āvertī, āversus, *to turn away, divert*

avidus, -a, -um, *greedy; eager, ardent*

avis, avis, m./f., *bird*

avus, -ī, m., *grandfather*

B

bacchor, -ārī, -ātus sum, *to celebrate the rites of Bacchus* (god of wine); *to act like a Bacchante* (a Bacchic celebrant), *rage, rave*

Bacchus, -ī, m., *Bacchus (the god of vegetation, the grapevine, and wine); by* METONYMY, *wine*

balteus, -ī, m., *shoulder-band, belt, baldric (for a sword or other weapon)*

barba, -ae, f., *beard*

bellum, -ī, n., *war*

bene, adv., *well*

bibō, bibere, bibī, *to drink*

bidēns, bidentis, m. and f., *sacrificial animal, sheep (called* **bidentēs** *because when young they have two prominent front teeth)*

bipennis, bipennis, f., *two-edged axe*

bis, adv., *twice*

bonus, -a, -um, *good*

bōs, bovis, m./f., *ox, cow*

brevis, -is, -e, *short;* **breviter,** *briefly*

C

cadō, cadere, cecidī, cāsūrus, *to fall*

caecus, -a, -um, *blind, blinded; dark, black, gloomy; unseen, hidden*

caedēs, caedis, f., *slaughter*

caedō, caedere, cecīdī, caesus, *to strike, beat; to kill, murder, slay*

caelestis, -is, -e, *in the sky, from the sky; celestial, heavenly, divine; as a noun, god, goddess*

caelicola, -ae, m./f., *inhabitant of heaven, heaven-dweller, god, goddess*

caelum, -ī, n., *sky, heaven*

caerulus (caeruleus), -a, -um, *blue; greenish-blue*

Caesar, Caesaris, m., *Caesar, emperor*

Calchās, Calchantis, acc. **Calchanta,** m., *Calchas (the leading Greek soothsayer in the Trojan War)*

calidus, -a, -um, *warm*

calor, calōris, m., *heat*

campus, -ī, m., *plain, field*

candēns, candentis, *shining, bright; white*

canis, canis, m./f., *dog, the lowest throw of knucklebones*

canō, canere, cecinī, cantus, *to sing, chant; to sing about, celebrate; to prophesy, foretell*

cantus, -ūs, m., *singing, song; music (of instruments), blast (of a horn)*

capessō, capessere, capessīvī, *to take hold of, grasp; to head for, go towards; to take charge of, undertake*

capiō, capere, cēpī, captus, *to take, catch, capture, seize*

captīvus, -ī, m., *captive, prisoner*

caput, capitis, n., *head*

Capys, Capyis, acc. **Capyn,** m., *Capys (a companion of Aeneas)*

carcer, carceris, m., *jail, prison, dungeon; sg. or pl., the barriers at the start of a race-course*

cardō, cardinis, m., *pivot, axis; hinge, socket (of a door)*

careō, carēre, caruī, caritūrus + abl., *to need, lack*

carīna, -ae, f., *keel, hull (of a ship); poetic (by* METONYMY), *boat, ship*

carpō, carpere, carpsī, carptus, *to pluck, gather, harvest; to seize; to eat away, erode, consume;* idiom, *with* **aurās,** *to draw breath*

cārus, -a, -um, *dear, beloved*

Cassandra, -ae, f., *Cassandra (daughter of Priam and Hecuba, she was was cursed by Apollo with always prophesying the truth but never being believed)*

castīgō (1), *to rebuke, reprimand*

castra, -ōrum, n. pl., *military camp*

cāsus, -ūs, m., *falling, fall; accident, chance; event; misfortune, disaster, risk*

caterva, -ae, f., *crowd*

causa, -ae, f., *reason*

cautēs, cautis, f., *rock, cliff, crag, reef*

caverna, -ae, f., *hollow cavity in the earth, cave, cavern; cavernous space*

cavus, -a, -um, *having a depression on the surface, concave; hollow; full of caves, cavernous, porous*

cēdō, cedere, cessī, cessūrus, + dat., *to yield to, give in to*

celer, -is, -e, *quick, swift*

cēlō (1), *to hide, conceal*

celsus, -a, -um, *high, lofty, tall*

centum, *a hundred*

Cerberus, -ī, m., *Cerberus (the three-headed dog of the Underworld)*

Cerēs, Cereris, f., *Ceres (goddess of grain and fruit, identified with the Greek*

Demeter); (by METONYMY) *wheat, bread, food*

cernō, cernere, crēvī, crētus, *to sift; to distinguish, separate; to see, perceive*

certāmen, certāminis, n., *contest*

certō (1), *to contend (for superiority), compete; to contend in battle, fight; to struggle, labor*

certus, -a, -um, *certain, unerring;* **certē,** adv., *certainly*

cervīx, cervīcis, f., *neck, back of the neck*

cervus, -ī, m., *stag, deer*

cessō, -āre, -āvī, -ātūrus, *to be idle, do nothing, delay, cease*

cēterus, -a, -um, *the rest (of), the other*

ceu, conj., introducing SIMILES, *in the same way as, as, like;* + subjunct., *as if*

Charōn, Charōnis, m., *Charon* (mythic ferryman of the Underworld, who conveyed the souls of the buried dead across the river Styx)

chorus, -ī, m., *chorus of singing and dancing; performers of a chorus; band of nymphs, worshippers, revelers*

cieō, ciēre, cīvī, citus, *to move, set in motion, stir up*

cingō, cingere, cīnxī, cīnctus, *to surround, encircle; to gird up one's dress* (for action); *to gird, equip*

cingulum, -ī, n., *belt, sword-belt* (often ornately embossed or plated)

cinis, cineris, m., *ashes, dust* (of the cremated body)

circum, prep. + acc., and adv., *around*

circumdō, circumdare, circumdedī, circumdatus, *to surround*

circumfundō, circumfundere, circumfūdī, circumfūsus, *to pour around;* pass., *to spread around/out, surround*

circumspiciō, circumspicere, circumspexī, circumspectus, *to look around*

circumvolō (1), *to fly/hover around; to encircle*

cithara, -ae, f., *lyre*

cīvis, cīvis, m./f., *citizen*

clam, adv., *secretly*

clāmō, -āre, -āvī, -ātūrus, *to shout*

clāmor, clāmōris, m., *shout, shouting*

clārus, -a, -um, *bright, shining, famous*

classis, classis, f., *class* (of citizens); *naval force, fleet*

claudō, claudere, clausī, clausus, *to shut, close; to shut in, enclose*

claustrum, -ī, n., *bolt, bar* (for a door or gate); *cage, prison; stalls* (on a racecourse)

clipeus, -ī, m., *shield.*

Cloanthus, -ī, m., *Cloanthus* (a Trojan)

Cōcȳtus, -ī, m., *Cocytus* (the Underworld's river of "lamentation"; the word itself, which is Greek, means "wailing")

coeō, coīre, coiī, coitus, irreg., *to come together, meet; to form an alliance*

coepī, coepisse, coeptus, defective vb. with chiefly perf. system forms, *to begin, commence, initiate*

cognōmen, cognōminis, n., *surname* (third or fourth name of a Roman)

cognōscō, cognōscere, cognōvī, cognitus, *to find out, learn, hear of*

cōgō, cōgere, coēgī, coāctus, *to compel, force*

colligō, colligere, collēgī, collēctus, *to gather together, collect, pick up*

collis, collis, m., *hill*

collum, -ī, n., often pl. for sg. in poetry, *neck*

colō, colere, coluī, cultus, *to cultivate, cherish*

color, colōris, m., *color, hue*

coluber, -brī, m., *snake, serpent*

columba, -ae, f., *pigeon, dove* (contrasted with other birds for their gentleness)

coma, -ae, f., often pl., *hair* (of the head)

comes, comitis, m./f., *companion*

comitor, comitārī, comitātus sum, *to accompany*

commendō (1), *to commit, entrust*

comminus, adv., *face to face, at close quarters*

commisceō, commiscēre, commiscuī, commixtus, *to mix together*

committō, committere, commīsī, commissus, *to bring together, entrust*

commoveō, commovēre, commōvī, commōtus, *to move, upset.* **commōtus, -a, -um,** *moved, excited* commūnis, -is, -e, *common*

compāgēs, compāgis, f., *binding, bond, tie; joint, seam*

compellō (1), *to address, speak to, call out to*

complector, complectī, complexus sum, *to embrace; to surround, enfold*

compleō, complēre, complēvī, complētus, *to fill, complete*

compōnō, compōnere, composuī, compositus, *to compose*

comprimō, comprimere, compressī, compressus, *to restrain, hold back, check*

concēdō, concēdere, concessī, concessus, *to go, go away, withdraw*

concidō, concidere, concidī, *to fall down*

concieō, conciēre, concīvī, concitus, *to stir up, rouse, set in motion*

concrēscō, concrēscere, concrēvī, concrētus, *to harden, become stiff*

concurrō, concurrere, concurrī, concursūrus, *to run together, rush up*

concursus, -ūs, m., *gathering, crowd, assembly*

concutiō, concutere, concussī, concussus, *to cause to vibrate, shake, agitate; to strike; to shake (emotionally), distress, upset*

condō, condere, condidī, conditus, *to put into, store (up); to hide; to found, establish*

cōnferō, cōnferre, contulī, collātus, *to bring together; to confer, bestow*

cōnfīdō, cōnfīdere, cōnfīsus sum, + dat., *to give trust (to), to trust*

congerō, congerere, congessī, congestus, *to bring together, collect, amass; to pile up, heap up* (with)

congredior, congredī, congressus sum, *to come together*

congressus, -ūs, m., *meeting*

coniciō, conicere, coniēcī, coniectus, *to throw, throw together; to figure out, guess*

coniugium, -ī, n., *marriage; husband, wife*

coniungō, coniungere, coniunxī, coniunctus, *to join*

coniūnx, coniugis, m./f., *husband, wife, spouse*

conlābor, conlābī, conlāpsus sum, *to collapse*

cōnor, -ārī, -ātus sum, *to try*

cōnscendō, cōnscendere, cōnscendī, cōnscēnsus, *to go on board* (a ship), *set out on* (the sea); *to climb to* (the top of), *ascend*

cōnscius, -a, -um, *sharing knowledge; inwardly aware, conscious; with a guilty conscience, guilty; confederate, allied;* as m. or f. noun, *accomplice, accessory*

cōnsequor, cōnsequī, cōnsecūtus sum, *to catch up to, to overtake*

cōnsīdō, cōnsīdere, cōnsēdī, *to sit down, settle; to sink, collapse*

cōnsilium, -ī, n., *plan*

cōnsistō, cōnsistere, cōnstitī, *to halt, stop, stand (at/on/in)*

cōnspectus, -ūs, m., *sight, view; appearance; contemplation*

cōnspiciō, cōnspicere, cōnspexī, cōnspectus, *to catch sight of, see*

cōnstituō, cōnstituere, cōnstituī, cōnstitūtus, *to decide*

cōnstō, cōnstāre, cōnstitī, *to stand together, take up a position, stand (up)*

cōnsulō, cōnsulere, cōnsuluī, cōnsultus, *to consult*

cōnsultum, -ī, n., *decree*

contendō, contendere, contendī, contentus, *to draw tight, stretch; to exert, strive; to hasten; to compete, contend*

conticēscō, conticēscere, conticuī, *to cease to talk, become silent; to be silent about*

contineō, continēre, continuī, contentus, *to confine, hold*

contingō, contingere, contigī, contāctus, *to be in contact with, touch;* **contigit,** impers. + dat. + inf., *to fall to one's lot* (to do something), *happen*

contrā, prep. + acc., *against, opposite, in front of, facing; in response/reply to;* adv., *on the other hand, at the same time, in turn*

contrārius, -a, -um, often + dat., *opposite, opposing; opposed, hostile*

cōnūbium, -ī, n., *intermarriage* (between two groups of people); *marriage, wedding* (a technical Roman word; often scanned as trisyllabic with SYNIZESIS of the -i-)

convellō, convellere, convulsī, convulsus, *to tug at, pull violently; to pull up, tear up; to undermine, tear down; to shake, batter*

conveniō, convenīre, convēnī, conventūrus, *to come together, meet, assemble*

convertō, convertere, convertī, conversus, *to turn around*

convīvium, -ī, n., *feast, banquet*

coorior, coorīrī, coortus sum, *to rise up, arise*

cōpia, -ae, f., *supply, abundance; body of men, band, (military) force; opportunity, freedom*

cor, cordis, n., *heart*

cōram, adv., *face to face, in one's presence, with/before one's own eyes*

cornū, -ūs, n., *horn, antler*

Coroebus, -ī, m., *Coroebus* (a Trojan hero and suitor of Cassandra)

corōna, -ae, f., *garland, crown*

corpus, corporis, n., *body*

corripiō, corripere, corripuī, correptus, *to seize hold of, snatch up, seize and carry off; to hasten upon, hasten over; to attack, overcome*

coruscō (1), *to shake, brandish; to quiver, tremble; to glitter, flash, gleam*

coruscus, -a, -um, *trembling, quivering; flashing, gleaming, glistening*

costa, -ae, f., *rib; flank, back* (of a body)

crēber, -bra, -brum, *at frequent intervals, closely spaced; frequent, repeated, constant; numerous, abundant; + abl., crowded/packed* (with), *full* (of)

crēdō, crēdere, crēdidī, crēditus + dat., *to trust, believe*

crēscō, crēscere, crēvī, crētus, *to be born* (+ abl., *from, of*); *to grow, increase*

Creūsa, -ae, f., *Creusa* (a daughter of Priam and Hecuba, Aeneas' wife and mother of Iulus/Ascanius)

crīmen, crīminis, n., *charge, accusation; misdeed, crime*

crīnis, crīnis, m., *lock of hair, tress;* pl., *hair* (of the head)

croceus, -a, -um, *(made) of saffron; saffron-colored, yellow, golden*

crūdēlis, -is, -e, *cruel*

cruentus, -a, -um, *stained with blood, bloody, bleeding*

cruor, cruōris, m., *blood, gore; bloodshed, slaughter*

culmen, culminis, n., *summit of a building, roof, rooftop; height, zenith*

culpa, -ae, f., *fault, blame*

cum, prep. + abl., *with*

cum, conj., *when, since, whenever, although*

cumba (cymba), -ae, f., *small boat, skiff*

cumulus, -ī, m., *heap, pile, mound; mass* (of water), *wave*

cūnctor, -ārī, -ātus sum, *to hesitate* (over/ about), *delay; to tarry, linger*

cūnctus, -a, -um, *all*

cupīdō, cupīdinis, f., *desire, lust*

cupiō, cupere, cupīvī, cupītus, *to desire, want*

cūr, adv., *why?*

cūra, -ae, f., *care, anxiety*

cūrō (1), *to look after, take care of; to care about*

currō, currere, cucurrī, cursūrus, *to run*

currus, -ūs, m., *chariot*

cursus, -ūs, m., *running, rushing; journey, course;* **cursū,** *at a run, quickly*

curvus, -a, -um, *curved; having many bends/ turns, winding*

cuspis, cuspidis, f., *sharp point, tip* (of a spear); *spear, lance*

custōs, custōdis, m./f., *guard*

Cyllēnius, -a, -um, *Cyllenian, of Mt. Cyllene* (a mountain in Arcadia where Mercury was born)

Cynthus, -ī, m., *Cynthus* (a mountain on the Aegean island of Delos, birthplace of Diana and Apollo)

Cytherēa, -ae, f., *the Cytherean, Venus* (the goddess was so called after the Aegean island of Cythera)

D

Daedalus, -ī, m., *Daedalus* (Athenian inventor compelled by the Cretan king Minos to design the labyrinth at Cnossus)

Danaī, Danaum or **Danaōrum**, m. pl., *Danaans* (descendants of Danaus, the name was commonly used of the Greeks in the Trojan War)

Dardania, -ae, f., *Dardania, Troy*

Dardanidēs, -ae, m., *descendant of Dardanus, Trojan*

Dardan(i)us, -a, -um, *Dardanian, of Dardanus* (son of Zeus and Electra, founder of Dardania in the Troad, and ancestor of Priam), *Trojan*

dē, prep. + abl., *down from, from, concerning, about*

dea, -ae, f., *goddess*

dēbellō (1), *to defeat, bring down in war*

dēbeō (2), *to owe;* + infin., (one) *ought*

dēcēdō, dēcēdere, dēcessī, dēcessūrus, *to go away; to die*

decem, *ten*

decet, decēre, decuit, impers., *it becoming, fitting; should*

dēcurrō, dēcurrere, dēcurrī, dēcursus, *to run down (from), hurry down*

decus, decoris, n., *honor, glory; something that adorns, ornament, decoration; grace, beauty*

dēdūcō, dēdūcere, dēdūxī, dēductus, *to show into, bring, escort, draw out, lead out of, spin*

dēfendō, dēfendere, dēfendī, dēfēnsus, *to defend*

dēferō, dēferre, dētulī, dēlātus, *to carry; to award, grant*

dēfessus, -a, -um, *tired*

dēficiō, dēficere, dēfēcī, dēfectus, *to let down, fail, fall short; to fall back, weaken, collapse*

dēfīgō, dēfīgere, dēfīxī, dēfīxus, *to fix by thrusting down, imbed; to keep (one's eyes, thoughts, etc.) fixed on, focus; to keep (one's eyes, etc.) rigidly fixed*

dēfungor, dēfungī, dēfūnctus sum, *to bring (some matter) to an end;* + abl., *to come to the end of, be done with, complete*

dēgener, dēgeneris, *base-born; degenerate, contemptible*

dehinc, adv., *thereupon, then*

dehīscō, dehīscere, *to split open, gape*

dēiciō, dēicere, dēiēcī, dēiectus, *to throw down;* pass., *to fall*

deinde, adv., *then, next*

dēlēctus, -a, -um, *chosen for excellence, hand-picked, select*

Dēlus, -ī, f., *Delos* (small island off the eastern coast of Greece)

dēlūbrum, -ī, n., *temple, shrine*

dēmēns, dēmentis, *out of one's mind, insane, mad, frenzied*

dēmittō, dēmittere, dēmīsī, dēmissus, *to send (down), let down, lower*

dēmum, adv., *at last, finally*

dēnique, adv., *at last, finally*

dēnsus, -a, -um, *dense, thick; crowded together, massed, closely packed*

dērigō, dērigere, dērēxī, dērēctus, *to direct, aim, guide, steer*

dēscendō, dēscendere, dēscendī, dēscēnsūrus, *to come/go down, climb down*

dēserō, dēserere, dēseruī, dēsertus, *to leave (behind), abandon*

dēsertus, -a, -um, *empty of people, deserted; left alone, lonely;* n. pl. as noun, *unfrequented places, wilderness*

dēsiliō, dēsilīre, dēsiluī, *to leap down*

dēsinō, dēsinere, dēsiī, dēsitus, *to stop*

dēsistō, dēsistere, dēstitī, *to leave off, desist, cease (from)* (+ abl., dat., or prep.)

dēspiciō, dēspicere, dēspexī, dēspectus, *to look down on/at; to look down upon, despise, scorn*

dēstruō, dēstruere, dēstrūxī, dēstrūctus, *to demolish, destroy*

dēsum, dēesse, dēfuī, dēfutūrus, *to be lacking/missing*

dēsuper, adv., *from above, up above*

dētineō, dētinēre, dētinuī, dētentus, *to detain, hold as a prisoner*

deus, deī, nom. and voc. pl., **deī, diī, dī,** dat. and abl. pl., **deīs, dīs,** m., *god*

dēveniō, dēvenīre, dēvēnī, dēventūrus, *to come to, arrive at*

dexter, -tra, -trum, *right; favorable*

dextra, -ae, f., *right hand*

dīcō (1), *to indicate, show; to give over, assign, devote, designate* dīcō, dīcere, dīxī, dictus, *to say, tell*

dictum, -ī, n., *utterance, word, speech*

Dīdō, Dīdōnis, acc. Dīdō, f., *Dido* (queen of Carthage and daughter of the Tyrian king Belus)

diēs, diēī, m. (f.), *day*

difficilis, -is, -e, *difficult*

diffugiō, diffugere, diffūgī, *to run away in different directions, scatter*

diffundō, diffundere, diffūdī, diffūsus, *to spread widely, scatter*

dignor, -ārī, -ātus sum, *to consider* (someone/acc.) *worthy* (of something/abl.)

dignus, -a, -um, *appropriate, suitable, worthy; deserving; deserved*

dīgredior, dīgredī, dīgressus sum, *to go away/ from, come/depart from, leave*

dīligō, dīligere, dīlēxī, dīlēctus, *to love, have special regard for*

dīmittō, dīmittere, dīmīsī, dīmissus, *to send away, allow to go away; to send off, dispatch*

dīripiō, dīripere, dīripuī, dīreptus, *to tear away, pull off; to plunder, rob*

dīrus, -a, -um, *awful, dire, dreadful*

Dīs, Dītis, m., *Dis* (lord of the Underworld in Roman religion)

discēdō, discēdere, discessī, discessūrus, *to leave, go away, depart*

discernō, discernere, discrēvī, discrētus, *to separate, mark off, divide; to decide, settle, resolve*

discō, discere, didicī, *to learn*

discrīmen, discrīminis, n., *dividing point; critical point, crisis; danger; difference, distinction; discrimination, decision*

disiciō, disicere, disiēcī, disiectus, *to break up and scatter, disperse; to dispel*

dispellō, dispellere, dispulī, dispulsus, *to drive apart, scatter, disperse*

dissimulō (1), *to conceal, disguise; to pretend* (that something is not what it is)

diū, adv., *for a long time*

dīva, -ae, f., *goddess*

dīvellō, dīvellere, dīvellī, dīvulsus, *to tear open/apart*

dīversus, -a, -um, *turned in different directions, from different directions; set apart, separated, distant, remote; different*

dīves, dīvitis, *rich*

dīvidō, dīvidere, dīvīsī, dīvīsus, *to divide*

dīvīnus, -a, -um, *divine*

dīvus, -ī, m., *god* (dīvum often = dīvōrum)

dō, dare, dedī, datus, *to give, grant*

doceō, docēre, docuī, doctus, *to teach*

doleō, -ēre, -uī, -itūrus, *to be sorry, be sad, be in pain, hurt*

Dolopes (-ēs), Dolopum, m. pl., *Dolopians* (a Thessalian tribe connected with Achilles' son Pyrrhus)

dolor, dolōris, m., *grief, pain*

dolus, -ī, m., *trick*

dominor, -ārī, -ātus sum, *to rule, be in control, dominate*

dominus, -ī, m., *master, owner*

domō, domāre, domuī, domitus, *to tame, subdue*

domus, -ūs, and domus, -ī, f., *house*

dōnec, conj., *until, as long as*

dōnum, -ī, n., *gift*

Dōricus, -a, -um, *Doric, of Doris* (a region in northern Greece), *Greek*

dubius, -a, -um, *uncertain, undecided, hesitant, wavering*

dūcō, dūcere, dūxī, ductus, *to lead, take, bring*

ductor, ductōris, m., *military commander, leader* (poetic for dux)

dulcis, -is, -e, *sweet* (in taste, smell); *not salty, fresh; delightful, dear*

dum, adv. and conj., *while, as long as; until*

duo, -ae, -o, *two*

dūrus, -a, -um, *hard, solid; hardy, strong, enduring; harsh, pitiless*

dux, ducis, m., *leader*

Dymās, Dymantis, m., *Dymas* (a Trojan)

E

ē, ex, prep. + abl., *from, out of*

ecce, interj., *look! look at . . . !*

edō, esse, ēdī, ēsus, irreg., *to eat*

ēdūcō, ēdūcere, ēdūxī, ēductus, *to lead out, to lead/raise up*

efferō, efferre, extulī, ēlātus, irreg., *to carry out, bring out*

effigiēs, -ēī, f., *statue, image*

effodiō, effodere, effōdī, effossus, *to dig up, dig out; to hollow out by digging*

effor, effārī, effātus sum, *to utter, say, speak*

effugiō, effugere, effūgī, *to flee, run away, escape*

effundō, effundere, effūdī, effūsus, *to pour out;* pass., *to spill*

egeō, egēre, eguī + gen. or abl., *to need, want; to be needy, indigent*

ego, pl. **nōs**, I, *we*

ēgredior, ēgredī, ēgressus sum, *to go out, leave, disembark*

ēgregius, -a, -um, *outstanding, excellent, splendid*

ēiciō, ēicere, ēiēcī, ēiectus, *to throw out, wash overboard*

ēlābor, ēlābī, ēlāpsus, *to slip out/ away from; to escape*

ēmicō, ēmicāre, ēmicuī, ēmicātūrus, *to dart forth, dash out, spring up*

ēmittō, ēmittere, ēmīsī, ēmissus, *to send out*

ēmoveō, ēmovēre, ēmōvī, ēmōtus, *to move out, remove; to dislodge*

emō, emere, ēmī, emptus, *to buy*

enim, conj., *for;* after **sed**, *indeed, in fact*

ēnsis, ēnsis, m., *sword*

eō, īre, iī or **īvī, itūrus**, irreg., *to go*

Ēous/Eōus, -a, -um, *of/relating to the dawn; eastern, oriental*

epulae, -ārum, f. pl., *banquet, feast*

eques, equitis, m., *horseman, cavalryman, rider*

equidem, adv., *for my part, personally speaking* (esp. with 1st pers.); *indeed, in truth*

equus, -ī, m., *horse*

Erebus, -ī, m., *Erebus, the Underworld*

ergō, conj./adv., *therefore*

Erīnys, Erīnyos, f., *Erinys, a Fury* (the spirit of revenge and destructive violence); *fury, frenzy*

ēripiō, ēripere, ēripuī, ēreptus, *to snatch from, rescue*

errō, -āre, -āvī, -ātūrus, *to wander, be mistaken*

error, errōris, m., *wandering, roaming; maze, deception, trick; confusion, mistake*

ēruō, ēruere, ēruī, ērutus, *to dig up, uproot; to lay low, destroy*

et, adv. and conj., *and, also;* **et . . . et**, conj., *both . . . and*

etiam, conj., *also, even*

Euboicus, -a, -um, *Euboean, of Euboea* (an Aegean island off the coast of Boeotia)

Eurus, -ī, m., *east (southeast) wind*

ēvādō, ēvādere, ēvāsī, ēvāsus, *to escape; to get through*

ēvertō, ēvertere, ēvertī, ēversus, *to overturn, upset*

ēvincō, ēvincere, ēvīcī, ēvictus, *to overcome, overwhelm*

ex or **ē**, prep. + abl., *from, out of*

exanimis, -is, -e, and **exanimus, -a, -um**, *lifeless, dead*

excēdō, excēdere, excessī, excessūrus, *to go out, leave*

excidium, -ī, n., *(military) destruction*

excidō, excidere, excidī, *to fall from, fall off, drop out*

excīdō, excīdere, excīdī, excīsus, *to cut out/ down; to hollow out, excavate; to cut/ break through*

excipiō, excipere, excēpī, exceptus, *to welcome, receive, catch; to follow after, succeed*

excitō (1), *to rouse, wake (someone) up*

exclāmō (1), *to exclaim, shout out*

excūdō, excūdere, excūdī, excūsus, *to hammer out, forge, fashion; to cause to be emitted by striking, strike out*

excutiō, excutere, excussī, excussus, *to shake off/out, knock off/out; to throw out, expel*

exeō, exīre, exiī or **exīvī, exitūrus**, *to go out*

exerceō (2), *to exercise, train*

exercitus, -ūs, m., *army*

exigō, exigere, exēgī, exāctus, *to drive out/ forth; to achieve, complete, carry out; to spend (time in); to find out*

eximō, eximere, exēmī, exēmptus, *to remove*

exitium, -ī, n., *destruction*

exitus, -ūs, m., *departure, exit; end, death*

exoptātus, -a, -um, *hoped for, much desired*

exorior, exorīrī, exortus sum, *to emerge, appear; to rise up, arise*

expediō (4), *to untie, unwrap; to make ready, prepare;* pass., *to be prepared, ready, make one's way*

experior, experīrī, expertus sum, *to test, try, experience*

expleō, explēre, explēvī, explētus, *to fill (up/ out); to complete, reach the end of*

explicō (1), *to explain*

explōrō (1), *to reconnoitre, inspect; to inquire into, ascertain*

exsanguis, -is, -e, *bloodless; pale*

exscindō, exscindere, exscidī, exscissus, *to cut off; to demolish, destroy*

exsequor, exsequī, exsecūtus sum, *to follow, go along with; to carry out, execute, perform*

exsilium, -ī, n., *exile, banishment*

exspectō (1), *to look out for, wait for*

exstinguō, exstinguere, exstīnxī, exstīnctus, *to extinguish, put out; to kill; to obliterate, annihilate*

exstruō, exstruere, exstruxī, exstructus, *to build*

exsultō (1), *to spring up, leap about; to exult*

exta, -ōrum, n. pl., *the inner organs of sacrificed animals (heart, lungs, liver)*

extemplō, adv., *without delay, at once, immediately*

extendō, extendere, extendī, extentus, *to hold out; to stretch out, extend, prolong*

extrā, prep. + acc., *outside*

extrēmus, -a, -um, *situated at the end, the end of; the rear of; last (part of); final; end (of life); extreme*

exuō, exuere, exuī, exūtus, *to take off, set aside; to strip (something, acc.) from (something, abl.)*

exuviae, -ārum, f. pl., *armor stripped from an enemy, spoils; mementos*

F

faciēs, -ēī, f., *appearance; sight, scene; form, shape, image; face, countenance*

facilis, -is, -e, *easy*

faciō, facere, fēcī, factus, *to make, do*

factum, -ī, n., *deed, act, action*

fallō, fallere, fefellī, falsus, *to deceive, trick; to disappoint; to elude, slip away from*

falsus, -a, -um, *false, deceitful*

fāma, -ae, f., *fame, reputation, story*

famēs, famis, abl. regularly with long -ē, i.e., **famē**, f., *hunger, starvation*

fās, indecl. n., *right, ordained (by divine law); morally right, fitting, proper*

fastīgium, -ī, n., *sharp point, tip; rooftop, top; high point*

fātālis, -is, -e, *fateful; destined, fated; deadly, fatal*

fateor, fatērī, fassus sum, *to acknowledge, accept; to admit guilt, confess*

fatīgō (1), *to tire out, weary, exhaust; to harass, assail*

fātum, -ī, n., *fate; death*

faucēs, faucium, f. pl., *throat; jaws*

fax, facis, f., *torch (used for light); torch (for setting fires), firebrand; light*

fēlix, fēlīcis, *lucky, happy, fortunate*

fēmina, -ae, f., *woman*

fēmineus, -a, -um, *of/relating to a woman/ women, female, womanly*

fenestra, -ae, f., *window*

fera, -ae, f., *wild animal, beast*

feriō (4), *to hit, strike, kill*

ferō, ferre, tulī, lātus, irreg., *to carry, bring, bear, say*

ferōx, ferōcis, *fierce*

ferrum, -ī, n., *iron; iron tool; sword; armed might*

ferus, -a, -um, *untamed, wild; savage, fierce, ferocious*

ferveō, fervēre, ferbuī, *to be intensely hot, to boil; to be active/busy, to seethe with activity*

fervidus, -a, -um, *intensely hot, boiling, burning; seething, blazing (with anger)*

fessus, -a, -um, *tired, weary, exhausted*

festīnō, -āre, -āvī, -ātūrus, *to hurry*

fēstus, -a, -um, *festival/feast (day)*

fētus, -a, -um, *having young offspring; pregnant; teeming, abounding*

fētus, -ūs, m., *birth; offspring; fruit*

fidēs, fideī, f., *good faith, reliability, trust, confidence*

fīdūcia, -ae, f., often + gen., *trust (in), reliance (on), confidence (in)*

fīdus, -a, -um, *faithful, loyal, devoted; trustworthy, reliable*

fīgō, fīgere, fīxī, fīxus, *to drive in, fix in, insert; to pierce, shoot* (with a weapon); *to set down, place firmly, plant*

fīlius, -ī, m., *son*

fīlum, -ī, n., *thread*

fingō, fingere, fīnxī, fictus, *to make, form, fashion, create; to make up, pretend*

fīnis, -is, m., *end;* pl., *borders, boundaries, territory*

fīō, fierī, factus sum, irreg., *to become, be made, be done, happen*

fīrmus, -a, -um, *strong, stout; solid; firm, determined; reliable, sure*

fīxus, -a, -um, *firmly established, unwavering, fixed*

flamma, -ae, f., *flame*

flammō (1), *to set fire to, burn, inflame*

flectō, flectere, flexī, flexus, *to bend, curve; to turn, redirect; to influence*

fleō, flēre, flēvī, flētus, *to weep, cry; to weep for, lament*

flētus, -ūs, m., *weeping, tears*

flōs, flōris, m., *flower*

flūctus, -ūs, m., *wave, billow, waters* (of the sea)

fluentum, -ī, n., usually pl., *stream, river*

fluō, fluere, flūxī, flūxus, *to flow, stream*

flūmen, flūminis, n., *river, stream*

fluvius, -ī, m., *stream, river*

foedō (1), *to make filthy, defile, pollute; to wound, mangle, mutilate*

foedus, -a, -um, *filthy, disgusting*

foedus, foederis, n., *agreement, treaty, league; compact, condition, bond*

folium, -ī, n., *leaf*

fōns, fontis, m., *spring, fountain, source;* often pl., *water* (from a spring), *waters* (of a sea, river)

for, fārī, fātus sum, *to speak, talk; to speak prophetically; to say, tell*

foris, foris, f., *door* (of a building); pl., *double-doors*

fōrma, -ae, f., *form, shape; beauty*

formīdō, formīdinis, f., *fear, terror, alarm*

fors, fortis, f., *chance, luck; destiny; chance happening, accident*

forsan, adv., *perhaps*

forte, adv., *by chance*

fortis, -is, -e, *brave*

fortūna, -ae, f., *fortune (good or bad)*

foveō, fovēre, fōvī, fōtus, *to keep warm; to comfort, soothe; to cherish* (a hope that, + acc. + inf.)

fragor, fragōris, m., *crash, noise, din*

frangō, frangere, frēgī, fractus, *to break*

frāter, frātris, m., *brother*

frāternus, -a, -um, *brotherly*

fremō, fremere, fremuī, fremitūrus, *to rumble, roar, growl; to grumble, cry out, clamor for*

frēnō (1), *to control horses with a bridle, rein in*

frēnum, -ī, n., (a horse's) *bridle, harness* (including the reins and bit)

fretum, -ī, n., *strait, channel*

frētus, -a, -um, + abl., *relying (on), trusting (to), confident (of)*

frīgidus, -a, -um, *cool, cold*

frīgus, frīgoris, n., *cold, cold weather; chill* (of the body, old age, death, fear); *weakness, numbness, torpor*

frondēns, frondentis, *covered with leaves, leafy*

frōns, frondis, f., *leafy part of a tree, foliage* (sometimes for wreathes or garlands)

frōns, frontis, f., *forehead; face*

frūstrā, adv., *in vain*

frustum, -ī, n., *scrap*

frūx, frūgis, f., *produce, fruit;* esp. pl., *grain*

fuga, -ae, f., *running away, flight*

fugiō, fugere, fūgī, fugitūrus, *to flee*

fugō (1), *to cause to flee, drive away, dispel*

fulgeō, fulgēre, fulsī, *to shine brightly, glitter, flash*

fulmen, fulminis, n., *lightning* (that strikes), *thunderbolt*

fulvus, -a, -um, *brown, tawny, sandy, yellow*

fūmus, -ī, m., *smoke*

fundāmentum, -ī, n., *substructure for a building, foundation*

fundō (1), *to lay the foundations of; to found; to give a firm base to, fix*

fundō, fundere, fūdī, fūsus, *to pour (out); to emit; to give birth to; to pour forth* (sounds), *utter freely; to rout, drive out; to lay low, slay; to spread (out), stretch (out)*

fūnis, fūnis, m., *rope, cable*

funus, -eris, n., *funeral, death*

furia, -ae, f., often pl., *avenging rage, fury; goddess of vengeance, Fury*

furiātus, -a, -um, *maddened, enraged*

furō, furere, *to be mad, be crazed; to rage*

furor, furōris, m., *frenzy*

fūrtim, adv., *stealthily*

fūrtum, -ī, n., *robbery, theft; stealth, deceit, trickery*

G

Gaetūlus, -a, -um, *Gaetulian, of the Gaetulians* (a tribe in northwest Africa)

galea, -ae, f., *helmet*

gaudeō, gaudēre, gāvīsus sum, *to be glad, rejoice*

gaudium, -ī, n., *joy*

gaza, -ae, f., *treasure*

gelidus, -a, -um, *cold, icy*

geminus, -a, -um, *twin; twofold, double*

gemitus, -ūs, m., *pained/sorrowful sound, groan, moan*

gemō, gemere, gemuī, gemitus, *to groan (at), lament*

gener, generī, m., *son-in-law*

genetrīx, genetrīcis, f., *mother, creator*

genitor, genitōris, m., *father; creator* (often applied to Jupiter and Neptune)

gēns, gentis, f., *family, clan, nation, tribe*

genū, -ūs, n., *knee*

genus, generis, n., *race, stock, nation; offspring; kind, type*

germāna, -ae, f., *sister*

germānus, -ī, m., *brother*

gerō, gerere, gessī, gestus, *to wear; to carry on, perform, do;* **bellum gerere,** *to wage war*

gestō (1), *to carry with one, carry about; to wear; to carry (in one's mind), harbor (thoughts, etc.)*

gignō, gignere, genuī, genitus, *to bring into being, create; to give birth to*

glomerō (1), *to form into a ball; to collect together into a mass, to accumulate; to collect into a crowd, mass together (often pass. in a reflex. sense)*

glōria, -ae, f., *fame, glory*

gnātus, -ī (alternate form of **nātus, -ī**), m., *son*

gradior, gradī, gressus sum, *to proceed, step, walk*

gradus, -ūs, m., *step, pace; step* (of a building), *stair, rung* (of a ladder)

Grāius, -a, -um, *Greek;* nom. pl. sometimes **Grāī,** *Greek*

grandō, grandinis, f., *hail*

grātus, -a, -um, + dat., *loved* (by), *pleasing* (to), *dear* (to), *grateful, thankful*

gravis, -is, -e, *heavy, serious; burdened*

graviter, adv., *heavily; gravely, grievously, seriously; intensely*

gressus, -ūs, m., *step, walk, course*

gurges, gurgitis, m., *eddy, whirlpool; stream, flood*

H

habēnae, -ārum, f. pl., *reins*

habeō (2), *to have, hold*

hāc, adv., *this way, in this direction;* **hāc . . . hāc,** *in this direction . . . in that, on this side . . . on that*

haereō, haerēre, haesī, haesus, *to stick, cling*

Halaesus, -ī, m., *Halaesus* (one of the Italian leaders opposing the Trojans' settlement in Latium)

harēna, -ae, f., *sand*

hasta, -ae, f., *spear*

haud, adv., *not, by no means*

hauriō, haurīre, hausī, haustus, *to drain*

Hector, Hectoris, acc. **Hectora,** m., *Hector* (oldest son of Priam and Hecuba, and Troy's most renowned hero in the Trojan War)

Hectoreus, -a, -um, *of Hector; Trojan*

Hecuba, -ae, f., *Hecuba* (wife of Priam and mother to many of his children)

herba, -ae, f., *small plant, herb;* sg. or pl., *grass*

hērēs, hērēdis, m., *heir*

hērōs, hērōos, m., *hero* (a legendary hero or a man with heroic qualities); often used as an appos. with adj. force, *heroic*

Hesperia, -ae, f., *Hesperia* (= *the land to the west,* i.e., Italy)

heu, interj., indicating dismay or sorrow, *alas*

Heus! *Hey there!*

hībernus, -a, -um, *of/belonging to/in winter*

hīc, adv., *here*

hic, haec, hoc, *this, the latter*

hiems, hiemis, f., *winter, wintry weather; rough weather, storm*

hinc, adv., *from this* (place, person, time, thing), *hence; next, then*

hodiē, adv., *today*

homō, hominis, m., *man*

honōr (honōs), honōris, m., *honor*

hōra, -ae, f., *hour*

horrendus, -a, -um, *terrible, fearful, horrendous*

horreō, horrēre, horruī, *to stand up, bristle, be rigid; to be unsightly, dreadful, gloomy; to shudder (at), shiver, be fearful*

horridus, -a, -um, *rough, bristly; wild, rugged; unkempt; grim, dreadful*

horror, horrōris, m., *standing on end, bristling* (of hair); *horror, dread*

hortor, -ārī, -ātus sum, *to encourage, urge*

hospes, hospitis, m., *friend, host, guest, a person related to one of another city by ties of hospitality*

hospitium, -ī, n., *entertainment of guests, hospitality; guest-host relationship; welcome, reception*

hostia, -ae, f., *sacrificial animal, sacrificial victim*

hostis, hostis, m/f., *enemy*

hūc, adv., *here, to here;* hūc illūc, adv., *here and there, this way and that*

humilis, -is, -e, *low, humble*

humō (1), *to bury, inter*

humus, -ī, f., *earth, ground*

hymenaeus, -ī, m., usually pl., *marriage, wedding*

Hypanis, Hypanis, m., *Hypanis (a Trojan)*

I

iaceō, iacēre, iacuī, iacitūrus, *to lie, be lying down*

iaciō, iacere, iēcī, iactus, *to throw*

iactō (1), *to throw, cast; to drive back and forth, toss about, torment; to talk/think about; to brag about, show off, flaunt oneself*

iaculor, -ārī, -ātus sum, *to throw a javelin; to shoot at, strike; to hurl, throw*

iam, adv., *now, already, soon*

iamdūdum, adv., *some time ago; for a long time, long since; now after all this time*

iānitor, iānitōris, m., *door-keeper, gate-keeper*

iānua, -ae, f., *door*

Ĭarbās, -ae, acc. Ĭarbān (trisyllabic), m., *Iarbas (king of the Gaetulians, a North African tribe)*

ibi, adv., *there*

īciō, īcere, īcī, ictus, *to strike* (with a weapon, missile, etc.)

ictus, -ūs, m., *thrust, blow; wound; force, impact*

īdem, eadem, idem, *the same*

ignārus, -a, -um, often + gen., *ignorant, unaware (of), unacquainted (with)*

ignāvus, -a, -um, *cowardly, lazy*

ignis, ignis, m., *fire*

ignōtus, -a, -um, *unknown, unfamiliar, strange;* as a substantive, *stranger*

īlex, īlicis, f., *holm-oak, ilex*

Īliacus, -a, -um, *of Ilium, Trojan*

Īlias, Īliadis, f., *Trojan woman*

īlicet, adv., *on the spot, immediately, straightaway*

Īlioneus, -ī, m., *Ilioneus (a Trojan warrior)*

Īlium, -ī, n., *Ilium (another name for the city of Troy)*

ille, -a, -ud, *that; he, she, it; the former; that famous*

illīc, adv., *there*

illūc, adv., *there, to that place;* hūc illūc, *here and there, this way and that*

imāgō, imāginis, f., *likeness, mask; image, shape, vision*

imber, imbris, m., *rain*

immānis, -is, -e, *savage, brutal; frightful; of enormous size, huge*

immemor, immemoris, + gen., *forgetful, heedless, unmindful*

immēnsus, -a, -um, *immeasurable, boundless; huge, immense*

immineō, imminēre, *to rise up, project, overhang, overlook, be overhead*

immittō, immittere, immīsī, immissus, *to send in, release*

immōtus, -a, -um, *unmoved, motionless; undisturbed; unchanged, unaltered*

impār, imparis, *unequal* (to, + dat.); *unevenly matched*

impellō, impellere, impulī, impulsus, *to strike (against); to drive, push, impel*

imperium, -ī, n., *empire, power*

impetus, -ūs, m., *attack*

impius, -a, -um, *wicked, immoral, impious*

impleō, implēre, implēvī, implētus, + abl. or gen., *to fill* (often used reflexively; i.e., *they are filled with = they fill themselves with*)

implicō, implicāre, implicāvī/implicuī, implicātus/implicitus, *to fold; to enfold, wrap around*

impōnō, impōnere, imposuī, impositus, *to place on, put*

imprimō, imprimere, impressī, impressus, *to apply with pressure, press (on/upon); to imprint, engrave* (with)

improbus, -a, -um, *morally unsound; shameless, wicked*

imprōvīsus, -a, -um, *unforeseen, unexpected*

īmus, -a, -um, *lowest, bottommost; lowest part of, bottom of; deepest, innermost*

in, prep. + abl., *in, on, among;* prep. + acc., *into, against, toward*

inānis, -is, -e, *empty; unoccupied, idle; meaningless, unimportant; vain, futile*

incautus, -a, -um, *incautious, unwary, unsuspecting*

incēdō, incēdere, incessī, *to go in, march in*

incendium, -ī, n., *fire*

incendō, incendere, incendī, incēnsus, *to burn, set on fire*

inceptum, -ī, n., *undertaking, enterprise; attempt, intention*

incertus, -a, -um, *not fixed, subject to chance; uncertain, unsure; (of a weapon) not firmly held*

incidō, incidere, incidī, incāsūrus, *to fall into/ onto*

incipiō, incipere, incēpī, inceptus, *to begin*

inclūdō, inclūdere, inclūsī, inclūsus, *to insert, enclose*

inclutus, -a, -um, *famous, renowned, celebrated*

incolumis, -is, -e, *unhurt, safe and sound*

incubō, incubāre, incubuī, incubitūrus, *to lie/recline (on); to brood (over); to swoop down (on)*

incultus, -a, -um, *uncultivated, wild*

incumbō, incumbere, incubuī, *to bend towards, lean on; to lie down upon; to press upon; to press on (with an activity), exert oneself*

incurrō, incurrere, incurrī, incursūrus, *to run into*

incūsō (1), *to blame, reproach; to complain of, condemn.*

inde, adv., *from there, then*

indignor, -ārī, -ātus sum, *to regard with indignation, resent*

indignus, -a, -um, *undeserving, unworthy; undeserved, unmerited*

indomitus, -a, -um, *untamed, unrestrained, wild*

indulgeō, indulgēre, indulsī, indultus, + dat., *to be indulgent/lenient (to); to indulge (in), give free rein (to); to show kindness, be generous (to)*

induō, induere, induī, indūtus, *to put on;* **indūtus, -a, -um,** *clothed, dressed in*

inermis, -is, -e, and **inermus, -a, -um,** *unarmed, defenseless*

iners, inertis, *lazy, sluggish; powerless, lifeless*

īnfandus, -a, -um, *unspeakable*

īnfēlīx, īnfēlīcis, *unproductive; inauspicious, disastrous; unfortunate, unlucky*

īnfēnsus, -a, -um, *bitterly hostile; angry, furious*

īnfernus, -a, -um, *lower, underground; of the Underworld, infernal*

īnferō, īnferre, intulī, illatus, irreg., *to bring in*

īnfestus, -a, -um, *hostile, warlike; threatening*

īnfigō, īnfigere, īnfīxī, īnfīxus, *to drive in, implant; to transfix, impale*

īnflectō, īnflectere, īnflexī, īnflexus, *to bend; to alter, change*

īnfundō, īnfundere, īnfūdī, īnfūsus, *to pour in/on/over; to pour down on*

ingemō, ingemere, ingemuī, *to utter a cry of pain/anguish, moan, groan*

ingēns, ingentis, *huge, big*

ingredior, ingredī, ingressus sum, *to go in, enter; to begin (to speak)*

inhumātus, -a, -um, *unburied*

iniciō, inicere, iniēcī, iniectus, *to throw into, thrust*

inimīcus, -a, -um, *unfriendly, inimical, hostile; harmful, injurious*

inīquus, -a, -um, *uneven, unequal; unjust, unfair*

iniūria, -ae, f., *unlawful conduct; injustice, a wrong; injury; insult*

innūptus, -a, -um, *unmarried, maiden, virgin*

inops, inopis, *lacking wealth, poor; re-sourceless, helpless;* + gen., *devoid (of), deficient* (in).

inquit, *(he/she) says, said*

inrumpō, inrumpere, inrūpī, inruptus, *to burst in*

inruō, inruere, inruī, *to rush in, dash in*

īnsānus, -a, -um, *of unsound mind, fren-zied, mad; crazed, tempestuous*

īnscius, -a, -um, *not knowing*

īnscrībō, īnscrībere, īnscrīpsī, īnscrīptus, *to write in, register*

īnsequor, īnsequī, īnsecūtus sum, *to follow closely, pursue, chase; to assault*

īnsidiae, -ārum, f. pl., *ambush; treachery, plot, trick*

īnsigne, īnsignis, f., *decoration; insignia*

īnsignis, -is, -e, *clearly visible, conspicuous; remarkable, noteworthy, outstanding*

īnsomnium, -ī, n., *sleeplessness; vision, dream*

īnsōns, īnsontis, *innocent, guiltless*

īnspiciō, īnspicere, īnspexī, īnspectus, *to examine*

īnstar, in acc. and nom. only, n., often + gen., *the equal, equivalent (of/to, in size, effect, moral worth)*

īnstaurō (1), *to repeat, start afresh, renew; to restore, revive*

īnstituō, īnstituere, īnstituī, īnstitūtus, *to establish*

īnstō, īnstāre, īnstitī, *to set foot on; to press on; to loom, threaten;* + dat., *to apply oneself (to), press on* (with)

īnstruō, īnstruere, īnstrūxī, īnstrūctus, *to build; to equip, fit out; to provide*

īnsula, -ae, f., *island*

īnsuper, adv., *on top, above; in addition, as well, besides*

intāctus, -a, -um, *untouched; undamaged; unharmed, unscathed; virgin*

intentus, -a, -um, *intent, eager*

inter, prep. + acc., *between, among*

intereā, adv., *meanwhile*

interior, interior, interius, *interior, inner (part of)*

interpres, interpretis, m., *intermediary, agent; spokesman, messenger*

intonō, intonāre, intonuī, *to thunder*

intorqueō, intorquēre, intorsī, intortus, *to bend back; to hurl*

intrā, prep. + acc., *inside*

intrō (1), *to enter, go into*

intus, adv., *within, inside*

inultus, -a, -um, *without recompense for injury, unavenged*

inūtilis, -is, -e, *useless, ineffectual*

invādō, invādere, invāsī, invāsus, *to as-sault, attack, invade*

inveniō, invenīre, invēnī, inventus, *to come upon, find*

invictus, -a, -um, *unconquered, undefeated; unconquerable, invincible*

invideō, invidēre, invīdī, invīsus, +dat., *to envy, be jealous of; to begrudge*

invidia, -ae, f., *ill will, envy, jealousy; dis-like, hatred*

invīsus, -a, -um, *hateful, hated, odious, disliked*

invītus, -a, -um, *unwilling, unwillingly*

invius, -a, -um, *pathless, trackless, that can-not be traveled, untraveled*

involvō, involvere, involvī, involūtus, *to enclose in a cover, wrap up, cover*

ipse, -a, -um, *himself, herself, itself, them-selves, very*

īra, -ae, f., *anger*

Īris, Īridis, f., *Iris (messenger of the gods, Juno in particular, and goddess of the rainbow)*

is, ea, id, *he, she, it; this, that*

iste, -a, -ud, *that (of yours); such (as you speak of/refer to); this*

ita, adv., *thus, so, in this way, in such a way;* **Ita vērō!** adv., *Yes! Indeed!*

Italus, -a, -um, gen. pl. m. **Italum,** *Italian;* m. as noun, *an Italian*

Ītalia, -ae, f., *Italy*

iter, itineris, n., *journey, route*

iterum, adv., *again, a second time*

Ithacus, -a, -um, *Ithacan, from Ithaca (a small island off the west coast of Greece, legendary home of Ulysses); as a noun, the Ithacan*

iuba, -ae, f., *mane; crest, plume*

iubeō, iubēre, iussī, iussus, *to order, bid*

iugālis, -is, -e, *of marriage, matrimonial*

iugum, -ī, n., *yoke (of a plow); ridge, cliff; bench*

Ĭūlus, -ī (trisyllabic) m., *Iulus (Ascanius' cognomen, connecting him to the Julian gens)*

iungō, iungere, iūnxī, iūnctus, *to join, yoke*

Iūnō, Iūnōnis, f., *Juno (queen of the gods, sister and wife of Jupiter; identified with the Greek Hera)*

Iuppiter, Iovis, m., *Jupiter (Roman equivalent of Zeus, king of the gods)*

iūrō (1), *to swear (as in an oath), swear by (+ acc.)*

iūs, iūris, n., *law; right, justice; privilege*

iussa, -ōrum, n. pl., *commands, orders*

iūstus, -a, -um, *just, fair*

Iūturna, -ae, f., *Juturna (river nymph, favorite of Juno, and sister of Turnus)*

iuvenis, iuvenis, m., *young man*

iuventa, -ae, f., *youth; youthfulness, youthful vigor*

iuventūs, iuventūtis, f., *(group of) young men, the youth*

iuvō, iuvāre, iūvī, iūtus, *to help, assist;* impers. + inf., *it helps, profits, avails (to do something)*

iūxtā, adv. and prep. + acc., *nearby, close by*

K

Karthāgō, Karthāginis, f., *Carthage (capital of the Phoenician settlement in North Africa, in modern Tunisia)*

L

labō, labāre, labāvī, labātūrus, *to stand unsteadily, be shaky, totter, give way*

lābor, lābī, lāpsus sum, *to slip, fall, stumble*

labor, labōris, m., *work, toil, task; suffering*

lacrima, -ae, f., *tear*

lacrimō (1), *to weep, cry*

lacus, -ūs, m., *lake, pond, pool; waters*

laedō, laedere, laesī, laesus, *to injure, harm; to displease, offend*

laetor, -ārī, -ātus sum, *to rejoice, be glad, be delighted*

laetus, -a, -um, *happy, glad*

laevus, -a, -um, *(on the) left; ill-omened, unfavorable, unpropitious*

lambō, lambere, lambī, *to lick*

languidus, -a, -um, *drooping, realxing, languorous*

Lāocoön, Lāocoöntis, m., *Laocoön (Laocoön, one of Priam's sons and a priest of Apollo)*

lapis, lapidis, m., *stone*

lāpsus, -ūs, m., *slipping, falling; gliding, sliding, slithering*

largus, -a, -um, *generous, bountiful; plentiful, copious*

lātē, adv., *over a wide area, widely, far and wide*

latebra, -ae, f., *hiding place; hole, lair (of an animal)*

lateō, latēre, latuī, *to hide, lie hidden, be concealed; to escape the notice of*

Latīnus, -a, -um, *Latin*

Latium, -ī, n., *Latium (the area of central Italy that included Rome)*

latrō (1), *to bark, howl*

lātus, -a, -um, *broad, wide; wide-open, gaping; extensive, widespread*

latus, lateris, n., *side (of a body or an object); flank (of an army)*

laudō (1), *to praise*

laurus, -ī, f., *laurel tree, bay tree*

laus, laudis, f., *praise, commendation*

Lausus, -ī, m., *Lausus (son of the Etruscan chieftain Mezentius, an ally of Turnus and the Rutulians)*

Lavīnium, -ī, n., *Lavinium (a large town south of Rome important during the early Republic)*

Lāvīnius, -a, -um, *Lavinian, of Lavinium*

laxō (1), *to open up, clear (out); to undo, loosen; to free, let go*

laxus, -a, -um, *spacious, roomy; loose, slack; wide open, gaping*

legō, legere, lēgī, lēctus, *to gather; to select, choose; to travel over; to read*

lēniō, lēnīre, lēniī, lēnītus, *to moderate; to calm, comfort*

lēnis, -is, -e, *slowly moving, gentle, light*

lentus, -a, -um, *slow; pliant, flexible*

leō, leōnis, m., *lion*

lētum, -ī, n., *death; destruction*

levis, -is, -e, *light; gentle*

levō (1), *to lift (up), raise; to support; to lift off, remove; to relieve, lighten*

lēx, lēgis, f., *law, statute*

lībō (1), *to pour a libation of, make an offering of; to touch lightly; with ōscula, to kiss gently*

lībrō (1), *to balance, poise; to aim, brandish*

Libya, -ae, f., *North Africa, Libya* (often = Carthage)

Libycus, -a, -um, *Libyan, of Libya* (a region of North Africa); *(North) African*

licet, licēre, licuit, impers., + dat., *it is allowed*

ligō (1), *to bind up*

līmen, līminis, n., *threshold, doorway*

līmes, līmitis, m., *strip of land* (marking a boundary), *boundary marker/stone; lane, path, course; line, track, trail*

lingua, -ae, f., *tongue, language*

linquō, linquere, līquī, *to leave*

lītō (1), *to gain favor/atone by sacrifice* (often + ABL. OF MEANS); *to offer* (in propitiation)

lītus, lītoris, n., *seashore, coast*

locō (1), *to place*

locus, -ī, m. (pl., loca, -ōrum, n.), *place*

longaevus, -a, -um, *of great age, aged*

longus, -a, -um, *long;* longē, adv., *far*

loquor, loquī, locūtus sum, *to speak, talk*

lōrica, -ae, f., *breastplate, cuirass*

lōrum, -ī, n., *leather strap, thong;* pl., (a horse's) *reins*

lūbricus, -a, -um, *slippery*

luctor, -ārī, -ātus sum, *to wrestle; to struggle (to escape), resist violently.*

luctus, -ūs, m., *grief, mourning*

lūcus, -ī, m., *(sacred) grove, woodland*

lūdō, lūdere, lūsī, lūsūrus, *to play*

lūmen, lūminis, n., *light, radiance; eye,* esp. pl.; *glance, gaze, sight, vision*

lūna, -ae, f., *moon*

lupa, -ae, f., *she-wolf*

lupus, -ī, m., *wolf*

lūstrō (1), *to move around* (a place); *to look around, see, survey;* with lūce etc., *to illuminate, light up*

lūx, lūcis, f., *light*

Lycius, -a, -um, *of Lycia* (a country in southern Asia Minor), *Lycian;* m. pl. as noun, *Lycians*

M

māchina, -ae, f., *machine; crane; siege-engine* (for breaking down or scaling city walls)

mactō (1), *to slay sacrificially, sacrifice*

maereō, maerēre, *to be sad, mourn, grieve*

maestus, -a, -um, *unhappy, sad, mournful; gloomy, stern, grim*

māgālia, māgālium, n. pl. (a Punic word), *huts, tents*

magis, comp. adv., *more*

magister, magistrī, m., *master, captain*

magnus, -a, -um, *big, great, large, loud* (voice, laugh)

maior, maior, maius, gen., maiōris, *bigger*

male, adv., *unpleasantly; badly, poorly; hardly, not at all*

mālō, mālle, māluī, irreg., *to prefer*

malus, -a, -um, *bad, evil*

mandātum, -ī, n., *order, instruction*

mandō (1), *to hand over, consign; to assign, entrust; to command, order*

maneō, manēre, mānsī, mānsūrus, *to remain, stay; to await*

mānēs, mānium, m. pl., *spirits of the dead*

manifestus, -a, -um, *detected in the act, flagrant* (of crimes); *evident, obvious; clearly visible*

manus, -ūs, f., *hand; band* (of men)

mare, maris, n., *sea*

marītus, -ī, m., *husband*

marmor, marmoris, n., *marble, block of marble*

Mārs, Mārtis, m., *Mars* (Italian god of agriculture and war, counterpart of the Greek Ares); *warfare, fighting*

Massȳlus, -a, -um, *Massylian, of the Massyli* (a North African tribe living west of Carthage)

māter, mātris, f., *mother*

māternus, -a, -um, *of/relating to a mother, maternal*

maximus, -a, -um, *biggest, greatest, very great, very large*

mē, *me*

meditor, -ārī, -ātus sum, *to ponder, meditate, contemplate, plan*

medius, -a, -um, *mid-, middle of*

mel, mellis, n., *honey*

melior, melior, melius, gen., **meliōris,** *better;* **melius,** adv., *better*

membrum, -ī, n., *part/organ of the body, limb, member;* pl., *body*

meminī, meminisse, imper., **mementō,** *to remember*

memor, memoris, *keeping in memory, mindful, unforgetting*

memorābilis, -e, *memorable*

memorō (1), *to speak, say; to speak of as, call, name; to tell about, narrate; to remind, call to mind*

mēns, mentis, f., *mind, heart; purpose, design; frame of mind, attitude; will*

mēnsa, -ae, f., *table*

mēnsis, mēnsis, f., *month*

mentior, mentīrī, mentītus sum, *to lie (about), deceive; to disguise; to assume/put on falsely* (as a disguise)

mentum, -ī, n., *chin*

mercor, -ārī, -ātus sum, *to buy, purchase*

Mercurius, -ī, m., *Mercury* (messenger god)

mereō (2), and **mereor, merērī, meritus sum,** *to receive as one's wage, earn; to merit, deserve*

meritum, -ī, n., *good deed;* pl., *services*

mēta, -ae, f., *mark, goal, turning-point*

metuō, metuere, metuī, metūtus, *to fear, be afraid of; to view with alarm*

metus, -ūs, m., *fear*

meus, -a, -um, *my, mine*

micō, micāre, micuī, *to move quickly to and fro, flash*

migrō, -āre, -āvī, -ātūrus, *to move one's home*

mīles, mīlitis, m., *soldier*

mīlle, indecl. adj., *thousand*

mina, -ae, f., *threat, menace*

Minerva, -ae, f., *Minerva* (Roman goddess of crafts, wisdom, and warfare, associated with Pallas Athena)

minimē, adv., *least*

minister, -trī, m., *servant, assistant; agent, accomplice*

ministrō (1), + dat., *to act as a servant (to) attend (to);* + acc., *to provide; to manage, look after, regulate*

minor, -ārī, -ātus sum, *to threaten, menace*

minor, minor, minus, gen., **minōris,** *smaller*

mīrābilis, -is, -e, *wonderful*

mīror, -ārī, -ātus sum, *to admire, wonder at, wonder*

mīrus, -a, -um, *wonderful, marvelous, strange*

misceō, miscēre, miscuī, mixtus, *to mix, stir up, throw into confusion*

Mīsēnus, -ī, m., *Misenus* (a famed trumpeter, and close comrade first of Hector, then of Aeneas)

miser, -a, -um, *unhappy, miserable, wretched*

miserābilis, -is, -e, *miserable, wretched*

misereōr, -ērī, -itus sum, + gen., *to pity*

miseror, -ārī, -ātus sum, *to view with compassion, feel sorry for, pity*

mittō, mittere, mīsī, missus, *to send, let go*

modo, adv., *only*

modus, -ī, m., *way, method, rhythmic/harmonious manner; limit, moderation*

moenia, moenium, n. pl., *walls*

mōlēs, mōlis, f., *mass, huge bulk*

mōlior, mōlīrī, mōlītus sum, *to work to bring about, work at, engineer, undertake, contrive; to build, construct*

mollis, -is, -e, *soft*

moneō (2), *to advise, warn*

monimentum, -ī, n., *memorial, reminder*

mōns, montis, m., *mountain, hill*

mōnstrō (1), *to show*

mōnstrum, -ī, n., *omen, sign, portent; monstrous event/thing/act; monster*

mora, -ae, f., *loss of time, delay*

morior, morī, mortuus sum, fut. part., **moritūrus,** *to die*

moror, -ārī, -ātus sum, *to delay, remain, stay*

mors, mortis, f., *death*

morsus, -ūs, m., *biting, bite; grip, hook*

mortālis, -is, -e, *subject to death, mortal*

mōs, mōris, m., *custom,* pl., *character;* **dē mōre,** idiom, *in accordance with custom, in the usual manner*

moveō, movēre, mōvī, mōtus, *to move, shake*

mox, adv., *soon, presently*

mūcrō, mūcrōnis, f., *point (of a sword or other implement); sword*

mulceō, mulcēre, *to touch lightly, caress; to soothe, pacify, calm*

multus, -a, -um, *much;* **multum,** adv., *greatly, much;* **multī, -ae, -a,** pl. *many*

mūnus, mūneris, n., *gift, service*

murmur, murmuris, n., *murmur, rumble*

mūrus, -ī, m., *wall*

Mūsa, -ae, f., *Muse (goddess of song and poetry)*

mūtō (1), *to change; to exchange*

Mycēnae, -ārum, f. pl., *Mycenae (a city in southern Greece, home of king Agamemnon, leader of the Greek forces in the Trojan War)*

Myrmidones (-ēs), Myrmidonum, m. pl., *Myrmidons (a tribe in Thessaly, led by Achilles in the Trojan War)*

N

nam, conj., *for*

namque, conj., *certainly, to be sure; for (explanatory and causal)*

nārrō (1), *to tell (a story)*

nāscor, nāscī, nātus sum, *to be born*

nāta, -ae, f., *daughter*

natō, -āre, -āvī, -ātūrus, *to swim*

nātus, -ī, m., *son*

nāvigō (1), *to sail*

nāvis, nāvis, f., *ship*

nāvita (= nauta), -ae, m., *sailor*

-ne, (indicates a question)

nē, conj. + subjunc., *in case, to prevent, to avoid, not to, so that . . . not*

nebula, -ae, f., *mist, fog; cloud* (of dust, smoke, etc.)

nec, conj., *and . . . not*

nectō, nectere, nexī, nexus, *to weave, interweave; to bind; to join together, connect*

nefandus, -a, -um, *unspeakable, wicked, impious*

nefās, n., indecl., *impious act, sacrilege; crime; portent, horror*

negō (1), *to deny, refuse*

nemus, nemoris, n., *woodland, forest; thicket; sacred grove*

Neoptolemus, -ī, m., *Neoptolemus* (the name means "new Ptolemy", or "new War"; son of Achilles, also known as Pyrrhus)

nepōs, nepōtis, m., *grandson; descendant*

Neptūnus, -ī, m., *Neptune* (brother of Jupiter, Juno, and Pluto, and god of the sea, horses, and earthquakes)

neque, conj., *and . . . not*

nēquīquam, adv., *in vain*

nesciō (4), *to be ignorant, not to know*

nescius, -a, -um, *not knowing, unaware, ignorant (of)*

neu, conj., *nor, or not; and (that) . . . not*

nex, necis, f., *murder, slaughter*

nī, conj. (= **nisi**), *unless, if not*

niger, -gra, -grum, *black*

nihil, *nothing*

nimbus, -ī, m., *rain-cloud, cloud; downpour, cloudburst, rain-storm*

nimium, adv., *too, too much, exceedingly, excessively*

nitēns, nitentis, *shining, bright, radiant*

nītor, nītī, nīxus or **nīsus sum,** *to rest one's weight on, lean on, tread upon; to be supported, be held up; to strain, struggle, grapple (with)*

nocturnus, -a, -um, *happening during the night*

nōdus, -ī, m., *knot (formed by tying); knot, node (of a tree); knotty problem, difficulty*

nōmen, nōminis, n., *name*

nōn, adv., *not*

nōndum, adv., *not yet*

noster, -tra, -trum, *our*

nōtus, -a, -um, *known, familiar*

Notus, -ī, m., *south wind*

novem, *nine*

novō (1), *to make something new, create, build; to change, alter*

novus, -a, -um, *new*

nox, noctis, f., *night*

nūbēs, nūbis, f., *cloud*

nūbilum, -ī, n., *cloud*

nūdō (1), *to strip bare, strip off; to uncover, expose (to view), reveal*

nūdus, -a, -um, *naked, nude; empty, deserted*

nūllus, -a, -um, *no, none*

Num . . . ? adv., *Surely . . . not . . . ?* (introduces a question that expects the answer "no")

nūmen, nūminis, n., *divine power, divine will, divine sanction; divinity, godhead; divine presence*

numerus, -ī, m., *number*

numquam, adv., *never*

nunc, adv., *now*

nūntius, -ī, m., *messenger; message*

nurus, -ūs, f., *daughter-in-law; young married woman*

nusquam, adv., *nowhere*

Nympha, -ae, f., *nymph, nature spirit*

O

ō, interj., *oh!,* (used with vocatives and in exclamations)

ob, prep. +acc., *on account of*

obeō, obīre, obiī, obitus, *to meet face to face, come up against; to enclose, border, surround; to take on, deal with; to die*

obiciō, obicere, obiēcī, obiectus, *to throw (in the way), put before; to present to*

oblīvīscor, oblīvīscī, oblītus sum, + acc. or gen., *to lose remembrance of, forget (about)*

obmūtēscō, obmūtēscere, obmūtuī, *to become incapable of speech, be dumbstruck; to become/remain silent*

obnīxus, -a, -um, *straining, exerting great effort; determined, resolute*

oborior, oborīrī, obortus sum, *to spring/ rise up, arise*

obruō, obruere, obruī, obrūtus, *to cover up; to overwhelm, overturn, sink*

obscūrus, -a, -um, *dim, dark, obscure; hidden, not visible; incomprehensible*

observō (1), *to watch, pay attention to*

obsideō, obsidēre, obsēdī, obsessus, *to besiege*

obstipēscō, obstipēscere, obstipuī, *to be dumbstruck, stunned, astounded*

obstō, obstāre, obstitī, obstātus, *to stand in the way of, obstruct, prevent*

obvius, -a, -um, *in the path of, in front of;* idiom with **sē ferre,** *to encounter*

occāsus, -ūs, m., *opportunity, chance; downfall, destruction*

occidō, occidere, occidī, occāsus, *to fall, collapse (in the way); to die*

occumbō, occumbere, occubuī, *to be laid low, meet with* (death); *to fall, die*

Ōceanus, -ī, m., *Ocean*

oculus, -ī, m., *eye*

ōdī, ōdisse, ōsus, defective vb. with chiefly perf. system forms, *to hate*

odium, -ī, n., *dislike, hatred*

offerō, offerre, obtulī, oblātus, *to present, offer, provide*

ōlim, adv., *once (upon a time), at some future time, one day*

Olympus, -ī, m., *Mt. Olympus* (mythical home of the gods on the border between Thessaly and Macedonia); *sky, heaven(s)*

ōmen, ōminis, n., *omen, augury, sign*

omnipotēns, omnipotentis, *all-powerful, omnipotent;* with **pater,** often = Jupiter

omnis, -is, -e, *all, the whole, every, each*

onerō (1), *to load*

onus, oneris, n., *load, burden*

opācus, -a, -um, *shady, darkened; dark, dim, gloomy*

operiō, operīre, operuī, opertus, *to hide, cover*

opīmus, -a, -um, *rich, plentiful, abundant;*

oppositus, -a, -um, *in front (of), facing, opposite; opposed, hostile*

opprimō, opprimere, oppressī, oppressus, *to overwhelm*

ops, opis, f., *power, ability; resources, wealth, riches* (often pl.); *aid, assistance*

optimus, -a, -um, *best, very good, excellent*

optō (1), *to wish; to choose, decide on*

opus, operis, n., *work, product, task; function, purpose;* **opus est** + abl., idiom, *there is need of* (something)

ōra, -ae, f., *border, edge; coast, shore; region, land*

orbis, orbis, m., *circle, any disc-shaped object;* **orbis terrārum,** *the circle of the lands, the whole earth*

Orcus, -ī, m., *Orcus, Dis* (the god of the Underworld); *the Underworld, Hades*

ordior, ordīrī, orsus sum, *to begin*

ōrdō, ōrdinis, m., *row, line, order, rank;* idiom, **ex ōrdine,** *in order*

oriēns, orientis, m., *the east, the orient*

orīgō, orīginis, f., *first appearance, beginning; birth; starting point*

Oriōn, Oriōnis, m., *Orion* (a hunter killed by Diana and transformed into a constellation); *the constellation Orion* (associated with stormy weather)

orior, orīrī, ortus sum, *to rise*

ornus, -ī, f., *flowering ash (tree)*

ōrō (1), *to beg, pray*

Orontēs, Orontī, acc. **Orontēn,** m., *Orontes* (a Lycian warrior)

Orpheus, -ī, m., *Orpheus* (legendary singer and husband of Eurydice)

ōs, ōris, n., *mouth, face, expression* (pl. common for s. in verse)

os, ossis, n., *bone*

ōsculum, -ī, n., *little mouth;* (most commonly) *kiss* or, pl., *lips*

ostendō, ostendere, ostendī, ostentus, *to show, point out*

ōstium, -ī, n., *door; opening; mouth* (of a river or harbor)

Othryadēs, -ae, m., *son of Othryas*

P

Palladium, -ī, n., *Palladium, statue of Pallas* (Athena/Minerva)

Pallas, Palladis, f., *Pallas (Athena), Minerva* (originally in Italy Minerva was goddess of household arts, but through identification with the Greek Athena a goddess of warfare as well)

Pallās, Pallantis, acc. **Pallanta,** m., *Pallas* (son of the Greek king Evander, who had established a settlement on one of the hills at Rome; Pallas became one of Aeneas' closest friends)

palleō, pallēre, *to be pale/bloodless; to have a pale color*

pallidus, -a, -um, *pale, colorless, pallid*

palma, -ae, f., *palm* (of the hand)

palūs, palūdis, f., *fen, swamp* (often applied to the murky waters of the Underworld)

pandō, pandere, passus, *to spread out, open out; to open (up); to reveal*

Panthūs, -ī, voc. **Panthū,** m., *Panthus* (a priest of Apollo at Troy)

pār, paris, often + dat., *matching, equal; similar (to), like*

parcō, parcere, pepercī, + dat., *to spare*

parēns, parentis, m./f., *parent*

pareō, parēre, paruī, paritūrus, + dat., *to obey*

pariēs, parietis, m., *wall* (of a house or room)

pariō, parere, peperī, partus, *to give birth to; to bring forth, produce; to create, procure, obtain, win*

Paris, Paridis, m., *Paris* (a Trojan prince, son of king Priam)

pariter, adv., *together, side by side; equally; in the same manner, alike; at the same time, simultaneously*

parō (1), *to prepare, get ready;* **parātus, -a, -um,** *ready, prepared*

pars, partis, f., *part, direction, region*

parvulus, -a, -um, *small, little*

parvus, -a, -um, *small*

pāscō, pāscere, pāvī, pāstus, *to feed, pasture* (domestic animals); pass., *to feed (on), graze (on)*

passim, adv., *widely scattered, here and there; in every direction*

passus, -a, -um, *extended, spread out, streaming, flowing*

pāstor, pāstōris, m., *shepherd*

pateō, patēre, patuī, *to open up, be open, lie open; to be visible, be revealed*

pater, patris, m., *father*

patēscō, patēscere, patēscuī, *to open (out); to be open to view; to be evident*

patior, patī, passus sum, *to suffer, endure; to allow, permit*

patria, -ae, f., *nation, native land*

patrius, -a, -um, *of a father, a father's; ancestral; of one's birthplace, native*

patruus, -ī, m., *uncle*

paucī, -ae, -a, *(a) few*

paulātim, adv., *gradually, little by little*

paulum, adv., *(a) little*

pauper, pauperis, *poor*

pavidus, -a, -um, *terror-stricken, frightened*

pavor, pavōris, m., *sudden fear, terror, fright*

pāx, pācis, f., *peace*

pectus, pectoris, n., *chest, breast, heart, mind, soul*

pecus, pecoris, n., *livestock, sheep and cattle, herd*

pedes, peditis, m., *one who goes on foot; footsoldier, infantryman;* idiom, **pedes īre,** *to go on foot*

pelagus, -ī, n., *sea, ocean*

Pelasgus, -a, -um, *Pelasgian, of the Pelasgians* (an ancient Aegean tribe); m. pl. as noun, *Pelasgians, Greeks*

Pēlīdēs, -ae, m., *son of Peleus* (king of Phthia and husband of Thetis), *Achilles; descendant of Peleus*

pellis, pellis, f., *skin, hide*

pellō, pellere, pepulī, pulsus, *to beat against, push; to drive away; to dispel*

Penātēs, Penātium, m. pl., *Penates* (gods who protected the Roman foodstore and, by extension, the household, the family, and the state)

pendeō, pendēre, pependī, *to be suspended, hang; to hang down* (upon/over)

penetrāle, penetrālis, n., *inner part, innermost recess; inner shrine; innermost part of a home, inner chamber*

penitus, adv., *from within; far within, deep down; far (away)*

penna, -ae, f., *wing; feather*

per, prep. + acc., *through, along, over*

peragō, peragere, perēgī, perāctus, *to do thoroughly, complete; to go through, deal with*

peragrō (1), *to travel over, wander throughout*

percutiō, percutere, percussī, percussus, *to strike; to beat, shake violently*

pererrō (1), *to wander through/over; to look over, think over/about*

pereō, perīre, periī, peritūrus, *to die, perish*

perferō, perferre, pertulī, perlātus, *to carry to (a place), carry (oneself) to = go to (a place); to tolerate, endure*

perficiō, perficere, perfēcī, perfectus, *to accomplish*

perfidus, -a, -um, *treacherous, false, deceitful*

Pergama, -ōrum, n. pl., *Pergama* (the citadel of Troy), *Troy*

pergō, pergere, perrēxī, perrēctūrus, *to make one's way, move on, proceed*

perīculum, -ī, n., *danger*

perlegō, perlegere, perlēgī, perlēctus, *to read through*

permittō, permittere, permīsī, permissus, *to send forth; to hand over, relinquish; to allow, permit*

perpetuus, -a, -um, *lasting, permanent*

persentiō, persentīre, persēnsī, persēnsus, *to perceive, realize; to feel deeply*

personō (1), *to resound, ring; to make resound*

perterritus, -a, -um, *frightened, terrified*

perveniō, pervenīre, pervēnī, perventūrus, + **ad** + acc., *to arrive (at), reach*

pēs, pedis, m., *foot*

petō, petere, petīvī, petītus, *to seek, look for, aim at, attack*

pharetra, -ae, f., *quiver*

Phoebus, -ī, m., *Phoebus Apollo* (god of the sun, civilization, and the arts, brother of Diana)

Phoenissus, -a, -um, *Phoenician, of Phoenicia* (country along the eastern Mediterranean coast, former home of Dido)

Phrygius, -a, -um, *Phrygian, of Phrygia* (in western Asia Minor); *Trojan*

Phryx, Phrygis, *Phrygian, of Phrygia* (in western Asia Minor), *Trojan*

pictūra, -ae, f., *picture*

pictus, -a, -um, *painted; embroidered* (in color)

pietās, pietātis, f., *dutiful respect, devotion* (to the gods, family, country)

pinguis, -is, -e, *fat, rich*

piō (1), *to cleanse by expiation, expiate*

pius, -a, -um, *dutiful, worshipful*

placeō (2), + dat., *to please*

placidus, -a, -um, *kindly, indulgent; calm, tranquil, peaceful; calming*

plācō (1), *to placate, conciliate; to calm; to appease.*

plaga, -ae, f., *open expanse, tract; region; net, trap* (used by hunters)

plangor, plangōris, m., *beating of the breast* (a sign of grief); *lamentation*

plēnus, -a, -um, *full*

plūrimus, -a, -um, *most, very much*

plūs, plūris, n. *more*

poena, -ae, f., *punishment, penalty;* **poenās dare,** *to pay the penalty, be punished*

Poenus, -ī, m., *Carthaginian*

polliceor, pollicērī, pollicitus sum, *to promise*

polus, -ī, m., (north and south) *pole; heaven, sky*

pondus, ponderis, n., *weight, mass*

pōne, adv., *in the rear, behind*

pōnō, pōnere, posuī, positus, *to put, place*

pontus, -ī, m., *sea*

populō (1), *to ravage, plunder*

populus, -ī, m., *people*

porta, -ae, f., *gate, entrance, opening*

porticus, -ūs, f., *portico, colonnade*

portitor, portitōris, m, *toll-collector, customs officer; ferryman*

portō (1), *to carry*

portus, -ūs, m., *harbor, port*

poscō, poscere, poposcī, *to ask for, demand*

possum, posse, potuī, irreg., *to be able*

post, adv., *after(ward), later*

post, prep. + acc., *after*

posterus, -a, -um, *next, following*

postis, -is, m., *door-post; doorway*

postquam, conj., *after*

potēns, potentis, *able, capable; strong, powerful*

potior, -īrī, -ītus sum, +abl., *to obtain, seize*

potius, adv., *rather*

praeceps, praecipitis, *rushing/falling headlong, rushing forward*

praeceptum, -ī, n., *order, instruction*

praecipiō, praecipere, praecēpī, praeceptus, + dat., *to instruct, order*

praecipitō (1), *to cause to fall headlong, hurl down;* intrans., *to fall headlong, plunge downward*

praecipuē, adv., *particularly, especially*

praeclārus, -a, -um, *distinguished, famous*

praecordia, -ōrum, n. pl., *chest, breast; heart* (as seat of the emotions)

praeda, -ae, f., *booty, plunder, spoil, loot; prey* (of a hunter, animal, etc.)

praemium, -ī, n., *payment; reward, prize*

praestāns, praestantis, *surpassing others, outstanding, excellent*

praestō, praestāre, praestitī, praestātus, *to excel, surpass;* + inf., *to be preferable, be better, be more important*

praetendō, praetendere, praetendī, praetentus, *to hold out; to extend across, stretch forth*

praetereā, adv., *besides, too, moreover*

praetereō, praeterīre, praeteriī or **praeterīvī, praeteritus,** irreg., *to go past*

praetexō, praetexere, praetexuī, praetextus, *to border, edge* (with); *to clothe, cloak, conceal* (with)

precor, precārī, precātus sum, *to pray (for), entreat*

prehendō (prēndō), prehendere, prehendī, prehēnsus, *to grasp, seize*

premō, premere, pressī, pressus, *to press, grip tightly; to press upon* (in pursuit); *to subdue, suppress, hold back; to tread upon, step on*

pretium, -ī, n., *price*

prex, precis, f., *entreaty, prayer*

Priamus, -ī, m., *Priam* (king of Troy)

prīmus, -a, -um, *first;* **prīmum,** adv., *first, at first*

prīnceps, prīncipis, m., *emperor, leader, leading citizen*

prīncipiō, adv., *at first, to start with*

prior, prior, prius, gen., **priōris,** *first (of two), previous;* **prius,** adv., *earlier, previously*

priscus, -a, -um, *of olden times, ancient*

priusquam, conj. + indic. or, introducing a cl. of purpose or anticipation, subjunct., *before, until* (often separated into two words by TMESIS, with one or more other words intervening)

prō, prep. + abl., *for, on behalf of, as*

probō (1), *to approve (of), commend; to assent to, sanction*

prōcēdō, prōcēdere, prōcessī, prōcessūrus, *to go forward*

procella, -ae, f., *violent wind, storm, gale, squall*

procul, adv., *in the distance, far off*

prōcumbō, prōcumbere, prōcubuī, prōcubitus, *to bend/lean forward; to fall forward/down*

prodeō, prōdīre, prōdiī, prōditūrus, irreg., *to come forth*

prōdō, prōdere, prōdidī, prōditus, *to put forward, project; to give birth to, produce; to give up, betray, reveal*

prōdūcō, prōdūcere, prōdūxī, prōductus, *to lead forth, produce; to prolong, extend*

proelium, -ī, n., *fight, battle*

prōficīscor, prōficīscī, prōfectus sum, *to set out, leave*

profor, profārī, profātus sum, *to speak out, hold forth*

profugus, -ī, m., *an exile*

profundus, -a, -um, *deep, bottomless; dense, profound; boundless*

prōgeniēs, -ēī, f., *offspring, progeny; race, family, lineage*

prōgredior, prōgredī, prōgressus sum, *to go forward, advance*

prohibeō (2), *to keep at a distance (from), keep away, exclude; to forbid the use/enjoyment of*

prōlēs, prōlis, f., *offspring, progeny; generation, race, breed*

prōmittō, prōmittere, prōmīsī, prōmissus, *to promise*

prōnuba, -ae, f., *bride's attendant*

prōnus, -a, -um, *face down*

propāgō, propāginis, f., *seedling, shoot* (of a plant); *offspring, progeny; race*

prope, adv. *near, nearby, nearly*

properō (1), *to hurry, hasten*

propinquō (1), often + dat., *to draw near (to), approach*

prōpinquus, -ī, m., *relative*

proprius, -a, -um, *one's own absolutely/in perpetuity; one's own property*

propter, prep. + acc., *on account of, because of*

prōra, -ae, f., *prow;* (METONYMY) *ship*

prōrumpō, prōrumpere, prōrūpī, prōruptus, *to burst forth, burst out*

prōsequor, prōsequī, prōsecūtus sum, *to follow, escort; to continue, proceed*

Prōserpina, -ae, f., *Proserpina* (the Greek Persephone, daughter of Ceres/Demeter, and goddess of the Underworld)

prōspiciō, prōspicere, prōspexī, prōspectus, *to see before one, see in front; to watch; to look forth/ahead (at)*

prōtinus, adv., *immediately*

proximus, -a, -um, *nearby*

pūbēs, pūbis, f., *adult population, company, band* (of able-bodied men); *youth, young men*

pudor, pudōris, m., *(sense of) shame; conscience*

puella, -ae, f., *girl*

puer, -ī, m., *boy*

pugna, -ae, f., *fight, battle*

pugnō, -āre, -āvī, -ātūrus, *to fight, resist*

pulcher, -chra, -chrum, *beautiful, pretty, handsome*

pulvis, pulveris, m., *dust*

Pūnicus, -a, -um, *Punic, Carthaginian*

puppis, puppis, acc. **puppim,** f., *stern of a boat;* (by METONYMY) *boat, ship*

purpureus, -a, -um, *purple, crimson*

pūrus, -a, -um, *spotless, clean, pure*

putō (1), *to think, consider*

Pygmaliōn, Pygmaliōnis, m., *Pygmalion* (brother of Dido and co-heir of the throne at Tyre)

Pyrrhus, -ī, m., *Pyrrhus* (the name means "fire" or "fire-red"; son of Achilles, also known as Neoptolemus)

Q

quā, adv., *where, by which route; by any chance, in any way*

quaerō, quaerere, quaesīvī, quaesītus, *to seek, look for, ask* (for)

quālis, -is, -e, interrog., *of what sort, what kind*; rel., *of which sort/ kind, (such) as, (just) as* (someone) *when she/he* (often, with or without the correlative **tālis**, introducing a SIMILE)

Quam . . . ! adv., *How . . . ! What a . . . !*

quam, adv., *than, as*

quamquam, conj., *although*

quandō, adv. and conj., *when; since*

quantus, -a, -um, *how big . . . ? how much . . . ? as much* (as); **Quantum . . . !**, adv., *How much . . . !*

quassō (1), *to shake repeatedly/violently; to batter, damage*

quater, adv., *on four occasions, four times; four times* (in degree)

-que, enclitic conj., *and*

quercus, -ūs, f., *oak-tree*

queror, querī, questus sum, *to complain* (of), *protest*

quī, quae, quod, *who, which, that*; after **sī, nisi, nē**, or **num**, *some (one/ thing), any(one/thing)*

Quī . . . ? Quae . . . ? Quod . . . ? interrog. adj., *What . . . ? Which . . . ?*

quia, conj., *since, because*

quīcumque, quaecumque, quodcumque, *whoever, whatever; no matter of what kind* (often depreciatory, *however small, inadequate*)

quid, adv., *why*

quidem, adv., *indeed*

quiēs, quiētis, f., *rest*

quiēscō, quiēscere, quiēvī, quiētūrus, *to rest, keep quiet*

quiētus, -a, -um, *at rest, asleep; restful, quiet, peaceful*

quīn, adv., *indeed, in fact; moreover, furthermore; why not*

quīnquāgintā, *fifty*

quippe, adv. and conj., *for, indeed, to be sure; of course, naturally* (often sarcastic)

Quirīnus, -ī, m., *Quirinus* (a god associated with Mars and identified with the deified Romulus)

Quis . . . ? Quid . . . ? *Who . . . ? What . . . ?*; after **sī, nisi, nē**, and **num**, *any, some*

quisquam, quicquam or **quidquam**, *any person, anyone, anything*

quisque, quaeque, quidque, *each (person/ thing)*

quisquis, quidquid, *whoever, whatever*

quō, adv., *there, to that place*; **Quo . . . ?** *Where . . . to*

quod, conj., *because*; with verbs of feeling, *that.*

quondam, adv., *formerly; in ancient times; in the future, in time to come; on occasion, at times* (common in SIMILES)

quoniam, conj., *since*

quoque, adv., *also*

quot, adv., *as many (as), How many . . . ?*

quotiēns, adv., *as often (as)*

R

rabidus, -a, -um, (of wild animals) *ravening, raging; rabid, mad; frenzied, wild*

rabiēs, -ēī, f., *savageness, ferocity* (of animals); *frenzy, madness*

radius, -ī, m., *ray* (of light); *pointed rod* (for drawing diagrams)

rāmus, -ī, m., *branch*

rapidus, -a, -um, *swiftly moving, rapid, quick*

rapiō, rapere, rapuī, raptus, *to snatch, seize*

raptō (1), *to carry away forcibly, drag violently* (off)

rārus, -a, -um, *loose, loosely woven; widely spaced, scattered, here and there*

ratiō, ratiōnis, f., *reasoning, reason; justification, purpose; manner, means*

ratis, ratis, f., *raft, boat, ship*

raucus, -a, -um, *hoarse; harsh-sounding, noisy, clanging*

recēdō, recēdere, recessī, recessus, *to draw back, retire, withdraw; to be set back, be secluded*

recēns, recentis, *of recent origin/occurrence; fresh, recently gathered*

recipiō, recipere, recēpī, receptus, *to receive, recapture*

reclūdō, reclūdere, reclūsī, reclūsus, *to open (up), lay open; to dig up; to reveal, uncover; to draw* (a sword)

recursō (1), *to come racing back, return again and again; to keep recurring* (to the mind)

recūsō (1), *to object, protest; to decline, refuse*

reddō, reddere, reddidī, redditus, *to give back, return; to reply*

redeō, redīre, rediī or **redīvī, reditūrus,** irreg., *to return, go back*

reditus, -ūs, m., *return*

redūcō, redūcere, reduxī, reductus, *to lead back, take back*

redux, reducis, *bringing/leading back* (home); *returning, restored*

referō, referre, rettulī, relātus, irreg., *to bring back, report, reply, write down*

refugiō, refugere, refūgī, *to shrink back, recoil*

refulgeō, refulgēre, refulsī, *to radiate light, shine brightly, gleam*

refūsus, -a, -um, *poured back, churned up, overflowed*

rēgīna, -ae, f., *queen*

regiō, regiōnis, f., *direction, line; region, locality, district*

rēgius, -a, -um, *royal, regal*

rēgnātor, rēgnātōris, m., *ruler, governor*

rēgnō (1), *to rule, govern, reign*

rēgnum, -ī, n., *kingdom*

regō, regere, rēxī, rēctus, *to rule; to guide, direct*

rēligiō, rēligiōnis, f., *religious feeling, religion; religious act/ritual/offering*

relinquō, relinquere, relīquī, relictus, *to leave behind*

reliquiae, -ārum, f. pl., *remnants, remains; survivors; vestiges, traces.*

rēmigium, -ī, n., *set of oars, oarage; oarsmen*

remittō, remittere, remīsī, remissus, *to send back*

removeō, removēre, remōvī, remōtus, *to remove, move aside*

remūgiō, remūgīre, *to moo in response; to respond with a booming noise, bellow back; to resound*

rēmus, -ī, m., *oar*

renovō (1), *to renew, revive*

reor, rērī, ratus sum, *to believe, think, imagine, suppose*

repellō, repellere, reppulī, repulsus, *to drive off, drive back*

rependō, rependere, rependī, repēnsus, *to weigh, balance; to pay/give (in return)*

repente, adv., *suddenly, in an instant*

reperiō, reperīre, repperī, repertus, *to find (out), discover*

repetō, repetere, repetīvī, repetītus, *to seek again; to pick up, recover*

repleō, replēre, replēvī, replētus, *to replenish, fill (up)*

repōnō, repōnere, reposuī, repositus or (by SYNCOPE) **repostus,** *to put back, replace; to restore; to put/store away; to put/lay down*

reportō (1), *to bring back*

reprimō, reprimere, repressī, repressus, *to hold in check, hold back*

requīrō, requīrere, requīsīvī, requīsītus, *to ask, inquire (about)*

rēs, reī, f., *thing, matter, situation, affair;* **rēs pūblica, reī pūblicae,** f., *republic, state*

reservō (1), *to reserve, hold back*

resīdō, resīdere, resēdī, *to take one's seat, be seated; to settle down, subside, grow calm*

resistō, resistere, restitī, + dat., *to pause, stop, halt; to resist*

resolvō, resolvere, resoluī, resolūtus, *to loosen, undo, relax; to unravel, solve; to break, violate*

respiciō, respicere, respexī, respectus, *to look back (at)*

respondeō, respondēre, respondī, respōnsūrus, *to reply*

respōnsum, -ī, n., *reply, answer*

restō, restāre, restitī, *to remain, linger; to be left, remain (to be done)*

retegō, retegere, retēxī, retēctus, *to uncover, lay bare; to make visible, reveal*

retrō, adv., *toward the rear, backwards; back again*

revīsō, revīsere, *to go and see again, revisit, return to*

revocō (1), *to recall, call back*

revolvō, revolvere, revoluī, revolūtus, *to roll back; to go over again*

rēx, rēgis, m., *king*

Rhīpeus, -ī, m., *Rhipeus (a Trojan warrior)*

rīdeō, rīdēre, rīsī, rīsus, *to laugh (at), smile*

rīma, -ae, f., *crack*

rīmōsus, -a, -um, *full of cracks, fissured*

rīpa, -ae, f., *bank*

rīte, adv., *properly*

rōbur, rōboris, n., *oak-tree; oak-wood (or any hard wood); firmness, strength*

rogō (1), *to ask*

rogus, -ī, m., *funeral pyre*

Rōma, -ae, f., *Rome;* **Rōmae,** *in Rome*

Rōmānus, -a, -um, *Roman*

roseus, -a, -um, *made of roses; rose-colored*

rota, -ae, f., *wheel*

ruīna, -ae, f., *collapse, ruin*

rumpō, rumpere, rūpī, ruptus, *to burst*

ruō, ruere, ruī, *to rush; to rush wildly, charge; to collapse;* trans., *to rush through/over*

rūpēs, rūpis, f., *steep rocky cliff, crag.*

rūrsus, adv., *again*

rūs, rūris, n., *country, country estate*

Rutulus, -a, -um, often m. as a noun, *Rutulian, of the Rutuli (an ancient Latin tribe)*

S

sacer, -cra, -crum, *sacred, hallowed, holy*

sacerdōs, sacerdōtis, m./f., *priest, priestess*

sacrō (1), *to make sacred, sanctify, consecrate*

sacrum, -ī, n. (often pl. with sg. meaning), *sacred object; sacrificial victim, offering; religious ceremony, rite*

saeculum, -ī, n., *age, era*

saepe, adv., *often*

saepiō, saepīre, saepsī, saeptus, *to surround, enclose; to envelop, cover*

saeviō, saevīre, saeviī, saevītūrus, *to behave ferociously, rage; to be violent*

saevus, -a, -um, *fierce, savage*

sagitta, -ae, f., *arrow*

sal, salis, m., *salt, wit*

salsus, -a, -um, *salted, salty*

saltem, adv., *at least*

saltus, -ūs, m., *woodland, grove, glade*

salum, -ī, n., *sea (in motion), swell, billow; open sea, deep*

salūs, salūtis, f., *safety; salvation, refuge*

sānctus, -a, -um, *holy, sacred*

sanguineus, -a, -um, *blood-stained*

sanguis, sanguinis, m., *blood; family*

Sarpēdōn, Sarpēdonis, m., *Sarpedon (son of Jupiter, a Lycian king and ally of the Trojans in the Trojan War)*

sat (= satis), adv. and indecl. adj./noun, *enough, sufficient(ly)*

satis, adv., *enough*

Sāturnius, -a, -um, *of Saturn (an ancient Roman god), of the Saturnian age (the first Golden Age); as an epithet of the gods, the m. usually = Jupiter, the f. = Juno*

saucius, -a, -um, *wounded; suffering*

saxum, -ī, n., *rock, boulder, stone*

scaena, -ae, f., *background (before which a play is performed), (natural) scenery; stage*

scandō, scandere, *to climb to the top of; to climb into; to tower over*

scelerātus, -a, -um, *accursed; criminal; sinful, atrocious*

scelus, sceleris, n., *crime*

scēptrum, -ī, n., *royal staff, sceptre; sovereignty, kingship*

scīlicet, adv., *naturally, surely; often ironic or indignant, to be sure, doubtless, surely not*

scindō, scindere, scidī, scissus, *to cut, split, carve, tear*

sciō (4), *to know*

scītor, -ārī, -ātus sum, *to seek to know, inquire about; to question (someone)*

scopulus, -ī, m., *projecting rock, crag, cliff, peak; boulder*

scūtum, -ī, n., *shield*

secō, secāre, secuī, sectus, *to sever, cut (with a knife, etc.); to cut into pieces; to* cut through, move rapidly through, cleave a path through

sēcrētus, -a, -um, *set apart, separate; withdrawn, remote, secluded*

secundus, -a, -um, *following; moving, coursing; compliant, favorable, propitious*

secūris, secūris, acc. **secūrim,** f., *axe*

securus, -a, -um, *carefree, unconcerned, heedless* (of)

secus, adv. (common with **haud** in similes), *otherwise, differently*

sed, conj., *but*

sedeō, sedēre, sēdī, sessūrus, *to sit*

sēdēs, sēdis, f., *seat, center* (of some activity); *abode, home*

sēditiō, sēditiōnis, f., *political strife, rebellion*

sēmita, -ae, f., *path, track, trail*

semper, adv., *always*

senātus, -ūs, m., *Senate*

senecta, -ae, f., *old age*

senex, senis, m., *old man*

senior, senior, (senius), *of a greater age, older;* often m. as substantive, *older man, old man*

sēnsus, -ūs, m., *sense, feeling*

sententia, -ae, f., *thinking, opinion, sentiment; purpose, intention; thought, idea*

sentio, sentīre, sēnsī, sēnsus, *to feel, notice, realize*

sepeliō, sepelīre, sepelīvī, sepultus, *to bury*

septem, indecl., *seven*

sepulcrum, -ī, n., *tomb*

sequor, sequī, secūtus sum, *to follow*

serēnus, -a, -um, *clear, bright*

Sergestus, -ī, m., *Sergestus* (a Trojan warrior)

sermō, sermōnis, m., *conversation, talk*

serō, serere, sēvī, satus, *to plant* (seeds), *sow; to give birth to, beget*

serta, -ae, f., *garland*

serviō, servīre, servīvī, servītūrus, + dat., *to serve*

servō (1), *to save, keep, protect*

seu or **sīve,** conj., *whether, or if;* as correlatives, *whether . . . or*

sex, indecl., *six*

sī, conj., *if*

Sibylla, -ae, f., *Sibyl* (a general name for the oracular priestesses of Apollo, the one at Cumae known as Deiphobe)

sīc, adv., *thus, in this way*

siccus, -a, -um, *dry*

Siculus, -a, -um, *of Sicily, Sicilian*

sīdō, sīdere, sīdī or **sēdī,** *to sit down; to come to rest, settle, land*

Sīdōnius, -a, -um, *Sidonian, of Sidon* (an important coastal city of Phoenicia)

sīdus, sīderis, n., *heavenly body, star, planet;* usually pl., *the heavens, stars*

signō (1), *to mark, inscribe; to mark, notice; to indicate, point out, show*

signum, -ī, n., *sign, signal*

silentium, -ī, n., *silence*

sileō, silēre, siluī, *to make no sound, be silent; to stop speaking, grow silent*

silex, silicis, m., *hard rock, stone, flint*

silva, -ae, f., *woods, forest*

similis, -is, -e, + dat., *like, similar (to)*

Simoīs, Simoentis, m., *Simois* (a tributary of the Trojan river Scamander)

simul, adv., *together, at the same time*

simul ac, conj., *as soon as*

simulācrum -ī, n., *likeness; image, statue; phantom, spectre*

simulō (1), *to pretend; to produce, simulate; to take the form of*

sīn, conj., *but if*

sine, prep. + abl., *without*

singulī, -ae, -a, *one each; every (single); individual*

sinister, -tra, -trum, *left*

sinistra, -ae, f., *left hand*

sinō, sinere, sīvī, situs, *to allow*

Sinōn, Sinōnis, m., *Sinon* (a Greek warrior)

sinus, -ūs, m., *fold* (of a garment), pl., *clothes; chest, breast, bosom; embrace; innermost part, heart* (of a place); *curve, bend; bay, gulf*

sistō, sistere, stetī, status, *to cause to stand, set (up); to halt, stop; to steady, stabilize*

sīve: see **seu**

socius, -a, -um, *associated, kindred, relted; allied, confederate*

socius, -ī, m., *companion, comrade; partner, colleague; ally*

sōl, sōlis, m., *the sun*

soleō, solēre, solitus sum, + infin., *to be accustomed* (to), *be in the habit of*

solidus, -a, -um, *made of the same material throughout, solid; firm, unyielding*

solium, -ī, n., *high-backed chair; royal chair, throne*

sōlor, -ārī, -ātus sum, *to give solace, comfort, console; to provide solace for*

solum, -ī, n., *base, bottom* (of a structure); *soil, ground, land, property*

sōlus, -a, -um, *alone*

solvō, solvere, solvī, solūtus, *to loosen, untie, dishevel; to release, let go of*

somnus, -ī, m., *sleep*

sonitus, -ūs, m., *sound*

sonō, sonāre, sonuī, sonitus, *to make a* (loud) *noise, sound; to echo, resound; to sound like, produce the sound* (of something)

sonus, -ī, m., *sound, noise; pronunciation, accent, tone*

sordidus, -a, -um, *dirty, grimy, filthy, unwashed*

soror, sorōris, f., *sister*

sors, sortis, f., *lot* (as used in divination); *destiny, fortune*

sortior, sortīrī, sortītus sum, *to draw lots; to choose by lot, select*

spargō, spargere, sparsī, sparsus, *to scatter, sprinkle, spatter; to spread*

spatium, -ī, n., *area, space; time* (i.e., time available for some purpose)

speciēs, -ēī, f., *spectacle, sight; look, appearance; impression*

spectāculum, -ī, n., *sight, spectacle*

spectātor, spectātōris, m., *spectator*

speculum, -ī, n., *mirror*

spēlunca, -ae, f., *cave*

spernō, spernere, sprēvī, sprētus, *to dissociate* (from); *to reject with scorn, spurn, disregard*

spērō (1), *to hope*

spēs, -eī, f., *hope, expectation*

spīrō (1), *to breathe; to pulse, throb; to live*

spoliō (1), *to strip; to rob, despoil, deprive* (someone, acc.) *of* (something, abl.)

spolium, -ī, n., *skin, hide* (of an animal); usually pl., *arms, weapons* (stripped from a fallen soldier), *spoils, booty*

spondeo, spondēre, spopondī, spōnsus, *to promise solemnly, pledge*

spōns, spontis, f., *will, volition*

spōnsa, -ae, f., *betrothed woman, bride*

spūmeus, -a, -um, *covered with foam, foamy, frothy*

spūmō (1), *to foam, froth, be covered with foam; to foam with saliva*

stabilis, -is, -e, *standing firm, steady; stable, immovable; lasting, enduring*

stabulum, -ī, n., *shelter for animals, stable, shed; lair, den*

stāgnum, -ī, n., *standing water, still water, pool, lagoon*

statuō, statuere, statuī, statūtus, *to set upright; to put up, erect, build*

sternō, sternere, strāvī, strātus, *to lay out on the ground, spread; to scatter, strew; to strike down, lay low, slay*

stīpō (1), *to compress, pack tight; to crowd* (around), *surround*

stō, stāre, stetī, statūrus, *to stand*

strātum, -ī, n., *coverlet, blanket, bedding; bed, couch* (esp. in pl.); idiom, **strāta viārum,** *paved roads*

strepitus, -ūs, m., *noise, clattering*

strīdō, strīdere, strīdī, *to creak, squeak, grate; to whistle, shriek, howl*

strīdor, strīdōris, m., *high-pitched sound* (depending on context, *squeak, creak, grating, screech; whistling, whirring, hissing; shriek, squeal*)

stringō, stringere, strīnxī, strīctus, *to draw*

struō, struere, strūxī, strūctus, *to set in place, arrange; to construct, build; to plan, contrive*

studium, -ī, n., *enthusiasm, study, pursuit*

stupeō (2), *to be amazed, gape* (at)

Stygius, -a, -um, *Stygian, of the Styx* (a mythic river in the Underworld); *of Hades, of the Underworld*

suādeō, suādēre, suāsī, suāsus, *to suggest, urge, advise* (often + inf. in poetry vs. the **ut** cl. common in prose)

sub, prep. + abl., *under, beneath; down in, down to; up to*

subdūcō, subdūcere, subdūxī, subductus, *to draw up, raise; to haul up, beach*

subeō, subīre, subiī, subitus, often + dat., *to go underneath; to support, carry, lift; to move/ rise up; to come up to, approach; to come up with assistance*

subiciō, subicere, subiēcī, subiectus, *to throw from below; to place underneath/below; to place* (someone/something) *under the control of*

subigō, subigere, subēgī, subāctus, *to drive* (from below); *to tame, subdue*

subitō, adv. *suddenly*

subitus, -a, -um, *sudden*

sublīmis, -is, -e, *high up, aloft*

subnectō, subnectere, subnexī, subnexus, *to bind* (one thing under another); *to bind up, tie up, fasten*

subrīdeō, subrīdēre, subrīsī, subrīsus, *to smile (at)*

subsistō, subsistere, substitī, *to stand firm; to halt* (in one's path), *stop short*

succēdō, succēdere, successī, successūrus, *to move to a position below, come to the foot of, stoop down to/beneath; to come up to, advance on*

successus, -ūs, m., *success, successful outcome*

succurrō, succurrere, succurrī, succursus, *to run quickly; to rush to the rescue* (of); *to come to mind, occur;* impers., *the thought occurs (that)*

sufferō, sufferre, sustulī, sublātus, *to lift up; to offer; to withstand, resist*

sufficiō, sufficere, suffēcī, suffectus, *to supply, provide; to imbue, stain*

suī (gen.), **sibi** (dat.), **sē** or **sēsē** (acc. and abl.), *himself, herself, oneself, itself, themselves*

sulcus, -ī, m., *furrow, trench*

sum, esse, fuī, futūrus, irreg., *to be*

summergō, summergere, summersī, summersus, *to (cause to) sink, submerge*

summittō, summittere, summīsī, summissus, *to surrender, submit* (to); *to moderate, allay*

summus, -a, -um, *very great, the greatest, the top of . . ., highest, supreme*

sūmō, sūmere, sūmpsī, sūmptus, *to take up, pick out, assume; to exact*

super, adv., *over, above; in addition, besides*

super, prep. + acc., *over, above*

superbus, -a, -um, *proud, arrogant, haughty*

superēmineō, superēminēre, *to stand out above, tower over*

superō (1), *to overcome, defeat; to survive*

supersum, superesse, superfuī, *to be above; to survive, remain*

superus, -a, -um, *above, upper, higher;* m. pl. as noun, *gods*

supplex, supplicis, *making humble entreaty, (as a) suppliant* (often used as a noun)

suprā, prep. + acc., *above*

suprēmus, -a, -um, *highest; farthest; last, final*

surgō, surgere, surrēxī, surrēctūrus, *to get up, rise*

suscipiō, suscipere, suscēpī, susceptus, *to catch from below, save (from falling); to support, hold up; to take up, have* (a child)

suspendō, suspendere, suspendī, suspēnsus, *to suspend, hang; to keep in suspense*

suspiciō, suspicere, suspexī, suspectus, *to look up at; to regard with mistrust, be suspicious of*

suus, -a, -um, *his, her, one's, its, their (own)*

Sychaeus, -ī, m., *Sychaeus* (deceased husband of Dido)

Syrtis, Syrtis, f., *Syrtis* (a sandy coastal region east of Carthage); often generalized in pl., *sandbanks, shoals*

T

tabulae, -ārum, f. pl., *tablets, records*

taceō (2), *to be quiet*

tacitus, -a, -um, *not speaking, silent, quiet*

taeda, -ae, f., *torch*

tālis, -is, -e, *such, like this, of this kind*

tam, adv., *so*

tamen, conj., *however, nevertheless, still, yet*

tandem, adv., *at last, at length*

tangō, tangere, tetigī, tāctus, *to touch*

tantum, adv., *only; so much*

tantus, -a, -um, *so great, such a big*

tardus, -a, -um, *slow*

Tartara, -ōrum, n. pl., *Tartarus, the Underworld*

Tartareus, -a, -um, *of Tartarus (the Underworld), Tartarean*

taurus, -ī, m., *bull*

tēctum, -ī, n., *roof, ceiling; roofed building, house, dwelling; shelter*

tegmen, tegminis, n., *cover, covering; armor, shield; skin, hide*

tegō, tegere, tēxī, tēctus, *to cover; to hide, conceal*

tēla, -ae, f., *web, fabric, loom*

tellūs, tellūris, f., *ground, earth; land, country*

tēlum, -ī, n., *weapon, spear*

temperō (1), *to exercise restraint, restrain oneself; to restrain, moderate, temper; to control, regulate*

tempestās, -tātis, f., *storm*

templum, -ī, n., *temple*

temptō (1), *to try*

tempus¹, temporis, n., *time*

tempus², temporis, n., *side of the forehead, temple*

tenāx, tenācis, *clinging, gripping; persistent, tenacious*

tendō, tendere, tetendī, tentus or tēnsus, *to extend (outward, upward), stretch out, spread out; to stretch back, pull tight, draw (a bow); to direct, aim (for), make one's way (toward)*

Tenedos, -ī, f., *Tenedos (an island a few miles off the coast of Troy)*

teneō, tenēre, tenuī, tentus, *to hold*

tenuis, -is, -e, *slender, thin*

ter, adv., *three times*

tergum, -ī, n., *back, rear; skin, hide*

terra, -ae, f., *earth, ground, land*

terreo (2), *to frighten, terrify*

terribilis, -is, -e, *frightening*

tertius, -a, -um, *third*

testor, -ārī, -ātus sum, *to call (someone, a deity) to witness; to swear by*

testūdō, testūdinis, f., *tortoise, turtle; shell of a tortoise; vaulted roof; tortoise formation (a military formation made by a line of soldiers with their shields locked above their heads), tortoise (a siege machine with a sloping roof)*

Teucer, -crī, m., *Teucer (father-in-law of Dardanus and ancestor of the Trojan kings)*

Teucrī, -ōrum, m. pl., *descendants of Teucer, Trojans*

texō, texere, texuī, textus, *to weave*

thalamus, -ī, m., *chamber, apartment; bedroom (of a married couple)*

Thȳbris, Thȳbridis, voc. **Thȳbri,** m., *the river Tiber (on which Rome was situated); Tiber (eponymous god of the river)*

tigris, tigris, m./f., *tiger*

timeō, -ēre, -uī, *to fear, be afraid of/to*

timor, timōris, m., *fear*

tollō, tollere, sustulī, sublātus, irreg., *to lift, raise*

torqueō, torquēre, torsī, tortus, *to twist tightly; to turn, roll; to hurl*

torus, -ī, m., *bed, couch (for reclining at a meal)*

tot, indecl. adj., *so many*

totidem, indecl. adj., *the same number (of), (just) as many*

totiēns, adv., *as often; so often*

tōtus, -a, -um, *all, the whole*

trabs, trabis, f., *trunk (of a tree); length of timber, beam*

tractābilis, -is, -e, *easy to handle/deal with, manageable; amenable, tractable*

trahō, trahere, trāxī, tractus, *to drag, pull*

trāiciō, trāicere, trāiēcī, trāiectus, *to throw across; to transfix, pierce*

trāns, prep. + acc., *across, through, over*

trānseō, trānsīre, trānsiī or trānsīvī, trānsitūrus, irreg., *to go across, cross, pass*

trānsferō, trānsferre, trānstulī, trānslātus, *to transport, transfer*

trānsmittō, trānsmittere, trānsmīsī, trānsmissus, *to send over, pass over; to go across, cross over*

tremefactus, -a, -um, *trembling (with fear)*

tremō, tremere, tremuī, *to tremble*

tremor, tremōris, m., *cause of fright, terror*

trepidō (1), *to panic; to rush around; to tremble*

trepidus, -a, -um, *alarmed, fearful, anxious; agitated; trembling, shaking*

trēs, trēs, tria, *three*

tridēns, tridentis, m., *trident*

tristis, -is, -e, *sad; grim, terrible*

Trītōn, Trītōnis, m., *Triton (an ocean divinity, son and attendant of Neptune)*

Trītōnius, -a, -um, *of lake Tritonis (in north Africa, near the birthplace of Athena/Minerva and sacred to her); as a noun, the Tritonian, Athena/Minerva*

triumphus, -ī, m., *triumphal procession; triumph, victory*

Trivia, -ae, *meeting place of three roads, crossroads; Trivia (epithet of Diana, Apollo's sister, in her capacity as goddess of crossroads and of the Underworld)*

Troia, -ae, f., *Troy*

Trōiānus, -a, -um, *Trojan*

Trōius, -a, -um, *of Troy, Trojan (often trisyllabic)*

Trōs, Trōis, nom. pl. **Trōes,** acc. pl. (a Greek form) **Trōas,** *a Trojan;* specifically Troy's eponymous founder, *Tros*

truncus, -ī, m., *body (of a man, excluding his head and limbs), trunk, torso; trunk (of a tree)*

tū, pl. **vōs,** *you*

tueor, tuērī, tuitus sum, *to look at; to watch over, protect*

tum, adv., *at that moment, then*

tumeō, tumēre, tumuī, *to be distended, swell, be swollen*

tumidus, -a, -um, *swollen, distended*

tumultus, -ūs, m., *uproar, commotion*

tumulus, -ī, m., *rounded hill, knoll, mound; burial mound, grave*

tundō, tundere, tutudī, tūnsus, *to strike with repeated blows, beat*

turba, -ae, f., *crowd, mob; cause of confusion/turmoil*

turbidus, -a, -um, *violently agitated, turbulent; troubled, gloomy; confused, disturbed*

turbō (1), *to agitate, stir up, disturb; to harass, attack; to confuse, alarm*

turbō, turbinis, m., *spinning object, top; whirlwind, tornado; whirlpool*

Turnus, -ī, m., *Turnus (prince of the Rutulians, and leader of the resistance to the Trojans' settlement in Italy)*

turpis, -is, -e, *foul, loathsome; ugly, unsightly; shameful, disgraceful*

turris, turris, acc. **turrim** or **turrem,** f., *tower (on a building or a city's walls)*

tūtus, -a, -um, *protected, secure, safe; free of danger, without risk*

tuus, -a, -um, *your (sing.)*

Tȳdīdēs, Tȳdīdae, voc. **Tȳdīdē,** m., *son of Tydeus, Diomedes (one of the foremost Greek leaders in the Trojan War)*

Tyndaris, Tyndaridis, acc. **Tyndarida,** f., *daughter of Tyndareus (king of Sparta and husband of Leda), Helen*

tyrannus, -ī, m., *tyrant, despot*

Tyrius, -a, -um, *Tyrian, of Tyre (a major city on the coast of Phoenicia)*

Tyros, -ī, f., *Tyre (capital of Phoenicia)*

U

ūber, ūberis, n., *woman's breast; animal's udder; fertile soil; abundant produce*

ubi, adv. and conj., *where, when*

ubīque, adv., *everywhere*

ulcīscor, ulcīscī, ultus sum, *to avenge*

Ulixēs, -ī, m., *Ulysses (Roman name for the Greek hero Odysseus, who was noted as much for his guile as for his valor)*

ūllus, -a, -um, *any*

ulterius, adv., *(any) further/longer*

ultimus, -a, -um, *farthest; last, final*

ultrā, adv. and prep. + acc., *further; beyond*

ultrō, adv., *in addition, besides, even; of one's own accord, on one's own initiative*

ūlulō (1), *to howl*

ulva, -ae, f., *sedge, rush (or other similar aquatic plants)*

umbra, -ae, f., *shadow, shade (of the dead)*

ūmeō, ūmēre, *to be moist/wet*

umerus, -ī, m., *shoulder*

ūmidus, -a, -um, *wet, moist, damp*

umquam, adv., *ever*

ūnā, adv., *together*

unda, -ae, f., *wave*

unde, adv., *whence, from where*

undique, adv. *on all sides, from all sides*

ūnus, -a, -um, *one; alone, only;* ūnā, *adv.,
together*

urbs, urbis, f., *city*

urgeō, urgēre, ursī, *to press, insist*

ūrō, ūrere, ussī, ustus, *to destroy by fire,
burn*

usquam, adv., *in any place, anywhere*

ūsus, -ūs, m., *use, purpose; utility*

ut or utī, conj. + indic., *as, when;* + subjunc., *so that, that, to; how*

ut prīmum, idiom, *as soon as*

uterque, utraque, utrumque, *each* (of two),
either (of two), *both*

uterus, -ī, m., *abdomen, belly; womb* (often
with reference to its contents, an unborn
child)

utinam, adv., used with subjunct. to
express wishes, *if only, would that, I wish
that*

V

vacuus, -a, -um, *empty, deserted*

vādō, vādere, *to advance, proceed, go*

vadum, -ī, n., *shallow, shoal; bottom* (of the
sea)

vagor, -ārī, -ātus sum, *to wander, roam; to
spread freely/unchecked*

valeō, -ēre, -uī, -itūrus *to be strong, be well*

validus, -a, -um, *powerful, strong, robust;
tough, sturdy*

vallēs, vallis, f., *valley*

vānus, -a, -um, *empty, insubstantial; illusory, meaningless; useless, (in) vain*

varius, -a, -um, *different, various, varied,
many-hued*

vāstus, -a, -um, *uncivilized, desolate; awe-
inspiring; immense, huge*

vātēs, vātis, m., *prophet, seer, soothsayer;
poet, bard*

-ve, enclitic conj., *or*

vehō, vehere, vexī, vectus, *to carry;* pass., *to
be carried, travel*

vel, adv. and conj., *or*

vēlum, -ī, n., *sail; sheet, awning, cloth;*
idiom, (ventīs) vēla dare, *to expose one's
sails (to the winds), to sail*

velut or velutī, *just as*

vēna, -ae, f., *blood-vessel, vein; vein, streak*
(in stone)

vēndō, vēndere, vēndidī, vēnditus, *to sell*

venia, -ae, f., *forgiveness, pardon; favor*

veniō, venīre, vēnī, ventūrus, *to come*

ventus, -ī, m., *wind*

Venus, Veneris, f., *Venus* (goddess of love
and generation, identified with the Greek
Aphrodite, mother of Aeneas)

verbum, -ī, n., *word, verb*

vereor, verērī, veritus sum, *to be afraid,
fear*

verrō, verrere, versus, *to sweep clean, sweep
away, sweep along*

versō (1), *to turn (around); to turn over in
the mind, ponder; to implement*

vertex, verticis, m., *whirlpool, eddy; whirlwind; crown of the head; summit, peak,
top*

vertō, vertere, vertī, versus, *to* (cause to)
turn, spin; to reverse, change

vērus, -a, -um, *true;* vērō, adv., *truly, really,
indeed*

Vesta, -ae, f., *Vesta* (goddess of the domestic hearth and protectress of families)

vester, -tra, -trum, *your* (pl.)

vestibulum, -ī, n., *entrance passage*

vēstīgium, -ī, n., *track, footprint, trace*

vestis, vestis, f., *clothing, garment, clothes*

vetō, vetāre, vetuī, vetitus, *to forbid, tell
not to*

vetus, veteris, *old*

via, -ae, f., *road, street*

vibrō (1), *to move quickly back and forth;
to dart out; to flicker*

victor, victōris, m., *conqueror, victor*

victōria, -ae, f., *victory*

victus, -ūs, m., *sustenance, nourishment,
food; way of life*

videō, vidēre, vīdī, vīsus, *to see*

vigeō, vigēre, viguī, *to be strong; to be influ-
ential/powerful; to flourish*

vigil, vigilis, *wakeful, watchful, vigilant*

vigil, vigilis, m., *guard, watchman, sentry*

vinciō, vincīre, vīnxī, vīnctus, *to fasten
(with bonds), tie (up)*

vincō, vincere, vīcī, victus, *to win, conquer,
overcome*

vinculum or **vinclum**, -ī, n., *chain, shackle; link, bond* (uniting people)

vīnum, -ī, n., *wine*

violō (1), *to do harm*

vir, virī, m., *man*

virga, -ae, f., *stick, rod, switch*

virgō, virginis, f., *maiden*

viridis, -is, -e, *green; covered with vegetation, verdant, grassy*

virtūs, virtūtis, f., *manliness, courage; merit, virtue, goodness*

vīs, vīs, acc. **vim**, abl. **vī**, f., *force, amount*; pl. **vīrēs**, *strength, military forces*

viscera, viscerum, n. pl., *vital organs*

vīsus, -ūs, m., *power of seeing, vision; gaze; a thing seen, a sight*

vīta, -ae, f., *life*

vītō (1), *to avoid*

vitta, -ae, f., *ribbon, headband*

vīvō, vīvere, vīxī, vīctūrus, *to live*

vīvus, -a, -um, *living*

vix, adv., *scarcely, with difficulty, only just*

vocō (1), *to call, invite*

volō (1), *to fly, move through the air; to move quickly, hurry, speed*

volō, velle, voluī, irreg., *to wish, want, be willing*

volucer, -cris, -cre, *flying; winged, swift*

voluntās, voluntātis, f., *will; good will, willingness, pleasure*

volutō (1), *to roll (forward); to turn over (in the mind), think about*

volvō, volvere, voluī, volūtus, *to move in a curved course, bring/turn around, roll; to unroll* (a scroll), *spin out* (a thread); *to turn around in the mind; to undergo*

vōs, *you* (pl.)

vōtum, -ī, n., *vow* (made to a god to do something in return for a granted prayer); *votive offering; prayer*

vōx, vōcis, f., *voice; utterance, speech, word*

vulgus, -ī, n., *common people, public; crowd, throng, mob; flock, herd;* **in vulgus** (**vulgum**), idiom, *to the public, publicly*

vulnus, vulneris, n., *wound*

vultus, -ūs, m., *face, expression*

X

Xanthus, -ī, m., *Xanthus* (the name of rivers in both Troy and Lycia)

Z

Zephyrus, -ī, m., *west wind*

VOCABULARY FREQUENCY LISTS

The selections from Vergil's *Aeneid* in this expanded edition of *A Song of War,* a total of 2,478 lines, contain 16,091 words, including 3,030 different words (counting only once the various forms of each verb, noun, etc.). The following frequency lists, containing those words occurring most often, should prove very helpful to students for vocabulary review (and to teachers for testing); included, in alphabetical order, are three lists: words occurring 20 or more times (142 items), those occurring 10-19 times (221), and those occurring 5-9 times (402). Students may wish to begin by mastering words in the first list (those occurring 20 or more times), and then move on in order to the remaining two. These lists were specially prepared for this text by David R. Pellegrino, whose interest in word frequency has led to the publications *Catullus Vocabulary Cards for AP Selections* and *Cicero and Horace Vocabulary Frequency Lists for AP Selections.*

20+ occurrences:

ā(ab) (55)
ac (atque) (113)
ad (85)
Aenēās (48)
aequor (23)
agmen (21)
alius (25)
altus (38)
amor (26)
animus (48)
ante (30)
āra (26)
arma (54)
arx (24)
at (ast) (31)
aura (23)
aut (78)
bellum (37)
caelum (39)
circum (29)
coniūnx (24)
corpus (31)
cum (conj.) (39)
cum (prep.) (27)
cūra (21)
Danaī (35)
dē (30)

deus (55)
dīcō (36)
dictum (27)
Dīdō (23)
dīvus (noun) (24)
dō (78)
domus (28)
dūcō (22)
dum (23)
ē (ex) (27)
ego (123)
eō, īre (45)
et (511)
fāma (22)
fātum (47)
ferō (64)
ferrum (23)
flamma (24)
for (33)
gēns (25)
hic (182)
hīc (40)
hinc (27)
hostis (21)
iam (77)
ignis (27)
ille (105)
in (180)
ingēns (43)

inter (25)
ipse (68)
is (20)
Iūnō (21)
Iuppiter (23)
labor (28)
līmen (25)
lītus (33)
locus (23)
lūmen (20)
magnus (73)
manus (36)
medius (42)
mēns (22)
meus (28)
miser (27)
moenia (23)
mors (20)
multus (45)
nātus (23)
nāvis (20)
nec (neque) (118)
nōn (79)
nōs (20)
noster (30)
nox (23)
nūmen (21)
nunc (52)
ō (30)

oculus (33)
omnis (78)
ōs, ōris (40)
pater (39)
pectus (39)
per (105)
petō (32)
possum (29)
Priamus (23)
prīmus (46)
-que (785)
quī (228)
quis (85)
rēgnum (36)
rēs (31)
rēx (26)
sanguis (27)
(any form of) sē (67)
sed (44)
sēdēs (24)
sequor (25)
sī (75)
sīc (56)
socius (noun) (24)
stō (26)
sub (40)
sum (154)
summus (28)
tālis (53)
tantus (37)
tēctum (24)
tēlum (34)
tendō (20)
teneō (35)
terra (47)
Teucrī (31)
tōtus (27)
Troia (36)
tū (113)
tum (47)
tuus (35)
ubi (25)
umbra (29)
unda (20)
ūnus (30)
urbs (60)
ut (utī) (40)
-ve (22)
veniō (42)

ventus (29)
via (22)
videō (67)
vincō (21)
vir (48)
vīs (24)
vocō (22)
vōx (28)

10-19 occurrences:

accipiō (15)
Achillēs (12)
adsum (14)
aethēr (10)
agō (19)
ait (15)
Anchīsēs (13)
annus (13)
antīquus (15)
antrum (10)
ārdeō (13)
arvum (12)
Ascanius (10)
aspiciō (15)
āter (16)
audeō (11)
audiō (17)
aurum (15)
bis (12)
cadō (12)
caecus (13)
capiō (17)
caput (16)
cāsus (11)
causa (11)
cavus (10)
cēdō (13)
centum (10)
cernō (18)
clāmor (15)
classis (17)
clipeus (11)
comes (17)
condō (13)
contrā (13)
cor (10)
corripiō (11)
crēdō (15)

crūdēlis (14)
cursus (18)
dea (17)
dēmittō (11)
dēserō (12)
dext(e)ra (noun) (19)
diēs (17)
dolor (14)
dolus (13)
dōnum (11)
dulcis (12)
dūrus (10)
ecce (10)
enim (13)
equidem (12)
equus (18)
ēripiō (14)
errō (15)
etiam (16)
extrēmus (10)
faciō (12)
fidēs (10)
fīnis (14)
flūctus (13)
forte (13)
fortis (10)
fortūna (16)
fuga (15)
fugiō (16)
fundō, -ere (11)
furō (17)
furor (12)
gemitus (16)
genitor (16)
genus (17)
gerō (10)
gravis (11)
habeō (10)
haereō (11)
haud (15)
heu (16)
homō (15)
hūc (12)
iactō (14)
īdem (12)
imāgō (11)
immānis (14)
imperium (15)
īmus (16)

incendō (11)

incipiō (10)

īnstō (10)

intereā (15)

īra (18)

iste (10)

Ītalia (18)

iubeō (13)

Iūlus (11)

iungō (10)

iussum (10)

iuvenis (12)

lābor, -ī (15)

lacrima (19)

laetus (17)

Latium (10)

latus (12)

lātus (11)

Libya (10)

longus (18)

lūx (13)

maneō (14)

mare (13)

metus (13)

misceō (16)

mittō (13)

mōns (15)

morior (15)

mortālis (10)

moveō (13)

mūrus (12)

nam (10)

namque (15)

-ne (-n) (17)

nē (18)

nōmen (18)

nōtus (11)

novus (14)

nūbēs (10)

nūllus (14)

optō (11)

opus (11)

ōra (19)

ōrō (18)

Pallās (m.) (13)

parēns (18)

parō (19)

pars (18)

patior (10)

patria (14)

patrius (12)

pelagus (14)

pēs (13)

Phoebus (10)

pietās (11)

poena (13)

pōnō (16)

pontus (10)

populus (12)

porta (16)

post (10)

postquam (10)

premō (19)

prīmum (adv.) (19)

prō (11)

puer (13)

pulcher (12)

puppis (10)

quā (17)

quaerō (15)

quālis (14)

quam (14)

quid (adv.) (11)

rapiō (14)

reddō (11)

referō (18)

rēgīna (18)

relinquō (19)

Rōmānus (10)

ruō (19)

saevus (14)

saxum (19)

servō (18)

seu (10)

sīdus (15)

silva (16)

simul (10)

sinō (10)

sōlus (11)

somnus (14)

soror (18)

sors (13)

spēs (17)

spolium (10)

sternō (10)

subeō (13)

super (17)

supplex (10)

surgō (14)

suus (17)

tacitus (10)

tamen (12)

tandem (17)

tantum (11)

tellūs (12)

templum (15)

tempus (15)

tergum (11)

terreō (10)

tollō (16)

tot (16)

trahō (17)

trīstis (12)

Troiānus (14)

Turnus (17)

Tyriī (12)

ūllus (16)

umerus (15)

vātēs (13)

Venus (12)

vērō (11)

vertex (13)

vertō (14)

vērus (11)

vester (14)

vinc(u)lum (10)

virgō (11)

vīta (13)

volō, velle (15)

volō, -āre (13)

volvō (18)

vōs (16)

vulnus (17)

vultus (14)

5-9 occurrences:

addō (9)

altum (9)

anima (9)

ars (9)

auris (9)

āvertō (9)

cingō (9)

coma (9)

Creūsa (9)

crīnis (9)

culmen (9)

cūnctus (9)

dux (9)

efferō (9)

ēnsis (9)

ergō (9)

fās (9)

fīgō (9)

geminus (9)

hasta (9)

Īliacus (9)

īnfēlīx (9)

inimīcus (9)

iuvō (9)

legō (9)

magis (mage) (9)

mōlēs (9)

mōs (9)

nemus (9)

ops (9)

orbis (9)

parvus (9)

quō (adv.) (9)

quondam (9)

rōbur (9)

sacer (9)

scopulus (9)

sedeō (9)

sonō (9)

spērō (9)

tegō (9)

ter (9)

Trōs (9)

ūnā (9)

vastus (9)

vix (9)

accendō (8)

Achātēs (8)

aciēs (8)

adversus (adj.) (8)

agnōscō (8)

alter (8)

arbor (arbōs) (8)

ārdēns (8)

aureus (8)

auxilium (8)

campus (8)

canō (8)

celer (8)

fremō (8)

fūnus (8)

futūrus (8)

Gra(i)ī (8)

Hector (8)

hērōs (8)

honōs (8)

impōnō (8)

inde (8)

inquam (8)

iterum (8)

Karthāgō (8)

lātē (8)

māter (8)

mīror (8)

mōlior (8)

mora (8)

moror (8)

nēquīquam (8)

obscūrus (8)

penātēs (8)

Pergama (8)

pius (8)

precor (8)

prius (8)

prōlēs (8)

quisquis (8)

quoque (8)

regō (8)

rīpa (8)

sacrō (8)

salūs (8)

sermō (8)

superbus (8)

superō (8)

Ulixēs (8)

velut (velutī) (8)

vestis (8)

vetus (8)

virtūs (8)

adfor (7)

aeger (7)

aequus (7)

aes (7)

āla (7)

Apollō (7)

artus (noun) (7)

asper (7)

attollō (7)

caedēs (7)

carīna (7)

celsus (7)

certus (7)

clārus (7)

claudō (7)

cōgō (7)

cruentus (7)

currus (7)

custōs (7)

Dardanius (7)

dīrus (7)

dīva (7)

ēvādō (7)

fīdus (7)

flūmen (7)

frūstrā (7)

inānis (7)

īnfandus (7)

iter (7)

lētum (7)

Libycus (7)

linquō (7)

locō (7)

longē (7)

loquor (7)

lūctus (7)

lūstrō (7)

memorō (7)

mereō (7)

misereor (7)

nefās (7)

nepōs (7)

omnipotēns (7)

pateō (7)

pendeō (7)

Phrygius (7)

poscō (7)

procul (7)

pugna (7)

quandō (7)

quīn (7)

recipiō (7)

revīsō (7)
rumpō (7)
scelus (7)
sine (7)
sinus (7)
solum (7)
solvō (7)
sonitus (7)
spūmō (7)
strīdō (7)
sūmō (7)
superī (7)
temptō (7)
thalamus (7)
tremō (7)
tueor (7)
tūtus (7)
ultrō (7)
unde (7)
varius (7)
vel (7)
vestīgium (7)
victor (7)
abeō (6)
ācer (6)
Achīvus (6)
adeō, adīre (6)
adloquor (6)
adytum (6)
aeternus (6)
aliquī (6)
almus (6)
āmittō (6)
aperiō (6)
appāreō (6)
armō (6)
astō (6)
autem (6)
bonus (6)
cārus (6)
certō (6)
cervīx (6)
circumdō (6)
colligō (6)
collum (6)
contingō (6)
cōnūbium (6)
cūnctor (6)

Dardanides (6)
decus (6)
doceō (6)
Eurus (6)
exanimis (exanimus) (6)
exuviae (6)
facilis (6)
factum (6)
fallō (6)
fastīgium (6)
fingō (6)
fluō (6)
frāter (6)
glōria (6)
harēna (6)
hiems (6)
horrendus (6)
iaceō (6)
impellō (6)
incumbō (6)
īnsidiae (6)
īnsignis (6)
iūs (6)
iuventūs (6)
lateō (6)
lēx (6)
lūcus (6)
maestus (6)
malum (6)
mānēs (6)
memor (6)
mīlle (6)
miseror (6)
mollis (6)
mōnstrō (6)
mūnus (6)
nimbus (6)
ob (6)
Olympus (6)
ōmen (6)
palma (6)
passim (6)
penitus (6)
portus (6)
postis (6)
proelium (6)
prōspiciō (6)
Pyrrhus (6)

quīcumque (6)
rāmus (6)
rapidus (6)
respiciō (6)
Rutulī (6)
sacerdōs (6)
sacrum (6)
saepe (6)
secō (6)
Sibylla (6)
sīve (6)
Stygius (6)
subitō (6)
tam (6)
timeō (6)
torqueō (6)
trabs (6)
turbō (noun) (6)
turbō (verb) (6)
undique (6)
valeō (6)
vehō (6)
vulgus (6)
accingō (5)
aditus (5)
Aeolus (5)
aequō (5)
aliter (5)
āmēns (5)
amīcus (adj.) (5)
amplector (5)
an (5)
Anna (5)
arceō (5)
Argī (5)
arrigō (5)
Ausōnius (5)
āvellō (5)
Calchās (5)
castra (5)
cieō (5)
compōnō (5)
cōnsīdō (5)
cōnsistō (5)
cōnspectus (5)
convellō (5)
coruscus (5)
crēber (5)

deinde (5)	indignor (5)	prior (5)
dēlūbrum (5)	ingredior (5)	prōdō (5)
dēmēns (5)	īnsequor (5)	quamquam (5)
dēnsus (5)	invīsus (5)	quisquam (5)
dīversus (5)	ita (5)	quod (5)
dīves (5)	iugum (5)	recēdō (5)
dubius (5)	iūxtā (5)	recēns (5)
effor (5)	laus (5)	regiō (5)
effundō (5)	levō (5)	rēgius (5)
ēgregius (5)	meminī (5)	remittō (5)
excipiō (5)	modo (5)	resolvō (5)
excutiō (5)	modus (5)	restō (5)
exspectō (5)	murmur (5)	ruīna (5)
extemplō (5)	Mycēnae (5)	rūrsus (5)
faciēs (5)	negō (5)	satis (sat (5)
fātālis (5)	nī (5)	secundus (5)
fateor (5)	nōdus (5)	septem (5)
ferus (5)	nympha (5)	sepulcrum (5)
fessus (5)	obstipēscō (5)	sōl (5)
flectō (5)	offerō (5)	soleō (5)
foedō (5)	ōstium (5)	statuō (5)
fōrma (5)	Pallas (f.) (5)	struō (5)
foveō (5)	pandō, -ere (5)	taurus (5)
frangō (5)	pār (5)	tempestās (5)
frīgus (5)	parcō (5)	torus (5)
fulgeō (5)	pariter (5)	trepidus (5)
fulmen (5)	pascō (5)	Trōius (5)
fulvus (5)	paucī (5)	turba (5)
gelidus (5)	pāx (5)	Tyros (5)
glomerō (5)	pereō (5)	uterus (5)
gradus (5)	pergō (5)	vēlum (5)
hauriō (5)	placidus (5)	verbum (5)
hospitium (5)	Poenī (5)	vitta (5)
ignārus (5)	portō (5)	vīvō (5)
ignōtus (5)	potēns (5)	vōtum (5)
Īlium (5)	prex (5)	

ACKNOWLEDGMENTS

MAPS

All maps by Richard A. LaFleur, Rachel Barckhaus, Tom Elliott, and Jeffrey Becker; copyright 2012, Ancient World Mapping Center. Please visit the AWMC via The University of North Carolina Chapel Hill website for additional information and free downloads.

PHOTOGRAPHS

Every effort has been made to secure permission and provide appropriate credit for photographic material. The publisher deeply regrets any omission and pledges to correct errors called to its attention in subsequent editions.

Unless otherwise acknowledged, all photographs are the property of Pearson Education, Inc.

Photo locators denoted as follows: Top (T), Center (C), Bottom (B), Left (L), Right (R), Background (Bkgd)

Cover ©NewsCom; **iv** The Art Gallery Collection/Alamy Images; **xii** extended loan from the collection of Giuliano Ceseri/Georgia Museum of Art, University of Georgia; **16** Alexander McKay's images, courtesy of Helen Jean McKay; **27** Suhail Halai; **29** Scala/Art Resource, NY; **31** Gilles Mermet /Art Resource, NY; **33** Erich Lessing/Art Resource, NY; **37** Scala/Art Resource, NY; **39** Erich Lessing/Art Resource, NY; **41** Alinari/Art Resource, NY; **43** Nimatallah/Art Resource, NY; **55** Réunion des Musées Nationaux/Art Resource, NY; **61** Archive Timothy McCarthy/ Art Resource, NY; **63** Gilles Mermet /Art Resource, NY; **71** Erich Lessing/Art Resource, NY; **75** Réunion des Musées Nationaux/Art Resource, NY; **77** Scala/Art Resource, NY; **79** Art Resource, NY; **81** Art Resource, NY; **83** Art Resource, NY; **85** Art Resource, NY; **87** Timothy McCarthy/Art Resource, NY; **89** Scala/Art Resource, NY; **91** Art Resource, NY; **99** Art Resource, NY; **109** Alexander McKay's images, courtesy of Helen Jean McKay; **113** Nimatallah/Art Resource, NY; **115** Réunion des Musées Nationaux/Art Resource, NY; **117** gift of Alfred H. Holbrook /Georgia Museum of Art, University of Georgia; **119** Art Resource, NY; **127** Marka/ SuperStock; **131** akg-images/British Library/NewsCom; **135** Alexander McKay's images, courtesy of Helen Jean McKay; **137** Réunion des Musées Nationaux/Art Resource, NY; **141** Art Resource, NY; **145** Art Resource, NY; **151** Erich Lessing/Art Resource, NY; **155** Suhail Halai; **161** Erich Lessing/Art Resource, NY; **165** Archive Timothy McCarthy /Art Resource, NY; **167** Georgia Museum of Art, University of Georgia; **171** Art Resource, NY; **175** Art Resource, NY; **179** Réunion des Musées

Nationaux/Art Resource, NY; **209** Réunion des Musées Nationaux/Art Resource, NY; **213** Scala/Art Resource, NY; **222** Réunion des Musées Nationaux /Art Resource, NY; **224** Scala/Art Resource, NY; **230** NewsCom; **237** Timothy McCarthy/Art Resource, NY; **239** Réunion des Musées Nationaux/Art Resource, NY; **243** Giraudon/Art Resource, NY; **258** Art Resource, NY; **261** Scala/Art Resource, NY; **267** Nimatallah/Art Resource, NY; **286** Art Resource, NY; **301** Giraudon/Art Resource, NY; **303** Art Resource, NY; **304** Giraudon/Art Resource, NY; **305** Suhail Halai; **311** NBay photos/Alamy Images; **313** Clore Collection, Tate Gallery, London/Art Resource, NY; **315** Alinari/Art Resource, NY; **317** Réunion des Musées Nationaux/Art Resource, NY; **323** Erich Lessing/Art Resource, NY; **329** Alexander McKay's images, courtesy of Helen Jean McKay; **335** Alexander McKay's images, courtesy of Helen Jean McKay; **336** Erich Lessing/Art Resource, NY; **339** Alexander McKay's images, courtesy of Helen Jean McKay; **347** RIA Novosti/Alamy Images; **349** Gordon Sinclair /Alamy Images; **357** Réunion des Musées Nationaux/Art Resource, NY; **361** Art Resource, NY; **363** Scala/Art Resource, NY; **370** Timothy McCarthy/Art Resource, NY; **376** bpk/Antikensammlung, SMB/Johannes Laurentius/Art Resource, NY; **380** Réunion des Musées Nationaux/Art Resource, NY; **388** Suhail Halai; **398** Scala/Ministero per i Beni e le Attività culturali/Art Resource, NY; **399** Réunion des Musées Nationaux/Art Resource, NY.

TEXT

Grateful acknowledgement is made to the following for copyrighted material:

65 *Climbing Parnassus* by Tracy Simmons, ISI Books; **168** *Pliny: Natural History,* Vol. **10** translated by D.E. Eicholz, Harvard University Press; **202** *The Aeneid of Vergil* translated by C. Day Lewis, Doubleday; **218** "Crazy to Hear the Tale Again (The Fall of Troy)" by A.E. Stallings from *Archaic Smile.* Used by permission; **245** *The Aeneid: Virgil* translated by Robert Fitzgerald, Random House, Inc.; **317** *The Lake of Dead Languages* by Carol Goodman, Ballantine Books (Random House); **325** *The Aeneid of Virgil* translated by Allen Mandelbaum, University of California Press.

Note: Every effort has been made to locate the copyright owner of material used in this textbook. Omissions brought to our attention will be corrected in subsequent editions.

NOTAE ET MEMORANDA

Notae et Memoranda